Research Anthology on Convergence of Blockchain, Internet of Things, and Security

Information Resources Management Association
USA

Volume III

Published in the United States of America by
   IGI Global
   Information Science Reference (an imprint of IGI Global)
   701 E. Chocolate Avenue
   Hershey PA, USA 17033
   Tel: 717-533-8845
   Fax: 717-533-8661
   E-mail: cust@igi-global.com
   Web site: http://www.igi-global.com

Library of Congress Cataloging-in-Publication Data

Names: Information Resources Management Association. editor.
Title: Research anthology on convergence of blockchain, internet of things,
  and security / Information Resources Management Association, editor.
Description: Hershey, PA : Information Science Reference, [2023] | Includes
  bibliographical references and index. | Summary: "This reference book
  describes the implementation of blockchain and IoT technologies to
  better protect personal and organizational data as well as enhance
  overall security, while explaining the tools, applications, and emerging
  innovations in security and the ways in which they are enhanced by
  blockchain and IoT"-- Provided by publisher.
Identifiers: LCCN 2022030165 (print) | LCCN 2022030166 (ebook) | ISBN
  9781668471326 (h/c) | ISBN 9781668471333 (eISBN)
Subjects: LCSH: Blockchains (Databases) | Computer networks--Security
  measures. | Internet of things. | Convergence (Telecommunication)
Classification: LCC QA76.9.B56 R474 2023 (print) | LCC QA76.9.B56 (ebook)
  | DDC 005.74--dc23/eng/20220815
LC record available at https://lccn.loc.gov/2022030165
LC ebook record available at https://lccn.loc.gov/2022030166

British Cataloguing in Publication Data
A Cataloguing in Publication record for this book is available from the British Library.

All work contributed to this book is new, previously-unpublished material. The views expressed in this book are those of the authors, but not necessarily of the publisher.

For electronic access to this publication, please contact: eresources@igi-global.com.

List of Contributors

Abbas, Syed / *IU India, India* 1084
Abdelhafidh, Maroua / *University of Sfax, Tunisia* 663
Abdelmajid, Nabih T. J. / *Higher Colleges of Technology, UAE* 382
Agbedanu, Promise / *University College Dublin, Ireland* 738
Agrawal, Ankit / *Department of Computer Science and Information Systems, Birla Institute of Technology and Science, Pilani, India* 873
Alam, Tanweer / *Islamic University of Madinah, Saudi Arabia* 258
AlKaabi, Saif Hamad / *Higher Colleges of Technology, UAE* 382
Ambhaikar, Asha / *Kalinga University, India* 852
Amin, Anang Hudaya Muhamad / *Higher Colleges of Technology, UAE* 382
Amjad, Mohammad / *Department of Computer Engineering, Jamia Millia Islamia University, New Delhi, India* 750
André da Costa, Cristiano / *Universidade do Vale do Rio dos Sinos - Unisinos, São Leopoldo, Brazil* 778
Ansari, Manzoor / *Jamia Millia Islamia, India* 1
Anwar, Taushif / *Pondicherry University, India* 1
Arora, Gagandeep / *ITS Engineering College, India* 142
B., Venmuhilan / *Sri Krishna College of Technology, India* 291
Balapuwaduge, Indika Anuradha Mendis / *Faculty of Engineering, University of Ruhuna, Sri Lanka* 1010
Bediya, Arun Kumar / *Jamia Millia Islamia University, India* 330
Ben Mnaouer, Adel / *Canadian University Dubai, UAE* 663
Bhatia, Ashutosh / *Department of Computer Science and Information Systems, Birla Institute of Technology and Science, Pilani, India* 873
Bhutani, Samarth / *Vellore Institute of Technology, Vellore, India* 768
Bollarapu, Manjula Josephine / *Koneru Lakshmaiah Education Foundation, India* 1309
Brown, Joseph / *City University of New York, USA* 818
Cai, Ting / *Sun Yat-sen University, China* 278
Cai, Yu / *Chongqing University of Posts and Telecom, China* 278
Cavalcanti, Carlos Frederico Marcelo da Cunha / *Federal University of Ouro Preto, Brazil* 986
Chaari, Lamia / *University of Sfax, Tunisia* 663
Chander, Bhanu / *Pondicherry University, India* 895
Charef, Nadia / *Canadian University Dubai, UAE* 663
Costa, Rogério Luís de C. / *CIC, Polytechnic of Leiria, Portugal* 67
D., Chandramohan / *Madanapalle Institute of Technology and Science, India* 931

de-Melo-Diogo, Marta / *ISEG, Lisbon School of Economics and Management, University of Lisbon, Portugal* 607

Dhasarathan, Chandramohan / *Madanapalle Institute of Technology and Science, India* 162

Dias, Ana Sofia / *ISEG, Lisbon School of Economics and Management, Portugal* 108

Edgar, Teresa / *University of Houston, USA* 1229

Ersoy, Mevlut / *Suleyman Demirel University, Turkey* 210

Ezhilmaran D. / *VIT University, India* 626

Feltus, Christophe / *Luxembourg Institute of Science and Technology, Luxembourg* 421

Ferreira, Célio Márcio Soares / *Federal University of Ouro Preto, Brazil* 986

Fischer, Gabriel Souto / *Universidade do Vale do Rio dos Sinos - Unisinos, São Leopoldo, Brazil* 778

Garrocho, Charles Tim Batista / *Federal University of Ouro Preto, Brazil* 986

Gaurav, Anup Bihari / *Maulana Azad National Institute of Technology, India* 841

Ghonge, Mangesh Manikrao / *Sandip Foundation's Institute of Technology and Research Centre, India* 1293

Goundar, Sam / *British University Vietnam, Vietnam* 162

Gupta, Govind P. / *National Institute of Technology, Raipur, India* 88

Gupta, Priti / *Banaras Hindu University, India* 1115

Gupta, Purnima / *Institute of Management Studies, Noida, India* 1128

Hiremath, Shruti Sangmesh / *Jayawantrao Sawant College of Engineering, India* 570

Hossain, Kaium / *Department of Computer Science & Engineering, Green University of Bangladesh, Dhaka, Bangladesh* 702

Hromada, Dominik / *FBM, Brno University of Technology, Czech Republic* 67

J. V., Anchitaalagammai / *Velammal College of Engineering and Technology, India* 247

Jahankhani, Hamid / *Northumbria University, London, UK* 1167

Jain, Esha / *The NorthCap University, Gurugram, India* 1037

Jain, Jay Kumar / *Sagar Institute of Research and Technology, India* 49

Jain, Varsha / *Bansal Institute of Science and Technology, Bhopal, India* 49

Jayasena, K. P. N. / *Sbaragamuwa University of Sri Lanka, Sri Lanka* 1205

Jayasena, K. Pubudu Nuwnthika / *Sbaragumuwa University of Sri Lanka, Sri Lanka* 1264

Jayatunga, Eranda Harshanath / *Faculty of Engineering, University of Ruhuna, Sri Lanka* 1010

Jurcut, Anca Delia / *University College Dublin, Ireland* 738

K., Sreelakshmi K. / *Department of Computer Science and Information Systems, Birla Institute of Technology and Science, Pilani, India* 873

Kalangi, Ruth Ramya / *Koneru Lakshmaiah Education Foundation, India* 1309

Kendzierskyj, Stefan / *Northumbria University, London, UK* 1167

Keshri, Shubham Kumar / *Banaras Hindu University, India* 588

Khalid Abdulqader Rashed Ahli, Sultan / *Higher Colleges of Technology, UAE* 382

Khanum, Saba / *Jamia Millia Islamia, India* 1

Khapre, Shailesh Pancham / *Amity University, Noida, India* 162, 931

Khedekar, Vilas Baburao / *VIT University, India* 570

Khieu, Brian Tuan / *San Jose State University, USA* 314

Kim, Henry / *blockchain.lab, York University, Canada* 402

Kiwanuka, Fred N. / *Higher Colleges of Technology, UAE* 382

Krishnan, Somayaji Siva Rama / *VIT University, India* 1193

Kumar, Abhishek / *Banaras Hindu University, India* 588, 1115

Kumar, K. Dinesh / *VIT University, Chennai, India* 193

Kumar, Pushpendra / *Maulana Azad National Institute of Technology, India* 841

Kumar, Rajendra / *Jamia Millia Islamia University, India* 330

Kumar, Sanjay / *National Institute of Technology, Raipur, India* 88

Kumar, Sunil / *Kalinga University, India* 852

Kumar, V. D. Ambeth / *Department of Computer Science and Engineering, Panimalar Engineering College, Anna University, Chennai, India* 1115

Kumar, Vinod / *Madanapalle Institute of Technology and Science, India* 133, 841

Lalotra, Gotam Singh / *Government Degree College for Women, Kathua, India* 133

Lamba, Jonika / *The NorthCap University, Gurugram, India* 1037

Laskowski, Marek / *blockchain.lab, York University, Canada* 402

Lin, Hui / *Sun Yat-sen University, China* 278

Lopes, Andreia Robert / *Hovione Farmaciencia, Portugal* 108

M., Thangavel / *Siksha 'O' Anusandhan (Deemed), India* 1058

Madhunamali, Poddivila Marage Nimasha Ruwandi / *Sabaragamuwa University of Sri Lanka, Sri Lanka* 1264

Madhunamali, ruwandi / *Sabaragamuwa University of Sri Lanka, Sri Lanka* 1205

Makka, Shanthi / *Birla Institute of Technology, Ranchi, India* 142

Mangrulkar, Ramchandra / *Dwarkadas J. Sanghvi College of Engineering, India* 1293

Manimaran, Praveensankar / *National Institute of Technology Puducherry, India* 37

Manoj, M. K. / *VIT University, India* 1193

Mkrttchian, Vardan / *HHH University, Australia* 556

Moh, Melody / *San Jose State University, USA* 314

Muthukumaran V. / *VIT University, India* 626

N., Ambika / *Department of Computer Applications, Sivananda Sarma Memorial RV College, Bangalore, India* 181, 647, 721

Nair, Siddharth M. / *Vellore Institute of Technology, Chennai, India* 1101

Noor, Mohd Azeem Faizi / *Jamia Millia Islamia, India* 1

Nunes Luís, Ângelo / *ISEG, Lisbon School of Economics and Management, University of Lisbon, Portugal* 607

Obaidat, Muath A. / *Center for Cybercrime Studies, City University of New York, USA* 818

O'Connor, Peadar / *Queensland University of Technology, Australia* 799

Oliveira, Ricardo Augusto Rabelo / *Federal University of Ouro Preto, Brazil* 986

P. R., Hemalatha / *Velammal College of Engineering and Technology, India* 247

P., Karthikeyan / *Thiagarajar College of Engineering, India* 1058

P., SivaRanjani / *Kongu Engineering College, India* 291

Paganelli, Andrea L. / *Western Kentucky University, USA* 1152

Paganelli, Anthony L. / *Western Kentucky University, USA* 1152

Pal, Kamalendu / *City, University of London, UK* 228, 349, 498, 525, 960, 1240

Palekar, Shailesh / *Queensland University of Technology, Australia* 799

Patil, Harsha Kundan / *Ashoka Center for Business and Computer Studies, Nashik, India* 488

Poluru, Ravi Kumar / *VIT University, India* 193

Popescu, Ionuț Octavian / *Northumbria University, London, UK* 1167

Pradeep, N. / *Bapuji Institute of Engineering and Technology, India* 1293

R., Sasikumar / *K. Ramakrishnan College of Engineering, India* 1058

Rabadão, Carlos / *CIIC, ESTG, Polytechnic of Leiria, Portugal* 67

Rahman, Mizanur / *Department of Computer Science & Engineering, Green University of*

Bangladesh, Dhaka, Bangladesh...702
Rajagopalan, Narendran / *National Institute of Technology, Puducherry, India* 21
Rajput, Dharmendra Singh / *VIT University, India*...570
Ramachandran, Muthu / *Leeds Beckett University, UK* 445
Ramesh, Varsha / *Vellore Institute of Technology, Chennai, India*.....................................1101
Ranaweera, Pasika Sashmal / *Faculty of Engineering, University of Ruhuna, Sri Lanka* 1010
Rao, K. V. S. N. Rama / *Koneru Lakshmaiah Education Foundation, India*...........................1309
Ravi, Chandrasekar / *National Institute of Technology Puducherry, India* 37
Ravi, Renjith V. / *MEA Engineering College, India* 1293
Righi, Rodrigo da Rosa / *Universidade do Vale do Rio dos Sinos - Unisinos, São Leopoldo Brazil*778
Roatis, Alexandra / *Aion Network, Canada* 402
Rodrigues, Vinicius Facco / *Universidade do Vale do Rio dos Sinos - Unisinos, São Leopoldo, Brazil* 778
Roy, Shanto / *Department of Computer Science & Engineering, Green University of Bangladesh, Dhaka, Bangladesh*..702
S., Kavitha / *Velammal College of Engineering and Technology, India*...............................247
S., Madumidha / *Sri Krishna College of Technology, India* 291
S., Murali / *Velammal College of Engineering and Technology, India* 247
S., Rakesh / *Galgotias University, India* 588
Sagar, B. B. / *Birla Institute of Technology, Mesra, India* 142
Sá-Moura, Bebiana / *ISEG, Lisbon School of Economics and Management, Portugal* 108
Santos, Leonel / *CIIC, ESTG, Polytechnic of Leiria, Portugal*...67
Saraf, Chitra Ramesh / *Ramrao Adik Institute of Technology, India* 1229
Satpathy, Shraddha P. / *Amity University, Noida, India* 931
Saurabh, Shantanu / *The Maharaja Sayajirao University of Baroda, India* 1115
Selvanambi, Ramani / *Vellore Institute of Technology, Vellore, India* 768
Sharma, Archana / *Institute of Management Studies, Noida, India* 1128
Sharma, Rinki / *Ramaiah University of Applied Sciences, Bangalore, India*..........................472
Sheikh, Anjum Nazir Qureshi / *Kalinga University, India*..852
Singh, Narendra / *GL Bajaj Insitute of Management and Research, Greater Noida, India* 1315
Singh, Pushpa / *KIET Group of Institutions, Delhi-NCR, Ghaziabad, India*..............................1315
Singhal, Achintya / *Banaras Hindu University, India*...588, 1115
Siountri, Konstantina / *University of Piraeus, Greece & University of the Aegean, Greece* 366
Skondras, Emmanouil / *University of Piraeus, Greece* 366
Smmarwar, Santosh Kumar / *National Institute of Technology, Raipur, India*...............................88
Sonawane, Prashant Madhav / *Jayawantrao Sawant College of Engineering, India*......................570
Sudhakara, M. / *VIT University, Chennai, India* 193
T., Puviyarasi / *Madanapalle Institute of Technology and Science, India* 162
T., Subanachiar / *Velammal College of Engineering and Technology, India* 247
Tavares, Jorge / *NOVA IMS, Universidade Nova de Lisboa, Portugal*....................................607
Thakur, Ramjeevan Singh / *Maulana Azad National Institute of Technology, India* 841
Turesson, Hjalmar K. / *York University, Canada* 402
Tyagi, Amit Kumar / *Vellore Institute of Technology, Chennai, India* 1101
U., Padmavathi / *National Institute of Technology, Puducherry, India* 21
Veauli, Komal / *Vellore Institute of Technology, Vellore, India* 768
Vengatesan, K. / *Sanjivani College of Engineering, Savitribai Phule University, India*.................588

Venkata Ramana R. / *Sri Venkateswara College of Engineering, Tirupati, India & Jawaharlal Nehru Technological University, Anantapur, India* 193

Venkata Rathnam T. / *Annamacharya Institute of Technology and Sciences, Tirupati, India & Jawaharlal Nehru Technological University, Anantapur, India* 193

Venkatachalam, Nagarajan / *Queensland University of Technology, Australia* 799

Vergados, Dimitrios D. / *University of Piraeus, Greece* 366

Vidhate, Amarsinh V. / *Ramrao Adik Institute of Technology, India* 1229

Waghmare, Sweta Siddarth / *Ramrao Adik Institute of Technology, India* 1229

Wani, Mrunal Anil / *Ramrao Adik Institute of Technology, India* 1229

Wu, Yuxin / *Guangdong Baiyun University, China* 278

Yadav, Ashok Kumar / *School of Computer and Systems Sciences, Jawaharlal Nehru University, New Delhi, India* 919

Yalcin, Cihan / *Suleyman Demirel University, Turkey* 210

Yüksel, Asım Sinan / *Suleyman Demirel University, Turkey* 210

Zeba, Sana / *Department of Computer Engineering, Jamia Millia Islamia University, New Delhi, India* 750

Table of Contents

Preface xx

Volume I

Section 1
Fundamental Concepts and Theories

Chapter 1
A Holistic View on Blockchain and Its Issues 1
Mohd Azeem Faizi Noor, Jamia Millia Islamia, India
Saba Khanum, Jamia Millia Islamia, India
Taushif Anwar, Pondicherry University, India
Manzoor Ansari, Jamia Millia Islamia, India

Chapter 2
Concept of Blockchain Technology and Its Emergence 21
Padmavathi U., National Institute of Technology, Puducherry, India
Narendran Rajagopalan, National Institute of Technology, Puducherry, India

Chapter 3
Introduction of Blockchain and Usage of Blockchain in Internet of Things 37
Chandrasekar Ravi, National Institute of Technology Puducherry, India
Praveensankar Manimaran, National Institute of Technology Puducherry, India

Chapter 4
A Novel Survey on Blockchain for Internet of Things 49
Jay Kumar Jain, Sagar Institute of Research and Technology, India
Varsha Jain, Bansal Institute of Science and Technology, Bhopal, India

Chapter 5
Security Aspects of the Internet of Things 67
Dominik Hromada, FBM, Brno University of Technology, Czech Republic
Rogério Luís de C. Costa, CIC, Polytechnic of Leiria, Portugal
Leonel Santos, CIIC, ESTG, Polytechnic of Leiria, Portugal
Carlos Rabadão, CIIC, ESTG, Polytechnic of Leiria, Portugal

Chapter 6
A Study on Data Sharing Using Blockchain System and Its Challenges and Applications 88
    Santosh Kumar Smmarwar, National Institute of Technology, Raipur, India
    Govind P. Gupta, National Institute of Technology, Raipur, India
    Sanjay Kumar, National Institute of Technology, Raipur, India

Chapter 7
Application of Technology in Healthcare: Tackling COVID-19 Challenge – The Integration of
Blockchain and Internet of Things 108
    Andreia Robert Lopes, Hovione Farmaciencia, Portugal
    Ana Sofia Dias, ISEG, Lisbon School of Economics and Management, Portugal
    Bebiana Sá-Moura, ISEG, Lisbon School of Economics and Management, Portugal

Section 2
Development and Design Methodologies

Chapter 8
Blockchain-Enabled Secure Internet of Things 133
    Vinod Kumar, Madanapalle Institute of Technology and Science, India
    Gotam Singh Lalotra, Government Degree College for Women, Kathua, India

Chapter 9
Consequent Formation in Security With Blockchain in Digital Transformation 142
    Shanthi Makka, Birla Institute of Technology, Ranchi, India
    Gagandeep Arora, ITS Engineering College, India
    B. B. Sagar, Birla Institute of Technology, Mesra, India

Chapter 10
Blockchain-Based Data Market (BCBDM) Framework for Security and Privacy: An Analysis 162
    Shailesh Pancham Khapre, Amity University, Noida, India
    Chandramohan Dhasarathan, Madanapalle Institute of Technology and Science, India
    Puviyarasi T., Madanapalle Institute of Technology and Science, India
    Sam Goundar, British University Vietnam, Vietnam

Chapter 11
A Reliable Hybrid Blockchain-Based Authentication System for IoT Network 181
    Ambika N., Department of Computer Applications, Sivananda Sarma Memorial RV College,
        Bangalore, India

Chapter 12
Towards the Integration of Blockchain and IoT for Security Challenges in IoT: A Review 193
    K. Dinesh Kumar, VIT University, Chennai, India
    Venkata Rathnam T., Annamacharya Institute of Technology and Sciences, Tirupati, India &
        Jawaharlal Nehru Technological University, Anantapur, India
    Venkata Ramana R., Sri Venkateswara College of Engineering, Tirupati, India & Jawaharlal
        Nehru Technological University, Anantapur, India
    M. Sudhakara, VIT University, Chennai, India
    Ravi Kumar Poluru, VIT University, India

Chapter 13
Adaptation of Blockchain Architecture to the Internet of Things and Performance Analysis 210
    Mevlut Ersoy, Suleyman Demirel University, Turkey
    Asım Sinan Yüksel, Suleyman Demirel University, Turkey
    Cihan Yalcin, Suleyman Demirel University, Turkey

Chapter 14
Blockchain Technology With the Internet of Things in Manufacturing Data Processing
Architecture... 228
    Kamalendu Pal, City, University of London, UK

Chapter 15
Current Trends in Integrating the Blockchain With Cloud-Based Internet of Things........................ 247
    Anchitaalagammai J. V., Velammal College of Engineering and Technology, India
    Kavitha S., Velammal College of Engineering and Technology, India
    Murali S., Velammal College of Engineering and Technology, India
    Hemalatha P. R., Velammal College of Engineering and Technology, India
    Subanachiar T., Velammal College of Engineering and Technology, India

Chapter 16
IoT-Fog-Blockchain Framework: Opportunities and Challenges 258
    Tanweer Alam, Islamic University of Madinah, Saudi Arabia

Chapter 17
Blockchain-Empowered Big Data Sharing for Internet of Things.. 278
    Ting Cai, Sun Yat-sen University, China
    Yuxin Wu, Guangdong Baiyun University, China
    Hui Lin, Sun Yat-sen University, China
    Yu Cai, Chongqing University of Posts and Telecom, China

Chapter 18
Integrating Blockchain and IoT in Supply Chain Management: A Framework for Transparency
and Traceability.. 291
    Madumidha S., Sri Krishna College of Technology, India
    SivaRanjani P., Kongu Engineering College, India
    Venmuhilan B., Sri Krishna College of Technology, India

Chapter 19
Cloud-Centric Blockchain Public Key Infrastructure for Big Data Applications.............................. 314
    Brian Tuan Khieu, San Jose State University, USA
    Melody Moh, San Jose State University, USA

Chapter 20
A Novel Intrusion Detection System for Internet of Things Network Security 330
    Arun Kumar Bediya, Jamia Millia Islamia University, India
    Rajendra Kumar, Jamia Millia Islamia University, India

Chapter 21
Information Sharing for Manufacturing Supply Chain Management Based on Blockchain
Technology.. 349
    Kamalendu Pal, City, University of London, UK

Chapter 22
Developing Smart Buildings Using Blockchain, Internet of Things, and Building Information
Modeling 366
    Konstantina Siountri, University of Piraeus, Greece & University of the Aegean, Greece
    Emmanouil Skondras, University of Piraeus, Greece
    Dimitrios D. Vergados, University of Piraeus, Greece

Chapter 23
Composite Identity of Things (CIDoT) on Permissioned Blockchain Network for Identity
Management of IoT Devices 382
    Anang Hudaya Muhamad Amin, Higher Colleges of Technology, UAE
    Fred N. Kiwanuka, Higher Colleges of Technology, UAE
    Nabih T. J. Abdelmajid, Higher Colleges of Technology, UAE
    Saif Hamad AlKaabi, Higher Colleges of Technology, UAE
    Sultan Khalid Abdulqader Rashed Ahli, Higher Colleges of Technology, UAE

Chapter 24
Privacy Preserving Data Mining as Proof of Useful Work: Exploring an AI/Blockchain Design 402
    Hjalmar K. Turesson, York University, Canada
    Henry Kim, blockchain.lab, York University, Canada
    Marek Laskowski, blockchain.lab, York University, Canada
    Alexandra Roatis, Aion Network, Canada

Volume II

Chapter 25
Reinforcement Learning's Contribution to the Cyber Security of Distributed Systems:
Systematization of Knowledge... 421
    Christophe Feltus, Luxembourg Institute of Science and Technology, Luxembourg

Chapter 26
SEF4CPSIoT Software Engineering Framework for Cyber-Physical and IoT Systems 445
    Muthu Ramachandran, Leeds Beckett University, UK

Section 3
Tools and Technologies

Chapter 27
Blockchain for Industrial Internet of Things (IIoT) 472
    Rinki Sharma, Ramaiah University of Applied Sciences, Bangalore, India

Chapter 28
Blockchain Technology-Security Booster 488
    Harsha Kundan Patil, Ashoka Center for Business and Computer Studies, Nashik, India

Chapter 29
Blockchain With the Internet of Things: Solutions and Security Issues in the Manufacturing
Industry 498
    Kamalendu Pal, City, University of London, UK

Chapter 30
Securing the Internet of Things Applications Using Blockchain Technology in the Manufacturing
Industry 525
    Kamalendu Pal, City, University of London, UK

Chapter 31
The Internet of Things and Blockchain Technologies Adaptive Trade Systems in the Virtual
World: By Creating Virtual Accomplices Worldwide 556
    Vardan Mkrttchian, HHH University, Australia

Chapter 32
Protection to Personal Data Using Decentralizing Privacy of Blockchain. 570
    Vilas Baburao Khedekar, VIT University, India
    Shruti Sangmesh Hiremath, Jayawantrao Sawant College of Engineering, India
    Prashant Madhav Sonawane, Jayawantrao Sawant College of Engineering, India
    Dharmendra Singh Rajput, VIT University, India

Chapter 33
Reliable (Secure, Trusted, and Privacy Preserved) Cross-Blockchain Ecosystems for Developing
and Non-Developing Countries 588
    Shubham Kumar Keshri, Banaras Hindu University, India
    Achintya Singhal, Banaras Hindu University, India
    Abhishek Kumar, Banaras Hindu University, India
    K. Vengatesan, Sanjivani College of Engineering, Savitribai Phule University, India
    Rakesh S., Galgotias University, India

Chapter 34
Data Security in Clinical Trials Using Blockchain Technology 607
    *Marta de-Melo-Diogo, ISEG, Lisbon School of Economics and Management, University of
        Lisbon, Portugal*
    Jorge Tavares, NOVA IMS, Universidade Nova de Lisboa, Portugal
    *Ângelo Nunes Luís, ISEG, Lisbon School of Economics and Management, University of
        Lisbon, Portugal*

Chapter 35
A Cloud-Assisted Proxy Re-Encryption Scheme for Efficient Data Sharing Across IoT Systems.....626
    Muthukumaran V., VIT University, India
    Ezhilmaran D., VIT University, India

Chapter 36
A Reliable Blockchain-Based Image Encryption Scheme for IIoT Networks 647
   Ambika N., Department of Computer Applications, Sivananda Sarma Memorial RV College,
      Bangalore, India

Chapter 37
A Survey of Blockchain-Based Solutions for IoTs, VANETs, and FANETs 663
   Maroua Abdelhafidh, University of Sfax, Tunisia
   Nadia Charef, Canadian University Dubai, UAE
   Adel Ben Mnaouer, Canadian University Dubai, UAE
   Lamia Chaari, University of Sfax, Tunisia

Chapter 38
IoT Data Compression and Optimization Techniques in Cloud Storage: Current Prospects and
Future Directions 702
   Kaium Hossain, Department of Computer Science & Engineering, Green University of
      Bangladesh, Dhaka, Bangladesh
   Mizanur Rahman, Department of Computer Science & Engineering, Green University of
      Bangladesh, Dhaka, Bangladesh
   Shanto Roy, Department of Computer Science & Engineering, Green University of
      Bangladesh, Dhaka, Bangladesh

Chapter 39
A Reliable IDS System Using Blockchain for SDN-Enabled IIoT Systems 721
   Ambika N., Department of Computer Applications, Sivananda Sarma Memorial RV College,
      Bangalore,, India

Chapter 40
BLOFF: A Blockchain-Based Forensic Model in IoT 738
   Promise Agbedanu, University College Dublin, Ireland
   Anca Delia Jurcut, University College Dublin, Ireland

Chapter 41
Identification of a Person From Live Video Streaming Using Machine Learning in the Internet of
Things (IoT) 750
   Sana Zeba, Department of Computer Engineering, Jamia Millia Islamia University, New
      Delhi, India
   Mohammad Amjad, Department of Computer Engineering, Jamia Millia Islamia University,
      New Delhi, India

Chapter 42
Security and Privacy for Electronic Healthcare Records Using AI in Blockchain 768
   Ramani Selvanambi, Vellore Institute of Technology, Vellore, India
   Samarth Bhutani, Vellore Institute of Technology, Vellore, India
   Komal Veauli, Vellore Institute of Technology, Vellore, India

Chapter 43
Use of Internet of Things With Data Prediction on Healthcare Environments: A Survey 778
    Gabriel Souto Fischer, Universidade do Vale do Rio dos Sinos - Unisinos, São Leopoldo, Brazil
    Rodrigo da Rosa Righi, Universidade do Vale do Rio dos Sinos - Unisinos, São Leopoldo Brazil
    Vinicius Facco Rodrigues, Universidade do Vale do Rio dos Sinos - Unisinos, São Leopoldo, Brazil
        Brazil
    Cristiano André da Costa, Universidade do Vale do Rio dos Sinos - Unisinos, São Leopoldo, Brazil
        Brazil

Chapter 44
Cyber Security and Cyber Resilience for the Australian E-Health Records: A Blockchain
Solution 799
    Nagarajan Venkatachalam, Queensland University of Technology, Australia
    Peadar O'Connor, Queensland University of Technology, Australia
    Shailesh Palekar, Queensland University of Technology, Australia

Section 4
Utilization and Applications

Chapter 45
Perspectives of Blockchain in Cybersecurity: Applications and Future Developments 818
    Muath A. Obaidat, Center for Cybercrime Studies, City University of New York, USA
    Joseph Brown, City University of New York, USA

Chapter 46
Conceptual Insights in Blockchain Technology: Security and Applications 841
    Anup Bihari Gaurav, Maulana Azad National Institute of Technology, India
    Pushpendra Kumar, Maulana Azad National Institute of Technology, India
    Vinod Kumar, Madanapalli Institute of Technology and Science, India
    Ramjeevan Singh Thakur, Maulana Azad National Institute of Technology, India

Chapter 47
Security for IoT: Challenges, Attacks, and Prevention 852
    Anjum Nazir Qureshi Sheikh, Kalinga University, India
    Asha Ambhaikar, Kalinga University, India
    Sunil Kumar, Kalinga University, India

Volume III

Chapter 48
Securing IoT Applications Using Blockchain 873
    Sreelakshmi K. K., Department of Computer Science and Information Systems, Birla Institute
        of Technology and Science, Pilani, India
    Ashutosh Bhatia, Department of Computer Science and Information Systems, Birla Institute
        of Technology and Science, Pilani, India
    Ankit Agrawal, Department of Computer Science and Information Systems, Birla Institute of
        Technology and Science, Pilani, India

Chapter 49
Blockchain Technology Integration in IoT and Applications 895
    Bhanu Chander, Pondicherry University, India

Chapter 50
Comprehensive Study on Incorporation of Blockchain Technology With IoT Enterprises................ 919
    Ashok Kumar Yadav, School of Computer and Systems Sciences, Jawaharlal Nehru
        University, New Delhi, India

Chapter 51
Optimization of Consensus Mechanism for IoT Blockchain: A Survey 931
    Shailesh Pancham Khapre, Amity University, Noida, India
    Shraddha P. Satpathy, Amity University, Noida, India
    Chandramohan D., Madanapalle Institute of Technology and Science, India

Chapter 52
Blockchain Technology for the Internet of Things Applications in Apparel Supply Chain
Management.. 960
    Kamalendu Pal, City, University of London, UK

Chapter 53
Blockchain-Based Industrial Internet of Things for the Integration of Industrial Process
Automation Systems 986
    Charles Tim Batista Garrocho, Federal University of Ouro Preto, Brazil
    Célio Márcio Soares Ferreira, Federal University of Ouro Preto, Brazil
    Carlos Frederico Marcelo da Cunha Cavalcanti, Federal University of Ouro Preto, Brazil
    Ricardo Augusto Rabelo Oliveira, Federal University of Ouro Preto, Brazil

Chapter 54
Blockchain Advances and Security Practices in WSN, CRN, SDN, Opportunistic Mobile
Networks, Delay Tolerant Networks 1010
    Eranda Harshanath Jayatunga, Faculty of Engineering, University of Ruhuna, Sri Lanka
    Pasika Sashmal Ranaweera, Faculty of Engineering, University of Ruhuna, Sri Lanka
    Indika Anuradha Mendis Balapuwaduge, Faculty of Engineering, University of Ruhuna, Sri
        Lanka

Chapter 55
Advanced Cyber Security and Internet of Things for Digital Transformations of the Indian
Healthcare Sector... 1037
    Jonika Lamba, The NorthCap University, Gurugram, India
    Esha Jain, The NorthCap University, Gurugram, India

Section 5
Organizational and Social Implications

Chapter 56
Blockchain Technology for IoT: An Information Security Perspective 1058
   Sasikumar R., K. Ramakrishnan College of Engineering, India
   Karthikeyan P., Thiagarajar College of Engineering, India
   Thangavel M., Siksha 'O' Anusandhan (Deemed), India

Chapter 57
Role and Impact of Blockchain in Cybersecurity 1084
   Syed Abbas, IU India, India

Chapter 58
Issues and Challenges (Privacy, Security, and Trust) in Blockchain-Based Applications 1101
   Siddharth M. Nair, Vellore Institute of Technology, Chennai, India
   Varsha Ramesh, Vellore Institute of Technology, Chennai, India
   Amit Kumar Tyagi, Vellore Institute of Technology, Chennai, India

Chapter 59
Security, Privacy, and Trust Management and Performance Optimization of Blockchain 1115
   Priti Gupta, Banaras Hindu University, India
   Abhishek Kumar, Banaras Hindu University, India
   Achintya Singhal, Banaras Hindu University, India
   Shantanu Saurabh, The Maharaja Sayajirao University of Baroda, India
   V. D. Ambeth Kumar, Department of Computer Science and Engineering, Panimalar
      Engineering College, Anna University, Chennai, India

Chapter 60
Blockchain Revolution: Adaptability in Business World and Challenges in Implementation 1128
   Archana Sharma, Institute of Management Studies, Noida, India
   Purnima Gupta, Institute of Management Studies, Noida, India

Chapter 61
Blockchain and the Research Libraries: Expanding Interlibrary Loan and Protecting Privacy 1152
   Anthony L. Paganelli, Western Kentucky University, USA
   Andrea L. Paganelli, Western Kentucky University, USA

Chapter 62
Millennials vs. Cyborgs and Blockchain Role in Trust and Privacy 1167
   Hamid Jahankhani, Northumbria University, London, UK
   Stefan Kendzierskyj, Northumbria University, London, UK
   Ionuț Octavian Popescu, Northumbria University, London, UK

Chapter 63
Decentralizing Privacy Using Blockchain to Protect Private Data and Challanges With IPFS 1193
    M. K. Manoj, VIT University, India
    Somayaji Siva Rama Krishnan, VIT University, India

Chapter 64
Blockchain and IoT Integration in Dairy Production to Survive the COVID-19 Situation in Sri
Lanka... 1205
    ruwandi Madhunamali, Sabaragamuwa University of Sri Lanka, Sri Lanka
    K. P. N. Jayasena, Sbaragamuwa University of Sri Lanka, Sri Lanka

Section 6
Managerial Impact

Chapter 65
Applying Blockchain Security for Agricultural Supply Chain Management 1229
    Amarsinh V. Vidhate, Ramrao Adik Institute of Technology, India
    Chitra Ramesh Saraf, Ramrao Adik Institute of Technology, India
    Mrunal Anil Wani, Ramrao Adik Institute of Technology, India
    Sweta Siddarth Waghmare, Ramrao Adik Institute of Technology, India
    Teresa Edgar, University of Houston, USA

Chapter 66
Security Issues of Blockchain-Based Information System to Manage Supply Chain in a Global
Crisis 1240
    Kamalendu Pal, City, University of London, UK

Chapter 67
Blockchain and IoT-Based Diary Supply Chain Management System for Sri Lanka 1264
    K. Pubudu Nuwnthika Jayasena, Sbaragamuwa University of Sri Lanka, Sri Lanka
    Poddivila Marage Nimasha Ruwandi Madhunamali, Sabaragamuwa University of Sri Lanka,
       Sri Lanka

Section 7
Critical Issues and Challenges

Chapter 68
A Comprehensive Review of the Security and Privacy Issues in Blockchain Technologies............ 1293
    Mangesh Manikrao Ghonge, Sandip Foundation's Institute of Technology and Research
       Centre, India
    N. Pradeep, Bapuji Institute of Engineering and Technology, India
    Renjith V. Ravi, MEA Engineering College, India
    Ramchandra Mangrulkar, Dwarkadas J. Sanghvi College of Engineering, India

Chapter 69

A Review on the Importance of Blockchain and Its Current Applications in IoT Security 1309
Manjula Josephine Bollarapu, Koneru Lakshmaiah Education Foundation, India
Ruth Ramya Kalangi, Koneru Lakshmaiah Education Foundation, India
K. V. S. N. Rama Rao, Koneru Lakshmaiah Education Foundation, India

Chapter 70

Blockchain With IoT and AI: A Review of Agriculture and Healthcare 1315
Pushpa Singh, KIET Group of Institutions, Delhi-NCR, Ghaziabad, India
Narendra Singh, GL Bajaj Insitute of Management and Research, Greater Noida, India

Index..xxiii

Preface

Security on the internet has never been more crucial as today an increasing number of businesses and industries conduct their vital processes online. In order to protect information and data, further study on emerging technologies, such as blockchain and the internet of things, is critical to ensure companies and individuals feel secure online and best practices are continuously updated.

Staying informed of the most up-to-date research trends and findings is of the utmost importance. That is why IGI Global is pleased to offer this three-volume reference collection of reprinted IGI Global book chapters and journal articles that have been handpicked by senior editorial staff. This collection will shed light on critical issues related to the trends, techniques, and uses of various applications by providing both broad and detailed perspectives on cutting-edge theories and developments. This collection is designed to act as a single reference source on conceptual, methodological, technical, and managerial issues, as well as to provide insight into emerging trends and future opportunities within the field.

The *Research Anthology on Convergence of Blockchain, Internet of Things, and Security* is organized into seven distinct sections that provide comprehensive coverage of important topics. The sections are:

1. Fundamental Concepts and Theories;
2. Development and Design Methodologies;
3. Tools and Technologies;
4. Utilization and Applications;
5. Organizational and Social Implications;
6. Managerial Impact; and
7. Critical Issues and Challenges.

The following paragraphs provide a summary of what to expect from this invaluable reference tool.

Section 1, "Fundamental Concepts and Theories," serves as a foundation for this extensive reference tool by addressing crucial theories essential to understanding the concepts and uses of blockchain, the internet of things, and security in multidisciplinary settings. Opening this reference book is the chapter "A Holistic View on Blockchain and Its Issues" by Profs. Mohd Azeem Faizi Noor, Saba Khanum, and Manzoor Ansari from Jamia Millia Islamia, India and Prof. Taushif Anwar from Pondicherry University, India, which covers a holistic overview of blockchain and argues about basic operations, 51% attack, scalability issue, Fork, Sharding, Lightening, etc. This first section ends with the chapter "Application of Technology in Healthcare: Tackling COVID-19 Challenge – The Integration of Blockchain and Internet of Things" by Ms. Andreia Robert Lopes from Hovione Farmaciencia, Portugal and Profs. Ana Sofia Dias and Bebiana Sá-Moura of ISEG, Lisbon School of Economics and Management, Portugal, which discusses IoT and blockchain technologies, focusing on their main characteristics, integration benefits, and limitations as well as identifying the challenges that need to be addressed.

Section 2, "Development and Design Methodologies," presents in-depth coverage of the design and development of blockchain and internet of things technologies for their use in security across different industries. This section starts with "Blockchain-Enabled Secure Internet of Things" by Prof. Vinod Kumar from Madanapalle Institute of Technology and Science, India and Prof. Gotam Singh Lalotra of Government Degree College for Women, India, which discusses the blockchain-enabled secure internet of things (IoT). This section ends with "SEF4CPSIoT Software Engineering Framework for Cyber-Physical and IoT Systems" by Prof. Muthu Ramachandran from Leeds Beckett University, UK, which proposes a systematic software engineering framework for CPS and IoT systems as well as a comprehensive requirements engineering framework for CPS-IoT applications which can also be specified using BPMN modeling and simulation to verify and validate CPS-IoT requirements with smart contracts.

Section 3, "Tools and Technologies," explores the tools and technologies used to implement blockchain and the internet of things for facilitating secure operations. This section begins with "Blockchain for Industrial Internet of Things (IIoT)" by Prof. Rinki Sharma from Ramaiah University of Applied Sciences, India, which presents the importance of blockchain in the industrial internet of things paradigm, its role in the different industrial internet of things applications, challenges involved, and possible solutions to overcome the challenges and open research issues. This section ends with the chapter "Cyber Security and Cyber Resilience for the Australian E-Health Records: A Blockchain Solution" by Profs. Shailesh Palekar, Nagarajan Venkatachalam, and Peadar O'Connor from Queensland University of Technology, Australia, which explores how blockchain can be a single digital option that can address both cybersecurity and cyber resilience needs of electronic health records.

Section 4, "Utilization and Applications," describes how blockchain and the internet of things are used and applied in diverse industries for various security applications, such as security. The opening chapter in this section, "Perspectives of Blockchain in Cybersecurity: Applications and Future Developments," by Profs. Muath A. Obaidat and Joseph Brown from City University of New York, USA, aims to provide a neutral overview of why blockchain has risen as a popular pivot in cybersecurity, its current applications in this field, and an evaluation of what the future holds for this technology given both its limitations and advantages. The closing chapter in this section, "Advanced Cyber Security and Internet of Things for Digital Transformations of the Indian Healthcare Sector," by Profs. Esha Jain and Jonika Lamba from The NorthCap University, India, reviews the need for cybersecurity amid digital transformation with the help of emerging technologies and focuses on the application and incorporation of blockchain and the internet of things (IoT) to ensure cybersecurity in the well-being of the business.

Section 5, "Organizational and Social Implications," includes chapters discussing the impact of blockchain and the internet of things on society including how they can be utilized for security purposes across industries. The chapter "Blockchain Technology for IoT: An Information Security Perspective" by Prof. Karthikeyan P. from Thiagarajar College of Engineering, India; Prof. Sasikumar R. of K. Ramakrishnan College of Engineering, India; and Prof. Thangavel M. from Siksha 'O' Anusandhan (Deemed), India presents a detailed investigation of various IoT applications with blockchain implementation. The closing chapter, "Blockchain and IoT Integration in Dairy Production to Survive the COVID-19 Situation in Sri Lanka," by Profs. ruwandi Madhunamali and K. P. N. Jayasena from Sabaragamuwa University of Sri Lanka, Sri Lanka, proposes a dairy production system integration with blockchain and IoT.

Section 6, "Managerial Impact," considers how blockchain and internet of things technologies can be utilized within secure business and management. The opening chapter, "Applying Blockchain Security for Agricultural Supply Chain Management," by Prof. Teresa Edgar from the University of Houston, USA and Profs. Amarsinh V. Vidhate, Chitra Ramesh Saraf, Mrunal Anil Wani, and Sweta Siddarth

Waghmare of Ramrao Adik Institute of Technology, India, provides an overview of blockchain technology and its potential in developing a secure and reliable agriculture supply chain management. The closing chapter, "Blockchain and IoT-Based Diary Supply Chain Management System for Sri Lanka," by Profs. K. Pubudu Nuwnthika Jayasena and Poddivila Marage Nimasha Ruwandi Madhunamali from Sabaragamuwa University of Sri Lanka, Sri Lanka, investigates how blockchain technology can be used in today's food supply chains to deliver greater traceability of assets.

Section 7, "Critical Issues and Challenges," presents coverage of academic and research perspectives on the challenges of using blockchain and the internet of things for various security applications across industries. Starting this section is "A Comprehensive Review of the Security and Privacy Issues in Blockchain Technologies" by Prof. N. Pradeep from Bapuji Institute of Engineering and Technology, India; Prof. Renjith V. Ravi of MEA Engineering College, India; Prof. Mangesh Manikrao Ghonge from Sandip Foundation's Institute of Technology and Research Centre, India; and Prof. Ramchandra Mangrulkar of Dwarkadas J. Sanghvi College of Engineering, India, which covers blockchain's security and privacy issues as well as the impact they've had on various trends and applications. The closing chapter, "Blockchain With IoT and AI: A Review of Agriculture and Healthcare," by Prof. Pushpa Singh from KIET Group of Institutions, Delhi-NCR, India and Prof. Narendra Singh of GL Bajaj Insitute of Management and Research, India, studies the literature, formulates the research question, and summarizes the contribution of blockchain application, particularly targeting AI and IoT in agriculture and healthcare sectors.

Although the primary organization of the contents in this multi-volume work is based on its seven sections, offering a progression of coverage of the important concepts, methodologies, technologies, applications, social issues, and emerging trends, the reader can also identify specific contents by utilizing the extensive indexing system listed at the end of each volume. As a comprehensive collection of research on the latest findings related to blockchain, the internet of things, and security, the *Research Anthology on Convergence of Blockchain, Internet of Things, and Security* provides business leaders and executives, IT managers, computer scientists, hospital administrators, security professionals, law enforcement, students and faculty of higher education, librarians, researchers, and academicians with a complete understanding of the applications and impacts of blockchain and the internet of things. Given the vast number of issues concerning usage, failure, success, strategies, and applications of blockchain and internet of things technologies, the *Research Anthology on Convergence of Blockchain, Internet of Things, and Security* encompasses the most pertinent research on the applications, impacts, uses, and development of blockchain and the internet of things.

Chapter 48
Securing IoT Applications Using Blockchain

Sreelakshmi K. K.

Department of Computer Science and Information Systems, Birla Institute of Technology and Science, Pilani, India

Ashutosh Bhatia

Department of Computer Science and Information Systems, Birla Institute of Technology and Science, Pilani, India

Ankit Agrawal

Department of Computer Science and Information Systems, Birla Institute of Technology and Science, Pilani, India

ABSTRACT

The internet of things (IoT) has become a guiding technology behind automation and smart computing. One of the major concerns with the IoT systems is the lack of privacy and security preserving schemes for controlling access and ensuring the security of the data. A majority of security issues arise because of the centralized architecture of IoT systems. Another concern is the lack of proper authentication and access control schemes to moderate access to information generated by the IoT devices. So the question that arises is how to ensure the identity of the equipment or the communicating node. The answer to secure operations in a trustless environment brings us to the decentralized solution of Blockchain. A lot of research has been going on in the area of convergence of IoT and Blockchain, and it has resulted in some remarkable progress in addressing some of the significant issues in the IoT arena. This work reviews the challenges and threats in the IoT environment and how integration with Blockchain can resolve some of them.

DOI: 10.4018/978-1-6684-7132-6.ch048

I. INTRODUCTION

The rapid advancements in networking technologies have led to an increased number of devices or things being able to connect to the Internet, which forms the Internet of Things, commonly known as IoT. Some of the leading IoT applications are Smart-grid, smart-homes, Industrial IoT, smart healthcare, etc. At a high-level, a typical IoT ecosystem consists of devices like sensors that collect data, actuators, and other devices that perform control and monitoring specific to the application area, communication infrastructure guided by the network protocols and local or centralized storage (cloud) that collects data from different devices and processes it for further analysis. The data generated by the various IoT devices is characterized by its vast volume, heterogeneity, and dynamic nature. Each device in an IoT environment has a unique identifier associated with it. A review work Colakovic and Hadialic (2018) gives a detailed and technical description of IoT and its enabling technologies. To build a sustainable IoT ecosystem that can adapt and perform well in a particular application area is a challenging task. With various smart solutions using a large number of devices, the problem of maintaining security for private or user data in the centralized cloud storage is a very tedious task that needs significant attention. The stakes are high if the private data falls into the hands of malicious entities. Another issue that draws concern is the resource and energy constraints of devices, which make it challenging to run massive cryptographic algorithms that strengthen the security of the data generated. The other challenges that need to be dealt with in specific situations such as a disaster are the fault tolerance and recovery of devices located at remote locations. Also, the diverseness in the IoT application areas and the uncertainty about the technology and the solutions offered creates a lack of trust in these solutions. Thus the need for a decentralized solution to ensure the security in an IoT ecosystem is an essential requirement of any IoT application.

The concept of Blockchain has been very active in cryptographic and security since its revelation in 2008. The remarkable advancements made in the Blockchain research have made cryptocurrencies a reality using BitCoin. The BitCoin with a current value of 5431.43 USD and holding around 5.7 million blocks is continuously increasing at a rapid rate with the help of more hashing power and mining pools. Software giants like Linux Foundation are already hacking the potential of Blockchain by researching on applications like HyperLedger (Blummer et al., 2018). With the Software industry predicting a promising future for the blockchain technology, it is essential that we investigate in detail the applicability of Blockchain in IoT to address the main security issues and how far it can be successful in solving them.

When Blockchain meets IoT, some of the expected benefits with this convergence are the building of trust between entities, completeness, consistency, and integrity of stored data, immutability or tamper-proof preservation of private data, reduction in expenses and thereby cheaper solutions, enhanced security and faster processing of Big Data.

The major objectives of the review work presented in this paper are:

- To investigate the security issues and challenges currently present in IoT applications.
- To highlight the decision criteria for applying Blockchain in IoT.
- To survey the scope of solutions that can be achieved through the convergence of Blockchain with IoT.
- To demarcate what IoT applications need and what distributed ledger technology (DLT) can offer.
- To present the state of the art in the integration of Blockchain with IoT.
- To identify and categorize IoT applications based on the issues addressed by Blockchain in the particular application area.

The rest of the paper is organized as follows: Section 2 discusses the security challenges in IoT, Section 3 presents the functioning of Blockchain, and Section 4 describes the need for using Blockchain in IoT. Section 5 discusses state of the art and the existing surveys and research that has gone in integrating Blockchain and IoT Blockchain; it analyses by taking some application domains of IoT where the application of Blockchain has succeeded in bringing trust and security among the different parties involved.

II. CHALLENGES AND SECURITY THREATS IN THE IOT ECOSYSTEM

Fig. 1 shows the primary security issues at different levels of IoT layered architecture. Safeguarding the device-level security of IoT objects is a cumbersome job considering the whole IoT assets and the possible vulnerabilities they hold. IoT applications should be developed, keeping in mind the design considerations such as storage space, computational power, physical security, communication bandwidth, cost, and latency. The total absence or the lack of regular firmware updates for the installed devices makes it easy for the attackers to exploit the weaknesses in them. The data generated by the devices can be leaked during transmission. The recently instigated Mirai botnet attack, which was one among the biggest distributed denial-of-service (DDoS) attacks in which malicious aggressors intruded into the network by manipulating IoT devices, which were poorly secured, emphasizes the need for strengthening the device-level security in the IoT domain (Fruhlinger, 2018). The low level of security and the high connectivity among the devices made it easy for the attackers to manipulate a few of the devices to obtain the data and make it dysfunctional. A malware named Mirai was installed in the IoT devices using network data from a "zombie network" through Telnet and elementary dictionary attack procedures. Those devices whose security was compromised became part of the botnet, which was then exploited to continue the DDoS attack.

To provide end-to-end host security at the transport layer, Transport Layer Security (TLS) and Datagram Transport Layer Security (DTLS) can be used, thus ensuring host anonymity. Nevertheless, the problem with solutions like TLS and VPNs is that it proves to be unsuitable for many applications because they are not scalable (Miraz,2019). The existing solutions suggest the usage of the Secure Socket Layer (SSL) protocol encrypts the user's data while relaying to the cloud storage. This can be used for ensuring secure communication between the devices and the cloud. At the application level, ensuring integrity becomes a significant problem as more and more data gets aggregated from different devices. However, in the IoT management level, as shown in Fig.1, while user-data resides in the cloud servers, there is a chance of it getting shared between or even sold to various companies, violating the user's rights for privacy and security and further driving public distrust. In most cases, the devices may require the end user's private data such as name, location, cell number, etc. or social media account information, which can expose a lot about the user to any malicious attacker who gets it. Thus, there is a lack of trust in the level of privacy offered by centralized infrastructures like a cloud. Ferrag et al. (2018) surveys a few privacy-preserving schemes and points out the technical flaws in them. The usage of privacy-aware ids during user-to-device and machine-to-machine communication is suggested in (Elrawy et al. 2018) for avoiding sensitive information tracking. Many researchers have proposed several security risk models and threat models for IoT. In Abdul-Ghani et al. (2018), IoT attacks have been systematically modeled, and the security goals have been analyzed. An attack taxonomy and the corresponding measures to tackle them have been listed. The attacks in the IoT environment have been broadly aligned as Physical-device based attacks, Protocol-based attacks, Data at rest-based attacks, and Application-based attacks.

Figure 1. Security Challenges at different levels of IoT layered architecture

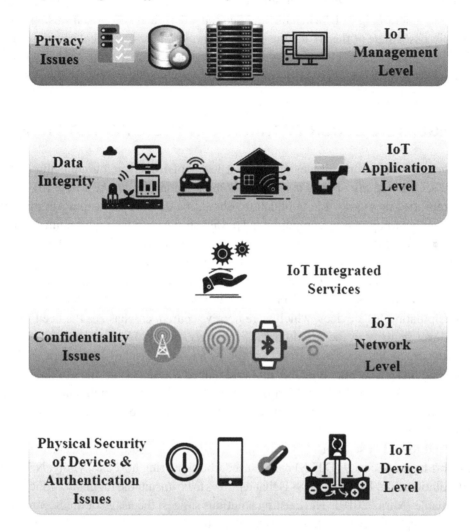

The work by Pongle and Chavan (2015) surveys the attacks on RPL and 6LoWPAN (IPv6 over Low-Power Wireless Personal Area Networks). In Kouicem et al. (2018), the authors have highlighted the significant challenges of deploying modern cryptographic mechanisms in different IoT applications as mobility, heterogeneity, resource constraints, lack of proper standardization, and scalability. In Elrawy et al. (2018), the authors have surveyed the intrusion detection systems (IDS) for IoT based systems. They claim that IDS can be a potential solution to reducing the network-level attacks on RPL (Routing Protocol for low power and lossy network). It has been shown that IDS can also reduce the chance of a DoS or DDoS attack that aims to disrupt the system by bombarding requests. Bassi et al. (2013) describes the trust factor as a fundamental quality of any IoT system, which depends mainly on the performance in M2M communications and the computational performance and interoperability of the IoT systems. A comprehensive solution to create a secure IoT environment should be an automatic data processing real-time platform that encompasses services like data encryption and authentication, thus promising data integrity, access control, privacy, and it should be scalable and less expensive. The ability to promptly detect and isolate the devices whose security has been compromised is a much-needed requirement to ensure device-level security in any IoT application. The emergence of Blockchain has paved the way for exploring its potential in providing some or all of these security services in the IoT system.

III. BLOCKCHAIN CONCEPTS

Although numerous papers have elaborated on the techniques and concepts of Blockchain and smart contracts, we must highlight the basics. Fernandez-Caramez and Fraga-Lamas (2018) gives a good description of the blockchain functioning.

A blockchain is a distributed ledger of immutable records that are managed in a peer to peer network. All the nodes in the network ensure the integrity and correctness of the Blockchain through consensus algorithms. This method of placing trust in a network of nodes strengthens the security of the Blockchain. Blockchains can be classified into public, private, or consortium based on whether the membership is permissioned or permissionless. In public blockchains, any user can become a member. There are no membership restrictions, and they are only pseudo-anonymous. Bitcoin and Ethereum are good examples of public blockchains. However, private blockchains are owned and operated by a company or organization, and any user who wants to join the network has to request for membership through the concerned people.

Thus there is only partial immutability offered. Private and consortium blockchains are faster in transaction processing compared to the public counterparts, due to the restricted number of members. Examples of some permissioned blockchains are HyperLedger (Fabric Blummer et al., 2018, Hyperledger, 2017) and R3 Corda (Brown et al., 2016). Some private blockchains impose read restrictions on the data within the blocks. Consortium blockchains are owned and operated by a group of organizations or a private community. Blockchain users use asymmetric key cryptography to sign on transactions. The trust factor maintenance within a distributed ledger technology (DLT), can be attributed to the consensus algorithms and the key desirable properties achieved thenceforth. Wüst and Gervais (2018) gives a good description of these properties. Some of them are Public Verifiability, Transparency, Integrity. The main terminologies in Blockchain are discussed below:

A.   Terminologies in Blockchain:

1.   *Blocks:* The transactions that occur in a peer-to-peer network associated with a blockchain are picked up from a pool of transactions and grouped in a block. Once a transaction has been validated, it cannot be reverted back. Transactions are pseudonymous as they are linked only to the user's public key and not to the real identity of the user. A block may contain several hundreds of transactions. The block-size limits the number of transactions that can be included in a block. Fig.2 shows the general structure of a block in a blockchain. A block consists of the version no., hash of the previous block, the Merkle root tree to trace the transactions in the block, hash of the current block, timestamp and nonce value. A blockchain starts with a genesis block.

2.   *Mining:* Mining is a process in which the designated nodes in the blockchain network called miners collect transactions from a pool of unprocessed transactions and combine them in a block. In mining, each miner competes to solve an equally difficult computational problem of finding a valid hash value with a particular no. of zeroes that is below a specific target. In Bitcoin mining, the number of

zeroes indicates the difficulty of the computation. Many nonce values are tried to arrive at the golden nonce that hashes to a valid hash with the current difficulty level. When a miner arrives at this nonce value, we can say that he has successfully mined a block. This block then gets updated to the chain.

3. ***Consensus:*** The consensus mechanism serves two main purposes, as given in Jesus et al. (2018): block validation and the most extensive chain selection. Proof-of-Work is the consensus algorithm used in Bitcoin Blockchain. The proof-of-stake algorithm is much faster than Proof-of-Work and demands less computational resources. The Ethereum blockchains use a pure proof-of-stake algorithm to ensure consensus. Besides Proof-of-Work, there are other consensus algorithms such as Proof of Byzantine Fault Tolerance (PBFT), proof- of activity, etc. Anwar(2018) presents a consolidated view of the different consensus algorithms. Proof-of-Work is a kind of a signature which indicates that the block has been mined after performing computation with the required difficulty level. This signature can be easily verified by the peers in the network to ensure a block's validity. The longest chain is always selected as the consistent one for appending the new block.

4. ***Smart Contracts:*** They are predefined rules deployed in the Blockchain network that two parties involved in a settlement must agree to priorly. Smart contracts were designed to avoid disagreement, denial, or violation of rules by the parties involved. They are triggered automatically in the Blockchain, on the occurrence of specific events mentioned in the rules.

Figure 2. Structure of a Block in a Blockchain

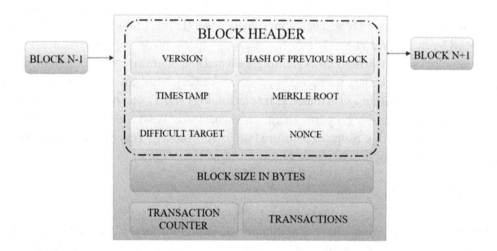

B.   Overall functioning:

Users connect to the Blockchain and initiate a transaction signed with their private key. This transaction is sent to a pool of transactions where it resides until it is fetched into a block by a miner. The miner then generates a new block after gathering transactions from the pool and computing the valid hash of the block. When a miner succeeds in generating a new block, the new block is broadcast to the nodes in the P2P network. All nodes in the network verify the block using a consensus algorithm, and upon successful validation, update it to their copy of the chain, and the transaction attains completion.

IV. WHY DO WE NEED BLOCKCHAIN IN IOT?

According to Agrawal et al. (2018), the major barricade in the decentralized environment of IoT is the lack of privacy and security of sensitive data that is transferred when connected devices communicate with each other or with the cloud. Data shared cannot be securely encrypted due to the lack of computational power and energy to run encryption algorithms. Thus ensuring data privacy and security is a requirement in any IoT application. The authors in Agrawal et al. (2018) have modeled a security solution using Smart Contracts and Blockchain to ensure continuously secured user-device communications in a smart city and smart home scenario. Using IoT hubs or edge nodes that enable the constrained device to connect to the Blockchain (Agrawal et al., 2018), thus mitigating the necessity to become full nodes, they have tackled the issue of resource and energy constraints. Also, in a distributed environment like blockchain possibility of detecting attacks and restraining further damage is easy since achieving consensus among peers is a necessary condition. Introducing Blockchain in IoT would eliminate the possibility of attacks like DDoS attack, device spoofing, impersonation, injecting malicious code, side-channel attacks, etc. Another reason is that the much-needed security services such as confidentiality, accountability, integrity, and availability come along when we use Blockchain to ensure trust in IoT data. M2M communication between IoT devices can be authenticated. Malicious nodes can be identified and isolated. Recently companies like Chronicle in San Francisco have started using blockchains in their pharmaceutical supply chain for delivering gene therapy drugs. Using a secure IoT platform, they can confirm the quality of drugs and ensure that they don't get damaged or go wrong while in transit. In Miraz (2019) the authors emphasize on the point, "Where IoT is often viewed as a convergence of operational technology (OT) and information technology (IT), Distributed Ledger Technology's (DLT) role as an enabler of the IoT lies in its ability to forge trust, not only at the product level but across an ecosystem of non-trusting constituents."

To determine whether Blockchain is essential in a particular IoT application domain, Ferrag et al. (2018) presents a flow diagram. The consolidated thoughts of it can be briefed as follows: If an IoT application requiring a decentralized security framework demands verification of records between multiple parties who do not trust each other nor a centralized third party and the documents need to be synchronized among these entities, then Blockchain can be applied to arrive at a presumed consensus. However, it should be noted that though the democratic blockchain platform can be used to limit the implications of attack by promoting easier detection, it cannot be taken as an ultimate solution to ensuring IoT security.

Blockchain should not be applied in IoT for merely performing transaction processing or as a substitute for a replicated database requirement. If a traditional database can solve the problem or if all participant trusts a centralized authority, then there's no need for Blockchain in such a scenario. Blockchain should not be used in applications where raw data needs to be gathered in real-time as these incur high latency overheads.

V. STATE OF THE ART AND EXISTING RESEARCH IN BLOCKCHAIN BASED IOT (BIOT)

Quite a lot of research papers have been written on the convergence of Blockchain with IoT. Blockchain technology, in its current form, cannot be directly absorbed into the IoT domain as most of the IoT applications operate in real-time, and the introduction of Blockchain increases latency, demands high computational power and bandwidth. However, some real implementations though at their nascent level Gundersen (2011) and Hanada et al. (2018) have shown results of a promising future that can be achieved through the convergence of the two technologies. Hence, research continues to delve deep into its use cases, such as the applicability of smart contracts to resolve the majority of the existing business matters like a violation or bypass of policies, forgery, frauds, etc. Many IoT applications may have the requirement of tracking and keeping the participating entities updated on the essential activities that occur in the system. A lot of discrepancies arise in business transactions while procuring products and services, e.g., selling counterfeit products or cheating a manufacturer by demanding payment before the completion of the required service, etc. These discrepancies can be taken care of using sensory data linked with smart contracts. With smart contracts, organizations can safely ascertain funds for current and future operations, the trust factor now being ensured. Bodkhe et al. (2020) survey various consensus algorithms and their applicability in a Cyber-physical system. They also address the challenges and security issues in various CPS application domains.

Dai et al. (2019) discuss the main opportunities that arise in the IoT ecosystem when it is converged with Blockchain, namely: Enhanced interoperability, improved security, traceability, and reliability of IoT data, Autonomic interactions of entities in IoT system. It also describes the architecture of Blockchain of things consisting of data sublayer, network sublayer, consensus sublayer, incentive sublayer, and service sublayer. Makhdoom et al. (2019) discuss methods, like Sharding to reduce transaction processing time, to overcome the challenges associated with the integration of Blockchain and IoT.

Hang and Kim (2019) introduce an IoT platform to assure data integrity of data sensed by IoT devices. It uses HyperLedger Fabric along with a proof of consensus method to achieve consensus. The solution is appropriate to be used in a resource-constrained environment. Rejeb et al. (2019) highlight the emerging research areas that arise with the integration of IoT with Blockchain as Scalability, Security, Immutability, and Auditing, Effectiveness and Efficiency of Information flows, Traceability and Interoperability and Quality

Maroufi et al. (2019) discuss the main challenges in blockchain and IoT integration. Its introduction helps to build a decentralized, scalable, secure, immutable ledger. The heterogeneity of IoT solutions is one of the main challenges involved with the convergence of the two technologies. Panarello et al. (2018) categorize the utility of Blockchain in smart environments into two: Device manipulation and data manipulation. Data manipulation uses Blockchain as a history keeping system, and device manipulation uses smart contracts to make autonomous decisions based on business logic.

Atlam et al. (2018) describe the comparison between Blockchain and IoT and elaborates on the benefits such as publicity, decentralization, resiliency, security, speed, cost minimization, immutability, and anonymity, of converging the two technologies. Yu et al. (2018) discuss various application domains for the integration of IoT and Blockchain and the main security challenges it solves in an IoT ecosystem. It also gives a view of the Blockchain and IoT integrated framework addressing each layer in the IoT architecture in detail.

Minoli and Occhiogrosso (2018) categorize the different frameworks for IoT blockchain integration into categories such as end-to-end blockchains, Analytics/storage-level, Gateway-level, Site-level, and Device level. A fast payment system for Blockchain backed edge IoT systems is proposed, which ensures security and reliability (Hao et al., 2018). The different phases of the protocol, such as Prepare Phase, Deposit Phase, Fast Payment Phase, Transfer Phase, are described. To prevent double spending problem, a Broker is designated with a pool of deposits. The Broker is responsible for The system ensures security and punishes Brokers. In case they violate the rules of the system.

Figure 3. Relationship between offerings of blockchain and security requirements

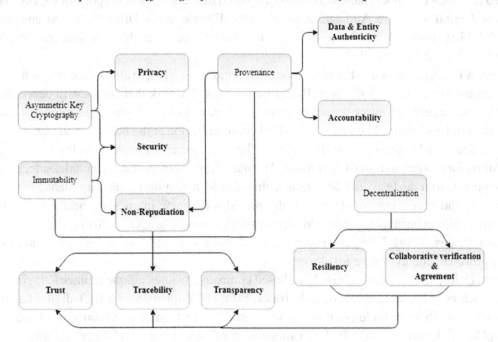

The potential of Blockchain to resolve problems in ensuring trust in the clinical trials in the healthcare industry has been discussed in many papers. Blockchain can not only provide automatized solutions but also establish trust among the different stakeholders such as patients, drug dealers, hospitals, and lab staff and also protect data privacy. According to Benchoufi and Ravaud (2017), Blockchain enables the patients to ensure trust in their private data through access control policies. A proof-of-concept methodology for collecting consent from the concerned people is explained in this context to enable differential privacy. Some of the companies that are currently working on converging the technologies of Blockchain and IoT are:

- Robonomics (Lonshakov et al., 2018): Robonomics platform implements DApp for smart cities and industries
- IoTeX (Dagher and Adhikari, 2018): It is an IoT-oriented blockchain platform that provides application-specific services such as scalability, isolating nodes, deploying applications.
- IoT Chain (Alphand et al.,2018): Uses a lite OS, the Practical Byzantine Fault Tolerance (PBFT), and CPS technology.
- Filament (2018) a startup that's working towards the goal of building a smart economy has their Blockchain solution kit that consists of hardware and software technologies which can be integrated into edge nodes and IoT devices to ensure a secure transaction execution environment (TEE) through Ethereum or HyperLedger blockchains. A hardware plug and play device has been built to enable tracking of events in autonomous vehicles such as vehicle tracking, charging, and making M2M payments. The main functional aspects associated with it are: assigning secret identities to IoT devices, hardware acceleration to reduce computational latency, manage M2M transactions, built-in quality assessment and compliance audit system and key management systems

used to connect to Blockchain and obtain Carbon credits, encryption support for ECDSA (Elliptic curve Digital Signature Authentication), ECDH (Elliptic curve Diffie Hellman) and SHA-256 with HMAC option. With this technology, IoT devices can securely communicate valid attested data, which can be verified.

- Xage: A California based cyber-security startup founded in 2016, exploits Blockchain for connecting industrial machines from oil-wells to smart meters. The perk that comes with decentralization is that the security of every device connected will have to be compromised to obtain control of the data in Blockchain. The security of M2M communication at the network and transport layer is secured as they happen over the Blockchain. The Xage Security Fabric provides a comprehensive solution for modern industrial operations. The main features of the fabric include: safeguarding all equipment from the latest IoT devices to vulnerable legacy systems, identity management, single sign-on, and access control. The company provides two new innovative mechanisms to ensure security: hierarchical tree system and super-majority consensus (Xage, 2019).
- Grid+ (Daley, 2019): Using the Ethereum blockchain, it grants consumers permission to access low powered, energy-saving IoT devices.
- Hypr (Daley, 2019): Being a New York-based company, it stores unique biometric login information such as palm, face, eye, a voice in Blockchain, and implemented a DLT digital key to allow homeowners to have single-point access to smart doors and smart entertainment centers.
- ShipChain (Lawrence, 2020): The Company combines a ship and trace platform based on Blockchain with information from near field communication (NFC) tags that observes and shares the temperature of goods throughout the supply chain, thus providing visibility and trust between producers, transporters, and consumers.
- Chronicled (Daley, 2019): The San Francisco based Company focuses on tracing and managing the supply chain for pharmaceuticals and food supply using Blockchain. It uses IoT enabled shipping containers and sensors for this.
- Netobjex (Daley, 2019): The Company created a standard mechanism for M2M communication for IoT devices. It uses IoToken to enable customers in a restaurant to pay their bill, and in drone delivery, it marks the point of delivery and the transaction for payment.
- Some of the companies like BIMCHAIN, Briq, ULedger, Hunter Roberts OEG & Gartner Builders, Probuild, Tata Steel, Lifechain by Costain are working towards the integration of Blockchain & IoT in the construction sector to improve verification of identities and keep track of the progress of their work (Mazhanda, 2019).
- Eight companies namely, Cisco, Asterix, Radiflow, Xage Security, Sumo Logic, BlackRidge Technology, TDi Technologies, Spherical Analytics, have been selected by the National Cybersecurity Center of Excellence (NCCoE) for working towards securing Industrial Internet of Things (IIoT). The main reasons for introducing Blockchain in IIoT is to secure M2M communication, authenticating, and authorizing a transaction.

Ellervee et al. (2017) presents a good comparison of some blockchains and describes the scope of Blockchain, clearly defining what Blockchain can do and what it cannot. Users and block validators or miners represent the actors in the Blockchain. It also describes the processes that occur in the system like network discovery, creating transactions, signing, issuing assets, mining, and assigning permissions, platforms (permissioned or permissionless), and data models. Fig. 3 represents the outline of how we can manipulate Blockchain to ensure security. The figure helps in understanding the relationship between offerings such as immutability, provenance, etc. and which aspect is needed to satisfy the specific security requirements in user applications.

In the following, we present some use-cases, that provide an overview of how Blockchain can be integrated into IoT. We have classified them based on the functional aspects of Blockchain that they utilize and present a sample system model wherever necessary. Some general issues, such as usage of Blockchain for authorization, access control, device identification, data security, secure M2M communication, have been mentioned in various research papers. However, their practical implementation is still in question. Hence these use cases are not discussed in detail.

A. Blockchain to ensure Privacy, Security, Non-Repudiation and Identification and Isolation of malicious nodes

Generally speaking, privacy is a primary concern in any IoT application. Here, we present some major IoT applications where the loss of confidentiality can result in catastrophes and describe how Blockchain can help in avoiding it. We have highlighted the lack of privacy in IoT and described its reasons in detail in Section II.

1) *Intelligent Transport System:* In an intelligent transport system (ITS), we have vehicles communicating with one another to exchange safety messages and navigation information in real-time such as road conditions, navigation information, traffic jams, accident cases, etc. When vehicles communicate with one another, they share information such as location and user's personal information to identify each other. Hence privacy-preserving schemes are required to protect such sensitive data. Similarly, messages circulated in the network can also be forged. To avoid this and improve trusted communication in VANETs, we look into the applicability of Blockchain in ITS and to what extent it succeeds in solving the problem of Privacy, Security, and Trust.

   System Model: The system model has been explained pertaining to the framework mentioned in Singh and Kim (2017). Here the actors are the vehicles. In this work, Blockchain has been put to use in a vehicular network of autonomous vehicles as a secure data-sharing framework. Here the distrust is between vehicles spreading the information and vehicles receiving this information and using it to perform actions such as taking a lane diversion. Certain vehicles have been designated as Miner nodes based on their willingness to contribute to the network. Consensus achieved in Blockchain helps to ensure trust in the navigation message disseminated and to decide which autonomous vehicle can cross an intersection. The framework implemented has negligible latency associated with it.

Other use-cases of Blockchain in ITS is for vehicle leasing, parts provenance, vehicle tax payment, ride-sharing, performing automatic payments at parking areas and fuel station, or charging station in case of electric vehicles.

The works in Li et al. (2018), Singh and Kim (2017) and Huang et al. (2018) present different methodologies by which Blockchain has been used in VANETS and intelligent transport systems for secure communication and transaction processing. In Singh and Kim (2017), the issues identified in smart vehicle communication are lack of trust, reliability, and data privacy. The authors have introduced a unique identifier called Intelligent Trust Point (IV-TP) similar to a Bitcoin id to ensure privacy in inter-vehicular communication. They have also brought out a proof of driving consensus protocol to maintain consensus. In Yuan and Wang (2016), the authors have elaborated on the design of a blockchain-based framework for ITS. They have presented a seven-layer conceptual model and considered the integration of Blockchain with ITS for creating a parallel transportation management systems (PTMS). A ride-sharing Dapp called La'zooz has also been exemplified. The authors of Lu et al. (2018) investigate the privacy-preserving schemes that can be applied in VANETs to ensure trust and anonymity. They have validated the entity-centric model, which is based on a reputation mechanism to judge the trustworthiness of a vehicle and data-centric model in which trust in the message propagated is computed through various metrics. Finally, they have used a protocol that places faith in a message using a mixture of these two techniques. They have formulated a proof of presence to arrive at a consensus. However, the model proposed by them assumes that the road-side units have adequate computing power. Hanada et al. (2018) studies a decentralized application (DApp) using Blockchain and smart contracts for automatic gasoline purchases in a smart transport system.

Table 1. Solutions Offered by Blockchain in Various Applications in IoT

Sl No.	IoT Application Domains	What Blockchain Offers								
		Identification & Isolation Of Malicious Nodes	Provenance	Security	Privacy	Traceability	Trust	Transparency	Non-Repudiation	Accountability
1	Smart city	✓	✓	✓			✓	✓		
2	Smart Grid		✓			✓	✓	✓	✓	✓
3	Smart Healthcare		✓	✓	✓	✓	✓	✓	✓	✓
4	Supply chain management		✓	✓		✓	✓	✓	✓	✓
5	Intelligent Transport Systems	✓	✓	✓	✓		✓	✓	✓	✓
6	Smart homes & Buildings	✓	✓		✓		✓		✓	
7	Industrial IoT & Smart Manufacturing		✓				✓		✓	

They have used smart contracts to counter the problems that affect the aspects of trust and transparency in the services provided by IoT applications.

For making this clearer, let's take the example of a fuel station that delivers its services based on smart contracts and IoT. Consider an interface between the fuel pump and the customer's car. The entities involved in the IoT ecosystem are the sensors that sense the level of fuel in the car and the fuel pump that stops when the fuel is filled. A DApp developed for

performing transactions between the IoT nodes can be deployed on the car kit and the fuel pump. The fuel station can then verify payment deposited, and based on this, it can circulate the fuel consumption details to a smart contract. A list of fuel stations based on the user's current location can be checked in the DApp for filling gas.

In Li et al. (2018), CreditCoin, a privacy-preserving incentive announcement network based on Blockchain, has been proposed to report traffic issues and accidents using VANETS. It includes two components: the announcement protocol and incentive mechanism. In this system, the users who complete successful missions are rewarded with credit coins, which actively allows consistent traffic incidents to be reported and verified.

Hîrţan et al. (2020) propose a reputation system that focuses on preserving the privacy of users in an Intelligent Transport System in the cities of San Francisco, Beijing, and Rome. It introduces a consensus mechanism for traffic data sharing, that uses the reputation of the node and the validated answer received from each node in the cluster to achieve consensus in a system of unreliable nodes.

The introduction of Blockchain in ITS helps tackle the privacy concern by introducing anonymity and dynamic heterogeneous key management schemes for ensuring the security of messages in transit.

2) **Smart Homes and Smart Buildings:**

System Model: A typical home network in smart homes of the future, consists of smart doors and gates, smart lights, smart walls, wearable devices, smart ventilation system, smart home appliances such as refrigerator, AC, Washing machine, etc., smart gardening system, smart surveillance and intrusion detection system (IDS), smart garage, smart washrooms and toilets, smart baby and old people tracker and smart whatnot. These devices communicate with each other and with the user to enhance comforts and living experience. Normally, a smart device in a home network may have shared users, and to personalize the experience, it may be configured with the user profile of its current user, and this data may be shared with other devices for understanding user's choices. However, this collaborative data collection and decision making in the home network comes at the cost of compromising privacy. Hence we use Blockchain to secure the communication between IoT devices. The data in the block consists of the data exchanged between devices, transaction information in case devices perform transactions with the outside world.

The private details of a user can be manipulated by attackers who hack into these devices to perform malicious activities. The stakes are high, including detecting the presence of people at home. Apart from this dangerous compromise in privacy, we

also need to take care of the security of devices as they relay information about the location of the smart home for various application purposes. Ensuring device security is another major challenge in a smart home ecosystem. Most vendors do not provide regular security updates for the firmware in smart devices, which leaves vulnerabilities. Hence it is necessary to confirm the security of the connected network of devices installed in a smart home be firmly ascertained. Even more critical is ensuring the security and privacy of devices in smart buildings where numerous employees work.

For this, Dorri et al. (2017) have proposed a scheme using shared keys with a particular lifetime to allow only trusted devices to communicate in a smart home network. Each device in the home network is registered with a home miner. The smart homes are connected to an overlay that enables provide hierarchical and distributed processing. Leiding et al. (2016) presents an access control mechanism that can be applied to Blockchain-based home networks where Security access managers (SAM) are used to identify malicious nodes and prevent them from generating any further transactions in the network. This strategy can be very useful to enable device-level trusted interoperability in smart homes and smart buildings and also in other use-case scenarios such as ITS, in general. Zhou et al. (2018) and Bastos et al. (2018), the authors have used smart contracts and Blockchain to bring about a secure solution for securing communication in a home network.

3) Smart Healthcare:

System Model: When we talk about smart healthcare, it is characterized by the vast volume of data from heterogeneous sources varying from wearable devices that track the personal health status of the user to the Doctor's diagnosis and evaluation data and prescriptions. Electronic Health Records are used to integrate and store all this data in digital form. However, since patients may visit different hospitals for different types of diseases and treatments, this data gets fragmented and inconsistent. If we use a central database to store and access this data, it invites security and privacy problems as the data may be accessed or modified by unauthorized parties. Many such cases are stated in papers where the patient data is sold to people in return for money and personal benefits. Hence there's a need for controlling access to such important information to ensure that patients receive proper healthcare services.

Numerous techniques have been proposed on Blockchain to promote a trusted medical data-sharing platform. Most solutions define a publisher-subscriber or patient-requester relationship between the communicating entities involved (Rifi et al., 2018, Shen et al., 2019). In Rifi et al. (2018), the author have proposed and implemented a method using edge servers to overcome the computational power constraint in a smart healthcare data collection network. They have defined the main actors in their network as publishers who are the patients whose health is monitored using sensors and subscribers who require the publisher's data to perform health monitoring and diagnosis. The subscribers who can have access to the health data are added by the publisher to their corresponding address. Thus only subscribers authorized by the publisher gain access to the health data. The patients are monitored within the premises of their smart home. The smart home has a local gateway that connects to an edge server for performing computationally intensive tasks. Using three types of smart contracts, namely: Publisher contract, client contract, and subscriber contract, they have defined the terms and permissions of each actor in the system. For ensuring privacy, the subscriber id and publisher id are verified. In MedChain, a Blockchain-based health data sharing system that uses session keys to safeguard the privacy is introduced (Rifi et al., 2018). In this, a healthcare provider collects data from the sensor devices and performs the mining process. Sessions are used to grant access to the requester of the data.

Ray et al. (2020) discuss Blockchain use cases in healthcare like accessing medical records, EHR claim and bill assessment, Clinical Research, Drug Supply Chain Management, IoBHealth, a dataflow architecture bringing together Blockchain and IoT is proposed, for accessing, storing and managing e-healthcare (EHR) data. Uddin et al. (2020) propose a three-layer architecture for leveraging Blockchain in eHealth services consisting of Sensing Layer, Edge processing layer, Cloud layer. A patient agent (PA) software implements a lightweight blockchain consensus mechanism and uses a task offloading algorithm for preserving privacy.

4) Smart Manufacturing and Industrial IoT:

System Model: The evolution of Industrial IoT (IIoT) and smart cognitive and autonomous robots, augmented reality technologies in the manufacturing sector has led to the emergence of the 4th Industrial revolution. This has created a huge impact on the manufacturing sector. Smart factories are becoming a reality with companies like Ubirch bringing automatization through smart strategies like a machine as a service, predictive maintenance, and verification of the condition of manufactured products. Smart devices aid manufacturing in design, manufacture maintenance, and supply of products. With IoT, the factory can be transformed into an ecosystem where everything is connected, well-monitored, secured and monetized. The advantages of this connected environment are: the quality of products can be ensured, and machines and services can be shared. In this shared, connected ecosystem, when machines engage in M2M communication, trust, security, and privacy become at stake. Hackers can target the surveillance or the machines for disrupting the factory operations.

Blockchain can be used to perform trusted communication and ensure privacy and security in the transactions performed in distributed manufacturing. Xu et al. (2019) and Liu et al. (2019) describe the security frameworks developed using Blockchain for IIoT. In Xu et al. (2019), a Blockchain-based Service Scheme is presented. A non-repudiation scheme is proposed, which works based on a homomorphic hash function to ensure whether a particular service promised is delivered or not. In Wan et al. (2019), presented a Blockchain-based security framework for ensuring privacy and security in a smart factory. They have given a layered division to the framework as the Sensing layer, Firmware layer, Management hub layer, Storage layer, and application layer. They have used a blacklist- whitelist mechanism to track and isolate malicious nodes and ensure privacy. They have shown how a lightweight private blockchain can be used to trace the operations of machines and M2M communications. They have combined two models: Bell-La Padula (BLP) model and Biba model to build the data security model using a dynamic identity verification mechanism.

B. Blockchain for Provenance, Accountability, Traceability, and Transparency

1) *Blockchain for Smart Grid:* Blockchains are used in Smart-Grid networks for secure trading of sustainable energy. The evolution of micro-grids and smart-grids have enabled small-scale production and selling of power. Provenance and accountability are the guiding factors that need to be brought into the transactions in the energy-trade microgrid network for efficient interoperability. *System Model:* The working of a smart-grid network in a city can be explained like this. Excess renewable energy such as solar energy or wind energy produced at homes can be stored in batteries, which can later be sold to other homes in the neighborhood or companies. A smart-meter installed keeps track of the energy units produced or consumed in real-time and relays this information to the energy distributor for monitoring and billing. With smart-grids becoming a reality, there is a need for a secure energy-trading platform to establish trust and track transactions that occur in the smart grid network.

The state of the art of applying Blockchain to micro-grids and smart-grids brings us to the Brooklyn Micro-grid solutions offered by LO3 Energy (Gundersen, 2011). The smart-contracts linked to the local grid are used to tokenize the extra energy and decide where to buy the electric power from. The energy sharing market consists of four main concepts: Tokenization, P2P Markets, Prosumers, and Community Micro-grids, and Energy-service Companies (CMESC). Tokenization involves converting surplus energy to energy credits. The P2P markets are a network of nodes established in the smart-grid between neighbors and prosumers to energy-producing companies. Prosumers are called so because of the dual role they play as producers and consumers in the energy trading system. In Pieroni et al. (2018), Blockchain is applied for securing communication, transactions, and tokenization of energy. A Smart energy blockchain application prototype has been implemented in the work that connects to the Blockchain in the P2P network. Li et al. (2017) has given a good demonstration of the smart-grid detailing the entities involved as Smart meters, energy nodes, and energy aggregators. Using a consortium blockchain, a unified blockchain for the energy credits transferred has been presented, which can be deployed in the Industrial IoT ecosystem. This enables the user to trace their transaction history and transact with trusted prosumers or companies efficiently. Daghmehchi Firoozjaei et al.(2020) propose a privacy-preserving hybrid blockchain framework called Hy-Bridge, which uses subnetworks that preserve the privacy of IoT users in a microgrid. It separates transactions of the power grid from those of the micro grid. It has three layers IoT user layer, platform layer, and enterprise layer.

2) ***Smart Cities:*** A waste management system for a future smart city is presented in Lamichhane et al. (2017), which is characterized by smart garbage bins(SGB) involving the sensors that detect and alerts the garbage collection service when the bin is full, actuators and smart locks to lock the SGBs. The different entities involved in the system are citizens, Municipality, Waste management operators who dispatch driverless vehicles that perform garbage collection, recyclers who recycle the waste to obtain rewards. Blockchain can be used to record operations and trace the transactions associated with garbage collection and recycling. In Nagothu et al. (2018), collaborative smart surveillance has been presented which uses access control rules specified in the smart contracts to restrict access of unauthorized nodes at fog level to connect to a cloud node containing Blockchain that stores surveillance data in various places in a smart city. In Nikouei et al. (2018), the authors have proposed an authentication scheme integrated into the Blockchain is used to share and aggregate the surveillance data in two trustless domains at the edge and fog level.

3) Smart Supply Chain Management:
System Model: A smart supply chain consists of smart objects which have a unique identity and are connected through wireless technologies. They can store information about their conditions like temperature, humidity, etc. and communicate to the Internet through wireless technologies. Then there are suppliers, distributors, transportation services, and consumers. In a conventional supply chain environment, the condition of the products is not traced at each checkpoint. Hence huge loss is encountered by the buyers. Sometimes products transported get tampered or replaced. Thus to ensure the security of manufactured products throughout the supply chain, we need an automated decentralized system that helps to track and assess the quality of product real-time.

Blockchain has been employed in a food supply chain system to overcome this problem. In Lin et al. (2018), Blockchain-based food traceability is proposed. This system enables to ensure food safety by tracking the food product and storing its condition at each stage. Through smart contracts which it establishes between buyer and seller, it provides a transparent system to the buyer, which allows them to verify and ensure the quality of the food they buy. Blockchain and IoT sensors together provide both parties provenance, traceability, trust, and transparency. Through this system, the seller can also identify at which stage in the supply chain the product suffered damage so that they can take remedial methods to avoid the same in the future. They can also determine whether the product has been tampered by scanning the RFID and tracing the sensor values collected, which are stored as metadata in the blocks. Table I summarizes the most relevant security services offered by Blockchain in each IoT application discussed so far.

VI. FUTURE WORK

The applications discussed in the previous section, depict a bright future for the convergence of Blockchain and IoT. However, the inclusion of Blockchain always introduces the probability of a 51% vulnerability. The papers surveyed predict this as far from the possible case. Lightweight algorithms being researched extensively might help in tackling energy and power constraints in IoT environments. However, there's a need for developing a unified blockchain framework for IoT applications. Also, though many initial research works claim that Blockchain is impregnable, there have been many incidents of breach of security of Blockchain like key tampering attacks, Sybil attack, etc. which have been elaborated in (Ferrag et al. 2018). Since the Blockchain in its current form cannot guarantee ultimate security, research needs to focus on identification and resolution of flaws so that developers can build more successful secure versions of Blockchain, which, when integrated with IoT, can provide a secure and safe environment for the application users.

VII. CONCLUSIONS

The IoT applications face a lot of challenges in terms of security, which can be solved using Blockchain. We have iscussed the major security issues in IoT and exemplified how the application of Blockchain can help in addressing these issues. Many research texts that were surveyed have applied Blockchain to IoT applications without actually ensuring whether it is necessary. Careful assessment needs to be done before applying Blockchain for a particular application. We have analyzed the need for using Blockchain in a particular application area. We have presented the decision criteria and mentioned where it can be used and what offerings it can provide and what it cannot. Also, we have explained a general system model and supportive use cases that can help in the integration and development of Blockchain-based secure IoT solutions.

REFERENCES

Abdul-Ghani, H. A., Konstantas, D., & Mahyoub, M. (2018). A comprehensive IoT attacks survey based on a building-blocked reference model. *International Journal of Advanced Computer Science and Applications*, 355-373.

Agrawal, R., Verma, P., Sonanis, R., Goel, U., De, A., Kondaveeti, S. A., & Shekhar, S. (2018, April). Continuous security in IoT using blockchain. In *2018 IEEE International Conference on Acoustics, Speech and Signal Processing (ICASSP)* (pp. 6423-6427). IEEE. 10.1109/ICASSP.2018.8462513

Alphand, O., Amoretti, M., Claeys, T., Dall'Asta, S., Duda, A., Ferrari, G., . . . Zanichelli, F. (2018, April). IoTChain: A blockchain security architecture for the Internet of Things. In 2018 IEEE Wireless Communications and Networking Conference (WCNC) (pp. 1-6). IEEE. doi:10.1109/WCNC.2018.8377385

Anchor, B. I. S. T. (2019). Taraxa White Paper.

Anwar, H. (2018). *Consensus Algorithms: The Root Of The Blockchain Technology*. Retrieved from https://101blockchains.com/consensus-algorithms-blockchain

Atlam, H. F., Alenezi, A., Alassafi, M. O., & Wills, G. (2018). Blockchain with Internet of Things: Benefits, challenges, and future directions. *International Journal of Intelligent Systems and Applications*, *10*(6), 40–48. doi:10.5815/ijisa.2018.06.05

Bassi, A., Bauer, M., Fiedler, M., & Kranenburg, R. V. (2013). *Enabling things to talk*. Springer-Verlag GmbH. doi:10.1007/978-3-642-40403-0

Bastos, D., Shackleton, M., & El-Moussa, F. (2018). *Internet of Things: A survey of technologies and security risks in smart home and city environments*. Academic Press.

Benchoufi, M., & Ravaud, P. (2017). Blockchain technology for improving clinical research quality. *Trials*, *18*(1), 335. doi:10.118613063-017-2035-z PMID:28724395

Bodkhe, U., Mehta, D., Tanwar, S., Bhattacharya, P., Singh, P. K., & Hong, W. C. (2020). A Survey on Decentralized Consensus Mechanisms for Cyber Physical Systems. *IEEE Access: Practical Innovations, Open Solutions*, *8*, 54371–54401. doi:10.1109/ACCESS.2020.2981415

Brown, R. G., Carlyle, J., Grigg, I., & Hearn, M. (2016). Corda: an introduction. *R3 CEV, 1*, 15.

Čolaković, A., & Hadžialić, M. (2018). Internet of Things (IoT): A review of enabling technologies, challenges, and open research issues. *Computer Networks*, *144*, 17–39. doi:10.1016/j.comnet.2018.07.017

Dagher, T. G. G., & Adhikari, C. L. (2018). *Iotex: A decentralized network for internet of things powered by a privacy-centric blockchain*. White Paper: https://whitepaper. io/document/131/iotexwhitepaper

Daghmehchi Firoozjaei, M., Ghorbani, A., Kim, H., & Song, J. (2020). Hy-Bridge: A hybrid blockchain for privacy-preserving and trustful energy transactions in Internet-of-Things platforms. *Sensors (Basel)*, *20*(3), 928. doi:10.339020030928 PMID:32050570

Dai, H. N., Zheng, Z., & Zhang, Y. (2019). Blockchain for internet of things: A survey. *IEEE Internet of Things Journal*, *6*(5), 8076–8094. doi:10.1109/JIOT.2019.2920987

Daley, S. (2019). *Blockchain and IoT: 8 examples making our future smarter*. Retrieved from https:// builtin.com/blockchain/blockchain-iot-examples

Dorri, A., Kanhere, S. S., Jurdak, R., & Gauravaram, P. (2017, March). *Blockchain for IoT security and privacy: The case study of a smart home. In 2017 IEEE international conference on pervasive computing and communications workshops (PerCom workshops)*. IEEE.

Ellervee, A., Matulevicius, R., & Mayer, N. (2017). A Comprehensive Reference Model for Blockchain-based Distributed Ledger Technology. In *ER Forum/Demos* (pp. 306-319). Academic Press.

Elrawy, M. F., Awad, A. I., & Hamed, H. F. (2018). Intrusion detection systems for IoT-based smart environments: A survey. *Journal of Cloud Computing*, *7*(1), 21. doi:10.118613677-018-0123-6

Fernández-Caramés, T. M., & Fraga-Lamas, P. (2018). A Review on the Use of Blockchain for the Internet of Things. *IEEE Access: Practical Innovations, Open Solutions*, *6*, 32979–33001. doi:10.1109/ACCESS.2018.2842685

Ferrag, M. A., Derdour, M., Mukherjee, M., Derhab, A., Maglaras, L., & Janicke, H. (2018). Blockchain technologies for the internet of things: Research issues and challenges. *IEEE Internet of Things Journal*, *6*(2), 2188–2204. doi:10.1109/JIOT.2018.2882794

Filament. (2018). *Blocklet USB Enclave Data Sheet*. Academic Press.

Fruhlinger, J. (2018). *The Mirai botnet explained: How teen scammers and CCTV cameras almost brought down the internet*. Retrieved from https://www.csoonline.com/article/3258748/the-mirai-botnet-explained-how-teen-scammers-and-cctv-cameras-almost-brought-down-the-internet.html

GSMAs Internet of Things Programme. (2018). *Opportunities and Use Cases for Distributed Ledger Technologies in IoT*. Academic Press.

Gundersen, T. (2011). *An introduction to the concept of exergy and energy quality*. Department of Energy and Process Engineering Norwegian University of Science and Technology, Version, 4.

Hanada, Y., Hsiao, L., & Levis, P. (2018, November). Smart contracts for machine-to-machine communication: Possibilities and limitations. In *2018 IEEE International Conference on Internet of Things and Intelligence System (IOTAIS)* (pp. 130-136). IEEE. 10.1109/IOTAIS.2018.8600854

Hang, L., & Kim, D. H. (2019). Design and implementation of an integrated IoT blockchain platform for sensing data integrity. *Sensors (Basel)*, *19*(10), 2228. doi:10.339019102228 PMID:31091799

Hao, Z., Ji, R., & Li, Q. (2018, October). FastPay: A Secure Fast Payment Method for Edge-IoT Platforms using Blockchain. In *2018 IEEE/ACM Symposium on Edge Computing (SEC)* (pp. 410-415). IEEE. 10.1109/SEC.2018.00055

Hîrţan, L. A., Dobre, C., & González-Vélez, H. (2020). Blockchain-based reputation for intelligent transportation systems. *Sensors (Basel)*, *20*(3), 791. doi:10.339020030791 PMID:32023997

Huang, X., Xu, C., Wang, P., & Liu, H. (2018). LNSC: A security model for electric vehicle and charging pile management based on blockchain ecosystem. *IEEE Access: Practical Innovations, Open Solutions*, *6*, 13565–13574. doi:10.1109/ACCESS.2018.2812176

Hyperledger Architecture Working Group. (2017). *Hyperledger Architecture* (Vol. 1). Introduction to Hyperledger Business Blockchain Design Philosophy and Consensus.

Jesus, E. F., Chicarino, V. R., de Albuquerque, C. V., & Rocha, A. A. D. A. (2018). A survey of how to use blockchain to secure internet of things and the stalker attack. *Security and Communication Networks*, *2018*, 2018. doi:10.1155/2018/9675050

Kouicem, D. E., Bouabdallah, A., & Lakhlef, H. (2018). Internet of things security: A top-down survey. *Computer Networks*, *141*, 199–221. doi:10.1016/j.comnet.2018.03.012

Lamichhane, Sadov, & Zaslavsky. (2017). *Smart Waste Management: An IoT and Blockchain based approach*. Academic Press.

Lawrence, C. (2020). *The Convergence of IoT and Blockchain is Transforming Industries*. Retrieved from https://www.codemotion.com/magazine/dev-hub/blockchain-dev/blockchain-and-iot-in-industry-use-cases/

Leiding, B., Memarmoshrefi, P., & Hogrefe, D. (2016, September). Self-managed and blockchain-based vehicular ad-hoc networks. In *Proceedings of the 2016 ACM International Joint Conference on Pervasive and Ubiquitous Computing: Adjunct* (pp. 137-140). ACM.

Li, L., Liu, J., Cheng, L., Qiu, S., Wang, W., Zhang, X., & Zhang, Z. (2018). Creditcoin: A privacy-preserving blockchain-based incentive announcement network for communications of smart vehicles. *IEEE Transactions on Intelligent Transportation Systems*, *19*(7), 2204–2220. doi:10.1109/TITS.2017.2777990

Li, Z., Kang, J., Yu, R., Ye, D., Deng, Q., & Zhang, Y. (2017). Consortium blockchain for secure energy trading in industrial internet of things. *IEEE Transactions on Industrial Informatics*, *14*(8), 3690–3700. doi:10.1109/TII.2017.2786307

Lin, J., Shen, Z., Zhang, A., & Chai, Y. (2018). Blockchain and IoT based Food Traceability System. *International Journal of Information Technology*, *24*(1), 1–16.

Liu, D., Alahmadi, A., Ni, J., Lin, X., & Shen, X. (2019). Anonymous reputation system for iiot-enabled retail marketing atop pos blockchain. *IEEE Transactions on Industrial Informatics*, *15*(6), 3527–3537. doi:10.1109/TII.2019.2898900

Lonshakov, S., Krupenkin, A., Kapitonov, A., Radchenko, E., Khassanov, A., & Starostin, A. (2018). *Robonomics: platform for integration of cyber physical systems into human economy*. White Paper.

Lu, Z., Liu, W., Wang, Q., Qu, G., & Liu, Z. (2018). A privacy-preserving trust model based on blockchain for VANETs. *IEEE Access: Practical Innovations, Open Solutions*, *6*, 45655–45664. doi:10.1109/ACCESS.2018.2864189

Makhdoom, I., Abolhasan, M., Abbas, H., & Ni, W. (2019). Blockchain's adoption in IoT: The challenges, and a way forward. *Journal of Network and Computer Applications*, *125*, 251–279. doi:10.1016/j.jnca.2018.10.019

Maroufi, M., Abdolee, R., & Tazekand, B. M. (2019). *On the convergence of blockchain and internet of things (iot) technologies*. arXiv preprint arXiv:1904.01936

Mazhanda, F. (2019). *How Blockchain and IoT Are Opening New Capabilities in the Construction Industry*. Retrieved from https://www.iotforall.com/iot-in-construction/

Minoli, D., & Occhiogrosso, B. (2018). Blockchain mechanisms for IoT security. *Internet of Things*, *1*, 1–13. doi:10.1016/j.iot.2018.05.002

Miraz, M. H. (2019). *Blockchain of Things (BCoT): The Fusion of Blockchain and IoT Technologies*. Cuhk Law.

Nagothu, D., Xu, R., Nikouei, S. Y., & Chen, Y. (2018, September). A microservice-enabled architecture for smart surveillance using blockchain technology. In *2018 IEEE International Smart Cities Conference (ISC2)* (pp. 1-4). IEEE. 10.1109/ISC2.2018.8656968

Nikouei, S. Y., Xu, R., Nagothu, D., Chen, Y., Aved, A., & Blasch, E. (2018, September). Real-time index authentication for event-oriented surveillance video query using blockchain. In *2018 IEEE International Smart Cities Conference (ISC2)* (pp. 1-8). IEEE. 10.1109/ISC2.2018.8656668

Panarello, A., Tapas, N., Merlino, G., Longo, F., & Puliafito, A. (2018). Blockchain and iot integration: A systematic survey. *Sensors (Basel)*, *18*(8), 2575.

Pieroni, A., Scarpato, N., Di Nunzio, L., Fallucchi, F., & Raso, M. (2018). Smarter city: Smart energy grid based on blockchain technology. *Int. J. Adv. Sci. Eng. Inf. Technol*, *8*(1), 298–306. doi:10.18517/ijaseit.8.1.4954

Pongle, P., & Chavan, G. (2015, January). A survey: Attacks on RPL and 6LoWPAN in IoT. In *2015 International conference on pervasive computing (ICPC)* (pp. 1-6). IEEE. 10.1109/PERVASIVE.2015.7087034

Ray, P. P., Dash, D., Salah, K., & Kumar, N. (2020). Blockchain for IoT-Based Healthcare: Background, Consensus, Platforms, and Use Cases. *IEEE Systems Journal*, 1–10. doi:10.1109/JSYST.2020.2963840

Rejeb, A., Keogh, J. G., & Treiblmaier, H. (2019). Leveraging the Internet of Things and Blockchain Technology in Supply Chain Management. *Future Internet*, *11*(7), 161. doi:10.3390/fi11070161

Rifi, N., Agoulmine, N., Chendeb Taher, N., & Rachkidi, E. (2018). Blockchain technology: Is it a good candidate for securing iot sensitive medical data? *Wireless Communications and Mobile Computing*, *2018*, 2018. doi:10.1155/2018/9763937

Security, X. (2019). *Next-Generation Industrial Cybersecurity Introduces Hierarchical-Tree and Conditional Consensus in Blockchain for the First Time.* https://www. globenewswire.com/news-release/2019/10/10/1928089/0/ en/Xage-Security-Reveals-New-Blockchain-Innovation-to-Protect-Trillions-of-Industrial-Devices-and-Interactions.html

Shen, B., Guo, J., & Yang, Y. (2019). MedChain: Efficient healthcare data sharing via blockchain. *Applied Sciences (Basel, Switzerland)*, *9*(6), 1207. doi:10.3390/app9061207

Singh, M., & Kim, S. (2017). *Intelligent vehicle-trust point: Reward based intelligent vehicle communication using blockchain.* arXiv preprint arXiv:1707.07442

Uddin, M. A., Stranieri, A., Gondal, I., & Balasubramanian, V. (2020). Blockchain Leveraged Decentralized IoT eHealth Framework. *Internet of Things*.

Wan, J., Li, J., Imran, M., Li, D., & Fazal-e-Amin. (2019). A blockchain-based solution for enhancing security and privacy in smart factory. *IEEE Transactions on Industrial Informatics*, *15*(6), 3652–3660. doi:10.1109/TII.2019.2894573

Wüst, K., & Gervais, A. (2018, June). Do you need a blockchain? In *2018 Crypto Valley Conference on Blockchain Technology (CVCBT)* (pp. 45-54). IEEE. 10.1109/CVCBT.2018.00011

Xu, R., Nikouei, S. Y., Chen, Y., Blasch, E., & Aved, A. (2019, July). Blendmas: A blockchain-enabled decentralized microservices architecture for smart public safety. In *2019 IEEE International Conference on Blockchain (Blockchain)* (pp. 564-571). IEEE. 10.1109/Blockchain.2019.00082

Xu, Y., Ren, J., Wang, G., Zhang, C., Yang, J., & Zhang, Y. (2019). A blockchain-based nonrepudiation network computing service scheme for industrial IoT. *IEEE Transactions on Industrial Informatics*, *15*(6), 3632–3641. doi:10.1109/TII.2019.2897133

Yu, Y., Li, Y., Tian, J., & Liu, J. (2018). Blockchain-based solutions to security and privacy issues in the Internet of Things. *IEEE Wireless Communications*, 25(6), 12–18. doi:10.1109/MWC.2017.1800116

Yuan, Y., & Wang, F. Y. (2016, November). Towards blockchain-based intelligent transportation systems. In *2016 IEEE 19th International Conference on Intelligent Transportation Systems (ITSC)* (pp. 2663-2668). IEEE. 10.1109/ITSC.2016.7795984

Zhou, Y., Han, M., Liu, L., Wang, Y., Liang, Y., & Tian, L. (2018). Improving IoT Services in Smart-Home Using Blockchain Smart Contract. *IEEE International Conference on Internet of Things (iThings) and IEEE Green Computing and Communications (GreenCom) and IEEE Cyber, Physical and Social Computing (CPSCom) and IEEE Smart Data (SmartData)*, 81-87. 10.1109/Cybermatics_2018.2018.00047

This research was previously published in Blockchain Applications in IoT Security; pages 56-83, copyright year 2021 by Information Science Reference (an imprint of IGI Global).

Chapter 49
Blockchain Technology Integration in IoT and Applications

Bhanu Chander

(iD) https://orcid.org/0000-0003-0057-7662

Pondicherry University, India

ABSTRACT

The Internet of Things (IoT) pictures an entire connected world, where things or devices are proficient to exchange a few measured data words and interrelate with additional things. This turns for a feasible digital demonstration of the existent world. Nonetheless, nearly all IoT things are simple to mistreat or compromise. Moreover, IoT devices are restricted in computation, power, and storage, so they are more vulnerable to bugs and attacks than endpoint devices like smartphones, tablets, and computers. Blockchain has remarkable interest from academics and industry because of its salient features including reduced dependencies on third parties, cryptographic security, immutability, decentralized nature, distributed nature, and anonymity. In the current scenario, blockchain with its features provides an anonymous framework for IoT. This chapter produces comprehensive knowledge of IoTs, Blockchain knowledge, security issues, Blockchain integration with IoT (BIoT), consensus, mining, message validation mechanisms, challenges, a solution, and future directions.

INTRODUCTION

The standard of Internet of Things (IoT) positioned solid way for a world where several days by day things interrelated and cooperate with the intrinsic atmosphere in order to gather knowledge for routine secure tasks. IoT is expanding its appliances at fast face some reports already predicated that IoT connectable devices (smartphones, laptops, tablets, etc.) will grow to 30 billion by 2020-22 moreover machine to machine connectivity also grow from 800 million to 3 billion, all of them allied with wide-ranging applications similar to healthcare management, transportation, smart society, justification, and automated robots. In support of trustworthy with broad network intensification, it is compulsory to fabricate ap-

DOI: 10.4018/978-1-6684-7132-6.ch049

propriate IoT protocols, architectures those can provide IoT services. At present IoT hang on centralized server-client prototype through Internet, but present prototype may not work in future because of rapidly growing devices usages, to overcome this fresh paradigm/prototype to be planned. Such as exposure entails, stuck between supplementary things, vigor against attacks, faultless authentication, data privacy and security, straightforward deployment and self-maintenance. These above-mentioned features obtain as a result of Blockchain (BC) the skill back-of-the Bitcoin crypto-currency scheme, studied to fascinating as well as critical for ensuring security and privacy for diverse applications in many domains-including the internet of things (Tiago et al., 2018; Mahadi et al., 2018; Ana Reyna et al., 2018).

Abstractly blockchain technology is a distributed database that holds proceedings of transactions which were collective among participated entities; every transaction is well-established by agreement of greater part of a group member, creating forged transactions unable to pass shared conformation. If one time a blockchain shaped and when established, it cannot be altered or modified. Blockchain technologies proficient to track, synchronize complete transactions and accumulate records/data from an outsized quantity of devices which make possible construction of applications that are entailing no central based cloud.

The hurried development of blockchain technology and blockchain involved appliances have begun to revolutionize the digital world's finances as well as financial services. At present, the appliances of blockchain raise from a financial transaction or insurance claim to issues in share trades and corporate bonds. In presumption, any-person any-place can utilize blockchain technology to broadcast information/data steadfastly. Blockchain technology is kind of distributed ledger knowledge that efficiently removes the central data point rather than most commonly used supply chains data structures. Here, distributed ledger knowledge/technology is the heart of blockchain mechanism, which offers validation method via a network of computers that make possible peer to peer transactions devoid-of the requirement for mediator/centralized authority to inform and maintain the information generated at the time of transactions. Each and every transaction in blockchain technology validated through a group of validated transaction operations, then after added as a new block to a previously existed chain of transaction operations, because of this reason it named as Block-chain. Once a transaction fixed, added to chain transaction it cannot be altered, deleted or modified. Notably there are two most successful blockchain networks available – public or permissionless blockchain networks – Each user can individually access and perform much like open-source network, permission blockchain networks – specific individuals or organizations use to conduct transaction operations (Deepak et al., 2018; Ana Reyna et al., 2018; Tiago et al., 2018).

Internet of Things (IoT) is one of the emerging topics in recent time in terms of technical, social and financial consequences. From the past decades, there is a significant development in the fields of wireless communication technology, information, and communication systems, industrial designs, and electromechanical systems encourage to progress new technology named as the Internet of things. The most important intention IoTs is to connect all or any devices to the internet or other connected devices. Internet of things is collection network of home appliances, physical devices, vehicular networks and other devices fixed with sensors, electronics, actuators moreover network connectivity which make-possibility for mentioned objects to gather/accumulate and exchange information/data. IoT works as a massive network of interconnected things, people those can collect and share resources about the way they are utilized and about the surrounding environment to them. Here each and everything/device typically identified with its corresponding computing system, however, is able to interoperate within the existing internet infrastructure (Deepak et al., 2018; Ana Reyna et al., 2018; Clemence et al., 2018).

TAXONOMY OF IOT SECURITY ISSUES

Internet of Things prototype covers, integrates numerous amounts of device collections from undersized implanted processing chips to outsized-end servers, at the same level IoT have to deal with defense troubles at dissimilar levels (Minhaj et al., 2018).

Physical and Data Link Layer Attacks

Both physical, as well as data link layers, execute key role to accumulate and organizing information at the starting phases of IoT services. Security at this stage concerned as the first level or low-level of security. Here some security issues of physical layers of hardware and data link layer of communication mentioned below.

1. **Insecure Physical Surface:** IoT consists of a wide variety of hardware devices, various physical factors composite severe exposures to accurate functioning of IoT devices. Unhealthy physical defense, software availability during physical interfaces, testing tools can probably demoralize nodes in the surrounding network.
2. **Insecure Initialization:** Proper initialization of IoT at preliminary level makes possibilities for appropriate functionality of complete organization without infringing as well as the distraction of network services. Secured physical level communications remove unauthorized receivers.
3. **Jamming Attacks:** Adversaries with a jamming attack on wireless-based sensor devices within IoT aim to decline communication arrangement through generating radio regularity signals without a definite procedure. These types of radio obstructions severely impact the network operations and disturb the legitimate entities sending and receiving procedures.
4. **Sleep Deprivation Attack:** Wireless sensor devices utilized in IoT are energy-constrained which makes them vulnerable to sleep deprivation attacks to stay away from the whole network. It will cause issues like battery exhaustion if there are a number of tasks to be carried out on a single sensor node.
5. **Sybil Attacks:** Adversaries with Sybil attacks generate fake identities to degrade IoT functionalities. And also starts aiming to decrease node or network resources power.

SECURITY SOLUTIONS FOR PHYSICAL AND DATA LINK LAYER ATTACKS

Jamming associated attacks for wireless sensor networks follow-on messages collision or overflows communication channel. (Young et al., 2011) detects jamming attacks by calculating the strength which is then used for extorting noised bases signals, after that evaluate with modified threshold values. (Xu et al., 2005) proposed jamming attack detection with packet delivery ratio. Cryptographic based error-correcting code presented by (Mounir et al., 2003). (Pecorella et al., 2016) designed a framework for secure physical layer communication where the smallest data rate is constituted among transfer and receiver to make sure the absences of adversaries. (Demirbas et al., 2006) designed a method against Sybil attacks, in their method detector nodes deployed to calculate the sender location at the time of message communication. One more message announcement with similar sender position but special sender personality indirect as Sybil attack. (Li et al., 2006) utilizes radio sign strength dimensions for MAC addresses for spot spoofing stacks. (Xiao et al., 2009) come with a new approach where the amount of uniqueness and extra parameters associated with channel evaluation, spot Sybil attacks.

Routing, Transport and Session Security Issues

Here some of the security issues mainly focused on communication, routing and session management of IoT devices are described below (Minhaj et al., 2018):

1. **Routing Attack:** The IPv6 routing procedures for LoWPAN are defenseless against numerous attacks through compromised nodes. The main reason for attacks is to decrease the resources of network devices.
2. **Sinkhole Attacks:** With the help of the sinkhole attack, attackers make sensor node more powerful than its adjoin nodes and try to transmit information through the attacker node then performs malicious activities on the network. Moreover, it transmits all packets of the selected region into the malicious node.
3. **Wormhole Attack:** In the wormhole attack, the attacker creates a short concentration link involving two segments of the network over that attacker replays network messages. This kind of attacks has rigorous implications include eavesdrop of service, privacy breach.
4. **Replay or Duplication Attacks:** Attacker intensions is interrupted message and try to retransmit the same message in upcoming time intervals so that bandwidth of the sensor network decreases. A modernization of packet portion fields at the 6LoWPAN layer could affect into the exhaustion of possessions, buffer run over as well as rebooting devices.
5. **End to End Security:** Transport layer provides a secure mechanism from end-to-end, so data from the initiator node to the receiver node in a consistent approach. To achieve the above-mentioned approach a well-dressed encrypted authentic mechanism to be applied that guarantees secure message communication and not breach privacy while working in an insecure channel.
6. **Buffer Reservation Attack:** In IoT, servicing node needs to preserve buffer gap used for a rebuild of arriving packets; here an invader might be utilizing it by transport imperfect packet fragments. This will lead to denial-of-service where legitimated fragments denied owing to the space engaged through imperfect packets send by the invader.
7. **Session Establishment:** The main intention is to take control of the session on transport layer with malicious nodes results in a denial-of-service attack. Moreover, the attacker impersonates the attacked node to prolong the session among two nodes.
8. **Authentication:** IoT is a collection of numerous devices and abusers, so key management process exploited to authenticate one with other devices or with abusers. Any kind of miss connection in security at network layer communication can represent the network to a great number of attacks. Convolution cryptographic mechanism ensures secure communication but concedes more energy from sensor nodes which have limited resource constraints.
9. **Privacy on Cloud-Based IoT:** Location privacy violation may deploy on cloud interrupt broadcasting system of IoT. malicious cloud services those employed on IoT based network can produce right to use confidential information being transmitted to the preferred target.
10. **Neighbor Discovery:** As discussed above IoT is a collection of devices so IoT designed architecture needs each and every connected device must be identified uniquely. Particularly message communication base authentication has to be secure, undertaking that the data correctly transmit

to a device in continuous communication. In neighbor discovery steps like address resolution and router discovery without suitable authentication may capture severe allegations.

Security Solution for Routing, Transport and Session Security Issues

The threats that take place from reply attacks due to the partition of packets in 6LoWPAN can deal through timestamp and nonce options. These packets are further given to 7LoWPAN version layer subsequent to segment packets. Both timestamp as well as nonce values employed for unidirectional as well as bi-directional packets correspondingly (Kim et al., 2008). (Riaz et al., 2009) projected a framework through secure neighbor discovery, key generation, data encryption, and authentication. Elliptic curve cryptography (ECC) engaged for secure node discovery, the encrypted data make sure node-to-node protection. (Dvir et al., 2011) designed a method for mitigating adversary attacks for the period of map-reading through IPv6 routing protocol for Low-power Lossy networks. The author constructs the directed acyclic graph through root to any gateways. (Weekly et al., 2012) designed a model to cope with sinkhole attacks. On behalf of rank confirmation consequent to Destination Information Object (DIO) message, in one-direction base hash-function employ mutually with a hash series task. In (Hu et al., 2005) authors incorporating symmetric key cryptographic algorithms to make safe nodes starting the attacked wireless nodes in a specific network. Authors in (Wang et al., 2008) describe a procedure to detect wormhole attacks in WSNs by calculating broadcasting distances estimated among neighbors. (Kothmayr et al., 2012) employed a method in favor of end-to-end safety with shared validation in the course of public-key cryptography. Authentication performed via authenticated platform module. Chips using RSA or exit on the trusted Platform module. Here RSA certificates are broadcast in X.509 design. (Park et al., 2016) employed a mutual validation scheme for safe and sound session supervision via asymmetric key-based encryption technique. In the planned system at first pick, an arbitrary number also achieve encryption and create a session key which was consequently utilized for encryption of one more arbitrary integer. The encrypted value is at that moment used for validation. In support of each fresh session, innovative session keys create exclusive of necessitating recurrence of parameters.

Application Layers Security Issues

IoT based application services helpless against some specific type attacks that are mentioned below.

1. **Insecure Interfaces:** In order to access IoT services mobile, web and cloud interfaces are employed but they vulnerable to dissimilar attacks that cloud rigorously distress the security and privacy of data.
2. **Middleware Security:** Middleware service in IoT planned to deliver message amongst mixed entities of IoT model that must be protected sufficient for the condition of services. Dissimilar interface atmospheres with middleware should be incorporated to endow with secure communication.
3. **CoAP Security with the Internet:** Constrained Application Protocol as web transfer protocol with various security models produces end-to-end safety measures. CoAP follows a special kind of encrypted message format of RFC-7252.

Security Solution for Application Layers Security Issues

(Liu et al., 2014) planned a scheme for middleware server which maintains data filtering throughout communication along with assorted IoT atmospheres. Projected middleware supports proficient method for naming, addressing and profiling across assorted surroundings. In (OneM2M 2014) authors presents a method for machine-to-machine communications in the IoT atmosphere, standard design with dissimilar layers for security. An energy-efficient security replica using public-key cryptography for IoT based CoAp is offered by (Sethi et al., 2012). It executes through an archetype that utilizes a Mirror proxy (MP) and Resources directory represents server-to-server request during sleep state and the list of assets on the server in that order. (Granjal et al., 2013) proposed another approach of secure message applications communicating through the internet using various CoAp securities. In (Brachmann et al., 2014) IoT based Ip networks, a protection model with 6LBR being used for message filtration in order to afford end-to-end security.

Table 1. Mapping of IoT layers with security issues/attacks and solutions

Layers	Security Issues/Attacks	Solutions
Physical and Datalink layers	• Sybil attacks • Sleep deprivation attacks • Jamming attacks • Insecure initialization • Insecure physical surface	• Signal strength measurements • Channel estimation • Multi-layer-based IDS • Compute packet delivery ratio • Encode packets with Error-correcting codes
Routing, Transport, Session layers	• Session establishment • Wormhole • Sinkhole • Reply attack • Authentication • Buffer reservation attack • Routing attack • Privacy on cloud • Neighbor discovery • End to end security	• Authenticate with ECC, HASH, RSA, SHA1, AES • Apply timestamp, Nonce values • Signature base identification, monitoring node behavior • Graph travels, Random walks on graphs, measuring signal strength
Application layer	• Middleware security • CoAP security with Internet • Insecure interfaces	• Key management among devices • Test the interface vulnerabilities with testing tools, firewalls • CoAP mapping, Mirror proxy, Resource directory • Restrict low passwords

BLOCKCHAIN SECURITY

Blockchain technology is one of the promising and emergent notions of decentralizes security. It professionally restores a variety of organizations economic transaction systems; moreover, based on mentioned sentences it has the capability of restoring heterogeneous business procedures of various industries. However, it ensures a scattered secured framework to assist exchange, allocation, and integration of information with all abusers and devices, so designers along with decision-makers have to explore it in-depth for its suitability in their respective industry and business appliances (Minhaj et al., 2018; Mahadi et al., 2018).

Blockchain noted as big revolution technology in the present era, in the year of 2008 idea of blockchain was originally initiated by well-known researcher namely Satoshi Nakamoto who executed digital currency famous as Bitcoin. Since decade's people involved in information transmit and transfer of money, property through an online transaction using internet connectivity. These transactions require a trusted third party who has taken responsibility for secured exchange and accountable for any kind of security violation. Coming to the blockchain paradigm, removes central authority among many parties performs fiscal and information transactions with the inclusion of immutable, decentralized public ledger. Here public ledger is a decentralized scattered database which was mutual among the entire network entities. Moreover, it is a cryptographically encrypted, everlasting and tamperproof witness of entire dealings that happen at any time among network entities (Figure 1). Participating entities can able to outlook transaction those associated with them any time they need. Nevertheless, at one time the transaction validated and linked with blockchain, it cannot be modified or deleted which turns blockchain undeniable and unalterable. Every transaction confirmed and verified by network entities through pre-defined confirmation or consent mechanisms without any kind of authentication from a central authority. There are numerous advantages with the mentioned sentences, reduces the cost of transmission and abolishes information loss due to single point malfunction because ledger copies distributed as well as synchronized across the network entities. Depending on data management and what actions can be preceded by abusers - blockchain separated into public, private and consortium blockchain. In a public blockchain, which is also acknowledged as a permission-less blockchain, anyone can join without need to take any permissions from third parties. Bitcoin, Litecoin and Ethereum are some instances of a public blockchain. In a private blockchain, a permissioned blockchain, the network owner has made a restriction on network access. In order to be a consortium and not a private chain, the participating companies must be uniformly concerned in the consensus and the decision-making processes of the chain. Technically, consortium chains can be simply executed using solutions such as parity (Tiago et al., 2018; Mahadi et al., 2018).

Figure 1. Pictorial representation of blockchain characteristics

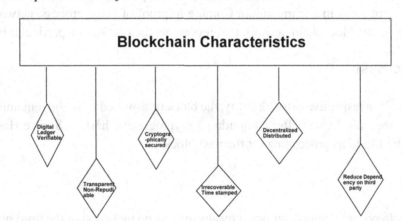

Consider a simple instance where a group of network entities allocating information and performing exchanges of assets. In place of a trusted third party, network entities make an agreement on a protocol that is to say consensus problem which guarantees for mutual trust, permits validated transaction from peer to peer basis. For the reason, this consensus protocol, digital signatures, proof of work, network entities, cryptographically generated hash values considered as building blocks for Blockchain technology. Here participating network entities could be persons, associations or organizations exchanges a replica of the ledger that contains relevant genuine transactions in chronological order. The public ledger is a collection of sequence blocks linked with their respective calculated hash values in sequential order to sustain data reliability and appropriateness. Each block contains set of transactions digitally sign by the possessor and verifies by the rest of the entities ahead of being added to the block (Deepal et al., 2018; Ana Reyna et al., 2018; Minhaj et al., 2018; Tiago et al., 2018).

Description of blockchain features mentioned below:

Digital Signature

Participating network entities try to implement a transaction and transmit across the network. For this entity who fabricates the transaction digitally sign on it by constantly hashing the public key for initiator confirmation and send out for transaction confirmation by other nodes.

Consensus

Consensus plays the main role in blockchain because blockchain entirely works on decentralization, no trustable third hand accountable for the safe transaction, management, and security attacks. New block after collecting transactions starts working on consensus protocol to recognize the verification of the transaction. Proof of work, proof of stake is essential consensus problems.

Proof of Work and Stake

Proof of work and Stake are confirmation methods for making sure the blockchain transactions. In proof of work, values explored from a pool of vales building the cryptographic hash value of the block, start with the N quantity of zeros in a competition. Coming to proof of stake process, network participants invest digital coins in the blockchain network that represents their stake in a particular block.

Cryptographic Hash

Proof of work done by a respective network entity, the block transmitted to all the remaining entities who allow it by add to their blockchain after computing a cryptographic hash as Secure Hash Algorithms, for the block Hash utilized as proceeding for the next block.

Centralized

Blockchain technology completely centralized means there is no inclusion of the third party in any kind of transaction. A public blockchain is decentralized; a private blockchain is fully centralized. Finally, consortium blockchain is moderately centralized.

Immutability

In public blockchain, transactions stored in dissimilar nodes in a dispersed manner hence is not feasible to tamper. Coming to private and consortium respective governing organizations may possibly tamper the blockchain.

Efficiency

Security as the major concern frontier of blockchain would be stricter if a large number of nodes takes part in the blockchain. It takes ample time to broadcast transactions and blocks. Hence, the result of transaction throughput is low in addition latency is high. With fewer consensus protocols blockchain could be more adequate.

Read Permission

All transaction in public blockchain visible publicly whereas read permissions depend on a private blockchain or consortium blockchain.

CONSENSUS, MINING, MESSAGE VALIDATION MECHANISMS IN BLOCKCHAIN

For accurate execution of Blockchain technology, "Consensus or agreement or Harmony" plays a very important role. The consensus is nothing but a mechanism that decides conditions to be satisfied to signal about an agreement has been accomplishing validations of the blocks to add with blockchain. This will remain you Byzantine Generals Problem, as it needs to make conformity regarding somewhat amongst numerous parties those not having faith on each-other. In crypto-currency, this computational trouble is associated with double-spend trouble, that compact with how to authenticate a little quantity of digital-based currency which was not at all utilized not including proper validation from a trusted third party that regularly maintains a record of all transactions of users. Providing equal consensus mechanism has controlled environment with consists all the miners have the same weights and decide according to the majority of votes. However, it will lead to a Sybil attack where unique abuser with numerous identities can intelligent to organize entire blockchain. In decentralized blockchain architecture, each abuser randomly preferred to insert block, although this random preference may easily vulnerable to attacks. Proof of Work consensus mechanisms proposed to avoid these kinds of attacks, where a node performs heavy work for the network there is a chance for it will not go under any attack. The mentioned work may involve some calculations until a satisfying solution may found. Just the once the mentioned problem is the answer, it is simple for the remaining nodes to validate that gained answer was acceptable. Nevertheless, these type of operations makes blockchain inadequate in energy expenditure, scalability, and throughput which was not applicable in an IoT network where it consists limited resources constrained devices, sensor nodes, etc. (Tiago et al., 2018).

Proof of Stake

In Proof of work (PoS) based blockchain, entities those have an additional contribution to the network has fewer concerned in any attack on it. Means miners need to verify repeatedly that they have a positive number of participations in the network. In view of the fact that those entities which have continuous participation have control over blockchain. For instance, Peers coin consensus algorithm which takes coinage as a preferred point. Those entities which have oldest, as well as largest groups of coins, would likely to mine a block. Furthermore, Proof of stake consensus problem requires limited computational power compared with proof of work (Peercoin, 2018).

Proof of Activity

Proof-of-Activity (PoA) consensus algorithm anticipated overcoming the limitations of the problem of Proof-of-stake based on stake age. It builds things even the node is not associated with the set-up; it encourages both ownership and action on the blockchain (Bentov et al., 2014).

Proof of Stake Velocity (PoSV)

Works based on perception regarding the velocity of money, implemented by Reddcoin. Concepts indicate how many times a unit of currency flows throughout a financial system and group of society members for a certain amount of time. As a rule, the higher the velocity of money the more transactions in which it is used and healthier the economy.

Transaction as Proof-of-Stake

It is somehow related to PoS. Usually, in PoS Selected nodes contribute for Consensus but in TaPoS every node created transactions supply to the safety of the network.

Delegated Proof-of-Stake

DPoS is related to PoS, in place of stockholders for selecting and certify blocks; they select certain delegates which can change block size and gaps to do it. By doing fewer nodes involved in block validation, the transaction will be performed faster than other schemes (DPoS 2018).

PBFT

PBFT consensus algorithms implemented to resolve the Byzantine Generals Problem in the view of asynchronous environments. For adding a new block to the chain, ledger selects the transactions that supported by at least 2/3 rd of all existing nodes (Castro et al., 1999).

Delegated BFT (DBFT)

It is considered as one of the variants of BFT, performs as a parallel method to DPoS. A number of selected nodes participated in voting to be the ones generate as well as authorize blocks.

Ripple Consensus Algorithm (RCA)

RCA planned to trim down the high latencies initiated in numerous blockchains which takes place in the employ of synchronous connections between nodes. Ripples server mainly lean on a most authenticated subset nodes while shaping consensus problem (Schwatz et al., 2014).

Stellar Consensus Protocol (SCP)

SCP is an initial achievement regarding consensus algorithm entitled as Federated Byzantine Agreement (FBA). Performs the same as PBFT but in place of nodes waits or a majority of all other nodes queries, SCP waits only for subset participants which consider being important (Miaziery et al., 2018).

BFTRaft

It is BFT consensus algorithm planned and designed based on Raft algorithm, trouble-free and straight-forward to understand in favor of everyone. BFTRaft combinations improve Raft method by building it towards Byzantine fault-tolerant and by amplifying its security next to diverse threats (Copeland et al., 2018).

Sieve

IBM based research group implement the Sieve consensus algorithm for hyper ledger-Fabric. The main objective behind the Sieve is run non-deterministic smart cards on permission base scenario. While developing sieve reproduces the procedure associated with non-deterministic smart contracts after that evaluates the outcome. For suppose if variance observed between outcomes achieved with the undersized quantity of processes, those sieved out, if variation excessive entire operation to be sieved out (Cachinc et al., 2016).

Tendermint

In tender mint consensus algorithm network entities acknowledged as validates moreover recommend blocks of transactions plus make a vote on them. Validation of block done in pre-vote as well as pre-commit. It can merely commit when more than 2/3 validations pre-commit in the round (Kwon et al., 2018).

Bitcoin-NG

Implemented as a variation of Bitcoin consensus protocol which is mainly designed to improve latency, scalability along with throughput (Eyal et al., 2016).

Proof of Burn

PoB harmony algorithm entails miners to explain a proof of their loyalty to mining, by means of burning a few crypto-currencies in the course of an unspendable address (Borge et al., 2017).

Proof of Personhood

PoP harmony/consensus method that constructs utilize ring signature moreover combined symbol to connect substantial to practical identities, in this approach secrecy conserved.

BLOCKCHAIN AND INTERNET OF THINGS INTEGRATION

The growing development in industrial scientific fields builds a new-fangled method known as the Internet of Things (IoT). IoT is converting and optimizing hand-based-operated processing's which made them as one of the parts in the Digital World where fabricated knowledge base data shows some outcome result. The fabricated data smooth the progression in smart applications enrichment and supervise quality life of citizens all the way in the course of the digitization services in modern cities. From past days cloud commuting technology contribute and produces analyzing results in real-time IoT services with essential functionality toward examine and progression information and finally spin into knowledgeable information (Ana et al., 2018: Diaz et al., 2016) On the other side, in many scenarios vulnerabilities has come to mind because lack of confidence level of systems. Cloud computing used as centralized architecture extensively added to the enlargement of IoT. Nevertheless, coming to data transmission and intelligibility they act as black boxes, more importantly, the applicants of IoT services do not know how and where the data/information which was produced by them is going to be used. Blockchain can able to improve the IoT with the help of faith sharing services, where information is trustworthy and can be observable.

Network participant's data resources talented to be recognized at any time furthermore data remain not able to be forfeited in due course and intensifying its safety measures. In some special scenarios where the IoT information must be steadily shared with numerous participants would symbolize a key riot. Furthermore, sharing consistent data could help the insertion of fresh applicants into the network and contribute to progress their services, acceptances. Hence, the utilization of blockchain can balance IoT through trustworthy and protected information. Many researchers found that IoT can significantly advantage from the functionality afforded by blockchain in addition help advanced future IoT technologies. There are soundless numerous research confront and open problems that to be considered in order to faultlessly utilize these two technologies mutually and this research focal point is still at the initial phase (Clemence et al., 2018; Deepak et al., 2018; Minhaj et al., 2018).

Blockchain – IoT Integration Models

Before the integration of blockchain with IoT, it is important to mention where transactions occur. Inside the IoT, among IoT - blockchain and hybrid blueprint are some of the integrations involved in IoT, blockchain (Ana et al., 2018; Khan et al., 2017) (See Figure 2).

IoT - IoT

Generally, IoT devices engage to discover other IoT devices and routing mechanisms. Here some pieces of IoT information accumulate in blockchain, which enables IoT communications to happen exclusive of blockchain technology involvement. This might be the greatest method within words of latency as well as security.

Figure 2. Symbolic demonstration of blockchain IoT integration models

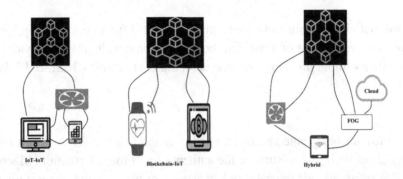

IoT - Blockchain

Here all transactions move all the way through blockchain, which facilitates an unchangeable record of interactions. It guarantees all selected interactions able to traceable as their particulars reserved in the blockchain. However, organizing each and every transaction in the blockchain would increase bandwidth and data usage.

Hybrid Method

In hybrid method some transaction operated in blockchain and remaining transaction organized and shared among IoT devices. But the problem occurs when which transaction should take place through blockchain and make a decision in the runtime environment. A faultless architectural combination of both IoT and blockchain influence the profits of blockchain furthermore improves real-time IoT exchanges. At present Fog computing introduction extends limitations of blockchain and IoT.

Here are some of the special improvements provided by the integration of Blockchain and IoT (Clemence et al., 2018; Deepak et al., 2018; Minhaj et al., 2018).

Decentralized and Scalability

In centralized schemes, few powerful network parts manage processing and storage space regarding information of numerous people. Shifts as central construction to decentralized distributed construction eliminate central points of malfunction and blockages. Decentralization can also improve error tolerance and structure scalability. It would trim down the IoT work pressure as well as progress IoT scalability (Ana et al., 2018; Veena et al., 2015).

Identity

Blockchain skill contestants are talented to distinguish each solitary device. Data feed into the structure is unchallengeable moreover individually identifies authentic information that was present by disseminated devices. Moreover, blockchain provides trust base distributed verification as well as the approval of devices for IoT appliances (Ana et al., 2018; Gan et al., 2017).

Autonomy

Improvement of IoT with blockchain technology make powerful future coming application features; it makes possibilities to development of smart autonomous resources, hardware services and capable to interact with each other without involving any servers (Ana et al., 2018; Chain, 2017; Filament, 2017).

Reliability

The information in IoT unchangeable and distributed over the blockchain. Network participants have complete authority about verifying, assurance the authenticity of the information. Machinery improvements make possible reliability and traceability key aspects of blockchain transport toward IoT (Ana et al., 2018).

Security

Security plays the main role while data in the transmission process, blockchain secures the transmission of data communications in the form of stored records. While transmitting messages blockchain validate them by smart contracts then only it treated as secured communication between two devices. With the help of blockchain technology present, secure protocols of IoT can be optimized (Ana et al., 2018; Modum, 2017; Filament, 2017).

Improves Market Services

Blockchain inclusion boosts the IoT eco-system services and market services. It improves IoT interrelationship and access IoT information toward blockchain (Modum, 2017).

Secure Operation

With the inclusion of blockchain, not able to forfeited data, code, storage will be securely and steadily operated towards IoT devices (Filament, 2017; Modum, 2017).

BLOCKCHAIN: IOT INTEGRATION CHALLENGES

Internet of Things integration with Blockchain technology is a tricky and challenging procedure. In view of the fact that the main intention of blockchain design is based on the internet state of affairs through commanding computers and this state of affairs is a faraway technique from IoT authenticity. All connections in blockchain digitally noticed so the devices talented to work. Currency has to be outfitted by this functionality.

Security

Internet of Things (IoT) is a collection of a heterogeneous network; its applications have to contract with different protection issues at special levels. Moreover, IoT scenario consists of various properties such as mobility of nodes, large scale environment, and wireless communication that affect security. Since numerous security attacks and their respective functions effects on IoT, this shows an indication to make even more complicated security for IoT. After performing several kinds of testing operations researchers found that Blockchain technology as suitable equipment to present and fulfill the much-desired protection improvement in IoT. Reliability of data is the most important challenge while integrating IoT with blockchain technology. Data in chains stays Immutable which is the main functionality of blockchain. For instance, while data reach your destination with corruption, blockchain settles as corrupt. Corrupted data in IoT application may raise more problems apart from malicious attacks. Sometimes devices and nodes not able to work properly because of this corrupted data; this problem cannot questionable until device went under examination tasks. In the view of the above-mentioned scenarios IoT devices as well as nodes comprehensively checked and tested prior to their amalgamation by blockchain technology. Moreover, it is better to incorporate practices on the road to notice machine malfunctions in a little time ahead of attacks take place (Ana et al., 2018; Roman et al., 2018; Lopez et al., 2017; Roman et al., 2013).

Anonymity and Data Privacy

Anonymity and privacy are the two most important terms in IoT applications. For a request, while IoT device is allied with any person as in e-health state, it is a situation where anonymity desires to be assured. Here device has the capability to hide individuality of person while transmitting individual data. In IoT privacy of data has multiple stages starting from collecting information, enlarges to the communications and finally reaches the application stage. Securing devices which means data which was secure and not easily accessible by other peoples with no proper consent is a challenge. Many types of research utilize numerous cryptographic techniques like IPsec, SSL, TLS, DTLS, symmetric and asymmetric encryption methods but these techniques need a large number of resources which are mostly not available in IoT devices. Applying Blockchain technology identity, anonymity problems will reduce to lighten process. Trust is one more key challenging task while integrating IoT with Blockchain technology (Liu et al., 2015; Wang et al., 2010; Fernandez et al., 2017).

Legal Issues

Blockchain, particularly in the view of virtual currencies, has made huge controversy regarding legitimacy and legality. Based on necessity and functioning, organize elements foremost the network blockchain approach in the structure of public, private along with consortium blockchains. IoT has well-framed features law and data privacy, protection issues. These laws will become more complicated when IoT added with new technologies like Blockchain. Those expansions of innovative laws and standards can relieve official recognition protection characteristics of devices (Ana et al., 2018).

Storage and Scalability

Blockchain technology not more appropriate if these two words are not included. IoT devices continuously accumulate a huge amount of data in real-time, this restraint symbolizes an enormous difficulty toward its integration by blockchain. In order to trim-down resources usage, present blockchain technologies implementations processed through a few transactions per second. This will potentially blockage for IoT usage with blockchain. Moreover, blockchain doesn't have the power to store data like IoT. Entire data which was accumulated in IoT is not so useful; at present some feature extracting or selecting methods like filters, compression methods which perform great actions. Data compression could reduce transmission, storage space and processing tasks regarding high volume IoT data. Here some focus also needs on blockchain consensus protocols which cause a bottleneck to improve bandwidth and reduce the latency of its communication thereby permit batterer transactions (Ana et al., 2018).

Smart Contracts

IoT has some benefits on or after employ of smart contracts which depend on approaches where contracts implemented at various levels. Theoretically, the contract is a set of code assignments with data positions that exist in definite blockchain tackles. Smart contracts offer secure along with a reliable system for IoT, by recording and managing all transactions. Smart contracts must take attention on heterogeneous and restraints nearby in the IoT. Filter and cluster methods could be harmonized via smart contracts toward facilitating appliances to deal with IoT depending on circumstance and requirements (Ana et al., 2018).

Consensus or Harmony

Blockchain has a wide variety of consensus algorithms those immutable and not thoroughly tested as much as necessary. By considering IoT applications restricted resource constraints of nodes as well as devices make them not eligible for taking part in consensus protocols. Mining is another challenge faced by IoT due to its limited resource constraints.

APPLICATIONS OF BLOCKCHAIN-IOT

Blockchain technology applicable to many fields, applicability starts from Bitcoin then after moving towards smart cards finally progress towards justice, efficiency applications. Bitcoin which is known as Blockchain 1.0 or Digital currency. It indicates mining, hashing, and public ledger, transaction assured software and digital currency that symbolizes a store, protocol value. Introduction of bitcoin greatly reduces the third-party online transaction charges which protect against price increases, bitcoin produce superior security than credit-cards. Blockchains smartcards implementation is also known as Blockchain 2.0 or Digital Economy that symbolizes financial and economic applications like payments of loans in traditional banking systems and transfers of bonds, stocks, derivatives, tiles, contracts, and assets in financial marketing. Smartcard contracts are essentially computer-based programs that can as a result of design complete the terms and conditions of an agreement. At the time of pre-arranged circumstance in a smart contract between two networks entities assemble then the contractual understanding can be mechanically prepared their payments as per the contract in transparent approach. Ethereum is one of the examples for Digital economy. Finally, Blockchain 3.0 or Digital society has numerous applications include science, public goods, identity, art, governance, health and various aspects of culture and communication. (See Figure 3)

Figure 3. Symbolic demonstration on Blockchain IoT applications

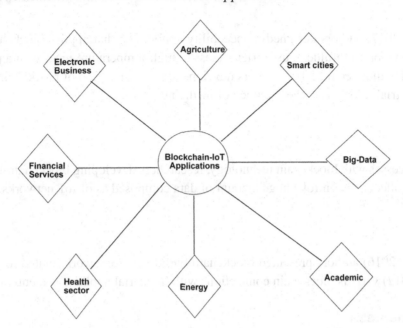

Financial Services

Implementation of Blockchain technology such as Bitcoin made tremendous changes in traditional financial as well as business services. It also makes attention to software companies and legal organizations. Peters et al have mentioned that blockchain has the capability to interrupt world banking working process like as settlement of financial assets etc. Risk management agenda has a major part in financial technology; it performs better with a combination of blockchain technology. Pilkington revealed the risk management agenda with blockchain that utilized to analyze investment risks. (Noyes 2016) build peer tot peer secure financial market by applying blockchain technology (Tiago et al., 2018; Zibin et al., 2018; Noyes, 2016).

Agriculture

IoT based agriculture appliances also engaged in Blockchain technology. For instance, many authors present traceability scheme to track food supplies, which is prepared in support of Radio frequency identification and blockchain technology (Tian et al., 2016; Tiago et al., 2018).

Energy Sector

The energy sector is also one of the applications of Blockchain to IoT. Authors (Lundqvist et al., 2017) design various methods based on blockchain with internet of energy where devices have to pay for services without any human interventions. In proposed methods smart chains that unite with a well-dressed socket which is proficient to pay for the energy consumed.

Healthcare

In (Bocek et al., 2017) authors designed a traceability application that applies blockchain technology to validate information truthfulness, user-friendliness to high-temperature records in a pharmaceutical stock chain. In (Hardjoin et al., 2016) authors developed the construction of blockchain base proposal for experimental trials along with the accuracy of medicine.

Big Data

Big data can successes with blockchain technology, researchers developing blockchain-based solutions that can handle collect and control a huge amount of data composed as of IoT networks.

Smart Cities

In (Biswas et al., 2016) authors presented blockchain-based IoT framework related to smart cities, in (Ahram et al., 2017) various blockchain connections with industrial appliances mentioned.

Electronic-Business

(Zhang 2015) designed IoT e-business model base on the blockchain, smart contract. Authors developed distributed autonomous corporations (DAC) like centralized operation unit which obtain as well as switch sensor data exclusive of any third party.

Academics

Academic reputation is important for a better society. (Sharples, 2015) designed a blockchain base scattered scheme for academic records as well as reputation. On the preliminary stage, every institution, as well as workers, provided with an opening reward of educational reputation currency. Institution/Organization can reward or transfer a few standing records to the staff, all records accumulate in blockchain so any kind of reputation changes can easily be detected.

Energy Saving

(Gogerty et al., 2011) designed blockchain-based green energy that encourages handling of renewable sources. Solarcoin distributed by sloarcoin foundation as long as solar energy generated by you, here solar coin is one type of digital currency incentive for solar power creators.

Safety, Privacy

Both safety and privacy defense important concern in IoT services. Inclusion of blockchain improves security and privacy in IoT based appliances. (Hardjoin et al., 2016) designed privacy-preserving method for IoT devices in a cloud environment. Authors also developed a method where devices to improve manufacturing attribution without any authentication from third-party.

FUTURE CHALLENGES, DIRECTIONS, AND ISSUES

Blockchain and Internet of Things exposed their prospective in production, commerce and academic (Tiago et al., 2018; Minhaj et al., 2018). Some of the future works based on existing literature survey are mentioned below.

Blockchain Construction

It is necessary to construct a complete trust base framework or infrastructure which able to carry-out every necessity to making use of blockchain in IoT services. For this reason, researchers need to develop numerous high rated methods which control inter-domain issues.

Complicated Technical Challenges

Both IoT and Blockchain reach their advanced levels but technically there still some issues to be solved such as privacy, security, scalability, cryptographic techniques development and stability requirements in BIoT appliances. Furthermore, blockchain technology various design, limitation issues in consensus protocols, implementations in smart cards and transaction capacities.

Rapid Testing

In the future when users may wish to merge blockchain and IoT systems. For this merger process, the initial pace will be make out which kind of blockchain fits for the user requirements; hence it is compulsory to create a system to test dissimilar blockchains.

Regulatory and Legal Aspects

Determining regulatory standards such as ownership, national and international jurisdiction are the principal problems to be solved beside technical challenges that can expand the promising value of BIoT.

Hardware Vulnerabilities

IoT is more vulnerable to hardware attacks because of low-cost and low-power devices. Routing, as well as packet preprocessing mechanisms, must be verified before employed in IoT. It is a tricky operation to detect vulnerabilities after network deployment so there is need of standard verification protocol which can exploit the IoT security.

Blockchain Vulnerabilities

Even though advanced methods proposed for IoT security, there is a chance for blockchain to be vulnerable. The consensus protocols depending on miners hashing rule can be concessional which allows the invader to maintain the entire blockchain. Effective mechanisms still are distinct to make sure the privacy of transaction dealings moreover stay away from attacks that might produce double-spending for the duration of transactions.

Interoperability of Security Protocols

In order to provide universal defense mechanisms for IoT, the designed protocols at special layers interoperate with each other for translation mechanisms. Inside that universal defense mechanism, each layers valuable arrangement of defense principles specific throughout consideration of architectural limitations.

Resource Limitations

IoT has a resource-constrained architecture which is the main issues to define a robust security mechanism. Conventional cryptographic procedures work with these limited resource constraints, moreover interchange of keys certificates as well as storage purpose more energy requirement is needed. Hence unbeaten execution of security, as well as message communication protocols in favor of IoT, needed which works efficiently in the limited energy-constrained devices, nodes.

Trusted Management and Software Update

IoT works with an outsized amount of devices for providing scalable and trusted management with a secure software update in outsized amount IoT devices is still one of the open research problems. Blockchain can ensure some of those security issues; on other hand blockchain technology suffers from scalability, key collision, and efficiency.

CONCLUSION

The purpose of the Blockchain concept has enlarged ahead of it's utilizing for Bitcoin production as well as transaction dealings. At present Blockchain along with its modifications are utilized to protect any type of transactions, rather It Human-To-Human or Machine-To-Machine connections. Blockchain adoption appears to be revolutionizing the IoT. This chapter inspects the up-to-date of blockchain-IoT equipment and projected important circumstances for BIoT appliances in areas like big-data, healthcare, financial services, agriculture, and energy management. Moreover, BIoT integration issues, challenges, applications, mining, and message validation methods explained. However, BIoT state of affairs facade specific technical requirements that vary from execution such as energy effectiveness in resource-constrained procedures or the requirement of precise structural design.

REFERENCES

Bentov, I., Lee, C., Mizrahi, A., & Rosenfeld, M. (2014, June). Proof of activity: Extending bitcoin's proof of work via proof of stake. In *Proceedings of the 9th Workshop on the Economics of Networks, Systems and Computation*, Austin, TX.

Blockchain of things. (2017). Available online: https://www.blockchainofthings.com (*Accessed 1 February 2018*)

Borge, M., Kokoris-Kogias, E., Jovanovic, P., Gasser, L., Gailly, N., & Ford, B. (2017, April). Proof-of-personhood: Redemocratizing permissionless cryptocurrencies. In *Proceedings of the IEEE European Symposium on Security and Privacy Workshop*, Paris, France.

Brachmann, M., Garcia-Morchon, O., Keoh, S.-L., & Kumar, S. S. (2012). Security considerations around end-to-end security in the IP-based internet of things. In *Proceedings 2012 Workshop on Smart Object Security, in Conjunction with IETF83*, pp. 1–3.

Cachin, C., Schubert, S., & Vukolic, M. (2016, December). Non-determinism in Byzantine´ fault-tolerant replication. In *Proceedings of the International Conference on Principles of Distributed Systems (OPODIS 2016),* Madrid, Spain.

Castro, M. & Liskov, B. (1999, February). Practical Byzantine fault tolerance. In *Proceedings of the Third Symposium on Operating Systems Design and Implementation,* New Orleans, LA.

Conzon, D., Bolognesi, T., Brizzi, P., Lotito, A., Tomasi, R., & Spirito, M. A. (2012). The VIRTUS middleware: An XMPP based architecture for secure IoT communications. In *Proceedings 2012 21st International Conference on Computer Communications and Networks, ICCCN*. doi:.6289309. pp 1-6.10.1109/ICCCN.2012

Copeland, C. & Zhong, H. (2018). *Tangaroa: A Byzantine fault tolerant raft*. Available at http://www.scs.stanford.edu/14au- cs244b/labs/projects/copeland_zhong.pdf

Demirbas, M. & Song, Y. (2006). An RSSI-based scheme for sybil attack detection in wireless sensor networks. In *Proceedings of the 2006 International Symposium on World of Wireless, Mobile and Multimedia Networks, WOWMOM '06,* IEEE Computer Society, Washington, DC, pp. 564–570. 10.1109/WOWMOM.2006.27

M. Díaz, C. Martín, B. Rubio. (2016). State-of-the-art, challenges, and open issues in the integration of internet of things and cloud computing. *Journal of Networks Computers*. pp. 99-117.

Dvir, A., Holczer, T., & Buttyan, L. (2011). VeRA - version number and rank authentication in RPL. In *2011 IEEE Eighth International Conference on Mobile Ad-Hoc and Sensor Systems*. pp. 709-714.

Eyal, I., Gencer, A. E., Sirer, E. G., & Van Renesse, R. (2016). Bitcoin-NG: a scalable blockchain protocol. In *Proceedings 13th USENIX Symposium on Networked Systems Design and Implementation (NSDI 16)*, Santa Clara, CA, pp. 45–59.

Eyal, I., Gencer, A. E., Sirer, E. G., & Van Renesse, R. (2016, March). Bitcoin-NG: A scalable blockchain protocol. In *Proceedings of the 13th USENIX Symposium on Networked Systems Design and Implementation*, Santa Clara, CA.

Fernandez-Gago, C., Moyano, F., & Lopez, J. (2017). Modelling trust dynamics in the internet of things. *Information Science, 396*, 72–82. doi:10.1016/j.ins.2017.02.039

Filament. (2017). Available at https://filament.com/

Gan, S. (2017). *An IoT Simulator in NS3 and a Key-Based Authentication Architecture for IoT Devices using Blockchain*. Indian Institute of Technology Kanpur.

Gmez-Goiri, A., Ordua, P., Diego, J., & de Ipiña, D. L. (2014). *Otsopack: Lightweight semantic framework for interoperable ambient intelligence applications* (pp. 460–467). Computer Human Behaviour. doi:10.1016/j.chb

Granjal, J., Monteiro, E., & Silva, J. S. (2013). Application-layer security for the WoT: Extending CoAP to support end-to-end message security for internet-integrated sensing applications. In *Proceedings International Conference on Wired/Wireless Internet Communication, Springer Berlin Heidelberg*, pp. 140–153. 10.1007/978-3-642-38401-1_11

Hu, Y.-C., Perrig, A., & Johnson, D. B. (2005). Ariadne: A secure on-demand routing protocol for ad hoc networks. *Wireless Networks*, *11*(1), 21–38. doi:10.100711276-004-4744-y

Khan, M. A. & Salah, K. (2018). IoT security: Review, blockchain solutions, and open challenges. *Future Generation Computer Systems*. pp. 395–411.

Khan, M. A., & Salah, K. (2017). *IoT security: Review, blockchain solutions, and open challenges. Future Generation Computer Systems.*

Kim, H. Protection against packet fragmentation attacks at 6LoWPAN adaptation layer. In *Proceedings 2008 International Conference on Convergence and Hybrid Information Technology*. . pp. 790-801.10.1109/ICHIT.2008.261

Kothmayr, T., Schmitt, C., Hu, W., Brnig, M., & Carle, G. (2012). *37th annual IEEE Conference on Local Computer Networks - Workshops.* doi:. pp. 964–972.10.1109/LCNW.2012.6424088

Kwon, J. (2018). Tendermint: Consensus without mining (v0.6). Available at https://tendermint.com/static/docs/tendermint.pdf

Larimer, D. (2018). *Transactions as proof-of-stake.* Available at https://bravenewcoin.com/assets/Uploads/TransactionsAsProofOfStake10.pdf

Li, Q., & Trappe, W. (2006). Light-weight detection of spoofing attacks in wireless networks. In Proceedings *2006 IEEE International Conference on Mobile Ad Hoc and Sensor Systems*, pp. 845–851. 10.1109/MOBHOC.2006.278663

Liu, C., Ranjan, R., Yang, C., Zhang, X., Wang, L., & Chen, J. (2015). Mur-dpa: Top-down levelled multi-replica merkle hash tree based secure public auditing for dynamic big data storage on cloud. *IEEE Transactions on Computers*, *64*(9), 2609–2622. doi:10.1109/TC.2014.2375190

Liu, C., Yang, C., Zhang, X., & Chen, J. (2015). External integrity verification for outsourced big data in cloud and IoT: A big picture. *Future Generation Computer Systems*, *49*, 58–67. doi:10.1016/j.future.2014.08.007

Liu, C. H., Yang, B., & Liu, T. (2014). Efficient naming, addressing and profile services in Internet-of-Things sensory environments. *Ad Hoc Networks*, *18*, 85–101. doi:10.1016/j.adhoc.2013.02.008

Lopez, J., Rios, R., Bao, F., & Wang, G. (2017). Evolving privacy: From sensors to the internet of things. *Future Generation Computer Systems*, *75*, 46–57. doi:10.1016/j.future.2017.04.045

Lundqvist, T. & De Blanche, A. (2017). Thing-to-thing electricity micro payments using blockchain technology. In *Proceedings of the Global Internet of Things Summit (GIoTS)*, Geneva, Switzerland, pp. 6-9.

Mazieres, D. (2018). *The stellar consensus protocol: A federated model for internet-level consensus.* Available at papers/stellar-consensus-protocol.pdf

Modum. (2017). Available at https://modum.io/

Noubir, G., & Lin, G. (2003). Low-power DoS attacks in data wireless LANs and countermeasures, SIGMOBILE Mob. *Computer Communication Review*, 7(3), 29–30. doi:10.1145/961268.961277

Noyes, C. (2016a). Bitav: Fast anti-malware by distributed blockchain consensus and feedforward scanning. *arXiv preprint arXiv:1601.01405*

OneM2M. (2017). Security solutions–OneM2M technical specification. Retrieved from http://onem2m.org/technical/latest-drafts

Ongaro, D. & Ousterhout, J. (2014, June). In search of an understandable consensus algorithm. In *Proceedings of USENIX Annual Technical Conference*, Philadelphia, PA.

Park, N., & Kang, N. (2016). Mutual authentication scheme in secure internet of things technology for comfortable lifestyle. *Sensors (Basel)*, 6(1), 20–20. doi:10.339016010020 PMID:26712759

Pecorella, T., Brilli, L., & Muchhi, L. (2016). The role of physical layer security in IoT: A novel perspective. *Information*, 7(3).

Peercoin official web page. Available at https://peercoin.net

Prisco, G. (2016) Slock. it to introduce smart locks linked to smart ethereum contracts, decentralize the sharing economy. Bitcoin Magazine. Nov-2015 [Online]. Available at https://bitcoinmagazine.com/articles/sloc-it-to-introduce-smart-locs-lined-to-smart-ethereum-contractsdecentralize-the-sharing-cconomy-1446746719.

Puthal, D., Malik, N., Mohanty, S. P., Kougianos, E., & Yang, C. (2018). Blockchain as decentralized security framework. *IEEE Consumer Electronics Magazine* March 2018. DPOS description on Bitshares. Available at http://docs.bitshares.org/ bitshares/dpos.html

Ren, L. (2018). Proof of stake velocity: Building the social currency of the digital age. Available at https://www.reddcoin.com/papers/PoSV. pdf

Reyna, A., Martín, C., Chen, J., Soler, E., & Díaz, M. (2018). On blockchain and its integration with IoT, Challenges and opportunities, *Future Generation Computer Systems*, 88, pp. 173-190.

Riaz, R., Kim, K.-H., & Ahmed, H. F. (2009). Security analysis survey and framework design for IP connected LoWPANs. In *Proceedings 2009 International Symposium on Autonomous Decentralized Systems*, pp. 1–6. 10.1109/ISADS.2009.5207373

Roman, R., Lopez, J., & Mambo, M. (2018). A survey and analysis of security threats and challenges. *Future Generation Computer Systems*, 78, 680–698. doi:10.1016/j.future.2016.11.009

Roman, R., Zhou, J., & Lopez, J. (2013). On the features and challenges of security and privacy in distributed internet of things. *Computer Networks, 57*(10), 2266–2279. doi:10.1016/j.comnet.2012.12.018

Schwartz, D., Youngs, N., & Britto, A. (2014). The ripple protocol consensus algorithm. *White paper, Ripple Labs.*

Sethi, M., Arkko, J., & Kernen, A. (2012). End-to-end security for sleepy smart object networks. In *Proceedings 37th Annual IEEE Conference on Local Computer Networks Workshops*, pp. 964–972.10.1109/LCNW.2012.6424089

Tiago, M. F.-C. & Fraga-Lamas, P. (2018). A review on the use of blockchain for the Internet of Things. *IEEE Transactions.*

Tian, F. (2016, June). An agri-food supply chain traceability system for china based on RFID & blockchain technology. In *Proceedings of the 13th International Conference on Service Systems and Services Management*, Kunming, China.

Veena, P., Panikkar, S., Nair, S., & Brody, P. (2015). Empowering the edge-practical insights on a decentralized internet of things. *IBM Institute for Business*, 17.

Wang, C., Wang, Q., Ren, K., & Lou, W. (2010). Privacy-preserving public auditing for data storage security in cloud computing. In *Proceedings INFOCOM, San Diego*, CA, IEEE, 2010, pp. 1–9. 10.1109/INFCOM.2010.5462173

Wang, W., Kong, J., Bhargava, B., & Gerla, M. (2008). Visualisation of wormholes in underwater sensor networks: A distributed approach. *Int. J. Secur. Netw., 3*(1), 10–23. doi:10.1504/IJSN.2008.016198

Weekly, K. & Pister, K. (2012). Evaluating sinkhole defense techniques in RPL networks. In *Proceedings of the 2012 20th IEEE International Conference on Network Protocols (ICNP)*, IEEE Computer Society, Washington, DC. . pp 1-6.10.1109/ICNP.2012.6459948

Xiao, L., Greenstein, L. J., Mandayam, N. B., & Trappe, W. (2009). Channel-based detection of sybil attacks in wireless networks. *IEEE Transactions on Information Forensics and Security, 4*(3), 492–503. doi:10.1109/TIFS.2009.2026454

Xu, W., Trappe, W., Zhang, Y., & Wood, T. (2005). The feasibility of launching and detecting jamming attacks in wireless networks. In *Proceedings of the 6th ACM International Symposium on Mobile Ad Hoc Networking and Computing, nMobiHoc '05*, ACM, New York, NY. . pp.46–57.10.1145/1062689.1062697

Young, M., & Boutaba, R. (2011). Overcoming adversaries in sensor networks: A survey of theoretical models and algorithmic approaches for tolerating malicious interference. *IEEE Communications Surveys and Tutorials, 13*(4), 617–641. doi:10.1109/SURV.2011.041311.00156

Zheng, Z., Xie, S., Dai, H.-N., Chen, X., & Wang, H. (2018). Blockchain challenges and opportunities: A survey. *International Journal of Web and Grid Services, 14*(4), 352. doi:10.1504/IJWGS.2018.095647

This research was previously published in Security and Privacy Issues in Sensor Networks and IoT; pages 231-263, copyright year 2020 by Information Science Reference (an imprint of IGI Global).

Chapter 50
Comprehensive Study on Incorporation of Blockchain Technology With IoT Enterprises

Ashok Kumar Yadav

(iD) https://orcid.org/0000-0002-7822-5870

School of Computer and Systems Sciences, Jawaharlal Nehru University, New Delhi, India

ABSTRACT

Unprecedented advancement in wireless technology, storage, and computing power of portable devices with the gigabyte speed of internet connectivity enables the possibility of communication among machine to machine. IoT has a different way to connect many nodes simultaneously to store, access, and share the information to improve the quality of life by the elimination of the involvement of human. Irrespective of unlimited benefit, IoT has so many issues that arise to eclipse IoT in reality because of its centralized model. Scalability, reliability, privacy, and security challenges are rising because of the huge numbers of IoT nodes, centralized architecture, and complex networks. Centralized architecture may lead to problems like a single point of failure, single way traffic, huge infrastructure cost, privacy, security, and single source of trust. Therefore, to overcome the issues of the centralized infrastructure of the IoT, the authors diverted to decentralized infrastructure. It may be the best decision in terms of performance, reliability, security, privacy, and trust. Blockchain is an influential latest decentralization technology to decentralize computation, process management, and trust. A combination of blockchain with IoT may have the potential to solve scalability, reliability, privacy, and security issues of IoT. This chapter has an overview of some important consensus algorithms, IoT challenges, integration of the blockchain with IoT, its challenges, and future research issues of a combination of blockchain and IoT are also discussed.

INTRODUCTION

The Internet of Things (IoT) is a most recent technology to connect and facilitate to communicate among numerous things simultaneously for providing different benefits to consumers that will change user's interaction with the technology. The concept of IoT is not new. "The Internet of Things has more potential

DOI: 10.4018/978-1-6684-7132-6.ch050

than the internet which changes the world, just as the internet did in the last few years (Hong-Ning Dai, Zibin Zheng, Yan Zhang, 2019). The core concept behind IoT is establishing a system to store all the data on the cloud without having the requirement of human efforts in collecting it. It is believed that the impact of IoT on the world will be immense in the upcoming years. Though the presence of IoT offers a cutting-edge opportunity in fully automated systems, traffic management, and solutions, it comes with certain limitations that we cannot ignore. IoT offers a universal model of sharing information to enhance society, enabling advanced services by interconnecting things based on existing wireless communication technologies. A study confirms approximate 60% of companies are already engaged in developing IoT projects. Recently more than 30% startups are at an early stage of deployment of IoT. More than 69% of these IoT based companies are now focusing problems like, how IoT operational cost can be reduced? Cisco says, 74% of organizations have failed with their IoT startups. It is happening due to the involvement of humans in IoT implementation, beyond the functional elements of sensors and network complexity. Data reliability, security, and privacy are rigorous issues in cloud-based IoT applications.

Heterogeneity, centralization, the complexity of networks, interoperability, privacy vulnerability, and security vulnerability are the root cause of security, privacy and reliability issues in IoT systems. To overcome problems of security, privacy, reliability, and the trust of the IoT system; there is a requirement of the new advanced techniques. The blockchain is one of the best emerging technology. It may ensure the privacy and security issues by using a public ledger, cryptographic and hash algorithms. Blockchain is an incorruptible decentralized digital public ledger of economical transactions that can be programmed to record not just only for financial transactions but also virtually everything which have value to facilitate data decentralization, transparency, tamper-proof, replicated ledger, immutability, and improved trust in peer to peer network. The blockchain has emerged as one of the major technologies that have the potential to transform the way of sharing the huge information. Improving trust in a peer - peer environment without the requirement of a trusted third party is a technological challenge to transform present scenarios of the society and industries. Decentralized and distributed nature, transaction verifiability, transparency and immutability features of blockchain can tackle challenges of IoT. Without considering the heavy computational load, delay, storage, bandwidth overhead of blockchain can lead to a new set of challenges in the integration of the blockchain with IoT (A. Baliga, 2017). Blockchain uses the technique of hash function, Merkle Tree, Nonce (to make the hash function harder to retrace) and others to provide Data Centralization, Transparency, Security and Privacy, Tamper proof replicated ledger, Immutable Ledger Non-Repudiation, irreversibility of records, Automation and Smart Contract, a new way of storing (M. Conoscenti, A. Vetro, and J. C. De Martin, 2016). Figure 1 shows the component of blockchain.

Issues of IoT are like security, privacy, scalability, reliability, maintainability. Blockchain has decentralizations, persistence, anonymity, immutability, identity and access management, resiliency, autonomy, apriority, cost-saving as attractive features.

These features may address challenges of IoT, Big data and machine learning. Blockchain pushes centralized network-based IoT to blockchain-based Distributed Ledger. Blockchain mainly can tackle scalability, privacy, and reliability issue in the IoT system. This chapter proposes a trusted, reliable and flexible architecture for IoT service systems based on blockchain technology, which facilitated self-trust, data integrity, audit, data resilience, and scalability (A. Panarello, N. Tapas, G. Merlino, F. Longo, & A. Puliafito, 2018).

The concept of Hashcash was suggested by Adam Back in 1997 (Z. Zheng, S. Xie, H. N. Dai, X. Chen, H. Wang, 2018). Hashcash is a mining algorithm used as Proof-of-Work Consensus algorithm (Used for Permission less blockchain Technology i.e. Bitcoin). It is used to restrain email and save such a system from Denial of service Attacks. Brute Force method is the only way to implement the Hashcash. The consensus algorithms are the heart of blockchain technology. The consensus algorithms are considered as the pillar of the blockchain network. Many consensus algorithms have been suggested to get system safe from any malicious activity in blockchain technology. Proof-of-Work, Proof-of-Stake, delegated proof of stake, Practical Byzantine Fault Tolerance are some of the popular consensus algorithms (D. Larimer, 2018). Basically, consensus ensures the attainment of logical decisions so, every peer should agree whether a transaction should be committed in the database or not (A. Panarello, N. Tapas, G. Merlino, F. Longo, & A. Puliafito, 2018).

CONSENSUS ALGORITHMS

The concept of PoW is used beyond blockchain. Ideally, the concept is to produce a challenge to a user, the user has to produce a solution which should show some proof of work being done against that challenge. Once it is validated the user accepted. It eliminates the entity that is slow or not capable enough to generate PoW In blockchain PoW is used to generate a value that is difficult to generate and easy to verify. To generate block hash there are n leading zeros. It will help in solution and known as a nonce. In PoW node having high power machine will perform more transaction to be committed and generate a new block. This will lead to higher incentives towards node utilizing more powerful machine in generating new blocks (Bentov, I., Gabizon, & M., 2016). In proof of work, miners are required to give a solution for the complex cryptographic hash problem. Miners compete with each other to become the first to find the nonce. The first miner solves the puzzle gets the reward. Mining in proof of work algorithm requires a lot of computing power and resources. Proof of work uses a huge amount of electricity and encourages mining pools which take the blockchain towards centralization (Z. Zheng, S. Xie, H. N. Dai, X. Chen, H. Wang, 2018). To solve these issues, a new consensus algorithm was proposed called Proof of Stake. A validator is chosen randomly to validate the next block. To become a validator, a node has to deposit a certain amount of coins in the network as a stake. This process is called staking/minting/forging. The chance of becoming the validator is proportional to the stake. The bigger the stake is, the higher the chances validate the block. This algorithm favors the rich stake. When a validator tries to approve an invalid block, he/she loses a part of the stake. When a validator approves a valid block, he/she gets the transaction fees and the stake is returned. Therefore, the amount of the stake should be higher than the total transaction fee to avoid any fraudulent block to be added. A fraud validator loses more coins than he/she gets. If a node does not wish to be a validator anymore, his/her stake as well as transaction fees are released after a certain period of time (not immediately as network needs to punish the node if he/she is involved in fraudulent block). Proof of Stake does not ask for huge amounts of electrical power and it is more decentralized. It is more environmentally friendly than Proof of Work. 51% attack is less likely to happen with Proof of Stake as the validator should have at least 51% of all the coins which is a very huge amount. Proof of Stake is performing for the more protective way and to use less usage of power to execute the transaction. Sometimes a person having the more cryptocurrency (i.e. Bitcoin) will have more probability to mine new block, but again, it was arising the problem of dominance when a person having 50 percent or more then it will have the highest probability to mine the block so the solution has been made in terms of some randomization protocol in which random nodes are selected to mine new block. Since it was also found that nodes are priory starting with PoW and then they move to PoS for better and smoother usage.

Since PoA can be considered as the combination of Proof-of-Stack (PoS) and Proof-of-Work (PoW). PoA modifies the solution for PoS. If any miner wants to commit some transactions in a block as to mine a new block, then if that miner wants to commit that mined block into the database, then most of every node sign the block for validation (D. Larimer, 2018). PoET algorithm suggests some common steps to select the miner that which would mine a new block. Each miner that had mined the prior block had waited for random time quantum to do so. Any miner which is proposing any new block to mine should wait for the random moment of time and it will be easy to determine whether any miner which is proposed for the new block to mine has waited for some time or not by making a determination that a miner has utilized a special CPU instruction set.

PBFT algorithm concerns when one or more node in any network becomes faulty and behave maliciously that results in improper communication among all nodes connected to that network. Such things result in a delay in functioning, whereas time is a very serious concern as we already are working in an asynchronous system where if at least one fault occurs then it would be impossible to solve the consensus problem. I will also generate discrimination in responses of various nodes. PBFT works for the permissions model. In practical Byzantine fault tolerance, state machine replication occurs at multiple nodes and the client will wait for an n+1 response from all nodes where n is the number of faulty nodes, but it isn't giving the proper solution for this because n+1 cannot determine the majority vote for the client. PBFT applies to the asynchronous system (M. Samaniego and R. Deters, 2016).

Generally, PBFT was attained after PAXOS and RAFT that both have maximum fault tolerance of $n/2 - 1$ among all nodes where n seems to be the number of faulty nodes (T. M. FernÃa̦ndez-CaramÃl's & P. Fraga-Lamas, 2018). Since PBFT is getting around 3n+1 response among all non-faulty nodes where n is determined as the faulty nodes. As we are discussing the state machine replication, then it is important to understand it. Delegated proof of stake is similar to PoS algorithm. It refers to more decentralized fashion in blockchain network and it also modifies the way by which energy can be utilized often very less in executing the proper manipulation. Now Delegated proof of stake is generally given the chances to stockholders to give their votes to whom they wanted to mine further coming block which should be committed in the database. Cryptocurrency holders will also have the opportunity to select the miner to mine a further block. Stockholders will choose the delegates which will be responsible for the mining of new block and somehow, some witnesses are also selected on an election basis by currency holders to perform proper manipulation like searching of nonce and validation of block etc. And what the delegates need to do is that they will decide how much incentives to be given to witnesses, and they will also decide the factors like block size, power, etc. And final decision will be made by stakeholders to what delegates will have proposed to them. Witnesses will change within some time duration or within a week. Witnesses should perform the transaction allotted within the given time duration. It's all about the reputation of witnesses, more they perform the transaction efficiently within the given time duration, more will be their chance to get selection again in the mining process by selectors (i.e. Cryptocurrency holders). DPoS is also increasing more decentralized fashion as what proposed in PoS was more in a centralized fashion to whom will have the higher amount of currency will have the more dominating effect in the whole network, but in DPoS it has been modified and made a system something distributed that is removing the centralization process (A. Baliga, 2017).

Table 1. Comparison of Permissioned Network Consensus Algorithms

BFT	RBFT	PBFT	PAXOS	RAFT
A closed network	A closed network	Synchronous	Synchronous	Synchronous
Used for business working based on smart contracts	Used for business working based on smart contracts	Smart contracts dependent	Smart contracts dependent	Smart contracts dependent
State machine replication is used	The proper authorities are handling, proper work	State machine replication is used	Sender, proposer and acceptor jointly work	Collecting selected ledger on some agreement to work
Good transactional throughput	Good transactional throughput	Greater transactional throughput	Greater transactional throughput	Greater transactional throughput
Byzantine faults	Byzantine faults (i.e. Hyperledger body)	Byzantine faults	Crash fault	Crash fault
Based on traditional notions	Based on traditional notions	It can bear f-1 tolerance	PAXOS can bear f/2-1 fault	RAFT can bear f/2-1 fault

Table 2. Comparison of Permissionless Network Consensus Algorithms

Proof of Work (PoW)	Proof of Stake (PoS)	Proof of Burn (PoB)	PoET
Used for industries working on a financial level	Used for industries working on a financial level	Used for industries working on a financial level	Used for industries working on a financial level
Using public key encryption (i.e. Bitcoin)	Using an RSA algorithm for encryption	RSA algorithm for encryption	RSA algorithm for encryption
Miners having higher work done after investing higher power will have higher probability to mine the new block	It is some election type selection of miners for the next block to be mined	PoB acquires some cryptocurrencies (wealth) to mine new block using virtual resource	A person spends some time and power to mine new block who finishes the first priority task will be the next miner
Power inefficient	Power efficient	Power efficient	Power efficient
An open environment	An open environment	An open environment	An open environment
Bitcoin script is used	Mostly Golong is used	Mostly Golong is used	

CHALLENGES OF BLOCKCHAIN TECHNOLOGY

Blockchain is an emerging technology that provides a way to record transactions in such a way that it ensures security, transparency, auditability, immutability, anonymity. Decentralization is one of the key features of blockchain technology because it can solve problems like an extra cost, performance limitations, and central point failure. Blockchain allows the validation of transactions through the nodes without authentication, jurisdiction or intervention done by a central agency, reduce the service cost, mitigate the performance limitations and eliminating the central point failure. Instead of transparency, blockchain can maintain a certain level of privacy by making blockchain addresses anonymous. It must be noted that the blockchain can only maintain pseudonyms. It may not preserve the full privacy. The features of blockchain-like decentralization, immutability, and transparency make it a suitable technology to integrate with IoT to provide a solution to the major challenges of IoT. Despite being a very efficient emerging technology for recording transactions, this technology still faces some challenges like storage and scalability. Long-chain may have a negative impact on the performance of IoT. It may increase the synchronization time for new users. Consensus protocol has a direct impact on the scalability of the blockchain. Besides this, blockchain technology also faces security weaknesses and threats. The most common attack is 51% or majority attack. In this situation, the consensus in the network can be controlled, especially those that centralized the consensus among fewer nodes. Double spending attack, race attack, denial of services and man in the middle attack are also some of the challenges faced by blockchain technology. Blockchain infrastructure is vulnerable to man in the middle kind of attack since they strongly depend on communication. In this attack, the attacker can monopolize the node's connections isolating it from the rest of the network (F. Atlam, A. Alenezi, M. O. Alassafi, G. B. Wills, 2018).

INTERNET OF THING (IoT)

We are entering an era where everything is going to be smart and is connected to each other through a network. All the different things around us is going to interconnect via wireless over the internet. These things are not only the computer and computing devices, but also the things we see and use in our daily life like, table, chair, dustbin, etc. The concept of interconnecting of things through internet, introduce a new buzzword "Internet of Things (IoT)". Now IoT is going to connect human to machine, machine to machine, human to things, things to machine and things to things. It means, things can communicate to things without any physical medium. Internet of Things is comprised of two terms Internet and Things. The Internet is the global system of interconnected computer networks that use the Internet Protocol suit to link the devices worldwide (A. Reyna, C. Martín, J. Chen, E. Soler, M. Díaz, 2018). The things in the internet of Things are not only the computers and computing devices, but also the real-world objects that are going to be transformed into intelligent virtual objects. The scope of this internet is going to expand beyond computers and computing devices, anything and everything in the real world is going to be connected with each other. IoT is going to provide advanced level services to the society and business enterprises. IoT is going to work as the basic building block for smart homes, smart cities, smart campus, smart dust, etc. IoT is a revolution in technical field in which computers, computing devices and real-world things are going to be interconnected, communicate with each other and generate a huge amount of data. Now IoT has considerable attention of researcher from industry and academics, that they must involve in research to overcome the challenges of IoT, to solve real application problems.

Challenges of IoT

Authentication, authorization and encryption are not enough tackling issues of IoT due to resource limited node. Instead of resource limited node, IoT systems are also vulnerable to malicious attacks. It is possible due to the failure of security firmware updates in time. So, major challenges in IoT are compatibility & interoperability of different IoT nodes. It requires nearly 40% to 60% effort. In IoT there are many nodes have very low computing power and their different working mechanism. IoT device uses different types of protocols. Identification & authentication of IoT devices are very difficult because of huge diversity and number of IoT devices. Currently, 20 billion devices are connected in IoT systems. Working with the IoT system is totally depends on the speed of internet connectivity. IoT needs a very high speed for the proper and efficient working of IoT. IoT system is not so applicable because the internet still not available everywhere in a seamless and appropriate speed. So, seamless and appropriate internet connectivity issues may be one of the biggest challenges in IoT deployment (J. Lin, W. Yu, N. Zhang, X. Yang, H. Zhang, and W. Zhao, 2017). Advancement of wireless technology, computing, and processing speed of the CPU, IoT makes human beings' life so easy and flexible but may generate huge amounts of structured, semi structured and structured data at very high speed and variation in a very short time (S. Muralidharan, A. Roy, N. Saxena, 2016). 80% of data generated by IoT system are unstructured data. Handling unstructured data may create a challenge to the deployment of IoT systems for real time applications. Conventional security & privacy approaches not applicable to IoT because of decentralized and resource constraints of the majority of IoT devices. By 2020, 25% of cyber-attacks will target IoT devices. And also 54% IoT device owners, do not use any third party too & 25% out of these do not even change the default password on their device. The device does not know neighbors in advance, no cooperative data exchange, the adversary can compromise device's data, energy-inefficient protocol, data capturing, intelligent analytics, and delivering value may create challenges for deploying the IoT systems. IoT nodes ask blockchain to store their state, manage multiple writers, and prevent from the need of a trusted third party (Hong-Ning Dai, Zibin Zheng, Yan Zhang, 2019).

IoT security and Privacy Solution

The Internet is the global system of interconnected computer networks that use the Internet Protocol suit to link the devices worldwide. Due to the worldwide interconnectivity of IoT device and resource constraint, the security of IoT is crucial issues. There are many solutions to resolve the security and privacy challenges from IoT. Some of the privacy solution is mentioned in the figure.

Integration of Blockchain with IoT

This is the era of peer to peer interaction. Unprecedented growth in IoT explores the new mechanism of storing, accessing and sharing information. This new mechanism of storing, accessing and sharing of information raises the issue of security, privacy and data availability. The centralized architecture of IoT enhanced the evolution of IoT, but creates the issue of single-point failure and also provide the entire control of the system to a few powerful authorized users. Blockchain is one of the latest emerging technology, which has the capabilities of a new way to store, access and share information in a decentralized and distributed system. Blockchain technology can be integrated with IoT to resolve the problem with IoT such as storing, accessing, sharing and central point failure. So, we can say that the use of blockchain may be a complement to the IoT with reliable and secure information. Blockchain may be defined as the key to solving scalability, reliability and privacy problems related to IoT paradigm.

Interaction of IoT with Blockchain can be mainly IoT-IoT, IoT-Blockchain and combination of IoT -IoT and IoT-Blockchain. In IoT-IoT data are stored in blockchain while its interaction takes place with the use of blockchain. It is a useful scenario where reliable IoT interaction with low latency is required. In IoT-Blockchain all interaction and their respective data go through blockchain, to collect an immutable and traceable record of interactions. It is helpful in scenarios like trade and rent to obtain reliability and security. In hybrid platform some interaction and data part are stored in blockchain and the remaining are directly shared between the IoT devices. This approach is a perfect way to leverage and benefit of both Blockchain and real-time IoT interaction. The interaction method can be chosen on a parameter such as a throughput, latency number of writers, a number of interested writers, data media, interactive media, consensus mechanism, security and resource consumption., Blockchain integration with IoT has the potential to overcome the challenges in the control IoT system (A. Reyna, C. Martín, J. Chen, E. Soler, M. Díaz, 2018).

Blockchain can improve the power of IoT by offering a trust, sharing service for reliability and tractability of information. Shifting from a cloud to a peer to peer network will resolve central points of failure. It also prevents few powerful companies to control the processing & storage of the information of a huge number of people also improve fault tolerance & system scalability. Blockchain specially designed for an internet scenario with high processing computer, it was far from the reality of IoT. Blockchain technology can be used to keep a track of connected IoT devices which can enable the process of transaction and coordination between devices. Blockchain technology can also be used to keep an immutable record of the history of smart devices in an IoT network, which will maintain the autonomy of peers without any requirement of the single authority (X. Liang, J. Zhao, S. Shetty, D. Li., 2017).

The fundamental issues of IoT such as security, privacy, scalability, reliability, maintainability can be solved by blockchain because blockchain provides many attractive features such as decentralization, persistence, anonymity, immutability, identity and access management, resiliency, autonomy, apriority, cost-saving. These features may address challenges of IoT, Big data and machine learning. Blockchain pushes network-based IoT to blockchain-based one. IoT system facing challenges such as heterogeneity of IoT system, poor interoperability, resource-limited IoT devices, privacy & security vulnerabilities. Blockchain can support the IoT system with the enhancement of heterogeneity, interoperability, privacy & security vulnerability. Blockchain can also improve the reliability & scalability of the IoT system. We can say blockchain can be integrated with the IoT system.

Advantages of integration of Blockchain with IoT

1. **Enhance interoperability** Heterogeneous type of data can be converted, process, extracted, compressed and finally stored in the blockchain.
2. **Improve security and privacy** IoT data transactions can be encrypted and digitally signed by cryptographic keys. Blockchain support automatic updating of IoT devices firmware to heal vulnerable breaches thereby improving the system security.
3. **Traceability and Reliability** All the historical transactions stored in the blockchain may be traceable because of anywhere, anytime verification. The immutability of blockchain helps in the reliability of IoT data due to the impossibility of temper blockchain stored information.
4. **Decentralization and use of public ledger** After integration of IoT with block chain, the central governing body is eliminated, which will remove the single point failure problem. Further, due to decentralization, the trust issue is also solved since the majority of the nodes in the network agree on the validation of a particular transaction. So, blockchain will provide a secure platform for IoT devices.

Challenges of integration of IoT with Blockchain

The integration of blockchain with IoT is secured around 99% from any attacker who belongs to the outside of the network or system. But when any miner becomes attacker or peers itself create their own virtual blockchain network to communicate and may start malicious activities. Since we update blockchain ledger regularly, and regular updating may lead to the problem of centralization. As time passes incentives are gradually decreasing due to limited available currency to pay the miners for mining. There may be a chance of not getting any incentive. To overcome the deficiency of currency blockchain authority may charge some fee to the node just like to trusted third party. İt will gain the concept of blockchain because one of the primary goals of blockchain is to reduce transaction charges. If we are discussing the permission-less model, then the first cryptocurrency comes in mind is Bitcoin. But a major problem with the permission-less model is one address of one user. A user can directly enter into the network and participate in a transaction that is very difficult to know the sender authentication by the receiver whereas digital signature is applied there to solve this problem. It also has the problem of 'how digital signatures can be identified or validated' whereas it may possibly use public key verification of the sender, but may have the problem of multiple addresses because public and private keys are changeable or dynamic in nature. Another point in a permission-less model is that if nodes are not active for almost 3 hours of time duration in the bitcoin network, then they would be disconnected from the same network.

Blockchain technology implementation has problem of scalability, block size, number of transactions per second, not applicable for high-frequency fraud. There may be a trade-off between block size and security. To improve the selfish mining strategy, miners can hide their mined block for more revenue in the future. There may be privacy leakage when users make transactions with their public key and the private key. A user real IP address could be tracked. The number of blocks is mined per unit time cannot fulfill the requirement of process of millions of transactions in a real-time fashion. What may be the maximum chain length and maximum number of miners? Is there any possibility to go for a centralized system using blockchain? Larger block size could slow down the propagation speed and may lead blockchain branch, small transactions can be delayed because miners give more performance to a high transaction fee technical challenge (T. M. FernÃa₎ndez-CaramÃl's & P. Fraga-Lamas, 2018).

To ensure the immutability and reliability of the information, blockchain is required to store all the transaction information for verification and validation. Due to storing all the transaction information and the exponential increase of storage limited IoT devices leads to a drastic increase in the size of Blockchain. This is the primary drawback of integration with IoT. Some of the blockchain implementations have the processing of very few transactions per second. But some real-time IoT applications need very high processing transactions per second. This may be also a major bottleneck of integrating IoT with blockchain. To resolve the issues of scalability of storage size, researchers are proposing a new optimized storage blockchain using the concept of removing old transaction records from the blockchain.

The biggest challenges in the integration of the blockchain with IoT are the scalability of the ledger and the rate of transaction execution in the blockchain. Huge number of IoT devices generate exponential transactions at a rate which current blockchain solution cannot handle. Implementing blockchain peers into IoT devices is very difficult because of resource constraints. Integration of IoT is limited by scalability and expensive computation and high transaction cost of public blockchain. Industries will face a lot of challenges after the integration of IoT with Blockchain such as the connection of huge numbers of IoT devices in the coming next five years, control and management of the huge number of IoT devices in a decentralized system. The integration of IoT with blockchain will raise a few questions for industries like how the industry will enable peer to peer communication between globally distributed devices, how the industry will provide compliance and governance for autonomous systems and how industry will address the security complexities of IoT landscape (M. Samaniego and R. Deters, 2016). Integration of blockchain with limited resource IoT devices is not suitable due to the lack of computational resources, limited bandwidth and they need to preserve power (H.N. Dai, Z. Zheng, & Y. Zhang, 2019).

Open Research Issues in Blockchain IoT (BCIoT)

Due to resource constraints of IoT devices, conventional big data analysis scheme may not apply to IoT. So, it is very difficult to conduct big data analysis in IoT blockchain systems. Security vulnerability and privacy mechanism are most important research areas in the fields of integration of the blockchain in IoT (R. Zhang & R. Xue, 2019).

IoT tries to make the system fully automated, but to ensure verifiability, authentication, and immutability of the blockchain requires an efficient incentive mechanism. Designing an efficient incentive mechanism is another area of research in the integration of the blockchain with IoT. The drastic increase in the complexity of the network and the addition of a huge number of IoT devices require an effective, scalable mechanism of integration of the blockchain with IoT. It is also one of the future research areas in the integration of blockchain with IoT.

CONCLUSION

Today, due to the emergence of IoT and Big data, the huge, diverse and critical information is available over the internet. The trust over the information is reduced drastically in IoT systems, causing an increase in security and privacy concern day-by-day of the industry and organizations. The integration of blockchain technology with IoT has the potential to change upcoming scenarios of society, industries, and organizations in the coming future. The Integration of blockchain with IoT is one of the emerging technologies for ensuring privacy and security by using cryptographic algorithms and hashing. In this book, chapter authors have discussed the basic consensus algorithms, comparison, and analysis of important consensus algorithms. This book chapter also have covered the basic concept of IoT, challenges of IoT. This chapter mainly have focused on possibility of Integration of blockchain with IoT, advantage, and challenges. In the future, the author will cover the different implementation platforms of integration of blockchain with IoT.

REFERENCES

Ali, M. S., Vecchio, M., Pincheira, M., Dolui, K., Antonelli, F., & Rehmani, M. H. (2019). Applications of Blockchains in the Internet of Things: A Comprehensive Survey. *IEEE Communications Surveys and Tutorials*, *21*(2), 1676–1717. doi:10.1109/COMST.2018.2886932

Atlam, Alenezi, Alassafi, & Wills. (2018). Blockchain with Internet of Things: Benefits, Challenges, and Future Directions. *International Journal of Intelligent Systems and Applications*.

Baliga. (2017). *Understanding blockchain consensus models*. Persistent Systems Ltd, Tech. Rep.

Bentov & Gabizon. (2016). Cryptocurrencies without proof of work. In *International Conference on Financial Cryptography and Data Security* (pp. 142-157). Springer. 10.1007/978-3-662-53357-4_10

Biswas, S., Sharif, K., Li, F., Nour, B., & Wang, Y. (2019). A Scalable Blockchain Framework for Secure Transactions in IoT. IEEE Internet of Things Journal, 6(3).

Conoscenti, M., Vetro, A., & De Martin, J. C. (2016). Blockchain for the internet of things: A systematic literature review. *3th International Conference of Computer Systems and Applications*, 1–6. 10.1109/AICCSA.2016.7945805

Dai, H.-N., Zheng, Z., & Zhang, Y. (2019). *Blockchain for Internet of Things: A Survey. IEEE Internet of Things Journal.*

Dai, H. N., Zheng, Z., & Zhang, Y. (2019). Blockchain for Internet of Things: A Survey. IEEE Internet of Things Journal, 6(5).

Fernandez-Caramals & Fraga-Lamas. (2018). A review on the use of blockchain for the internet of things. *IEEE Access, 6.*

Larimer. (2018). *Delegated proof-of-stake consensus*. Academic Press.

Larimer, D. (2018). DPOS Consensus Algorithm – The Missing Whitepaper. *Steemit*. Available: https://steemit. com/dpos/dantheman/dpos-consensus-algorithm-this-missingwhite-paper

Liang, X., Zhao, J., Shetty, S., & Li, D. (2017). Towards data assurance and resilience in IoT using blockchain. *IEEE Military Communications Conference (MILCOM)*. 10.1109/MILCOM.2017.8170858

Lin, J., Yu, W., Zhang, N., Yang, X., Zhang, H., & Zhao, W. (2017). A survey on internet of things: Architecture, enabling technologies, security and privacy, and applications. *IEEE Internet of Things Journal*, 4(5), 1125–1142. doi:10.1109/JIOT.2017.2683200

Liu, B., Yu, X. L., Chen, S., Xu, X., & Zhu, L. (2017). Blockchain based data integrity service framework for IoT data. In *IEEE International Conference on Web Services (ICWS)*. IEEE. 10.1109/ICWS.2017.54

Muralidharan, S., Roy, A., & Saxena, N. (2016). An Exhaustive Review on Internet of Things from Korea's Perspective. *Wireless Personal Communications*, 90(3), 1463–1486. doi:10.100711277-016-3404-8

Panarello, A., Tapas, N., Merlino, G., Longo, F., & Puliafito, A. (2018). Blockchain and IoT integration: A systematic survey. *Sensors (Basel)*, 18(8), 2575. doi:10.339018082575 PMID:30082633

Reyna, A., Martín, C., Chen, J., Soler, E., & Díaz, M. (2018). On blockchain and its integration with IoT Challenges and opportunities. *Future Generation Computer Systems*, 88, 173–190. doi:10.1016/j.future.2018.05.046

Samaniego, M., & Deters, R. (2016). Blockchain as a service for IoT. *IEEE International Conference on Internet of Things (iThings) and IEEE Green Computing and Communications (GreenCom) and IEEE Cyber, Physical and Social Computing (CPSCom) and IEEE Smart Data (SmartData)*, 433–436. 10.1109/iThings-GreenCom-CPSCom-SmartData.2016.102

Song, J. C., Demir, M. A., Prevost, J. J., & Rad, P. (2018). Blockchain design for trusted decentralized iot networks. In *13th Annual Conference on System of Systems Engineering (SoSE)*. IEEE. 10.1109/SYSOSE.2018.8428720

Viriyasitavat, W., & Li Da Xu. (2019). Blockchain Technology for Applications in Internet of Things—Mapping from System Design Perspective. IEEE Internet of Things Journal, 6(5).

Zhang, R., & Xue, R. (2019). Security and Privacy on Blockchain. *ACM Computing Surveys*, *1*(1).

Zheng, Z., Xie, S., Dai, H. N., Chen, X., & Wang, H. (2018). Blockchain challenges and opportunities: A survey. *International Journal of Web and Grid Services*, *14*(4), 352. doi:10.1504/IJWGS.2018.095647

This research was previously published in Opportunities and Challenges for Blockchain Technology in Autonomous Vehicles; pages 22-33, copyright year 2021 by Engineering Science Reference (an imprint of IGI Global).

Chapter 51
Optimization of Consensus Mechanism for IoT Blockchain:
A Survey

Shailesh Pancham Khapre
Amity University, Noida, India

Shraddha P. Satpathy
Amity University, Noida, India

Chandramohan D.
Madanapalle Institute of Technology and Science, India

ABSTRACT

The essence of blockchain is a decentralized distributed ledger system; the IoT is formed by accessing and interconnecting a large number of heterogeneous terminals and has a natural distributed feature. Therefore, the combination of the two IoT blockchains is widely optimistic. At the same time, due to the heterogeneity of IoT sensing terminals, limited computing storage, and data transmission capabilities, the IoT blockchain is facing greater challenges, among which cryptographic consensus technology has become a key issue. In this chapter, based on the summary of the current blockchain consensus algorithm, applicability to the IoT-blockchain has been analyzed, the application status of several major IoT-blockchain platforms and consensus mechanisms have been introduced, and also the IoT-blockchain research progress on optimization of consensus mechanism has been expounded. Looking forward to the optimization techniques of the IoT blockchain, potential research directions have been summarized.

DOI: 10.4018/978-1-6684-7132-6.ch051

INTRODUCTION

With the advent of IoT (Khodadadi *et.al*, 2017), information sensing equipment is widely used in smart communities, smart agriculture, smart transportation, shared economy, and other fields to promote comprehensive interconnection and integration of man-machine-things. IoT research institutions predict that by the end of 2020 (Ashton, 2009), the number of IoT terminal devices will increase to 26 billion.

The main access control methods in the Internet of Things environment are: role-based access control RBAC, attribute-based access control ABAC, access control based on usage control model UCON, and capability-based access control CapABC. The aforementioned RBAC, ABAC and UCON IoT solutions rely on a centralized server-client architecture to connect to cloud servers via the Internet. In order to meet the growth, the decentralized architecture CapABC was proposed to create a large-scale P2P wireless sensor network. CapABC achieves lightweight distributed control, dynamics, and scalability, but CapABC cannot guarantee security or user privacy. Compared with the traditional Internet, IoT architecture expands network connections to a richer physical space. In view of its massive heterogeneous and resource-constrained IoT terminal, data sharing, privacy protection, intrusion detection, access control, and cross-domain authentication and other problems (Wang *et.al*, 2019, Kouicem *et.al*, 2018), traditional security technologies with large computing requirements and high deployment costs cannot be directly applicable to the IoT platform, we need to find new security solutions.

As shown in Figure 1, from the past closed centralized framework to the open cloud centralized architecture, and the next step is to distribute cloud functions to multiple nodes, blockchain technology can play a big role in the next trend effect.

Figure 1. The IoT architecture of the past, present and future

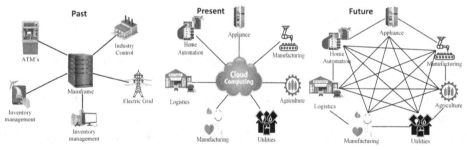

Blockchain is a decentralized distributed technology, a peer-to-peer distributed ledger based on cryptographic algorithms. The blockchain technology extracted from the underlying architecture of Bitcoin can be applied to the transfer of value between any media that does not require mutual trust, thereby spawning a general blockchain application platform such as Ethereum and hyperledger (Qi-feng *et.al*, 2017). Blockchain has the basic characteristics of decentralization, tamper-proof information, open and transparent data, and three guarantee mechanisms: consensus mechanism, smart contract, and asymmetric encryption. Blockchain technology can solve the following challenges in large-scale IoT systems: Most IOT solutions are still expensive because of the high cost of deploying and maintaining central clouds and servers. When the supplier does not provide the above facilities, these costs are transferred to the middleman. Maintenance is also a big issue, when software needs to be regularly updated for millions of smart devices. After the Snowden leak, it is difficult for IOT adopters to trust other technology partners, give them access and control, and allow them to collect and analyze user data. Therefore, privacy and anonymity should be the core of the future development of IOT. The closed source code also leads to a lack of trust. To increase trust and security, transparency is important, so open source solutions should be taken into consideration when developing next-generation IOT solutions.

As shown in Figure 2, the blockchain can generally be divided into six parts: data layer, network layer, consensus layer, incentive layer, contract layer, and application layer (Sun *et.al*, 2018).

Figure 2. The typical layered structure of Blockchain

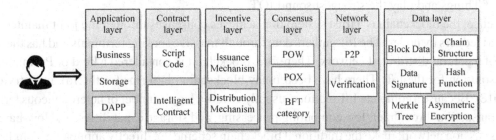

What Blockchain can Accomplish for IOT?

1. Reduce Operating Costs

Blockchain technology focuses on the point-to-point direct connection of data to be transmitted, rather than through the central processing unit. This distributed computing method can handle hundreds of millions of exchanges. At the same time, it can also make full use of nodes distributed in different locations around the world to develop hundreds of millions of idle computing power, storage capacity and network resources, which are used for transaction processing on the Internet of Things, which is costly for calculation and storage. The amplitude is reduced.

2. Reduce Security Risks

The core problem of IoT security is the lack of original mutual trust mechanism between devices. In the early stage of the development of the Internet of Things, all devices need to be verified with the data of the Internet of Things center. Once the central database collapses, it will cause great damage to the entire Internet of Things.

What is gratifying is that in a distributed blockchain network, a new mechanism can be provided to ensure that consensus can be maintained between devices without the need to go to the data center for verification. In this way, even if one or more nodes on the Internet of Things are compromised, the data on the overall network is still reliable and safe.

3. Efficient and Intelligent Network Operation Mechanism

Since the blockchain has a decentralization and consensus mechanism, on the Internet of Things, cross-system data transmission will be transferred from the upper layer to the underlying blockchain. In this way, the complexity of IoT applications can be greatly reduced. The Internet of Things will also evolve into the era of "Internet of Things" and build a new world on the chain.

The combination of blockchain technology and the Internet of Things can eliminate the verification and certification links between nodes, directly build a communication bridge for multiple contacts, and improve network operation efficiency. At the same time, the decentralized consensus mechanism based on the blockchain can also ensure the security and privacy of the Internet of Things and facilitate the transmission of real information. In view of this, the blockchain will definitely come together with the Internet of Things and play the strongest sound IOT.

In essence, the blockchain is a trust system that achieves consensus through the joint maintenance of distributed ledgers by nodes. The IoT gathers data through massive sensing terminals and has the characteristics of a natural distributed network. Therefore, blockchain is considered a kind of Promising basic security solution for the IoT. There have been many blockchain platforms for the IoT industry (Pan & Yang, 2018). Because a complete IoT platform usually covers a large number of heterogeneous terminals, its high transaction throughput, low computing processing, and storage capabilities, and low-bandwidth data transmission network make the traditional blockchain scheme not directly applicable. A lightweight optimized blockchain system must be studied. Among them, the direct factor affecting the throughput of the blockchain is the cryptographic consensus mechanism. In fact, the consensus mechanism usually consists of two parts, one part is the cryptographic algorithm required to reach consensus, namely the consensus algorithm; the other part is the rules for reaching consensus, the consensus rules. The consensus algorithm belongs to the basic application research of cryptography, and its innovative breakthrough faces great challenges. Therefore, how to improve the blockchain data layer, network layer, application layer, and optimize the traditional consensus rules, and how to make the consensus mechanism more applicable to the IoT application environment has become the focus of current research and development.

This chapter outlines the research on IOT Blockchain Consensus algorithms, how Blockchain and IOT can help each other to outcome the shortcoming's in smart applications, author describes the basic working of Blockchain Consensus Mechanism followed by the development status of IOT-Blockchain Consensus Mechanism, author then describes and analyze the hybrid IOT-Blockchain architecture. At the end author outline the research prospects of optimization of consensus mechanism in IOT Blockchain.

Basics of Blockchain Consensus Algorithm

With the popularity and the development of blockchain technology, more and more consensus algorithms have been proposed. In order to enable readers to have a deeper understanding of different consensus algorithms, this section gives a mainstream of the blockchain consensus process Model. It should be noted that this model is not a general model and may not cover all types of consensus processes, but it can reflect the core ideas of most mainstream consensus algorithms.

The blockchain system is built on the P-2-P network. P denotes the collection of all nodes, which is generally split up into ordinary nodes that produce data or transactions, which are accountable for verifying, packaging, and updating the data or transactions generated by ordinary nodes(). The set of "miner" nodes for mining operations (denoted as M), the two types of nodes may have an intersection; usually, miner nodes will all participate in the consensus competition process, and specific representative nodes will be elected in specific algorithms to replace them Participate in the consensus process and compete for accounting rights. The collection of these representative nodes is recorded as D; the accounting node selected through the consensus process is recorded as A. The consensus process is repeated in rounds, and each round of the consensus process generally re-selects the accounting node of the round.

The core of the consensus process is the "master election" and "accounting" two parts. In the specific operation process, each round can be divided into leader election, block generation, data validation and chaining. (Chain Updation, that is, accounting) 4 stages. As shown in Figure 3, the input of the consensus process is the transaction or data generated and verified by the data node, and the output is the encapsulated data block and the updated blockchain .The 4 stages are executed cyclically, and each round of execution will generate a new block.

Figure 3. A basic model of blockchain consensus processes

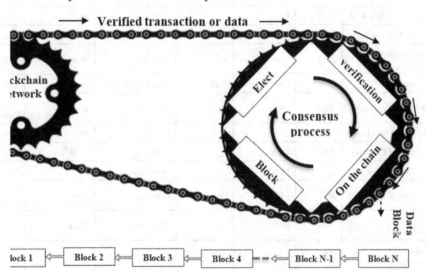

Phase 1: Master election. Master election is the core of the consensus process, that is, the process of selecting accounting node A from the set of all miner nodes M: We can use the formula $f(M) \rightarrow A$ to represent the master election process, where the function f represents the specific implementation of the consensus algorithm. Generally speaking, $|A| = 1$, that is, the only miner node is finally selected for accounting.

Phase 2: Block building. The accounting node selected in the first phase packages the transactions or data generated by all nodes P in the current time period into a block according to a specific strategy, and broadcasts the generated new block to all miners Node M or its representative node D. These transactions or data are usually sorted according to various factors such as block capacity, transaction fees, transaction waiting time, etc., and then packaged into new blocks in order. Block-building strategy is the key to the performance of the blockchain system Factors are also a concentrated manifestation of the strategic behavior of miners such as greedy transaction packaging and selfish mining.

Phase 3: Verification. After the miner node M or representative node D receives the broadcasted new block, they will each verify the correctness and rationality of the transaction or data encapsulated in the block. If the new block obtains the majority of verification/representative nodes If approved, the block will be updated to the blockchain as the next block.

Phase 4: On-chain. The accounting node adds the new block to the main chain to form a complete and longer chain from the genesis block to the latest block. If there are multiple fork chains in the main chain, you need to According to the main chain discrimination criteria stipulated by the consensus algorithm, one of the appropriate branches is selected as the main chain.

Table 1. Comparison of blockchain consensus algorithms

Classification	Consensus algorithm	Proposed time	Calculation overhead	Tolerance of malicious nodes	Degree of decentralization	Manageability	Application
Proof of consensus	POW(Proof of Work)	1999	Large	<1/2	Complete	Weak	Bitcoin, Permacoin
	POS(Proof of Stake)	2011	Moderate	<1/2	Complete	Weak	Peercoin
	DPos (Delegated Proof of Stake)	2013	Low	<1/2	Complete	Weak	EOS
	Ouroboros	2017	Low	<1/2	Semi-Centralised	Strong	Cardno
	POA(Proof of Activity)	2014	Large	<1/2	Semi-Centralised	Strong	Ethereum private chain, Oracles Network
	PoB(Proof of Burn)	2014	Large	<1/2	Semi-Centralised	Strong	Slimcoin
	POC(Proof of Capacity)	2016	Large	—	Complete	Weak	File Sharing
	PoD(Proof of Devotion)	—	Medium	—	Semi-Centralised	Strong	Nebula Chain
	PoE((Proof of Existence)	2016	Unknown	—	Complete	Weak	HeroNode, DragonChain
	PoI (Proof of Importance)	2015	Low	—	Complete	Weak	NEM
	PoR (Proof of Retrievability)	2014	Low	<1/4	Complete	Weak	File Sharing
	PoET (Proof of Elapsed Time)	2017	Low	<1/2	Semi-Centralised	Strong	Sawtooth Lake
	PoP (Proof of Publication)	2012	Large	<1/4	Complete	Weak	BitCoin
Byzantine consensus	PBFT	1999	low	<1/3	Semi-Centralised	Strong	Super Ledger
	Raft	2013		—	Semi-Centralised	Strong	etcd
Directed Acyclic Graph	DAG	—	low	—	Complete	Weak	IoTA

As the core of the blockchain, the consensus algorithm mainly has two characteristics: Firstly, consistency, removing the k end blocks of the blockchain to make the block prefixes saved by trusted nodes the same; secondly, effectiveness, transaction information published by trusted nodes will be recorded in the blockchain by other trusted nodes. Table 1 compares the commonly used traditional blockchain consensus from the aspects of classification, proposed time, computational consumption, tolerance of malicious nodes, degree of decentralization, manageability, and application. For example, in the proof consensus, the PoW mechanism applied by Bitcoin obtains the authority of accounting by calculating the accurate Nonce value, which consumes a lot of computing power, and Permacoin uses PoW to provide data preservation services (Miller *et.al*, 2014); In the Byzantine consensus, PBFT (Castro *et.al*, 2002 & Androulak *et.al*, 2018) is applied to the super ledger and can tolerate 1/3 of the wrong nodes. The Byzantine-based consensus also includes Quorum / Update (Abd-El-Malek *et.al*, 2005), Hybrid Quorum (Cowling *et.al*, 2006), FaB (Martin *et.al*, 2005), Spinning (Martin *et.al*, 2005), Robust BFT SMR (Veronese *et.al*, 2009) and Aliph (Clement et.al, 2009), etc.; Others are different from the traditional chain structure, with transaction as the granularity of block-free consensus DAG (directed acyclic graph) (Popov, 2018), this new type of blockchain topology provides new thinking for consensus research.

The consensus mechanism currently used in the cloud blockchain still cannot achieve a perfect balance in terms of computing power consumption, supervisability, decentralization, and security. However, in the field of IoT, massive heterogeneous terminal devices have limited computing and storage capabilities, relatively complex network architecture, and strong expansion requirements. As a result, the current consensus is not fully applicable to the IoT.

IOT-BLOCKCHAIN CONSENSUS MECHANISM APPLICATION STATUS

Examples of deep integration of blockchain and IoT are still in continuous innovation and practice phase. The IoT realizes communication calculation and data transmission and interaction in a peer-to-peer open network environment through sensor nodes, protocols, and other related technologies. Each terminal device can serve as a node of the district chain and participate in the consensus maintenance of the blockchain network. The following will explain the status of projects based on the IoT blockchain from two aspects: the project overview of the IoT blockchain consensus mechanism and the analysis of consensus advantages and disadvantages.

Project Overview of Consensus Mechanism

The IoT blockchain project optimizes and improves the existing consensus algorithm, and uses the main sub-chain and computing power chips to help strengthen the consensus rules, thus reducing the contradictions in the application of the IoT in the blockchain. The existing IoT blockchain systems mainly include IoTA, IoTEX, μNEST, and EOSIoT.

IoTA

IoTA (Popov, 2018) is a new type of transaction settlement blockchain system designed for the IoT. Different from the traditional chain-type blockchain, IoTA adopts a Tangle (DAG) architecture inside. No transfer fees are required for transfers, which is extremely scalable. As the number of nodes increases, the stability of the system increases. In the DAG system, new transactions need to be verified through two historical transaction pointers. The elimination of miner settings in this mechanism can prevent the blockchain from being threatened by computing power and double attacks. At the same time, changes in the consensus mechanism effectively improve transaction efficiency and throughput, and most double-spend attacks will be caught by the system and immediately stopped. DAG's network topology also gives users a clearer and more concise model architecture. Although PoW still consumes computing power as part of DAG, the advantages of a new blockchain based on DAG data structure are emerging, and the IoTA project has also been recognized and developed rapidly.

However, high TPS (transactions per second, the number of transactions per second) will bring the following problems: In Tangle, the time from a transaction to the confirmation is unknown. In addition, high performance will bring low security, and attackers can attack the network through lower computing costs (Lathif *et.al*, 2018).

IoTEX

The IoTEX project has good scalability, privacy, and isolation. As shown in figure 4, in terms of architecture, the project adopts a chain-in-chain form that includes a root chain and a sub-chain, and the chain structure of ledgers is still used internally. In terms of function, the root chain is a public chain, which plays a management role on the child chain; in terms of scalability, the sub-chain can design different extensions according to needs to adapt to the diversity of IoT functions; in terms of security, the attack of the sub-chain does not affect the operation of the root chain; in terms of value, data between sub-chains can also be transferred through the root chain.

Figure 4. IoTEX root chain sub-chain structure diagram

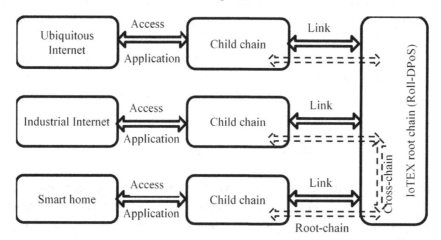

In the IoTEX project, the consensus mechanism is a random consensus mechanism that can be verified based on random functions (Roll-DPoS) (Fan & Chai, 2018). IoTEX is based on the Byzantine Fault Tolerance Algorithm (PBFT), which votes for nodes, settles quickly, and builds an efficient and scalable blockchain. In terms of node selection, in order to improve efficiency, the system randomly selects group nodes according to the RDPoS algorithm. Compared to DPOS, Roll-DPoS draws on the Algorand algorithm (Gilad *et.al*, 2017) for random node selection, so that each node has the opportunity to participate in consensus building and avoid node isolation.

Application of IoTEX to the IoT, the changes in the architecture can adapt to the distributed environment of the IoT, it also enhances the randomness of consensus, but it has not responded to the disadvantages of low power consumption, poor storage capacity, and small communication bandwidth of IoT devices.

μNEST

The μNEST project is quite different from the above two. The project uses the DPoS consensus mechanism. Although DPoS has improved PoS and optimized the verification efficiency and block production speed, it is still helpless against the current situation of low energy consumption and high concurrency in the IoT, and the internal token mechanism is not applicable in the field of IoT. The μNEST team through the research on cryptography and the application of high-performance hardware reduced the consumption of computing power in the consensus mechanism, improve the computing power of IoT devices so that blockchain programs can run stably on IoT devices. Currently, the project is still under development.

EOSIoT

EOSIoT is an extension of the IoT of the EOS project. Through the RFID system, RFID electronic tags can be sent to the EOS chain, which is used in new supply chains, manufacturing, tracking, and access control. The project is different from the above using physical devices as nodes, retaining the existing architecture of blockchain and IoT, and providing EOS-based blockchain services for IoT systems through smart contracts. EOS adopts DPoS consensus mechanism.

Advantages and Disadvantages of the Consensus Mechanism

Table 2 combines the above projects on the consensus mechanism to summarize and compare the applicability of existing IoT blockchain technologies. The application of consensus mainly depends on the performance, scalability, and security of IoT devices. μNEST and EOSIoT use DPoS consensus, and the existing token mechanism has little effect in the field of IoT, so the scalability is poor. Among them, in the μNEST project, the hardware is used to enhance device performance and optimize the efficiency of the consensus algorithm. The IoTEX project adopts the main sub-chain form, which has strong scalability and is suitable for various IoT fields. However, the inherent weakness of IoT devices has not been greatly improved. The storage method of the chain ledger still limits the low power consumption and weak storage. The IoTA project adopts a novel DAG consensus. Although the performance has been improved and it is easy to expand, when the number of nodes is too small, the degree of decentralization is much lower than the chain structure blockchain, resulting in low security, risks such as untimely transaction verification.

For other consensus that is not used by the project, PoW has high security in an open network, but the huge computing resource requirements are not realistic to implement in IoT devices, so PoW consensus is not adopted in the project. Compared with PoW consensus, PoS consensus can significantly reduce energy consumption, but it still needs to consume a certain amount of computing resources for mining, and it still has certain operating pressure for low-power IoT devices. While increasing the number of nodes, PBFT will reduce the performance of the entire network and cannot improve reliability. Therefore, most of the consensus algorithms and rules currently used still have room for improvement in the field of IoT.

Table 2. Advantages and disadvantages of the project and its consensus

Project Name	Consensus algorithm	App types	Disadvantages	Advantage	Scalability	Security	Performance
μNEST EOSIoT	DPoS	Public chain	The degree of decentralization is low, and internal consensus relies on tokens. Representation is not strong when there are few nodes.	The efficiency is better than PoW and PoS. The block generation speed is faster	Weak	Strong	Higher
IoTEX	Roll-DPoS	Public chain	Depending on the token, the method of selecting representative nodes may not be suitable for completely decentralized scenarios	By randomly selecting nodes, each node has the opportunity to participate in the accounting process	Stronger	Strong	Higher
IoTA	DAG	Public chain	No global ordering, does not support strong oneness, efficient implementation is more complicated	High throughput, no central control for asynchronous communication	Strong	Weak	High

RESEARCH ON OPTIMIZATION OF IOT BLOCKCHAIN CONSENSUS MECHANISM

Through the above analysis and comparison, the application of the consensus mechanism in the IoT is still insufficient. Combining the characteristics of the IoT environment, academia has put forward many optimization solutions. As shown in Table 3, through consensus algorithm improvement, data layer optimization, and architecture service optimization, the consensus rules are strengthened to help the IoT- blockchain.

Improvements in Consensus Algorithms

The consensus algorithm needs to rely on the computing power of the nodes, and the new blocks generated at the same time are synchronized to all nodes through the consensus rules for backup. In the field of the IoT, there are far more mass heterogeneous devices than the Internet environment, and the computing power and throughput are limited by itself and the operating environment. In addition, there are problems such as easy intrusion, easy to simulate, and easy tampering, which increase the hidden dangers of traditional consensus in the field of IoT. The method of using hardware to increase computing power in μNEST is not suitable for all devices. Therefore, how to optimize the consensus mechanism is crucial in node selection, reducing complexity, and improving security and throughput. The Enhanced intelligent consensus model is shown in Figure 5 and selects normal nodes to construct consensus by detecting node data to improve security.

Table 3. Current status and characteristics of research on consensus mechanism optimization of IoT-blockchain

Application direction	Related work	Overview	Performance advantages
Consensus algorithm improvement	Improved Algorithm based on trust PoW (Huang *et.al*, 2019)	Evaluate the trustworthiness of nodes and adjust the mining difficulty of each node through the coefficient	Increase the computing power consumption of malicious nodes, so that they do not get the right to keep accounts, and at the same time reduce the probability of selecting malicious nodes, increasing fault tolerance
	Fault-tolerant optimization based on PBFT (Salimitari *et.al*, 2019)	Use outlier detection algorithms to divide malicious nodes through data.	The consensus algorithm is layered, the first layer uses anomaly node detection algorithm to detect and distinguish malicious nodes, the second layer carries out PBFT consensus. Enhanced fault tolerance.
	DRL boosts consensus mechanism (Liu et.al, 2019)	Use deep reinforcement learning for block generation and other adjustments.	Apply DRL technology to block generation and adjustment, and dynamically adjust the system to achieve balance and efficiency
	DAG main chain sub-chain combination (Jiang et.al. 2018)	DAG-based main chain sub-chain form distinguishes domain and block	The main subchain form of DAG effectively increases the throughput of the blockchain, while reducing the storage of block data.
Data layer optimization	Blockchain system based on data compression (Kim *et.al*, 2019)	Compress the data blocks in the blockchain to reduce storage space and ease the storage pressure of the device.	Greatly enhance the storage capacity of the device and reduce the performance problems caused by the small storage space of the device.
	High-performance data read-write architecture based on FPGA memory module (Sakakibara *et.al*, 2017)	Make an external storage module, and request a high-performance storage module instead of a server during the communication process.	The high-performance storage module effectively improves the reading and writing of data, reduces the performance consumption of data during transmission, and improves the efficiency of consensus.
	Data optimization through edge computing (Casado-Vara *et.al*, 2018)	Verify data quality through a combination of edge computing and distributed computing.	In the blockchain architecture, the edge computing layer is proposed to improve data quality and error data detection, and enhance the consensus fault tolerance rate.
Architecture Service Optimization	IoT+Blockchain Architecture and Services (Sagirlar *et.al*, 2018 & Dorri - *et.al*, 2017)	Combine different layers in the blockchain with different layers in the IoT to build a new architecture	The integration of the architecture circumvents the shortcomings of the IoT, and combines the two to form a stable new structure, so that the blockchain can be applied to the IoT.

Figure 5. Enhanced Intelligent Consensus Model

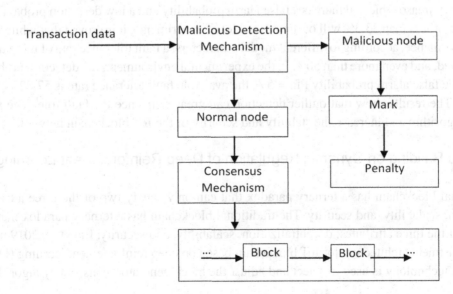

Malicious Detection Boosts Consensus Mechanism

The trust-based PoW mechanism (Huang *et.al*, 2019) can effectively enhance the security of the blockchain network. In this mechanism, whether a node is malicious is measured by two parts, the positive part, and the negative part. These two parts can be adjusted by configuring weights. The positive part is obtained by calculating the number of effective transactions and the number of transaction verifications; the negative part is determined by the joint effect of the time for the node to perform malicious actions and the penalty coefficient, there are two types of penalty coefficients, one is to identify the node as a lazy node, that is, to contribute less in the consensus process, the other is to identify the node as a double-spend node, that is, to send malicious transactions such as repeated transactions. These two penalty coefficients will be dynamically adjusted according to the actual situation. The verification of the mechanism by the Raspberry Pi proves that the node judged as malicious will set a higher penalty coefficient, resulting in a larger difficulty value, and the time for the node to run the PoW consensus algorithm will be much longer than that of the normal node. At the same time, when simulating a malicious attack on a node, the coefficient of the passive response part will immediately increase. In this way, the 51% fault tolerance rate of the traditional PoW is enhanced, and the malicious node will never get the authority to keep accounts. (Huang *et.al*, 2019). Node selection through this method can effectively reduce the performance consumption of non-malicious nodes, and at the same time, increase the computational complexity of malicious nodes' PoW algorithm, which is conducive to the stability and robustness of the consensus algorithm under the IoT blockchain system.

Based on hyperledger fabric and consensus protocol PBFT, (Salimitari *et.al*, 2019) proposed a malicious detection mechanism to improve the fault tolerance of IoT blockchain. Through data collection of IoT devices, a data matrix D is formed, and two probability values are obtained through outlier detection algorithm and low-rank subspace recovery model training data matrix D: Detection probability Pd and false alarm probability Pfa to determine abnormal nodes. In this consensus mechanism, the anomaly node detection algorithm runs as the first-level consensus in each node in the form of a script to verify the compatibility of new data and discard suspicious data. The algorithm will no longer select the node with malicious data as the accounting node to generate the blockchain, enhancing the fault tolerance of the second layer of consensus PBFT. In the experiment, it was found that only when the outlier detection setting is very unreasonable and there is a false alarm probability and a low detection probability, a fault tolerance rate of less than 33.3% will occur. After a lot of experiments, it is proved that while improving network performance, according to different model parameters, a fault tolerance rate of more than 33.3% can be obtained, and even more than 50%. In the experimental environment, the detection probability Pd = 46% and the false alarm probability Pfa = 5%, the available fault tolerance rate is 57.82% (Salimitari *et.al*, 2019). The results show that outlier detection can greatly enhance the fault tolerance rate of the consensus algorithm and increase the stability and security of the IoT blockchain network.

Consensus Building on Dynamic Regulation of Deep Reinforcement Learning

The traditional blockchain has a ternary paradox that can only satisfy two of the three attributes: decentralization, scalability, and security. The traditional blockchain has a ternary paradox that can only satisfy two of the three attributes: decentralization, scalability, and security. Liu et.al, 2019 proposed a dynamic adjustment architecture for IoT blockchain based on deep reinforcement learning (DRL) technology. DRL technology is used to select and adjust the block generator, consistency algorithm, block size and block generation interval, internally combined with PBFT, Zyzzyva (Kotla *et.al*, 2007) and Quorum (Aublin *et.al*, 2015) proposed a new fault-tolerant consensus to achieve a dynamic balance of scalability, decentralization, security, and throughput.

The scheme uses Gini coefficient, block delay, and error tolerance rate to represent decentralization, throughput, and security, and uses deep reinforcement learning (mainly Q-Network) for training to obtain appropriate parameters to select the appropriate block generation node, consensus algorithm, block size, and block generation interval.

After `a lot of experiments, by comparing with the existing unmodified system, the proposed scheme has higher performance and throughput (Liu et.al, 2019), which effectively proves that the design improves the performance of the IoT-Blockchain, and the dynamic adaptation to the distributed heterogeneous architecture of the IoT.

DAG Segmentation Technology to Improve the Consensus Rule

As a new blockchain architecture, there are many improvements and optimizations based on DAG. Different from the traditional DAG in Section 3.1.1 and the main chain model based on the traditional chain structure in Section 3.1.2, Jiang *et al.* 2018 complemented the advantages of DAG and the main chain, and proposed a DAG-based cross-chain solution. The scheme is based on the main sub-chain architecture of directed acyclic graphs. Nodes in a domain jointly maintain a ledger to form a sub-chain. At the same time, the sub-chain is connected to the main chain in the form of an alliance chain for management and maintains the main chain ledger. This kind of scheme connects different nodes to the main chain after fragmenting consensus, which solves the situation that consensus is difficult to establish due to a large number of devices in the IoT environment, and reduces the network consumption caused by large-scale ledger synchronization. After a lot of experiments, running in different memory and different processor-server environments, compared with traditional blockchain, the throughput of this architecture has been significantly improved, at the same time, in the storage of block information, the sub-chain only stores block data in specific areas, and the storage capacity is much smaller than the main chain, reducing the storage pressure of the main chain nodes and sub-chain nodes.

Data Layer Optimization

The IoT collects, stores data, and provides centralized services from various types of terminal devices. If the server is attacked, there is a risk of data leakage. In order to solve the problem of centralized data storage, blockchain technology was introduced, but the low storage capacity of lightweight devices has led to the blockchain consensus mechanism not being able to operate for a long time. At the same time, various sensors in the sensing layer of the IoT generate a large amount of real-time data. If the entire chain is stored by the blockchain, it will exert great pressure on the nodes and the network.

Block Compression Mechanism Saves Storage Space

Combining consensus rules, compressing early data to ensure the consistency of the blockchain, and reducing the storage of block data is a way to solve the storage limitations of IoT devices. Kim *et al.* 2019 proposed a block compression storage method to increase the storage space of the device. The uninterrupted operation of IoT devices will generate massive real-time data. Such data has the characteristics of large data volume and a short validity period. The effective compression of the pre-blocks under the premise of ensuring the establishment of the blockchain consensus can ensure the storage capacity of the lightweight IoT devices in the blockchain network. After the IoT device node joins the network, it is required to synchronize the storage capacity of the node to the entire network, improving the PBFT consensus, as shown in Figure 6.

Figure 6. Block compression model (Fan & Chai, 2018)

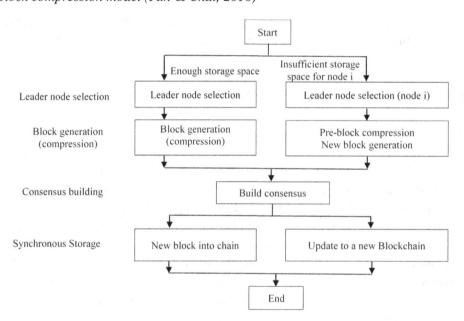

In the process of selecting the Leader node for transaction block, through the evaluation of the storage capacity of its own equipment; if it is less than the set threshold, the consensus mechanism is established normally: if it is greater than the set threshold, the data compression program is started to compress the original block, that is, a new block is generated by Hash operation, the hash value of the parent block of the new block is the compressed block hash value, and the network-wide node synchronization operation is performed on the compressed block and the newly generated block, and the network-wide node is updated to a new blockchain. Based on the comparison between the blockchain model based on block compression and the traditional blockchain model, as the number of nodes increases, the block delay increases by less than 1, and the average storage space of each data block in the blockchain decreases by nearly 63%. After running for a period of time, the compressed model reduces the total storage space by about 63% and tends to be stable (Kim *et.al*, 2019). Although the compression algorithm consumes a certain amount of block time, data compression combined with consensus effectively solves the problem of insufficient data storage space in IoT devices.

High-Performance Cache and Edge Computing Increase Throughput

There is still a contradiction between the heterogeneous data of IoT devices and low communication bandwidth. The transmission delay of a large amount of heterogeneous data in low-bandwidth channels will inevitably greatly affect the operation of the blockchain consensus algorithm and affect the establishment of consensus. Sakakibara *et.al*, 2017, proposed a high-performance cache device to improve the read and write performance. Hardware cache module is added made of an external high-efficiency read-write device to the IoT. Store transaction information in the cache module, reduces the workload of the server, and improve the storage capacity of physical devices in the IoT blockchain. In the network, if there is target data in the cache, it is directly read in the cache module, otherwise, it is obtained from the node. Use cache technology to reduce the resource consumption of data and improves throughput. After extensive experiments, it is seen that IoT blockchain using the cache module shows throughput several times smaller than the one without using it. As the transaction volume increases, throughput shows an inversely proportional curve and gradually converges to stabilize, while the hit rate of the data in the cache shows a proportional trend with the increasing number of transactions, continuously increasing (38). This shows that the application of the cache module can effectively reduce the increase in throughput caused by heterogeneous data transmission in the IoT blockchain, and reduce the load on the device caused by low-bandwidth communications. At the same time, a distributed cooperative algorithm based on game theory can also be used (Huang *et.al*, 2019), which improves the security of incoming data and improves network throughput by improving data quality and performing error data detection in network edge devices.

ARCHITECTURE OPTIMIZATION SERVICES

Blockchain + IoT

General IoT-Blockchain Architecture

The architecture is the combination of a traditional 5 layer Blockchain system with the existing IoT system (Lao et.al, 2020). Figure 7 shows the general 5 layers of IoT Blockchain Architecture. The IoT Blockchain's physical layer has the same functionality as the IoT physical layer. It consists of IoT devices related to application scenarios like home devices, mobile phones, Car sensors, etc. The second layer in IoT Blockchain architecture i.e. the network layer is similar to the traditional blockchain network layer. This layer is responsible for overall communication among the entities involved in the system, i.e. internetworking, routing, and multicasting. Blockchain functions i.e. data storage, data sharing, and consensus are the part of Blockchain layer. The main purpose of the IoT Blockchain middle layer is to manage blockchain, service integration, and to provide additional security services. The topmost layer i.e. the application layer of IoT Blockchain is similar to the IoT system and Blockchain system application layer, the purpose of the application layer is to provide user interaction, abstraction service, and API services.

Figure 7. General IoT Blockchain Architecture

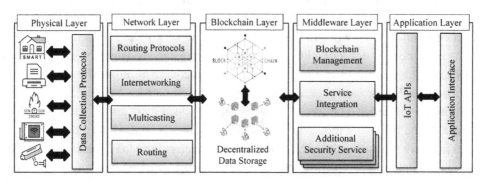

In this architecture, the IoT device generates data, and Blockchain is responsible for securely storing the data in a secure distributed environment to avoiding malicious modifications. Conversely, all previous data can be easily retrieved with any loss of information. Still, IoT Blockchain is in an early stage of development. Before starting with the architecture optimization let us summarize the current status of IoT-Blockchain Applications and their Architectures. Table 4 differentiates different IOT-Blockchain applications with Blockchain technology, Consensus, services, and IoT devices. All these applications follow the same architecture as described in figure 5. These applications are further divided into two types as per their field application.

Table 4. Comparison between different IoT-Blockchain applications

IoT-Blockchain	*Blockchain*	*Consensus*	*Service*	*IoT devices*
Slock.it (sloct.it 2018)	Ethereum	PoW	Commission shop	Electronic lock
ElectriCChain (ectriCChain 2018)	SolarCoin	PoS	Process data of solar panel	Solar panel
LO3 Energy (O3 2018)	Public blockchain solution	PoW	Solar energy marketplace	Grid Edge, Solar plane
LeewayHertz (LewayHertz)	Public blockchain	PoW	IoT-blockchain solutions	Robots, Audio devices
Xage (Xage 2018)	Fabric	Fabric consensus	Security service	Broker, Enforcement Point
Filament (Filament. 2018)	Hardware-based Consortium Blockchain	PoW	Transaction service to embedded IoT	Blocklet USB Enclave, Blocklet Chip
UniquID (UniquID 2018)	Litecoin	PoW	Integrated service to IoT and blockchain	Sensors, Actuators, Appliances
Atonomi (Atonomi 2019)	Atonomi	Atonomi consensus	IoT-blockchain solutions	Smart devices, Smart home
JD.com (JDChain 2019)	BFT blockchain	BFT	Blockchain platform	IoT devices

1. **Specific Application:** Standalone applications that use IoT and Blockchain in their operations. The application layer and the physical layer perform as core layers. The middle layers act as a supporting layer that is responsible for storage and communication. IoT Device and the application protocol defines the nature and function of IoT Blockchain application.

2.   **Application Platform as a Service:** it is the support software that integrates everything in IoT Blockchain System. Developers are provided with direct access to the management platform, which provides developers to manage connected devices, configure communication protocols, and also control data flow. The middleware layer acts as a core layer defining the nature and functionality of the application service. The application layer and physical layer components are not specified in this kind of service.

Hybrid Blockchain+IoT

Combining different layers of the blockchain and the IoT a new architecture (Sagirlar *et.al,* 2018 & Dorri *et.al,* 2017) is formed, it is different from the way in which the blockchain is used as a cloud service to provide services to edge devices through smart contracts in Section 3.1.4. As shown in Figure 8, the IoT device nodes in the network are interconnected through network devices such as gateways and routers, at the same time, data storage warehouses are built locally and in the cloud to solve data storage issues for IoT devices.

Figure 8. The architecture of Hybrid blockchain+IoT

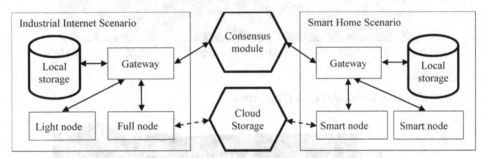

In a node network, nodes with high-performance computing capabilities and high-availability storage capacity are set as full nodes, and nodes with low power consumption and weak storage capacity are set as light nodes. Full nodes have the ability to participate in maintaining the ledger, establish consensus with other full nodes, and synchronize the ledger; light nodes do not participate in the maintenance of the ledger, and only synchronize the header information of the block (for example, when a new block appears in the blockchain network, the light node download only the block header and send a Merkel certificate request in a specific state). Under such an architecture, blockchain and the IoT are organically combined, and devices exist as light nodes of the blockchain to jointly maintain a network.

The DDoS attack for stress simulation was carried out in which a set of light nodes repeatedly transmitted data to full nodes. Figure 9 shows the CPU usage of the victim node, it was observed that even though the victim's CPU was almost exhausted, it successfully managed to perform blockchain task without halting or crashing even under heavy load from the attacker. Figure 10 shows the CPU usage of the attacker node, it was observed that nearly 100% of the CPU was exhausted, even though the Attacker node was able to generate transaction load without crashing. The second test was carried out with the varying number of sub-blockchains, it was observed that sub-blockchain having more full nodes the resources usage is averaged with longer consensus rotations. Table 5 shows the performance of the sub-blockchain with varying numbers of full nodes. After the simulation, the architecture can effectively solve the problem of the IoT devices that were not able to meet the blockchain computing power requirements and account storage, and also provide new ideas for the combination of blockchain and IoT.

Figure 9. Full node (Victim node) Cpu Utilization

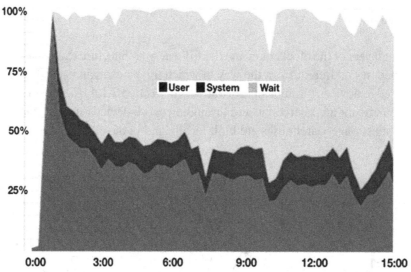

Figure 10. Light node (Attacker node) Cpu Utilization

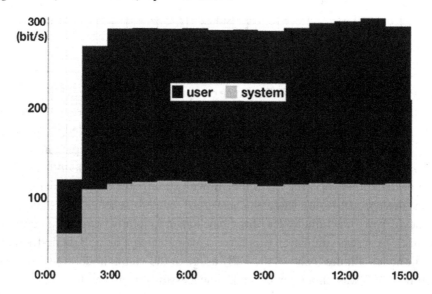

Table 5. Performance of sub-blockchain with varying number of full nodes

Resource Utilized	20 nodes	40 nodes	100 nodes	200 nodes
Avg. CPU	6.5%	5.1%	2.7%	1.9%
Avg. Memory	110 Mb	106 Mb	105 Mb	104 Mb
Avg. Network	8.2 Kb/s	6.5 Kb/s	4.1 Kb/s	2.1 Kb/s
Avg. Packets	10.1 /s	9.3/s	6.8/s	4.2/s

Blockchain+ IoT+AI

Blockchain + AI+IOT provides a decentralized AI method to share information in cryptographically secured, trusted, and signed manner, it also provides decision-making capabilities for IoT devices in IoT applications. A hierarchically layered structured architecture is proposed consisting of 4 layers of intelligence (S.K. Singh *et.al*, 2019). Figure 11 shows the new Blockchain +IoT+AI. As shown in the figure each layer is enabled with AI, AI at each level is responsible to sense devices, analyzes and processes data, and sends a response to upper or lower layers. At the cloud intelligence layer, AI is associated with data centers that are connected to Blockchain which provide decentralized and secure data for IoT applications. Different consensus protocols can be used in different layers for convergence of Blockchain+AI+IoT for scalability and security. S.K. Singh *et.al*, 2019 further evaluated the architecture in 2 ways, "blockchain-driven AI for IoT" and "AI-driven Blockchain for IoT" depending on the IoT services.

Figure 11. Blockchain+AI+IoT Architecture

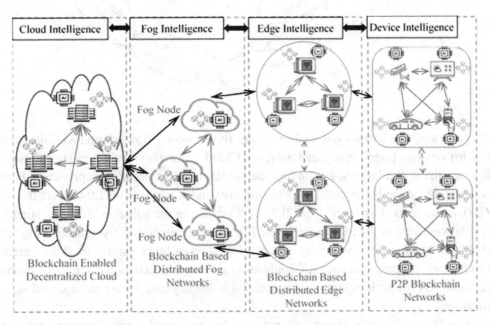

AI-driven Blockchain for IoT, i.e., Integration of AI to mitigate the limitation of Blockchain for IoT such as high transaction cost, Complexity, network size, etc. Conversely, to mitigate the limitation of AI for IoT such as artificial trust, AI effectiveness, data sharing, explainable AI, security, and privacy, Blockchain is integrated into the IoT system. Figure 12 and figure 13 shows the classified limitations from Blockchain-driven AI and AI-driven Blockchain for IoT respectively.

Figure 12. Limitations of Blockchain-driven AI for IoT

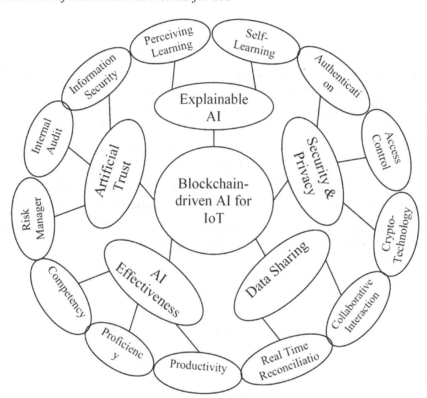

S.K. Singh et.al, 2019 carried out analysis using the proposed Blockchain+AI+IoT Architecture (Table 6) on IoT devices, Edge Layer, Fog Layer, and Cloud Layer with parameters considering security and privacy, accuracy, and latency. By finding the similarity index security & privacy was measured and it was found that at the IoT device layer the similarity index varies from 1.0-0.01, at the edge layer it was 0.62-0.4, and at the Fog layer it was 0.9-0.1. Comparing the values with the existing research, accuracy is showing 72% at the IoT device layer, 75% at edge computing layer, 90% at fog computing layer, and 68% at the cloud computing layer. It was found when blockchain is used the Latency value came out to be high as compared with IoT application without blockchain. Hence it can be concluded that Blockchain+AI+IoT architecture obtains acceptable latency with high precision and security in a decentralized way.

The blockchain can also provide services such as data tamper resistance, data traceability, and trust credentials to the IoT through smart contracts. In such applications, the IoT does not participate in the maintenance of the blockchain.

Figure 13. Limitations of Blockchain-driven AI for IoT

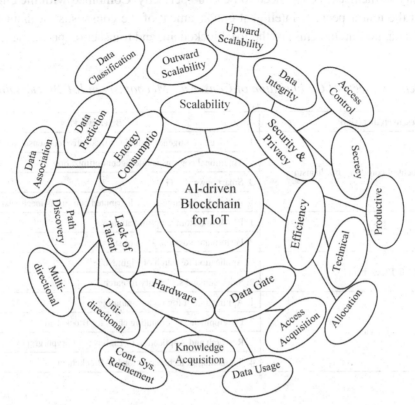

Table 6. Performance of sub-blockchain with varying number of full nodes

Layers	Parameters					
	Security & Privacy(SI)		Accuracy (%)		Latency(ms)	
	Min.	Max.			Min.	Max.
Device Layer	0.01	1.0	72		56	57
Edge Layer	0.4	0.6	75		56	58
Fog Layer	0.1	0.9	90		0	11
Cloud Layer	-	-	68		-	-

Research Prospects of Optimization of Consensus Mechanism in IoT Blockchain

From the above description table 7, we can see that the combination of IoT and blockchain is mainly limited by the computing power, storage capacity, and throughput of the device. In view of the current blockchain consensus scalability is poor, huge computing power consumption, transaction confirmation efficiency is low, node fault tolerance and performance is difficult to balance, etc., when the IoT and the blockchain are combined, how to choose a consensus algorithm that conforms to the IoT scenario, how to specify a consensus rule that conforms to the IoT business scenario, how to ensure the security, stability, and scalability of the network still need to be done perfectly. Combined with the current research, Table 5 looks at the four aspects of intelligent enhancement of the consensus mechanism, reasonable optimization of data, new architecture of the IoT-blockchain, and transaction performance.

Table 7. Research Prospects of Optimization of Consensus Mechanism in IoT Blockchain

Research direction	Brief overview
Intelligent enhancement of consensus mechanism	1. Artificial intelligence combined innovative consensus mechanism
	2. Traditional consensus intelligent optimization
	3. Smart power DAG
	4. Research on a large-scale distributed consensus mechanism
Reasonable optimization of data	1. Block data storage optimization
	2. Performance optimization of storage mode
New Architecture of IoT Blockchain	1. Application Research of Light Node
	2. Sidechain and scalability research
Improved transaction performance	1. Application of fog node computing
	2. Development of computing chips for Blockchain
	3. Research and Application of Lightweight cryptography
	4. Segmentation technology for IoT-Blockchain

Intelligent Enhancement of Consensus Mechanism

Artificial intelligence is a manual method that simulates, extends, and expands human intelligence. Through data mining, analysis, and training, it realizes the scientific technology of machine intelligence. The combination of blockchain and artificial intelligence provides directions for the internal enhancement of the blockchain and the intelligentization of external governance. The combination of artificial intelligence and the IoT blockchain consensus mechanism is mainly expanded in the following aspects.

Artificial Intelligence Combined Innovative Consensus Mechanism (Salah et.al, 2019).

The current consensus is mainly selected from the proof consensus and the Byzantine consensus, and cannot be fully applied to the special environment of the Internet of Things, combining the characteristics of high real-time data requirements and a large amount of data in the Internet of Things, a new AI-based consensus mechanism is created based on the quality of the learning model, the effective optimization of search strategies, and data quality.

Traditional Consensus Intelligent Optimization

Using deep reinforcement learning's perception and decision-making ability, intelligently improve the computing power consumption and Leader node selection of traditional consensus, in order to achieve the purpose of reasonably distributing the computing power of the IoT-Blockchain, enhancing network fault tolerance, and strengthening the decentralized features.

Smart Power DAG (Pervez et.al, 2018)

The new consensus mechanism model of a directed acyclic graph is still in the development stage, using AI technology to strengthen DAG's shortcomings in transaction confirmation and security is also a direction that requires in-depth research.

Research on a Large-scale Distributed Consensus Mechanism.

The IoT is essentially a large distributed system, the network topology caused by massive nodes is intricate. a multi-layer consensus mechanism can be established through research on the distributed consensus mechanism, so that different regions can establish consensus and then move up to consensus until the entire network reaches consensus, in order to achieve the purpose of reducing throughput and alleviating the limitation of computing power consumption.

Reasonable Optimization of Data

Due to the limitation of throughput, the blockchain cannot adapt to the real-time big data environment of the IoT. Therefore, the following research can be performed on the data.

Block Data Storage Optimization (Taylor et.al, 2019)

IoT device data has real-time characteristics, some of the early data entered into the chain are useless except for the establishment of a consensus mechanism. Therefore, how to reasonably delete the ledger data stored in the blockchain without affecting the establishment of the consensus mechanism, so that the block ledger data can continuously store data that can be deeply studied.

Performance Optimization of Storage Mode

Due to the low storage capacity of IoT devices, it is possible to study in-depth how to improve the existing storage mode, use the caching mechanism or improve block storage middleware, enhance the read and write capabilities of block data, and adapt to the low bandwidth data transmission network of the IoT.

New Architecture of IoT Blockchain

The disadvantages of low computing power and small storage space of the IoT limit the blockchain technology to be fully applied to the IoT environment, but the layered combination of the two can still provide strong assistance for the IoT. Mainly from the following aspects.

Application Research of Light Node (Reilly et.al, 2019)

The characteristic of light nodes is that only the data of the block header is synchronized, and the blockchain architecture based on light nodes and full nodes can be built on IoT devices with different storage performance, and the establishment of a consensus mechanism and the synchronous storage of blocks can be reasonably performed.

Sidechain and Scalability Research (Zhou et.al, 2020)

Through the side chain technology, the field of IoT blockchain application is effectively expanded to achieve more flexible user customization. How to design side chains, how to strengthen extended attributes, and how to realize data interaction between sidechains are the future research directions.

Improved Transaction Performance

Transaction performance is one of the constraints that the blockchain cannot be effectively used in the field of IoT. In the face of the massive data environment of the IoT, the throughput of the blockchain cannot be completely satisfied. Therefore, to improve the throughput of the blockchain, the following directions can be studied.

Application of Fog Node Computing (Xiong et.al, 2020)

Fog computing is a new computing paradigm, sink storage and calculations to a location close to data generation, establishing a local small cloud at the end of the IoT to achieve localized computing or storage, reduce the bandwidth consumption of messages, reduce the computing pressure of the central node, and speed up the establishment of a consensus mechanism.

Development of Computing Chips for Blockchain

The low computing performance of the device is mainly limited by the performance of the processor, and a computing chip for the blockchain can be developed to increase the compatibility of the IoT and the blockchain.

Research and Application of Lightweight Cryptography (Sfar et.al, 2017)

Blockchain is the application of cryptography, it is one of the research focuses to use safe and lightweight passwords to replace the original high-consumption passwords and to improve operational efficiency.

Segmentation Technology for IoT Blockchain (Tong et.al, 2019)

The principle of sharding is to split a large database into small pieces of data and store the pieces on different servers. Combining the consensus mechanism with sharding technology can effectively improve the consistency of the blockchain consensus-building speed.

CONCLUSION

As one of the key areas for future development, the IoT is combined with the blockchain that has the characteristics of decentralization, data tampering, and collective maintenance, or it will have a disruptive impact on the trusted and secure access of massive heterogeneous terminal devices and data security management, becoming one of the indispensable technologies for changing the future. As can be seen from the new research, in the direction of enhancement of consensus mechanism, reasonable optimization of data, a new architecture of IoT blockchain, and improvement of transaction performance, there are still urgent problems to be solved in the combination of IoT and blockchain. It is worth further research.

REFERENCES

O3. (2018). *LO3 Energy The Future of Energy*. Retrieved from https://lo3energy.com/

Abd-El-Malek, M., Ganger, G. R., Goodson, G. R., Reiter, M. K., & Wylie, J. J. (2005). Fault-scalable Byzantine fault-tolerant services. *Operating Systems Review, 39*(5), 59–74.

Androulaki, E., Barger, A., Bortnikov, V., Cachin, C., Christidis, K., Caro, A. D., Enyeart, D., Ferris, C., Laventman, G., Manevich, Y., Muralidharan, S., Murthy, C., Nguyen, B., Sethi, M., Singh, G., & Smith, K., SornIoTti, A., Stathakopoulou, C., Vukolic, M., Cocco, S.W., & Yellick, J. (2018). Hyperledger fabric: a distributed operating system for permissioned blockchains. In *The Thirteenth EuroSys Conference*. New York: ACM Press.

Ashton, K. (2009). *That "Internet of Things" Thing: In the Real World Things Matter More than Ideas*. RFID Journal.

Atonomi. (2019). *Atonomi—Bringing Trust and Security to IoT*. Retrieved from https://atonomi.io/

Aublin, P., Guerraoui, R., Knezevic, N., Quéma, V., & Vukolic, M. (2015). The Next 700 BFT Protocols. *ACM Trans. Comput. Syst., 32*, 12:1-12:45.

Back, A., Corallo, M., Dashjr, L., Friedenbach, M., Maxwell, G., Miller, A., Poelstra, A., Timón, J., & Wuille, P. (2014). *Enabling Blockchain Innovations with Pegged Sidechains*. Academic Press.

Bentov, I., Lee, C., Mizrahi, A., & Rosenfeld, M. (2014). Proof of Activity: Extending Bitcoin's Proof of Work via Proof of Stake (Extended Abstract). *SIGMETRICS Perform. Evaluation Rev., 42*, 34–37.

Casado-Vara, R., Prieta, F.D., Prieto, J., & Corchado, J.M. (2018). Blockchain framework for IoT data quality via edge computing. *BlockSys'18*.

Castro, M., & Liskov, B. (2002). Practical byzantine fault tolerance and proactive recovery. *ACM Transactions on Computer Systems, 20*, 398–461.

Chen, L., Xu, L., Shah, N., Gao, Z., Lu, Y., & Shi, W. (2017). *On Security Analysis of Proof-of-Elapsed-Time (PoET)*. SSS.

Clark, J., & Essex, A. (2011). CommitCoin: Carbon Dating Commitments with Bitcoin. *IACR Cryptol. ePrint Arch., 2011*, 677.

Clement, A., Wong, E. L., Alvisi, L., Dahlin, M., & Marchetti, M. (2009). *Making Byzantine Fault Tolerant Systems Tolerate Byzantine Faults.* NSDI.

Courtois, N. (2014). *On The Longest Chain Rule and Programmed Self-Destruction of Crypto Currencies.* ArXiv, abs/1405.0534.

Cowling, J.A., Myers, D.S., Liskov, B., Rodrigues, R., & Shrira, L. (2006). HQ replication: A hybrid quorum protocol for byzantine fault tolerance. *OSDI '06.*

Dorri, A., Kanhere, S.S., Jurdak, R., & Gauravaram, P. (2017). *LSB: A Lightweight Scalable BlockChain for IoT Security and Privacy.* ArXiv, abs/1712.02969.

ectriCChain. (2018). *ElectriCChain The Solar Energy Blockchain Project for Climate Change and Beyond.* Retrieved from https://www.electricchain.org/

Eyal, I., Gencer, A. E., Sirer, E. G., & Renesse, R. V. (2016). *Bitcoin-NG: A Scalable Blockchain Protocol.* NSDI.

Fan, X., & Chai, Q. (2018). Roll-DPoS: A Randomized Delegated Proof of Stake Scheme for Scalable Blockchain-Based Internet of Things Systems. In *Proceedings of the 15th EAI International Conference on Mobile and Ubiquitous Systems: Computing, Networking and Services.* ACM Press.

Filament. (2018). *Filament's Industrial Internet of Things Blockchain Solution Wins 2018 IoT Innovator Award.* Retrieved from https://globenewswire.com/news-release/2018/09/26/1576581/0/en/Filament-s-Industrial-Internet-of-Things-Blockchain-Solution-Wins-2018-IoT-Innovator-Award.html

Gilad, Y., Hemo, R., Micali, S., Vlachos, G., & Zeldovich, N. (2017). Algorand: Scaling Byzantine Agreements for Cryptocurrencies. In *Proceedings of the 26th Symposium on Operating Systems Principles.* ACM Press.

Huang, J., Kong, L., Chen, G., Wu, M., Liu, X., & Zeng, P. (2019). Towards Secure Industrial IoT: Blockchain System With Credit-Based Consensus Mechanism. *IEEE Transactions on Industrial Informatics, 15,* 3680–3689.

JDChain. (2019). *JD Enterprise Blockchain Service.* Retrieved from http://blockchain.jd.com/blockchain_store/pc/index.html#/BlockChainTrace

Jiang, Y., Wang, C., Huang, Y., Long, S., & Huo, Y. (2018). A Cross-Chain Solution to Integration of IoT Tangle for Data Access Management. *2018 IEEE International Conference on Internet of Things (iThings) and IEEE Green Computing and Communications (GreenCom) and IEEE Cyber, Physical and Social Computing (CPSCom) and IEEE Smart Data (SmartData),* 1035-1041.

Khodadadi, F., Dastjerdi, A. V., & Buyya, R. (2017). Internet of Things: An Overview. ArXiv, abs/1703.06409.

Kiayias, A., Russell, A., David, B.M., & Oliynykov, R. (2016). Ouroboros: A Provably Secure Proof-of-Stake Blockchain Protocol. *IACR Cryptol. ePrint Arch., 2016,* 889.

Kim, T., Noh, J., & Cho, S. (2019). SCC: Storage Compression Consensus for Blockchain in Lightweight IoT Network. *2019 IEEE International Conference on Consumer Electronics (ICCE),* 1-4.

Kotla, R., Alvisi, L., Dahlin, M., Clement, A., & Wong, E. L. (2007). *Zyzzyva: Speculative byzantine fault tolerance*. TOCS.

Kouicem, D. E., Bouabdallah, A., & Lakhlef, H. (2018). Internet of things security: A top-down survey. *Computer Networks*, *141*, 199–221. doi:10.1016/j.comnet.2018.03.012

Lao, L., Li, Z., Hou, S., Xiao, B., Guo, S., & Yang, Y. (2020). A Survey of IoT Applications in Blockchain Systems: Architecture, Consensus, and Traffic Modeling. *ACM Computing Surveys*, *53*, 1–32.

Lathif, M. R., Nasirifard, P., & Jacobsen, H. (2018). CIDDS: A Configurable and Distributed DAG-based Distributed Ledger Simulation Framework. In *The 19th International Middleware Conference (Posters)*. New Yew: ACM Press.

LewayHertz. (2019). *Blockchain Development for Startups and Enterprises | USA | UAE*. Retrieved from https://www.leewayhertz.com/

Liu, M., Yu, F. R., Teng, Y., Leung, V. C., & Song, M. (2019). Performance Optimization for Blockchain-Enabled Industrial Internet of Things (IIoT) Systems: A Deep Reinforcement Learning Approach. *IEEE Transactions on Industrial Informatics*, *15*, 3559–3570.

Martin, J., & Alvisi, L. (2005). Fast Byzantine Consensus. *IEEE Transactions on Dependable and Secure Computing*, *3*, 202–215.

Miller, A., Juels, A., Shi, E., Parno, B., & Katz, J. (2014). Permacoin: Repurposing Bitcoin Work for Data Preservation. *2014 IEEE Symposium on Security and Privacy*, 475-490.

Miller, A., Juels, A., Shi, E., Parno, B., & Katz, J. (2014). Permacoin: Repurposing Bitcoin Work for Data Preservation. *2014 IEEE Symposium on Security and Privacy*, 475-490.

Nakamoto, S. (2009). *Bitcoin: A Peer-to-Peer Electronic Cash System*. Academic Press.

NOMURA. (2016). *Survey on Blockchain Technologies and Related Services*. FY2015 Report.

Pan, J., & Yang, Z. (2018). Cybersecurity Challenges and Opportunities in the New "Edge Computing + IoT" World. *SDN-NFV Sec'18*.

Pervez, H., Muneeb, M., Irfan, M., & Haq, I. U. (2018). A Comparative Analysis of DAG-Based Blockchain Architectures. *2018 12th International Conference on Open Source Systems and Technologies (ICOSST)*, 27-34.

Popov, S. (2018). *The Tangle*. https://assets.ctfassets.net/r1dr6vzfxhev/2t4uxvsIqk0EUau6g2sw0g/45eae33637ca92f85dd9f4a3a218e1ec/IoTa1_4_3.pdf

Qi-feng, S., Cheqing, J., Zhao, Z., Weining, Q., & Ao-ying, Z. (2017). *Blockchain: Architecture and Research Progress*. Academic Press.

Reilly, E., Maloney, M., Siegel, M., & Falco, G. (2019). An IoT Integrity-First Communication Protocol via an Ethereum Blockchain Light Client. *2019 IEEE/ACM 1st International Workshop on Software Engineering Research & Practices for the Internet of Things (SERP4IoT)*, 53-56.

Sagirlar, G., Carminati, B., Ferrari, E., Sheehan, J. D., & Ragnoli, E. (2018). Hybrid-IoT: Hybrid Blockchain Architecture for Internet of Things - PoW Sub-Blockchains. *2018 IEEE International Conference on Internet of Things (iThings) and IEEE Green Computing and Communications (GreenCom) and IEEE Cyber, Physical and Social Computing (CPSCom) and IEEE Smart Data (SmartData)*, 1007-1016.

Sakakibara, Y., Nakamura, K., & Matsutani, H. (2017). An FPGA NIC Based Hardware Caching for Blockchain. *HEART2017*.

Salah, K., Rehman, M. H., Nizamuddin, N., & Al-Fuqaha, A. (2019). Blockchain for AI: Review and Open Research Challenges. *IEEE Access: Practical Innovations, Open Solutions*, 7, 10127–10149.

Salimitari, M., Joneidi, M., & Chatterjee, M. (2019). *An Outlier-aware Consensus Protocol for Blockchain-based IoT Networks Using Hyperledger Fabric.* ArXiv, abs/1906.08177.

Sfar, A. R., Natalizio, E., Challal, Y., & Chtourou, Z. (2017). A roadmap for security challenges in the Internet of Things. *Digital Communications and Networks*, 4, 118–137.

Singh, S. K., Rathore, S., & Park, J. H. (2019). BlockIoTIntelligence: A Blockchain-enabled Intelligent IoT Architecture with Artificial Intelligence. *Future Generation Computer Systems*.

sloct.it. (2018). *slock.it A Blockchain Company*. Retrieved from https://slock.it/

Sun, Y. Z., Fan, L., & Hong, X. (2018). Technology Development and Application of Blockchain: Current Status and Challenges. *Chinese Journal of Engineering Science*, 20(2), 27–32. doi:10.15302/J-SSCAE-2018.02.005

Taylor, P. J., Dargahi, T., Dehghantanha, A., Parizi, R. M., & Choo, K. R. (2019). *A systematic literature review of blockchain cyber security*. Digital Communications and Networks.

Tong, W., Dong, X., Shen, Y., & Jiang, X. (2019). A Hierarchical Sharding Protocol for Multi-Domain IoT Blockchains. *ICC 2019 - 2019 IEEE International Conference on Communications (ICC)*, 1-6.

Underwood, S. (2016). Blockchain beyond bitcoin. *Communications of the ACM*, 59, 15–17.

UniquID. (2018). *UniquID Incorporation Blockchain Identity Access Management*. Retrieved from https://uniquid.com/

Veronese, G. S., Correia, M., Bessani, A. N., & Lung, L. C. (2009). Spin One's Wheels? Byzantine Fault Tolerance with a Spinning Primary. *2009 28th IEEE International Symposium on Reliable Distributed Systems*, 135-144.

Wang, X., Zha, X., Ni, W., Liu, R. P., Guo, Y. J., Niu, X., & Zheng, K. (2019). Survey on blockchain for Internet of Things. *Computer Communications*, *136*, 10–29. doi:10.1016/j.comcom.2019.01.006

Xage. (2018). *Home Page of Xage Security*. Retrieved March 20, 2019 from https://xage.com/

Xiong, Z., Feng, S., Wang, W., Niyato, D., Wang, P., & Han, Z. (2019). Cloud/Fog Computing Resource Management and Pricing for Blockchain Networks. *IEEE Internet of Things Journal*, 6, 4585–4600.

Yang, F., Zhou, W., Wu, Q., Long, R., Xiong, N. N., & Zhou, M. (2019). Delegated Proof of Stake With Downgrade: A Secure and Efficient Blockchain Consensus Algorithm With Downgrade Mechanism. *IEEE Access: Practical Innovations, Open Solutions, 7,* 118541–118555.

Zheng, Z., Xie, S., Dai, H., Chen, X., & Wang, H. (2017). An Overview of Blockchain Technology: Architecture, Consensus, and Future Trends. *2017 IEEE International Congress on Big Data (BigData Congress),* 557-564.

Zhou, Q., Huang, H., Zheng, Z., & Bian, J. (2020). Solutions to Scalability of Blockchain: A Survey. *IEEE Access: Practical Innovations, Open Solutions, 8,* 16440–16455.

Chapter 52
Blockchain Technology for the Internet of Things Applications in Apparel Supply Chain Management

Kamalendu Pal

(iD) https://orcid.org/0000-0001-7158-6481

City, University of London, UK

ABSTRACT

Adoption of the internet of things (IoT) and blockchain technology opens new opportunities of business process automation in apparel supply chain management. The IoT technology helps to capture real-time information from different aspects of garment manufacturing activities by using radio frequency identification (RFID) tags and sensors. Blockchain technology is an emerging concept of computing that enable the decentralized and immutable storage of business transactions. In combination with IoT, blockchain technology can enable a broad range of application scenarios to enhance business value and trust. This chapter presents some of the blockchain-based IoT technology applications in apparel business processes. Moreover, the chapter provides a classification of threat models, which are considered by blockchain protocols in IoT networks. Finally, the chapter provides a taxonomy and a side-by-side comparison of the state-of-the-art methods towards secure and privacy-preserving blockchain technologies concerning the blockchain model, specific security goals, performance, and limitations.

INTRODUCTION

Apparel (i.e. textile and clothing) industry is an integral part of the world economy and society (Pal & Ul-Haque, 2020) (Pal, 2020). In recent decades, global apparel manufacturing businesses are inclined to worldwide activities due to the economic advantage of the globalization of product design and development (Pal, 2020a). In a typical textile and clothing supply chain is the sequence of organizations – their facilities, functions, and activities – that involved in producing and developing a product or service.

DOI: 10.4018/978-1-6684-7132-6.ch052

The sequence begins with raw materials purchase from selective suppliers and products are made at one or more manufacturing plants (Pal, 2019). Then these products are moved to intermediate collection points (e.g., warehouse, distribution centers) to store temporarily to move to next stage of supply chain and ultimately deliver the products to intermediate-users or retailers or customers (Pal, 2017) (Pal, 2019). The path from supplier to the customer can include several intermediaries – such as wholesalers, warehouse, and retailers, depending on the products and markets. Also, global apparel supply chains becoming increasingly heterogeneous and complicated due to a growing need for inter-organizational and intra-organizational connectedness, which is enabled by advances in modern technologies and tightly coupled business processes. Hence, information has been an important strategic asset in apparel business operational management. The apparel business networks are also using the information systems to monitor the supply chain activities ((Pal & Ul-Haque, 2020).

As a result, many global textile and clothing businesses are investing in new information and communication technology (ICT) to harness the smooth information sharing ability in supply chain operations (Pal & Ul-Haque, 2020). With the recent progress in Radio Frequency Identification (RFID) technology, low-cost wireless sensor hardwires, and world wide web technologies, the Internet of Things (IoT) advance has attracted attention in connecting global apparel business activities and sharing operational business information. These technologies promise to reshape the modus operandi of modern supply chains through enhanced data collection as well as information sharing and analysis between collaborating supply chain stakeholders. In this way, IoT technology supports the capability to connect and integrate both digital and physical business world. The process is quite simple: (i) collect data from real-world objects, (ii) communicate and aggregate those data into information, and (iii) present clear results to systems or users so that decisions can be made or object behaviour adapted.

Different research groups analysed IoT technology deployment-related issues in SCM and logistics (Atzori et al., 2018) (Gubbi et al., 2013). Particularly, a group of researchers reviewed the energy management in smart factories and concluded that IoT powered manufacturing can improve supply chain competitiveness through more effective tracking of the flow of materials, and leading to improvements in the effectiveness and efficiencies of important business processes (Shrouf et al., 2014). The other important characteristics of IoT-based systems (e.g. sharing precise and timely information related to production, quality assurance, distribution, and logistics) are also reported in the context of multi-party supply chains (Chen et al., 2014) (Cui, 2018) (Yan-e, 2011). Also, the use of IoT applications inside the production plant can increase the visibility of parts and processes, and by extension, using IoT devices along the supply chain can help to boost productivity, reduce operational costs, and enhance customer satisfaction (Deloitte, 2017).

Despite the increasing applicability of IoT applications in supply chains, there are many challenges for the use of this technology. For example, IoT-related technical issues experienced when operating at the ecosystem level, such as security, authenticity, confidentiality, and privacy of all stakeholders (Tzounis et al., 2017). Academics and practitioners consider privacy and security issues are mainly related to the vulnerability of IoT system applications. Existing security solutions are not well suited because current IoT devices may consume huge amounts of energy and often these devices need substantial information processing overhead (Dorri et al., 2017). Besides, problems such as physical tampering, hacking, and data theft might increase trust-related issues within apparel network information exchange business partners (Kshetri, 2017). Therefore IoT applications must be secure against external security attacks, in the perception layer, secure the aggregation of data in the network layer and offer particular protections that only authorized entities can access and change data in the application layer.

Moreover, most of the IoT devices are limited in power, data processing capability, and memory resources due to their small sizes and low inherent design cost. Academics and practitioners are urging to design IoT devices and their protocols in a way to design to be resource-efficient and meanwhile perform real-time data processing (Pal, 2020), keep connectivity and protect the security and privacy of the transmit data using IoT data communication network. Besides, IoT data reliability can be achieved by using distributed information processing methods which execute a verification process among all its participants to ensure that data remain immutable and untampered. Considering these technical issues and realizing the basic characteristics of today's blockchain technology now offers several potential solutions to address known disadvantages related to IoT applications in apparel business networks.

A blockchain is a distributed network for orchestrating transactions, value, and assets between peers, without the assistance of intermediaries. It is also commonly referred to as a 'ledger' that records transactions. The blockchain technology helps to record transactions or any digital interaction that is designed to be secure, transparent, highly resistance to outages, auditable, and efficient. These characteristics provide impetus to blockchain-based IoT architecture for secure data processing in a distributed environment. In order words, IoT-based information systems to improve their IoT networked infrastructure to blockchain complimented technology. It is a distributed ledger which managed by a peer-to-peer (P2P) network to provides internode communication and verifying new blocks. Once data is recorded in the blockchain, it cannot be modified without modification of all subsequent blocks and that needs a consensus of the network majority. A convergence of IoT and blockchain technologies can lead to a verifiable, secure, and robust mechanism of storing and managing data processed by smart connected devices. This network of connected devices will be able to interact with their environment and make decisions without any human intervention. However, integrating blockchain technology in IoT-based information systems will enhance security, data privacy, and reliability of IoT devices, it creates a new set of challenges.

This chapter presents how apparel businesses can leverage IoT applications in combination with blockchain technology to streamline their apparel business supply chains business information. When combined, these enabling technologies will help global textile and clothing companies to overcome problems related to data acquisition and integrity, address security challenges, and reduce information asymmetry. This chapter will demonstrate areas of disadvantages towards safety and privacy in blockchain technology. The rest of this chapter is organized as follows. Section 2 presents an introduction of IoT and its applications in apparel industry. It includes IoT applications in apparel supply chain management, and drawbacks of IoT applications in apparel supply chain. Section 3 describes blockchain technology in apparel supply chain management applications. Section 4 explains blockchain applications for the IoT. Section 5 describes the background related security and privacy for enterprise computing and research challenges. Then Section 6 reviews some of the threat models for blockchain technology. Finally, Section 7 concludes the chapter by discussing relevant research issues.

INTERNET OF THINGS AND ITS APPLICATIONS IN APPAREL INDUSTRY

The idea of the IoT was first created in 1999 by Kevin Ashton (Keertikumar et al., 2015). The IoT technology has been used in apparel industries for different business process automation purpose. Sensing Enterprise (SE) is an attribute of an enterprise or a network that allows it to react to business stimuli originating on the Internet. This area of computing has come into focus recently on the enterprise automation, and there are handful of evidences of the successful use of this technology in supply chain operations. IoT based information system aims to improve organizational communication and collaboration activities. In recent decades, World Wide Web technologies are getting prominence for business use and the number of Internet-based IoT services are increasing rapidly for supply chain communities. These services, which human users can access using devices. The main form of communication is human-to-human. IoT attempts to not only have humans communicating through the Internet but also have objects or devices. These things are to be able to exchange information by themselves over the Internet, and new forms of Internet communication would be formed: human-to-things and things-to-things. In this way, IoT refers to an information network that connects sensors on or in physical objects (*'things'*) ranging from consumer goods, pallets of goods to everyday tools, and industrial machinery.

Simplistically, the IoT technology is characterized by three types of visions:

1. **Things Oriented Vision**: This vision is supported by the fact that this technology can track anything using sensors. The advancement and convergence of micro-electronical systems technology, wireless communications and digital electronics has resulted in the development of miniature devices having the ability to sense, compute and communicate wirelessly in an effective way. The basic philosophy is uniquely identifying an object using specifications of Electronic Product Code (EPC). It is important to note that future of 'Things Oriented Vision' will depend upon sensor technology evolution for accurate sensing (without any error) and its capabilities to fulfil the "thing" oriented other issues.

2. **Internet Oriented Vision**: This vision is based upon the need to make smart objects which are connected. To take full advantage of the available Internet technology, there is a need to deploy large-scale, platform-independent, wireless sensor network infrastructure that includes data management and processing, actuation, and analytics. Cloud computing promises high reliability, scalability, and autonomy to provide ubiquitous access, dynamic resource discovery and composability required for the next generation Internet of Things applications.

3. **Semantic Oriented Vision**: This vision is powered by the fact that the number of sensors which are used in the apparel industry is huge and the data that these IoT infrastructures collect is massive. Thus, the industry needs to process this data in a meaningful way to form value-added services using semantic technologies (e.g. ontology, knowledge-based reasoning), which are efficient, secure, scalable, and market-oriented computing.

In this way, the IoT application builds on three pillars, related to the ability of smart objects to (i) be identifiable (anything identifies itself), (ii) to communicate (anything communicates), and (iii) to interact (anything interacts) – either among themselves, building networks of interconnected objects, or with end-users or other entities in the network.

Furthermore, cloud computing and the more recent concept of fog computing (i.e., a decentralized computing structure, extending the concept of cloud computing through the local performance of computation, storage and communication through so-called 'edge devices') provides computing resources and scalability to connect, store and analyse IoT data (often labelled as big data) received from connected devices and sources including WSNs, global positioning systems (GPS), GPRS, and geographic information systems (GIS). The analysis of IoT data can assist firms to sense and then respond to situations in real-time and may lead to automation or value-creating predictive analytics capabilities (Tzounis et al., 2017). Moreover, through the connection of a heterogeneous set of hardware devices, (e.g., sensors) IoT streamlines critical business processes through the capture of data, such as the identification of human operators and environmental variables (e.g., temperature, humidity, vibration, air currents). IoT devices are often deployed to sense the physical world, communicate over a wireless signal and to actuate based on predefined conditions.

According to Barreto et al. (Barreto et al., 2017), the three distinguishing features of IoT are context, omnipresence and optimization. The context describes the capability of IoT to provide real-time monitoring, to interact, and to enable instant response to specific situations that are controlled. Omnipresence lies in the pervasiveness of the technology and its broad applicability, while optimization refers to the specific functionalities and characteristics each physical object has (Witkowski et al., 2017). These features pave the way for novel and innovative IoT use cases among exchange partners within both simple and complex supply chains and open new business opportunities.

IoT Applications in Apparel Supply Chain Management

The application of IoT promises significant improvements in supply chain performance and operational efficiency. The benefits result primarily from real-time information exchange, which can reduce time wastage caused by the bullwhip effect (Wang et al., 2008) (Zhou, 2012). Moreover, IoT can help to revolutionize supply chains by improving operational efficiencies and creating revenue opportunities. Three of the areas that can benefit from IoT deployment include (1) inventory management and warehouse operations, (2) production and manufacturing operations, and (3) transportation operations (See Table 1). For example, smart forklifts and racks, and novel usage of *smart glasses* (i.e. wearable devices equipped with sensors and camera technologies to locate objects in the warehouse), monitoring cameras, and other intelligent warehouse management software.

Also, in warehouse operations – reusable assets (e.g. inventory storage totes and pallets) can be attached with IoT enabled tags or devices that help in guiding and directing the warehouse pickers to their storage locations. In this way, IoT technologies not only help to automate the operational activities in the warehouses, but they reduce human intervention (and error) linked with manual storage management. This advantage results from using industrial-grade RFID-tags and RFID-readers that send a radio signal to identify correctly tag-embedded on pallets, totes, or the product cartons leading to a reduction in the time spent in collecting, recording, and retrieving business operational data.

IoT technologies are also used in apparel production and manufacturing activities. Apparel manufacturing processes consist of spinning and knitting. Spinning is the conversion of fibers into yarn, while knitting is a process of making fabric by intermeshing a series of loops of one or more yarn. It generally contains three major phases, i.e., producing raw materials, processing materials, and making clothes. Industrial machines with embedded sensors can be monitored in real-time and controlled by smart instruments, such as microcomputers, microcontrollers, microprocessors, and intelligent sensors. IoT-based solutions can enhance operational control over the processing capacity, set-up time, and throughput. Therefore, IoT-based technologies usage can lead to more efficient machine utilization, reduction of bottlenecks in production and can help in optimizing production planning and scheduling at varying levels within an apparel business. As a result, this enhanced insight into key manufacturing processes will enable stronger collaboration and value co-creation with suppliers as well as improved machine-to-machine and machine-to-human interaction.

Moreover, when it comes to transportation activities in apparel supply chain management, IoT-based technology can also provide potential advantages. For example, a GPS (Global Positioning System) helps to position vehicles (e.g. trucks) from remote distribution centers and to optimize both routing and delivery time. In a greater extent, GPS, RFID technology, and attached sensors increase the in-transit visibility by precisely localizing vehicles on public roads or at shipping terminals through large scale mapping, traffic data collection and analysis. The data gathered from these IoT devices will help to improve the forecasting of delivery times, fleet availability, and routing efficiency (Waller & Fawcett, 2013). Moreover, these devices can be used for enhancing the sharing of under-utilized resources among vehicles in the parking space or on the road (Barreto et al., 2017).

Table 1. IoT Levers in Apparel Supply Chain Business

Inventory Management and Warehouse Operations	
Enablers	**Processes**
• Smart racks • Smart glasses • Monitoring cameras • Smart forklifts • Smart warehouse management system (SWMS)	• Route optimization, elimination of in-process collisions • Fast, cost-efficient, and flexible operations • Better handling of items that are hard to reach (i.e., items that are difficult to detect on the shelf or racks) • Real-time visibility of inventory levels • Avoidance of stockouts • Agility and fast responsiveness to inadequacies (e.g., misplacement of items) • Workspace monitoring (e.g., for security purposes) • Stock keeping units (e.g., pallets) recognition • Simultaneous threat detection and scanning for imperfections
Production and Manufacturing Operations	
Enablers	Processes
Embedded machine sensors Machine analytics	• Real-time condition monitoring • Predictive maintenance: Detection of physical stress levels, pileups, and prevention of failures • Improved measurement of throughput, setup-time, and overall productivity • Enhancement of both machine-to-machine and machine-to-human interactions
Transportation Operations	
Enablers	Processes
GPRS sensors RFID tags Routers GPS satellites	• Continuous visibility of products along the supply chain • Real-time shipment tracking • Remote sensing (e.g., temperature, humidity, vibrations) • Improve activity bottlenecks and outdoor traffic, transport mobility, road, and driver safety • Maximizing fuel efficiency and optimize routing strategies

Drawbacks and Threats of IoT Applications in Apparel Supply Chain

Apparel manufacturing process consists of spinning and knitting. Spinning is the conversion of fibers into yarn, while knitting is a process of making fabric by intermeshing a series of loops of one or more yarn. The use of IoT-based applications in the apparel supply chain has proved to be effective in operational efficiency. The IoT technology addresses different apparel manufacturing chain challenges including the growing business need to improve supply chain information transparency and improve the integrity of production data and the identity of products (i.e., the right products, at the right time, in the right place, incorrect quantity, and at the right price). In this way, as IoT systems generate massive volumes of data across the apparel network business environment, and this data often resides in silos, which are often the potential for security and privacy-related risks.

There are different types of IoT security issues need to be addressed and these include IoT device trust, access control, data integrity, physical tampering, and user privacy. An IoT technology deployment survey concluded that 70 percentage of IoT devices are vulnerable due to encryption-related issues, unprotected interfaces, and inappropriate authorization (Lee & Lee, 2015). In highlighting different privacy and security issues, a group of researchers (Cam-Winget et al., 2016) comment on the recent system security solutions are insufficient due to scalability issues in processing and analyzing data generated from huge networks of heterogeneous IoT-based devices and the need to fulfil real-time requirements. Proper security and privacy approaches are considered unusable to IoT-based information system environment due to their dynamic topology and distributed nature. In addition, the current Internet architecture with its server-based computing platform might not be able to deal with an enormous number of devices and vast amounts of data because individual servers may pose a single point of failure for cyber-attacks and physical damage. For example, IoT devices are at risk from DDoS attacks, data theft, and remote hijacking. Also, Marjani and colleagues (Marjani et al., 2017) argue that some IoT-based applications lack a service level agreement (SLA) to safeguard 'Personally Identifiable Information' (PII) demanded by privacy laws. Therefore, it can have a negative influence on data integrity. Hence, system security may suffer in privacy protection for both individuals and enterprises (Suresh et al., 2014).

Moreover, apparel supply chain business partners may have concerns regarding the physical security and confidentiality of product information as it moves along the enterprise value chain. Even though IoT-based information system helps supply chain exchange partners to validate and verify the authenticity of items in the supply chain; there are still some concerns about the vulnerability of IoT devices to counterfeiting, cloning, and fraudulent practices, such as unauthorized access, tampering, and manipulation of content. For example, if RFID tags are compromised, it may be possible to bypass security measures and to introduce new vulnerabilities during automatic verification processes (Kumar & Iyengar, 2017). In addition, the manual retrieval and storage of information regarding unique tag identities in a centralized database enables the reproducing or forging of this information at any time (Lin et al., 2017). Hence, it is difficult to identify counterfeit products accompanied by misleading provenance histories (Hua et al., 2018).

At the end, centralized systems may pose a disadvantage for IoT-based system deployments in the apparel manufacturing business for traceability operations. The existence of centralized business organizations may lead to mistrust, which may curb the futuristic enhancement of supply chains (Tse et al., 2017). A centralized approach for data storing and processing can lead to several business risks and operational problems related to data integrity, security, and privacy. For example, cloud-based solutions for monitoring IoT data may be subject to manipulation and privacy legislation issues that arise when exporting substantial amounts of confidential and highly sensitive information to external services in other jurisdictions (Khetri, 2017) (Kamilaris et al., 2019). Moreover, these solutions may create obscurity and enhance information asymmetry between supply chain exchange partners. An additional factor is that centralized information systems act as a black box, and the collaborating business nodes do not know how their data is stored, managed, utilized, and secured (Galvez et al., 2018). Blockchain technology can help to alleviate several of these problems.

BLOCKCHAIN TECHNOLOGY IN APPAREL BUSINESS

Since the innovation of Bitcoin, a digital cryptocurrency, in 2008 (Nakamoto, 2008), blockchain technology has positioned itself in the focal point of interest among a diverse range of researchers and practitioners. Blockchain is a decentralized ledger that stores all transactions that have been made on top of a peer-to-peer (P2P) network in a secure, verifiable, and transparent way. The main advantage of blockchain over the existing technologies is that it enables the two parties to make transactions over the Internet securely without the interference of any intermediary party. The omission of the third party can reduce the processing cost while improving the security and efficiency of transactions.

Due to the considerable amount of benefits that blockchain can bring in information processing, this technology is expanding its applicability to new territories such as supply chain management, and logistics management. Today, blockchain also stands as a gatekeeper in the emerging "trust economy", in which the global apparel supply chain operates to serve its suppliers and customers. The efficiency of a global apparel supply chain relies on trust between the different stakeholders and the interaction between blockchain and IoT technologies can assist in increasing the traceability and reliability of information along with the business network. To achieve this strategic objective, the IoT technology should be integrated with enterprise resource planning (ERP) and point of sales (POS) systems of apparel business to be able to share and monitor real-time information at each stage, as shown in Figure 1.

Globally, blockchain technology offers a way to record transactions or any digital interaction that is designed to be secure, transparent, highly resistant to outages, auditable, and efficient. In other words, the blockchain technology has introduced an effective solution to the IoT based information systems security. A blockchain enhance IoT devices to send data for inclusion in a shared transaction repository with the tamper-resistant record and enables business partners to access and supply IoT data without the intervention of central control and management, which creates a digital fusion.

Figure 1. RFID tagging level at different stages in the apparel manufacturing network

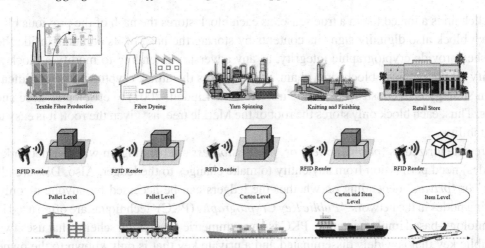

Therefore, blockchain is now a vital and important technology for different enterprise applications in the apparel business. In simple, a '*blockchain*' is a particular type of data structure used in some distributed manner (known as '*distributed ledger*' - DL) which stores and transmits data in packages called '*blocks*' that are connected in a digital '*chain*'. The idea of distributed ledger originated from the concept of '*shared ledger*'. A shared ledger can be a single ledge with *layered permissions* or a distributed ledger, which consists of multiple ledgers maintained by a distributed network of nodes (or *business activities*). Distributed Ledger Technology (DLT) refers to a novel and fast-evolving approach to recording and sharing data across multiple data stores (or ledgers). This technology allows for transactions and data to be recorded, shared, and synchronized across a distributed network of different network participants. Blockchains employ '*cryptographic*' and algorithmic methods to record and synchronize data across a network in an '*immutable manner*'. A simple diagrammatic representation of blockchain is shown in Figure 2.

Figure 2. Basic blockchain representations

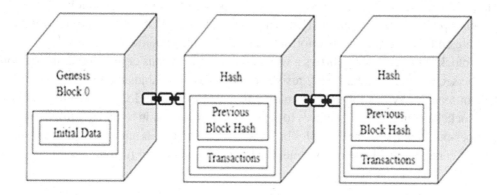

A blockchain is a linked list in a true sense, as each block stores the hash of the previous block in its chain. Each block also digitally signs its contents by storing the hash of its contents inside the block. These hashes provide cryptographic integrity, as any adversary intending to modify a block needs to also modify all the previous blocks in a chain, which makes the attack cryptographically infeasible. A key design strategy is to construct a Merkle tree (Katz & Lindell, 2007) to efficiently store and verify the hashes. Thus, each block only stores the root of the Merkle tree, as, given the root, it is easy to verify the immutability.

DLs are categorized as '*permissioned*' or '*permissionless*', depending on whether network participants (nodes) need permission from any entity to make changes to the ledger. Also, DLs are classified as '*public*' or '*private*' depending on whether the ledgers can be accessed by anyone or only by the participating nodes in the network. '*Public Key Cryptography* (PKC)' techniques are often used in blockchain technology-based implementation. PKC is an asymmetric encryption scheme that uses two sets of keys: a public key that is widely disseminated and a private key that is only known to the owner. PKC can be used to create digital signatures and is used in a wide array of applications, such as '*HyperText Transmission Protocols*' (HTTPs) used in the Internet operation, for authentication in critical applications and also in chip-based payment cards.

Figure 3. Design steps of a decentralized blockchain application

Distributed Ledger Technology (*acronym*: DLT)   Ledger records ALL transactions   'key/value' database with current state (optional)

Decentral peer-to-peer network of nodes   Public key-cryptography without central authority   Any transaction added is validated by multiple entities

Transactions in a blockchain system are identical to their traditional database counterparts. These transactions are issued by the clients to the servers of the blockchain system. These transactions act on the data stored on all the participating servers. In its vanilla form, a blockchain transaction could be visualized as a set of reading/write operations performed on each node of a replicated distributed database. To determine an ordering for all the incoming transactions, each blockchain application employs a consensus protocol, and some of the important steps in the blockchain technology is shown in Figure 3.

In a blockchain-based infrastructure, every node of the chain maintains a local copy of transaction information. This copy, which is identical to the original copy and updated in the global information sheet as it is distributed within the database with well-built constancy support. In this database, once data is entered within the blockchain ledger, then no one is capable to change this data in the future and this mechanism is known as *tamperproof*. However, a systematic effort is required towards building a *reliable* blockchain-based information infrastructure. The main features of these systematic efforts are as follows: (i) Blockchain Protocols for Commitment: The *protocol of commitment* makes sure that valid transaction from apparel business processes are committed and stored in the blockchain information storage with appropriate *validation mechanism* and within a *stipulated time*; (ii) Consensus: Consensus consists of two functions: First, it allows blockchain to be updated while ensuring that every block in the chain is valid as well as keeping participants incentivized and second, it prevents any single entity from controlling or crashing the whole blockchain system. The consensus aim is to create a distributed network without central authorities with participants who do not necessarily need to trust each other. The consensus is an essential part of blockchain technology. Each node runs a programmed mechanism, called a consensus. The consensus is the process by which nodes agree on how to update the blockchain because of a set of transactions. Achieving consensus ensures most of the nodes in the network have validated the same set of transactions; (iii) Security: Safety is an important aspect of the blockchain-based transaction processes. All the data within the blockchain ecosystem needs to be secured, and tamper-proof. This ensures that there are no malicious nodes within the blockchain-based enterprise ecosystem; (iv) Privacy and Authenticity: Privacy in blockchain enables the client/user to perform transactions without leaking its identification information in the network; and (v) Smart Contracts: In 1994, Nick Szabo (Szabo, 1994) presented the basic concept of a smart contract. It is a self-executable code that runs on the blockchain to facilitate, perform, and enforce the terms of an agreement. Thus, smart contracts guarantee low transaction fees, high-speed, precision, efficiency, and transparency, compared to traditional systems that require a trusted third party to enforce and execute the terms of an agreement.

In recent years, the blockchain technology ushering a huge range of industrial applications and many comparable information exchange schemes have been developed for different types of industrial business process automation purpose.

BLOCKCHAIN APPLICATIONS FOR THE IoT

The blockchain technology is used in different application areas in SCM. Some of these applications are described in this section.

Applications in Supply Chain

Academics and practitioners identified industrial business processes, particularly supply chain and logistics management, are important areas for deploying IoT based information system applications (Atkore et al., 2018) (Gubbi et al., 2013). IoT based industrial information systems can enhance the competitiveness of enterprise through more effective tracking of the flow of raw materials, leading to improve the effectiveness and efficiencies of business processes (Shroud et al., 2014). In the context of globalized business practice, with multiple collaborating-partners based supply chains, IoT-based applications enhance to facilitate the sharing of more precise and timely information relevant to production, quality control, distribution and logistics (Chen et al., 2014). However, researchers expressed their concern regarding standalone IoT-based applications along with global supply chain management (Pal, 2020). The main concerns were raised on the issues of standalone IoT systems security and privacy.

Different hybrid information system architectures (e.g. IoT with blockchain, cloud based IoT and blockchain technology) have been proposed by the research community. A blockchain enhances IoT-based applications tamper-resistant characteristics. In recent years, different blockchain-based information management systems have been reported by researchers. For example, IBM has developed a new blockchain-based service that is designed to track high-value items through complex supply chains in a secure cloud-based application system (Kim, 2016). Another exemplary industrial application is a fine-wine Provence-tracking service, known as the Chai Wine vault, developed by London-based Company Ever ledger (Finextra, 2016) in business-partnership with fine-wine expert Maureen Downey. An innovative anti-counterfeit application, called Block Verify, is designed and deployed for tracking anti-counterfeit products (Hulse apple, 2015) to create a sustainable business world. A start-up company from Finland (i.e. Kouvola) in partnership with IBM, developed a smart tendering application for the supply chain management. The reported application is built on an automatic blockchain-based smart contract (Banker, 2016). Another blockchain-based smart contract, called SmartLog, the application was launched by Kouvola in recent years (AhIman, 2016).

In recent decades, due to globalization manufacturing supply chain networks are going through an evolutionary change through continued digitization of its business practices. These global manufacturing chains are evolving into value-creating networks where the value chain itself turns into an important source of competitive advantage. At the same time, developments are in progress to integrate blockchain technology with other innovative technological solutions (e.g. IoT-based applications, cloud-based solutions, and fog computing-based automation), leading to novel structures of modern manufacturing supply chains, new types partnerships, holistic mechanisms of collaboration and value-enhancing applications for the global business.

Applications in Vehicles Management

The IoT-based Vehicles (or Transport) management is an emerging application area where the convergence of IoT on blockchain technologies are playing a significant role. This type of application permits the integration of vehicles into the new era of the IoT to establish smart communication between vehicles and heterogeneous networks such as vehicle-to-vehicle, vehicle-to-road, vehicle-to-human, and vehicle-to-everything. In recent years, researchers are trying to use blockchain technology to internet-of-vehicle (IoV) applications. Using decentralized security model, a group of researchers (Huang et al., 2018) designed a blockchain ecosystem model, known as LNSC (Lighting Network and Smart Contract), for electric vehicle and charging pile management. The LNSC model uses elliptic curve cryptography to calculate hash functions of electric vehicles and charging piles. To avoid the location tracking in the IoV, a group of researchers (Dorri et al., 2017) proposed a decentralized privacy-preserving architecture, where overlay nodes manage the blockchain. Also, the hash of the backup storage is stored in the blockchain.

Lei and fellow researchers (Lei et al., 2017) reported a research project that uses a blockchain-based dynamic key management for vehicular communication systems. This system is based on a decentralized blockchain structure, and the third-party authorities are removed, and the key transfer processes are verified and authenticated by the security manager network. In this way, with the rapid development of IoT and embedded technologies, drivers can access various services. However, these services are vulnerable to potential attacks such as replay, impersonation and session key disclosure attacks because they are provided through public channels. Many traditional cryptographic algorithms such as RSA also are suitable for vehicular networks because a vehicle is equipped with resource-constrained sensors.

Applications on the Internet of Things Devices Management

In IoT, devices management relates to security solutions for the physical devices, embedded software, and residing data on the devices. Internet of Things (IoT) comprises "Things" (or IoT devices) which have remote sensing and / or actuating capabilities and can exchange data with other connected devices and applications (directly or indirectly). IoT devices can collect data and process the data either locally or send to centralized servers or cloud-based application back-ends for processing. A recent on-demand model of manufacturing that is leveraging IoT technologies is called Cloud-Based Manufacturing (CBM); and it enables ubiquitous, convenient, on-demand network access to a shared pool of configurable manufacturing resources that can be rapidly provisioned and released with minimal management effort or service provider interaction.

But attackers seek to exfiltrate the data of IoT devices by using the malicious codes in malware, especially on the open-source Android platform. Gu et al., (Gu et al., 2018) introduced a malware detection system based on the consortium blockchain, named CB-MDEE, which is composed of detecting consortium chain by test members and public chain by users. The CB-MDEE system uses a soft-computing based comparison technique and more than one marking functions to minimise the false-positive rate and improve the identification ability of malware variants. A research group (Lee et al., 2017) uses a firmware update scheme based on the blockchain technology, to safeguard the embedded devices in the IoT system.

Applications in Internet of Things Access Management

Access control is a mechanism in computer security that regulates access to the system resources. The current access control systems face many problems, such as the presence of the third-party, inefficiency, and lack of privacy. These problems can be addressed by blockchain, the technology that received major attention in recent years and has many potentials. Jemel and other researchers (Jemel & Serhrouchni, 2017) report a couple of problems in centralized access control systems. As there is a third party, which has access to the data, the risk of privacy leakage exists. Also, a central party is in charge to control the access, so the risk of a single point of failure also exists. This study presents an access control mechanism with a temporal dimension to solve these problems and adapts a blockchain-based solution for verifying access permissions. Attribute-based Encryption method (Sahai & Waters, 2005) also has some problems such as privacy leakage from the private key generator (PKG) (Hur & Noh, 2011) and a single point of failure as mentioned before. Wang and collegues (Wang, et al.,2018) introduce a framework for data sharing and access control to address this problem by implementing decentralized storage.

Based on the data management and the type of applications, blockchain can be classified either as private (permission) or public (permissionless). Both classes are decentralized and provide a certain level of immunity against faulty or malicious users for blockchain technology. The main differences between private and public blockchains lie in the execution of the consensus protocol, the maintenance of the ledger, and the authorization mechanism to join the distributed network.

Recently, there is a huge amount of investment from the industries, as well as a significant interest from academia to solve major research challenges in blockchain technologies. For example, the consensus protocols are the major building blocks of the blockchain technologies, thus, the threats targeting the consensus protocols become a significant research issue in the blockchain.

BLOCKCHAIN SECURITY AND PRIVACY ISSUES

Blockchain technology offers an approach to storing information, executing transactions, performing functions, and establishing trust is a secure computing without centralized authority in a networked environment. From data management point of view, a blockchain is a distributed database, which logs an evolving list of transaction records by organizing them into a hierarchical chain of blocks. From security perspective, the blockchain is created and maintained using a peer-to-peer overlay network and secured through intelligent and decentralized utilization of cryptographic techniques. Many consider blockchain as a technology breakthrough for cryptography and cybersecurity, with use cases ranging from globally deployed procurement systems in textile and clothing industries, to smart contracts, to global product transportation management over the Internet of Things, and so forth. Although blockchain has received growing interest in the academia and industry in the recent years, the security and privacy of blockchains continue to be at the center of the debate when deploying blockchain in different industrial applications.

Key Security Risk Areas of Blockchain

The main areas of security on blockchain technology are: (i) Ledger, (ii) Consensus Mechanism, (iii) Networking Infrastructure, (iv) Identity Access Management, and (v) Cryptography. A diagrammatic representation is shown these risk areas in Figure 4.

Ledger: The ledger is used to register all transactions and changes in the status of the data. The ledger is distributed by smart design and shared between the blockchain participating nodes. Two challenging problems (or hazards) generally threaten the applicability of the ledger technology in blockchain applications: (a) unauthorized entry into the ledger; and (b) unauthorized (or improper, or illegal) operations on recorded ledger data.

Consensus Mechanism: A consensus mechanism is a protocol (i.e. set of rules) to ensure that all the participants in the blockchain network are complying with the agreed rules for day-to-day operations. It makes sure that the transactions originate from a legitimate source by having every participant consent to the state of the distributed ledger. The public blockchain is a decentralized technology, and no centralized authority is in place to regulate the required act. Therefore, the network requires authorizations from the network participants for the verification and authentication of any activities that occur in the blockchain network. The whole process is done based on the consensus of the network participants, and it makes the blockchain a trustless, secure, and reliable technology for digital transactions. Distinct consensus mechanisms follow different principles, which enables the network participants to comply with those rules. Several consensus mechanisms have been introduced considering the requirements of secure digital transactions. However, proof of work (PoW), proof of stake (PoS), and delegated proof of stake (DPoS) are the few consensus protocols used by the industries. In this way, the blockchain relies on the distributed consensus mechanism to establish mutual trust. However, the consensus mechanism itself has vulnerability, which can be exploited by attackers to control the entire blockchain. Although a few approaches, e.g., (Muhammad et al., 2018), have been introduced in blockchains to deter and prevent attacks, due to the inherent characteristics of openness, the PoW-based permissionless blockchain networks may not be completely secure.

Network Infrastructure: The network infrastructure is required for both blockchain and Distributed Ledger Technology (DLT). The network infrastructure threats can be detected in the case of nodes being stopped by malicious attacker by using good anticipatory mechanisms. In August 2016, nearly 120,000 Bitcoin (over US $60mn at the time) were stolen from Bitfinex (Nagaraj & Maguire, 2017). Based in Hong Kong, Bitfinex is one of the world's largest digital and cryptocurrency exchanges. The incident exploited security vulnerabilities within individual organizations. The blockchain network itself remained fully functional and operated as envisioned. The incident may have been prevented had there been a detailed end-to-end review of security, using scenarios, meaning there would have been a higher chance of identifying risks up front and being able to mitigate them at that point.

Identity Access Management: Privacy in blockchain enables the client/user to perform transactions without leaking its identification information in the network. The blockchain transparency compromises data privacy even though there is no direct relationship between transactions and individuals. They can reveal the user identity by checking, auditing, and tracing each transaction from the system's very first transaction. Also, blockchain technology uses numerous techniques to achieve the highest level of privacy and authenticity for transactions. As information is coming from different users within the blockchain industrial ecosystem, the infrastructure needs to ensure every user privacy and authenticity.

Blockchain-based information system often employs a combination of public and private key to securely encrypt and decrypt data.

Cryptography: The records on a blockchain are secured through cryptography. Network participants have their own private keys that are assigned to the transactions they make and act as a personal digital signature. If a record is altered, the signature will become invalid and the peer network will know right away that something has happened. However, there could be software bugs and glitches in cryptography coding. These could include anything from coding mistakes by developers, poor implementations of an underlying flaw in the cryptography routines. Even experienced programmers can make a mistake in putting together tried and tested cryptographic tools so that they are not secure. Hackers can take advantages of this weakness.

Figure 4. Various Security Risk Areas of Blockchain

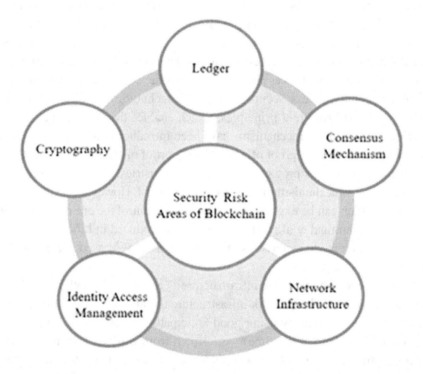

Safety is an important aspect of the blockchain-based transaction processes. All the data within the blockchain ecosystem needs to be secured, and tamper-proof. This ensures that there are no malicious nodes within the blockchain-based enterprise ecosystem. This is because, as mentioned earlier, the data inserted into a public ledger or inside the blockchain is now distributed to individual users and everyone maintains their local copy of the blockchain. In that local copy, that individual cannot tamper but upgrade the data and retransmit the data within the network. But for the transaction to be validated, the other nodes should be convinced that the broadcasted information is not malicious, and the system security is ensured.

THREAT MODELS FOR BLOCKCHAIN

This section explains the threat models that are considered by the blockchain protocols in IoT networks. Threat agents are mostly malicious users whose intention is to steal assets, break functionalities, or disrupt services. However, threat agents might also be inadvertent entities, such as developers of smart contacts who unintentionally create bugs and designers of blockchain applications who make mistakes in the design or ignore some issues.

Threats facilitate various attacks on assets. Threats arise from vulnerabilities at the network, in smart contracts, from consensus protocol deviations or violations of consensus protocol assumptions, or application-specific vulnerabilities. Countermeasures protect owners from threats. They involve various security and safety solutions and tools, incentives, reputation techniques, best practices, and so on. Risks are caused by threats and their agents and may lead to a loss of monetary assets, a loss of privacy, a loss of reputation, service malfunctions, and disruptions of services and applications (i.e., availability issues).

The owners of the blockchain-based information systems wish to minimize the risk caused by threats that arise from threat agents. This section presents five types of attacks: *identity-based attacks*, *manipulation-based attacks*, *cryptanalytic attacks*, *reputation-based attacks*, and *service-based attacks*. A diagrammatic representation of these attacks is shown in Figure 5.

Identity-Based Attacks

The emergence of DLT based upon a blockchain data structure, has given rise to new approaches to identity management that aim to upend dominant approaches to providing and consuming digital identities. These new approaches to identity management (IdM) propose to enhance decentralization, transparency and user control in transactions that involve identity information. In identity-based attacks, the attacker forge identity to masquerade as authorized user, to get access to the system and manipulate it. Again, identity-based attacks can be broadly classified into four different types, and they are namely: Key attack, Replay attack, Impersonation attack, and Sybil attack.

Key attack: In blockchain technology, certificates and identities are validated and protected in Hyperledger Fabric by asymmetric cryptography. How each participant chooses to store and protect their private key is up to them. There are a wide range of wallets and management methods available as there is no cohesive management scheme required by Hyperledger Fabric. An outside attacker obtaining private key(s) could lead to any number of attacks. In this section an example has been used where the attack is defined in the context of a system combining electric vehicles and charging piles, as follows: "If the private key of an electric vehicle that has been used for longtime leaks, the attacker can impersonate this electric vehicle to deceive others" (Huang et al., 2018). To deal with this attack, LNSC (Lightning Network and Smart Contract) protocol (Huang et al., 2018) provides a mutual authentication mechanism between the electric vehicles and charging piles. To this end, it employs the elliptic curve encryption to calculate the hash functions, and hence it ensures resiliency against the key leakage attack.

Replay attack: A replay attack is usually a scheme that is utilized during a fork of a blockchain. For example, an attacker might copy an existing transaction and then attempt to resubmit it to the blockchain as if it were a new transaction. A hacker may also attempt to resubmit the transaction if a hacker has your digital signature and because your original transaction was valid. If the attacker succeeds in resubmitting this rogue transaction, they will receive the wallet transactions twice. This attack aims to spoof the identities of two parties, intercept their data packets, and relay them to their destinations without modification. To resist this attack, LNSC (Huang et al., 2018) uses the idea of elliptic curve encryption to calculate the hash functions. On the other hand, BSein (blockchain-based system for secure mutual authentication) (Lin et al., 2018) uses a fresh one-time public/private key pair, which is generated for each request, to encrypt the message and compute the Message Authentication Code (MAC). In this way, the replay attack can be detected.

Impersonation attack: An adversary tries to masquerade as a legitimate user to perform unauthorized operations. As presented in Table II, three methods are proposed to protect against this attack. The idea of elliptic curve encryption to calculate the hash functions is proposed by LNSC protocol (Huang et al., 2018). Wang et al. (Wang et al., 2018) propose a distributed incentive-based cooperation mechanism, which protects the user's privacy as well as a transaction verification method of the node cooperation. The mechanism hides the user's privacy information within a group and ensures their protection from the impersonation attack. BSein (Lin et al., 2018), on the other hand, uses the idea of attribute-based signatures, i.e., only legitimate terminals can generate a valid signature, and hence any impersonation attempt will be detected when its corresponding authentication operation fails.

Sybil attack: A sybil attack is when an attacker creates multiple accounts on a blockchain to deceive the other blockchain participants. This behaviour is like folks who troll on social media by creating multiple accounts to accomplish their silly behaviour. A sybil attack could be quite like a phishing attack where an imposter pretends to be someone such as your boss asking you for your network password. Preventing sybil attacks is considered straightforward in the sense that you need to pay attention to who your wallet funds are being sent to. These types of attacks should not be an issue on a permissioned blockchain since the members are clearly identified and wallets are not normally used. Under this attack, an adversary creates many fake identities. By performing many interactions in the network, the adversary can gain a large influence within the community, i.e, increasing/decreasing the reputation of some agents. TrustChain (i.e. capable of creating trusted transactions among strangers without central control) (Otte et al., 2017) addresses this issue by creating an immutable chain of temporally ordered interactions for each agent. It computes the trustworthiness of agents in an online community with Sybil-resistance by using prior transactions as input. It ensures that agents who use resources from the community also contribute back.

Manipulation-Based Attacks

They involve unauthorized access and tamper of data. In this category, four attacks are classified, namely: False data injection attack, Tampering attack, Overlay attack, and Modification attack

False data injection attack: This attack aims to compromise the data integrity of the control system to make it take wrong control decisions. Liang et al. (Liang et al., 2018) consider the meter node as a private blockchain network. Also, the interactions among the nodes are based on a consensus mechanism, which consists of executing a distributed voting algorithm. Each node can verify the integrity of the received data. The latter is considered correct when a positive agreement is reached.

Tampering attack: The adversary may tamper the bitcoin transactions of the bitcoin addresses, amounts and other information after signing. To prevent this attack, Wang et al. (Wang et al., 2017) use a public-key cryptosystem that is compatible with the existing Bitcoin system. They propose adding the homomorphic Paillier encryption system to cover the plaintext amounts in transactions, and the encrypted amounts will be checked by the Commitment Proof.

Overlay attack: It means that the attacker adds a forgery encrypted amount to the original encrypted amount under the receiver's public key. In (Wang et al., 2017), this attack is detected as every transaction is embedded with a timestamp to mark its uniqueness. Different inputs under the same trader can be distinguished and linked to the different transactions, and hence resistance against the overlay attack is ensured.

Modification attack: It consists in modifying the broadcast transaction or the response message. To deal with this attack, LNSC (Huang et al., 2018) uses the idea of elliptic curve encryption to calculate the hash functions. BSeIN (Lin et al., 2018), on the other hand, employs the attribute signature and the MAC.

Man-in-the-middle attack: An attacker by spoofing the identities of two parties can secretly relay and even modify the communication between these parties, which believe they are communicating directly, but in fact, the whole conversation is under the control of the attacker. To resist this attack, BSeIn (Lin et al., 2018) provides secure mutual authentication. In (Huang et al., 2018), LNSC provides mutual authentication by using elliptic curve encryption (Kumanduri & Romero, 1998) (Washington, 2008) to calculate the hash functions.

Cryptanalytic Attacks

They aim to break the cryptographic algorithm and expose its keys. In (Yin et al., 2018) the quantum attack is investigated in the blockchain. This attack is designed to solve the elliptic curve digital logarithm, i.e., derive the private key from the elliptic curve public key. In this way, an adversary can sign unauthorized transactions and forge the valid signature of users. To deal with this issue, Yin et al. (Yin et al., 2018) use the idea of lattice-based signature scheme., which allows deriving many sub-private keys from the seed in the deterministic wallet of blockchain.

Reputation-Based Attacks

An agent manipulates his reputation by changing it to a positive one. In this category, we can find the following attacks, namely: Hiding Blocks attack, and Whitewashing attack.

Hiding Blocks attack: Under this attack, an agent-only exposes transactions that have a positive impact on his reputation and hides the ones with a negative reputation. In (Otte et al., 2017), an immutable chain of temporally ordered interactions for each agent. Since each record has a sequence number, any agent in the network can request specific records of others. The requested agents cannot refuse to provide their records. Otherwise, other agents will stop interacting with them.

Whitewashing: When an agent has a negative reputation, it can get rid of its identity and make a new one. There is no way to prevent this behaviour. However, it is suggested in (Otte et a., 2017) to give lower priorities to the agents of new identities when applying the allocation policy.

Service-Based Attacks

They aim either to make the service unavailable or make it behave differently from its specifications. Under this category, we can find the following attacks:

Figure 5. Classification of threat models for blockchain

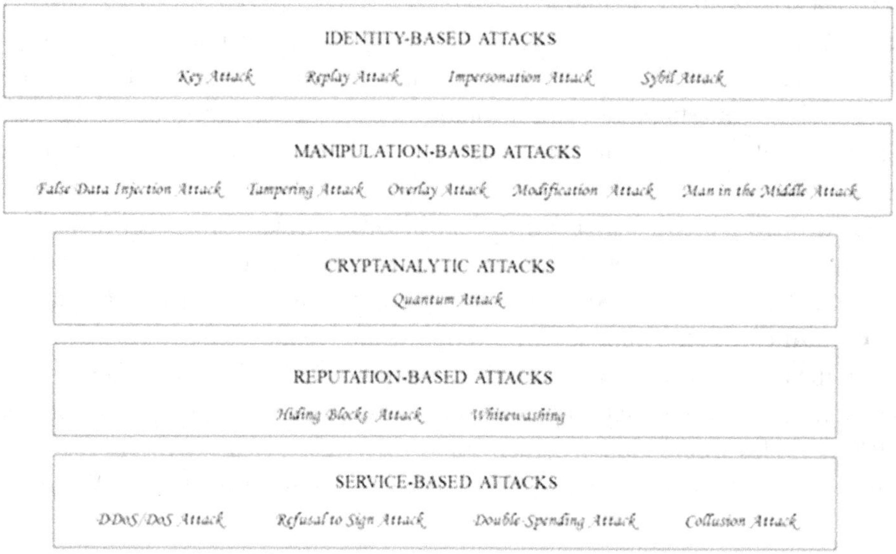

DDoS/DoS attack: A distributed denial-of-service (DDOS) attack is an extremely common type of a network attack against a website, a network node, or even a membership service provider. This DDOS attack is essentially initiated by many multiples (possibly thousands) of remote nodes, and then coordination is used to start their attacks. Essentially, a DDOS attack occurs when multiple systems flood a network resource with what are known as connection requests, messages, or other types of communication packets. The goal of this type of attack is to slow down or crash the system. The concentrated attack and subsequent shut down of the system results in a "denial of service" for legitimate users. Denial of Service (DoS) and DDoS are common security problems. DoS attacks on connectivity of consensus nodes may result in a loss of consensus power, thus preventing consensus nodes from being rewarded. For validating nodes, this attack leads to a disruption of some blockchain dependent services. It involves sending a huge number of requests to cause the failure of the blockchain system. The idea of distributed SDN architecture is proposed by DistBlockNet protocol in (Sharma et al., 2017). CoinParty (Ziegeldorf et al., 2018) proposes the idea of decentralized mixing service. Liu et al. (Liu et al., 2018) employ a ring-based signature with the Elliptic Curve Digital Signature Algorithm (ECDSA). The resilience against DoS in BSeIn (Lin et al., 2018) is achieved by limiting the block size, checking the maximum number of attribute signatures for the transaction input, and using '*multi-receivers*' encryption technique to provide confidentiality for authorized participants.

Refusal to Sign attack: A malicious agent can decide to not sign a transaction that is not in his favour. Although preventing this attack is not possible, punishment measures can be taken against the refusal agents. It is proposed in (Otte Et al., 2017) to not interact with the malicious agent or split the transactions into smaller amounts. If an agent refuses to sign a transaction, the interaction is aborted.

Double-spending attack: It means that the attackers spend the same bitcoin twice to acquire extra amounts. In (Wang et al., 2017), the Timestamp and the Proof-of-Work mechanism is used. In (Aitzhan & Svetinovic, 2016), a multi-signature transaction is employed, where a minimum number of keys must sign a transaction before spending tokens.

Collusion Attack: Nodes can collide with each other and behave selfishly to maximize their profit. In (He et al., 2018), an incentive mechanism and pricing strategy are proposed to thwart selfish behaviours.

CONCLUSION

Today's textile and clothing supply chain face significant volatility, uncertainty and complexity imposed by a dynamic business environment. Changes in customer buying pattern – the demand for a lower price, higher service levels, mobile commerce and so on – necessitate customer intelligence and varying fulfilment models. These have introduced significant stress on apparel manufacturing supply chain networks, compelling clothing businesses to revisit their supply chain design strategies. It includes the deployment of appropriate information systems that enhance supply chain execution. In such scenarios, enterprise information systems architecture plays a very important role.

This chapter explains and summarizes some of the main issues of apparel manufacturing supply chain management system. IoT is a smart worldwide network of interconnected objects, which through unique address schemes can interact with each other and cooperate with their neighbors to reach common goals. The data obtained from the IoT applications along apparel business processes can make operational decision-making much easier. However, standalone IoT application systems face security and privacy-related problems.

Existing security solutions are not necessarily suited for IoT due to high energy consumption and processing overhead. With rapid growth in the number of connected IoT device, many obstacles arise that may slow down the adoption of the IoT across different apparel business processes automation. Firstly, the market for IoT devices and platforms is fragmented, with many standards and many vendors. Secondly, there are concerns about interoperability, as the solution implemented often tend to create new data silos. IoT device data often stored in the cloud securely, but they are not protected against compromised integrity devices or tampering at the source. In contrast, the blockchain is an emerging technology that can help with IoT systems resiliency. The blockchain build trust between IoT devices and reducing the risk of tampering with cryptographic techniques.

Security and business organizational issues tend to enhance the need to build an apparel manufacturing supply chain management system leveraging blockchain ledger technology. Regardless of the particularities of the specific textile manufacturing supply chain-related application, blockchain can offer a wide range of advantages. By registering and documenting a product's (e.g. cotton, fiber, textile cloths) lifecycle across the manufacturing supply chain nodes increases the transparency and the trust of the participating business partners.

Finally, the chapter tries to emphasize the security and privacy related issues of blockchain-based technology deployment. Then the chapter concludes by presenting five different types of threat models, namely - identity-based attacks, manipulation-based attacks, cryptanalytic attacks, reputation-based attacks, and service-based attacks in the context of blockchain technology.

The idea of a permissioned blockchain presents many hopeful solutions to development and integration of smart apparel supply chain operations. In practice however many more efforts need to be conducted to security of permissioned blockchains before they can be a realistic implementation. In the future the current research moves on to a more in-depth approach to permissioned blockchain security, whether an analytical or experimental analysis. The attack surface of the membership service provider (MSP) needs to be analyzed comparatively and rigorous proofs need to be built to numerically quantify the threats that accompany permissioned blockchain. Further work is encouraged in comparative analysis of key management systems to find a best fit system for permissioned blockchain. In addition, there still exist several challenging research areas, such as resiliency against combined attacks, dynamic and adaptable security framework, compliance with GDPR (General Data Protection Regulation), and energy-efficient mining related issues.

On 25 May 2018, the GDPR became enforceable in the European Union (EU) region. This has a paradoxical effect on blockchain data in general and should be strongly considered when implement any blockchain identity solution within the EU region. In this way, enforcing data privacy and protecting user data is no longer optional in Europe. However, it should be noted that the text of the GDPR documentation is void of both technical and non-technical implementation details necessary to achieve GDPR compliance. This constitutes a significant research gap that this research aims to fill in the future.

REFERENCES

AhIman, R. (2016). *Finish city partners with IBM to validate blockchain application in logistics.* https://cointelegraph.com/news/finish-city-partners-with-ibm-to-validate-blockchain-application-in-logistics

Aitzhan, N. Z., & Svetinovic, D. (2016). Security and Privacy in Decentralized Energy Trading through Multi-signatures, Blockchain and Anonymous Messaging Streams. *IEEE Transaction on Dependable and Secure Computing*, 1.

Atzori, L., Iera, A., & Morabito, G. (2018). The Internet of Things: A survey. *Computer Networks*, *54*(15), 2787–2805. doi:10.1016/j.comnet.2010.05.010

Banker, S. (2016). *Will blockchain technology revolutionize supply chain applications?* https://logisticsviewpoints.com/2016/06/20/will-block-chain-technology-revolutionize-supply -chain-applications/

Barreto, L., Amaral, A., & Pereira, T. (2017). Industry 4.0 implications in logistics: An overview. *Procedia Manufacturing*, *2017*(13), 1245–1252. doi:10.1016/j.promfg.2017.09.045

Cam-Winget, N., Sadeghi, A.-R., & Jin, Y. (2016). INVITED: Can IoT be Secured: Emerging Challenges in Connecting the Unconnected. *Proceedings of the 53rd Annual Design Automation Conference (DAC '16)*. 10.1145/2744769.2905004

Chen, R., Guo, J., & Bao, F. (2014). Trust management for service composition in SOA-based IoT systems. *Proceedings of the 2014 IEEE Wireless Communications and Networking Conference (WCNC)*, 3444–3449. 10.1109/WCNC.2014.6953138

Cui, Y. (2018). Supply Chain Innovation with IoT. In Multi-Criteria Methods and Techniques Applied to Supply Chain Management. Intech Open. doi:10.5772/intechopen.74155

Deloitte. (2017). *Digital Procurement: New Capabilities from Disruptive Technologies*. Deloitte Development LLC.

Dorri, A., Kanhere, S. S., Jurdak, R., & Gauravaram, P. (2017). Blockchain for IoT security and privacy: The case study of a smart home. *Proceedings of the 2017 IEEE International Conference on Pervasive Computing and Communications Workshops (PerCom Workshops)*.

Finextra. (2016). *Everledger secures the first bottle of wine on the blockchain*. https://www.finextra.com/pressaritcle/67381/everledger-secures-the-first-bottle-of-wine-on-the-blockchain

Galvez, J. F., Mejuto, J. C., & Gandara, J. S. (2018). Future challenges on the use of blockchain for food traceability analysis. *Trends in Analytical Chemistry, 107*, 222–232. doi:10.1016/j.trac.2018.08.011

Garg, S., Gentry, C., Halevi, S., Sahai, A., & Waters, W. (2013). *Attribute-Based Encryption for Circuits from Multilinear Maps*. Academic Press. doi:10.1007/978-3-642-40084-1_27

Gu, J., Sum, B., Du, X., Wang, J., Zhuang, Y., & Wang, Z. (2018). Consortium Blockchain-Based Malware Detection in Mobile Devices. *IEEE Access: Practical Innovations, Open Solutions, 6*, 12118–12128. doi:10.1109/ACCESS.2018.2805783

Gubbi, J., Buyya, R., Marusic, S., & Palaniswami, M. (2013). Internet of Things (IoT): A vision, architectural elements, and future directions. *Future Generation Computer Systems, 29*(7), 1645–1660. doi:10.1016/j.future.2013.01.010

He, Y., Li, H., Cheng, X., Liu, Y., Yang, C., & Sun, L. (2018). A Blockchain based Truthful Incentive Mechanism for Distributed P2P Applications. *IEEE Access: Practical Innovations, Open Solutions, 6*, 1–1. doi:10.1109/ACCESS.2018.2821705

Hua, J., Wang, X., Kang, M., Wang, H., & Wang, F. (2018). Blockchain based Provenance for Agricultural Products: A Distributed Platform with Duplicated and Shared Bookkeeping. *Proceedings of the IEEE Intelligent Vehicles Symposium (IV)*. 10.1109/IVS.2018.8500647

Huang, X., Xu, C., Wang, P., & Liu, H. (2018). LNSC: A security model for electric vehicle and charging pile management based on blockchain ecosystem. *IEEE Access: Practical Innovations, Open Solutions, 6*, 13565–13574. doi:10.1109/ACCESS.2018.2812176

Hulse Apple, C. (2015). *Block Verify uses blockchains to end counterfeiting and making world more honest*. https://cointelegraph.com/news/block-verify-uses-blockchains-to-end-counterfeiting-and-make-world-more-honest

Hur, J., & Noh, D. K. (2011). Attribute-based access control with efficient revocation in data outsourcing systems. *IEEE Transactions on Parallel and Distributed Systems, 22*(7), 1214–1221. doi:10.1109/TPDS.2010.203

Jemel, M., & Serhrouchni, A. (2017). Decentralized access control mechanism with temporal dimension based on blockchain. In *2017 IEEE 14th International Conference on e-Business Engineering (ICEBE)*. IEEE.

Kamilaris, A., Fonts, A., & Prenafeta-Boldv, F. X. (2019). The rise of blockchain technology in agriculture and food supply chain. *Trends in Food Science & Technology, 91*, 640–652. doi:10.1016/j.tifs.2019.07.034

Katz, J., & Lindell, Y. (2007). *Digital Signature Schemes. In Introduction to Modern Cryptography*. Chapman & Hall/ CBC Press. doi:10.1201/9781420010756

Keertikumar, M., Shubham, M., & Banakar, R. M. (2015). Evolution of IoT in smart vehicles: An overview. *Proceedings of the International Conference on Green Computing and Internet of Things (ICGCIoT)*, 804–809. 10.1109/ICGCIoT.2015.7380573

Kim, N. (2016, July). IBM pushes blockchain into the supply chain. *Wall Street Journal.*

Kshetri, N. (2017). Can Blockchain Strengthen the Internet of Things? *IEEE IT Professional, 19*(4), 68–72. doi:10.1109/MITP.2017.3051335

Kumanduri, R., & Romero, C. (1998). *Number Theory with Computer Applications.* Prentice Hall.

Kumar, M. V., & Iyengar, N. C. S. N. (2017). A Framework for blockchain technology in rice supply chain management. *Advanced Science and Technology Letters, 146,* 125–130. doi:10.14257/astl.2017.146.22

Lee, B., & Lee, J. H. (2017). Blockchain-based secure firmware update for embedded devices in an Internet of Things environment. *The Journal of Supercomputing, 73*(3), 1152–1167. doi:10.100711227-016-1870-0

Lee, I., & Lee, K. (2015). The Internet of Things (IoT): Applications, investments, and challenges for enterprises. *Business Horizons, 58*(4), 431–440. doi:10.1016/j.bushor.2015.03.008

Liang, G., Weller, S. R., Luo, F., Zhao, J., & Dong, Z. Y. (2018). Distributed Blockchain-Based Data Protection Framework for Modern Power Systems against Cyber Attacks. *IEEE Transactions on Smart Grid,* 1–1.

Lin, C., He, D., Huang, X., Choo, K. K. R., & Vasilakos, A. V. (2018). Bsein: A blockchain-based secure mutual authentication with fine-grained access control system for industry 4.0. *Journal of Network and Computer Applications, 116,* 42–52. doi:10.1016/j.jnca.2018.05.005

Lin, I. C., Shin, H., Liu, J. C., & Jie, Y. X. (2017). Food traceability system using blockchain. *Proceedings of the 79th IASTEM International Conference.*

Liu, Y., Liu, X., Tang, C., Wang, J., & Zhang, L. (2018). Unlinkable Coin Mixing Scheme for Transaction Privacy Enhancement of Bitcoin. *IEEE Access: Practical Innovations, Open Solutions, 6,* 23261–23270. doi:10.1109/ACCESS.2018.2827163

Mahjabin, T., Xiao, Y., Sun, G., & Jiang, W. (2017). A survey of distributed denial-of-service attack, prevention, and mitigation techniques. *International Journal of Distributed Sensor Networks, 13*(12), 155014771774146. doi:10.1177/1550147717741463

Muhammad, S., Aziz, M., Charles, K., Kevin, H., & Laurent, N. (2018). Countering double spending in next-generation blockchains. IEEE ICC 2018.

Nakamoto, S. (2008). Bitcoin: A Peer-to-Peer Electronoic Cash Aystem, 2008.

Nagaraj, K., & Maguire, E. (2017). *Securing the Chain.* KPMG International. https://assets.kpmg.com/content/dam/kpmg/xx/pdf/2017/05/securing-the-chain.pdf

Otte, P., de Vos, M., & Pouwelse, J. (2017, Sept.). TrustChain: A Sybil-resistant scalable blockchain. *Future Generation Computer Systems.*

Paillisse, J., Subira, J., Lopez, L., Rodriguez-Natal, A., Ermagan, V., Maino, F., & Cabellos, A. (2019). *Distributed Access Control with Blockchain.* Academic Press.

Pal, K. (2017). Supply Chain Coordination Based on Web Services. In H. K. Chan, N. Subramanian, & M. D. Abdulrahman (Eds.), *Supply Chain Management in the Big Data Era* (pp. 137–171). IGI Global Publication. doi:10.4018/978-1-5225-0956-1.ch009

Pal, K. (2019). Algorithmic Solutions for RFID Tag Anti-Collision Problem in Supply Chain Management. *Procedia Computer Science*, 929-934.

Pal, K. (2020). Information Sharing for Manufacturing Supply Chain Management Based on Blockchain Technology. In Cross-industry Use of Blockchain Technology and Opportunities for the Future. IGI Global.

Pal, K. (2020a). Ontology-Assisted Enterprise Information Systems Integration in Manufacturing Supply Chain. In Handbook of Research on Developments and Trends in Industrial and Material Engineering. IGI Global.

Pal, K., & Ul-Haque, A. (2020). Internet of Things and Blockchain Technology in Apparel ManufacturingSupply Chain Data Management. *Proceeding of 11th International Conference on Ambient Systems, Networks and Technologies (ANT-2020).*

Rejeb, A. (2018). Blockchain Potential in Tilapia Supply Chain in Ghana. *Acta Tech. Jaurinensis*, *11*(2), 104–118. doi:10.14513/actatechjaur.v11.n2.462

Sahai, A., & Waters, B. (2005). Fuzzy identity-based encryption. In *Annual International Conference on the Theory and Applications of Cryptographic Techniques*. Springer.

Sharma, P. K., Singh, S., Jeong, Y. S., & Park, J. H. (2017). DistBlockNet: A Distributed Blockchains-Based Secure SDN Architecture for IoT Networks. *IEEE Communication Management*, *55*(9), 78–85. doi:10.1109/MCOM.2017.1700041

Shrouf, F., Ordieres, J., & Miragliotta, G. (2014). Smart factories in Industry 4.0: A review of the concept and of energy management approached in production based on the Internet of Things paradigm. *Proceedings of the IEEE International Conference on Industrial Engineering and Engineering Management*, 679–701. 10.1109/IEEM.2014.7058728

Szabo, N. (1994). *Smart Contracts*. Available online: https://archive.is/zQ1p8

Tse, D., Zhang, B., Yang, Y., Cheng, C., & My, H. (2017). Blockchain application in food supply information security. *Proceedings of the IEEE International Conference on Industrial Engineering and Engineering Management (IEEM 2017)*, 1357–1361. 10.1109/IEEM.2017.8290114

Tzounis, A., Katsoulas, N., Bartzanas, T., & Kittas, C. (2017). Internet of things in agriculture, recent advances and future challenges. *Biosystems Engineering*, *164*, 31–48. doi:10.1016/j.biosystemseng.2017.09.007

Waller, M. A., & Fawcett, S. E. (2013). Data science, predictive analytics, and big data: A revolution that will transform supply chain design and management. *Journal of Business Logistics*, *34*(2), 77–84. doi:10.1111/jbl.12010

Wang, Q., Qin, B., Hu, J., & Xiao, F. (2017, Sept.). Preserving transaction privacy in bitcoin. *Future Generation Computer Systems*.

Wang, S., Zhang, Y., & Zhang, Y. (2018). A blockchain-based framework for data sharing with fine-grained access control in decentralized storage systems. *IEEE Access: Practical Innovations, Open Solutions, 6,* 38437–38450. doi:10.1109/ACCESS.2018.2851611

Wang, S. J., Liu, S. F., & Wang, W. L. (2008). The simulated impact of RFID-enabled supply chain on pull-based inventory replenishment in TFT-LCD industry. *International Journal of Production Economics, 112*(2), 570–586. doi:10.1016/j.ijpe.2007.05.002

Washington, L. C. (2008). *Elliptic Curves: Number Theory and Cryptography* (2nd ed.). Chapman & Hall/CRC. doi:10.1201/9781420071474

Witkowski, K. (2017). Internet of Things, Big Data, Industry 4.0 - Innovative Solutions in Logistics and Supply Chains Management. *Procedia Engineering, 2017*(182), 763–769. doi:10.1016/j.proeng.2017.03.197

Yan-e, D. (2011). Design of intelligent agriculture management information system based on IoT. *Proceedings of the 2011 Fourth International Conference on Intelligent Computation Technology and Automation, 1,* 1045–1049. 10.1109/ICICTA.2011.262

Yin, W., Wen, Q., Li, W., Zhang, H., & Jin, Z. (2018). An Anti-Quantum Transaction Authentication Approach in Blockchain. *IEEE Access: Practical Innovations, Open Solutions, 6,* 5393–5401. doi:10.1109/ACCESS.2017.2788411

Zhou, Z. (2012). Applying RFID to reduce bullwhip effect in a FMCG supply chain. In *Proceedings of the Advances in Computational Environment Science* (pp. 193-199). Springer.

Ziegeldorf, J. H., Matzutt, R., Henze, M., Grossmann, F., & Wehrle, K. (2018). Secure and anonymous decentralized Bitcoin mixing. *Future Generation Computer Systems, 80,* 448–466. doi:10.1016/j.future.2016.05.018

KEY TERMS AND DEFINITIONS

Block: A block is a data structure used to communicate incremental changes to the local state of a node. It consists of a list of transactions, a reference to a previous block and a nonce.

Blockchain: In simple, a blockchain is just a data structure that can be shared by different users using computing data communication network (e.g. peer-to-peer or P2P). Blockchain is a distributed data structure comprising a chain of blocks. It can act as a global ledger that maintains records of all transactions on a blockchain network. The transactions are time stamped and bundled into blocks where each block is identified by its *cryptographic hash.*

Blockchain Headers: The block header is dependent on the combination of messages in the block. It lists the transaction(s), the time at which the list was made, and a reference back to the hash of the most recent block.

Cryptography: Cryptography is the science of keeping communications private. It is the study of methods of sending messages in disguised form so that only the intended recipients can remove the disguise and read the message. Blockchain's transactions achieve validity, trust, and finality based on cryptographic proofs and underlying mathematical computations between various trading partners.

Decentralized Computing Infrastructure: These computing infrastructures feature computing nodes that can make independent processing and computational decisions irrespective of what other peer computing nodes may decide.

Hashing: Software causes the block header to be "hashed". Hashing is the process by which a grouping of digital data is converted into a single number, called a hash. The number is unique (effectively a "digital fingerprint" of the source data) and the source data cannot be reverse engineered and recovered from it.

Immutability: This term refers to the fact that blockchain transactions cannot be deleted or altered.

Internet of Things (IoT): The internet of things (IoT), also called the internet of everything or the Industrial Internet, is now technology paradigm envisioned as a global network of machines and devices capable of interacting with each other. The IoT is recognized as one of the most important areas of future technology and is gaining vast attention from a wide range of industries.

Provenance: In a blockchain ledger, provenance is a way to trace the origin of every transaction such that there is no dispute about the origin and sequence of the transactions in the ledger.

Smart Contract: Smart contracts are made from software coding and can self-perform autonomously. Depending on a range of factors, they may sometimes amount to binding contracts in the legal sense or otherwise affect legal relationships between parties.

Supply Chain Management: A supply chain consists of a network of *key business processes* and facilities, involving end users and suppliers that provide products, services, and information. In this chain management, improving the efficiency of the overall chain is an influential factor; and it needs at least four important strategic issues to be considered: supply chain network design, capacity planning, risk assessment and management, and performances monitoring and measurement.

Time-Stamped: A time stamp is associated with each block and this allows all participants to know when a transaction recorded by a blockchain occurred. This is likely to be particularly useful when it is necessary to prove transacting history (for example – legal or regulatory reasons).

Transparency: In a fully permissionless blockchain, all messages (including – when consensus has been reached – when they have been included on a blockchain as blocks) sent by participants are visible to all other participants.

Warehouse: A warehouse can also be called storage area and it is a commercial building where raw materials or goods are stored by suppliers, exporters, manufacturers, or wholesalers, they are constructed and equipped with tools according to special standards depending on the purpose of their use.

Chapter 53
Blockchain–Based Industrial Internet of Things for the Integration of Industrial Process Automation Systems

Charles Tim Batista Garrocho
https://orcid.org/0000-0001-8245-306X
Federal University of Ouro Preto, Brazil

Célio Márcio Soares Ferreira
Federal University of Ouro Preto, Brazil

Carlos Frederico Marcelo da Cunha Cavalcanti
Federal University of Ouro Preto, Brazil

Ricardo Augusto Rabelo Oliveira
https://orcid.org/0000-0001-5167-1523
Federal University of Ouro Preto, Brazil

ABSTRACT

The industrial internet of things is expected to attract significant investment to the industry. In this new environment, blockchain presents immediate potential in industrial IoT applications, offering several benefits to industrial cyber-physical systems. However, works in the blockchain literature target environments that do not meet the reality of the factory and do not assess the impact of the blockchain on industrial process requirements. Thus, this chapter presents an investigation of the evolution of industrial process automation systems and blockchain-based applications in the horizontal and vertical integration of the various systems in a supply chain and factories. In addition, through an investigation of experimental work, this work presents issues and challenges to be faced for the application of blockchain in industrial processes. Evaluations and discussions are mainly focused on aspects of real-time systems in machine-to-machine communication of industrial processes.

DOI: 10.4018/978-1-6684-7132-6.ch053

INTRODUCTION

Industry 4.0 refers to the fourth industrial revolution that transforms industrial manufacturing systems into Industrial Cyber-Physical Systems (ICPS), introducing emerging paradigms of information and communication, such as the Internet of Things (Serpanos & Wolf, 2018). By 2025, investments in the Industrial Internet of Things (IIoT) in the world should reach US$ 950 billion (Grand View Research [GVR], 2019). The forecasts are that investment in this market will grow by 30% during the forecast period. All this because the IIoT insertion in the factory brings excellent benefits, such as the possibility of increasing productivity by 30%.

IIoT devices have unique features such as low processing and memory, low bandwidth for data transmission, and limited autonomy (Sisinni, Saifullah, Han, Jennehag, & Gidlund, 2018). With the popularization of these devices and faced with such restrictions, it was necessary to develop new types of communication protocols designed to address these limitations. Generally, the protocols used work with the Publish-Subscribe paradigm, which allows data to be available to multiple consumers. Also, some devices may communicate with each other, either directly or through some intermediary, which is called Machine-to-Machine (M2M) communication (Kshetri, 2017).

M2M communication has shown immediate potential in industrial applications (Bartodziej, 2017). However, M2M communication based on the Publish-Subscribe paradigm uses a communication model through an intermediate node that becomes a point of failure. Also, M2M communication latency can affect the time requirements of real-time systems, compromising deadlines. Intending to establish a decentralized Peer-to-Peer (P2P) network and without the need for a reliable intermediary, several works are introducing blockchain-based smart contracts in various industrial environments. The main benefits pointed out in these works are safe, traceable, and independent communication of processes.

Blockchain-based ICPS can benefit from the vertical integration of Industrial Process Automation Systems (IPAS), creating an IIoT data flow from the production level by sensors/actuators to the short- and long-term decision-making levels by corporate servers/workstations. However, advances in recent blockchain and other technologies (hardware and software) do more harm than good when the ICPS needs to meet tight time constraints. The execution time of an ICPS depends on the context, which leads to uncontrollable variability. In addition, programming languages are generally Turing complete, which makes the runtime undecidable (Lee, 2005). Besides, industrial plant updates with new equipment that are expensive and unrealistic for small and medium industries and will replace that equipment that already work perfectly.

Although it is possible to find much research in the literature on blockchain-based smart contracts in the literature, this technology in the industrial field is still in its early stages. In particular, Lin and Liao (2017) initiate a discussion on blockchain-based smart contract platforms in the industrial environment. Reyna, Martín, Chen, Soler, and Díaz (2018) investigated the possibility of blockchain integration with IIoT and presented issues and challenges. The work of Nawari and Ravindran (2019) discusses the potentials and limitations of the application of smart contracts in the architecture, engineering and construction sectors. Alladi, Chamola, Parizi, and Choo (2019) present challenges and research on blockchain applications for IIoT.

However, most existing research suffers from the following limitations: there is no convergence of blockchain and smart contracts with the horizontal and vertical hierarchy of IPAS; There is no study explicitly discussing blockchain and smart contracts for real-time systems, but this topic is of great importance for the development of industry 4.0. Therefore, although blockchain-based smart contracts can benefit the horizontal and vertical hierarchy of IPAS, there are also several challenges to be faced before potentials can be fully unlocked. Therefore, this book chapter aims to present research on the advances, challenges and open research issues of blockchain-based smart contracts in IPAS.

In view of the previous work, we intend in this chapter of the research book: (i) to provide a conceptual introduction to IPAS, real-time systems, blockchain and smart contracts in Section 2; (ii) present an analysis of the potential for incorporating blockchain in sector 4.0 from IPAS applications, and a survey of the works that carry out the horizontal and vertical integration of IPAS in Section 3; (iii) present and discuss problems and challenges regarding the integration of IPAS from the blockchain in Section 4. Finally, Section 5 presents the final considerations.

BACKGROUND

Today, at the beginning of the fourth industrial revolution, the role of industrial networks is becoming increasingly crucial as they are expected to meet new and more demanding requirements in any new operating contexts (Wollschlaeger, Sauter, & Jasperneite, 2017). A notable example in this regard is the widespread adoption of IIoT, which requires a fast and reliable worldwide connection of industrial equipment. This scenario requires securing connectivity to even the most remote field devices through proper communication systems and interfaces.

IIoT networks are used to monitor conditions, manufacturing processes, predictive maintenance, and decision making. These networks have typical configurations, traffic and performance requirements that make them distinct and different from traditional communication systems generally adopted by general purpose applications in homes and businesses. Thus, IIoT networks are designed to meet the requirements derived from their various fields of application. The most critical requirements are time, reliability and flexibility (Felser, 2005).

IPAS Hierarchy and Synchronicity Requirements

Unlike many network protocols and information systems already widely adopted in homes and businesses, M2M communication protocols and process control systems are designed for specific industry environments. As shown in Figure 1, IPAS are typically based on a five-level hierarchy, widely known in the automation area as the IPAS pyramid (Mehta & Reddy, 2014). These systems are generally adopted by continuous industrial processes such as oil and gas distribution, power generation and management, chemical processing and treatment of glass and minerals.

At the bottom of the IPAS pyramid, the field devices level contains sensors and actuators controlled by process control level that consists of devices such as Programmable Logic Controller (PLC) and Distributed Control System (DCS) that provide an interface for Internet Protocol (IP)-based network communication at the supervision level (Vitturi, Zunino, & Sauter, 2019). At the supervisory level, processes are monitored and executed by shop floor workers through systems like the Supervisory Control and Data Acquisition (SCADA). Finally, in the top of the IPAS pyramid, there is corporate and plant management and sending process-related data to the cloud, trough systems like the Manufacturing Execution System (MES) and Enterprise Resource Planning (ERP).

IPAS comprises many nodes, logically positioned at various hierarchical levels and distributed over large geographic areas (Sharma, 2016). Many servers are used to horizontally integrate the supply chain, and also Human Machine Interface (HMI) computers are used for interaction between man and the level of control. In this context, blockchain can decentralize or support decision making in internal processes of a factory and external processes in a supply chain. This approach can make industrial automation systems fully decentralized and automated.

Real-Time Systems

Real-Time Systems are applications in which the deadline to execute tasks is critical. According to Nilsson, Bernhardsson, and Wittenmark (1998), control systems evolved to a state where they are distributed and controlled using the network. Hence, there is a delay related to network flow. Therefore, an essential challenge in the integration of real-time systems in interconnected environments is the communication aspect.

As presented in Figure 1, at the bottom of the pyramid, the processes are mostly synchronous and real-time critical. The practices presented in the top of the pyramid are goal-oriented and mainly asynchronous. The systems at the bottom of the pyramid are mostly synchronous, with soft or hard real-time constraints. In modern industrial approaches, this brings challenges in communication aspects with the concepts of the ICPS (Jeschke, Brecher, Meisen, Özdemir, & Eschert, 2017) and the IIoT (Tao, Cheng, & Qi, 2017).

Cyber-Physical Systems are the enablers of the new industrial era (Colombo, Karnouskos, Kaynak, Shi, & Yin, 2017). These systems are expected to integrate the processes from shop-floors to the business decisions. Also, they are expected to create a link from the customers to the suppliers. Jeschke et al. (2017) enforce that the industry 4.0 concept is a proposition of a fourth industrial revolution based on Internet connections, allowing the integration and cooperation of manufacturing machines. This scenario represents a challenge as the industrial processes rely on synchronous and real-time driven elements. Real-time processing is a system-level requirement in the novel Internet-connected industrial devices (Pinto, Gomes, Pereira, Cabral, & Tavares, 2017).

Tao et al. (2017) affirm that these modern paradigms represent novel information technologies applied in the industrial manufacturing processes. Nevertheless, they enforce that the interconnection is still a challenge, as the equipment is usually heterogeneous, the deployment is not so quick, and the online service generation still does not have a fixed framework. Finally, it is expected that the latency related to network integration becomes a challenge in novel industrial applications. O'Donovan, Gallagher, Bruton, and O'Sullivan (2018) assert that this aspect creates a natural conflict given the difference from decentralized decision-making processes and reliable real-time control.

Blockchain and Smart Contracts

IIoT devices used in locations that are expected to have a long lifespan need to work on an infrastructure that supports this functionality without exposing them to vulnerabilities. Machines that exchange goods or services need the support of M2M transactions; notably, those dealing with financial or other critical resources, require trust and, to be viable, need to operate risk-free and fault-tolerant (Hill, Al-Aqrabi, Lane, & Aagela, 2019). Some blockchain features make it a potential tool for securing M2M communications as it allows the use of a decentralized and trusted P2P network because network nodes do not need a trusted intermediary to exchange messages with each other or with a central authority (Fernández-Caramés & Fraga-Lamas, 2019).

Figure 1. IPAS hierarchy levels and synchronicity requirements

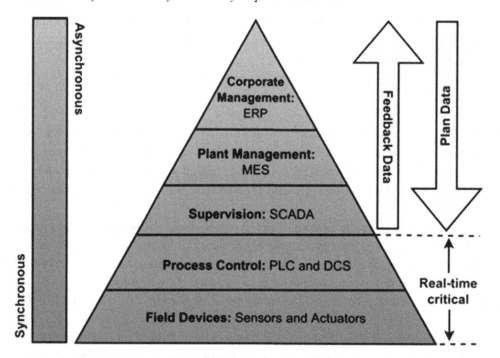

Several works related to the area of security and privacy in M2M communication are introducing concepts of this area in practice in IIoT environment (Zhong et al., 2019). However, classic countermeasures against threats adopted by general-purpose networks (e.g., firewalls, encryption techniques, and intrusion detection systems) can negatively affect the performance of industrial networks. Besides, such countermeasures based on centralized infrastructure requires more significant investment and makes the network prone to failure as all nodes in the network need a reliable central intermediate node to exchange messages with each other.

The blockchain is a decentralized P2P network with no points of failure and has excellent fault tolerance, which transactions on the cannot be deleted or changed. Blockchain is highly scalable, and all transactions are encrypted, making them secure, and auditable. At the heart of this technology, there are the consensus algorithms, which are protocols for obtaining agreements between nodes distributed across the network (Banerjee & Choo, 2018). Consensus algorithms are designed to achieve reliability in a network that involves multiple untrusted nodes. Proof of Work (PoW), Proof of Stake (PoS), Proof of Authority (PoA), and Practical Byzantine Fault Tolerant (PBFT) are the most used algorithms.

Blockchain can be permissionless or permissioned. In permissionless approach, transactions are validated by public nodes. In permissioned blockchain, transactions are validated by a select group of nodes approved by the blockchain's owner. Permissioned systems tend to be more scalable and faster, but are more centralized. Permissionless systems are open for all nodes to participate and thus provide a more decentralized approach where the trade-off is speed and scalability. Generally, on public blockchain networks, to increase network security and stability, consensus algorithms apply a mining process that requires effort from participants in the public network. As for a private network, where all nodes are known and configured individually, there is no inherent need to incentivize miners in a private/permissioned blockchain.

Platforms and Technologies

Bitcoin, the best-known digital currency uses a blockchain-based permissionless distributed ledger that maintains the transaction history (Zheng, Xie, Dai, Chen, & Wang, 2018). After the bitcoin, new blockchain-based applications emerged. Among them, the smart contract is a computer protocol intended to digitally facilitate, verify, or enforce the negotiation or performance of a contract. Smart contracts can transact between different nodes without the intermediation of a third-party entity or agent. Ethereum, Hyperledger (Fabric, Sawtooth), and Corda are popular smart contract platforms that are contributing significantly to the generation of Decentralized Applications (DApps) (Voulgaris, Fotiou, Siris, Polyzos, Jaatinen, & Oikonomidis, 2019). As illustrated in Figure 2, DApps queries the blockchain network through a network peer that executes the smart contract for ledger access.

Ethereum, Hyperledger Fabric, and Hyperledger Sawtooth are flexible, while Corda was designed specifically for the financial sector. Ethereum was designed to make DApps easily understandable and simple to implement. But Ethereum's permissionless mode of operation and the DApps' simplicity of understanding lead to scalability and privacy issues. Hyperledger Fabric solves performance scalability and privacy issues by permissioned mode of operation and specifically by using a PBFT algorithm and fine-grained access control. In addition to having the features of Hyperledger Fabric, Hyperledger Sawtooth relies on parallel transaction processing, which leads to a low latency time for the transaction commit (Dinh, Liu, Zhang, Chen, Ooi, & Wang, 2018).

When defining which platform to use in the industrial environment, the strict time requirements involved in real-time systems must be taken into account. In this context, Hyperledger Fabric and Sawtooth should be adopted for the following reasons: highly modular platform that separates the main system from the application level; supports permissionless and permissioned Infrastructure; allows parallel processing of transactions; compatibility of smart contracts with the public and private network of Ethereum; connectable consensus mechanisms; supports languages such as Rust and C++ for implementing smart contracts, which allows for shorter execution times; and tolerant of Byzantine faults.

Each factory has its private blockchain, where field devices enforce their contracts at a large industrial plant. In a supply chain, one factory can influence the processes of another factory. Thus, smart contracts can define process actions according to external demands. However, smart contracts cannot connect to external data feeds. To address this problem, the Decentralized Oracle Network (DON), a much-needed layer of the trustless future the crypto space, is building. DON, a chain link, connect smart contracts to any external piece of data in a trusted way (Pedro, Levi, & Cuende, 2017). This retrieval of data from the real world is done following the rules of a protocol that incentivizes all nodes, to tell the truth, and punishes them for lying.

CONVERGENCE OF BLOCKCHAIN-BASED IIOT AND IPAS

Blockchain technology is currently in its second stage. As shown in Figure 1, blockchain 1.0 was primarily adopted by Bitcoin to solve issues related to cryptocurrencies and decentralized payments. Blockchain 2.0 has focused on market-wide decentralization and is used to transform assets through smart contracts, creating value through the emergence of alternatives to Bitcoin. By 2020, blockchain 3.0 is expected to enable real-time transactions, scalability, and unlimited decentralized storage for critical industrial application environments.

Figure 2. Blockchain-based smart contracts operation overview

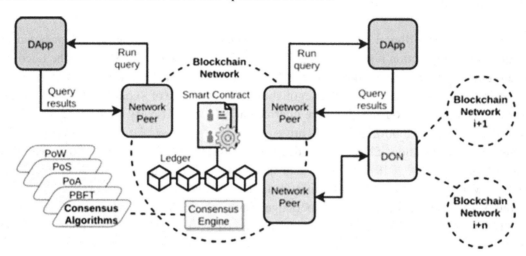

Figure 3. Development of blockchain

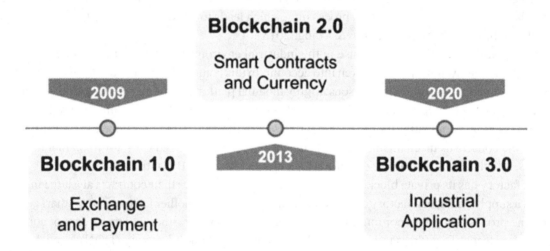

Industry 4.0 technologies can benefit from the use of smart contracts, but their application also presents challenges in several ways. Deploying a blockchain today can help cloud-based solutions provide redundancy for storage needs, while at the same time this local blockchain deployment is currently challenging replication on IIoT nodes due to memory and computing constraints. Also, there is a connectivity problem, as field devices (sensors and actuators) use specific networks and protocols like Modbus and ISA100 (Zhao, 2020), while the blockchain network requires an IP-based network.

Therefore, blockchain platforms must be strategically positioned from the IPAS supervisory level, as it is the last layer of IP-based communication, necessary for interaction with the blockchain network. In this way, the levels of corporate management, factory management and supervision now interact in a decentralized way through smart contracts. The blockchain network must act as middleware, in which smart contracts mediate communication between different levels of IPAS, providing an interface for all levels (Garrocho, Ferreira, Junior, Cavalcanti, & Oliveira, 2019).

Most factories currently belong to a supply chain and therefore require communication and negotiation with other factories. No manufacturer is an island, so a digitally connected supply chain is a cornerstone of any industry 4.0 discussion. Working safe and semi-automated with supply chain partners is just a concept, but with smart contracts, this scenario can finally be conceived (Alladi et al., 2019). In this context, analysis and discussion become critical to assess the role and impacts of blockchain-based smart contracts technology in the industrial environment.

Following the Kitchenham (2004) protocol, a survey was carried out covering the terms blockchain and industry. The results of this research were organized into three subsections: in the first subsection, the authors present blockchain-based applications according to the levels of the IPAS hierarchy; finally, in the second subsection, the authors present several works that propose the horizontal and vertical integration of the IPAS hierarchy.

Blockchain-Based Applications in IPAS

Despite the challenges, blockchain-based smart contracts have enormous potential to leverage industry 4.0 scenarios, considering the robustness that M2M communication will add to this new environment (Ferreira, Oliveira, Silva, & Cavalcanti, 2020). This scenario introduces a new era of efficiency, safety, intelligence, and a level playing field for industrial supply chains. In this context, it is possible to identify the following scenarios for the application of blockchain in industry environment:

- **Corporate Management:** is a level of long-term decision making through resource planning. This level can enhance the internal processes through:
  - **Voting system:** In corporate environments of a factory there are moments of choice, in which smart contracts can preserve voters' privacy and increase accessibility, providing transparent, safe and economical voting systems (Dagher, Marella, Milojkovic, & Mohler, 2018).
  - **Online audit:** Through an intelligent audit structure, smart contracts can solve problems of resource sharing difficulties, risks of exposure to privacy, illegal invocation of data and system consistency in the traditional audit mode (Yu, Yan, Yang, & Dong, 2019).
  - **Temporary work contracts:** Smart contracts can guarantee respect for the rights of all actors involved in temporary work in a factory. It guarantees employees fair and legal compensation for job performance and also protection of the employer for inappropriate employee attitudes (Pinna & Ibba, 2018).
  - **Insurance processes**: Different parts of the value chain need to initiate, maintain and close various types of policies in their businesses. In this environment, it is essential that there is a distributed platform based on smart contracts that can execute transactions in insurance processes between the parts of the value chain (Raikwar, Mazumdar, Ruj, Gupta, Chattopadhyay, & Lam, 2018).
- **Plant Management:** is a level of analysis and short-term decision making of processes. At this level, supply chain logistics is an essential process within the industry and requires interaction with other factories. This level can enhance the internal processes through:
  - **Manufacturing on demand**: In the manufacturing services market, users can, through smart contracts, create pre-established machine agreements where they perform standalone requests to other machines directly to take advantage of manufacturing services on an on-demand model (Nguyen & Ali, 2019).

- **Subscription services**: Consumers can purchase services that require the participation of more than one manufacturer or machine, this subscription governed by a smart contract allows ordering and manufacturing or service to order through transactions between machines (Oktian, Witanto, Kumi, & Lee, 2019).
- **Stakeholder quality and reputation**: Smart contracts can make machines automatically place orders and trade with other machines, based on reputations on available vendor public quality parameters such as delivery time and ratings provided by other customers (Cha, Chen, Su, & Yeh, 2018).

- **Supervision:** is a level that allows the operator to interact and monitor with field devices (sensors and actuators) through an interface provided by the devices (PLC and DCS) of process control level. This level can enhance the internal processes through:
  - **Autonomy**: Using blockchain, devices can interact with each other without the involvement of any intermediary. It can pave way to develop device-agnostic IIoT applications, like economic autonomous agents (Kapitonov, Lonshakov, Krupenkin, & Berman, 2017).
  - **Machine diagnostics and maintenance**: Intelligent machine diagnostics and self-service can enable monitoring autonomy, enabling preventative and diagnostic actions on issues such as refueling station orders and replacement requests from maintenance service providers (Stodt, Jastremskoj, Reich, Welte, & Sikora, 2019).
  - **Inventory control**: Smart contracts can be responsible for reporting details such as manufacturing date models and other machine identifying data. These details can be read by machines that have smart contracts that coordinate audit or inventory control transactions (Zhu & Kouhizadeh, 2019).

- **Process Control:** this level is made up of automation devices such as PLC and DCS that derive ideal process parameters from the different sensors. This level triggers the actuators as per the processed sensor signals. This level can enhance the internal processes through:
  - **Traceability**: Smart contracts can help track M2M interactions, making the process and asset traceability easier, enabling a complete record of the production process. This traceability would make it easier to identify defective products by analyzing the entire production chain from the history of M2M interactions. In a supply chain application, for example, it is even possible to know who owns the asset and when it is delivered (Shih & Yang, 2019).
  - **Immutable log**: All transactions and states logged in the blockchain are immutable. Blockchain is considered a ledger because it is analogous to the book where the accountant records the inputs and outputs of a company. In a ledger, the sheets and the books themselves are numbered and the releases made there unchanging. One of the goals of a ledger is to record, without the possibility of tampering, the movement of the company, i.e., the log of the input and output records. Blockchains are called ledgers for logging undelete transactions in a distributed manner and are of fundamental importance in logging M2M messages sent in an industrial environment (Hang & Kim, 2019).

- **Field Devices**: is a level lowest automation hierarchy level and is made up of field devices such as actuators and sensors. The field devices have a core task of transferring machines and processes data to the next level for monitoring and analysis. This level can enhance the internal processes through:

- ◦ **Authenticity**: It may be necessary to prove the authenticity of a particular device. Information such as manufacturer, specifications, date of manufacture, expiration date, maintenance dates can be stored in smart contracts on the blockchain, for stock or possession, reducing and even eliminating physical certificates. This ability to verify authenticity can further improve process security and reliability. In this new context, forgery and tampering can be mitigated during the production process and, consequently, in interactions between devices (Rehman, Javaid, Awais, Imran, & Naseer, 2019).
- ◦ **Identity**: The use of blockchain allows for better identification of each device. Moreover, it can also provide a trusted means for authentication and authorization of IIoT devices (Hasan, AlHadhrami, AlDhaheri, Salah, & Jayaraman, 2019).

Most blockchain and smart contract technologies today have throughput and latency constraints on their operation, which require some time to reach consensus and for transactions to be carried out effectively. The works of process control level do not take into account the stringent requirements imposed by industrial systems, such as real-time systems (Candell, Kashef, Liu, Lee, & Foufou, 2018). This scenario points to a significant problem for many applications in the IPAS hierarchy that need to react in real-time or near real-time to data and events collected from field devices. This scenario may justify the few works at lower levels of the IPAS hierarchy.

Blockchain-Based Integration in IPAS

One of the concepts of industry 4.0 is to have greater integration between processes and sectors in factories exchanging information in a faster and more efficient way for faster decision making in order to increase productivity, decrease losses, optimize resources and lead to digital transformation into the industries. Therefore, systems integration is one of the pillars of industry 4.0 and aims to connect the different areas of an industry, in order to extract data and information that will be used to make continuous improvements throughout the production process and related support areas (Xu, Xu, & Li, 2018).

Each process of the factory dynamics generates and is supplied with data. In an environment without integration, there is the job of capturing all the information generated by one stage of the manufacturing process and supplying the next, this is often done manually, inefficiently and analogically. The lack of integrated systems also means that management levels have a much greater job of analyzing whether what is being manufactured really matches the demand received and whether suppliers and distributors are aligned with this production (Pérez-Lara, Saucedo-Martínez, Marmolejo-Saucedo, Salais-Fierro, & Vasant, 2018).

As the processes are diverse and involve different agents in a factory, the concept of integration aligned to industry 4.0 was divided into horizontal and vertical integration. As shown in Figure 4, horizontal integration concerns the entire production chain: from suppliers to customers, while vertical integration integrates the functions to be developed within the factory. To achieve the best results, there must still be an interaction between vertical and horizontal integrations to unite processes and optimize production as a whole.

Figure 4. Horizontal and vertical integration of industry

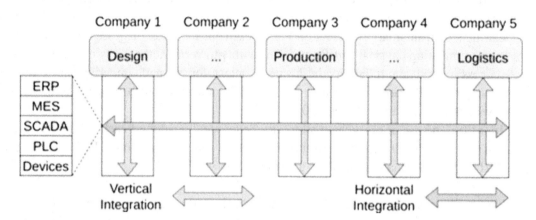

Horizontal Integration

For the factory, horizontal integration represents synchrony, loss reduction, consequently a saving of resources as the demand of suppliers is adjusted to the demand of customers, without waste during the process. Besides, the higher quality of the products represents a lower level of return and increases the consumer confidence index towards the factory, which generates customer loyalty. Also, with delivery control and distribution monitoring, it is possible to be sure that deadlines are met and also to generate data to predict more accurate deliveries.

Traditionally, horizontal integration occurs through manufacturing execution systems, product life cycle management and company resource planning. However, the aforementioned platforms cannot allow connection with other partners or customers in the industry (thus requiring additional integrations, which are generally very expensive and use ad-hoc protocols). Besides, there is a complex relationship between the strategic and operational goals of the different levels of manufacturing systems that inhibit the realization of an intelligent manufacturing system.

A factory needs to deploy networks to connect smart production systems horizontally. Market analysis, supplier management, even production, logistics and distribution, horizontal integration helps sectors to work with more harmony and synchronization, optimizing resources while also integrating market analysis into the manufacturing process (Pérez-Lara et al., 2018). Therefore, industry 4.0 requires higher levels of integration, essential to automate data exchange in factories, communication with suppliers and customers and, finally, their field devices.

When automation is inserted in the connectivity of the horizontal integration, the information can be collected and sent automatically from the various systems implanted in a factory to any of the relevant parts of the value chain. This automation reduces the time for decision making and also reduces the number of intermediate elements (such as employees) and bureaucracy (documents and physical contracts). In this context, blockchain-based smart contracts can help with horizontal integration, providing common and reliable data or money exchange points through which various smart entities in the factory can interact (Di Vaio & Varriale, 2020).

Blockchain is ideal for enhancing supply chain manufacturing processes thanks to decentralized transactions and its data management capabilities. The information exchanged in the supply chain requires a record of transactions and an indication of ownership in order to provide transparency of the processes, to be inviolable, so that they can be trusted by all parties involved. Currently it is possible to find several blockchain works aimed at horizontal integration in the supply chain, such as: collaborative development of electronic power devices (Yan, Duan, Zhong, & Qu, 2017), enhance composite materials industry (Mondragon, Mondragon, & Coronado, 2018), services as enterprise smart contracts (Bagozi, Bianchini, De Antonellis, Garda, & Melchiori, 2019),

Despite the various advantages presented by horizontal integration through blockchain and smart contracts, its adoption is a challenge mainly for traditional industries due to their difficulty in accepting changes and also the high costs of this horizontal integration from blockchain (Ko, Lee, & Ryu, 2018). The final cost of deploying a blockchain includes not only the costs related to software integration, but also the cost of the time required to understand the underlying business processes and define accurate and flexible smart contracts.

Vertical Integration

The vertical integration provides for the connection of the specific systems used at each of the IPAS levels, connecting the data, making the influence flow between all hierarchical levels more quickly and efficiently, reducing the time for decision making and improving the management process industrial. Therefore, vertical integration is in place when inside the factory the employees, computers, manufacturing machines are linked with each other, communicate automatically with each other, and their interaction exists not only in the real world but also in virtual reality, in the model of the entire system.

Vertical integration makes the traditional IPAS pyramid view disappear. The same goes for several systems and applications across these various levels. Other systems such as ERP, MES, and SCADA will dramatically change while still others will be replaced by rapidly emerging applications in the scope of Industrial IoT platforms (Frank, Dalenogare, & Ayala, 2019). In this context of automation and systems integration, the vertically integrated company in Industry 4.0 gains a crucial competitive advantage by being able to respond appropriately and quickly to changes in market signals and new opportunities.

Industry 4.0 aims for a highly flexible and digitized industrial production model that is smarter and more reliable than today's possibilities. This requires vertical integration of different operations in one manufacturing to promote a reconfigurable intelligent factory. Using raw data as an asset from which value can be created to support business and manufacturing decisions has motivated many scientists to explore the challenges of how to exploit that value. In this context, works like (Pal, Vain, Srinivasan, & Ramaswamy, 2017) introduce optimization models to schedule maintenance operations using formal methods. However, this approach does not indicate how raw data can be collected and transmitted to the top of the PAS hierarchy.

To integrate IoT into the manufacturing process, some work (Alexakos & Kalogeras, 2017; Alexakos, Anagnostopoulos, Fournaris, Koulamas, & Kalogeras, 2018; Shirazi, 2019) presents approaches that combine field device networking and high-level multi-agent systems that contribute to vertical integration. However, the evaluation of such proposals was by simulation only, and it is not considered the impact of IP-based networks that can occur on real-time system deadlines. Other works (Garcia, Irisarri, Perez, Estevez, & Marcos, 2016; Calderón Godoy & González Pérez, 2018; Llamuca, Garcia, Naranjo, Rosero, Alvarez-M, & Garcia, 2019; Liu, Vengayil, Lu, & Xu, 2019), based on the Open Platform Communications Unified Architecture (OPC-UA) protocol, presents vertical integration architectures whose temporal requirements of real-time systems can be met. However, the need for expensive equipment (unrealistic for small and medium industries) and a server to intermediate communication between the components of these architectures makes such architectures vulnerable in the event of a centralized server failure.

Aiming at making communication and decision making decentralized, a lot of works is applying blockchain technologies in the industry. Blockchain-based smart contracts are being applied across supply chains to improve decision making in control and management processes (Kapitonov, Berman, Lonshakov, & Krupenkin, 2018; Petroni, de Moraes, & Gonçalves, 2018), trusted data generation and privacy (Liang, Shetty, Tosh, Zhao, Li, & Liu, 2018), reliable communication, and between end-user and service provider (Schulz & Freund, 2018; Vatankhah Barenji, Wang, Huang, & Guerra-Zubiaga, 2019). However, such approaches aim at horizontal communication between companies and/or customers. Aiming for vertical integration of the PAS hierarchy, the works (Leang, Kim, & Yoo, 2018; Maw, Adepu, & Mathur, 2019) feature blockchain-based architectures for cyber-physical systems.

The approaches proposed by the works (Leang et al., 2018; Maw et al., 2019) are intended only to monitor data from field devices controlled by the PLC and to record this information on the blockchain to generate an unchanging history. The works (Smirnov & Teslya, 2018; Gallo, Nguyen, Barone, & Van Hien, 2018; Isaja & Soldatos, 2018; Lee, Azamfar, & Singh, 2019; Petroni, Reis, & Gonçalves, 2019) have similar approaches in which the objective is to use blockchain-related technologies to control processes involving devices and businesses. However, the process control of these architectures is implemented through smart contracts, where the execution time is variable (either by network latency or by committing transactions on the blockchain network), making processes unsafe and prone to failures to meet deadlines in real-time systems.

ISSUES AND CHALLENGES IN BLOCKCHAIN-BASED IPAS INTEGRATION

In the previous sections, the authors presented the main aspects of IPAS, blockchain, and smart contracts. The authors presented industrial applications based on the blockchain according to the level of the IPAS hierarchy. Also, the authors introduced the fundamental concepts of blockchain-based smart contracts, conjecturing about their use in replacing a classic approach to the IPAS hierarchy. In this section, the authors discussed the critical issues and challenges in applying and integrating blockchain-based smart contracts platforms in the IPAS hierarchy. Table 1 summary the issues and challenges in blockchain-based IPAS integration.

In the previous section, the authors showed that the integration of IPAS based on blockchain and smart contracts needs investments for a new reality of the hardware and software equipment infrastructure. In this new context, the general agreement in the blockchain-based IIoT ecosystem requires that all stakeholders (both at horizontal and vertical levels) commit to investing and using this new equipment. Therefore, finding low-cost blockchain solutions is a big challenge, as mentioned earlier, small and medium-sized companies/factories are quite resistant to change. In addition, companies should not invest and support these changes because they lack standards for such technologies in the industrial sphere and equipment that demonstrates high durability.

In addition to the problem of investment in infrastructure, there is another problem of investment in staff qualification. Automation engineers and technicians are familiar with the use of ladder logic and do not understand the scripting language, so they feel comfortable working with today's easy-to-use, reliable, proven functional and necessary industrial process control systems. Therefore, while new technologies allow for higher levels of scalability, traceability, integration, manufacturing capacity and autonomous collaboration with other systems, the lack of skills and understanding to explore IIoT and blockchain will bring challenges. In this context, new professions (with skills of industrial process control, blockchain, smart contracts, and contracts and rights) must emerge in order to fill and integrate this gap in the industrial environment.

Although small and medium industries avoid changing their plant of industrial equipment that works perfectly, there will be a natural change in this context soon. This is because IIoT focuses on the development of information throughout the supply chain, optimizing resources and benefiting the productive processes, where equipment, machinery, and suppliers are connected in a network. IIoT allows managers to perceive the loss of productivity and operational processes in advance, making production decisions, contingencies, safety and costs in real time, through an artificial model complemented by IoT, which is why it was introduced in Industry 4.0 (Oztemel & Gursev, 2020).

According to Maqbool Khan et al. (2017), industrial automation is becoming complex gradually, and the data generated in manufacturing alters to big data. Robots, sensors, actuators, switches, industrial devices, and M2M communication are the ore of big data in Industry 4.0. Heavy usage of IIoT brought an immense commute in the era of industries. Industry 4.0 is a blend of modern smart technology and systems which creates a deluge of data, which is quite challenging to handle with classical tools and algorithms. Therefore, in addition to the problems of investment in infrastructure and qualification of the professional team, there is a significant challenge in the transfer and storage of large amounts of IIoT data between the various systems of the IPAS hierarchy.

Recently, big data analysis tools have been proposed for Industry 4.0, which aim to facilitate the cleaning, formatting, and transformation of industrial data generated by systems by different levels of IPAS hierarchy (Rehman, Yaqoob, Salah, Imran, Jayaraman, & Perera, 2019). However, localization and data processing becomes a significant challenge, as the centralized communication architectures used have high network traffic and high latency, due to the large volume of IIoT data. For decentralized communication architectures, the impact on network traffic and latency is greater due to the consensus among nodes of a blockchain network.

Industry 4.0 technologies can benefit from the use of blockchain, but their application also presents challenges in many ways. Deployment a blockchain today can help cloud-based solutions provide redundancy for storage needs, while at the same time this local blockchain deployment is currently challenging to replicate on IIoT nodes due to its memory constraints and computational. In this context, several blockchain approaches to IIoT define the blockchain network above the IIoT device layer (Seok, Park, & Park, 2019; Wan, Li, Imran, & Li, 2019). However, it is essential to assess the impact of this new blockchain layer on the transfer, storage, and control of IIoT data to the other layers above the blockchain network.

In the vast majority of recent approaches to cyber physical systems, the blockchain network is deployed from the level of process control devices in the IPAS hierarchy, allowing integration between synchronous and asynchronous systems. However, in this new context, synchronous IIoT applications acquire new features (data encryption, transaction creation, generation and storage of public and private keys) that can negatively influence the energy consumption of IIoT field devices that are deployed for long periods of time (Barki, Bouabdallah, Gharout, & Traore, 2016). Thus, new encryption schemes and techniques or new lightweight, efficient and robust encryption algorithms must be designed with the aim of reducing energy consumption in IIoT devices.

Another significant challenge in adopting connected IPAS multilayer systems is the integration of asynchronous systems (DER, MER, and SCADA) with process control (PLC and DCS) and real-time oriented synchronous field devices (IIoT devices such as manufacturing machines). In many situations, these IIoT devices have very severe time constraints. For this matter, communication is an essential aspect in which the main challenge is to establish a framework or middleware that allows integration with asynchronous decisions from the top levels of the IPAS hierarchy with synchronous communication on the bottom levels of the IPAS hierarchy. Such blockchain-based solutions that guarantee execution, control, monitoring and decision-making without influencing the real-time systems deadlines, can provide a breakthrough in industry 4.0.

Some recent work, through the results of experimental evaluations, points out that there are problems related to the high and variable blocking time when changing a state in the blockchain network, from the request (made by a requesting client device) to a blockchain node to the commit of the transaction which is the confirmation among all blockchain nodes that the state has been inserted or changed in the ledger (Pongnumkul, Siripanpornchana, & Thajchayapong, 2017; Vatcharatiansakul & Tuwanut, 2019). These results show that the problem is due to the standard operation of the blockchain and its consensus algorithms. Thus, designing fast and reliable consensus algorithms is the key to enabling critical, real-time process controls for IIoT devices. However, seeking the low latency and reliability of a consensus algorithm at the same time is a challenging task. The problem is further compounded by slower and less reliable wireless connectivity compared to wired connections assumed in traditional consensus algorithms (Tramarin, Mok, & Han, 2019).

Table 1. Summary of issues and challenges in blockchain-based IPAS integration

	Issue	Challenge
Ability	Automation technicians and engineers are not professionally qualified or even encouraged to work with blockchain and smart contracts.	Find ways to encourage automation teams to build on the new skills required by blockchain incorporation, or identify new professions based on blockchain, automation and rights.
Investment	The current infrastructure required for the implementation of the blockchain network requires large investments in which not every company or factory is willing to participate and invest.	Find alternatives to reduce investment costs in infrastructure with new platforms and blockchain equipment in a way that guarantees the inclusion of small and medium industries.
Storage	It is necessary to store all IIoT data for application of mining and other techniques, however, storage on the blockchain network can overload the network and devices.	Find IIoT data storage alternatives in a way that does not compromise the blockchain network and guarantees data authenticity and security.
Energy	Encryption algorithms negatively influence the energy consumption of IIoT devices that are deployed for long periods of time.	Find alternatives to encryption schemes or create new lighter, more efficient and more robust encryption algorithms that meet the requirements of IIoT devices.
Time	The time required to complete the insertion of a transaction in the blocks of a blockchain network is high for real-time systems that require 10 to 100 ms times.	Find alternatives to reduce transaction processing time on the blockchain network to incorporate all industrial processes like real-time systems.
Deadline	There is a great jitter in the total time for the transaction process between all nodes of the blockchain network, in which it can compromise the deadlines of the industrial processes.	Find alternatives to reduce the jitter of transaction processing time on the blockchain network to ensure the deadlines of industrial processes.
Scalability	The including transactions in blocks in the blockchain network is serial, not allowing parallel requests by industrial applications.	Find alternatives to increase the number of transaction requests to the blockchain network carried out by the industrial processes.
Mobility	The mobility of IIoT devices reduces opportunities for communication with the blockchain network, negatively influencing synchronous industrial processes.	Find alternatives to ensure the communication of IIoT devices with the blockchain network, even with failures in the communication generated by the mobility of these devices.

Communication latency and jitter are very sensitive in the lower layers of the IPAS pyramid. Such delays can mainly influence the monitoring and control of industrial processes. Monitoring, carried out at the supervisory level by shop floor operators, is less sensitive, however, deadlines from data collection to visualization by HMI cannot be changed, with risks of compromising the entire product process. At the process control level, the control performed by PLC is highly sensitive, with low latency and strict deadlines, here a single deadline break can compromise the entire production process chain. Therefore, current blockchain platforms and smart contracts are not suitable for this environment, requiring the design and development of new technologies that do not compromise the strict requirements of the industrial systems of the lower levels of the IPAS pyramid.

In order not to affect the time and strict deadlines of industrial process control systems, some approaches store IIoT data outside the blockchain network and reduce latency with new paradigms. Recent works in the literature apply concepts of fog and edge computing in M2M communication approaches, in which gateways based on the MQTT protocol are used close to field devices as a communication bridge for IIoT data collection and IIoT data hashing only for storage on the blockchain network (Fernández-Caramés & Fraga-Lamas, 2019). However, gateways can increase the delay in delivering sensor and actuator data to higher levels of IPAS, compromising decision making.

In addition to the problems of high and variable block time, other results of experimental evaluations have shown that some blockchain platforms such as Ethereum do not allow parallel operations to be performed (Schäffer, di Angelo, & Salzer, 2019). However, serial execution seems to be necessary: smart contract sharing state and smart contract programming languages have serial semantics in the current operation of the Ethereum system and its four testnets. Although several works in the literature present new ways to enable miners and validators to execute smart contracts in parallel, this is still an open problem in this area of research (Saraph & Herlihy, 2019).

Introducing parallelism into blockchain is a challenging task. There is currently an effort in which the classic blockchain architecture is extended to a more sophisticated architecture based on Directed Acyclic Graphs (DAG) (Bai, 2018) and other programming languages used to write smart contracts with mechanisms of concurrency control as presented in modern languages. These approaches lead to parallel transaction validation, which reduces block time by allowing M2M communication closer to real-time requirements. However, DAG increases the complexity of the implementation, and there is no DAG-based solution yet that supports the execution of smart contracts.

Most existing IIoT security systems operate as a set of individual tools and are neither automated nor integrated. Currently, there is a growing consensus about the potential of linking blockchain to IIoT devices (Dai, Zheng, & Zhang, 2019). However, some important questions remain open: Where should blockchain nodes be hosted and located? Hosting blockchain directly on resource-constrained IIoT devices is inadvisable in the literature for the following reasons: lack of computational resources for encryption and basic tasks such as mining; lack of sufficient bandwidth for ledger replication and maintenance; energy saving required.

Another important issue is the mobility of the field devices. With IIoT devices in constant motion, communication with the blockchain network will face high dynamism and, consequently, large amounts of connectivity failures (Lucas-Estañ, Sepulcre, Raptis, Passarella, & Conti, 2018). This scenario will contribute to the reduction of communication opportunities with the blockchain network, increasing the communication delay in the interaction of IIoT devices and blockchain network. Also, if the process control is in the blockchain network layer or higher layers, production may be compromised.

Finally, newer generations of IIoT devices are expected to be equipped with better hardware specifications, which will allow direct communication with smart contracts, reducing communication latency. In this context, the blockchain-based smart contract is expected to operate within an environment in which it must adapt its capabilities to the context of the IIoT devices. This scenario will contribute to the viability of the Pervasive Computing paradigm (Weiser, 1991), where devices run applications and integrate seamlessly with field devices.

CONCLUSION

In a complex industrial ecosystem, several entities are integrated to create, collect, process, transmit and store IIoT data. Industries are resistant to changes in their processes, however, due to rapid advances in technology and innovations in business models, blockchain is expected to be widely applied to the shop floor. In this article, we approach blockchain and IIoT integration from an industrial perspective. A survey of blockchain-based IIoT applications from an industrial process automation and control perspective were presented and discussed. The main applications and challenges are addressed. We also analyzed the research challenges and future trends associated with blockchain-enabled IIoT.

The current use and adoption of blockchain-based smart contracts in Industry 4.0 is in its early stages, as this is an area that has a lot to explore. The cataloged solutions show that most of the related approaches are designed for specific processes designed to automate horizontal IPAS communication. The challenges in horizontal integration are mainly related to the difficulty of changes in processes that work perfectly and a high investment in infrastructure necessary for the new blockchain-based approaches.

On the other hand, vertical blockchain-based integration of IPAS is still in its early stages, in which current approaches do not take advantage of the current manufacturing, supervision and control systems widely used in the industry. Besides, current approaches do not take into account the strict time and deadline requirements related to industrial processes, making the introduction of these approaches on the shop floor unfeasible. In this context, the authors presented several research opportunities and challenges related to blockchain and industrial integration systems.

Finally, it is important to list that there are still many experimental studies to evaluate the behavior of the blockchain network in an industrial environment. Also, such assessments allowed for a deeper analysis of the real application of blockchain in industrial systems, mainly for process control systems that are quite time sensitive. In this context, new consensus algorithms and blockchain platforms are needed to meet the requirements of the industrial environment.

ACKNOWLEDGMENT

We acknowledge the support of the Brazilian research agencies National Council for Scientific and Technological Development (CNPq) and Coordination for the Improvement of Higher Education Personnel (Capes), the Minas Gerais State Research Foundation (FAPEMIG), the Federal Institute of Minas Gerais (IFMG), and the Federal University of Ouro Preto (UFOP).

REFERENCES

Alexakos, C., Anagnostopoulos, C., Fournaris, A., Koulamas, C., & Kalogeras, A. (2018, May). IoT integration for adaptive manufacturing. In *2018 IEEE 21st International Symposium on Real-Time Distributed Computing (ISORC)* (pp. 146-151). IEEE. 10.1109/ISORC.2018.00030

Alexakos, C., & Kalogeras, A. (2017, May). Exposing MES functionalities as enabler for cloud manufacturing. In *2017 IEEE 13th International Workshop on Factory Communication Systems (WFCS)* (pp. 1-4). IEEE. 10.1109/WFCS.2017.7991966

Alladi, T., Chamola, V., Parizi, R. M., & Choo, K. K. R. (2019). Blockchain Applications for Industry 4.0 and Industrial IoT: A Review. *IEEE Access: Practical Innovations, Open Solutions, 7*, 176935–176951. doi:10.1109/ACCESS.2019.2956748

Bagozi, A., Bianchini, D., De Antonellis, V., Garda, M., & Melchiori, M. (2019, July). Services as enterprise smart contracts in the digital factory. In *2019 IEEE International Conference on Web Services (ICWS)* (pp. 224-228). IEEE. 10.1109/ICWS.2019.00046

Bai, C. (2018, November). State-of-the-art and future trends of blockchain based on DAG structure. In *International Workshop on Structured Object-Oriented Formal Language and Method* (pp. 183-196). Springer.

Banerjee, M., Lee, J., & Choo, K. K. R. (2018). A blockchain future for internet of things security: A position paper. *Digital Communications and Networks, 4*(3), 149–160. doi:10.1016/j.dcan.2017.10.006

Barki, A., Bouabdallah, A., Gharout, S., & Traore, J. (2016). M2M security: Challenges and solutions. *IEEE Communications Surveys and Tutorials, 18*(2), 1241–1254. doi:10.1109/COMST.2016.2515516

Bartodziej, C. J. (2017). The concept industry 4.0. In *The concept industry 4.0* (pp. 27–50). Springer Gabler. doi:10.1007/978-3-658-16502-4_3

Calderón Godoy, A. J., & González Pérez, I. (2018). Integration of sensor and actuator networks and the SCADAsystem to promote the migration of the legacy flexible manufacturing system towards the industry 4.0 concept. *Journal of Sensor and Actuator Networks, 7*(2), 23. doi:10.3390/jsan7020023

Candell, R., Kashef, M., Liu, Y., Lee, K. B., & Foufou, S. (2018). Industrial wireless systems guidelines: Practical considerations and deployment life cycle. *IEEE Industrial Electronics Magazine, 12*(4), 6–17. doi:10.1109/MIE.2018.2873820

Cha, S. C., Chen, J. F., Su, C., & Yeh, K. H. (2018). A blockchain connected gateway for BLE-based devices in the internet of things. *IEEE Access: Practical Innovations, Open Solutions, 6*, 24639–24649. doi:10.1109/ACCESS.2018.2799942

Colombo, A. W., Karnouskos, S., Kaynak, O., Shi, Y., & Yin, S. (2017). Industrial cyberphysical systems: A backbone of the fourth industrial revolution. *IEEE Industrial Electronics Magazine, 11*(1), 6–16. doi:10.1109/MIE.2017.2648857

Dagher, G. G., Marella, P. B., Milojkovic, M., & Mohler, J. (2018). *BroncoVote: secure voting system using Ethereum's blockchain*. Academic Press.

Dai, H. N., Zheng, Z., & Zhang, Y. (2019). Blockchain for internet of things: A survey. *IEEE Internet of Things Journal*, *6*(5), 8076–8094. doi:10.1109/JIOT.2019.2920987

Di Vaio, A., & Varriale, L. (2020). Blockchain technology in supply chain management for sustainable performance: Evidence from the airport industry. *International Journal of Information Management*, *52*, 102014. doi:10.1016/j.ijinfomgt.2019.09.010

Dinh, T. T. A., Liu, R., Zhang, M., Chen, G., Ooi, B. C., & Wang, J. (2018). Untangling blockchain: A data processing view of blockchain systems. *IEEE Transactions on Knowledge and Data Engineering*, *30*(7), 1366–1385. doi:10.1109/TKDE.2017.2781227

Felser, M. (2005). Real-time ethernet-industry prospective. *Proceedings of the IEEE*, *93*(6), 1118–1129. doi:10.1109/JPROC.2005.849720

Fernández-Caramés, T. M., & Fraga-Lamas, P. (2019). A review on the application of blockchain to the next generation of cybersecure industry 4.0 smart factories. *IEEE Access: Practical Innovations, Open Solutions*, *7*, 45201–45218. doi:10.1109/ACCESS.2019.2908780

Ferreira, C. M. S., Oliveira, R. A. R., Silva, J. S., & da Cunha Cavalcanti, C. F. M. (2020). Blockchain for Machine to Machine Interaction in Industry 4.0. In *Blockchain Technology for Industry 4.0* (pp. 99–116). Springer. doi:10.1007/978-981-15-1137-0_5

Frank, A. G., Dalenogare, L. S., & Ayala, N. F. (2019). Industry 4.0 technologies: Implementation patterns in manufacturing companies. *International Journal of Production Economics*, *210*, 15–26. doi:10.1016/j.ijpe.2019.01.004

Gallo, P., Nguyen, U. Q., Barone, G., & Van Hien, P. (2018, September). DeCyMo: Decentralized Cyber-Physical System for Monitoring and Controlling Industries and Homes. In *2018 IEEE 4th International Forum on Research and Technology for Society and Industry (RTSI)* (pp. 1-4). IEEE.

Garcia, M. V., Irisarri, E., Perez, F., Estevez, E., & Marcos, M. (2016). OPC-UA communications integration using a CPPS architecture. In IEEE Ecuador technical chapters meeting (pp. 1-6). doi:10.1109/ETCM.2016.7750838

Garrocho, C., Ferreira, C. M. S., Junior, A., Cavalcanti, C. F., & Oliveira, R. R. (2019, November). Industry 4.0: Smart Contract-based Industrial Internet of Things Process Management. In Anais do IX Simpósio Brasileiro de Engenharia de Sistemas Computacionais (pp. 137-142). SBC.

Grand View Research. (2019, June). *Industrial internet of things (iiot) market size, share trends analysis report by component, by end use (manufacturing, energy power, oil gas, healthcare, logistics transport, agriculture), and segment forecasts, 2019 - 2025*. Retrieved from https://www.grandviewresearch.com/industry-analysis/industrial-internet-of-things-iiot-market

Hang, L., & Kim, D. H. (2019). Design and implementation of an integrated IoT blockchain platform for sensing data integrity. *Sensors (Basel)*, *19*(10), 2228. doi:10.339019102228 PMID:31091799

Hasan, H., AlHadhrami, E., AlDhaheri, A., Salah, K., & Jayaraman, R. (2019). Smart contract-based approach for efficient shipment management. *Computers & Industrial Engineering*, *136*, 149–159. doi:10.1016/j.cie.2019.07.022

Hill, G., Al-Aqrabi, H., Lane, P., & Aagela, H. (2019, January). Securing Manufacturing Business Intelligence for the Industrial Internet of Things. In *Fourth International Congress on Information and Communication Technology* (p. 174). Springer Singapore.

Isaja, M., & Soldatos, J. (2018, May). Distributed ledger technology for decentralization of manufacturing processes. In *2018 IEEE Industrial Cyber-Physical Systems (ICPS)* (pp. 696-701). IEEE.

Jeschke, S., Brecher, C., Meisen, T., Özdemir, D., & Eschert, T. (2017). Industrial internet of things and cyber manufacturing systems. In *Industrial internet of things* (pp. 3–19). Springer. doi:10.1007/978-3-319-42559-7_1

Kapitonov, A., Berman, I., Lonshakov, S., & Krupenkin, A. (2018, June). Blockchain based protocol for economical communication in industry 4.0. In *2018 Crypto valley conference on blockchain technology (CVCBT)* (pp. 41-44). IEEE.

Kapitonov, A., Lonshakov, S., Krupenkin, A., & Berman, I. (2017, October). Blockchain-based protocol of autonomous business activity for multi-agent systems consisting of UAVs. In *2017 Workshop on Research, Education and Development of Unmanned Aerial Systems (RED-UAS)* (pp. 84-89). IEEE. 10.1109/RED-UAS.2017.8101648

Khan, M., Wu, X., Xu, X., & Dou, W. (2017, May). Big data challenges and opportunities in the hype of Industry 4.0. In *2017 IEEE International Conference on Communications (ICC)* (pp. 1-6). IEEE. 10.1109/ICC.2017.7996801

Kitchenham, B. (2004). Procedures for performing systematic reviews. Keele University.

Ko, T., Lee, J., & Ryu, D. (2018). Blockchain technology and manufacturing industry: Real-time transparency and cost savings. *Sustainability*, *10*(11), 4274. doi:10.3390u10114274

Kshetri, N. (2017). Can blockchain strengthen the internet of things? *IT Professional*, *19*(4), 68–72. doi:10.1109/MITP.2017.3051335

Leang, B., Kim, R. W., & Yoo, K. H. (2018, July). Real-Time Transmission of Secured PLCs Sensing Data. In *IEEE International Conference on Internet of Things and IEEE Green Computing and Communications and IEEE Cyber, Physical and Social Computing and IEEE Smart Data* (pp. 931-932). 10.1109/Cybermatics_2018.2018.00177

Lee, E. A. (2005). Absolutely positively on time: What would it take? *Computer*, *38*(7), 85–87. doi:10.1109/MC.2005.211

Lee, J., Azamfar, M., & Singh, J. (2019). A blockchain enabled Cyber-Physical System architecture for Industry 4.0 manufacturing systems. *Manufacturing Letters*, *20*, 34–39. doi:10.1016/j.mfglet.2019.05.003

Liang, X., Shetty, S., Tosh, D. K., Zhao, J., Li, D., & Liu, J. (2018). A Reliable Data Provenance and Privacy Preservation Architecture for Business-Driven Cyber-Physical Systems Using Blockchain. *International Journal of Information Security and Privacy*, *12*(4), 68–81. doi:10.4018/IJISP.2018100105

Lin, I. C., & Liao, T. C. (2017). A survey of blockchain security issues and challenges. *International Journal of Network Security*, *19*(5), 653–659.

Liu, C., Vengayil, H., Lu, Y., & Xu, X. (2019). A cyber-physical machine tools platform using OPC UA and MTConnect. *Journal of Manufacturing Systems*, *51*, 61–74. doi:10.1016/j.jmsy.2019.04.006

Llamuca, J. D., Garcia, C. A., Naranjo, J. E., Rosero, C., Alvarez-M, E., & Garcia, M. V. (2019, November). Integrating ISA-95 and IEC-61499 for Distributed Control System Monitoring. In *Conference on Information Technologies and Communication of Ecuador* (pp. 66-80). Springer.

Lucas-Estañ, M. C., Sepulcre, M., Raptis, T. P., Passarella, A., & Conti, M. (2018). Emerging trends in hybrid wireless communication and data management for the industry 4.0. *Electronics (Basel)*, *7*(12), 400. doi:10.3390/electronics7120400

Maw, A., Adepu, S., & Mathur, A. (2019). ICS-BlockOpS: Blockchain for operational data security in industrial control system. *Pervasive and Mobile Computing*, *59*, 101048. doi:10.1016/j.pmcj.2019.101048

Mehta, B. R., & Reddy, Y. J. (2014). *Industrial process automation systems: design and implementation*. Butterworth-Heinemann.

Mondragon, A. E. C., Mondragon, C. E. C., & Coronado, E. S. (2018, April). Exploring the applicability of blockchain technology to enhance manufacturing supply chains in the composite materials industry. In *2018 IEEE International conference on applied system invention (ICASI)* (pp. 1300-1303). IEEE. 10.1109/ICASI.2018.8394531

Nawari, N. O., & Ravindran, S. (2019). Blockchain and the built environment: Potentials and limitations. *Journal of Building Engineering*, *25*, 100832. doi:10.1016/j.jobe.2019.100832

Nguyen, D. D., & Ali, M. I. (2019, June). Enabling On-Demand Decentralized IoT Collectability Marketplace using Blockchain and Crowdsensing. In *2019 Global IoT Summit (GIoTS)* (pp. 1-6). IEEE.

Nilsson, J., Bernhardsson, B., & Wittenmark, B. (1998). Stochastic analysis and control of real-time systems with random time delays. *Automatica*, *34*(1), 57–64. doi:10.1016/S0005-1098(97)00170-2

O'donovan, P., Gallagher, C., Bruton, K., & O'Sullivan, D. T. (2018). A fog computing industrial cyber-physical system for embedded low-latency machine learning Industry 4.0 applications. *Manufacturing Letters*, *15*, 139–142. doi:10.1016/j.mfglet.2018.01.005

Oktian, Y. E., Witanto, E. N., Kumi, S., & Lee, S. G. (2019, February). BlockSubPay-A Blockchain Framework for Subscription-Based Payment in Cloud Service. In *2019 21st International Conference on Advanced Communication Technology (ICACT)* (pp. 153-158). IEEE. 10.23919/ICACT.2019.8702008

Oztemel, E., & Gursev, S. (2020). Literature review of Industry 4.0 and related technologies. *Journal of Intelligent Manufacturing*, *31*(1), 127–182. doi:10.100710845-018-1433-8

Pal, D., Vain, J., Srinivasan, S., & Ramaswamy, S. (2017, September). Model-based maintenance scheduling in flexible modular automation systems. In *2017 22nd IEEE International Conference on Emerging Technologies and Factory Automation (ETFA)* (pp. 1-6). IEEE. 10.1109/ETFA.2017.8247738

Pedro, A. S., Levi, D., & Cuende, L. I. (2017). *Witnet: A decentralized oracle network protocol*. arXiv preprint arXiv:1711.09756.

Pérez-Lara, M., Saucedo-Martínez, J. A., Marmolejo-Saucedo, J. A., Salais-Fierro, T. E., & Vasant, P. (2018). Vertical and horizontal integration systems in Industry 4.0. *Wireless Networks*, 1–9.

Petroni, B. C. A., de Moraes, E. M., & Gonçalves, R. F. (2018, August). Big Data Analytics for Logistics and Distributions Using Blockchain. In *IFIP International Conference on Advances in Production Management Systems* (pp. 363-369). Springer. 10.1007/978-3-319-99707-0_45

Petroni, B. C. A., Reis, J. Z., & Gonçalves, R. F. (2019, September). Blockchain as an Internet of Services Application for an Advanced Manufacturing Environment. In *IFIP International Conference on Advances in Production Management Systems* (pp. 389-396). Springer. 10.1007/978-3-030-29996-5_45

Pinna, A., & Ibba, S. (2018, July). A blockchain-based Decentralized System for proper handling of temporary Employment contracts. In *Science and information conference* (pp. 1231–1243). Springer.

Pinto, S., Gomes, T., Pereira, J., Cabral, J., & Tavares, A. (2017). IIoTEED: An enhanced, trusted execution environment for industrial IoT edge devices. *IEEE Internet Computing*, *21*(1), 40–47. doi:10.1109/MIC.2017.17

Pongnumkul, S., Siripanpornchana, C., & Thajchayapong, S. (2017, July). Performance analysis of private blockchain platforms in varying workloads. In *2017 26th International Conference on Computer Communication and Networks (ICCCN)* (pp. 1-6). IEEE. 10.1109/ICCCN.2017.8038517

Raikwar, M., Mazumdar, S., Ruj, S., Gupta, S. S., Chattopadhyay, A., & Lam, K. Y. (2018, February). A blockchain framework for insurance processes. In *2018 9th IFIP International Conference on New Technologies, Mobility and Security (NTMS)* (pp. 1-4). IEEE. 10.1109/NTMS.2018.8328731

Rehman, M., Javaid, N., Awais, M., Imran, M., & Naseer, N. (2019, December). Cloud based secure service providing for IoTs using blockchain. *IEEE Global Communications Conference (GLOBCOM)*. 10.1109/GLOBECOM38437.2019.9013413

Rehman, M. H. U., Yaqoob, I., Salah, K., Imran, M., Jayaraman, P. P., & Perera, C. (2019). The role of big data analytics in industrial Internet of Things. *Future Generation Computer Systems*, *99*, 247–259. doi:10.1016/j.future.2019.04.020

Reyna, A., Martín, C., Chen, J., Soler, E., & Díaz, M. (2018). On blockchain and its integration with IoT. Challenges and opportunities. *Future Generation Computer Systems*, *88*, 173–190. doi:10.1016/j.future.2018.05.046

Saraph, V., & Herlihy, M. (2019). *An Empirical Study of Speculative Concurrency in Ethereum Smart Contracts*. arXiv preprint arXiv:1901.01376.

Schäffer, M., di Angelo, M., & Salzer, G. (2019, September). Performance and scalability of private Ethereum blockchains. In *International Conference on Business Process Management* (pp. 103-118). Springer. 10.1007/978-3-030-30429-4_8

Schulz, K. F., & Freund, D. (2018, July). A multichain architecture for distributed supply chain design in industry 4.0. In *International Conference on Business Information Systems* (pp. 277-288). Springer.

Seok, B., Park, J., & Park, J. H. (2019). A Lightweight Hash-Based Blockchain Architecture for Industrial IoT. *Applied Sciences (Basel, Switzerland)*, *9*(18), 3740. doi:10.3390/app9183740

Serpanos, D., & Wolf, M. (2018). Industrial internet of things. In *Internet-of-Things (IoT) Systems* (pp. 37–54). Springer. doi:10.1007/978-3-319-69715-4_5

Sharma, K. L. S. (2016). *Overview of industrial process automation*. Elsevier.

Shih, C. S., & Yang, K. W. (2019, September). Design and implementation of distributed traceability system for smart factories based on blockchain technology. In *Proceedings of the Conference on Research in Adaptive and Convergent Systems* (pp. 181-188). 10.1145/3338840.3355646

Shirazi, B. (2019). Cloud-based architecture of service-oriented MES for subcontracting and partnership exchanges integration: A game theory approach. *Robotics and Computer-integrated Manufacturing*, *59*, 56–68. doi:10.1016/j.rcim.2019.03.006

Sisinni, E., Saifullah, A., Han, S., Jennehag, U., & Gidlund, M. (2018). Industrial internet of things: Challenges, opportunities, and directions. *IEEE Transactions on Industrial Informatics*, *14*(11), 4724–4734. doi:10.1109/TII.2018.2852491

Smirnov, A., & Teslya, N. (2018, July). Robot Interaction Through Smart Contract for Blockchain-Based Coalition Formation. In *IFIP International Conference on Product Lifecycle Management* (pp. 611-620). Springer. 10.1007/978-3-030-01614-2_56

Stodt, J., Jastremskoj, E., Reich, C., Welte, D., & Sikora, A. (2019, September). Formal Description of Use Cases for Industry 4.0 Maintenance Processes Using Blockchain Technology. In *10th IEEE International Conference on Intelligent Data Acquisition and Advanced Computing Systems: Technology and Applications (IDAACS)* (Vol. 2, pp. 1136-1141). IEEE. 10.1109/IDAACS.2019.8924382

Tao, F., Cheng, J., & Qi, Q. (2017). IIHub: An industrial Internet-of-Things hub toward smart manufacturing based on cyber-physical system. *IEEE Transactions on Industrial Informatics*, *14*(5), 2271–2280. doi:10.1109/TII.2017.2759178

Tramarin, F., Mok, A. K., & Han, S. (2019). Real-time and reliable industrial control over wireless LANs: Algorithms, protocols, and future directions. *Proceedings of the IEEE*, *107*(6), 1027–1052. doi:10.1109/JPROC.2019.2913450

Vatankhah Barenji, A., Li, Z., Wang, W. M., Huang, G. Q., & Guerra-Zubiaga, D. A. (2019). Blockchain-based ubiquitous manufacturing: A secure and reliable cyber-physical system. *International Journal of Production Research*, 1–22.

Vatcharatiansakul, N., & Tuwanut, P. (2019, July). A performance evaluation for Internet of Things based on Blockchain technology. In *2019 5th International Conference on Engineering, Applied Sciences and Technology (ICEAST)* (pp. 1-4). IEEE. 10.1109/ICEAST.2019.8802524

Vitturi, S., Zunino, C., & Sauter, T. (2019). Industrial communication systems and their future challenges: Next-generation Ethernet, IIoT, and 5G. *Proceedings of the IEEE*, *107*(6), 944–961. doi:10.1109/JPROC.2019.2913443

Voulgaris, S., Fotiou, N., Siris, V. A., Polyzos, G. C., Jaatinen, M., & Oikonomidis, Y. (2019). Blockchain Technology for Intelligent Environments. *Future Internet*, *11*(10), 213. doi:10.3390/fi11100213

Wan, J., Li, J., Imran, M., Li, D., & Fazal-e-Amin. (2019). A blockchain-based solution for enhancing security and privacy in smart factory. *IEEE Transactions on Industrial Informatics*, *15*(6), 3652–3660. doi:10.1109/TII.2019.2894573

Weiser, M. (1991). The Computer for the 21st Century. *Scientific American*, *265*(3), 94–105. doi:10.1038cientificamerican0991-94 PMID:1675486

Wollschlaeger, M., Sauter, T., & Jasperneite, J. (2017). The future of industrial communication: Automation networks in the era of the internet of things and industry 4.0. *IEEE Industrial Electronics Magazine*, *11*(1), 17–27. doi:10.1109/MIE.2017.2649104

Xu, L. D., Xu, E. L., & Li, L. (2018). Industry 4.0: State of the art and future trends. *International Journal of Production Research*, *56*(8), 2941–2962. doi:10.1080/00207543.2018.1444806

Yan, Y., Duan, B., Zhong, Y., & Qu, X. (2017, October). Blockchain technology in the internet plus: The collaborative development of power electronic devices. In *IECON 2017-43rd Annual Conference of the IEEE Industrial Electronics Society* (pp. 922-927). IEEE.

Yu, Z., Yan, Y., Yang, C., & Dong, A. (2019, March). Design of online audit mode based on blockchain technology. *Journal of Physics: Conference Series*, *1176*(4), 042072. doi:10.1088/1742-6596/1176/4/042072

Zhao, Q. (2020). Presents the Technology, Protocols, and New Innovations in Industrial Internet of Things (IIoT). In *Internet of Things for Industry 4.0* (pp. 39–56). Springer. doi:10.1007/978-3-030-32530-5_3

Zheng, Z., Xie, S., Dai, H. N., Chen, X., & Wang, H. (2018). Blockchain challenges and opportunities: A survey. *International Journal of Web and Grid Services*, *14*(4), 352–375. doi:10.1504/IJWGS.2018.095647

Zhong, S., Zhong, H., Huang, X., Yang, P., Shi, J., Xie, L., & Wang, K. (2019). *Security and Privacy for Next-Generation Wireless Networks*. Springer International Publishing. doi:10.1007/978-3-030-01150-5

Zhu, Q., & Kouhizadeh, M. (2019). Blockchain technology, supply chain information, and strategic product deletion management. *IEEE Engineering Management Review*, *47*(1), 36–44. doi:10.1109/EMR.2019.2898178

This research was previously published in Blockchain and AI Technology in the Industrial Internet of Things; pages 163-186, copyright year 2021 by Engineering Science Reference (an imprint of IGI Global).

Chapter 54

Blockchain Advances and Security Practices in WSN, CRN, SDN, Opportunistic Mobile Networks, Delay Tolerant Networks

Eranda Harshanath Jayatunga

ⓘD https://orcid.org/0000-0001-9435-7761

Faculty of Engineering, University of Ruhuna, Sri Lanka

Pasika Sashmal Ranaweera

ⓘD https://orcid.org/0000-0002-4484-2002

Faculty of Engineering, University of Ruhuna, Sri Lanka

Indika Anuradha Mendis Balapuwaduge

ⓘD https://orcid.org/0000-0003-1792-2645

Faculty of Engineering, University of Ruhuna, Sri Lanka

ABSTRACT

The internet of things (IoT) is paving a path for connecting a plethora of smart devices together that emerges from the novel 5G-based applications. This evident heterogeneity invites the integration of diverse technologies such as wireless sensor networks (WSNs), software-defined networks (SDNs), cognitive radio networks (CRNs), delay tolerant networks (DTNs), and opportunistic networks (oppnets). However, the security and privacy are prominent conundrums due to featured compatibility and interoperability aspects of evolving directives. Blockchain is the most nascent paradigm instituted to resolve the issues of security and privacy while retaining performance standards. In this chapter, advances of blockchain technology in aforesaid networks are investigated and presented as means to be followed as security practices for pragmatically realizing the concepts.

DOI: 10.4018/978-1-6684-7132-6.ch054

INTRODUCTION

All the discussed variants of this chapter are the pioneer technologies that govern the emerging communication based services and their applications. These directives were formed to address lacking aspects of different existing technologies with an improved perspective for elevating performance standards. Though, each distinct directive has limitations in security, where application of cumbersome but tamper-proof security mechanisms would obviously degrade the performance of them. Thus, there is a clear trade-off between latency and applicable security level. In addition, similar to most existing communication technologies or protocols, verifiable security is only credible with Trusted Third Parties (TTPs), or certificate authorities. Blockchain, in contrast, offers a decentralized approach that eliminates the TTP dependency. Moreover, the transparent yet tamper-proof mechanism in blockchain is enabling it to be adopted for diverse applications to secure their transactions. Thus, this chapter is focusing on the technologies of WSN, oppnets, SDN, CRN, and DTNs for adopting blockchain to their security limitations. The chapter is mainly categorized into the sections of WSN, SDN, CRN, DTN and oppnets, where various prevailing blockchain adaptations are discussed summarizing the best security practices.

BACKGROUND

Wireless Sensor Networks (WSNs) are basically ad hoc networks, amalgamating small devices embedded with sensing capabilities deployed to monitor physical activities in the surrounding area of interest. These sensor nodes should have the characteristics of large coverage area, monitoring with high precision, self-organization, random deployment and fault-tolerance, etc. Due to the possibility of providing low cost solutions, nowadays Wireless Sensor Networks (WSNs) are getting more and more attention in many real-world applications. However, the dense deployment of many sensor nodes cause unique security challenges in its management. In the meantime, adaptation of many security protocols to overcome those challenges are not straightforward because of inherent limits for energy consumption at sensor nodes as well as availability of lower memory and storage space. Therefore, it is timely important researchers to discuss the trade-off between resource consumption minimization and security maximization in WSNs.

Flexibility is the key feature of Software Defined Networks (SDNs) that elevate its standards beyond the conventional networking infrastructures (Kreutz, Ramos, & Verissimo, 2013). This concept offers advanced network management capabilities to the network administrator by enabling configuration of networking instances independent of the hardware layer. Infact, diversification exhibited in networking devices and their plethoric aggregate are contriving compatibility and interoperability debacles. In SDN, homogeneity of the both core and access networks are improved with standardizing the hardware specifications; and higher reliance on hardware based processing is transformed into an autonomous processing approach with software integration (Kumar et al., 2017). In fact, SDN envisages solutions for complex issues in traditional networking topologies and routing algorithms by integrating intelligence to the control plane. In addition, this is a paradigm shift for network operators that eases their issues with hardware layer and the ability to advance networking features with novel requirements to broadened avenues. Apart from flexibility, main benefits of SDN can be specified as: cost effectiveness (monetary), centralization, higher throughput, dynamic nature that support higher mobility, low communication latency, optimum network utilization, rapid and efficient load-balancing, fault tolerance, and adaptable/ context-aware security (Tomovic, Pejanovic-Djurisic, & Radusinovic, 2014; Jaballah, Conti, & Lal, 2019; Scott-Hayward, O'Callaghan, & Sezer, 2013).

Recently, research in the field of wireless communications has been focusing on the Fifth Generation (5G) cellular systems. Meanwhile, the 5G and beyond wireless network designers face challenging demands such as more capacity, higher data rates, lower latency, better connectivity for a massive number of users, lesser cost and energy, and more importantly improved quality of experience (QoE) (Munsub Ali, Liu, & Ejaz, 2020). Moreover, with the increase in the number of communication devices, the requirement for higher bandwidth is essential. However, with the limited and expensive radio spectrum resources, allocation of new frequency bands is an extremely difficult task. Therefore, efficient management of the spectrum under dynamic policies has recently become a prospective research topic.

Although Internet access has evolved as one of basic primary needs of humans, still there are many rural areas that do not have any network connectivity or sometimes intermittent. These scenarios demand the development of distributed networking techniques in an opportunistic manner to provide atleast some level of service with ad-hoc networks. Consequently, these Opportunistic Networks (oppnets) integrate diverse communication, computation, sensing, storage and other devices and resources in the surrounding. The initial set of nodes associated with an oppnet are called seed nodes. Once other nodes are invited to become potential helpers for the original oppnet, this seed oppnet nurtures into an expanded oppnet while persisting various security concerns.

The integration of blockchain with IoT provides many benefits to build a secure, trusted and robust communication prospects. But the challenge is to identify the most suitable location in placing blockchain for current IoT settings. With the amalgamation as third party to keep data in centralized data centers and later a fog layer to offload the traffic burden from the data centers, the current IoT is a three tier architecture namely IoT devices layer, Fog layer and the cloud layer. Generally, the incoming requests for access level can be divided as real-time, non-realtime and delay tolerant. Delay tolerant networks are helpful in addressing issues related to lack of infrastructure, stationary nodes and connectivity in today's heterogeneous networks by storing and forwarding facilities. Nevertheless, these networks require new authentication and trust establishing mechanisms to ensure that no adversary parties can destroy the privacy in time dependent delay tolerant network routes.

SECURITY CONCERNS IN DIVERSE NETWORKS

Security Lapses in Wireless Sensor Networks

The attacks in WSNs can be classified as host-based and network-based attacks. In host-based attacks, adversary parties always compromise with the users in the network to reveal information such as passwords or keys about the sensor nodes. This is achieved by breaking the software running on the sensor nodes or tampering the hardware to extract the program code, data and keys stored at sensor nodes. Whilst network-based attacks include all the attacks related to information transmission and/or deviations crafted on the intended functioning of protocols. The summary of inherent four-fold attacks such as interruption, interception, modification and fabrication with respect to different layers in ISO-OSI layer are shown in Table 1 (Chowdhury & Kader, 2013).

Hence, the security requirements of WSNs can be identified under four disciplines namely Confidentiality, Integrity, Authentication and Availability (CIAA). For any network, the data authenticity is required to guarantee the identities of communicating nodes whether the data has been originated from a reliable source. In the presence of malicious nodes in the network, the data at transit nodes can be tampered, altered or changed by adversaries. In order to ensure the data integrity, normally a code of message integrity is used. Since radio access technologies are open resources, sometimes passive attackers can eavesdrop messages or discover secrets in surveillance applications by collecting secret data through other compromised nodes. Consequently, encryption standards should be defined in advance to keep the confidentiality among nodes. Ultimately, the availability shall determine whether a node has the ability to use the resources and the network to transmit data (Zia & Zomaya, 2006).

Table 1. Plausible security threat in WSNs based on ISO-OSI layered architecture

Layer	Attack	Plausible Security Threat
Physical layer	Jamming	An adversary party attempts to disrupt the operation of the network by broadcasting a high-energy signal
	Tampering	Extract cryptographic keys from the captured node, tamper with its circuitry, modify the program codes or even replace it with a malicious node.
Data link layer	Continuous channel access (Exhaustion)	A malicious node disrupts the MAC protocol by continuously requesting or transmitting over the channel
	Collision	Two nodes attempt to transmit on the same frequency simultaneously
Network layer	Sinkhole	An adversary party attempts to attract almost all the traffic of other nodes through a compromised node
	Sybil	A single node attempts to demonstrate multiple identities for all other nodes in the network
	Wormhole	A low latency link is created between two portions of a network thus an attacker is able to tunnel messages to confuse the routing protocol
	Hello flood	Disrupts the process of neighbor discovery by broadcasting HELLO packets
	Acknowledge flooding	Acknowledgements are used by many link layer network routing algorithms to choose the next hop to overcome reliability issues in the network. Acknowledgments spoofing results in packets being lost when travelling along such links.
	Sniffing	An adversary node is placed in the proximity of sensor grid for interception or listen-in
Transport layer	Injects false messages and energy drain attacks	Normally sensor nodes are resource-constrained entities. As a result, attackers attempt to use compromised nodes to inject fabricated reports to generate a large amount of traffic in the network
	Flooding	An attacker generates new connection requests repeatedly to reach a maximum limit until others get exhausted
	De-synchronization	Disrupts an existing connection
Application layer	False nodes	Addition of a malicious node by an adversary party to inject malicious data as well as to lure other nodes to capture data.
	Node subversion	Revealing its information by a compromised node including disclosure of cryptographic keys thus affects the whole network.

Security Lapses in Software Defined Networks

As Figure 1 indicates, conventional networks are mainly partitioned into access or local, edge, and core networks; where the nodes or devices operating at each level are different in terms of their build, system specifications (processing, storage, memory, energy requirement, access interfaces and amounts), financial cost, operating cost, embedded protocols, and operational complexity. In fact, the complexity of the devices are dependent on the layer in which the device is operating in the Open System Interconnection (OSI) or TCP/IP protocol stacks. Typically, local network devices are operating at Layer 2 (Data-Link) while edge and core network devices are extending to the rest of the layers above Layer 2 (Network to Application in OSI). Directives such as Multi-Protocol Labeled Switching (MPLS), and Virtual Private LAN Service (VPLS) have been introduced to improve the packet forwarding efficiency and security at edge and core networks (Liyanage, Ylianttila, & Gurtov, 2016). Upgrading the holistic network into such directives require the replacement of networking nodes, so that they are compatible with the pursuing updates. This is an obvious drawback with the existing networks that restricts the application of advancements to real-world networks. In addition, control/signalling information, and data forwarded through the network are carried through separate channels; which make bandwidth utilization arduous due to the dedicated signalling channels. Traffic load balancing has become a static and standalone process that can be monitored and administered only via the control channels remotely. Since the load balancing algorithms/ mechanisms/ protocols should be executed at the device level, managing the control signals and statistics has become overly de-centralized beyond the acceptable controlling domains. This is an important aspect of novel services that require more control over the traffic management with the prescribed Quality of Service (QoS) and Quality of Experience (QoE) classifications.

Figure 1. Comparison of conventional and SDN networks

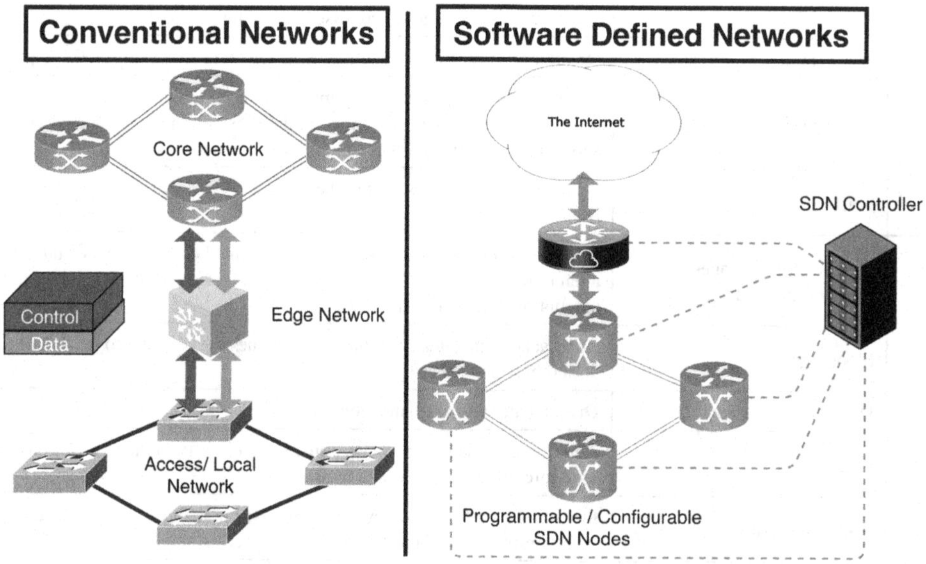

The SDN architecture is categorized into 3 layers or planes as illustrated in Figure 2. Application layer launches the applications and services specified in the networking context. The application instances are generating the flow rules and convey the requirements to the controller via the Northbound Application Programming Interfaces (APIs) or plugins (Feghali, Kilany, & Chamoun, 2015). The infrastructure layer consists of network elements that have a controller logic embedded to it. As specified above, these network elements can be configured into different network functions. The control layer is the most important aspect of this architecture that centralizes the complete network. The controller is responsible for the functions of network visualization, service provisioning, network management, and trac engineering. These functions are carried out by the Network Operating System (NOS) and an instance of each network service is deployed at the controller. High-level policies can be formed at the controller supporting security and dependability (Kreutz et al., 2013). OpenFlow (OF) protocol is employed to establish the communication channel between the controller and the network elements while NOX, POX, Faucet, Floodlight, ONOS, Open vSwitch, Cherry and Beacon are most commonly used controllers. The controller is reaching the network elements via the resource abstraction layer from southbound APIs. In addition to the three common layers, there is a management and administration layer that interacts with all other layers. In fact, management abstraction layer is interacting with: application layer on Service Level Agreements (SLAs) for each service instance, control layer for updating configuration policy and monitoring performance, and infrastructure layer for setting up and launching network elements.

Figure 2. Typical SDN architecture

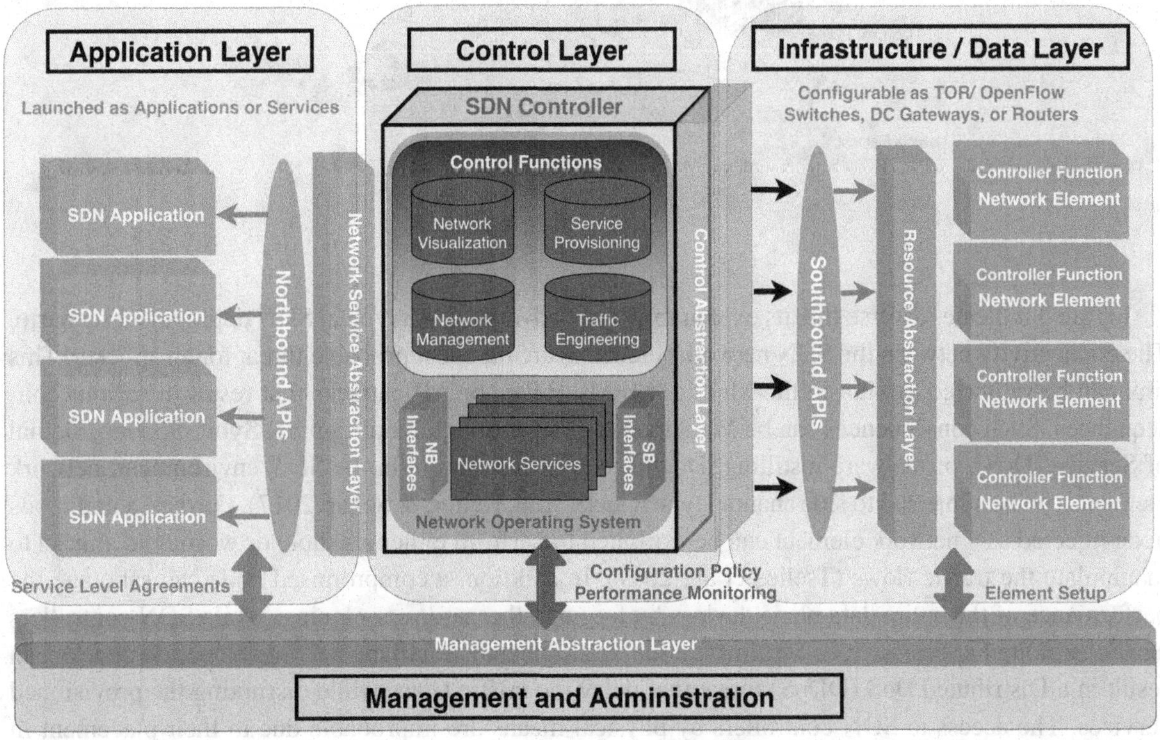

The same benefits of SDN, network programmability and centralized control logic, are exposing the IT networks towards nascent threats (Kreutz et al., 2013). The allowance granted for application layer entities to engage with control plane elements (i.e. for improving the flexibility) is exposing the rest of the architecture towards unauthorized access control, and malicious network rule insertion threats (Tselios, Politis, & Kotsopoulos, 2017). Centralized nature of the paradigm is compromising the holistic network in case the SDN controller becomes infiltrated. The softwarized approach in SDN is no longer operating standalone network devices, where connected nature is improving the odds for adversaries to instill malicious content or interpose such links (Aujla et al., 2020). Since conventional networks were mostly based proprietary devices as in Cisco, Juniper, and NEC, the attackers were tasked with revealing vulnerabilities specific to each vendor. This is an arduous task, which meant one revealed vulnerability is only applicable to devices of a specific vendor. Though with SDN, for maintaining compatibility and interoperability, a generic standardization and a set of protocols should be utilized. This fact is increasing the vulnerability level of the SDN, where Advanced Persistent Threats (APTs) can be targeted to gain access.

Figure 3. Threats in a typical SDN deployment

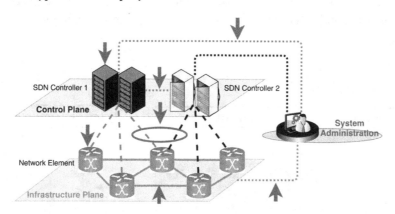

Figure 3 indicates diverse threats exploitable by an adversary in a typical SDN deployment scenario. The connectivity between the SDN networks elements are the most probable threat for an attacker. This link can be subjected to Man-in-the-Middle (MitM), Relay, or APT attacks that result in various consequences. Such consequences can be Malicious code injection, Eavesdropping, Sybil, Spoong, Denial of Service (DoS), or malware instilling. Due to its dynamic nature in the SDN environment, network elements can be subjected to side channel type attacks (Liu, Reiter, & Sekar, 2017). Further, a malicious node injected as a network element can be exploited to perform either sinkhole or wormhole attacks to manipulate the traffic flows (Tselios et al., 2017). In addition, a compromised node can sabotage the performance of the entire data plane devices by forging other nodes or cloning; while SDN controllers can be exploited appearing as a legitimate node. Multiple and simultaneous impersonation attacks can result in a Distributed DoS (DDoS) threat that delay the traffic flows while disrupting the provisioned services. The access to SDN controllers by physical means are improbable due to their placement in secure premises. Their access can be gained from exploiting the vulnerabilities of the OF protocols. Appearing as a legitimate network device and authenticating to secure the access is an obvious approach for any attacker. Once the access is gained, the SDN controller can be overloaded via DoS type attacks. Further, a compromised network controllers can delude the controllers in other domains. A resourceful attacker capable of launching an impersonation attack as the administrator can infiltrate both control and infrastructure planes. The main issue with the SDN environment is its lack of trust and accountability model for guaranteeing security of consumers.

Security Lapses in Cognitive Radio Networks

According to the spectrum utilization statistics, a large amount of spectral resources in all over the world are still either partially or completely unused at different times across geographical areas, and therefore, inefficient. Although different technologies and techniques have been identified as solutions for spectrum underutilization in future wireless networks, integration of cognitive radio (CR) technology will provide an effective solution for spectrum scarcity issues faced in the future 5G and beyond networks (Hindia et al., 2020). The main objective of CR technology is to sense the spectrum from the real time environment and discover the non-utilized spectrum. Cognitive radio networks (CRNs) are intended to be able to opportunistically exploit those spectrum holes in order to adapt their radio parameters accordingly. To facilitate this task, CR needs accurate and reliable spectrum sensing.

Figure 4. Main components in a CR node

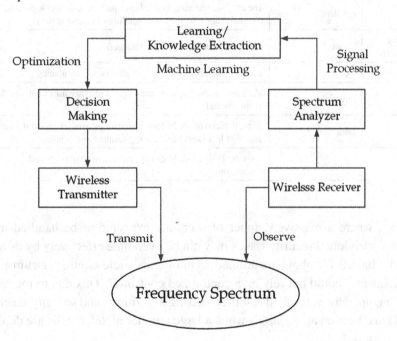

Therefore, a cognitive radio transceiver consists of different components to implement those functionalities as shown in Figure 4. In order to detect the channel occupancy of licensed users and to find vacant or available channels for unlicensed access spectrum analyzer is used. For an effective identification of available and occupied spectrum bands efficient signal processing techniques need to be supported in a CR node. Based on the analyzed spectrum details, CR node's learning and knowledge extraction unit functions to identify spectrum usage patterns of licensed users by adopting machine learning techniques. From this correct identification, the decision on accessing the spectrum has to be made by the decision making unit by applying optimization theory.

In a CRN, CRs have the capability of adapting their transmission parameters according to the environmental conditions and make changes based on their communication capabilities. However, the security is susceptible in case of wireless networks compared to wired networks. Spectrum management and sensing in CRNs involve various control messages. During this process, malicious users may eavesdrop on those information, thereby leading to the serious statistical information leakage of both licensed and unlicensed users. Consequently, malicious activities need to be prevented within the CRN. For instance, a malicious secondary user can eavesdrop other users' signal information and based on that, pretend a false interference level. On the other hand, some malicious secondary users may masquerade as a primary user to obtain the resource of a given channel by using Physical layer attacks (Nanthini S., Hemalatha, Manivannan, & Devasena, 2014). A summary of several security issues, network layers involved, as well as possible reasons for those issues are listed in Table 2.

Table 2. Security issue in CRNs

Attack Type	Target Layer	Reason/Description
Jamming (Primary user or secondary user)	Physical	The attacker maliciously sends out packets to hinder legitimate participants in a communication session from sending or receiving data
Increase interference by malicious nodes	Network	When negotiating with malicious nodes
Ripple effect	Network	Due to incorrect information about channel occupancy
Primary user emulation attack (PUE)	Physical	Malicious secondary user emulating a primary user to obtain the resources of a given channel
Spectrum sensing data falsification	Data Link	The CR receivers make false spectrum-sensing decision if an attacker sends incorrect local spectrum sensing results to its neighbors
Lion attack	Transport	Uses the PUE attack to disrupt the Transmission Control Protocol (TCP) connection

In 5G networks, where a massive number of users are expected to be handled in heterogeneous networks, the above mentioned security issues may not be overcome effectively by using existing cryptographic methods. Indeed for above mentioned technological fields, the spectrum management and the security mechanisms should not rely on a centralized controller. This due to the fact that the fixed spectrum allocation, operator controlled resource sharing algorithms and security mechanisms will not be scalable for 5G and beyond applications when a large number of small cells are deployed to support Millions of mobile users.

BLOCKCHAIN ADVANCES AND SECURITY PRACTICES IN DIVERSE NETWORKS

Blockchain Advances for Enhancing Security in WSNs

Malicious node detection and isolation in the application layer, key management and secure routing implementations in network layer, and link layer encryption performed at the data link layer are the most commonly available techniques. In addition, use of adaptive antennas and spread spectrum techniques have been considered as physical layer solutions. However, in the current IOT paradigm, WSNs are open, distributed and dynamic multi-hop routing technology is used to transmit aggregated data from integrated sensor nodes to a central location via agreed routing protocol. Hence, it is required many judgments on security, privacy, connectivity and data requirements. The existing cryptography mechanisms are simply capable of detecting and defending node compromise to some extent. On the other hand, multi-hop routing is exposed to several malicious or selfish attacks solely depends on encryption algorithm and authentication mechanism. When there is a malicious attack, conventional routing algorithms cannot distinguish a malicious node from other routing nodes. The malicious node can discard packets thus creates a data "black hole" in the network. Hence, a trusted, decentralized and self-organizing third-party intermediary is mandatory to overcome the aforesaid security issues.

Consequently, blockchain is perceived as a decentralized or distributed network that is capable of Peer-to-Peer Networking (PPN), Distributed File Sharing (DFS) and Autonomous Device Coordination (ADC) functions, allowing the IoT systems to track the massive number of connected and networked devices. Mainly it enhances the privacy and reliability of IoT systems having robust transactions among devices in coordination.

Blockchain Based Malicious Node Detection in WSNs

Threats generated in WSNs follow two customs as the external attacker to the network or an internal node which becomes malicious after being invaded. Therefore, malicious node detection is key in WSNs to assure the security in operation. It has been comprehended using either based on developing trust models or based on introducing new WSN protocols. In the former method, trust models were developed by accounting trust values with neighbor-weight trust determination (NWTD) algorithm, D-S (Dempster-Shafer) evidence theory or fuzzy based multi-attribute trust model, etc. Enhanced LEACH protocol to detect energy consumption, distance and malicious nodes to ensure the robustness, and new multi-valued trust routing protocol (MTR) are some examples for new protocols used for malicious detection (She, et al., 2019). Despite the behavioral-based trust models that can be used to monitor the network and detect malicious nodes, they are still exposed to malicious attacks due to inaccurate location estimates. In order improve the accuracy as well as to record the detection process of malicious nodes for later traceability, a hybrid blockchain based trust evaluation method of behavioral- and data-based has been proposed in (Kim, et al., 2019) as shown in Figure 5. This rejects malicious sensor nodes in network and thus enhances trust relationships among beacon nodes. First, a trust value of each beacon node is computed taking into account the metrics such as closeness, honesty, intimacy and frequency of interaction and then it is broadcast to base stations to generate blockchain of trust values. The beacon values with least trust values are discarded eventually. Simulated results reveal that the proposed algorithm outperforms the existing algorithms in terms of False Positive Rate (FPR), False Negative Rate (FNR) and Average Energy Consumption (AEC) though most trusty beacon nodes were used to estimate localization process of unknown nodes. However, it is recommended that Bayesian statistics, Maximum likelihood estimation, reinforcement learning based trust evaluation and the complexity associated with the length of blockchain should be tested further to determine the completeness of the method.

Figure 5. Hybrid blockchain-based trust management model

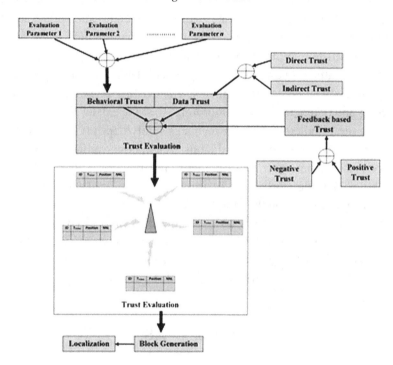

Trusted Routing Schemes Using Blockchain and Reinforcement Learning

In order to enhance the trustworthiness among routing nodes, conventional WSNs use cryptographic systems, trust management, centralized routing decisions, etc. Although many researchers have suggested third-party intermediaries or management centers to resolve the security issues, most of the routing schemes in multi-hop distributed WSNs are failed to identify untrusted behaviors of routing nodes dynamically. Meanwhile, there is still no effective way to prevent malicious node attacks. Therefore, as a trusted, decentralized, self-organizing ledger system, the blockchain has shown improved solutions for the security and fairness. By replacing the traditional public key infrastructure (PKI) with a blockchain protocol, Gómez-Arevalillo et al. has proposed blockchain based public key management framework (SBTM) to remove central authentication and to provide a decentralized inter-domain routing system. Smart blockchain based contract routing (BCR) has been used in (Ramezan & Leung, 2018) to record routing nodes with malicious behaviors and thus to help routing nodes for finding trusted routes. However, it seems that there is no assurance to stop packet forwarding to a malicious node that claims with a BCR token. Therefore, there is a need for developing routing algorithms with self-adaptive nature. Therefore, Yang et al. has proposed a trusted routing scheme using blockchain together with reinforcement learning to improve the credibility of routing information. In here, proof of authority (PoA) blockchain is used for easy traceability and to avoid any tampering while the reinforcement learning model is used select more trusted route dynamically.

Blockchain Based Data Provenance in WSNs

The nature of deploying a larger number of sensor nodes in unattended or even adversarial environments lead WSNs to be vulnerable for network failures and attacks. Therefore, it is essential to keep track of packets among sensor nodes to evaluate the trustworthiness, probe adversarial conducts and detect communication failures. The data provenance normally records the data origin trace back information of a packet in accordance with both ownership and the actions taken on them. However, the provenance size of a packet significantly grows with the number of transmission hops in a selected WSN path, thus creating issues in battery life, communication bandwidth, etc. Consequently, it is required to develop data provenance schemes itself or outside the host WSN.

A lightweight blockchain technique to empower against tampering has been proposed in (Tiberti, et al., 2020) to detect compromised nodes. In this approach, the sensor network consists of several motes and a sink node, a constrained node which serves as the gateway towards the external networks. In the monitoring process, the sink node collects and stores data from other nodes before forwarding them to other networks. A blockchain based hash computation is used to provide an immutable and tamper-resistant storage at the sink node. Another compression free blockchain based data provenance scheme (BCP) has been proposed in (Zeng,et al., 2018) where provenances are stored distributively on the high performance nodes (H-nodes) deployed above or nearby the network along the packet path. Base stations can retrieve the provenance on demand through a query process.

Although non-repudiation and non-tampering properties can be adopted with blockchain based schemes in WSNs, the implementation of these schemes is still a challenge due to resource-limited edges. A green blockchain framework for big data sharing in collaborative edges to overcome the challenges arising from the properties of edge computing has been proposed by Chenhan Xu et al. They have divided the framework into four layers, Application Programming Interface (API) layer, cache layer, blockchain layer, and storage layer based on the reduced computational, storage, and network resource requirements for big data sharing in collaborative edges as shown in Figure 6. The key findings of the this works are; 1) PoC (Proof-of-Collaboration) based consensus mechanism with low computation complexity which provided low computation capacity, 2) blockchain transaction filtering and offloading scheme that can significantly reduce the storage overhead, and 3) new types of blockchain transaction (i.e., Express Transaction) and block (i.e., Hollow Block) to enhance the communication efficiency.

All the above research works have considered applying data provenance within the network or at the edge of the network. However, mission-critical applications such as industrial control, smart grids, and security and surveillance systems are still preferred for cloud-centric IoT networks. In order to guarantee a high level of trustworthiness for data and to make accurate and timely decisions, a secure data provenance framework for cloud-centric IoT network with public blockchain smart contracts has been proposed in (Ali, et al., 2018). In this framework, the cryptographic hash of the device metadata is stored in the blockchain whereas actual data is stored in the cloud. These multiple smart contracts positioned in the blockchain are used to guarantee the data provenance in the cloud thus allowing more and more dense deployment of IoT devices. Table 3 summarizes some of the key research literature used to enhance the security aspects of WSNs with blockchain technology.

Figure 6. Layered architecture for blockchain framework in WSNs

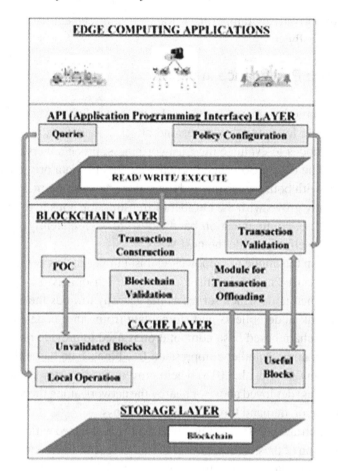

Advancements of Blockchain for Securing SDN

The consensus to verify/validate and append to the tamper-proof ledger makes blockchain the most promising solution for trust and accountability issues in the SDN deployments. In fact, blockchain is enabling SDN to operate without a third-party trust agent in a decentralized peer-to-peer nature. The main issue of the SDN networks is its vulnerability for trac based attacks such as wormhole or sinkhole threats that are perpetrated through manipulation of traffic headers due to its over reliance on softwarized controlling. Flow rules tables, its content, updating process, and specifics of the OF protocol and its integration issues with TLS and TCP protocols are vulnerable aspects of SDN. Thus, securing such factors that relate to routing and trac engineering processes with instilled traceability and verification capabilities is a prime requisite. Blockchain being a data structure that its elements (i.e. blocks) are linked or chained with cryptographic hashes imprinted on timestamps and a record of all the transactions conducted in the ledger (Tselios et al., 2017). This approach makes the blockchain immutable and incorruptible. Such features of the blockchain technology are well suited for securing flow/ routing tables, and protocol mechanisms that offer a transparent and rapid applying abilities. Thus, this subsection is explicating various approaches blockchain can be applied for securing SDN.

Table 3. Blockchain based security practices for WSNs

Reference	Blockchain Based Security Practice	Preventable Security Threats/ Attacks	Feature of the Solution
She, et al., 2019)	A malicious node detection blockchain trust model (BTM)	Data tampering, Malicious node detection	Uses hash values and hash pointers to connect the previous block thus to meet the needs of blockchain integrity
(Kim, et al., 2019)	Base station generates blockchain with trust values of individual beacon nodes for trust management.	Malicious node detection	Interactions and collaborations among beacon nodes are used to evaluate trust values based on node location information, node behavioral trust and data trust
(Yang et al., 2019)	Queries network state information through blockchain	Tracing and tampering of routing information	Preliminary obtains the routing information of routing nodes on the blockchain and uses reinforcement learning to improve the routing security
(Ramezan & Leung, 2018)	A decentralized Ethereum blockchain-based contractual routing (BCR)	Blackhole and Greyhole attacks by malicious devices	Routing protocol for the IoT with much lower routing overhead
(Cui, et al., 2020)	A consortium blockchain with the PoA consensus mechanism to be jointly managed by several authoritative nodes	False nodes, Node subversion	Decentralized network with high provenance security including integrity and authenticity
(Ali, et al., 2018)	A hybrid blockchain model consists of both local blockchain and public blockchain	Collisions, Flooding, De-synchronization	Adaptation of the network to eliminate private blockchain nodes that need to be authenticated to join the network, while are at different base stations
(Haseeb, et al., 2019)	A trustworthy device registration and identity provenance smart contracts via blockchain	Discrepancies in the traffic behavior	Ensures the device integrity and provenance in cloud-centric IoT network
(Xu, et al., 2019)	A blockchain transaction filtering and offloading scheme that can significantly reduce the storage overhead	Traffic issues	Longer network lifetime with lightweight secure data routing between mobile IoT devices based on WSNs

Blockchain for SDN Node Identity Verification

Injecting malicious packets into a traffic flow of the OF switch is a most common infiltration method for SDN attackers. In (Aujla et al., 2020), flow tables and packets are secured using permissioned blockchain where the function of contriving blocks and aggregating into a chain are restricted to the controller. This approach is extended to verify and validate the OF switches' identity in the authentication phase using zero knowledge proof concept. The switch identities are linked into a blockchain. This research further demonstrates prevention of DoS/ DDoS attacks perpetrated at the immediate connected nodes at the infrastructure plane, finally targeting the controller. The final solution can be visualized as blockchain as a service approach for SDN.

A Blockchain Layer for SDN Architecture

A monolithic blockchain based security mechanism is proposed by (Jiasi, Jian, Jia-Nan, & Yue, 2019), that decentralizes the SDN control plane to avoid single point of failure while guaranteeing authenticity, traceability, and accountability. In the proposed architecture, a blockchain layer is appended in between the control and data planes; where Attribute Based Encryption (ABE) is employed for interactions with the application plane and One-pass High Performance Diffie-Hellmann (HOMQV) protocol is utilized for interactions between the blockchain layer and the data plane. This blockchain layer is creating a secure zone for all the transactions conveying within control and data planes.

Applying Blockchain for SDN Flow Rules Tables

Load balancing is a key aspect of SDN, where the conveyed control statistics and network states should be secured in transit. The (Faizullah, Khan, Alzahrani, & Khan, 2020) proposes a permissioned blockchain based approach for securing the load balancing process of SDN, that enables it as a suited solution for Internet of Things (IoT) applications. The SDN flow rules tables are secured with blockchain based transactions. A flow rule table update process is used to evaluate the proposed system where accuracy, scalability, security, and efficiency are compared with public blockchain based and OF based SDN; where the proposed system proved to be better performing.

The DistBlockNet scheme proposed in (Sharma, Singh, Jeong, & Park, 2017) is a novel method for updating the flow rules table employing blockchain with a verification strategy. Version verification, validation, and downloading the flow rules table to the IoT devices can be achieved with this system. One of the major concerns of SDN is its reliance on administrator manual engagement for reviewing and applying proliferating amounts of security policies and recommendations. DistBlockNet offers adaptability towards the considered threat landscape, where complete autonomous decision making and application can be realized in the real-time context. Each SDN controller-local network view is composed of OrchApp, controller, and shelter components. Both OrchApp and Shelter modules are focusing on security attacks perpetrated at application and data layers. In terms of functionality, OrchApp is responsible for access controlling with threat intelligence; while shelter is updating the flow rules table in a distributed blockchain network. Thus, application of blockchain in this solution is focused on the trac policy within the SDN controller network.

Blockchain Enabled SDN Approaches for Emerging Applications

Emerging technologies such as Internet of Vehicles (IoV) or Vehicle-to-Vehicle (V2V) have considered applying SDN based networking infrastructure to achieve the envisaged requirements stated under 5G based use cases. The architecture proposed in (Gao et al., 2019) employs SDN to manage the networking within the fog zones and mobile access networks for Vehicular Ad-Hoc Network (VANET) deployments. The data extracted from the on-board units are forwarded to the backhaul or cloud, via the fog zones in the edge equipped with radio resources. The SDN model enables the softwarized trac handling of fog zones utilizing the OF protocol and leveraging the capacity of the fiber optic backhaul link. Blockchain is adopted for handling authentication, access control, data management, and policy management in the control plane. The block structure is formulated with timestamp and Merkle root embedded in the header while transaction stats are encapsulated as a separate eld. This solution contrives a trust model for VANET peers that enable rapid and secure communication.

Handover process is an inconvenient aspect of any mobile or wireless networks that exposes the radio channels for interception intended adversaries. This is an unavoidable factor of such networks that require re-authentication of the mobile device at each handover instance. The issue becomes severe when corresponding wireless cells become heterogeneous, where authentication mechanisms and protocols are distinct for each underlying technology. Therefore, (Yazdinejad, Parizi, Dehghantanha, & Choo, 2019) proposes a SDN based internal network for tackling the heterogeneous nature with 5G while a blockchain approach is adopted for securing the handover mechanism. A blockchain centre where Ethereum based ledger technology is employed, handles the authentication control incorporation with the SDN controller. The primitives generated for each mobile device are recorded at the blockchain centre where they can be leveraged to verify its identity during a handover administered by the SDN controller. This approach eliminates the requirement for re-authentication and discourages infiltrations.

Various methods are adopted for integrating blockchain for SDN networks as perceived in the previous sub section. Classification of such approaches is imperative for realizing the successful adaptation of these two technologies in a pragmatic context. Thus, Table 4 specifies the classified best practices for blockchain enabled SDN implementations.

Table 4. Blockchain based security practices for SDNs

Applicable SDN Layer	Reference	Blockchain Based Security Practice	Preventable Security Threats/ Attacks	Features of the Solution					
				Adaptability	Flexibility	Authenticity	Accountability	Traceability	Intrusion Detection
Application	(Steichen et al, 2017)	Blockchain firewall application for SDN	Virus, malware, warms						×
Control	(Faizullah et al., 2020) (Sharma et al., 2017)	Employing blockchain to secure flow rules tables and their update process	Traffic engineering	×	×		×	×	
	(Gao et al., 2019)	Authentication, access control, and data management of VANETs	attacks, wormhole, sinkhole	×	×	×	×	×	
	(Yazdinejad et al., 2019)	Securing mobile handover process in heterogeneous networks	Intervening attacks such as MitM, Relay, APT	×	×	×	×	×	
Infrastructure/ Data	(Jiasi et al., 2019)	Introducing a blockchain layer between control and data layers	DoS/ DDoS attacks on controller, impersonation threats	×	×	×	×	×	
	(Aujla et al., 2020)	Blockchain for OF switch identity verification	Malicious node injection, rouge node			×	×	×	

Advancements of Blockchain for CRNs

Meanwhile Blockchain technology is introduced as an effective solution for security issues in wireless networks which consists of distributed databases that can be securely and iteratively updated. Blockchain technology implements a distributed ledger: a secure decentralized form of a database where no single party has control (Werbach, 2018). Thus, blockchains can be considered as tamper resistant digital ledgers implemented in a distributed manner without a central source.

Note that the records stored on blockchain's distributed ledger can be related to any data type. Then, information about spectrum access rights and spectrum usage and their dynamic changes can be recorded on this distributed ledger. Meanwhile, the spectrum can be dynamically managed using smart contracts. Consequently, with respect to a CRN, they enable CR users to record spectrum sensing details and QoS requirements and true identities in a shared ledger within the relevant group of CRNs, such that under normal operation of the blockchain network no information can be changed in malicious ways.

Secure Blockchains for DSA in Moving CRNs

In (Kotobi & Bilen, 2018), a blockchain verification protocol is proposed and evaluated as a technique for enabling and securing spectrum sharing in CRNs. In order to verify and secure spectrum sharing between mobile CRs a decentralized blockchain database is maintained. The general concept behind this proposed work is that spectrum licensees announce the auction of a particular spectrum band to the other parties, i.e., secondary users. For this, a common control channel is utilized to advertise the available channels and the auction information. The bidder(s) who won the bid can purchase the corresponding spectrum via a virtual currency known as Specoins. By making the blockchain or through direct exchange, secondary users can receive this currency. For instance, A CR can earn Specoins via updating the blockchain by utilizing its processing power. In addition, the proposed scheme permits conversion of real currency into Specoins by considering the secondary users who have a large amount of data to transmit however without enough Specoins.

Secondary users' transactions using Specoins are recorded in the blockchain. Note that this distributed database is visible by all participating parties according to the blockchain concept. The nodes which can update the database are known as miners. Once the secondary network transactions occur, it is updated by miners. After that the blockchain is used to validate the transactions. According to the simulation results obtained, the proposed blockchain-based spectrum allocation scheme in (Kotobi & Bilen, 2018) outperforms the conventional CR systems, in terms of the amount of transmitted data. However, this throughput improvement is achieved at a cost of higher power consumption. An interesting observation made in (Kotobi & Bilen, 2018) is that the proposed scheme can provide a higher throughput than the existing schemes even at the presence of fading conditions. This study provides a basic way of looking into the application of blockchains over the CRNs. It needs further improvement in terms of power consumption of battery-powered devices.

A CR Technique for Blockchain-Enabled IoV

Vehicular ad-hoc networks (VANETs) enable communication among on-road vehicles to provide safety to drivers in a vehicular environment by collecting and sharing traffic status with other vehicles. Since future VANETs are equipped with cognitive sensors and intelligent communication units, CRN-based Internet of vehicle (IoV) will provide a smart solution for high reliable and safety vehicular communications. Since secure communication is an essential feature to achieve high reliability, in (Rathee et al., 2020), a decision-making technique is developed to provide the security to IoV during spectrum sensing and information transmission using CRNs. Therein, in order to maintain transparency among the vehicles during data sharing, a Blockchain mechanism has been used.

In (Rathee et al., 2020), a fusion center (FC) is adopted to collect the spectrum sensing data of cognitive users (CUs). The FC analyzes the security and privacy measures of submitted data reports. In addition, the FC conducts an independent assessment of CUs' performance, analyzing the availability of ideal channels. The decision-making model can be represented hierarchically as shown in Figure 7 consisting of this decision-making scheme known as Technique for Order Preference by Similarity to the Ideal Solution (TOPSIS), and Blockchain framework. In this figure, ⟦CUij⟧_ denotes the *j*th security parameter of *i*th CU. In the blockchain part, the records from each CU is stored on a network which will be further traced and analyzed by all the users. Therein, the records and data modifications by intruders can be identified by legitimate CUs. In order to increase the number of miners who perform the block verification, the proposed decision model provides various incentives in the form of extra credits or high trust ability.

According to the simulation results analyzed based on a real-world dataset of San Francisco, the detection rate of malicious IoT devices is significantly higher when the proposed method is adopted than to a baseline (existing) method. The main reason for having a higher detection rate could be the identification process of legitimate IoT devices based on various interaction parameters such as interaction frequency, energy consumption, and the positive and negative interactions by legitimate or malicious devices and transmission time. Moreover, the results in (Rathee et al., 2020) shows that denial-of-service (DoS) threats can easily be measured by the proposed method through the blockchain mechanism. Due to the fact that the proposed approach is based on blockchain in the back-end the impact of the intrusion is also limited as the devices are unable to delete or alter the data. Furthermore, it is shown that when the network consists of a large number of IoT devices, the proposed phenomenon can provide better performance due to the parametric evaluation.

Figure 7. Hierarchical model of Blockchain-based IoV proposed in (Rathee et al., 2020)

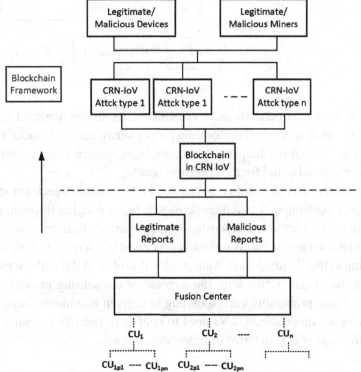

Blockchain Enabled Cooperative Spectrum Sensing

The application of blockchain technology over radio spectrum sensing is studied in (Weiss et al., 2019). Therein, a cooperative-sensing-based dynamic spectrum access (DSA) scheme for CRNs which is enabled by blockchain is proposed. The proposed DSA scheme includes a protocol that includes a time-slotted operation by the SUs to get an access to the available spectrum. An SU needs to perform the both roles, i.e., as a sensing node and as a miner or a verifier in the proposed blockchain network. In order to perform the miner's task, SU nodes gather up a large number of records of spectrum sensing and utilization as can fit into a block, and go through a mathematical computation to validate the block and combine it to the chain of previous blocks. Interestingly, the paper proposes a cooperative spectrum sensing mechanism for the secondary network where the final sensing result is concluded by analyzing the individual sensing results of all contributing SUs. Therein, majority rule is applied to determine the channel availability for a particular spectrum band.

Figure 8. Operation of CRN in each time slot as proposed in (Weiss et al., 2019)

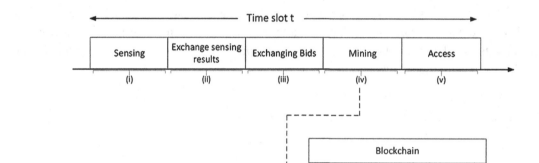

As shown in Figure 8, the cooperative spectrum sensing details are recorded in a blockchain after exchanging bids for spectrum access and performing proper verifications. In order to motivate the SUs to perform mining tasks, SUs who participate in the cooperative spectrum sensing will be rewarded with tokens that can be later utilized to bid for the spectrum access.

As already pointed out, when blockchains are enabled in the dynamic spectrum access, it is observed an increase of the power consumption as a major cost to achieve a higher throughput of CR networks. To further analyze this cost, a metric called sensing-mining energy efficiency is introduced in (Weiss et al., 2019) which measures the average transmission rate per unit of energy consumption used for sensing and mining. According to the obtained simulation results, it is observed that the sensing-mining energy efficiency does not grow monotonically with the increase of the sensing probability of SUs. Indeed, an optimal value of sensing probability corresponding to a given maximum energy efficiency can be noticed. Therefore, blockchain-enabled CRNs need to configure spectrum sensing related parameters of CRs without causing higher cost in terms of power consumption.

Deep Reinforcement Learning in CR-based Blockchain Networks

Different from the previously discussed research work, (Luong et al., 2019) proposes a deep reinforcement learning approach to derive an optimal transaction transmission policy for the secondary users in a CR-based blockchain network. Due to the lack of transparency and traceability as well as the limited security, traditional ways of maintaining IoT data in a CRN will not help to achieve 5G level service requirements. Therefore, to avoid those drawbacks, (Luong et al., 2019) adopts blockchain technology for collecting, storing, and processing the sensing data from the SUs. However, in order to make optimal decisions, only blockchain enabled secure mechanisms may not be sufficient. Consequently, the authors proposed a deep neural network (DNN) and Q-learning based machine learning approach to take optimal transmission decisions and channel selection.

In the proposed network model, an SU selects required channels and sends a transaction message which contains sensing data of the SU and a transaction fee that the SU is willing to pay to the blockchain mining pool via a base station. On the other hand, the adopted reinforcement learning method learns the environment with the objective of maximizing the number of successful transaction transmissions and minimizing the channel cost and the transaction fee. Furthermore, considering more practical situations, (Luong et al., 2019) does not completely neglect double-spending attacks in which transactions in a block can be maliciously modified during the transmission. During the performance evaluation, it can be noticed that the proposed machine learning approach enables the SU to achieve the higher number of successful transaction transmissions under a lower cost.

CRNs are susceptible for different kinds of threats and security problems that will affect the performance of the network. With blockchain technology, new security practices can be realized in the management of this CR spectrum. The goal of this section is to investigate the utility of blockchain in CRNs by referring to recently performed research work. A summary of the above discussed blockchain-based security practices in CRNs is listed in Table 5.

Table 5. Blockchain-based security practices in CRNs

Applicable Layer in CRNs	Reference	Blockchain Based Security Practices	Preventable Security Threats/ Attacks
MAC	(Weiss et al., 2019)	Eliminate the need for trusted third party for spectrum sensing	Tampering of sensing data
MAC, Network	(Kotobi & Bilen, 2018)	Blocking the access for malicious users to the network	Single-point attacks
Application, Network	(Rathee et al., 2020)	Secure data sharing process among each other and validate the legitimacy of new users	Denial-of service (DoS) attack, False report generation, Malicious nodes identification
Application, MAC	(Luong et al., 2019)	Enhance the security and guarantees the data integrity	Double-spending attack is analyzed, however, did not overcome completely

Blockchain Advances and Security Practices in DTNs

R.H. Memon et al. has proposed a blockchain-based DualFog-IoT architecture which segregates the Fog layer as Fog Cloud Cluster and Fog Mining Cluster. In here, the Fog Cloud Cluster entertain real-time and non real-time application requests similar to existing IoT architecture whereas Fog Mining Cluster is dedicated to perform the mining operations and to maintain the distributed ledger for delay tolerant blockchain application requests as shown in Figure 9.

Figure 9. Model for DualFog-IoT architecture

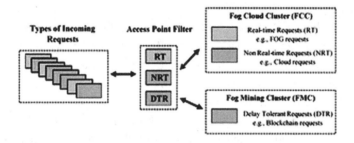

In machine-to-machine (M2M) communication, machine-type communication Devices (MTDs) are connected and communicated without any human intervention. Therefore, applications such as intelligent meters, environmental monitoring and e-health systems can allow relatively longer delays in data traffic. As an example, deploying smart meters may require data uploads or downloads that happen periodically. However, since the MTDs are equipped with limited battery power, data computing tasks cannot be cached, processed and executed solely on the local devices. Therefore, the best option to offload some of the storage and computation requirements at the edge of the network. On the other hand, security and reliability is also a prime concern for sensitive data of MTDs. Meng Li et al has proposed a joint optimization framework to make optimal decisions about caching servers and computing servers as well as to ensure the security in M2M communication networks based on dueling deep Q-network (Li,et al., 2020).

Blockchain Advances and Security Practices in OPPNETs

Normally, the mobile IoT oppnets are frequently suffer from to bandwidth and latency issues in cloud computing mainly due to poor wireless connectivity between the device and cloud. Rather than depending solely on centralized cloud platforms, it is vital to seek solutions that is plausible execute same network operations or services closer to the devices. Referring to that, an opportunistic collaborative mobile IoT design has been proposed in (Chamarajnagar & Ashok, 2018), to provide distributed computing solutions at the edge of the mobile IoT network using the blockchain framework. Similar to the previous work, in order to meet the stringent latency and bandwidth requirements of next-generation mobile networks, Fog-based Radio Access Network (F-RAN) has been proposed in (Jijin, Seet, & Joo Chong, 2019). However, this is not entirely identical to conventional F-RAN and virtual Fog Access Points (v-FAP) or service nodes formed dynamically with devices placed at the local edge are monitored by pre-defined physical or seed nodes. The integrations of Opportunistic Fog RAN (OF-RAN) with blockchain smart contracts guarantees the verifiable automation of physical processes at edge nodes.

FUTURE RESEARCH DIRECTIONS

It is evident that state-of-the art of blockchain technologies have made a huge impact to enhance the security in field such as healthcare, logistics, smart cities or energy management. However, these blockchain based IoT settings demand numerous technical requirements that differ from implementation of crypto-currencies to different aspects like energy efficiency of resource-constrained hardware or the need for specific architectures. Hence, it still needs to discover innovative research directions regarding seamless authentication, data privacy, easy deployment and self-maintenance along with safeguarding blockchain based networks against security attacks as stated below.

- **Data Management and Privacy, and Security Solutions:** The traditional online payments are usually visible to only transacting parties and to a distributor. But, since all transactions are shared by users in blockchain technique, it needs to ensure the privacy of transactions while nurturing the transparency.
- **Energy Efficiency:** Generally, blockchain based transactions use power-hungry mining processes and request more power requirement to setup point-to-point (P2P) links among edge devices. Therefore, ensuring the energy efficiency in blockchain based applications are utterly important characteristic.
- **Multi-chain Management:** The possibility of dealing multiple networks simultaneously would enable to provide more flexibility in network management.
- **Sustainability of the Blockchain Protocols:** More and more protocol suits are requisite to attract the claims of diverse applications by optimizing the throughput and latency of blockchain networks while regulating the blockchain size, bandwidth and infrastructure required.
- **Big Data and Artificial Intelligence:** The adaptation of artificial intelligence solutions backed by blockchain can be used to exploit smart contracts as well as routing autonomous drones for allowing real-time implementations.

CONCLUSION

Modern and future communication networks will grow up to billions of interactions among machines and sensors. Moreover, future wireless networks are becoming increasingly heterogeneous and complicated due to a growing need for ubiquitous access for various data sources, which is enabled by advances in modern technologies. Since those networks highly utilize the existing wireless sensor technologies, inherently it remains exposed to privacy as well as security threats. Wireless nodes in SDNs, WSNs as well as CRNs characteristically are considered to be prone to attacks such as distributed denial-of-service. Moreover, intelligent wireless nodes in those networks are mostly controlled on cloud environments. Such centralized architecture also undergoes single point of failure and further adds to vulnerability.

However, prevention of the drawbacks associated with security, privacy and vulnerability aspects has become one of the main challenges for those networks. This chapter explores existing studies which discuss how to add blockchains to distributed systems implemented in SDNs, WSNs and CRNs which can make network operations more secure, autonomous, flexible, and profitable. Blockchain provides those networks security, anonymity, and data integrity without the involvement of a third party.

In addition, blockchain applications over delay tolerant and opportunistic mobile networks are also discussed in brief. The research works presented in this chapter show that blockchain can serve as a method to log data in a form highly resistant to tampering and as a way to combat the introduction of malicious users into SDN, WSN and CRN networks.

REFERENCES

Ali, S., Wang, G., Bhuiyan, M. Z. A., & Jiang, H. (2018). Secure data provenance in cloud-centric internet of things via blockchain smart con-tracts. In 2018 IEEE Smart-world, Ubiquitous Intelligence Computing, Advanced Trusted Computing, Scalable Computing Communications, Cloud Big Data Computing, Internet of People and Smart City Innovation (smart-world/scalcom/uic/atc/cbdcom/iop/sci) (pp. 991-998). Academic Press.

Aujla, G. S., Singh, M., Bose, A., Kumar, N., Han, G., & Buyya, R. (2020). BlockSDN: Blockchain-as-a-service for software defined networking in smart city applications. *IEEE Network*, *34*(2), 83–91. doi:10.1109/MNET.001.1900151

Chamarajnagar, R., & Ashok, A. (2018). Opportunistic mobile Iot with blockchain based collaboration. In *2018 IEEE Global Communications Conference* (pp. 1-6). 10.1109/GLOCOM.2018.8647756

Chowdhury, M., Kader, M. F., & Asaduzzaman, A. (2013). Security issues in wireless sensor networks: A survey. *International Journal of Future Generation Communication and Networking*, *6*(5), 97–116. doi:10.14257/ijfgcn.2013.6.5.10

Cui, Z., Xue, F., Zhang, S., Cai, X., Cao, Y., Zhang, W., & Chen, J. (2020). A hybrid blockchain-based identity authentication scheme for multi-WSN. *IEEE Transactions on Services Computing*, *13*(2), 241–251. doi:10.1109/TSC.2020.2964537

Faizullah, S., Khan, M. A., Alzahrani, A., & Khan, I. (2020). *Permissioned blockchain-based security for SDN in IoT cloud networks.* arXiv preprint arXiv:2002.00456.

Feghali, A., Kilany, R., & Chamoun, M. (2015). SDN security problems and solutions analysis. In *2015 International Conference on Protocol Engineering and New Technologies of Distributed Systems* (pp. 1-5). Academic Press.

Gao, J., Agyekum, K. O.-B. O., Sifah, E. B., Acheampong, K. N., Xia, Q., Du, X., & Xia, H. (2019). A blockchain-SDN-enabled Internet of vehicles environment for fog computing and 5G networks. *IEEE Internet of Things Journal*, *7*(5), 4278–4291. doi:10.1109/JIOT.2019.2956241

Gómez-Arevalillo, A. de la R., & Papadimitratos, P. (2017). Blockchain-based Public Key Infrastructure for Inter-Domain Secure Routing. In *International Workshop on Open Problems in Network Security* (pp. 20-38). Academic Press.

Haseeb, K., Islam, N., Almogren, A., & Ud Din, I. (2019). Intrusion prevention framework for secure routing in wsn-based mobile internet of things. *IEEE Access: Practical Innovations, Open Solutions*, 7, 185496–185505. doi:10.1109/ACCESS.2019.2960633

Hindia, M. N., Qamar, F., Ojukwu, H., Dimyati, K., Al-Samman, A. M., & Amiri, I. S. (2020). On platform to enable the cognitive radio over 5G networks. *Wireless Personal Communications*, 113(2), 1241–1262. doi:10.100711277-020-07277-3

Jaballah, W. B., Conti, M., & Lal, C. (2019). *A survey on software-defined vanets: benets, challenges, and future directions.* arXiv preprint arXiv:1904.04577.

Jiasi, W., Jian, W., Jia-Nan, L., & Yue, Z. (2019). *Secure software-defined networking based on blockchain.* arXiv preprint arXiv:1906.04342.

Jijin, J., Seet, B., & Joo Chong, P. H. (2019). Blockchain enabled opportunistic fog-based radio access network: A position paper. In *2019 29th International Telecommunication Networks and Applications Conference* (pp. 1-3). Academic Press.

Kim, T., Goyat, R., Rai, M. K., Kumar, G., Buchanan, W. J., Saha, R., & Thomas, R. (2019). A novel trust evaluation process for secure localization16 using a decentralized blockchain in wireless sensor networks. *IEEE Access: Practical Innovations, Open Solutions*, 7, 184133–184144. doi:10.1109/ACCESS.2019.2960609

Kotobi, K., & Bilen, S. G. (2018). Secure blockchains for dynamic spectrum access: A decentralized database in moving cognitive radio networks enhances security and user access. *IEEE Vehicular Technology Magazine*, 13(1), 32–39. doi:10.1109/MVT.2017.2740458

Kreutz, D., Ramos, F. M., & Verissimo, P. (2013). Towards secure and dependable software-defined networks. In *2nd ACM SIGCOMM Workshop on Hot Topics in Software Defined Networking* (pp. 55-60). 10.1145/2491185.2491199

Kumar, R., Hasan, M., Padhy, S., Evchenko, K., Piramanayagam, L., Mohan, S., & Bobba, R. B. (2017). End-to-end network delay guarantees for real-time systems using SDN. In *2017 EEE Real-Time Systems Symposium* (pp. 231-242). 10.1109/RTSS.2017.00029

Li, M., Yu, F. R., Si, P., Wu, W., & Zhang, Y. (2020). Resource optimization for delay-tolerant data in blockchain-enabled iot with edge computing: A deep reinforcement learning approach. *IEEE Internet of Things Journal*, 7(10), 9399–9412. doi:10.1109/JIOT.2020.3007869

Liu, S., Reiter, M. K., & Sekar, V. (2017). Flow reconnaissance via timing attacks on SDN switches. In *2017 IEEE 37th International Conference on Distributed Computing Systems* (pp. 196-206). 10.1109/ICDCS.2017.281

Liyanage, M., Ylianttila, M., & Gurtov, A. (2016). *Improving the tunnel management performance of secure VPLS architectures with SDN. 2016 13th IEEE Annual Consumer Communications & Networking Conference.*

Luong, N. C., Anh, T. T., Binh, H. T. T., Niyato, D., Kim, D. I., & Liang, Y.-C. (2019). Joint transaction transmission and channel selection in cognitive radio based blockchain networks: A deep reinforcement learning approach. In *IEEE International Conference on Acoustics, Speech and Signal Processing* (pp. 8409-8413). 10.1109/ICASSP.2019.8683228

Memon, R. A., Li, J. P., Nazeer, M. I., Khan, A. N., & Ahmed, J. (2019). Dualfog-Iot: Additional fog layer for solving blockchain integration prob-lem in Internet of things. *IEEE Access: Practical Innovations, Open Solutions*, 7, 169073–169093. doi:10.1109/ACCESS.2019.2952472

Munsub Ali, H., Liu, J., & Ejaz, W. (2020). Planning capacity for 5G and beyond wireless networks by discrete fireworks algorithm with ensemble of local search methods. *EURASIP Journal on Wireless Communications and Networking*, 185, 1–24.

Nanthini, S. B., Hemalatha, M., Manivannan, D., & Devasena, L. (2014). Attacks in cognitive radio networks (CRN) - a survey. *Indian Journal of Science and Technology*, 7(4), 530–536. doi:10.17485/ijst/2014/v7i4.18

Ramezan, G., & Leung, C. (2018). A Blockchain-Based Contractual Routing Protocol for the Internet of Things Using Smart Contracts. *Wireless Communications and Mobile Computing*, 4029591, 1–14. Advance online publication. doi:10.1155/2018/4029591

Rathee, G., Ahmad, F., Kurugollu, F., Azad, M. A., Iqbal, R., & Imran, M. (2020). *CRT-BIoV: A cognitive radio technique for blockchain-enabled Internet of vehicles. IEEE Transactions on Intelligent Transportation Systems*.

Sharma, P. K., Singh, S., Jeong, Y.-S., & Park, J. H. (2017). Distblocknet: A distributed blockchains-based secure SDN architecture for IoT networks. *IEEE Communications Magazine*, 55(9), 78–85. doi:10.1109/MCOM.2017.1700041

She, W., Liu, Q., Tian, Z., Chen, J., Wang, B., & Liu, W. (2019). Blockchaintrust model for malicious node detection in wireless sensor networks. *IEEE Access: Practical Innovations, Open Solutions*, 7, 38947–38956. doi:10.1109/ACCESS.2019.2902811

Steichen, M., Hommes, S., & State, R. (2017, September). ChainGuard—A firewall for blockchain applications using SDN with OpenFlow. In 2017 Principles. Systems and Applications of IP Telecommunications. Academic Press.

Tiberti, W., Carmenini, A., Pomante, L., & Cassioli, D. (2020). A light weight blockchain-based technique for anti-tampering in wireless sensor networks. In *2020 23rd Euromicro Conference on Digital System Design* (pp. 577-582). Academic Press.

Tselios, C., Politis, I., & Kotsopoulos, S. (2017). Enhancing SDN security for IoT-related deployments through blockchain. In *2017 IEEE Conference on Network Function Virtualization and Software Defined Networks* (pp. 303-308). 10.1109/NFV-SDN.2017.8169860

Weiss, M. B. H., Werbach, K., Sicker, D. C., & Bastidas, C. E. C. (2019). On the application of blockchains to spectrum management. *IEEE Transactions on Cognitive Communications and Networking*, 5(2), 193–205. doi:10.1109/TCCN.2019.2914052

Werbach, K. (Ed.). (2018). *The blockchain and the new architecture of trust*. MIT Press. doi:10.7551/mitpress/11449.001.0001

Xu, C., Wang, K., Li, P., Guo, S., Luo, J., Ye, B., & Guo, M. (2019). Making big data open in edges: A resource-efficient blockchain-based approach. *IEEE Transactions on Parallel and Distributed Systems*, *30*(4), 870–882. doi:10.1109/TPDS.2018.2871449

Yang, J., He, S., Xu, Y., Chen, L., & Ren, J. (2019). A Trusted Routing Scheme Using Blockchain and Reinforcement Learning for Wireless Sensor Networks. *Sensors (Basel)*, *19*(4), 970. doi:10.339019040970 PMID:30823560

Yazdinejad, A., Parizi, R. M., Dehghantanha, A., & Choo, K.-K. R. (2019). Blockchain-enabled authentication handover with ecient privacy protection in SDN-based 5G networks. *IEEE Transactions on Network Science and Engineering*.

Zeng, Y., Zhang, X., Akhtar, R., & Wang, C. (2018). A blockchain-based scheme for secure data provenance in wireless sensor networks. In *2018 14th International Conference on Mobile Ad-hoc and Sensor Networks* (pp. 13-18). 10.1109/MSN.2018.00009

Zia, T., & Zomaya, A. (2006, October). Security issues in wireless sensor networks. In *2006 International Conference on Systems and Networks Communications (ICSNC'06)* (pp. 40-40). 10.1109/ICSNC.2006.66

ADDITIONAL READING

Banerjee, M., Lee, J., & Choo, K.-K. R. (2018). A blockchain future for internet of things security: A position paper. *Digital Communications and Networks*, *4*(3), 149–160. doi:10.1016/j.dcan.2017.10.006

Casino, F., Dasaklis, T. K., & Patsakis, C. (2019). A systematic literature review of blockchain-based applications: Current status, classification and open issues. *Telematics and Informatics*, *36*, 55–81. doi:10.1016/j.tele.2018.11.006

Chanson, M., Bogner, A., Bilgeri, D., Fleisch, E., & Wortmann, F. (2019). Blockchain for the IoT: Privacy-preserving protection of sensor data. *Journal of the Association for Information Systems*, *20*(9), 1274–1309. doi:10.17705/1jais.00567

Dai, H., Zheng, Z., & Zhang, Y. (2019). Blockchain for internet of things: A survey. *IEEE Internet of Things Journal*, *6*(5), 8076–8094. doi:10.1109/JIOT.2019.2920987

Jiasi, W., Jian, W., Jia-Nan, L., & Yue, Z. (2019). Secure software-defined networking based on blockchain.

Minoli, D., & Occhiogrosso, B. (2018). Blockchain mechanisms for IoT security. *Internet of Things*, *1-2*, 1–13. doi:10.1016/j.iot.2018.05.002

Mohsin, A., Zaidan, A., Zaidan, B., Albahri, O., Albahri, A., Alsalem, M., & Mohammed, K. (2019). Blockchain authentication of network applications: Taxonomy, classification, capabilities, open challenges, motivations, recommendations and future directions. *Computer Standards & Interfaces*, *64*, 41–60. doi:10.1016/j.csi.2018.12.002

Raju, S., Boddepalli, S., Gampa, S., Yan, Q., & Deogun, J. S. (2017). Identity management using blockchain for cognitive cellular networks. *In 2017 IEEE International Conference on Communications* (p. 1-6) 10.1109/ICC.2017.7996830

KEY TERMS AND DEFINITIONS

Consensus Mechanism: An agreement in relation to a single data value made by all members in a group of a blockchain based system such as with crypto-currencies.

Crypto-Currency: This a digital currency which is used to acquire services through online. Therfore, a decentralized ledger is used to verify and execute online transactions securely.

Data Provenance: A piece of metadata or records that can be used to trace the validity of source data including all transition steps from the origin to the current location.

Fog Computing: This enables computing functions at the edge of network or closer to the source of data, as a result, it allows to get rid of the necessity for cloud based storing requirement.

Reinforcement Learning: An area of Machine learning used by software agents to maximize or determine the best possible solution based on cumulative reward in a specific environment.

Software-Defined Networking: This a centralized controller that enables the management of network functions using software applications by separating the control plane by the data plane.

Spectrum Sensing: A periodic monitoring process regarding a specific frequency band to determine whether to identify status of the presence or absence of primary users.

Chapter 55
Advanced Cyber Security and Internet of Things for Digital Transformations of the Indian Healthcare Sector

Jonika Lamba
The NorthCap University, Gurugram, India

Esha Jain
https://orcid.org/0000-0002-0152-8566
The NorthCap University, Gurugram, India

ABSTRACT

Cybersecurity is not just about fortification of data. It has wide implications such as maintaining safety, privacy, integrity, and trust of the patients in the healthcare sector. This study methodically reviews the need for cybersecurity amid digital transformation with the help of emerging technologies and focuses on the application and incorporation of blockchain and the internet of things (IoT) to ensure cybersecurity in the well-being of the business. It was found in the study that worldwide, advanced technology has been used in managing the flow of data and information, India should focus on maintaining the same IT-enabled infrastructure to reduce causalities in the nation and on the other hand improve administration, privacy, and security in the hospital sector. Depending on the network system, resource allocation, and mobile devices, there is a need to prioritize the resources and efforts in the era of digitalization.

INTRODUCTION

As per available reports spending of the Indian government on healthcare is estimated to be 1.5% of the total GDP which is low as far as the population of the nation is considered. The spending of the government in the healthcare sector is too low in comparison to other nations. The healthcare sector theaters a pivotal part in the accomplishment and prosperity of a nation, so the government should devote

DOI: 10.4018/978-1-6684-7132-6.ch055

considerable resources to the upliftment of the living conditions of people. The government has taken various steps to improve the present condition of the healthcare sector by framing policies such as the National Health Policy 2017 focused on plummeting infant mortality rate and providing access to good quality healthcare services to the people of the nation. The current situation in the country is alarming and the COVID-19 pandemic had forced nations to rethink the present health care infrastructure as the government alone will not be able to cope up with the present situation (Jain & Lamba, 2020). It need support from the big industrialists to fasten the process of developing the infrastructure for the COVID-19 patients. The time has come where a nation can sustain only based on investment in the well-being care sector due to drastic changes in the environment, pollution level, and modern living habits. The well-being care sector is one of the most important pillars of the Indian economy as it supports the rest of the sectors in smooth functioning.

A healthy nation will be able to face any pandemic and will emerge out of being a winner in the period of disguise. The health care sector is one of the most important pillars of the Indian economy as it supports the rest of the sectors in smooth functioning. A healthy nation will be able to face any pandemic and will emerge out of being a winner in the period of disguise. With the advancement in information and technology, every sector has get influenced to some extent. The need for data management and organization has paved the way for evolving know-hows such as Blockchain and the Internet of Things (IoT) (Miraz et al., 2020; Aich et al., 2019). Blockchain is the technology that integrates healthcare and data. The distinguishing features of blockchain such as transparency, data attribution, accurate and reliable reporting and data analytics help in resolving rigorous data management issues in clinical trials (Omar et al., 2020; Rathee, 2020; Fekih & Lahami, 2020; Fekih et al., 2020). The healthcare sector shown tremendous improvement such as patient retention, data integrity, privacy and regulatory compliances due to adoption of blockchain advanced application. The peculiarities of advanced technology such as Blockchain and how it improved the operations in the healthcare domain with the assistance of its key features and innovative applications. The major risks and opportunities related to technology adoption have also been discussed in the study.

The impact of COVID 19 on the economy of different countries has been studied and it was analyzed that COVID 19 had seriously impacted the healthcare sector (Attia et al. 2019; McGhin et al., 2019; Epiphaniou et al. 2019; Hasselgren et al., 2020). The use of advanced tools and applications such as Artificial Intelligence (AI), Internet of Things (IoT), Unmanned Aerial Vehicles (UAVs) and Blockchain etc., helps in reducing the influence of contagion on the environment (Chamola et al., 2020).

The Healthcare sector is the most important domain of a nation's prosperity. Data and health integration can solve many difficult problems in the healthcare sector. It facilitates exchange and dealings in the database that can be shared across authorized operators. It is peer-to-peer disseminated ledger know-how. It consists of majorly three components which are namely distributed network, shared record, and digital transaction. Blockchain technology ensures that no one can change any information or record and that can be done with the permission of all authorized operators in the system. Blockchain is the most used technology to assemble scattered data and at the critical time, it serves its purpose at best (Abdellatif et al., 2020; Ray et al., 2020). This technology has brought many changes in the well-being sector and in the way, data is managed in the hospital industry. The availability of crucial data at the right point in time has saved many lives (Alladi et al., 2019). Looking at the outdated healthcare infrastructure, emerging technologies have raised the expectations from blockchain and the Internet of Things (Hussein et al., 2019). Emerging technologies such as the Internet of Things (IoT), blockchain, artificial intelligence, machine learning, and big data all together have brought a drastic change in data compilation and management (Abdullah & Jones, 2019). These technologies help in maintaining the confidentiality of patients and provide access to a secure platform for the exchange of information. Step by step implementation of these evolving technologies will brighten the future of the healthcare sector in the long run. Maintaining the privacy of patients and the exchange of transactions between hospitals lead to the proper treatment of patients with less time frame. This helps in the organization of patients' records such as their chronicles related to laboratory tests, patient history of ailment, surgery records, medicine ledger, disease registries, and lab results, etc. With the help of master keys patients, records can be grasped in a quick manner that will facilitate the management of data on the other hand. Blockchain technology has the budding to renovate the hospital sector and bring revolutionary changes which will be beneficial for both patients and hospitals. Though it is quite costly to integrate with the existing infrastructure it is expected that its benefits will outweigh outlays in the extended run. It will also have a promising future in supply change management and claim settlement. Evolving technologies such as big data, the internet of things (IoT), blockchain, and machine learning will together have the potential to bring digital transformation in every sphere of the healthcare industry. Blockchain technology can renovate medical trials, SCM, remedy supply administration, and avert frauds in the healthcare business (Kumar & Mallick, 2018; Akram et al., 2020).

REVIEW OF LITERATURE

Martin et al. (2017) stated that digital transformation in the healthcare sector has huge potential for improving the level of services for the patients. The cyber security threats such as ransomware highlighted the significance of the cyber security to ensure safety of patient records. Due to the inherent limitations of healthcare sector, this sector encounters the largest cyber risk in its security position. The healthcare sector is the soft and easy target for the attackers due to loopholes in its security mechanism and it offers plenty of valuable data.

Pilkington (2017) examined the requirement of distributed ledger technology in the hospital and medicine segment after encountering the problems with private and public enterprises for retrieving data related to patients. The distributed ledger technology has acknowledged the remarkable role for the organization and compilation of electronic health records (Bell et al., 2018). The study aroused the fast-mounting demand for medical equipment by the consumers and figure out the role of public-private relationships for designing blockchain technologies for the health care sector.

Rose (2017) stated that online medicine ordering i.e., telemedicine is not a new concept in the nation but the outburst of COVID 19 has made this mobile health concept very much popular. The concept of mhealth has led to wider integration of hospitals and patients and resulted in wider reach and participation (Celesti et al., 2020). The chapter focused on the alarming usage of electronic media and health apps in the period of novel coronavirus which will help to overcome the fear of infection due to physical interaction between people (Kalla et al., 2020; Ahmad et al., 2021). The study explored the upsurge in the concept of mhealth and what are its developments, and what kind of opportunities are being offered by this emerging concept in the medical industry. The challenges and threats posed by this concept were also covered by the study.

Teoh & Mahmood (2017) stated that the digital economy is possible with the help of cyber security. The cyber space is becoming very challenging and there are new advancements with each passing day. This calls for the enactment of National cybersecurity strategy (NCSS) to protect the digital economy in the phase of drastic online transformation (Brunetti et al., 2020). The adoption of NCSS is not mandatory but it will help in continuous growth and prosperity in the online world.

Rabah (2018) said that data is the new blood in the economy. Data management is required in every field whether it is healthcare, manufacturing, retail, food, transport, service, operational and agriculture, etc. and demand for professionals in big data is also increasing day by day. It played a crucial role in identifying the needs of consumers and supplying requisite goods at the best price to remain ahead of their competitors. Developing knowledges such as the, blockchain, artificial intelligence, Internet of Things (IoT), machine learning, and big data all together have brought a drastic change in data compilation and management. This will lead to a promising industrial revolution. The study focused on the implementation of evolving technology in healthcare and any other domains it answered many questions related to the application of technology in the fast-changing era of digitalization. Data is the basis of evolving artificial intelligence and helps in the growth of every sector of the economy.

Attia et al. (2019) focused on security architecture in the field of IoT and blockchain for reviewing the healthcare applications. Various appropriate examples have been used to validate this framework at design level. In advanced technology framework, devices are connected and information needs to be placed in a highly secure environment.

Abraham et al. (2019) examined that Healthcare sector is most vulnerable to cyber security. The cyber risk due to malware, ransomware, hacking and phishing, etc,. pose serious threats in the operation of healthcare sector. The United States (US) healthcare domain found that due to excessive legality and discordant systems, application of cyber security has become difficult. The governance, securities laws, compliance regulations futher complicate the challenge of cyber security into the system.

Dai et al. (2019) dicussed about the opportunities and challenges of IoT in the technology driven environment. There are number of loopholes noticed in the IoT applications such as privacy, security, decentralization and deprived interoperability. The study also discussed how blockchain adoption helped in overcoming the challenges caused by IoT.

Epiphaniou et al. (2019) explored the peculiarities of advanced technology such as Blockchain and how it improved the operations in the healthcare domain with the assistance of its key features and innovative applications. The major risks and opportunities related to technology adoption have also been discussed in the study.

Meske et al. (2019) examined the possibilities of online shoving in medical clinics and reasoned that computerized poking in medical clinics can decidedly impact the utilization of innovation, new worth creation, the difference in structures, and subsequently monetary elements of advanced change, supporting guardians as well as overseers.

Ricciardi et al. (2019) found that the influence of the digitalization process has been thoughtful, and it is projected to be more thoughtful in nearby future (Jain & Lamba, 2021). The study evaluated whether health care services contributed in a significant manner to the goals of health care processes and systems. Optimally decision should be taken at which level digital services should be introduced based on the evidence from the medical industry.

Alam (2020) emphasized how blockchain can be fruitful in the mobile health (mhealth) of patients. Patients nowadays are more knowledgeable and need to know all information related to their health on a real-time basis and this would empower them. The blockchain phenomena will boost mobile health and its applications and usage. The combination of the Internet of Things (IoT) and blockchain will provide a unique identification number to the connected device in the framework including mobile and medical devices. This will be helpful for the patients to monitor their health and reduce the cost of physically visiting the hospitals. In a nutshell, the adoption of emerging advancements in the field of technology will provide relief and comfort to effectively monitor patient's health problems and it will also benefit the doctors and hospital staff to perform their duties while maintaining integrity in the system.

Chamola et al. (2020) inspected the impression of COVID 19 on the budget of diverse countries and it also analyzed that COVID 19 had seriously impacted the healthcare sector. The use of advanced tools and applications such as, Internet of Things (IoT), Unmanned Aerial Vehicles (UAVs), Artificial Intelligence (AI) and Distributed expertise etc., helps in reducing the influence of pandemic on the economy.

El-Gazzar & Stendal (2020) studied the advantages and challenges faced by the health care sector with the application of blockchain technology and how the innovation in the information and technology sector enhanced the exchange of patient-sensitive data and empowered the patients and found that adoption of this distributed ledger technology may raise the problems of the health care sector instead of solving them. It was found that there is a requirement of using more cases to understand the sharing of information with the health care domain (Khezr et al., 2019).

Fekih & Lahami (2020) examined that blockchain technology applications in the medicine and well-being domain. The research in this sector is emerging rapidly. The advanced technology is used for patient monitoring, reviewing drug supply chain and sharing the electronic medicinal histories. The study also focused on the limitations of blockchain also.

Mathy et al. (2020) studied the influence of digitalization on the supply chain of the hospital industry. The digitalization of the supply chain had raised concerns for decision-makers in the healthcare sector. These are usually valued with techniques such as return on investments, Health technology assessments (HTA), etc. The introduction of ADS (automated dispensing system) in French hospital central pharmacy with a posteriori evaluation from the opinion of hospitals. It has led to hidden cost assuagement which does not generate any cash flow i.e., financial flow and it has not been valued. When they are given weightage, the results changed dramatically, as the profitability changes from negative to positive. Importance should be given to these hidden costs and gains as they had a drastic impact on the evaluation of the organization's impact.

Moro Visconti & Morea (2020) explored the influence of making digital the smart hospital project financing (PF) promoted by pay-for-performance (P4P) inducements. Electronic stages facilitate the exchange of information between different agents. Submission to healthcare public-private firms (PPPs) has importantly led to the steadiness of electronic stages with the well-being problems and the intricacy of the shareholder's interface. Digital savings can be very useful for all the stakeholders and it has proved beneficial in the digitalization of supply chains and is significantly contributing towards a patient-centric approach. Digitalization of the medicine sector will be beneficial for surveillance of infectious disease, supplement massive healthcare intervention, provide timely and accurate data, and helps in the decongestion of hospitals during the COVID 19 period.

Omar et al. (2020) explored the prospects in the well-being domain wide the applications of Blockchain technology. The distinguishing features of blockchain such as transparency, data attribution, accurate and reliable reporting and data analytics help in resolving rigorous data management issues in clinical trials. The healthcare sector shown tremendous improvement such as patient retention, data integrity, privacy and regulatory compliances due to adoption of blockchain advanced application.

Ratthe (2020) discussed about the wide applications of IoT such as healthcare, agriculture, public safety, smart phones and smart homes. The IoT is now considered as IoE "Internet of Everything". It has undertaken a drastic revolution in the field of advanced technology. It has a promising future ahead.

Singh & Singh (2020) studied the integration of blockchain and the Internet of Things (IoT) in the agriculture and healthcare sector predominantly. With emerging advancements and innovations these technologies will transform the food and healthcare industry (Kumar et al., 2018). It was discovered that 20% of papers are accessible in agriculture and 14% obtainable in the hospital sector that integrated blockchain with AI and IoT. It will help in managing healthcare and nutrition stock chain administration (Farouk et al., 2020).

Srivastava et al. (2020) The technology of the Internet of Things (IoT) has increased the usage of blockchain applications in the well-being sector. The aim is to reap maximum benefits from the request of blockchain in the well-being domain. The sphere of blockchain has reached many sectors besides the financial sector, the chapter focused on IoT applications specifically in the well-being sector by making use of distributed ledger expertise (Clauson et al., 2018). This is a challenging area of research as per today's scenario and the chapter dealt with positive attributes of this technology and what will be its future implications has been discussed in detail in the study. The author emphasized exploring this new horizon and IoT integration with the blockchain.

Tripathi et al. (2020) found that blockchain helped to overcome the failure of privacy and security-related issues. The study explored the technical and communal hurdles while adopting Smart Healthcare Systems (SRS) by exploring the views of experts and operators and observed the role of blockchain as the remarkable to facilitate the security and veracity of the system (Mistry et al., 2020).

Caldarelli et al. (2021) intended to inspect and overwhelmed the barricades to the extensive acceptance of blockchain technology and reinforced the impression that the blockchain explanation could be an appreciated add-on in maintainable supply chains. However, a high thoughtful knowledge of technology and widespread statement with patrons is obligatory for fruitful incorporation.

Foster et al (2021) stated the remarkable advancement in the field of technology and how it is going to decide the survival and growth in the wake of digitalization in the future. The technologies have been become agile such as blockchain, Machine learning, IoT, Virtual Reality have fostered the digital transactions in the country. These tools are going to decide the which sector will flourish in the 2021. Innovations and research in education industry are shaping the future of the nation.

Kamble et al. (2021) acknowledged intrant heaviness, companion willingness, apparent practicality, and seeming comfort of use as the most persuading aspects for blockchain acceptance.

Mathivathanan et al. (2021) recognized the espousal barricades and showed that the absence of commercial consciousness and acquaintance with distributed expertise on what it can deliver for upcoming supply chains, are the greatest powerful barricades that obstruct blockchain espousal. These barricades delay and influence trades choice to create a blockchain-enabled supply chain and that other barricades act as subordinate and related variable star in the implementation procedure.

Sharma & Joshi (2021) recognized barricades in the direction of the implementation of distributed technology in Indian hospital and well-being industry and recommended that low-slung consciousness linked to permissible subjects and little provision from upper level of organization have supreme pouring control.

OBJECTIVE OF THE STUDY

The aim of the study is as follows:

Primary Objectives

- To study the need for cyber-security amid digital transformation with the aid of emerging technologies.
- To study the application and combination of blockchain and the Internet of Things (IoT) for ensuring cyber-security in the healthcare industry.

Secondary Objectives

- To study the various innovations in the healthcare sector concerning technology adoption.
- To study the worldwide applications and developments of blockchain in the well-being domain.
- To study measures to mitigate cyber risk in wake of digitalization.

RESEARCH METHODOLOGY

This article methodically reviews the present literature published in peer-reviewed journals related to the application of blockchain and the Internet of Things (IoT) in the healthcare industry to overcome cyber risk in the period of digitalization. The information gathered in this study has been taken from authentic sources of secondary data collection including past studies. The study is a descriptive analysis of need for cyber-security amid digital transformation with the support of emerging technologies and the integration of blockchain and the Internet of Things (IoT) in the hospital sector and also throw some light on the worldwide applications of blockchain in the healthcare domain to ensure security and integrity in the phase of digital transformation.

USE OF DIGITAL TECHNOLOGY IN HEALTHCARE SECTOR

Technology has become the most important need of every sector. The technologies in the healthcare domain have wide applications from hospital administration applications to surgery and cancer research to eradicate the flaws in the system and make the patient experience with the hospital as pleasant as possible and improve overall efficacy in the well-being business (Jain, 2020).

Administrative

The use of IoT and blockchain has organized the administrative work in hospitals. The AI applications help in calculating the waiting time for a patient and also ask preliminary questions which makes it easier for the doctors and professionals to pact with patients in an operative manner. This has led to the more efficient and effective functioning of hospitals in the country.

Surgical Treatment

The use of machine learning, and robotics has been widely used in surgical procedures. During the COVID-19 period (Chamola et al., 2020) robotics has helped a lot in discharging services to patients and eradicate the chances of catching an infection. Robots are assisting doctors from minor surgeries to open-heart operations. Healthtech had a bright future ahead and the pandemic situation made the need for further advancement in the field of robotics. Augmented Reality (AR) is also helping doctors in explaining concepts to patients more clearly.

Medicine Development

Medicine and drug development is an important area of research and this has become all the way more vital due to the emergence of a pandemic. Healthcare and pharmaceutical companies are using artificial intelligence and paving new methods of drug development. It has simplified the process of drug development and reduce the period as well leading to the optimal drug. The patients and drug suitability can be checked via artificial intelligence.

Fitness

A healthy body is a must for keeping other things workable. There has been advancement in the number of applications that guide people on how to keep themselves healthy including wearables to keep a record of several steps in a day, sleep schedule measurement, weight reducing tips, etc.

Fault Reduction and Diagnostics

Early detection of disease can save millions of lives so the integration of Healthtech in the field of diagnosis is of paramount importance. Integration of technology in the field of genetics, pathology, diagnosis fields helped in the early detection of deadly diseases such as cancers and provided solutions with accuracy to treat can patients.

Psychological Well-Being

In today's era keeping your mind healthy is of paramount importance in one's life. Due to the continuously changing environment and increasing competition, it has become vital to pay attention to mental health. Disease such as depression, PTSD, Alzheimer's, etc. are arousing so there is a need to tackle these problems by inventing telemedicine apps where patients can access counselors online and exposure therapies can also be helpful to revive patients from depression.

APPLICATIONS OF DIGITAL TECNOLOGY IN THE HEALTHCARE SECTOR

- **Eradicating Centralization:** With the emergence of blockchain in technological advancement things changed drastically, earlier only authorized representatives had access to the repository of patient information but the introduction of blockchain led to decentralization where every user can access the information available on digital or cloud platform without any authorization and hurdles.
- **Enhanced data security and confidentiality:** The usage of blockchain leads to the removal of concerns related to data security and privacy concerns as they transform the exchange process,

now information is accessible in an encrypted format only which is difficult to decode. Moreover, the use of master and primary keys leads to the chronological arrangement of data and enhanced the security of patient records and details.

- **Control over patient records and ownership:** The patient's consent should be taken before using their treatment records. Using blockchain technology patients can monitor where data has been used and what are replications of that. The patients possess the ultimate control over their records and should not part on their privacy at any cost.

- **The atmosphere of Trust:** The step-by-step adoption of blockchain in the health care sector ensures the integrity of the system while sharing information. The uncluttered and see-through features of blockchain boost the trust and help various stakeholders of the health care sector in the implementation of numerous applications of data compilation, arrangement, retrieval, and management.

- **Claim Verification:** The use of blockchain in the healthcare domain has simplified the process of claim adjudication as it will make the process of verifying documents of patients much easier and reliable.

- **Data Accessibility:** The data stored on multiple nodes in the blockchain is easily available on the available to all the entitled users and their chances of data theft or loss are also minimal due to the security framework developed by blockchain and IoT technology and there will no corruption on part of data accessibility.

NEED FOR CYBERSECURITY IN PHASE OF DIGITAL TRANSFORMATION

The pace of digitalization in the market today calls for security issues as well, the emerging cyber-crimes such as hacking of websites, bank frauds, ATM card fraud, Call center fraud and Napster case etc., arose the fear of cyber threat in the business (Srivastava ct al., 2020). The benefits offered by digitalization are numerous but challenges also need to be addressed on an immediate basis. In data driven society security of information needs to be maintained, to secure trust of public in technology. Recently the data of Dominos company related to credit card information of customers have been leaked which possess the threat to personal information of the customers. The advanced research in cyber security is providing tools and mechanism to control the menace of digital frauds. There have been several laws enacted at national and international level to control the menace of frauds by technocrats. The advancement in the IT sector is commendable but it offers certain challenges and threats also. These applications include Augmented Reality (AR), Big Data, Blockchain, Robotics and Virtual Reality and many more. There is a need for controlling cyber risk by strict application of security measures in the system and appointment of Chief Information Security Officer to maintain the safety of dealings in the business. The malicious activities need to be curbed to better use the leading advancement in the information technology sector. It need to be focused that no digital transformation should be taken without understanding its security implications. The Healthcare sector is a data enrich sector which is more lucrative to cyber attackers to impede the security of the system.

CYBER SECURITY ROADMAP

- **Consider Cyber Security Risk:** Recognize core and assignment perilous roles and formulate an reservior of susceptible assets and allot a risk influence score to each susceptible asset.
- **Escalating cybersecurity risk and measures:** Evaluate the adverse consequences linked with diverse outbreak set-ups. Then estimate the outlay of suggested risk reduction measures such as prevention, recognition and retrieval and use of erudite analytics to guess the likelihood of adverse consequences and allied outlay.
- **Collaborating cybersecurity activities and results:** Upsurge transparency about cybersecurity strategy and measures. Adapt communications and attain a certain level of shared understanding and accord on inferences of cybersecurity events.

EMERGING MEDICAL DEVICES IN THE ERA OF DIGITALIZATION

The upsurge of digitization has taken over the world. All the evolving technologies like Cloud-based solutions, the Internet of Things (IoT) and Artificial Intelligence (AI), and many others are serving individuals animate a healthier and relaxed lifespan. The service division has been promoted a lot from digitization especially in the health care industry.

Patient-Generated Health Data (PGHD): It is a healthcare mobile application that provides information related to symptoms, lifestyle, the healing process, disease, treatment history, habits, and many more. It provides a critical analysis of the patient's disease history and helps in reducing the number of visits to a clinic.

Wearable Devices: Digital wearable devices always provide continuous nursing of health. It provides facilities such as quality of sleep, heart rate, steps walked, and more. They are widely used in the North American region.

Communication Channels: The recent developments in communication technology helps in keeping updated on all details related to their treatment such as instant messaging, emergency calls (SOS Signals), real-time video calls, and many more. By incorporating all these facilities in a mobile application companies are planning to offer real-time sustenance to patients in the time of need.

Geolocation: It is one of the distinguishing features of every mobile health application. It allows patients to locate nearby hospitals' addresses, clinics, and medical stores. It also has a provision in case of emergency when the patient is unable to locate his current location then he can make emergency calls. During the COVID 19 phase, it helps to locate COVID hot spots during the pandemic phase. It helps in fighting against the deadly virus. For instance, the government of the nation has developed an app named "Aarogya Setu" that uses geolocation and Bluetooth data to aware the users in the case of COVID 19 patients adjacent.

Contact Tracing: To combat the spread of this deadly virus infection and the practice of returning to a new world of normal requires the use of contact tracing. It helps in silent tracking of the COVID 19 patients and alerts the people promptly regarding any of their contacts who tested positive of this deadly disease.

Internet of Things (IoT): It has provided significant assistance in the era of digitalization; it helps in the collection of data from the connected devices and transmits it to the health care service provider. It can be vigilant for the doctors as they will be informed if anything wrong happens to a patient or any values crosses the threshold limits. The problem of depression has been well monitored by the usage of these technologies.

Cloud-based Solutions: EMR (Electronic Medical Records) have been integrated with EHR (Electronic Health Records) with cloud-based solutions that allow easy access to the patient treatment history, their recovery process, medical bills, insurance plans, and many more. With the emergence of cloud-based solutions and infrastructure, hospitals and healthcare companies promise to render better services at a relative lessor cost.

ELEMENTS OF ADVANCED BLOCKCHAIN TECHNOLOGY

- **Distributed Ledger Technology:** Blockchain is a record of all transactions in a peer-to-peer system. It is a dispersed ledger technology that ensures that everyone in the network has access to the information without any delay.
- **Encryption of Information:** The use of blockchain ensures that information is encrypted and leads to secure transfer of information. In short, it maintains the integrity and security of the data.
- **No need for Third Party:** All the authorized users in the system can directly share information amongst themselves that reduces the need for any third-party organization to authenticate the dealings.
- **Smart Contracts:** It permitted the agreement on additional business logic and automatic enforcement of the expected behavior of dealings or assets embodied in blockchain technology.

CYBER THREATS IN THE DIGITAL TRANSFORMATION OF HEALTHCARE SECTOR

- **Ransomware:** With the help of this malware the wrongdoers are trying to stop users from accessing their systems or data and even to delete their files unless a fees is paid to attackers.
- **Information theft for Impact:** Now a days there is common practice of stealing the data and information just for the sake of publicity stunts such as in case of high profile people, politicians and celebrities their health data is used for publicity purpose.
- **Stealing data for financial gains:** The attackers steal the information such personal information including names, address, credit card details, etc to use them for unethical monetary gains.
- **Denial of Service attacks:** It often used by attacker to cause disruption in the network by blocking the network with artificial requests, blackmail and activism.
- **Phishing:** It is a common fraud technique where a link is send over email and the victim by clicking on the link gives the way to intruder to access his/her system. Due to this victim faces huge financial loss.
- **Malevolent attacks:** These types of attacks can lead to complete or partial loss od data related to customers, accounts and financial dealings leading to serious regulatory desecrations.

WORLDWIDE ADVANCED TECHONLOGY APPLICATIONS IN HEALTHCARE SECTOR

Factom

It is widely used in information technology and enterprise system in Austin, Texas. It develops products that assist the healthcare sector to store data related to patients on the organization's blockchain that is available to hospital staff and operators only. Only authorized people can access the information stored in the Factom security chip. It laboring blockchain distributed technology for data handling and store information in a secured manner digitally.

Medicalchain

It is widely used in maintaining health records electronically and blockchain assists that only in London, England. It ensures the privacy of patients as outsiders cannot access the patient's confidential information and doctors, professionals and laboratories can access information from a record origin as well. With the help of blockchain, they can maintain the information from the origin and protect the confidentiality of patients.

Guardtime

It is used in cybersecurity in Irvine, California. It is being applied in the healthcare sector for cybersecurity applications. It is very much helpful for government and healthcare companies to integrate blockchain with cybersecurity applications.

Simplyvital Health

This company is using decentralized technology in the healthcare domain in Watertown, Massachusetts. It provides an open database where pertinent information is stored and made available to health care professionals for further research in the healthcare industry. Patients' information can be accessed in a time-effective manner and information can be shared for obtaining coordination.

Coral Health Research and Discovery

It employs blockchain to speed up the process of administration, care process and automate other health operations queries and improve the resulting information. It led to smart contracts between patients and professionals in the medical industry.

Robomed

This company does the task of gathering information related to patients with the help of AI and share the information gathered with healthcare benefactors. It is put up in Moscow, Russia, and used blockchain technology to securely access and share information with professionals and healthcare operators only.

Patientory

It focused on maintaining the confidentiality of patient's data in Atlanta. Georgia. It provided end-to-end encryption of data and information. All patient's information has been placed under one roof from where all doctors, professionals, surgeons can retrieve the information as per their requirement by employing blockchain technology.

RECENT DEVELOPMENTS IN BLOCKCHAIN TECHNOLOGY

- **Blockchain As a Service (BaaS):** This trend has been made famous more in 2020 as blockchain has been integrated with start-up ventures. The users can make their online products with the assistance of blockchain. These products can take the form of decentralized applications and smart contracts, all the more it offers services that don't require blockchain infrastructure. Companies such as Microsoft and Amazon making blockchain applications need of the hour to remain competitive.
- **Coalesced Blockchain Transfers to the Center Phase:** It is one of the latest and demanding trends in blockchain technology. The case used has been increased with the help of federated blockchain. It led to decentralization where diverse authorities can control nodes of blockchain. It has sped up the processing speed and will provide a more customized outlook.
- **High Demand of Stablecoins:** To stabilize the volatility in the cryptocurrencies blockchain stable coins will be in high demand in the year 2021.
- **Blockchain Networks:** These networks have fastened the process of exchange of data and sharing of information from one network to another integrated via blockchain.
- **Lucrative to Government Organizations:** Government agencies are required to monitor a huge volume of data, blockchain applications will reduce the burden of storage by providing a separate database for a specific activity. The adoption of distributed ledger technology will improve the functioning of government departments.
- **Blockchain integration with Artificial Intelligence:** The combination of blockchain and artificial intelligence can boost the machine learning concept and blockchain can make AI more understandable and comprehensive. It can trace why conclusions are reached in machine learning and enhance the application domain of emergent technology.

MEASURES TO MITIGATE CYBER RISK IN WAKE OF DIGITALIZATION

Depending on the nature of business, complexity of dealings and usage of network, the measures should the adopted to prevent cyber risk in light of digitalization in the economy.

- Identification of the risk at the initial phase helps in prevention of a big problem from originating. Depending on the network system, allocation of resources and mobile devices, there is a need to prioritize the resources and effort in wake of digitalization.

- The practice of restricting the permission to access the system is one of the common ways to mitigate cyber risk. Use of passwords and proper administration will help in achievement of cyber security in the system.
- Encryption devices makes sure that data that is private and confidential is not available to people outside the organization domain.
- Use of proper software and firewall applications serve the purpose of cyber security in digital transactions.
- Periodic monitoring of the system also helps in maintaining security of the system in the network and often ensure smooth functioning of the system as well. The information security manager should be alert all the time to ensure the integrity and trust in the system.
- A proper response strategy also helps in overcoming the severity of cyber-attacks. The strategy helps in fetching legal remedies and reduces the monetary impact of unwanted dealings in the system.
- There is need for timely backup and customized training for ensuring reliability and integrity at all stages of organization.
- The vetting needs to be done for cloud service providers to ensure compliance with auditing standards such as SAS 70 and FIPS 200.
- Deploying AI automated structures that proactively notice and prevent outbreaks on web and devices.
- A risk management regimes needs to be set up and embedded into cybersecurity of the business dealings

MAJOR FINDINGS OF THE STUDY

- The introduction of advanced tehnology in digital world led to decentralization where every user can access the information available on digital or cloud platforms without any authorization and hurdles.
- The digital transformation led to smart contracts between patients and professionals in the medical industry.
- Cybersecurity ensures the privacy of patients as outsiders cannot access the patient's confidential information and doctors, professionals and laboratories can access information from a record origin as well.
- Digital wearable devices always provide continuous nursing of health. It provides facilities such as quality of sleep, heart rate, steps walked, and more.
- The step-by-step adoption of blockchain in the well-being sector ensures the integrity of the system while sharing information. The uncluttered and see-through features of blockchain boost the trust and help various stakeholders of the health care sector in the implementation of numerous applications of data compilation, arrangement, retrieval, and management.
- Emerging technologies such as the Internet of Things (IoT), blockchain, artificial intelligence, machine learning, and big data all together have brought a drastic change in data compilation and management. These technologies help in maintaining the confidentiality of patients and provide access to a secure platform for the exchange of information.

- Internet of Things (IoT) has provided significant assistance in the era of digitalization; it helps in the collection of data from the connected devices and transmits it to the health care service provider.
- Government agencies are required to monitor a huge volume of data, blockchain applications will reduce the burden of storage by providing a separate database for a specific activity.
- It is very much helpful for government and healthcare companies to integrate blockchain with cybersecurity applications.
- It is highly recommended to maintain adequate documentation on the technical standards followed and aspired to be followed by the businesses and that need to be driven by adequate policy and top managerial employees. It further suggested that top and senior management should be guided by a competent and professional Chief Inforamtion Security Officer.
- Identification of the risk at the initial phase helps in prevention of a big problem from originating. Depending on the network system, allocation of resources and mobile devices, there is a need to prioritize the resources and effort in wake of digitalization.
- The use of blockchain in the healthcare domain has simplified the process of claim adjudication as it will make the process of verifying documents of patients much easier and reliable.
- The use of master and primary keys leads to the chronological arrangement of data and enhanced the security of patient records and details.

SOLUTIONS AND RECOMMENDATIONS

The healthcare sector is very soft target of the malicous attackers so security needs to be fostered at every level of business transactions. It is highly recommended to maintain adequate documentation on the technical standards followed and aspired to be followed by the businesses and that need to be driven by adequate policy and top managerial employees. It further suggested that top and senior management should be guided by a competent and professional Chief Inforamtion Security Officer. The information security manager should be alert all the time to ensure the integrity and trust in the system.he following security measures should be pracrices such as use of proper software and firewall applications that serve the purpose of cyber security in digital transactions and continous monitoring of the system also helps in maintaining security of the system in the network and often ensure smooth functioning of the system as well. A proper response strategy also helps in overcoming the severity of cyber-attacks. The strategy helps in fetching legal remedies and reduces the monetary impact of unwanted dealings in the system. There is need for timely backup and customized training for ensuring reliability and integrity at all stages of organization.

FUTURE RESEARCH DIRECTIONS

The cybercrime is a universal challenge, the present study mainly discussed about the cyber security threats, measures and digital advancement in the healthcare sector. There is scope for other sectors to analyse the cyber security impications in the era of digitalization. The effective cybersecurity must become an vital part of healthcare domain and further guidelines and compliance actions should be subject of imminent research tactics.

CONCLUSION

Cybersecurity is not just about protection of data it has wide implications such as maintaining safety, privacy, integrity, trust of the patients in the healthcare sector. The need for data management and organization has paved ways for advanced technologies such as Blockchain and the Internet of Things (IoT). The Healthcare sector is the most important domain of a nation's prosperity. Data and health integration can solve many difficult problems in the healthcare sector. It facilitates exchange and dealings in the database that can be shared across authorized operators. Advanced technology such as Blockchain is peer-to-peer disseminated ledger know-how. It consists of majorly three components which are namely distributed network, shared record, and digital transaction. The healthcare industry has undergone various reforms since the evolution of blockchain and Internet of Things (IoT) technology came into the picture. The emergence of these techniques has led to a drastic improvement in the field of Hospital administration, Medicine development, Surgery, Mental Health, and cybersecurity, etc. During the COVID 19 phase, the most affected sector was healthcare where technological advancement was much needed. Robotics helped the nations to face this pandemic with strength.

The technologies in the healthcare domain have wide applications from hospital administration to surgery and cancer research to eradicate the flaws in the system and make the patient experience with the hospital as pleasant as possible and improve overall efficiency in the healthcare industry. Emerging technologies such as the Internet of Things (IoT), blockchain, artificial intelligence, machine learning, and big data all together have brought a drastic change in data compilation and management. This will lead to a promising industrial revolution. The study focused on the implementation of evolving technology in the healthcare sector. Worldwide, blockchain technology has been used in managing the flow of data and information and ensuring security in the system, India should focus on maintaining the same blockchain-enabled infrastructure to reduce causalities in the nation. The adoption of these techniques has led to the secure transfer of information and helped in maintaining the confidentiality of patient's health records.

"Healthcare is an important sector of Indian Economy. Both government and technocrats should work together in the best possible manner by exploiting emerging technologies so that it leads to improvement of healthcare services and the well-being of the nation."

ACKNOWLEDGMENT

This study received no explicit grant from any funding agency in the public, commercial, or not-for-profit divisions.

REFERENCES

Abdellatif, A. A., Al-Marridi, A. Z., Mohamed, A., Erbad, A., Chiasserini, C. F., & Refaey, A. (2020). Health: Toward secure, blockchain-enabled healthcare systems. *IEEE Network*, *34*(4), 312–319. doi:10.1109/MNET.011.1900553

Abdullah, T., & Jones, A. (2019, January). eHealth: challenges far integrating blockchain within healthcare. In *2019 IEEE 12th International Conference on Global Security, Safety and Sustainability (ICGS3)* (pp. 1-9). IEEE.

Abraham, C., Chatterjee, D., & Sims, R. R. (2019). Muddling through cybersecurity: Insights from the US healthcare industry. *Business Horizons*, *62*(4), 539–548. doi:10.1016/j.bushor.2019.03.010

Ahmad, R. W., Salah, K., Jayaraman, R., Yaqoob, I., Ellahham, S., & Omar, M. (2021). The role of blockchain technology in telehealth and telemedicine. *International Journal of Medical Informatics*, *148*, 104399. doi:10.1016/j.ijmedinf.2021.104399 PMID:33540131

Aich, S., Chakraborty, S., Sain, M., Lee, H. I., & Kim, H. C. (2019, February). A review on benefits of IoT integrated blockchain-based supply chain management implementations across different sectors with case study. In *2019 21st international conference on advanced communication technology (ICACT)* (pp. 138-141). IEEE. 10.23919/ICACT.2019.8701910

Akram, S. V., Malik, P. K., Singh, R., Anita, G., & Tanwar, S. (2020). Adoption of blockchain technology in various realms: Opportunities and challenges. *Security and Privacy*, *3*(5), e109. doi:10.1002py2.109

Alam, T. (2020). mHealth Communication Framework using blockchain and IoT Technologies. *International Journal of Scientific & Technology Research*, *9*(6).

Alladi, T., Chamola, V., Parizi, R. M., & Choo, K. K. R. (2019). Blockchain applications for industry 4.0 and industrial IoT: A review. *IEEE Access: Practical Innovations, Open Solutions*, *7*, 176935–176951. doi:10.1109/ACCESS.2019.2956748

Attia, O., Khoufi, I., Laouiti, A., & Adjih, C. (2019, June). An IoT-blockchain architecture based on hyperledger framework for health care monitoring application. In *NTMS 2019-10th IFIP International Conference on New Technologies, Mobility and Security* (pp. 1-5). IEEE Computer Society.

Bell, L., Buchanan, W. J., Cameron, J., & Lo, O. (2018). Applications of blockchain within healthcare. *Blockchain in Healthcare Today*, *1*(8).

Brunetti, F., Matt, D. T., Bonfanti, A., De Longhi, A., Pedrini, G., & Orzes, G. (2020). Digital transformation challenges: Strategies emerging from a multi-stakeholder approach. *The TQM Journal*, *32*(4), 697–724. doi:10.1108/TQM-12-2019-0309

Caldarelli, G., Zardini, A., & Rossignoli, C. (2021). Blockchain adoption in the fashion sustainable supply chain: Pragmatically addressing barriers. *Journal of Organizational Change Management*, *34*(2), 507–524. doi:10.1108/JOCM-09-2020-0299

Celesti, A., Ruggeri, A., Fazio, M., Galletta, A., Villari, M., & Romano, A. (2020). Blockchain-based healthcare workflow for tele-medical laboratory in federated hospital IoT clouds. *Sensors (Basel)*, *20*(9), 2590. doi:10.339020092590 PMID:32370129

Chamola, V., Hassija, V., Gupta, V., & Guizani, M. (2020). A comprehensive review of the COVID-19 pandemic and the role of IoT, drones, AI, blockchain, and 5G in managing its impact. *IEEE Access: Practical Innovations, Open Solutions*, *8*, 90225–90265. doi:10.1109/ACCESS.2020.2992341

Clauson, K. A., Breeden, E. A., Davidson, C., & Mackey, T. K. (2018). Leveraging blockchain technology to enhance supply chain management in healthcare: an exploration of challenges and opportunities in the health supply chain. *Blockchain in Healthcare Today, 1*(3), 1-12.

Dai, H. N., Zheng, Z., & Zhang, Y. (2019). Blockchain for Internet of Things: A survey. *IEEE Internet of Things Journal, 6*(5), 8076–8094. doi:10.1109/JIOT.2019.2920987

El-Gazzar, R., & Stendal, K. (2020). Blockchain in health care: Hope or hype? *Journal of Medical Internet Research, 22*(7), e17199. doi:10.2196/17199 PMID:32673219

Epiphaniou, G., Daly, H., & Al-Khateeb, H. (2019). Blockchain and healthcare. In *Blockchain and Clinical Trial* (pp. 1–29). Springer. doi:10.1007/978-3-030-11289-9_1

Farouk, A., Alahmadi, A., Ghose, S., & Mashatan, A. (2020). Blockchain platform for industrial healthcare: Vision and future opportunities. *Computer Communications, 154*, 223–235. doi:10.1016/j.comcom.2020.02.058

Fekih, R. B., & Lahami, M. (2020, June). Application of blockchain technology in healthcare: a comprehensive study. In *International Conference on Smart Homes and Health Telematics* (pp. 268-276). Springer.

Foster, I., Lopresti, D., Gropp, B., Hill, M., & Schuman, K. (2021). *A National Discovery Cloud: Preparing the US for Global Competitiveness in the New Era of 21st Century Digital Transformation.* arXiv preprint arXiv:2104.06953.

Hasselgren, A., Kralevska, K., Gligoroski, D., Pedersen, S. A., & Faxvaag, A. (2020). Blockchain in healthcare and health sciences—A scoping review. *International Journal of Medical Informatics, 134*, 104040. doi:10.1016/j.ijmedinf.2019.104040 PMID:31865055

Hussein, A. H. (2019). Internet of things (IOT): Research challenges and future applications. *International Journal of Advanced Computer Science and Applications, 10*(6), 77–82. doi:10.14569/IJACSA.2019.0100611

Jain, E. (2020). Digital Employability Skills and Training Needs for the Indian Healthcare Industry. In *Opportunities and Challenges in Digital Healthcare Innovation* (pp. 113–130). IGI Global. doi:10.4018/978-1-7998-3274-4.ch007

Jain, E., & Lamba, J. (2020). Covid-19: Economic Hardship and Financial Distress in Indian Economy. *International Journal of Disaster Recovery and Business Continuity, 11*(3), 3081–3092.

Jain, E., & Lamba, J. (2021). Management and Digitalization Strategy for Transforming Education Sector: An Emerging Gateway Persuaded by COVID-19. In Emerging Challenges, Solutions, and Best Practices for Digital Enterprise Transformation (pp. 69-83). IGI Global.

Kalla, A., Hewa, T., Mishra, R. A., Ylianttila, M., & Liyanage, M. (2020). The role of blockchain to fight against COVID-19. *IEEE Engineering Management Review, 48*(3), 85–96. doi:10.1109/EMR.2020.3014052

Kamble, S. S., Gunasekaran, A., Kumar, V., Belhadi, A., & Foropon, C. (2021). A machine learning based approach for predicting blockchain adoption in supply Chain. *Technological Forecasting and Social Change, 163*, 120465. doi:10.1016/j.techfore.2020.120465

Khezr, S., Moniruzzaman, M., Yassine, A., & Benlamri, R. (2019). Blockchain technology in healthcare: A comprehensive review and directions for future research. *Applied Sciences (Basel, Switzerland), 9*(9), 1736. doi:10.3390/app9091736

Kumar, N. M., & Mallick, P. K. (2018). Blockchain technology for security issues and challenges in IoT. *Procedia Computer Science, 132*, 1815–1823. doi:10.1016/j.procs.2018.05.140

Kumar, T., Ramani, V., Ahmad, I., Braeken, A., Harjula, E., & Ylianttila, M. (2018, September). Blockchain utilization in healthcare: Key requirements and challenges. In *2018 IEEE 20th International Conference on e-Health Networking, Applications and Services (Healthcom)* (pp. 1-7). IEEE.

Martin, G., Martin, P., Hankin, C., Darzi, A., & Kinross, J. (2017). Cybersecurity and healthcare: How safe are we? *BMJ (Clinical Research Ed.), 358*. doi:10.1136/bmj.j3179 PMID:28684400

Mathivathanan, D., Mathiyazhagan, K., Rana, N. P., Khorana, S., & Dwivedi, Y. K. (2021). Barriers to the adoption of blockchain technology in business supply chains: A total interpretive structural modelling (TISM) approach. *International Journal of Production Research*, 1–22.

Mathy, C., Pascal, C., Fizesan, M., Boin, C., Délèze, N., & Aujoulat, O. (2020, July). Automated hospital pharmacy supply chain and the evaluation of organisational impacts and costs. In Supply chain forum: An international journal (Vol. 21, No. 3, pp. 206-218). Taylor & Francis.

McGhin, T., Choo, K. K. R., Liu, C. Z., & He, D. (2019). Blockchain in healthcare applications: Research challenges and opportunities. *Journal of Network and Computer Applications, 135*, 62–75. doi:10.1016/j.jnca.2019.02.027

Meske, C., Amojo, I., Poncette, A. S., & Balzer, F. (2019, July). The Potential Role of Digital Nudging in the Digital Transformation of the Healthcare Industry. In *International Conference on Human-Computer Interaction* (pp. 323-336). Springer. 10.1007/978-3-030-23538-3_25

Miraz, M. H. (2020). Blockchain of things (BCoT): The fusion of blockchain and IoT technologies. In *Advanced Applications of Blockchain Technology* (pp. 141–159). Springer. doi:10.1007/978-981-13-8775-3_7

Mistry, I., Tanwar, S., Tyagi, S., & Kumar, N. (2020). Blockchain for 5G-enabled IoT for industrial automation: A systematic review, solutions, and challenges. *Mechanical Systems and Signal Processing, 135*, 106382. doi:10.1016/j.ymssp.2019.106382

Moro Visconti, R., & Morea, D. (2020). Healthcare digitalization and pay-for-performance incentives in smart hospital project financing. *International Journal of Environmental Research and Public Health, 17*(7), 2318. doi:10.3390/ijerph17072318 PMID:32235517

Omar, I. A., Jayaraman, R., Salah, K., Yaqoob, I., & Ellahham, S. (2020). Applications of blockchain technology in clinical trials: Review and open challenges. *Arabian Journal for Science and Engineering*, 1–15.

Pilkington, M. (2017). Can blockchain improve healthcare management? Consumer medical electronics and the IoMT. *Consumer Medical Electronics and the IoMT.*

Rabah, K. (2018). Convergence of AI, IoT, big data and blockchain: a review. *The Lake Institute Journal, 1*(1), 1-18.

Rathee, G., Sharma, A., Saini, H., Kumar, R., & Iqbal, R. (2019). A hybrid framework for multimedia data processing in IoT-healthcare using blockchain technology. *Multimedia Tools and Applications*, 1–23. doi:10.100711042-019-07835-3

Rathee, P. (2020). Introduction to Blockchain and IoT. In *Advanced Applications of Blockchain Technology* (pp. 1–14). Springer. doi:10.1007/978-981-13-8775-3_1

Ray, P. P., Dash, D., Salah, K., & Kumar, N. (2020). Blockchain for IoT-based healthcare: Background, consensus, platforms, and use cases. *IEEE Systems Journal.* Advance online publication. doi:10.1109/JSYST.2020.2963840

Ricciardi, W., Pita Barros, P., Bourek, A., Brouwer, W., Kelsey, T., Lehtonen, L., Anastasy, C., Barros, P., Barry, M., Bourek, A., Brouwer, W., De Maeseneer, J., Kringos, D., Lehtonen, L., McKee, M., Murauskiene, L., Nuti, S., Ricciardi, W., Siciliani, L., & Wild, C. (2019). How to govern the digital transformation of health services. *European Journal of Public Health, 29*(Supplement_3), 7–12. doi:10.1093/eurpub/ckz165 PMID:31738442

Rose, K. J. (2017). Mobile Health: Telemedicine's Latest Wave but This Time It's for Real. In L. Menvielle, A. F. Audrain-Pontevia, & W. Menvielle (Eds.), *The Digitization of Healthcare.* Palgrave Macmillan. doi:10.1057/978-1-349-95173-4_9

Sharma, M., & Joshi, S. (2021). Barriers to blockchain adoption in health-care industry: an Indian perspective. *Journal of Global Operations and Strategic Sourcing.*

Singh, P., & Singh, N. (2020). Blockchain With IoT and AI: A Review of Agriculture and Healthcare. *International Journal of Applied Evolutionary Computation, 11*(4), 13–27. doi:10.4018/IJAEC.2020100102

Srivastava, A., Jain, P., Hazela, B., Asthana, P., & Rizvi, S. W. A. (2021). Application of Fog Computing, Internet of Things, and Blockchain Technology in Healthcare Industry. In *Fog Computing for Healthcare 4.0 Environments* (pp. 563–591). Springer. doi:10.1007/978-3-030-46197-3_22

Srivastava, G., Parizi, R. M., & Dehghantanha, A. (2020). The future of blockchain technology in healthcare internet of things security. *Blockchain Cybersecurity, Trust and Privacy*, 161-184.

Teoh, C. S., & Mahmood, A. K. (2017, July). National cyber security strategies for digital economy. In *2017 International Conference on Research and Innovation in Information Systems (ICRIIS)* (pp. 1-6). IEEE. 10.1109/ICRIIS.2017.8002519

Tripathi, G., Ahad, M. A., & Paiva, S. (2020, March). S2HS-A blockchain based approach for smart healthcare system. In Healthcare (Vol. 8, No. 1, p. 100391). Elsevier.

This research was previously published in the Handbook of Research on Advancing Cybersecurity for Digital Transformation; pages 353-372, copyright year 2021 by Information Science Reference (an imprint of IGI Global).

Section 5
Organizational and Social Implications

Chapter 56
Blockchain Technology for IoT:
An Information Security Perspective

Sasikumar R.
https://orcid.org/0000-0002-4656-6662
K. Ramakrishnan College of Engineering, India

Karthikeyan P.
https://orcid.org/0000-0003-2703-4051
Thiagarajar College of Engineering, India

Thangavel M.
https://orcid.org/0000-0002-2510-8857
Siksha 'O' Anusandhan (Deemed), India

ABSTRACT

In the internet era, data is considered to be the primary asset, and the host or applications in a network are vulnerable to various attacks. Traditional network architectures have centralized authority to provide authentication, authorization, and access control services. In this case, there is a possibility of data mishandling activities from the valuable information available in the given network application. To avoid this type of mishandling, a new technology came into existence known as blockchain. Implementing blockchain technology in the internet of things (IoT) will ensure data integrity, stability, and durability. The authors present a detailed investigation of various IoT applications with blockchain implementation. Blockchain-based mechanisms will improve the security aspects in the traditional network applications related to IoT like insurance policies claiming, personal identification, and electronic health records.

DOI: 10.4018/978-1-6684-7132-6.ch056

1. INTRODUCTION

The world recognizes Internet of Things (IoT) in the year 1999 by the British technology pioneer Kevin Ashton. It is the interconnected device, which is capable of gathering different types of data from various locations and communicate among themselves. It communicates and transfers data among the things in peer to peer (P2P) manner. While enriching P2P communication, the workload among the things in the network will share with its neighbours. Involved devices may have differences in size, memory capacity, and processing capabilities. The main objectives of Internet-of-Things are 1) To gather valuable information from deployed location 2) Transform that information to centralized place without data loss 3) Above mentioned process is done without human intervention. IoT devices can be any devices that are capable of collecting and transforming data. For example, Smartwatches, Smartphones, Medical equipment, Environmental monitoring devices, Agricultural equipment, and many more. Communication among IoT devices is transmitted through a connected network topology.

Figure 1. IoT device example for Home automation

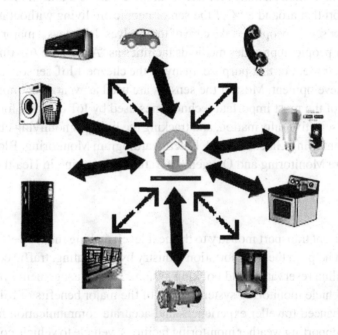

IoT is not a new technology; it is a combination of various traditional technologies like Wireless Sensor Network (WSN), Cloud computing, Big data analytics, Radio-Frequency Identification (RFID), Location-based services, and Automation. Internet of Things mainly deals with constraint devices. So it is unable to fulfil all the requirements like Storage capacity, Execution speed, Captured data Transferring capabilities, and Energy. In this case, Cloud computing will play a major part in IoT devices to provide a huge amount of memory for storage.

Every year millions of devices are connected through IoT across the globe. When thinking about millions of devices connected over the internet, People has to think about various issues with respect to information. Data integrity has to be improved and does redundancy should be minimized to maximize the storage capacity and increase the performance of data processing. Heterogeneity is one of the major issues while dealing with billions of devices, solution is cloud storage.

Constrained Application Protocol (CoAP) was proposed to solve the problem faced by constrained heterogeneous devices. To solve the energy consumption issues, Ultra Wideband technology has been used. With help of Blockchain technology, we can ensure the security and data reliability of IoT data.

1.1 Applications of IoT

Internet of Things comes forward in the day to day life activity, because of fast computing capabilities and accurateness of the result. In the following section, we are going to discuss some of the major applications of IoT (Lo.S.K et.al, 2019), which will take the majority of the part in our daily lifestyle.

a) Healthcare

A recent report from the United Nations predicted that there will be 2 billion older people by 2050, and many researchers report that around 89% of the senior people are living without help from their family. So it's very difficult for senior people to take care of themselves. IoT plays a major role in the Healthcare filed mainly for senior people, it provides medicals facilities as "Anywhere Anytime" to make them safe and comfortable in their life. For that purpose, many of the cheapest IoT sensors in the form of cost and size involved in this development. Most of the sensors are used as wearable, implanted, and ecological manner. RFID is one of the most important technologies used by IoT devices, for communicating with other devices, storing sensitive information, and tracking the living or nonliving objects in the world. An IoT sensor helps to identifying Glucose Level, Electrocardiogram Monitoring, Blood Pressure Monitoring, Body Temperature Monitoring and Oxygen Saturation Monitoring in Healthcare.

b) Transportation

IoT can change the current transport industry to the next level, making them by efficient use of data generated from sensors. It helps in the transportation industry by facilitating, traffic control system, Vehicle health monitoring, online reservation and booking system, Fleet management system, Self-controlling vehicle, and remote vehicle monitoring system. Some of the major benefits of IoT based transportation are: 1) It provides enhanced traveller experiences and accurate communication facilities. 2) It ensures safety to traveller by supporting weather monitoring facilities, vehicle to vehicle communication, current traffic, and health of vehicles. 3) Reduced energy utilization based on demand and supply mechanism. 4) This allows tracking real-time vehicle speed and location. 5) This ensures public safety assurance, disaster response, and rescue management.

c) Smart Cities

A smart city is considered by many researchers and corporate due to its inherent intelligence in trade with indescribable resource utilization and environment. Smart Cities require integrated intelligent sensors to operate efficiently (Jaoude et.al, 2019). Just imagine the integration of sensors to operate with energy consumption meter, water supply, traffic flows and parking, environmental pollution monitoring, security cameras on the street, supermarket, public transportation facilities, waste management system, and more.

d) Supply Chain Management

It is a process of tracking the raw materials from an organization to delivering a product to the customer. It enables the timely delivery of the product to the customer and improvement of accuracy. It reduces the investment cost for both manufacturers and retailers. SCM has three flow of its process: 1) Materials and Product flow 2) Information flow 3) Finance flow. Integration of IoT with supply chain management provides, where goods are available and how they are stored, when those goods will reach specified location, real-time inventory visibility, and monitoring. Some of the use cases are: Manufactures can detect faulty materials using IoT enabled cameras, Food retailers can check the temperature and humidity of place where food is currently available, Farmer can detect the soil condition to decide the optimum time to plant or harvest.

1.2 IoT Data Breach/Theft Attacks in Identified Applications

a) Smart Healthcare

IoT sensors play a major role in the smart healthcare application to monitor and take necessary action for patient health conditions. Those devices do their routine activities like patient health information collection and transforming those data to the storage location for taking necessary action. It is important to be acquainted with security requirements, vulnerabilities, and countermeasures. Here, it is possible to affect the overall process of healthcare by stealing/modifying the health data of the patient by the adversary (Tang.W et.al, 2019). Based on the above information attack can be classified into the following categories:

- **Denial of Services** – The attacker purposely creates unnecessary traffic in the communication channel to disturb the data transmission in the network. In the other side, accessing the protected information without having proper access rights. These activities will lead to insecurity for the patient information and improper treatment.
- **Router Attack** – Data transmission route plays a vital role in the medical field. In the Healthcare system, many of the sensors are based on wireless. During transmission, the attacker may create unnecessary traffic, which leads to unnecessary delay.
- **Selective Forwarding Attack** – This type of attack is very dangerous to the healthcare filed. In this type, the attacker will hack one or more sensors in the system. After compromising the sensor he/she will drop some of the packets, remaining information will pass on to the servers. This will misguide the treatment of the patient.

b) Transportation

IoT brings many advantages to the transportation system and also brings some challenges while implementing smart transportation (Wang.K et.al, 2018). Organization can track the following: Speed of the vehicle, live location using GPS, Transports idle condition. The following section includes challenges of Transportation:

- **Limited Connectivity** – Number of connectivity increases, many of the vehicles are not having capabilities to update their sensors software up-to-date, which leads to malfunctioning of devices.
- **Security breaches** – When increasing number of devices, it is tedious task to manage and monitor the entire devices. We must protect all the data generated by enormous number of appliances in the network.
- **Access control and Device authentication** - Access control mechanism should be adopted with users communicating with these sensors. This access control is based on a dynamic approach (i.e) User's List. Sensors must transmit data to authenticated devices in an encrypted format.
- **Network Attacks** –The attacker can stop the entire communication of the network. Due to network attacks transportation cost will increase, more fuel utilization, which reduces the safety of traveller.
- **Insufficient privacy protection** – Personal records are stored in the devices, it may be used by unauthorized users.

c) Smart Cities

Fast growth in the implementation of IoT helps to form the connected network in the smart cities, starting from smart meter to building, from traffic signals to parking lots and from garbage collection to the environmental pollution monitoring systems. There are many numbers of potential vulnerabilities and malicious activities (Falco.G et.al, 2018). Here we have pointed out common security threats and data breaches:

- **Eavesdropping** – Many numbers of sensors and its communication involved in the smart cities. Eavesdropping captures the network traffic and trying to listen to multiparty communication to trap the configuration information.
- **SQL Injection Attack** – Attacker trying to insert SQL query on the client request to the application for performing an insert or delete or modifying the original data available in the database.
- **Distributed Denial of Service** – The attacker tries to send multiple requests from end sensor/user to utilize the more bandwidth of the network for overloading. In such case, entire network will become slower.

d) Supply Chain Management

IoT is being used in many industries to secure supply chain management. Communication happening in the form of 1) interaction between device and supplier 2) supplier to supplier 3) device to device (Omitola et.al, 2018). Security is essential in any form of electronic communication including IoT devices and infrastructures. IoT devices and infrastructure may face several attacks, if those attacks are not handled appropriately it leads, danger to human, physical damages, and operational disturbances. The vulnerabilities of IoT based supply chain are:

- **People, Policy and Procedure vulnerability** – Policy and procedures are formulated by the organization. People involving in the process are trained to follow the framed policies and procedures. Inefficient approach and system take into security risk.
- **Software/firmware vulnerabilities** – All the components involved in the supply chain process are based on software. Software design, development, and deployment must be carefully intended. Errors in any one of the stages will allow the adversaries to access Supply Chain System.
- **Tampering proof of Work** –In between at any point of operation, the original information can be modified to misuse the entire operation.
- **Mal-hardware insertion** – In the assembly section of the product, the hardware may function improperly. It leads to disturbance of the entire process also it may happen due to internal attack.

1.3 IoT Security Essentials for Identified Applications

a) Smart Healthcare

One of the most important devices used by healthcare for data communication and storage is RFID. It enables communication between RFID-tags and RFID-readers. The following security requirements must be provide for communication.

1. **Mutual Authentication**- Before enabling communication between the sender and receiver, the process must ensure the mutual authentication between parties.
2. **Confidentiality and Anonymity**- The confidential information stored on the sensing device must be kept securely. Before transmitting, the information should be encrypted using any lightweight cryptography algorithms to ensure confidentiality.
3. **Self Healing** – Devices used for monitoring patient data may fail due to hardware failure or low energy. In this case, network devices should be capable to handle current situation.
4. **Computational Limitations** – IoT sensors are constrained devices, so these devices must be providing lightweight security mechanisms to minimize resource consumption and maximize security.
5. **Data Freshness** – Sensors and devices generated data must be a very recent one for providing better treatment.

b) Transportation System

Integration of transportation with IoT provides accurate communication facilities and location information, superior customer services, improved life of vehicle, accurate understanding and information of transits, autonomous vehicles, reduces traffic, and improved fuel utilization. To achieve the above advantages, the system needs following security essentials:

1. **Physical security, Access control, and Security measure** – Traffic and Vehicle management systems need proper Access-control mechanisms to restrict unauthorized access. Physical security is essential for both physical assets and digital assets.
2. **Developing Secure and Private Communication channel** – To avoid cyberattack on the public communication channel need to develop secure communication channel. In V2V communication,

attacker can compromise the digital assets of the transport. To avoid such attacks need encryption-based communication channels.

c) Smart Cities

IoT technology and wireless connectivity together brings technology-enabled cities in the human lifecycle. This moves traditional city life into next-generation intelligent cities (Shen.M et.al, 2019). Following security requirements are necessary to implement smart cities:

1. **Firmware integrity and Security Boot** – Security boot is an approach, It utilizes cryptographic code for signing techniques. It ensures the code is executed by a device that data generated other authorized devices or trusted parties.
2. **Security Monitoring and Analysis** – In this approach, it captures the entire data from the end device to transforming information over the communication channel for analysis of the security violation. Once the malicious activities detected, the entire network policies should be executed to quarantines affected devices/users.
3. **Secure Authentication and Access Control** –The main objective of this Authentication should be to determine the right user on the right device at right time.
4. **Availability and Integrity** – Smart cities works based on real-time data. Without these data not possible to operate smart-city functionalities.

d) Smart Supply-chain

All major logistics providers and investors are faced with cybersecurity risk at securing the private data, investing time, resources. Due to security attacks, logistics providers and suppliers will face the loss of private information, increasing of investing cost, and increase process time. So it's time to address the cyber-security on supply-chain.

1. **Protection against Software/Firmware vulnerabilities** –Hackers could be embedded in their malware into this firmware; it works as spying on our device activity. So its role in the hardware industry to resist their hardware against malware and provide regular updates to their devices.
2. **Prevention against People/Policy/Procedure vulnerability** – Providing effective training to the staff on the latest cybersecurity risk and how to protect against them.
3. **Detection of malfunction hardware-** Devices may be executing vulnerable instruction due to failure condition or deployment of unauthorized devices inside network/software issue.
4. **Device Connectivity issue** – Before implementing any services on the network must be analyzed. Whenever adopting a new device to the network, the performance and security must be consulting with technology providers for moving devices in a too-long way.

1.4 Blockchain Technology Need in Identified Applications

This section describes how blockchain technologies provide a smart way for identified above applications (Miraz.M.H et.al, 2020).

a) Smart Healthcare

Implementing blockchain technology in the healthcare application will support to provide many advantages. It addresses for various attacks, availability and exchange of patient information.

- **Health Information Exchange and Interoperability** - In the traditional method of treatment, Electronics Health Records (EHR) limit within the particular sickbay alone, not easily share with others. As a result, a patient faces a lot of challenges in the sharing of authorized data to other consulting doctors (Zhou.T et.al 2019). Blockchain technology enables a new way of sharing authorized information worldwide. With the help of the distributed nature of blockchain technology, it provides patient information to consulting doctors even though it faces DoS attack. It ensures the availability of data at any point in time.
- **Secure and Trustable EHR sharing -** Blockchain enables timestamp-based data sharing and monitoring of clinical information with the help of Proof-of-Concept consensus protocols.
- **Information Privacy –** Even though blockchain is distributed in nature and information is publicly available, it uses the asymmetric strong cryptographic algorithm for ensuring the privacy of stored information. Private Keys helps to get data from blockchain for valid users. Mainly it uses homomorphic encryptions like Zero-Knowledge Proofs and zk-SNARKs.

b) Transportation Application

Blockchain has solutions to the transportation system faced over many decades; it supports organizational cost-saving and internet-based accurate tracking of transportation orders. Due to inefficient existing transportation methods, many companies are ready to join in blockchain-based transportation and logistics industry.

- **Reliability of Tracking** –Current systems do not support providing these data due to manipulation or false impression. Blockchain technology provides immutable data storage for increased reliability.
- **Tracking vehicle performance history** – The performance of vehicle can be monitor from unaltered transaction ledger.
- **Vehicle to Vehicle communication** – Many companies are already implementing v2v communication, which enables one vehicle can share its information to other for safety aspects and fuel efficiency. This information can be stored in the blockchain to enlarge the transportations industry to the next level.
- **Cut Costs and Eliminate Middlemen** – Quite possibly the most powerful methods of blockchain technology is "Smart-contract", which eliminates the middle man in the progress and self-executing instructions, based on the some conditions.

c) Smart Cities Application

Transformation of traditional cities into the next milestone with the help of the IoT. These systems require a database to store and manipulated the data generated by the above technology. In this case, blockchain will help well than a traditional database to improve the efficiency, security, and transparency of the operations.

- **Integrity over the information** – In this technology, integrity can be enforced by implementing the encryption technique over the communicating.
- **Direct communications** – Blockchain makes communication between the public and government/authorities directly without any intermediaries. This process will speed up communication, reduces waiting or approval times.
- **Increased Transparency and efficient management** – Entire operation happening in this progress will be transparent to the public and government, so no one can modify the value or process.
- **Real-Time information** – This technology enables the availability of real-time information over the network. In the distributed ledger, any authorized user can access real-time information with their identity.

d) Smart Supply Chain Management

Traditional supply-chain traceability methodology does not guarantee consistency, transparency, scalability, and accuracy of entire process. In the flow of supply-chain, every time resources move from one hand to another hand need to create a block on the blockchain to store material information, timestamp information, cost of a product from raw materials to product delivery. Blockchain technology provides more accuracy and transparency.

- **Interoperability** –Information sharing reduces delays and avoids fraudulent activities. All the progress in the supply chain can be tracked in real-time, it reduces the deficiency rate.
- **Tamper-proof Records and Smart-Contracts** – Anyone trying to tamper in supply chain records can detect easily. Smart contracts are automatically triggered based on need in the supply will reduce the waiting time and simplify the work.
- **Preventing Data-breach** – Supply chain has security risk at manufactured goods containment to stealing due to unproductive transparency. Blockchain technology helps to prevent implementing transparency from all corners.

2. BACKGROUND

Researchers say About 31 billion devices are connected via IoT in the year 2021. Every year this number will increase tremendously. Many research says, by the year 2025 one trillion devices will be connected to IoT. The author says this count will become very high if the internet world implements 5G technology. While discussing numerous devices generated data, it needs to be maintained with high security and privacy. In traditional methodologies, the centralized method used for maintaining that confidential information. It may be vulnerable to unauthorized access and data unavailability. Each node is possible of failure, it leads to data unavailability due to DoS attack. Cyberattack is the major problem, the originality of data can be modified by Attacker, and it creates very serious issues in the future. To address the above problems, blockchain technology play major role in that.

2.1 What Is Blockchain?

Blockchain technology is immutable, distributed in nature, and provides better reliability and availability of information. Blockchain is a public ledger, anyone can read the values of a block in a chain, but none of them will allow doing the modification. One member in the network will create a block for storing transactions, this block will be verified by other members on the same network. Once the network members agreed the above block will be added to the existing chain. Block stores various transaction details like timestamp, participating member's details. To distinguish one block from others, it uses a unique code called "hash". Hashes are a unique code generated by special cryptography algorithms. Initially this technology successfully implemented on the various Crypto-currencies. Table-1 lists outs the Applications where this technology has been applied for providing better performance. Here we mentioned familiar applications; it can extend many more applications too.

Table 1. Applications of blockchain technology

Sl No.	Name of the Applications
1.	Cryptocurrency
2.	Finance Sector's
3.	Internet of Things
4.	Smart Appliances
5.	Healthcare
6.	Government Land Registration Process
7.	Certification maintenance by Universities
8.	Supply-chain management sector

2.2 Working Principles of Blockchain

Blockchain is nothing but a sequence of blocks working together, helps to store data with immutable characteristics. To link or insert a new block to the chain following four activities to happen (Reiff, Feeb-2020). First, to create a block transaction should be happened, which states that some operation must take place in the event. Second, the above transactions must be approved by other members of the network. Third, once approved by the network members particular block will be inserted onto the existing chain with a unique identity. Fourth, this block will be reflected in every member's chain. Every block on the chain will get unique hash value, these hash not only depending on the current block transactions also it includes previous block hash value. Blockchain itself renews its structure for every 10 minutes.

2.3 Components Blockchain and Its Functionalities

A blockchain is a type of spreadsheet holding transaction details. The hash value is a combination of numbers and alphabets. In cryptocurrency, the size of the block will be 1MB. When a user creates a new transaction, that Tx will be recorded (called as mined) on a particular block with the help of consensus algorithms. A block on a blockchain can hold 4-7 transaction. The size of the block can be increase to a larger one; the block can hold more number of transactions in a block.

Table 2. Components in blockchain structure

Name of the Components	Description
Hash value of the Block	Hash value of the current Block
Previous Hash value	Hash value of the Previous Block
Nonce	Random number, Helps to achieve the target value
Block Number	It denotes the order of the block in the current chain
Timestamp	Date and Time of Block creation
Transaction Details	Transaction information

Each transaction has its unique identification number within this block. Figure-2 shows the structure of the Blockchain (Nofer.M et.al, 2017).

Every block contains the following particulars in it:

1. **Hash value of block:** By using hash algorithm this value is generated for every block. While generating a hash value for a particular block, it uses data in the block and previous block hash value.
2. **Previous hash value:** It maintains a hash value of the previous block in a network. The previous hash value of Genesis block is "00000000".
3. **Nonce:** Nonce is expanded as "Number only used once". It is a random number used by a blockchain to increase the difficulty level and helps for improving security.
4. **Timestamp:** Date and Time are monitored with the help of an internal clock. It ensures the transactions "proof of integrity". The transaction timestamp should be within some intervals. Otherwise completed work will be removed from the block.
5. **Transaction details:** It keeps the record of the transaction in a particular block.

Figure 2. Structure of blockchain

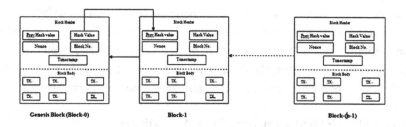

The initial block of any blockchain network is called "Genesis Block". When calculating a hash value for this block, it takes an argument for the hash algorithm is data of this block and "00000" as the previous hash value. Every block in the chain refers to the hash value of the previous block. Miners want to mine a new block need to satisfy the target value within the stipulated time. A consensus algorithm helps to mine a new block in the blockchain structure.

2.4 Merkle Tree

Blockchain has many numbers of blocks and each block has its transaction. In this case, it is very difficult to verify all the transactions. The verification process alone consumes more execution time and storage capacity. To resolve those issues, the Merkle tree has implemented in Blockchain technology. This mathematical model executes the verification process as soon as possible and produces with high accuracy. It uses some of the familiar hashing algorithms like MD5/SHA-3/SHA-256. Every transaction is paired with some other transaction to form the Merkle root, follows the concept of the binary tree. Each node must have two leaves and every transaction will generate its encrypted value using Hash algorithm. Once encrypted value achieved, then the leaves are paired to make a new root for those transactions. This process will be continued until the single root is achieved. This scenario will be shown in Figure-3.

Figure 3. Structure of Merkle Tree Root

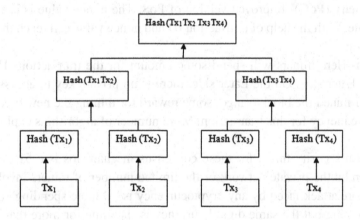

2.5 Consensus Protocols

It is a decision making process on the blockchain network. Many of the members are involved in this chain. Now the question is, who is going to use the available memory space for their transaction? In this structure, no one has a higher priority or highest share than other members. The objective of this technology is, to provide an immutable distributed ledger without a central Administrator/owner. So now everyone has equal priority or rights among themselves.

In this case, more than one people want to mine a transaction in a particular block, which will be resolved by consensus algorithms. The aim of this protocol is, to offer the following credentials to the members:

- Equal rights
- Co-Operation

- More members participation
- Decision making
- Conclusion

Various types of consensus algorithms available for blockchain technology. Algorithms can be decided depending upon the Application domain, Availability of resources, Time consideration, and processing speed. The performance of the mining process is measured based on the hash rate. Most familiar consensus algorithms are listed here (Lo.S.K et.al, 2019):

1. **Proof-of-Work(PoW)** - Anyone can mine a new block if miners will be capable of solving the puzzle within the stipulated period. More than one person solved the puzzle within the period, the mining process allowed based on their mining power.
2. **Proof-of-Stake(PoS)** –In this method, who has more coin with their wallet, chances of mining are very high.
3. **Byzantine Fault Tolerance-** During the voting time some nodes may become failure or malfunctioning. In this situation, this method will help us to continue the mining process without any delay.
4. **Proof-of-Activity(PoA)-** It inherits the characteristics of PoW and PoS.
5. **Proof-of-Capacity (PoC)-** Improved version of PoS. The nonce value is used for achieving the target hash value. With the help of transaction ID and nonce value can reach the target hash within the time duration.
6. **Proof-of-Burn-** Here miners will spend some amount for the transaction. This amount will be credited to the Eater side. On the Eater side, there is no private key to access those burnt coins. Once the miner mined the block can get some reward for mining the new block. In future miners able to get more money for this transaction. More number of algorithms explains in the Table 3.

The most common security threat for these consensus mechanisms is a 51% attack. In this type of attack will happen on the private network or the limited number of miners involved during mining process. And one more attack faced by any cryptocurrency is "Double spending" (Lee.Y et.al, 2020). Double spending, nothing but the same digital currency is spending for more than one transaction, to different purposes. To solve this issue, transactions will be placed in the mining pool for execution, (i.e) unconfirmed transactions. The first transaction will be validated, on the confirmation, it will be placed on the block. The second transaction will be invoked from the unconfirmed transaction, and then it will be rejected due to invalid.

2.6 Smart Contracts

The smart contract is a system protocol, which is digital facilitation to execute, verify, negotiation, and improving the performance of Blockchain technology without any intermediate authorities (Christidis.K et.al, 2016). Defined as "a computerized transaction protocol that executes the terms of a contract". This concept initially used by Bitcoin communities for transferring currencies. It needs permissioned, prewritten statement with an exact sequence of execution. Execution order must be mentioned very carefully, otherwise, execution will happen with the wrong answer. Generally, a contract has two attributes namely "state" and "value". It works like "IF...THEN" statement. Once the triggering statements are agreed by community members, it will be broadcast into the network and inserted into the particular block in the chain.

In addition to that, we can include the "WHEN" condition on the execution statements, can be Timestamp (or) particular state. According to the execution model of smart contracts stages are categorized into:

1.   Discovery and Negotiation
2.   Learning and self-description
3.   Deployment and Development
4.   Execution, Billing and Penalty services
5.   Termination

Figure 4. Life-cycle of Smart contracts

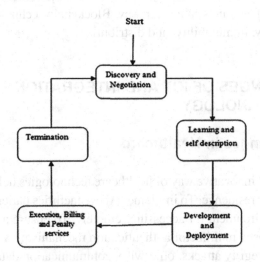

2.6.1 Challenges of Smart Contracts

Smart contracts work on distributed ledger, faces a lot of problems during executions of its predetermined instructions. Here, we have listed some of major issues:

1.   **Mining order of transaction on the Block** - Every block has its own number of transactions in it. During simultaneous transaction, the miner can alter that order of transaction for writing on a block. It leads to invalidating the forthcoming valid transaction.
2.   **Transaction leads to an unhandled exception** – Both caller and callee must be ensured the successful execution of the contract. If not checked properly, this will become the unhandled exception.
3.   **Immutable bugs** - Stored information's are ineradicable. Suppose any improper implementation happened after the execution of contracts, it is unable to revoke the work.
4.   **Performance issue** – Memory utilization is very high, possible to create bottleneck due to make multiple copies, Limited scalability.

5.   **Privacy issue** – In this approach, both contract information and transaction data are publicly available.

2.7 Blockchain for IoT Applications

Blockchain is considered an innovative technology for smart healthcare domains. This technology helps to improve the availability, security, and privacy or transparency of healthcare system. IoT based healthcare technology would be a more powerful and successful one. This technology helps to add force to traditional smart transportation systems. To eradicate fault or scam and improve security and privacy, IBM introduced blockchain-based transportation. A smart city uses digital technology to improve the effective functioning, share the information for quality improvement. Blockchain-based smart cities, sense and manage the data securely and effective utilization of resources in an economic way. The main objectives of supply-chain systems are to satisfy the customer requirements with quality and accuracy, cost reduction, traceability of products in a safer way. Blockchain technology facilitates for a supply-chain system with traceability, immutability, and distribution.

3. SECURITY CHALLENGES OF IOT AND INTEGRATION OF BLOCKCHAIN TECHNOLOGY

3.1 IoT Security Challenges in Healthcare

Dhillon et.al (2018) proposed innovative way of healthcare technologies helps the patient can have their healthcare services from their residence. To implement these facilities patient medical information must be recorded on the cloud environment for accessing remotely. To ensure authentication and efficiency the authors proposed ECC based multifactor authentication mechanism. A proposed system checks the timestamp to protect from integrity attacks, otherwise, communication data will be getting altered. By providing a unique private key to the communication parties system will protects from DoS and DDoS attacks. IoT based cloud storage is an open environment for all, it is easy for compromise attack, this architecture facilitates mutual authentication between Medical expert and cloud server to resist compromise attacks.

Duraiswamy et.al (2019) proposed security architecture for protecting patient data against cyber-attacks and improve performance. In this system, authentication helps to continuously monitor the patient even in the nonclinical situation. Architecture designed for protects from both passive and active attacks. Mutual authentication used to resist tampering or unauthorized access to patient records. A session key, unique pseudo-identity, sequence number, and hashing mechanism used for protection from various cyber-attacks.

Deebak et.al (2019) applied Anonymous Biometric Authentication Scheme for resolving privacy issue. Healthcare systems are vulnerable to an insider attack, forgery attack, user anonymity attack, and various cyber-attacks. One-way hash function approaches used to avoid legitimate user attack, for privacy concerns. The proposed system uses symmetric key based biometric to prevent illegal access to a user's identification. This session key is derived from the mathematical calculation as independently.

Tang.W et.al (2019) implements a data aggression scheme for collecting patient's medical information and provides confidentiality, protection against various cyber attacks. This system combines the "Boneh-Goh-Nissim Cryptosystem and Shamir Secret Sharing" to maintain data secrecy and fault tolerance. The proposed architecture provides fault tolerance of healthcare data using the shared secret key and sub secret key.

3.2 IoT Security Challenges in Smart Transportation

Wang.K et.al (2018) proposed a new approach for avoiding jamming and eavesdropping attack between sensors and remote controllers. This system simulated using two algorithms "stochastic algorithm with feedback and renewed intelligent simulated annealing". Here two antenna models used for transmission: Single antenna model and Multi-antenna model. Usually, Malicious jammers select optimal power strategies to increase the side effect of any sensors. Proposed architecture applies a stochastic algorithm with feedback algorithms to select an appropriate optimal strategy to avoid jamming and eavesdropping.

Riahi Sfar.A et.al (2019) enforces game theory-based approaches between actors to enable privacy and protect against various attacks. The main aim of this system is to protect against location tracking of vehicles and break forward secrecy. It consists of two actors involved in the data transformation. Players are "Data Holder" (DH) and "Data Requestor" (DR).

Chen.Q et.al (2019) proposed this model for reducing accident happens due to threads and physical individual protection. Proposed system use "Driver behaviours prediction & S2 module", this module designed based on biometric access control. An attacker can steal this biometric information from drivers, so to avoid these attacks proposed model uses the following machine learning algorithms: Hidden Markov Model, K-means clustering cross-validation, and support vector machine. Machine learning algorithm helps to become aware of authorized driver's characteristics and behavioural.

Eiza.M et.al (2017) describes and presented various threats and its countermeasures of automated vehicles. Automotive vehicles are operated with various sensors and electronics boards embedded with programming code. The attacker can exploit the systems through USB, Bluetooth, DSRC, OBD, and many more. To protect from various types of attacks providing one solution is not possible. So this operation can be done with multiple layers concepts. Secure OTA approach proposed for updating the most recent patches required by sensors.

3.3 IoT Security Challenges in Smart Cities

Falco.G et.al (2018) model uses, Heart of the smart cities is CCTV, electric grids, water networks, and transportation systems. All the sensors must be work properly and taken care should be done against cyber attacks. Many governments are feeling that smart city components are under high risk and difficult to identify which component affected by what types of vulnerabilities. To overcome these issues the authors proposed AI-based techniques to generate the automated generation of the tree to identify the risk and structures. The objective of the tree is to trace the affected device and leaves of the attacked system. The main advantage of this model is time consumption compared to manual tree generation.

Xu.C et.al (2019) proposes a strategy against DDoS attack in a smart city is SDNFV. The objective is to reduce the load of the Software-Defined Network. To protect against DDoS, attack model is defined into three modules "Attack trigger module", "attack detection module", and "attack backtracking module". Responsible for attack trigger module is, while abnormal transmission happens in the communication it sends an alert message to attack detection module. The attack detection module detects the traffic flow and forwarded it to the backtracking model. The backtracking module identifies the source generating DDoS attack.

Mohammad.N (2019) proposed a model to identify various cyber-security vulnerability and then assessed properties of those vulnerabilities. This system comprises of the three-layered model. In the first layer, ensures authentication and encryption process to avoid unauthorized access. But in this layer not protects from component level attacks. In addition to first layer activity, the second layer provides some of the tools and firewalls to protect and monitor malicious activity. The third layer called attack defense module plays an important role in cyber attacks. This model designed based on Markov Decision Process (MDP) because of the dynamic nature of attackers.

Badii.C et.al (2020) implements a framework called Snap4City. This framework provides full-stack security from IoT Devices to cloud storage including IoT edge. Authentication is ensured with the help of the Single Sign-On (SSO) module, which is a centralized approach. On the edge, the part has powerful processing capabilities, which take care connections and authentication works. Snap4City provides authentication and authorization using a user registry. This user registry managed by LDAP and CRM.

3.4 IoT Security Challenges in Supply-Chain Management

Omitola et.al (2018) used the iPhone/Apple supply chain for identifying vulnerabilities and attacks. The authors classified vulnerabilities into four categories depending upon the IoT ecosystem. Those are policy and procedure vulnerabilities, software vulnerabilities, network vulnerabilities, and gateway vulnerability. Likewise, attacks are classified into malicious insertion, exploitation of vulnerabilities, and Noncyber attacks. Insertion of malicious viruses can be done at any point in the supply chain lifecycle. These attacks are not possible to detect until proper observation of entire activities. The exploitation of malware may affect in the commercial sectors.

Chamekh.M et.al (2018) proposes a architecture to improve the issues of P2P communication using Merkel-Tree, it helps to improve scalability and key management. Proposed architecture designed using a hierarchical structure. In structure, each company can be built its own tree and nodes. While creating a node, each node will get a unique hash through that the hosting company can identify every node in the supply chain system. The tree structure has two identity Intra tree and Inter Tree. Each tree can be in a different phase in a different tree.

Hiromoto.R.E et.al (2017) designed a architecture using DANN. This machine-learning algorithm helps to analyze the behaviours of the system. These categories into two sub-networks, the First model represents normal data, and the second one used to become aware of abnormal behaviours caused by vulnerabilities. DANN is embedded with the hardware. It helps to monitor temperature instability, heat generation of components, component vibration including cryptography attacks. A Synchronous LGDM approach used to generate a data flow precedence graph helps to predict the balancing data flow in the supply chain.

Zhou.W et.al (2018) uses, RFID based framework for healthcare supply, to learn and progress automatically based on the environmental deviations. The reasons for motivating the authors to develop RFID based framework, healthcare appliances need to be track and trace from manufacturing to retailing for improving accuracy, protect from the theft of costly medical equipment and avoid from fake products. In this framework, the authors analyzed a simple RFID Reader authentication protocol. This protocol is lightweight and rapid execution, but not provides sufficient security.

3.5 Implementation of Blockchain Technology for IoT Enabled Healthcare Application

Xu.J et.al (2019) identified that Healthcare application implemented using IoT technology, it has storage constraints due to constrained devices, so it needs centralized third party storage devices for managing healthcare information, which makes user lose control over their data and leads to privacy leakage. It uses two chain mechanisms based on blockchain technology. One chain for keeping user information and another chain keeps doctor's data. To protect patient information used AES symmetric key-based encryption and for managing doctor's information, they used the asymmetric key-based Merkle tree approach. The advantage of this model ensures tamper resistant and avoids data crashes.

Griggs et.al (2018) identified from existing system, availability of EHR's does not guarantee, alteration of healthcare record and leakage are possible. In proposed model, Healthcare application is implemented on a smart contract using Ethereum, this approach is based on permissioned. Proposed model provides immutability, availability of EHR's is guaranteed, transparency. To ensure the privacy of patient information, this model doesn't make any association between patients and their data. Patients are still monitored remotely without compromising privacy.

Zhou.T et.al (2019) identified many issues on the traditional system. In existing, difficult to share EHR's of patients due to that information is stored in a distributed manner. Traditional system uses third-party and cloud-based storage structures for maintaining EHR, these approaches are vulnerable to various attacks. Proposed architecture, the encrypted medical data are stored in multiple blocks for ensuring privacy. Consensus identity-based Verifiable Random Function used for verification of node locally to avoid DDoS and Sybil attacks.

Zhang.A et.al (2018) pointed out, sharing of EHR are enrich accuracy of diagnosis. Security and privacy preservation are critical issues in the traditional system. The authors proposed a system depending on Private Blockchain and Consortium Blockchain. Private Blockchain is responsible for maintaining Personnel Health Information and the responsibility of consortium blockchain keeps secured index of PHI. Implementation of blockchain ensures immutability, so this model protects from the alteration of information. In the proposed model encrypted PHI is stored in a private blockchain. These records can be accessed only by authorized users, it ensures security on data.

3.6 Implementation of Blockchain Technology for IoT Enabled Smart Transportation System

Zheng.D et.al (2019) indicates that authentication and privacy are major concerns on VANET. In existing, it's difficult to control from internal forged and reply attacks. This advanced model used blockchain, to provide a solution for the above attack and also afford decentralized traceable vehicles. All the transactions are stored in the blockchain using a Hash algorithm. If an adversary/malicious tries to tamper the recorded data, he/she need to regenerate all the hashes in the network. So it is not possible to do the above work, it avoids tampering of Road Side Unit record. Each transaction has its transaction-id, vehicle communication happens using this id, the transaction with an inaccurate random number is discarded for protecting from reply attack.

Zeng.P et.al (2020) proposed a system for analysis and verification of security filed in smart traffic lights. In blockchain-based traffic, the information management system needs to prove the authenticity of the ledger to add new records since it avoids a ghost attack on the traffic system. Also, these distributed storage mechanisms avoid from various attacks.

Zhang.X et.al (2019) proposed a system based on Digital Signature using the ECC for ensuring reliability and integrity on VANET. The proposed architecture ensures the following security requirements: 1) Blockchain based system avoids malicious attacks in the centralized storage. 2) The digital signature-based authentication mechanism used for protecting from brute force. 3) All the vehicles need to verify before recording data on the storage, it guarantees the integrity. Liang.X et.al (2018) addresses the solution for IoT based smart cities security vulnerabilities. The blockchain technologies use public key algorithms ECC and SHA, it avoids leakage of information and cryptographic vulnerabilities.

3.7 Implementation of Blockchain Technology for IoT Enabled Smart Cities

Lee.Y et.al (2020) applies BC in home gateway, Gateway plays a major role, the gateway is vulnerable to various security threats such as reliability, availability, and cyber attacks. To address the above security vulnerabilities the authors proposed Blockchain technology to prevent DDoS attacks in smart home applications; it is not possible to attack all the nodes in the chain.

Xie.J et.al (2019) designed structure to smart city for improve the lifestyle of urban people using modern ICT. The characteristics of smart cities are: citizen's lifestyle improvement, effective utilization power consumption and transportation, environmental protection, traffic management, and many more. Here authors identified the following features of blockchain on smart-cities: Transparency and resource utilization protects from single point of failure and immutability nature.

Shen.M et.al (2019) proposed architecture called "SecureSVM". This architecture using a machine learning algorithm called SVM. To employ homomorphism cryptosystem for secure data sharing implements polynomial multiplication and comparison approaches. To protect from various threat model systems uses the "Known Cipher-Text Model" and "Known Background Model". This approach improves the efficiency and accuracy of the privacy system.

Biswas.K et.al (2016) presented a security framework for communication in smart cities. This framework has three different layers: Physical layer- is vulnerable to security attacks since the lack of encryption. Proposed architecture implements multiple vendors agreed on communications to avoid above security threats. In communication, the layer needs application-specific protocols for improved privacy. The final layer is the database layer, to protect from unauthorized manipulation of data, can use permissioned and permissonless blockchain.

3.8 Implementation of Blockchain Technology for IoT Enabled Supply Chain Management

Gao.Z et.al (2018) designed construction for maintaining supply chain hierarchies. But it is difficult to manage distributed nature and fraudulent activity. To ensure these, the authors proposed the "Two-step block consortium mechanism based on hybrid decentralized ledger". The proposed system needs two types of ledger 1)Reservation Ledger 2)Data Ledger to record the supply chain activity. RL is used to store users and helpers information whereas in DL stores the entire supply chain information. An attacker cannot modify or tamper the records since RL is implemented based on the PoW consensus algorithm. This system uses SSL enabled communication between two parties, it avoids from eavesdropping or tampering of the message.

Mao.D et.al (2019) proposed a model using smart contract-based consortium blockchain called FTSCON. It implements Online Double Auction algorithms for eliminating competition among merchants. This system uses the following mechanisms to improve the security. 1) To provide robust and scalable architecture uses p2p communication. 2) All the transactions are recorded on the block encrypted using the hash algorithm. 3) For privacy protection, this model uses only public key without revealing the private key.

Toma.C et.al (2018) dived the entire process into two parts. The first part consists of two smart-contracts; the first contract maintains a set of rules between product and seller, second contracts used to store exact information about the clients. The second part used to analyze the good's purchase information stored on the blockchain. With help of transaction key details are stored on blockchain. Once information recorded on the chain, in future it cannot modify, it prevents tampering of information.

Dasaklis.T.K et.al (2019) proposed a "forensics-by-design supply chain traceability framework with audit trails" for ensuring reliability, security, and resilience. Proposed system implements the token concept by using Bill-of-Material hierarchical list. Still, the proposed architecture needs to be addressed for assessing scalability in large scale applications.

4. SOLUTIONS AND RECOMMENDATIONS

This section provides how blockchain will help with the above application.

4.1 Benefits of Blockchain Technology Implementation for Smart Healthcare Application

Healthcare application requires high quality of services to provide better solutions and accuracy with the latest technological developments. Arya (2019) says the current approach does not provide sufficient security and flexibility on patient records and medical equipment. Novel technology helps in the following way:

- **Improving Medical Record Access**- Accessing a patient's medical history is difficult in the traditional healthcare system. Blockchain helps to access accurate medical history and reduce time consumption.
- **Securing Patients Health Records** – All information about the patients and other medical details will be stored in distributed with security.
- **Avoids Counterfeit Drugs** – In blockchain technology, all the information is secure and transparent. It helps to reduce the supply of counterfeit drugs and equipment to the patient and medical organization.

4.2 Benefits of Blockchain Technology Implementation for Smart Transportation System

Blockchain technology helps to eliminate the transparency issue in the transportation and logistics system (Chen.s et.al. 2020). This digital auditing guarantees accuracy and protects from the modification of recorded information. In addition to this:

- **Brings Trust and Data Transparency** – All the processes are transparent and accurate including price, ownership, and other processes.
- **Improved Traceability and Trackability** – Live transaction and location can be verified and tracked from anywhere. Transport status, location, and history of travel can be transparent.
- **Accelerated payment, better security, and reduction of fraud** – Automatic schedule can be done for the payment with help of smart contract.

4.3 Benefits of Blockchain Technology Implementation for Smart Cities

Blockchain technologies can be applied in smart cities in many aspects. In consideration with the categories benefits of blockchain technologies listed in the following:

- **Personal Data Storage** – With the rapid development of technology innovations, individual data also get increased rapidly. Blockchain technology helps to store and maintain personal data with security, transparency, and immutability.
- **Data Access Control** –Blockchain technology helps to provide an access control mechanism, which data requester can know they have access rights or not.
- **Effective Resource Utilization** - Recent years many countries face a lot of difficulties to use resources effectively. Blockchain technology provides solutions for the above difficulties.

4.4 Benefits of Blockchain Technology Implementation for Smart Supply-chain Management

The supply chain application covers many entities in the product lifecycle. Blockchain technologies help to maintain the product information from the raw material to delivery (Infopulse, 2019).

- **Transparent and controlled transactions** – It eliminates third-party involvement, and then result will be transparent and time-saving.
- **Preapproved Transaction Fees** – When making Swift based inter-bank transactions, the amount will be deducted only after completion of the transaction. But in the blockchain amount can be approved priorly.
- **Auditability and Reliability** - All the transaction details are maintained up to date on the blockchain.

4.5 Challenges of Blockchain Technology Implementation for Smart Healthcare Application

Many of the organization requests to implement blockchain-based healthcare technologies. But still, very few organizations are ready for implementation, due to new technology, and still difficult to understand the entire operation. Most of the people are not willing to share their Healthcare report to others. The following points discuss the additional challenges:

- **Storage Capability** – Healthcare organization includes Patients Healthcare Records, images, lab reports, and documents. New technology required huge storage capacity.

- **Data ownership Rules and Regulations** - In this technology eliminate the concept of a single owner of any data or information, so it leads to it difficult to frame the rules and regulations.

4.6 Challenges of Blockchain Technology Implementation for Smart Transportation System

Blockchain works efficiently when integration with smart contracts, it enforces communication clarity between parties, rules, and regulations. Still, it faces some of the challenges:

- **Infrastructure**- Blockchain-based specific infrastructure helps to improve the performance of the transportation system. Still, the specific infrastructure is in the investigation phase.
- **Computational Overheads** – The rapid growth of internet vehicles increases, it will create communication overhead. IoT based sensors are constrained devices, not capable to handle an increased number of vehicles and requests.

4.7 Challenges of Blockchain Technology Implementation for Smart Cities Application (Montori.F, 2018)

The following challenges are there to implement blockchain technology with smart cities.

- **Security and Privacy** – Blockchain provides privacy for the stored data, but these data cannot stay completely anonymous since distributed nature this technology.
- **Throughput**- This technology successfully implemented on crypto-currencies, but while focusing on throughput it supports a maximum of 7 transactions per second, in Ethereum supports 15 transactions per second. But this throughput is not sufficient in the current digital world;
- **High implementation cost** – The cost can be categories into two types. Design cost and Operational Cost, Design cost states that one-time implementation cost, and operational cost required to maintaining smart cities. All the aspects of blockchain technology require high cost.

4.8 Challenges of Blockchain Technology Implementation for Smart Supply-chain Management

All the technologies have to address challenges to adapt to any applications. Blockchain technology also has certain technological challenges while integrating with supply chain management (Mondal.S, 2019).

- **Technical issues** – Currently available infrastructure is only capable to store limited transaction details. This limits number of transactions and information storage. Another one is, digital technologies require constant updates.
- **Policymaking process**- All the industry/organization needs to support for this technology is short of policies, inadequate learning, and guidance platforms.

5. CONCLUSION

Blockchain technology comes with a decentralized and immutable environment. By default, this technology protects from tamper-proof, increases transparency, fast processing among multiple devices, and increased stability. With the help of millions of devices Internet of Things brings innovative technologies development to this world. By integrating Blockchain with IoT can monitor and track all the devices involved in many IoT based applications. Blockchain uses cryptographic algorithms for ensuring privacy and security to the world. Blockchain can afford valuable and resourceful in real-time applications while integrating with IoT. This technology brings consensus algorithms to ensure the work is done by authentication and protects from unauthorized activity. And another important concept is smart contracts, transactions can be created based on some constraints for reducing the intermediary, minimize time and cost consumption. Most familiar crypto-currencies like Etherum and Bitcoin face scalability issues and so it's difficult to handle IoT generated a large volume of data. The main limitation of blockchain technologies are, it requires a huge amount of energy and computing resources, very limited number of the transaction can be executed, in some situation economically and practically unviable.

REFERENCES

Deebak, B.D., Al-Turjman, F., Aloqaily, M., & Alfandi, O. (2019). An Authentic-Based Privacy Preservation Protocol for Smart e-Healthcare Systems in IoT. *IEEE Access.* . doi:10.1109/ACCESS.2019.2941575

Dhillon, P., & Kalra, S. (2018). Multi-factor user authentication scheme for IoT-based healthcare services. *Journal of Reliable Intelligent Environments*, 4(3), 141–160. Advance online publication. doi:10.100740860-018-0062-5

Duraiswamy, S. (2019). End to end lightweight mutual authentication scheme in IoT-based healthcare environment. *Journal of Reliable Intelligent Environments*, 6(1), 3–13. Advance online publication. doi:10.100740860-019-00079-w

Falco, G., Viswanathan, A., Caldera, C., & Shrobe, H., (2018). A Master Attack Methodology for an AI-Based Automated Attack Planner for Smart Cities. *IEEE, 6*, 48360-48373.

Gao, Z., Xu, L., & Chen, L. (2018). CoC: A Unified Distributed Ledger Based Supply Chain Management System. *J. Comput. Sci. Technol., 33*, 237–248. . doi:10.1007/s11390-018-1816-5

Griggs, Ossipova, O., Kohlios, C. P., Baccarini, A. N., Howson, E. A., & Hayajneh, T. (2018). Healthcare Blockchain System Using Smart Contracts for Secure Automated Remote Patient Monitoring. *Journal of Medical Systems*, 42(7), 130. Advance online publication. doi:10.100710916-018-0982-x PMID:29876661

Hashem Eiza, M., & Ni, Q. (2017). Driving with Sharks: Rethinking Connected Vehicles with Vehicle Cybersecurity. *IEEE Vehicular Technology Magazine*, 12(2), 45–51. doi:10.1109/MVT.2017.2669348

Hiromoto, R. E., Haney, M., & Vakanski, A. (2017). A secure architecture for IoT with supply chain risk management. *IEEE International Conference on IDAACS*, 431-435.

Infopulse (2019, Oct. 7). *Blockchain in Supply Chain Management: Key Use Cases and Benefits.* https://medium.com/@infopulseglobal_9037/blockchain-in-supply-chain-management-key-use-cases-and-benefits-6c6b7fd43094

Lee, Y., Rathore, S., Park, J. H., & Park, J. H. (2020). A blockchain-based smart home gateway architecture for preventing data forgery. *Hum. Cent. Comput. Inf. Sci.*, 10(1), 9. doi:10.118613673-020-0214-5

Liang, X., Shetty, S., & Tosh, D. (2018). Exploring the Attack Surfaces in Blockchain Enabled Smart Cities. *IEEE International Smart Cities Conference*, 1-8. 10.1109/ISC2.2018.8656852

Lo, S. K. (2019). Analysis of Blockchain Solutions for IoT: A Systematic Literature Review. *IEEE Access : Practical Innovations, Open Solutions, 7*, 58822–58835.

Mao, D., Hao, Z., Wang, F., & Li, H. (2019). Novel Automatic Food Trading System Using Consortium Blockchain. *Arabian Journal for Science and Engineering*, 44(4), 3439–3455. doi:10.100713369-018-3537-z

Miraz, M.H. (2020). Blockchain of Things (BCoT): The Fusion of Blockchain and IoT Technologies. *Studies in Big Data, 60.*

Mohammad, N. (2019). A Multi-Tiered Defense Model for the Security Analysis of Critical Facilities in Smart Cities. *IEEE, 7*, 152585-152598.

Mondal, S., Wijewardena, K. P., Aruppuswami, S., Kriti, N., Kumar, D., & Chahal, P. (2019). Blockchain Inspired RFID-Based Information Architecture for Food Supply Chain. *IEEE IoT Journal*, *6*(3), 5803–5813.

Montori, F., Bedogni, L., & Bononi, L. (2018). A Collaborative Internet of Things Architecture for Smart Cities and Environmental Monitoring. *IEEE IoT Journal*, *5*(2), 592–605.

Nofer, M., Gomber, P., & Hinz, O. (2017). Blockchain Bus. *Inf Syst Eng*, *59*, 183–187. doi:10.100712599-017-0467-3

Omitola, T., & Wills, G. (2018). Towards Mapping the Security Challenges of the Internet of Things (IoT) Supply Chain. *Procedia Computer Science*, *126*, 441–450. doi:10.1016/j.procs.2018.07.278

Reiff, N. (2020, Feb. 1). *Blockchain Explained*. https://www.investopedia.com/terms/b/blockchain.asp

Riahi Sfar, A., Challal, Y., Moyal, P., & Natalizio, E. (2019). A Game Theoretic Approach for Privacy Preserving Model in IoT-Based Transportation. *IEEE Transactions on Intelligent Transportation Systems*, *20*(12), 4405–4414. doi:10.1109/TITS.2018.2885054

Shen, M., Tang, X., Zhu, L., Du, X., & Guizani, M. (2019). Privacy-Preserving Support Vector Machine Training Over Blockchain-Based Encrypted IoT Data in Smart Cities. *IEEE Internet of Things Journal*, *6*(5), 7702–7712.

Shen, M., Tang, X., Zhu, L., Du, X., & Guizani, M. (2019). Privacy-Preserving Support Vector Machine Training Over Blockchain-Based Encrypted IoT Data in Smart Cities. *IEEE IoT Journal*, *6*(5), 7702-7712.

Tang, W. Ren, T., Deng, K., & Zhang, Y. (2019). Secure Data Aggregation of Lightweight E-Healthcare IoT Devices With Fair Incentives. *IEEE IoT Journal*, *6*(5), 8714-8726.

Toma, C., Talpiga, B., Boja, C., Popa, M. I., & Zurini, M. (2018). Secure IoT Supply Chain Management Solution Using Blockchain and Smart Contracts Technology, Innovative Security Solutions for Information Technology and Communications. *Lecture Notes in Computer Science, 11359*. https://blog.usejournal.com/how-can-blockchain-healthcare-solution-benefits-hospitals-and-patients-43fa6ce485a3

Wang, K., Yuan, L., Miyazaki, T., Chen, Y., & Zhang, Y. (2018). Jamming and Eavesdropping Defense in Green Cyber–Physical Transportation Systems Using a Stackelberg Game. *IEEE Transactions on Industrial Informatics*, *14*(9), 4232–4242. doi:10.1109/TII.2018.2841033

Xie, J., Tang, H., Huang, T., Yu, F. R., Xie, R., Liu, J., & Liu, Y. (2019). A Survey of Blockchain Technology Applied to Smart Cities: Research Issues and Challenges. *IEEE Communications Surveys and Tutorials*, *21*(3), 2794–2830. doi:10.1109/COMST.2019.2899617

Xu, C., Lin, H., Wu, Y., Guo, X., & Lin, W. (2019). An SDNFV-Based DDoS Defense Technology for Smart Cities. *IEEE Access: Practical Innovations, Open Solutions*, *7*, 137856–137874. doi:10.1109/ACCESS.2019.2943146

Xu, J., Xue, K., Li, S., Tian, H., Hong, J., Hong, P., & Yu, N. (2019). Healthchain: A Blockchain-Based Privacy Preserving Scheme for Large-Scale Health Data. *IEEE Internet of Things Journal*, *6*(5), 8770–8781. doi:10.1109/JIOT.2019.2923525

Zeng, P., Wang, X., Li, H., Jiang, F., & Doss, R. (2020). A Scheme of Intelligent Traffic Light System Based on Distributed Security Architecture of Blockchain Technology. *IEEE Access: Practical Innovations, Open Solutions*, 8, 33644–33657. doi:10.1109/ACCESS.2020.2972606

Zhang, A., & Lin, X. (2018). Towards Secure and Privacy-Preserving Data Sharing in e-Health Systems via Consortium Blockchain. *Journal of Medical Systems*, 42(8), 140. doi:10.100710916-018-0995-5 PMID:29956061

Zhang, X., & Chen, X. (2019). Data Security Sharing and Storage Based on a Consortium Blockchain in a Vehicular Ad-hoc Network. *IEEE Access: Practical Innovations, Open Solutions*, 7, 58241–58254. doi:10.1109/ACCESS.2018.2890736

Zheng, D., Jing, C., Guo, R., Gao, S., & Wang, L. (2019). A Traceable Blockchain-Based Access Authentication System With Privacy Preservation in VANETs. *IEEE Access: Practical Innovations, Open Solutions*, 7, 117716–117726. doi:10.1109/ACCESS.2019.2936575

Zhou, T., Li, X., & Zhao, H. (2019). Med-PPPHIS: Blockchain-Based Personal Healthcare Information System for National Physique Monitoring and Scientific Exercise Guiding. *Journal of Medical Systems*, 43(9), 305. doi:10.100710916-019-1430-2 PMID:31410583

Zhou, W., & Piramuthu, S. (2018). IoT security perspective of a flexible healthcare supply chain. *Information Technology Management*, 19(3), 141–153. doi:10.100710799-017-0279-7

KEY TERMS AND DEFINITIONS

Consensus Algorithm: Enforces teamwork and security among multiple nodes in distributed environment.

Electronic Health Records: Digital format of patient's medical information.

Immutability: The transactions of blockchain are consistent, unaltered, and unmodifiable.

Mining: Process of adding new block in a blockchain by solving mathematical problem.

Proof of Work: Submitted work need to be agreed by all other participants in a network.

Quality of Service: Can manage privacy, transparency, speed, and accuracy of blockchain transaction.

Smart Contract: Agreement based self-executing computer programs.

Smart Meter: Enabling two-way communication among sensors without human intervention.

This research was previously published in Enabling Blockchain Technology for Secure Networking and Communications; pages 175-200, copyright year 2021 by Information Science Reference (an imprint of IGI Global).

Chapter 57
Role and Impact of Blockchain in Cybersecurity

Syed Abbas
IU India, India

ABSTRACT

Blockchain is a staggering innovation with possibilities to change business, particularly in developing business sector global partnerships. Blockchain innovation is a circulated and decentralized record framework that can record exchanges between various PCs. The innovation is viewed as a solid online protection convention because of its abilities of showing any injustice and giving sureness in the trustworthiness of exchanges. The blockchain is another creative innovation that is in the period of being taken on by associations for overseeing records.

INTRODUCTION TO BLOCKCHAIN

Data that we store and cycle on the web is expanding and the trustworthiness of the information has gotten one of the difficulties for computerized capacity and correspondence. The blockchain is another imaginative innovation which could take care of the basic issues of information respectability (Yaga et al., 2018). As indicated by National Institute of Standards and Technology (NIST), "Blockchains are alter apparent and alter safe computerized records carried out in a circulated style (i.e., without a focal storehouse) and as a rule without a focal power (i.e., a bank, organization, or government) (Tikhomirov et al., 2018) (Swan, 2015)." The possibility of blockchain came from the paper distributed by Stuart Haber in 1991. He distributed a paper called "How to Time-Stamp a Digital Document", where he had referenced about the need of time stepping a record to affirm when it was made and adjusted for the trustworthiness of the information (Iansiti & Lakhani, 2017). The Blockchain which is a progressive innovation set to change the eventual fate of figuring and upset a few ventures with more inventive arrangements. It is open, permanent and conveyed consequently basically material in numerous conditions. The innovation acquired huge allure from the ascent of digital forms of money however it sees applications in numerous different areas another than finance. The Blockchain may be be inexactly interpreted as a

DOI: 10.4018/978-1-6684-7132-6.ch057

few cryptographically tied squares. A square alludes to an information compositions with threesome segments; information (Crosby, 2016). In like way, there's a inquire for reliance 'tween squares which may be utilized to guarantee the trustworthiness of the total Blockchain. Must be the data in any of the squares change, its hash will be changed moreover. This will induce a turning impact where the hashes of the coming with regards to squares will wrapped up invalid. This is frequently the explanation exchanges on the Blockchain are enduring. This framework can be exceptionally valuable in offering online protection arrangements in dangerous regions like IoT gadgets, organizations and information stockpiling and transmission. Toward this objective, we will fundamentally analyze existing works and studies on blockchain network protection and utilize our experiences to foster new headings (Cachin, 2016).

BACKGROUND

The blockchain is made of up interconnected squares which have put away the data about the exchange with the hash worth of the past block. Every one of the squares in blockchain will have the hash worth of the past square and that load of squares are connected all together. Each square of the blockchain will have data put away, not many of the terms put away on the square are recorded underneath (Zheng et al., 2018) (Li et al., 2020):

- **File:** Index will have the data with respect to the area of a square inside the blockchain. Every one of the squares will have a file esteem which implies the area of that square in that blockchain.
- **Hash:** Hash is the special worth that is utilized for quick arrangement of information in the blockchain.
- **Previous Hash:** All the squares on the blockchain will have the put away the has data of the past block connected to them.
- **Timestamp:** Timestamp will have the data about when the square was made.
- **Transaction:** This recorded will save the data about the exchange executed on the blockchain.

The main square on the blockchain is called beginning square and this square won't have the hash a worth put away of the past block, from that point onward, every one of the squares made will have the data has a worth of the past block. Assuming somebody attempted to alter the information inside the square of blockchain, it will change the hash worth of blockchain and will make every one of the squares after that invalid, since the hash esteem saved money on the square won't coordinate with the past block (Li, 2017) (Mengelkamp et al., 2018).

Figure 1. Blockchain structure

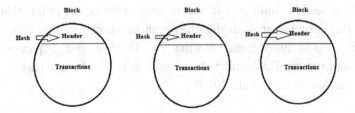

Figure 1 shows the overall construction of the blockchain, there are three squares displayed on the figure where the main square is called beginning square.

The principal block stores the data about exchange executed and stores the hash. Since the beginning square is the primary square on the blockchain, it won't have the hash worth of the past block (Khan et al., 2018). The subsequent square will have a hash worth of the principal block and the data about the exchange and the third square will have the hash worth of the subsequent square and the exchange subtleties. Prefer as such, every new square produced on the blockchain will have the hash worth of the past block and the data about the exchange executed during that time (Gao & Nobuhara, 2017) .

This is the overall construction of blockchain without the savvy contract on them like Bitcoin. On the off chance that the blockchain is intended to help savvy contract, they will have an alternate construction and more space on the square for putting away data with respect to the shrewd agreement. In the event that we take an illustration of Ethereum, which is a blockchain with Smart Contract support, it has an alternate structure. Ethereum creates has for every exchange and it will choose a couple and again it will produce another hash for those chose sets, and it will make the leftover has root. Ethereum square will have three Merkle tree in its header and capacity of these trees are to keep up with the condition of the square, keep up with the exchange and to keep up with the receipts. Diverse blockchain may have their own construction however these are the overall design of blockchain with or without the brilliant agreement support (Aste et al., 2017).

There are cardinal generality correspondence calculations, PoW and PoS. A verification of the work agreement involves the approval of a square by hubs showing that they have accomplished some work and gone to an arrangement of the outcomes (Taylor et al., 2019a) (Gill et al., 2019) . Coming up next is an illustration of a PoW agreement calculation:

1. The organization groups exchanges from clients in a memory pool
2. Diggers competition to confirm every exchange in the pool
    a. Settle an unpredictable riddle to check exchange
    b. Propose result to the organization check
        i. Assuming Correct, then broadcast right response to different diggers
        ii. Else

    Redo computation
3. First excavator with right answer gets compensated
4. The memory pool is confirmed and added as a square to the Blockchain . The flowchart for the calculation is as per the following:

One more critical component in the Blockchain is the scattered model of recordkeeping. Center points in a Blockchain association can store all of the data in the association accepting they need to. Various center points do this as it is basic during either for understanding or reference purposes (Sharma et al., 2017). This ensures that there is no bound together amassing of data10. Any adversary that endeavors to mull over Blockchain needs to mull over immense level of the center points that store the decentralized pieces of data. This is on the grounds that the organization checks the squares of information put away in decentralized areas to discover the ones that vary from the rest. Typically, the greater part has the right or positive information. The high level components in Blockchain make it ideal for the present online protection needs (Mkrttchian et al., 2019).

Figure 2. Flowchart POW algorithm

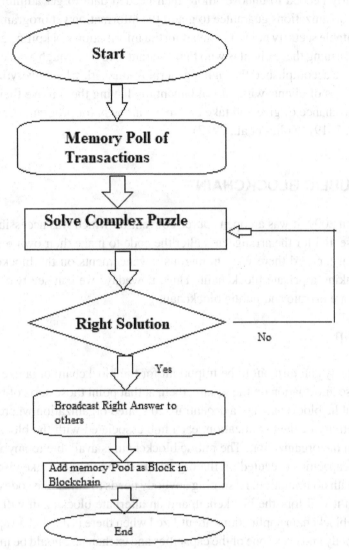

One of the manners in which Blockchain can be incorporated into online protection is for the improvement of instruments that can forestall extortion and fraud. Clients are continually confronting the danger of unapproved admittance to and change of information. This is on the grounds that numerous clients have brought together information stockpiling. It is hence simple for a programmer to break the information stockpiling area and alteration the information with noxious expectations. Blockchain forestalls such cases with its appropriated stockpiling of information. Touchy information, for example, political decision results could, in this way, be put away in great many PCs whereby each will have a duplicate of the information. Except if the programmer can think twice about huge number of PCs with the duplicates of information, the break and alteration of only a couple of PCs won't influence the remainder of the information in the organization. Essentially, Blockchain can be utilized to discourage data fraud. As clarified by NASDAQ, the present information robbery episodes are brought about by helpless information the executives (How Blockchain Can Fight Fraud Based on Know-Your-Customer Data, 2019).

Clients are regularly needed to uncover more than needed data to get administrations from many organizations. These organizations guarantee to guard the information yet programmers generally wind up discovering exploitable security holes and invading the information stockpiling areas. Blockchain can forestall fraud by confirming that a client is who they guarantee to be through a decentralized personality framework. This can be accomplished through a general framework where everything associations can confirm the personalities of clients without fundamentally having them move their delicate subtleties. This will diminish the chance of give and take and make it costly for programmers to take client information (Casino et al., 2019) (Kolias et al., 2017).

PRIVATE AND PUBLIC BLOCKCHAIN

When bitcoin began in 2009, it was an open source convention which was accessible to everybody and anybody could be essential for the arrange and alter the code to make their own rendition of the blockchain. From that point forward there were numerous advancements on the blockchain and there was a requirement for making a private blockchain. Thus, nowadays we can see two various types of the blockchain, and they are private and public blockchain.

Public Blockchain

In the event that anybody can turn out to be important for the blockchain organize and have the option to peruse and compose information on the square, then, at that point those sorts of blockchain are called public blockchain. Public blockchain are a decentralized shared organization where no one controls the information or the activity of the organization, each hub associated with the blockchain network have equivalent consent on the organization. The public blockchain is available to anybody so anybody can see every one of the capacities executed on the organization and they can likewise be the piece of the blockchain network with no limitation. Assuming anybody needs to adjust the codes and capacities from the public blockchain it will fork the blockchain and an alternate blockchain will be framed from the changed code. Public blockchain applications are utilized when there is need of an application that ought to be available to anybody and every one of the capacities and exchanges should be made straightforward. Digital currencies are perhaps the most mainstream utilizations of the public blockchain and Bitcoin, Ethereum, Litecoin, Monero are not many instances of cryptographic forms of money utilizing public blockchain innovation (Trautman & Ormerod, 2016).

Private Blockchain

At some point there may be a prerequisite to make a blockchain network accessible just for specific clients, all things considered, we can limit the entrance of blockchain to general society and make it accessible just for certain whitelisted clients. In the event that the blockchain isn't available to people in general and accessible just for specific clients then it is known as a private blockchain. For the most part association utilizes private blockchain for the inside utilization of association when there is no need of making the information accessible to people in general. Private blockchain doesn't permit people in general to peruse or compose information from the blockchain and they can't be essential for the blockchain data set. Private blockchain may have better execution contrasted with the public blockchain because of the predetermined number of hubs and more modest exchange. In any case, it is less secure than public blockchain in light of the fact that one can undoubtedly alter the data in blockchain and fork the organization, one can adjust the code whenever to meet their requirements. In open blockchain, it is almost difficult to alter the information on blockchain except if we control over half of the hubs. However, private blockchain doesn't have that security highlight, which makes it less secure than public blockchain. R3, EWF, B3i, and Corda are not many of the instances of the private blockchain (Kshetri, 2017).

METHODOLOGY

This examination will utilize the subjective investigation of auxiliary information to assess the appropriateness of Blockchain innovation in the present network protection industry. It will zero in on a recent report through with by Taylor et al. Which is assessed 30 ongoing exploration concentrates on Blockchain network protection. In the first place, it will take a gander at the most recent executions of the developing Blockchain innovation in online protection. Second, it will take a gander at the techniques accessible for sending Blockchain online protection arrangements. The fundamental focus points from the exploration discoveries and proposals from the dissected papers will be utilized to frame a conversation on how Blockchain can bear the cost of safety in the present IT client conditions (Xie, Ding, Yang, & Wang, 2019) (Yeoh, 2017).

OUTCOMES

The pie graph beneath sums up the discoveries whereby IoT, organization, information, public key framework (PKI), and information protection guarantee the majority of the new Blockchain security executions:

Figure 3. Almost analyze blockchain security application fields

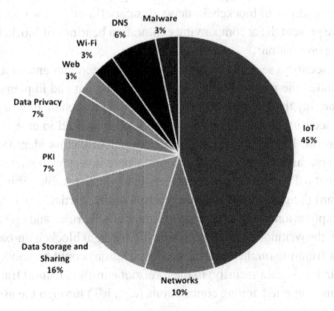

Since there are correct as of now nine billion such contraptions. These contraptions have slight security arrangements and various are being hacked and picked into botnet frameworks. One such botnet mastermind included IoT contraptions is the Mirai Botnet which has been used with tall speeds of advance against massive targets like Dyn DNS, one of the Internet's most noteworthy zone title target associations (Cha et al., 2018). At last, there is gigantic thought towards Blockchain security reply for data insurance. Most of the examinations are surveying strategies for getting before long conspicuous information through an overall Blockchain confirmation plot. This will dishonor the prerequisite for customers to send their information to affiliations, taking everything into account, the affiliations will check customers through the Blockchain.

The second focal point of the exploration is the means by which the Blockchain innovation can be utilized to further develop network safety. Despite the fact that the current security arrangements offer estimable degrees of assurance to IT assets, they are as yet inclined to disappointment.

Passing by the data given by the pie diagram over, the principle focal point of numerous scientists is the manner by which Blockchain can further develop the security stood to IoT gadgets, information, and organizations. The most security threat is unapproved get to and control of the contraptions. Blockchain security courses of action can help with directing get to control and data sharing for all IoT contraptions all the more effectively. A Blockchain security course of activity may be set up to guarantee solid client recognizable confirmation, affirmation, and information move. It may work by keeping scattered records around the trusted in fundamental affiliations and social occasions to avoid unapproved get to. Cutting edge affiliations may be set to be permitted reasonable in case perpetual the famous affiliations cast a vote or certify the unused client. Along these lines, an IoT contraption, for case, an IP camera in a house will reasonable convey consent to trusted in contraptions of the family. On the off chance that a program build endeavors to encourage to the camera, the Blockchain course of activity will prevent get to until most of the acknowledged contraptions vote to permit the computer program build to encourage to the camera (Viriyasitavat et al., 2019).

The utilization cases examined exhibited the expanding reason ability of the Blockchain innovation in network protection (Fernández-Caramés & Fraga-Lamas, 2018). Despite the fact that there were different regions investigated, the three featured regions are generally fundamental in the cutting edge IT climate.

Future examination headings of blockchain network safety Based on the consequences of this study and our perceptions, we present the accompanying exploration bearings of blockchain for digital protection that value further examination:

Blockchain for IoT security: security in IoT networks has been guaranteed as a squeezing need of the business and has gotten the most extreme need for development and implementation, regardless of flow research shows the way that pretty much every article on blockchain digital protection in the writing brings up that the security of IoT frameworks could be revitalized in case it is upheld with blockchain innovation. However, little is known and examined about factors identified with choices about and practicality to take on this innovation, and how and where it very well may be deliberately put into utilization to cure current IoT security chances/dangers in an unmistakable setting, considering the creative mind and afterward the production of future vectors in this particular space (Gupta et al., 2018). Subsequently, future exploration needs to foster some quantifiable rules and apparatuses that can assist with filling this clear in the writing. Besides, proposing lightweight blockchain-based solutions for asset compelled IoT gadgets (running on the edge of the organization) could be another space of additional exploration. Blockchain for AI data security: in the forefront enrolling natural framework, data is gotten from various sources and imparted among contraptions (e.g., IoT) through the associations. Man-made cognizance (AI) and its subordinates have been used as vital resources for examine and manage the got data to achieve practical intuition in keeping an eye on security issues. In spite of the way that AI is amazing and can be secured with scattered figuring, misdirecting assessment would be delivered when polluted or deceitful data is intentionally or startlingly planned by a malevolent outcast ward on adversarial information sources. Blockchain as a commended record progression might possibly be used in various spaces of the web. Blockchain tries to reduce exchange possibilities and cash related shakedown, sum up from its characteristics like decentralization, demonstrate and lastingness for guaranteeing the validness, faithfulness what's more, decency of information. The sidechain advancement (Taylor et al., 2019b) has most actually arisen as a different chain added to the fundamental chain, in contrasting and exchanges, to help the difficulties (fundamentally execution) perceived with fundamental blockchains. Before long, we envision a scattered multi-blockchain environment, in which unmistakable rule secures and sidechains work to team up with one another totally different circumstances. In any case, the down to earth parts of sidechains stay insufficiently comprehended, and various essential examination questions are still to be examined (Miller, 2018).

CYBERCRIMES COME IN DIFFERENT FORMS

A portion of the kinds of cybercrimes as articulated by (Nurse, 2019) (Ventures, 2019) are as per the following:

1. Saltines: Criminals with expectation of making misfortune the casualty to fulfill some enemy of social thought processes or for no particular reason.
2. Programmers: Criminals that obtain entrance into the PC framework or information base of casualties to get individual data stowed away in those PC frameworks.
3. Clowns: These crooks execute stunts on others with no expectation of a specific or durable damage.
4. Profession crooks: These lawbreakers embrace cybercrime as their vocation and make part or the entirety of their pay from wrongdoing. In various cases, they structure union with others or work inside coordinated groups like the mafia.
5. Digital psychological oppressors: They assault sites, telephone directories, mail records, and others by sending malware, similar to Trojans, infections, worms and such to casualties to upset their information base. Their motivation is to debilitate the data innovation framework of nations, making them inconsistent for forthcoming financial backers and people who wish to turn out to be important for such casualty country's IT framework.
6. Digital bulls: This set hassles casualties through the web. They send abusive sends, horrendous posts and offer such expressions through the web which makes provocation in any structure the person in question.
7. Salami aggressors: They assault through web for the commissions. Their primary point is to make a little modification in single cases which become unseen by and large. For instance a bank representative secures and embeds a program into bank's workers which deducts limited quantity from the record of each client consequently, such demonstration is by and large unseen, however the general increase by.

FUTURE EXPLORATION HEADINGS OF BLOCKCHAIN DIGITAL PROTECTION

In light of the consequences of this overview and our perceptions, we present the accompanying exploration headings of blockchain for digital protection that worth further examination:

Blockchain for IoT security: security in IoT networks has been asserted as a squeezing need of the business and has gotten the most extreme need for development and implementation, notwithstanding flow research shows the way that pretty much every article on blockchain network safety in the writing brings up that the security of IoT frameworks could be renewed in case it is upheld with blockchain innovation. However, little is known also, examined about factors identified with choices about and plausibility to embrace this innovation, and how and where it tends to be methodicallly put into utilization to cure current IoT security hazards/dangers in a reasonable setting, taking into consideration the creative mind and afterward the making of future vectors in this particular area. Along these lines, future exploration needs to foster a few quantifiable rules and instruments that can assist with filling this clear in the writing. Besides, proposing lightweight blockchain-based arrangements for asset obliged IoT gadgets (running o Blockchain for AI information security: in the cutting edge registering biological system,data is gotten from various sources and sent among contraptions (e.g., IoT) through the associations. Man-made mental ability (AI) and its subordinates have been used as basic resources for inspect and measure the got data to achieve effective speculation in watching out for security issues. Notwithstanding the way that AI is amazing and can be secured with flowed figuring, precarious examination would be delivered when destroyed or deceitful data is deliberately or surprisingly organized by a malignant pariah subject to badly arranged data sources. Blockchain as a well known record advancement might potentially be used in different spaces of the web. Blockchain attempts to decrease trade possibilities and money related deception, inferable from its characteristics like decentralization, undeniable status and perpetual quality for ensuring the validness, trustworthiness additionally, decency of data. Exactly when the credibility and resolute nature of data can be ensured, more secure and solid outcomes can be conveyed by AI. A future assessment heading could be the examination of Sidechain security: The sidechain development (Mahajan et al., 2011; Manzoor et al., 2019) has most actually emerged as an alternate chain joined to the standard chain, in comparing with trades, to moderate the troubles (essentially execution) related to principal blockchains. Before long, we envision a scattered multi-blockchain organic framework, in which unmistakable essential chains what's more, sidechains work to collaborate with each other in various circumstances. Notwithstanding, the viable parts of sidechains remain inadequately comprehended, furthermore, manyy crucial exploration questions are still to be discussed. For model, How do these sidechains set up security defaults to forestall assaults? How should blockchain clients be guaranteed of the trustworthiness and classification of their information through sidechains? Responding to these inquiries is essential for the future examinations to have a more supported blockchain network safety research (Siboni et al., 2019). Delivering open-source programming and dataset, and drawing in with local area: blockchain network protection research is cracked between the scholarly world and the designer local area. To overcome this issue, endeavors are needed by scholastic specialists to deliver more open-source applications, apparatuses, and dataset to be locked in by the business local area also, new companies. Indeed, there is an enormous local area who are intrigued in blockchain examination (confirmed by the ubiquity of open-source instruments for example, bitcoin-abe (Wang et al., 2019) or BlockBench (Xie, Ding, Yang, & Wang, 2019) for example), so scholastic specialists ought to effectively include the local area in the turn of events, approval, and upkeep of their exploration results.

VARIOUS SERVICES USING BLOCKCHAIN TECHNOLOGY

They are now different administrations utilizing blockchain innovation in the accompanying fields (Kan et al., 2018) (Kim et al., 2018):

- Finance: Bitcoin and other virtual monetary standards can be a utilization case for blockchains. Different monetary administrations including settlement, security of the exchange, cases, and others are applying the blockchain innovation. Wave is one these applications.
- Reward and devotion focuses: Blockchains can upgrade prize and dependability focuses. GyftBlock is a stage dependent on blockchain innovation, and it empowers start to finish abilities of gift vouchers.
- Communication: Getgems worker is an interpersonal interaction administrations (SNS) that awards virtual money (GMZ tokens) to SNS's clients when the clients peruse the commercials. Clients can trade advanced tokens inside the SNS.
- Asset Management: Ownership and move of resources and properties are significant occasions, so they ought to be unchanging; thusly, blockchain innovation can be helpful around here counting land enlistment and property enrollment. Factom is a stage, which guarantees genuineness, trust, and unchanging nature dependent on blockchain innovation.

ADVANTAGES AND DISADVANTAGES OF IMPLEMENTING BLOCKCHAIN TECHNOLOGY

Advantages of Blockchain Implementation Perceivability

One of the center explanations behind SC failures is helpless start to finish exchange. Blockchain gives constant data about the beginning of exchange and status of every exchange between various inventory network individuals. Offered the chances of sensor approaches and the IOTs, any quantifiable circumstance, for example, every information point in the Supply Chain can be followed. This element assists clients with further developing precision of information improving aggregate arranging and execution and furthermore forestalls hazard the board measures (Elhoseny & Hassanien, 2019).

Respectability

By having the common record, clear and changeless records, blockchain innovation gives practicableness to follow resources back to their start strategy. Data on module and spot of beginning is valuable to guarantee authenticity and guarantees honesty of resources that include product and administrations. This practicableness upholds responsible sourcing and allows analyst work to forestall item fake and different tricky activities. Also, Blockchain innovation facilitates work in worldwide exchange by making certain legitimacy customs freedom (Singh et al., 2020).

Virtualization

Virtualization expands the use of IT resources by fostering a coherent portrayal of programming identified with each actual equipment. Tokenization of actual SC resources i.e., specialized gear and inventories, follow a similar procedure. Virtualization assists with further developing agreement adaptability and empowers redistribution of relating hazards in inventory network the executives. Virtualization of IT equipment would empower further developed limit use of SC resources since abundance limits could be adapted (Konstantinidis et al., 2018).

Money

Considering any exchange universally, applications which are right now intended to work monetary store network the board are a characteristic „fit? for blockchain innovation. Parallelly, there are 2 varying sorts of systems which are liked by specialists. ? Blockchain innovation facilitates the multi-level and multi-party cash exchanges. Machine-driven exchanges and tokenized cash empower subsidizing of resources from blockchain parties that conjointly diminishes financing costs. Because of this, Supply Chain resources could be collateralized by presenting token frameworks (Dwivedi et al., 2020).

Trustless Exchange

At the point when individuals are engaged with monetary tasks, two distinct parties can without much of a stretch work the trading of money with no oversight or interference of an untouchable.

Enabled Customers

Customers are engaged with top-nature of data inside blockchain. The information inside blockchain is finished, solid, advantageous, precise and open. Each party is answerable for each and every party among their data and business transactions (Ali et al., 2018).]

Interaction Decency

Each party inside the blockchain organization can consider that cash trades will be executed in an extremely exact manner, as the show calls ousting the prerequisite for the confided in outsiders (Kurt Peker et al., 2020).

Straightforwardness and Constancy

Every one of the exchanges are extremely durable in blockchain innovation. Any type of exchange whether changed or switched is displayed to all or any party, which suggests that they can't be changed or deleted.

Quicker Transactions

Blockchain empowers quicker exchanges. As of now, bank exchanges can without much of a stretch require over one day for clearing request drafts and checks. In case Blockchain is executed, all exchanges between banks can be done in a brief time frame. Clients can undoubtedly get to Electronic Banking, Mobile Banking, UPI and so on for any kind of exchange even from distant areas (Tiwari & Batra, 2021) (Bera et al., 2021).

Disadvantages of Carrying Out Blockchain

Absence of Mindfulness

Many individuals are as yet uninformed of Blockchain innovation and its applications. As initial step, a simple system ought to be ready and individuals ought to be taught about Blockchain, and trust ought to be worked to carry out and test it in their own spaces. Channels or correspondence organization ought to be worked to make mindfulness. For a wide use of Blockchain we ought to consistently be prepared to determine difficulties like managing speed, confirmation strategy and data limits (Abdellatif et al., 2021).

Exclusive Expectations of Innovation

Application designers who pick Blockchain innovation ought to profoundly investigate and consider coordinating blockchain with other non-blockchain frameworks.

Overseeing Dangers of Progress

It is the obligation of blockchain clients to think about arrangements without influencing any current deal (Bodkhe et al., 2020).

Updating of Guideline and Enactment

Rules, laws, guidelines and enactments are worked by a few gatherings for clients and business parties. Be that as it may, by having the goal to guarantee guideline and enactment prerequisites, blockchain innovation faces a few difficulties in execution. Guidelines ought to be outlined to execute blockchain innovation as a vital piece of the monetary market(Esposito et al., 2021).

High Initial Capital Expense

Considering the expense engaged with blockchain innovation set up, however the working and exchange cost is by all accounts less, introductory capital expense is high and obstruction.

Control, Security and Protection

Protection and security are two of the key boundaries considered before any clients carry out blockchain innovation. They ought to be kept educated regarding these issues preceding setting up the trust utilizing their private data to a blockchain arrangement. As to the perceptions made on digital protection worries on blockchains, it is prescribed to screen the encryptions completely by the gatherings engaged with blockchain network (Mamta et al., 2021) (Nguyen et al., 2021).

Huge Energy Utilization

The blockchain innovation utilizes a ton of electric energy, which is a test to be looked by numerous nations.

CONCLUSION

Blockchain innovation proceeds to advance and conceive the fewer purpose suits in the cutting edge world-wide. Extraordinary of the practical regions where it has been considered and applied is network protection. The Blockchain system makes it significantly commonsense in tending to the current security challenges in districts like IoT contraptions, organizations, and data in transmission and capacity. The paper has surveyed the significance of the Blockchain development agreeing to the point of see of 45 pros checked. It has been seen that most Blockchain security researchers are centering a ton on the gathering of Blockchain security for IoT contraptions. Near by this, other noteworthy spaces of Blockchain security are organizations and data. As seen within the discussion, the Blockchain innovation can be utilized to induce IoT contraptions through more tried and true affirmation and data move components. These can keep software engineers from entering into these contraptions which routinely transport with defenseless security courses of action. The development can moreover be utilized to tie down systems by utilizing the unbending system to hinder unapproved affiliations and communication. Ultimately, Blockchain can get information in transmission and capacity through encoded blocks which must be opened by the conveying parties and are not inclined to control. More use cases are being concentrated yet these three have become the dominant focal point. It is suggested that future analysts investigate the common sense of a solitary Blockchain which may be utilized to the foster security arrangements since a large portion of the current arrangements utilize distinctive Blockchains subsequently hampering reconciliation.

Blockchain can be utilized in different areas like man-made reasoning, medical care, modern control framework, finance, IoT gadgets and for government employments. It can tackle the issue of a weak link and can forestall the most well-known assaults like Distributed Denial of Administration (DDoS). Solid encryption and carefully designed innovation of blockchain can be utilized to foster a safe application.

REFERENCES

Abdellatif, A. A., Samara, L., & Mohamed, A. (2021). MEdge-chain: Leveraging edge computing and blockchain for efficient medical data exchange. *IEEE Internet of Things Journal.*

Ali, S., Wang, G., Bhuiyan, M. Z. A., & Jiang, H. (2018). Secure data provenance in cloud-centric internet of things via blockchain smart contracts. *Proceedings of the 2018 IEEE SmartWorld, Ubiquitous Intelligence & Computing, Advanced & Trusted Computing, Scalable Computing & Communications, Cloud & Big Data Computing, Internet of People and Smart City Innovation (SmartWorld/SCALCOM/ UIC/ATC/CBDCom/IOP/SCI)*, 991–998. 10.1109/SmartWorld.2018.00175

Aste, T., Tasca, P., & Di Matteo, T. (2017). Blockchain technologies: The foreseeable impact on society and industry. *Computer, 50*(9), 18–28. doi:10.1109/MC.2017.3571064

Awad, A. I., Furnell, S., Hassan, A. M., & Tryfonas, T. (2019). Special issue on security of IoT-enabled infrastructures in smart cities. *Ad Hoc Networks*, *92*, 92. doi:10.1016/j.adhoc.2019.02.007

Battula, S. K., Garg, S., Naha, R. K., Thulasiraman, P., & Thulasiram, R. (2019). A micro-level compensation-based cost model for resource allocation in a fog environment. *Sensors (Basel)*, *19*(13), 2954. doi:10.339019132954 PMID:31277474

Bera, A., Das, A. K., & Sutrala, A. K. (2021). Private blockchain-based access control mechanism for unauthorized UAV detection and mitigation in internet of drones environment. *Computer Communications*, *166*, 91–109. doi:10.1016/j.comcom.2020.12.005

Bodkhe, U., Tanwar, S., Parekh, K., Khanpara, P., Tyagi, S., Kumar, N., & Alazab, M. (2020). Blockchain for industry 4.0: A comprehensive review. *IEEE Access: Practical Innovations, Open Solutions*, *8*, 79764–79800. doi:10.1109/ACCESS.2020.2988579

Cachin, C. (2016). Architecture of the hyperledger blockchain fabric. *Workshop on distributed crypto-currencies and consensus ledgers, 310*(1), 4.

Casino, F., Dasaklis, T. K., & Patsakis, C. (2019). A systematic literature review of blockchain-based applications: Current status, classification and open issues. *Telematics and Informatics*, *36*, 55–81. doi:10.1016/j.tele.2018.11.006

Cha, S.-C., Chen, J.-F., Su, C., & Yeh, K.-H. (2018). A blockchain connected gateway for BLE-based devices in the internet of things. *IEEE Access: Practical Innovations, Open Solutions*, *6*, 24639–24649. doi:10.1109/ACCESS.2018.2799942

Challa, S., Wazid, M., Das, A. K., Kumar, N., Reddy, A. G., Yoon, E. J., & Yoo, K. Y. (2017). Secure signature-based authenticated key establishment scheme for future IoT applications. *IEEE Access: Practical Innovations, Open Solutions*, *5*, 3028–3043. doi:10.1109/ACCESS.2017.2676119

Crosby, M. (2016). Blockchain technology: Beyond bitcoin. *Applied Innovation, 2*, 6-10.

Dwivedi, Amin, & Vollala. (2020). Blockchain based secured information sharing protocol in supply chain management system with key distribution mechanism. *Journal of Information Security and Applications, 54*.

Elhoseny, M., & Hassanien, A. E. (2019). An encryption model for data processing in WSN. In Dynamic Wireless Sensor Networks (pp. 145–169). Springer. doi:10.1007/978-3-319-92807-4_7

Esposito, C., Ficco, M., & Gupta, B. B. (2021). Blockchain-based authentication and authorization for smart city applications. *Information Processing & Management*, *58*(2), 102468. doi:10.1016/j.ipm.2020.102468

Fernández-Caramés, T. M., & Fraga-Lamas, P. (2018). A review on the use of blockchain for the internet of things. *IEEE Access: Practical Innovations, Open Solutions*, *6*, 32979–33001. doi:10.1109/ACCESS.2018.2842685

Gao, Y., & Nobuhara, H. (2017). A proof of stake sharding protocol for scalable blockchains. *Proceedings of the Asia-Pacific Advanced Network.*, *44*, 13–16.

Gill, S. S., Tuli, S., Xu, M., Singh, I., Singh, K. V., Lindsay, D., Tuli, S., Smirnova, D., Singh, M., Jain, U., Pervaiz, H., Sehgal, B., Kaila, S. S., Misra, S., Aslanpour, M. S., Mehta, H., Stankovski, V., & Garraghan, P. (2019). Transformative effects of IoT, blockchain and artificial intelligence on cloud computing: Evolution, vision, trends and open challenges. *Internet of Things*, *8*, 100118. doi:10.1016/j. iot.2019.100118

Gupta, Y., Shorey, R., Kulkarni, D., & Tew, J. (2018). The applicability of blockchain in the Internet of Things. *2018 10th Int. Conf. Commun. Syst. Networks*, 561-564. 10.1109/COMSNETS.2018.8328273

Hammi, M. T., Hammi, B., Bellot, P., & Serhrouchni, A. (2018). Bubbles of trust: A decentralized blockchain-based authentication system for IoT. *Computers & Security*, *78*, 126–142. doi:10.1016/j. cose.2018.06.004

How Blockchain Can Fight Fraud Based on Know-Your-Customer Data. (2019). Available: https://www. nasdaq.com/articles/how-blockchain-can-fight-fraud-based-know-your-customer-data-2019-02-11

Iansiti, M., & Lakhani, K. R. (2017). The truth about blockchain. *Harvard Business Review*, *95*(1), 118–127.

Jayaraman, P. P., Yang, X., Yavari, A., Georgakopoulos, D., & Yi, X. (2017). Privacy preserving internet of things: From privacy techniques to a blueprint architecture and efficient implementation. *Future Generation Computer Systems*, *76*, 540–549. doi:10.1016/j.future.2017.03.001

Kan, L., Wei, Y., Muhammad, A. H., Siyuan, W., Linchao, G., & Kai, H. (2018). A multiple blockchains architecture on inter-blockchain communication. *2018 IEEE International Conference on Software Quality, Reliability and Security Companion (QRS-C)*. 10.1109/QRS-C.2018.00037

Khan, K. M., Arshad, J., & Khan, M. M. (2018). Secure digital voting system based on blockchain technology. *International Journal of Electronic Government Research*, *14*(1), 53–62. doi:10.4018/ IJEGR.2018010103

Kim, S., Kwon, Y., & Cho, S. (2018). A survey of scalability solutions on blockchain. *2018 International Conference on Information and Communication Technology Convergence (ICTC)*. 10.1109/ ICTC.2018.8539529

Kolias, C., Kambourakis, G., Stavrou, A., & Voas, J. (2017). DDoS in the IoT: Mirai and other botnets. *Computer*, *50*(7), 80–84. doi:10.1109/MC.2017.201

Konstantinidis, I., Siaminos, G., Timplalexis, C., Zervas, P., Peristeras, V., & Decker, S. (2018). Blockchain for business applications: a systematic literature review. In *Business Information Systems* (pp. 384–399). Springer. doi:10.1007/978-3-319-93931-5_28

Kshetri, N. (2017). Can blockchain strengthen the internet of things? *IT Professional*, *19*(4), 68–72. doi:10.1109/MITP.2017.3051335

Kurt Peker, Y., Rodriguez, X., Ericsson, J., Lee, S. J., & Perez, A. J. (2020). A cost analysis of internet of things sensor data storage on blockchain via smart contracts. *Electronics (Basel)*, *9*(2), 244. doi:10.3390/ electronics9020244

Li, W. (2017). Securing proof-of-stake blockchain protocols. In Data Privacy Management, Cryptocurrencies and Blockchain Technology. Springer. doi:10.1007/978-3-319-67816-0_17

Li, X., Jiang, P., Chen, T., Luo, X., & Wen, Q. (2020). A survey on the security of blockchain systems. *Future Generation Computer Systems*, *107*, 841–853. doi:10.1016/j.future.2017.08.020

Mahajan, P., Setty, S., Lee, S., Clement, A., Alvisi, L., Dahlin, M., & Walfish, M. (2011). Depot: Cloud storage with minimal trust. *ACM Transactions on Computer Systems*, *29*(4), 12. doi:10.1145/2063509.2063512

Mamta, Gupta, Li, Leung, Psannis, & Yamaguchi. (2021). Blockchain-assisted secure fine-grained searchable encryption for a cloud-based healthcare cyber-physical system. *IEEE/CAA Journal of Automatica Sinica*.

Manzoor, A., Liyanage, M., Braeke, A., Kanhere, S. S., & Ylianttila, M. (2019). Blockchain based proxy re-encryption scheme for secure IoT data sharing. *2019 IEEE International Conference on Blockchain and Cryptocurrency (ICBC)*. 10.1109/BLOC.2019.8751336

Mengelkamp, E., Notheisen, B., Beer, C., Dauer, D., & Weinhardt, C. (2018). A blockchain-based smart grid: Towards sustainable local energy markets. *Computer Science-Research and Development*, *33*(1), 207–214. doi:10.100700450-017-0360-9

Miller, D. (2018). Blockchain and the internet of Things in the industrial sector. *IT Professional*, *20*(3), 1518. doi:10.1109/MITP.2018.032501742

Mkrttchian, V., Gamidullaeva, L. A., Vertakova, Y., & Panasenko, S. (2019). New tools for cyber security using blockchain technology and avatar-based management technique. In *Machine Learning and Cognitive Science Applications in Cyber Security* (pp. 105–122). IGI Global. doi:10.4018/978-1-5225-8100-0.ch004

Nguyen, G. N., Viet, N. H. L., Elhoseny, M., Shankar, K., Gupta, B. B., & El-Latif, A. A. A. (2021). Secure blockchain enabled cyber-physical systems in healthcare using deep belief network with ResNet model. *Journal of Parallel and Distributed Computing*, *153*, 150–160. doi:10.1016/j.jpdc.2021.03.011

Nurse, J. R. C. (2019). *Cybercrime and You: How Criminals Attack and the Human Factors That They Seek to Exploit. In The Oxford Handbook of Cyberpsychology*. OUP.

Sharma, P. K., Moon, S. Y., & Park, J. H. (2017). Block-VN: A distributed blockchain based vehicular network architecture in smart city. *JIPS*, *13*(1), 184–195.

Siboni, S., Sachidananda, V., Meidan, Y., Bohadana, M., Mathov, Y., Bhairav, S., Shabtai, A., & Elovici, Y. (2019). Security testbed for IoT devices. *IEEE Transactions on Reliability*, *68*(1), 23–44. doi:10.1109/TR.2018.2864536

Singh, A., Parizi, R. M., Zhang, Q., Choo, K.-K. R., & Dehghantanha, A. (2020). Blockchain smart contracts formalization: Approaches and challenges to address vulnerabilities. *Computers & Security*, *88*, 101654. doi:10.1016/j.cose.2019.101654

Swan, M. (2015). *Blockchain: Blueprint for a new economy*. O'Reilly Media, Inc.

Taylor, P. J., Dargahi, T., Dehghantanha, A., Parizi, R. M., & Choo, K. K. (2019a). A systematic literature review of blockchain cyber security. *Digital Communications and Networks.*, *12*(5), 1–14.

Taylor, P. J., Dargahi, T., Dehghantanha, A., Parizi, R. M., & Choo, K.-K. R. (2019b). A systematic literature review of blockchain cyber security. *Digital Communications and Networks*. Advance online publication. doi:10.1016/j.dcan.2019.01.005

Tikhomirov, S., Voskresenskaya, E., Ivanitskiy, I., Takhaviev, R., Marchenko, E., & Alexandrov, Y. (2018). Smartcheck: Static analysis of ethereum smart contracts. *2018 IEEE/ACM 1st International Workshop on Emerging Trends in Software Engineering for Blockchain*, 9–16.

Tiwari, A., & Batra, U. (2021). IPFS enabled blockchain for smart cities. *International Journal of Information Technology*, *13*(1), 201–211. doi:10.100741870-020-00568-9

Trautman, L. J., & Ormerod, P. C. (2016). Corporate Directors' and Officers' Cybersecurity Standard of Care: The Yahoo Data Breach. *Am. UL Rev.*, *66*(1), 1231.

Ventures, C. (2019). *2019 official annual cybercrime report.* https://www.herjavecgroup.com/the-2019-officialannual-cybercrime-report

Viriyasitavat, W., Da Xu, L., Bi, Z., & Pungpapong, V. (2019). Blockchain and internet of things for modern business process in digital economy—The state of the art. *IEEE Transactions on Computational Social Systems*, *6*(6), 1420–1432. doi:10.1109/TCSS.2019.2919325

Wang, X., Zha, X., Ni, W., & Ren, P. L. (2019). Survey on blockchain for internet of things. *Computer Communications*, *136*, 10–29. doi:10.1016/j.comcom.2019.01.006

Xie, L., Ding, Y., Yang, H., & Wang, X. (2019). Blockchain-based secure and trustworthy internet of things in SDN-enabled 5G-VANETs. *IEEE Access: Practical Innovations, Open Solutions*, *7*, 56656–56666. doi:10.1109/ACCESS.2019.2913682

Xie, L., Ding, Y., Yang, H., & Wang, X. (2019). Blockchain-based secure and trustworthy internet of things in SDN-enabled 5G-VANETs. *IEEE Access: Practical Innovations, Open Solutions*, *7*, 56656–56666. doi:10.1109/ACCESS.2019.2913682

Yaga, D., Mell, P., Roby, N., & Scarfone, K. (2018). *Nistir 8202 blockchain technology overview. National Institute of Standards and Technology.* US Department of Commerce.

Yeoh, P. (2017). Regulatory issues in blockchain technology. *Journal of Financial Regulation and Compliance.*, *25*(2), 196–208. doi:10.1108/JFRC-08-2016-0068

Zheng, Z., Xie, S., Dai, H. N., Chen, X., & Wang, H. (2018). Blockchain challenges and opportunities: A survey. *International Journal of Web and Grid Services*, *14*(4), 352–375. doi:10.1504/IJWGS.2018.095647

This research was previously published in Blockchain Technologies and Applications for Digital Governance; pages 105-126, copyright year 2022 by Information Science Reference (an imprint of IGI Global).

Chapter 58
Issues and Challenges (Privacy, Security, and Trust) in Blockchain–Based Applications

Siddharth M. Nair
Vellore Institute of Technology, Chennai, India

Varsha Ramesh
Vellore Institute of Technology, Chennai, India

Amit Kumar Tyagi
iD https://orcid.org/0000-0003-2657-8700
Vellore Institute of Technology, Chennai, India

ABSTRACT

The major issues and challenges in blockchain over internet of things are security, privacy, and usability. Confidentiality, authentication, and control are the challenges faced in security issue. Hence, this chapter will discuss the challenges and opportunities from the prospective of security and privacy of data in blockchain (with respect to security and privacy community point of view). Furthermore, the authors will provide some future trends that blockchain technology may adapt in the near future (in brief).

1. INTRODUCTION

Blockchain introduced the world's most famous cryptocurrency concept, bitcoin (Tomov, 2019). It is an improvement on the ideals of a peer to peer network and creates a universal data set which can be trusted by all users despite the fact that they do not trust each other. It creates a database or a record of transactions that are shared, trusted and protected, where stable and encrypted copies of data are saved on every node in the system. Financial incentives like native network tokens are applied onto the system to make it more immune to faults and collision.

DOI: 10.4018/978-1-6684-7132-6.ch058

Blockchain has been useful in other sectors of technology. For example, it has been implemented in IoT to improve security and efficiency of IoT based devices. For example, in the agriculture industry, research shows that Blockchain allows food to be tracked from farms to supermarkets in a few seconds. So, it helps in reducing illegal harvesting and shipping scams (Hackernoon, n.d.a). It is also used to keep tabs on overflowing commodities. This works on the principle that data tampering cannot take place using Blockchain, thereby making hacking difficult. Using Blockchain in IoT has its own issue. Data mining in Blockchain needs a large amount of computation and processing power. Most IoT devices do not have the required power to do so.

Blockchain is also hinted to be able to improve security and efficiency in cyber physical systems. For example, studies show that Blockchain can be used in autonomous automobile industry. A Blockchain based database can be used to store the identity information of newly created vehicles (Dorri, Steger, Kanhere et al, 2017). Thus, the information of newly created vehicles can be stored securely in an E-wallet. The data stored cannot be tampered with and will be cryptographically verified. This will enable the vehicle to communicate with a number of networks and thus pay bills, tolls, fines autonomously.

Blockchain technology has been used in social media and networks, to fix many issues. On social media, fake news spreads as quickly as good content. Blockchain helps in fighting fake news using its ledger system. Content and identification can be verified at any time. This also makes collection of data a lot simpler. Blockchain also makes it possible to track data and monitor user interaction with the content. This helps social media channels estimate the likes, shares and views more accurately.

In recent times, the popularity of crowdsourcing systems has increased massively despite the certain privacy issues and challenges faced by it. Blockchain based crowdsourcing systems were employed to solve the problem of small value transactions in crowdsourcing (Li et al., 2019). Similarly, the acquisition and computation of data using some sensing devices to share the gathered data, also known as crowdsensing has been growing in popularity in recent times. Blockchain, being a distributed database in which data cannot be tampered, has the right characteristics to improve the security of crowdsensing applications.Another important where Blockchain is used is the cloudlet (Xu et al., n.d.). Cloudlet is a group of computer systems designed to swiftly render cloud computing resources to the users to enhance the performance of multimedia applications. The security and integrity of the offloaded data that are processed by cloudlets have to be preserved especially with the increasing user requirements of migrating tasks. The characteristics of Blockchain prove to be favorable in these circumstances.

Blockchain is also used to improve security and trust in fog, edge and cloud computing. Fog computing is a decentralized computing foundation in which data, computation, storage and applications are placed some place between the cloud and the source of data. Fog computing has a distributed architecture and requires a technique to protect network resources and transactions. Similarly, edge is a distributed structure in which data is computed at the edge of the network where generation of data takes place instead of computing it in a centralized data processing repository.Cloud computing, is a technology that makes computing services like database, storage, software and analytics available on the internet. For these purposes, an equally distributed security structure is required. Blockchain is a distributed ledger in which data cannot be tampered. So, it creates distributed trust and security.

Note that many useful/ possibleapplications of blockchain have been discussed in **(Sawal et al., 2019)**. Hence, now the remaining part of this chapter is organized as:

- Section 2 discusses related work Blockchain technology and Blockchain enabled applications

- Section 3 discusses motivation behind this work, interested/ useful facts/ points behind writing this chapter.
- Section 4 discusses importance and benefits of Blockchaintechnology in current era, i.e., useful to society or citizens/ business (i.e., in present and future).
- Section 5 discusses many critical issues towards existing Blockchain based applications.
- Section 5 discusses several tools, methods,existing algorithms, available for Blockchain based applications.
- Further, section 7 discusses/ provides several opportunities for future researchers (with identifying several research gaps towards Blockchain based applications).
- Section 8 provides an open discussion with discussing that "Is really Blockchain technology is the necessity of future technology, or just a trend"?
- In last in section 9, this chapter will be concluded in brief.

2. RELATED WORK

In this chapter, we use block chain technology to analyze some of the different applications. We also address the problems of security and privacy, as well as the approaches suggested.

Blockchain in finance: Initially Blockchain was established as a framework for the common decentralized digital currency Bitcoin. In many digital currencies like Altercoin, Peercoin, Ethereum (Wood, 2014), Karma (Vishumurthy et al., 2003), Hashcash(Back, n.d.) and BinaryCoin, Blockchain off late is used. Although they use different consensus algorithms to verify and validate blocks, the majority of digital currencies are based on a blockchain structure. (Tschorsch & Scheuermann, 2016) examines in detail the bitcoin currency and the financial blockchain and points out that the biggest import of the blockchain in the financial sector, which is the use of smart contracts. In any organization security related issues are more concentrated. Organization that uses Block chain is the one which ensures authorization among parties to access accurate data. The main goal of blockchain is to give warranty for data secure and data access. Blockchain guarantees data integrity based on its basic immutability and traceability characteristics. The merging of sequential hashing and encryption makes it extremely difficult to manipulate blockchain data for any user or nodes in the network. The right to be forgotten guarantees the user's privacy in any network, which is particularly important in terms of data immutability. The main challenge is to ensure that the right is applied in a technology based on no content loss. Also, blockchain provides many solutions.

Blockchain in healthcare: In the healthcare sector, Blockchain should be transparent and scalable, protected and data protection should be preserved. The health care blocks primarily contain medical records, reports and images. (Linn & Koo, 2016) Discusses the healthcare blockchain in context and has demonstrated that the data have storage impacts and performance limitations. Each user would have a copy of every individual's health record in the network while data is stored in Bitcoin-patterned blockchains. This is not an acceptable method of storing and bandwidth-intensive system for processing. It generates a waste of network resources and data transmission issues. We have to implement a system that Access Control Manager for data management and processing to incorporate the use of blockchains in the healthcare sector. Only an index or list of all the authorized user information are in the actual blockchain. It operates like a metadata catalog about patients and locations and stores the data for an authorized user to access. The data is encrypted, time-stamped, and retrieved by a unique identifier to increase data access efficiency. In blockchain data repositories called data lakes all health-related data is stored. Data in data lakes is encrypted and digitally signed for privacy purposes, and only authenticated users are allowed to access them.

Blockchain in Defense: The defense has to dependent on cyber-physical systems and their data stored in it, to overcome highly congested environments in the future. The current cyber defense appears to be turbulent and progressive improvements fall short of the growing cyber threat. Blockchain technology overturns the cyber security paradigm, which reduces the probability of data compromise by its untrustworthy, transparent and fault-tolerant. (Barnas, n.d.) discusses the need of blockchain technology in global defense in detail. The core elements in blockchain functioning such as secure hashing, backlinked data structure and consent mechanism play a major role in attributing the blockchain security factor. Since any authorized Network user can access the network data, the confidentiality of data is a major problem with blockchain security. This can be overcome through data encryption and access control maintenance by stored in blockchains. Blockchain may be used by acting as operational or support roles in the defense application.

Cyber defense: It's a low-cost, high-paid blockchain technology. First, blockchain ensures the widespread perception of all digital events by transmitting them to all network nodes and then employs various consensus algorithms to validate and verify. Once the data is stored it cannot be manipulated. If the information is altered or modified, it will be time-marked again and a record will be maintained. One can image, hash and secure modern weapons and component information in the database and continuously track them with blockchain devices. The specifics are mentioned in (Tirenin & Faatz, 1999).

3. MOTIVATION

For building a secure cyber infrastructure in above discussed (mentioned) applications like cloudlet, cyber physical systems, internet of things, we need to provide some innovation, reliable mechanism to protect our/ device communication (data). Blockchain is the best ever solution for achieving a certain level of security and building trust among users in this current (smart) era. It is because, till no attack has been faced on a Blockchain network, on Bitcoin (a popular cryptocurrency).There are few chances (possibility)that Blockchain will be fail for (in) providing a secure communication (to industries). There are many uses of blockchain are introducing now days in manysectors like agriculture, transportation, manufacturing, smart grids, etc., but every application cannot use (digest) Blockchain technology easily. There are various issues like time required for authentication, lesser privacy preservation, etc., raised in Blockchain technology. Also, there is a possibility of 51 percent attack on a Blockchain network or blockchain based applications.

Hence, this section discusses reason/ our motivation behind writing this chapter. Now, next section will discuss scope and importance of this work or Blockchain concept in many applications/ technology components in near future.

4. SCOPE OF THE WORK/ BLOCKCHAIN BASED APPLICATIONS IN PRESENT AND FUTURE

We are at the culmination of a historical change in technology that is making a massive impact in the technology. In this chapter, we will discuss how Blockchain has made an impact, making an impact and will make an impact in the future.

The emergence of Blockchain: Twenty years ago, a company called Netscape released the whole software of the navigator of internet, this movement kickstarted the concept of open source and hence coined the same as 'open source'. Without the concept of open source, Blockchain would have nerve started.

A computationally practical solution for time stamping digital documents such that it could not be backdated or tampered with was the need of the hour. This issue is being resolved by the system which uses a cryptographically secured chain of blocks to store the time stamped documents. In 1992, Merkle trees were incorporated into the design to make it more efficient by allowing several documents to be collected into one block.This technology was not made use of for a brief period of time and the had been taken down in 2004, four years before the inception of bitcoin.In 2004, cryptographic activist Hal Finney introduced a system called RPoW,Reusable Proof ofWork (Changelly, n.d.), the system worked by receiving a non-exchangeable hash cash-based proof of work token and in return created an RSA-signed token that could then be transferred from client to client. RPow solved the double spending problem by keeping the ownership of tokens registered on a trusted server that was designed to allow users throughout the world to verify its correctness and integrity in real time.RPoW can be considered as an early prototype and a significant early step in the history of cryptocurrencies.In late 2008 a white paper introducing a decentralized peer to peer electronic cash system called bitcoin-was posted to a cryptography mailing list by a person or group using the pseudonym. Based on the hashcash proof of work algorithm, but rather than using a hardware trusted computing function like the RPoW, the double spending protection in bitcoin was provided by a decentralized peer to peer protocol for tracking and verifying the transactions.In short,Bitcoins are 'mined' for a reward using the proof work mechanism by individual miners and then verified by the decentralized nodes in the network. However, it was not very well appreciated. Hence, a scripting functionality called smart contracts came up. Note that Smart contracts are decentralized Turing machine, they can be also known as complete virtual machine.

Moving Beyond the Hype

Blockchain 1.0 is the present reality of Blockchain while Blockchain 2.0 is a new paradigm of collectivity and Blockchain 3.0 are the self-organizing networks (decentralized governance). Also, now a days Blochain 4.0 is in ternds for distributed and decentralized applications(**Sawal et al., 2019**). In Blockchain 1.0, the entire network agreed with consensus about the records, in Blockchain 2.0, the entire network consents to the records, the agreements over the records and the execution of those agreements. In terms of analogy, Blockchain 1.0 **OS** some sort of public ledger, then Blockchain 2.0 is a public computer, a decentralized computer. United nations are actually contemplating about adding the right to internet access to the Human Rights. In the future, a completely transparent entry of data will be available which will be audited by everyone. For example, Estonia (Rivera et al., 2017) is known for being innovative in their governance, they already implemented a digital ID and online voting for the citizens and they are now moving forward as one of the first countries in the world to issue their own cryptocurrency, it is coined as East corn. One important key point of Blockchain is digital assets which is nothing but decentralized tokens which has given rise to 'icos', i.e. initial coin offerings and this technology is used for centrally crowd funding money for Blockchain products but Blockchain is more similar to a digital IPO. There is an already a movement towards the decentralization of opinion and the decentralization of coordination. In Blockchain 3.0, shares of the network will be distributed to the participants, according to their contribution; the value of their contribution as perceived by other peers in that network, in last Blockchain 4.0 belongs to Dapps (Decentralized Applications).

Hence, this section discusses scope of the blockchain technology or block based applications to people/ society. Further, section will discuss several open issues in existing Blockchain based applications (in detail).

5. OPEN ISSUES IN BLOCKCHAIN BASED APPLICATIONS

Analogically quoting, like 'Every coin has two sides', similarly, 'the power to authenticate digital information and its transparent nature' has its downfalls. Often the power is misused and fake news spreads which leads to cyber-attacks. The key concern to Blockchain is how to design a system which is resistant to fraudulent behavior. How to incentivize people to participate in their best professional way? And how to maximally align everyone's interests (Hackernoon, n.d.b)?

a) The First and foremost concern is the mounting attention and engagement into renowned social networking sites. Platforms like Facebook and twitter use marketing strategies to increase their growth, however certain consumers prefer to underplay their identity.

b) The second issue is sending wrong information. This becomes a major issue when the information sent is confidential and to an unknown server who can use it to his advantage.

c) The third issue is crypto jacking, it is the type of malware, although they don't directly steal money from the members, they decrease the efficiency rate of the system which opens the door for criminals to access hostile codes which causes unwanted problems for the users.

d) The fourth issue is selfish miners, who increase their productivity or rewards by keeping their blocks private and not revealing their true identity making the whole process incomplete.

e) The fifth issue is the fact that the block data is searched using the index method, the block does not contain the hash value of the next block; it should be looked into as it resembles a linked list.

f) The sixth issue is only according to a study, an attacker can realize illegal gain with only 25% operating capability through a malicious mining process instead of 51%.

g) The seventh issue is the bitcoin wallet, it has become the attackers main subject to seek.It leads to hacking attacks and thefts, weak spots are being exploited

h) The eighth issue is double spending, this issue has been pertaining for a while now and irreversibility of data makes the transaction invalid

i) The ninth issue is the software used and how secure it is. As efficient as it is, it is not free from small bugs which makes huge transaction errors.

j) The tenth issue is they have proposed to protect the personal key by using a hardware token, which again might be misused or mishandled

k) The eleventh issue is by creating unwanted collisions which are timestamp attacks and also by cannibalizing the data.

l)   The next issue is falsifying the ledger, this is a very critical issue as it changes the whole blueprint of the information sent.

m)   The thirteenth issue is that the base foundation of the Blockchain, that is, the technology which is being made use of must be verified and cross checked.

Note that some useful issues and challenges towards blockchain based applications have been discussed in **(Hassan et al., 2019)** and in table 1 (refer appendix A). Hence, this section discusses or list about existing all open issues available in blockchain based applications. Now, next section will provide a summary on existing tools, method and algorithms for available Blockchain based applications.

6. TOOLS, METHODS AND ALGORITHMS FOR BLOCKCHAIN BASED APPLICATIONS

Blockchain is renowned for its application in cryptocurrencies like Bitcoin and Ethereum but it has the ability and potential to evolve many industries such as agriculture, finance, healthcare, defense etc. Blockchain is one of the fastest growing technologies on the planet. Thus, with its scaling importance and usage, the need for simple tools to develop Blockchain applications has risen. There are many Blockchain development tools available at the moment. A few of the most widely used tools are (Hackernoon, n.d.c),

a. Remix IDE

This is an uncomplicated tool which is based on the browser and is used to produce and deploy smart contracts. Smart contracts are an integral part of cyber physical systems and cryptocurrencies like Ethereum use Remix IDE tool to create and deploy smart contracts into the Blockchain. This tool is used with the help of the programming language 'Solidity', where it can write, debug, test and deploy smart contracts

b. Solc

Solidity is a programming language used to create smart contracts. The syntax of this programming language has a certain similarity to JavaScript. The generated script has to be converted into a format which can be read by Ethereum. This is where the Solc tool comes into play

c. Solium

Security is of utmost importance when it comes to developing Blockchain applications. The generated Solidity code must be free from all sorts of security loopholes. A tool has been developed to format the generated Solidity code and resolve all the security issues in them. This tool is called Solium. It checks if the code is formatted and also checks the vulnerability of the code.

d. Blockchain as a Service

This is a tool created to offer solutions based on the cloud to construct, host and utilize Blockchainapplications on the Blockchain, wherein the service provider from the cloud controls operations to develop a flexible and operational foundation. This benefits the companies and the individuals who want to utilize the Blockchain technology but have had trouble in implementing it because of technical difficulties or operational expenses.

e. Metamask

This is a tool that acts as a link or a connection between EthereumBlockchain and web browsers like Firefox and Chrome. It works as an extension to the browser. It is extensively used for storing keys for Ether and ERC20. This tool is also used for selling tokens. It links with various Ethereum testing networks to make it an exemplary tool for developers.

As discussed above and in (Sawal et al., 2019), Blockchain is a decentralized, distributed, and open digital ledger in which transactions are registered by users across many computers such that a record cannot be tampered with, without the modification of all the blocks on the Blockchain along with the consensus of the network. The mechanism by which nodes are added to the end of the Blockchain, along with checking the validity of records, is called the Blockchain algorithm. The algorithm in Blockchain is used to validate signatures, approve balances, check is a created block is valid or not, establish how miners are allowed to validate a block, authorize the method to report a block to move, define the consensus of the network. The different Blockchain algorithms are,

i. Consensus Algorithm (Bach et al., 2018)

These algorithms are complicated but very useful when it comes to running a node or to purchase coins. They deliver reliability on those particular networks in which many nodes are present such that they adhere to the said protocols. Consensus in a Blockchain is defined by the nodes, not the miners. The chain with most work defines the consensus. If the Blockchain forks and the Proof of Work changes, there will not be any mining power left to secure it. Nodes accept, verify and replicate the transactions. The also verify and replicate the blocks along with serving and storing in the Blockchain. The proof of work algorithm is defined by the nodes and not the miners.

- Proof of Work: This is the first consensus algorithm established for a Blockchain. This algorithm is used to authenticate transactions and create new blocks onto the Blockchain. Proof of work is based on the competition of miners against each other to authenticate transactions and get remunerated. Digital tokens are sent to each user in a network. In a decentralized ledger, all transactions are aggregated into blocks. During this process, the validation of transactions should be done carefully.
- Proof of Stake: This algorithm was designed to solve some issues in the Proof of Work algorithm. It states that a user can verify or mine block transactions based on the number of coins they hold. Thus, the more coins a user has, the more mining power he/she will possess.
- Delegated Proof of Stake: This is a consensus algorithm that preserves conclusive agreements on the facts across the network, verifies transactions and acts like a digital republic.This algorithm uses voting which takes place in real time, along with reputation consideration to attain consensus. Among all the consensus protocols, this is the least centralized, thus making it the most inclusive
- Practical Byzantine Fault tolerance: This is a system for a dispersed network to attain consensus in the Blockchain, even if some nodes are fake or malicious. According to this, for a transaction to be

confirmed, an agreement on the subject must be made by most nodes. Basically, it is the hallmark of the Blockchain to confirm a particular transaction even if some nodes do not approve it.

- Raft Consensus: This algorithm works on two basic principles which are as follows. In a term, one leader only can be chosen. Also, a leader cannot append or erase entries in the log, only the new entries can be appended by it. This algorithm is used when the number of servers is relatively less. The servers are assigned as leader, follower and candidates. The followers acknowledge the requests sent by the leaders. During the start of each term, all the candidates contest for the position of the leader.

ii. Mining Algorithms

Mining of data has three major segments namely, Clustering, Sequence Analysis and Association Rules. The analysis of a collection of data to create a collection of grouping laws by which future data is classified is called Clustering or Classification. The examination of patterns that transpire in a particular sequence is called Sequence Analysis. An association rule is a law which dictates particular association rules and relationships between a collection of objects in a database.

iii. Traceability Chain Algorithm (Chen, 2018)

Traceability confirms the start and working following a transaction when in the background, additional data is also being accumulated to enhance the performance of internal processes and to plan the ventures of every node in the chain. The purpose of this algorithm is to obtain traceability decisions swiftly. Due to the presence of an inference mechanism, this algorithm operates quicker than a consensus algorithm. Traceability in Blockchain is responsible for supporting and enhancing the coordination that is possessed by the chain so that more data can be collected about the location and status of the transactions taking place and this information can be used by the nodes to plan the rest of its ventures. Using this algorithm, every single digital asset used in the Blockchain can be traced. This algorithm involves marking of nodes so that they can be identified easily. With the flow of information electronically, many scans are run so that data retrieval can be done efficiently. Links are established so that sharing of data between different chains can be made efficient.

Hence, this section discusses many existing tools, methods and algorithms for blockchain based applications in detail. Now, next section will provide some useful and future reserch directions for future reserchers (towards possible blockhain based applications).

7. FUTURE RESEARCH DIRECTIONS USING BLOCKCHAIN APPLICATIONS

Blockchain is a technology that has taken the world by storm. It has shown its prospects in various industries. This section discusses a few possible future directions of this technology.

a) Big Data (Karafiloski & Mishev, 2017): The combination of big data and Blockchain has shown an immense amount potential. The couple can be used for the management of data as well as the analysis of data. For the management of data, Blockchain can be used to save valuable data as it is a distributed, decentralized and a secure ledger for records. It can also verify the authenticity of the data as the information stored in the Blockchain cannot be tampered with. For analysis of data, the different transactions taking place on the Blockchain could be analysed to detect patterns of trade. Using this, an algorithmic assumption of the trading patterns of the users of the Blockchain would be available.

b) Artificial Intelligence (Marwala & Xing, n.d.): Blockchain technology has had many developments in recent times and research suggests that the technology has a massive scope in the field of artificial intelligence. Artificial intelligence could resolve many hurdles present in Blockchain technology. For instance, a trusted third party is required in Blockchain to check if a particular condition is fulfilled for a contract. Artificial intelligence could help remove the need for a trusted third party. A virtual third party could be created which would learn from the background and educate itself. This way, all conflicts would be resolved. Blockchain can also be used to make sure that Artificial intelligence devices do not misfire. As the information in Blockchain cannot be tampered with there can be no changes made to the protocols which the devices will have to adhere to.

c) Testing of Blockchains: In recent times, new kinds of Blockchains have been created and several hundred different cryptocurrencies have been recorded. But some Blockchain developers may fake the execution of their Blockchain to draw investors and gain huge amounts of money. Also, when a person wants to incorporate Blockchain into their business, they need to know which type of Blockchain to use so that it is suitable for their needs. This is where Blockchain testing comes in handy. For example, the need for different characteristics of a Blockchain like throughput, scalability, verification speed or crash fault tolerance has to be judged and administered into the application accordingly. Thus, Blockchains can be used for testing as well.

Hence, this section provides a several future research directions with blockchain technology with many new emerging areas/sectors. Now, next section will provide an open discussion, which will tell that blockchain is really necessary for future or not with providing some useful facts.

8. AN OPEN DISCUSSION: BLOCKCHAIN BASED APPLICATIONS IS A NECESSITY OR JUST A TREND

According to what we have seen in the paper so far, it will be right to say that Blockchain based applications was a trend when the concept of Blockchain kicked in but now it's become a necessity. Blockchains revolution was a beginning, which means to continue it, change is the only guarantee to revolutionize it. The applications become internally self-organizing which reduces the number of faults, since the information is stored in a database, we can use logistics to update ourselves with the best routes, traffic analysis and the best schedule which can be efficiently produced. In this way, the transportation can be greatly improvised. The most advanced form of Blockchain which is used in Blockchain application is steemBlockchain (Davidson et al., 2018), steem can be compared to a real estate system, it is basically *open-source immutable database which distributes resources in a decentralized way*. With resources like steem, you can post content which can never be deleted, in Facebook, they own our data and can remove the same, usingsteemBlockchain no one can remove our account without our consent. Thus, Blockchain will impact every facet of our life in the near future.

Hence, this section discusses about an open discussion, i.e., provide an opinion with some basic facts which prove that Blockchain is necessity of future technology. It will be used in many sectors and businesses for improving profit and building trust in (of) the same. Now next section will conclude this work in brief with some future remarks.

9. SUMMARY

Now a days, Blockchain network is growing and using by many industries/ organizations. In near future, blockchain technology will change every possible business in next few years (10 or 20) due to having its unique features of decentralization, distributed (or using no intermediary). Blockchain is an open, decentralized ledger, can transform business and society. Blockchain based transformation can be made with (in) short-term reality. Some popular advantages of using blockchain (using proof of work) in manipulations (like cloudlet, internet of things, cloud computing, edge computing, etc.) are great transparency, enhanced security, improved traceability, increased efficiency, and speed (with reduced cost). For future, work, we need to improve blockchain technology or removing several implications of blockchain transformation. A technology should be adopted by many and affordable (accessible) and should not harm environment (basic fundamentals of human being)/ nature. With blockchain technology, we can create a disruptive/ sustainable life (reduce negative impact of blockchain to our life/ business).

REFERENCES

Azaria, A., Ekblaw, A., Vieira, T., & Lippman, A. (2016). MedRec: Using Blockchain for Medical Data Access and Permission Management. *2016 2nd International Conference on Open and Big Data (OBD)*, 25-30. 10.1109/OBD.2016.11

Bach, L. M., Mihaljevic, B., & Zagar, M. (2018). Comparative analysis of blockchain consensus algorithms. *2018 41st International Convention on Information and Communication Technology, Electronics and Microelectronics (MIPRO)*, 1545-1550. 10.23919/MIPRO.2018.8400278

Back. (n.d.). *Hashcash-a denial of service counter-measure*. Academic Press.

Barnas. (n.d.). *Blockchains in national defense: Trustworthy systems in a trustless world*. Blue Horizons Fellowship, Air University, Maxwell Air Force Base.

Changelly. (n.d.). https://changelly.com/blog/what-is-blockchain

Chen. (2018). A traceability chain algorithm for artificial neural networks using T–S fuzzy cognitive maps in blockchain. *Future Generation Computer Systems*, *80*(March), 198–210.

Davidson, De Filippi, & Potts. (2018). Blockchains and the economic institutions of capitalism. *Journal of Institutional Economics*, *14*(4), 639–658.

Dorri, A., Kanhere, S. S., Jurdak, R., & Gauravaram, P. (2017). Blockchain for IoT security and privacy: The case study of a smart home. *2017 IEEE International Conference on Pervasive Computing and Communications Workshops (PerCom Workshops)*, 618-623. 10.1109/PERCOMW.2017.7917634

Dorri, A., Steger, M., Kanhere, S., & Jurdak, R. (2017). Blockchain: A Distributed Solution to Automotive Security and Privacy. *IEEE Communications Magazine*, *55*(12), 119–125. Advance online publication. doi:10.1109/MCOM.2017.1700879

Hackernoon. (n.d.a). https://hackernoon.com/how-will-blockchain-agriculture-revolutionize-the-food-supply-from-farm-to-plate-f8fe488d9bae

Hackernoon. (n.d.b). https://hackernoon.com/how-blockchain-is-solving-the-biggest-problems-in-social-networking-87e4e0753e39

Hackernoon. (n.d.c). https://hackernoon.com/top-12-blockchain-development-tools-to-build-blockchain-ecosystem-371a1b587248

Hassan, M. U., Rehmani, M. H., & Chen, J. (2019). Privacy preservation in blockchain based IoT systems: Integration issues, prospects, challenges, and future research directions. *Future Generation Computer Systems*, *97*, 512-529.

Investopedia. (n.d.). https://www.investopedia.com/terms/1/51-attack.asp

Karafiloski, E., & Mishev, A. (2017). Blockchain solutions for big data challenges: A literature review. *IEEE EUROCON 2017 -17th International Conference on Smart Technologies*, 763-768. 10.1109/EUROCON.2017.8011213

Kogias. (2019). Toward a Blockchain-Enabled Crowdsourcing Platform. *IT Professional, 21*(5), 18-25.

Li, M., Weng, J., Yang, A., Lu, W., Zhang, Y., Hou, L., Liu, J.-N., Xiang, Y., & Deng, R. H. (2019, June 1). CrowdBC: A Blockchain-Based Decentralized Framework for Crowdsourcing. *IEEE Transactions on Parallel and Distributed Systems*, *30*(6), 1251–1266. doi:10.1109/TPDS.2018.2881735

Linn, L. A., & Koo, M. B. (2016). Blockchain for health data and its potential use in health it and health care related research. In *ONC/NIST Use of Blockchain for Healthcare and Research Workshop*. ONC/NIST.

Lu, Wang, Qu, Zhang, & Liu. (n.d.). A Blockchain-Based Privacy-Preserving Authentication Scheme for VANETs. *IEEE Transactions on Very Large-Scale Integration (VLSI) Systems*.

Marwala & Xing. (n.d.). *Blockchain and Artificial Intelligence*. https://arxiv.org/ftp/arxiv/papers/1802/1802.04451.pdf

Mohanta, B. K., Panda, S. S., & Jena, D. (2018). An Overview of Smart Contract and Use Cases in Blockchain Technology. *2018 9th International Conference on Computing, Communication and Networking Technologies (ICCCNT)*, 1-4. 10.1109/ICCCNT.2018.8494045

Rivera, R., Robledo, J. G., Larios, V. M., & Avalos, J. M. (2017). How digital identity on blockchain can contribute in a smart city environment. *2017 International Smart Cities Conference (ISC2)*, 1-4. 10.1109/ISC2.2017.8090839

Sanghi, N., Bhatnagar, R., Kaur, G., & Jain, V. (2018). BlockCloud: Blockchain with Cloud Computing. *2018 International Conference on Advances in Computing, Communication Control and Networking (ICACCCN)*, 430-434. 10.1109/ICACCCN.2018.8748467

Sawal, N., Yadav, A., & Tyagi, D. (2019). *Necessity of Blockchain for Building Trust in Today's Applications: An Useful Explanation from User's Perspective*. Available at SSRN: https://ssrn.com/abstract=3388558

Taylor, Dargahi, Dehghantanha, Parizi, & Choo. (2019). A systematic literature review of blockchain cyber security. *Digital Communications and Networks*.

Tirenin, W., & Faatz, D. (1999). A concept for strategic cyber defense. *Military Communications Conference Proceedings*, 458–463. doi: 10.1109/MILCOM.1999.822725

Tomov, Y. K. (2019). Bitcoin: Evolution of Blockchain Technology. *2019 IEEE XXVIII International Scientific Conference Electronics (ET)*, 1-4.

Tschorsch & Scheuermann. (2016). Bitcoin and beyond: A technical survey on decentralized digital currencies. *IEEE Communications Surveys & Tutorials, 18*, 2084-2123. doi: .2535718 doi:10.1109/COMST.2016

Vishumurthy, V., Chandrakumar, S., & Sirer, E. G. (2003). Karma: A secure economic framework for peer-to-peer resource sharing. *Proceedings of the 2003 Workshop on Economics of Peer-to-Peer Systems*.

Wood, G. (2014). Ethereum: A secure decentralizedgeneralised transaction ledger. *Ethereum Project Yellow Paper, 151*, 1–32.

Xu, X. (2018). An Energy-Aware Virtual Machine Scheduling Method for Cloudlets in Wireless Metropolitan Area Networks. *2018 IEEE International Conference on Internet of Things (iThings) and IEEE Green Computing and Communications (GreenCom) and IEEE Cyber, Physical and Social Computing (CPSCom) and IEEE Smart Data (SmartData)*, 517-523. 10.1109/Cybermatics_2018.2018.00110

Xu, X., Chen, Y., Yuan, Y., Huang, T., & Zhang, X. (n.d.). Blockchain-based cloudlet management for multimedia workflow in mobile cloud computing. *Multimedia Tools and Applications*. Advance online publication. doi:10.100711042-019-07900-x,2019

KEY TERMS AND DEFINITIONS

Bitcoin: Bitcoin is a digital or virtual currency developed in 2009 that allows instant transactions easier by using peer-to-peer technology.

Blockchain: A process in which records are maintained on several computers connected in a pair-to-pairs network of transactions in Bitcoin or other cryptocurrency.

Cloud Computing: On-demand computer system resources available without direct active user management, especially data storage and computing power.

Cryptocurrency: Digital currency used to control authentication techniques for the generation of currency units and the confirmation of transactions, working without a central banking authority.

Ethereum: It is the smart contract (scripting) operating system and open source, public, distributed computing platform based on blockchain.

Internet of Things: Interconnect computer devices embedded in everyday objects via the Internet to enable data to be transmitted and received.

APPENDIX A

Table 1. A Taxonomy of Blockchain Based Applications

APPLICATION	CHARACTERISTICS	ADVANTAGES	DISADVANTAGES	RESEARCH CHALLENGES	OPEN ISSUES	SOLUTIONS TO THE CHALLENGES
CYBER PHYSICAL SYSTEMS (Taylor et al., 2019)	Aims to synchronise the realistic world with computational space of the internet	It helps in identifying the potential aspects of Blockchain to include and boom technologies of Blockchain 4.0	The components which fail exhibit this unusual behaviour which arises when you send conflicting information to different parts of the system	The need to include an explicit focus on the cybersecurity	Security and availability is still an ongoing issue	Increasing resilience, robustness and reliability to save against cyberattacks
IOT (Dorri, Kanhere, Jurdak et al, 2017)	Blockchain prevents duplication and personal thefts	The information is sent to trusted resources and the ledger grants information after a lot of analyzation by different groups of resourceful parties	Often false alerts are sent and the sensors are not that powerful to adapt information	There is less transparency and the end to end visibility has to be taken into account	The risk of losing data and gaining other unimportant data makes it an unambiguous situation	
Vehicular Ad Hoc Network(VANET) (Lu et al, n.d.)	Effectively gives a solution to maintain the trust between the VANET entities.	Blockchain is used to quantify the available of the anonymous entities, this helps in valuation of VANET	The processing time is more than the actual time required	The identity of the owner should not be disclosed	The privacy of the location has to be taken into account	VANET time, Effective distance between the systems, Connectivity rate and privacy should be maintained
COMPUTING (Sanghi et al, 2018)	Helps in transporting data, processing and storing data is done by Blockchain.	The traceability of the entitiescloud is improved using Blockchain.	There are a lot of unauthorised service providers who have vendors which send false information and there is no one cross checking	The time taken to take massive amounts of data is impossible to handle	Monitoring the data keeping the time in check becomes very difficult and the cost of transferring the complex data requires a lot of money	A data portability is necessary where they cannot switch and send data without restraints, they should be no lock in period for switching data
SMART PROPERTY (Mohanta et al, 2018)	A non-physical property which cannot be accessed all the time is solved by authentication using an ownership key, the device used a trustable sourceof time	It decreases the risk of running into fraud, reduces taxes and fees and disables the possibility of duplicates.	The key is in a physical form, for example, a car key and a sim card which makes it very difficult to transfer information or copy information.	In a smart property it will function only if you enter the right pin code, so if the phone has no battery or the phone is disabled, accessing the device becomes difficult	The dividends are not divided equally and the cost is not equally distributed.	The Blockchain solves this issue by a 'replace and replicate a lost protocol'.
MEDICAL FIELDS (Azaria et al., 2016)	Used in transparently tracking prescription medicines	It is very useful in identifying the right medicine using serial or batch numbers to ensure that the consumers get the right medicine	There may be cases when the expiry data might be reached while the medicine is till being delivered	A large amount of time is taken to deliver the medicines and the effective cost increases	Due to high security and technological advances, the service technician won't be able to access the medicines or won't be sure of which medicine to send	Maintaining regular compliance and a ledge for transport and access of medicines and feasibility is required
CROWDSOURCING (Kogias, 2019)	Uses the idea of a third party to fulfil the exchange between the shared data and in return the rewards are gained as information exchange	Its legal and has structural restrictions	It is vulnerable to manipulate huge amount of data	Leveraging the Blockchain to infuse incentives but can't reveal the confidential inputs of incentive mechani	They have the access to generate their own ids which gives malicious workers to create fake ids and hence forge ideas and signatures	Data confidentiality and transparency and identification if users is a necessity.
CLOUDLET [32]	Cloudlet acts as a high end platform that can run the virtual machines	It support low-latency secure, anonymous, and always-within an on-demand data-sharing scenario	The necessity to be online and offline simultaneously is a necessity	It is still ambiguous about whether to choose the blocks according to proof of work or delegated proof of work	The transaction is fee based and it is based on the stipulated time duration Thus,time is directly proportional to fees	A bridge is required to connect the different types of models to maintain and support the chains

Chapter 59
Security, Privacy, and Trust Management and Performance Optimization of Blockchain

Priti Gupta
Banaras Hindu University, India

Abhishek Kumar
Banaras Hindu University, India

Achintya Singhal
ⓘ https://orcid.org/0000-0003-0242-2031
Banaras Hindu University, India

Shantanu Saurabh
The Maharaja Sayajirao University of Baroda, India

V. D. Ambeth Kumar

Department of Computer Science and Engineering, Panimalar Engineering College, Anna University, Chennai, India

ABSTRACT

Blockchain provides innovative ideas for storing information, executing transactions, performing functions, creating trust in an open environment, etc. Even though cryptographers, mathematicians, and coders have been trying to bring the most trustable protocols to get authentication guarantee over various systems, blockchain technology is secure with no central authority in an open network system because of a large distributed network of independent users. If anyone tries to change the blockchain database, the current hash will also change, which does not match with the previous hash. In this way, blockchain creates privacy and trust in digital data by removing malleability attacks. In this chapter, security and privacy on the blockchain has been focused. The safety and privacy of blockchain are mainly engrossed on two things: firstly, uncovering few attacks suffered by blockchain systems and, secondly, putting specific and advanced proposals against such attacks.

DOI: 10.4018/978-1-6684-7132-6.ch059

INTRODUCTION

Why Blockchain – does it secure? Can we trust on it?

Blockchain technology has been called the one of the greatest innovations since the internet. Blockchain is a peer-to-peer distributed ledger or public registry that permanently records transactions in a way that cannot be erase or update. Blockchain is designed to use a cryptographic hash and timestamps so that record cannot be change once they are created. This makes easier for the blockchain experts to inspect record ledger or registry to determine the facts of any given transactions or to detect attempts to tamper with the ledger.

Blockchain is secure. 'Secure' doesn't means to hide information but it simply means that nobody going to tamper records on the blockchain. Even if somebody does attempt to fraudulently alter records, original records will still exist on the valid ledger and can be pinned down by comparing information on duplicate records.

Billions of people in the world who can't trust intermediaries such as banks, and other legal system for transactions or accurate record keeping. Particularly, Blockchain are useful in these cases to provide trust and assurance to people when transacting with one another. Centralized databases and institutions work when there is trust in the system of regulations, laws, government and people. Even sometimes, this trust is betrayed, causing people to lose money and assets. Blockchain is a decentralized database which remove the need of centralized institutions and databases. With all people connected to the blockchain network having access to the blockchain ledger in a way they can view and validate transactions which create transparency and trust. Although blockchain removed intermediaries to maintain the trust between the people involved in the transactions. The removal of intermediaries improved transparency and decentralized structure of the blockchain (Mark Gates, 2017).

Figure 1. Blockchain architecture diagram

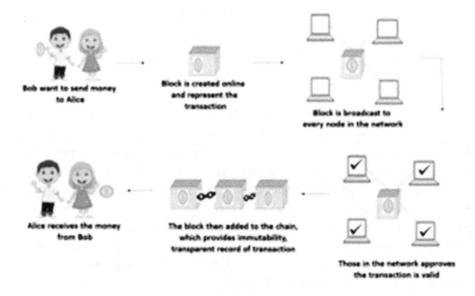

WHY BLOCKCHAIN?

There are many problems faces by the current system like:

- Banks and other third parties charge fees for transferring money.
- Mediating cost increases transaction costs.
- System is lacking transparency.
- System is lacking fairness.
- Financial exchanges are slow so checking and low-cost wire services take many days to complete it.
- Central authority can misuse their power and can create money as per their own will.

We need a system which solve the above problems:

- System which eliminate the need of intermediaries for making transaction cost nil or negligible.
- System which is transparent in order to avoid manipulation.
- System which is tamper resistant in order to avoid misuse.
- System which enhances transaction execution speed and can facilitate instant reconciliation.
- System in which creation of currency is not in control of any central authority.
- System which is regulated to maintain the value of the currency.

STRUCTURE OF BLOCKCHAIN

Blockchains are composed of three core components. They are:

1. Block: A block is like a page of a ledger in which listing of transactions is done periodically. A block is composed of a header and a list of transactions. First block is called Genesis block. For every blockchain the size, period, and triggering event for blocks is different. Chain of blocks is an immutable data structure where each next block contains a hash of the previous block. Result of this hashing is the chain of blocks is immutable. We cannot alter or delete a block from the middle of the chain without rebuilding all the blocks above, because a minor change will require a rebuild of all blocks (Hori K. et al., n.d.).
2. Chain: A hash act as glues for linking one block to another. The hash depends upon the data in the block, as data is change hash will also change. The Secure Hash Algorithm (SHA) is one of the cryptographic hash functions used in blockchains. Practically, think hash as a digital fingerprint of data that is used to lock it in place within the blockchain (Hori K. et al., n.d.).
3. Network: The network is composed of "full nodes". Each node contains a complete record of all the transactions that were ever recorded in that blockchain (Hori K. et al., n.d.).

PERMISSIONED VS. PERMISSIONLESS BLOCKCHAIN

Based on the access control layer built into the blockchain nodes, properly permissioned blockchain networks differ from permission less blockchain networks. Permissioned blockchain are secure because it restricts those actors one who contribute to the consensus of the system state where in permission less blockchain, since the network is open, anyone can participate and contribute in the consensus. In context of privacy, permissioned blockchain allows only actors who have rights to view the transactions. A permission less blockchain is a shared database where everyone can read everything, but no single user has control to write.

VARIOUS PLATFORMS FOR IMPLEMENTING BLOCKCHAIN

§   Ethereum: An open blockchain platform proposed in 2013 by Vitalik Buterin. It provides public blockchain to develop smart contracts and decentralized applications. Ethers are currency tokens in Ethereum.

§   Multichain: A platform that helps users to establish a private blockchains that can be used by the organizations for financial transactions.

§   Hydra chain: It is an open source platform which is joint development effort of Brainbot technologies and the Ethereum project that supports the creation of scalable blockchain based applications and private blockchain networks. The supporting language for Hydrachain is python.

§   Hyperledger: It is a cooperative open source effort designed to promote cross-industry blockchain technologies.

§   Openchain: It is an open source distributed ledger technology which suited for organizations wishing to issue and manage digital assets in secure, robust and scalable way.

§   IBM Bluemix: It is built on top of the Hyperledger project and offers additional security and infrastructure facilities for enterprises.

§   Chain: It is a blockchain platform that runs on the open-source chain protocol. It is used to issue and transfer financial assets on a permissioned blockchain infrastructure.

§   IOTA: Blockless distributed ledger which is scalable, lightweight and for the first time ever makes it possible to translate value without any fees.

FEATURES OF A BLOCKCHAIN PLATFORM

To evaluate a given blockchain platform the following features are important:

1.   Programmability: What are the particular languages for programming?
2.   Scalability: How many nodes can blockchain produce? Is there any upper limit?
3.   Upgradability. What is the developer's track record for improving and upgrading the blockchain?
4.   Transactions manageability: Is all transactions transparent in real time?
5.   Visibility. Do you have a complete perspective on the blockchain activity?
6.   Affordability. What is the cost of transmitting this technology?
7.   Security. What is the documented standard of trust in the safety of the blockchain?

8. Speed/Performance. What are the upper limits for speed in validating transactions?
9. High Availability. What is the uptime's track record?
10. Extensibility. Would you be able to expand the fundamental blockchain functionality with a variety of add-ons?
11. Interoperability. Does it inter-operate well with other blockchains or related technologies?
12. Open Source. Is the code open source? What is the level of collaboration level and contributions from a variety of developers?

PRIVACY OF THE BLOCKCHAIN

Privacy is of utmost significance on the Blockchain organization of agencies. Blockchain use asymmetric cryptography to maintain privacy between transactions.

- Public and private keys

A key component of privacy in blockchains is using private and public keys. Both keys are random strings of number and related cryptographically. It is impossible for the user to know the other user's private key. This results in privacy and protection from the hackers. Each user has an address to send and receive assets on the blockchain. These addresses are derived from the public key using hash function. Users can see earlier transactions and activity that has occurred on the blockchain because networks are shared to all participants. Past transactions of senders and receivers are represented by their addresses. Public addresses do not disclose the personal information rather it suggested that public address is not use by the user more than once. This approach neglects the chances of hacking by tracing a particular address' past transaction to avoid the leak of information (Hasib Anwar, 2018).

Suppose Alice send cryptocoins to Bob on the blockchain. Actually, Alice is sending the hash version of public key. Bob knows their private key, and every user of blockchain knows their private key. Bob should not share their private key with other user otherwise cryptocurrencies will be stolen by that particular user. Public and private key are large integer numbers therefore it is represented by separate Wallet Import Format (WIF). Private key is used to derive the public key by complicated mathematical algorithm. Public key is then transformed with a hash function to produce the address that other people can see. Then Bob receive cryptocoins that Alice sends to his address.

We can derive public key from private key using mathematical algorithm. But we can't derive private key from public key by reverse key generator. The process of reversing the process is even more complex that the world's most powerful computer would need more than 40000000000000000000000000000000 0(31 zeros) years to complete the calculations.

- Peer-to-peer(P2P) network

The Blockchain technology depends on a peer-to-peer computer network comprised of its clients' computer. Blockchain's peer-to-peer infrastructure combined with its immutability (unchangeable of data), transparency, and removal of "mid men" make it a best platform for the business and exchange of any worthy asset.

Figure 2. Transformation of private key to public key

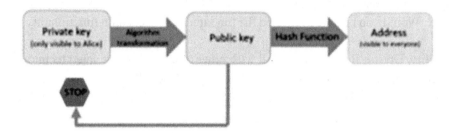

In the blockchain architecture, user's computer work as nodes; they share a record that gets updated or, altered through peer-to-peer replication. Whenever a transaction happens, each node gets the information about transactions from other nodes. Because nodes act as both sender and receiver, nodes can send transactions as well. The data which is transacted synchronized across the network of blockchain as it is transferred.

- Zero-knowledge proofs (ZKP)

Zero knowledge is a technique by which prover proofs to verifier that he knows the key or secret without saying anything about the secret. It means that one party proofs to other party that information is true without revealing the exact information.

Figure 3. Peer-to-peer

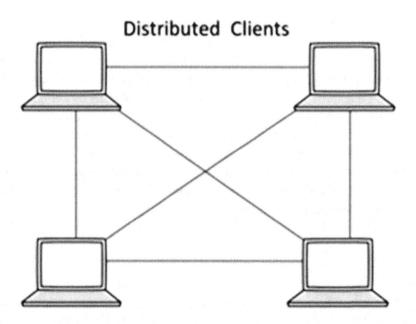

Zero knowledge encryption is of two types –

1. Interactive zero knowledge proof: It is a zero-knowledge proof with interaction between prover and verifier.
2. Non-interactive zero knowledge proof: It is a zero-knowledge proof without interaction between prover and verifier.

Where can Zero-knowledge proofs be use?

- Messaging: In messaging end-to-end encryption is required for securing the private messages. With the help of ZKP, no one could hack the message because it provides end-to-end trust without leaking any personal information.
- Authentication: ZKP does not allow any user to access any complex document.
- Complex documentation: It help to convey sensitive information like validation data with additional security.
- Sharing data: ZKP helps in sharing data without any intermediaries.
- Security for sensitive information: ZKP provide high security to the sensitive information like banks statements, or credit card.
- Storage Privacy: ZKP provide highly protection to the stored data which help from the theft.

Comparison of Blockchain Privacy Systems

- Private Blockchain: Private Blockchain is different from public blockchain. In Public blockchain, all transactions and records are publicly accessible. Public blockchains offer full decentralisation. Examples of public blockchain are: Bitcoin, Ethereum, Dash, Factom. A private blockchain is also known as permissioned blockchain. It has restrictions on one who can access it and participate in transactions. So private blockchain network requires an invitation and can be validated by either the network starter or by a set of rules put in place by the network starter. Examples of private blockchain are: Multichain, Blockstack ("IntelliPaat Blogs", n.d.).
- Consortium Blockchain: It is hybrid of public and private blockchain. It is public because the blockchain is being shared by different nodes and it is private because the nodes that can access the blockchain is restricted. It controlled by a consortium of members. Only predefined set of nodes have access to write the data or block. Examples of consortium blockchain are: Ripple, R3 ("IntelliPaat Blogs", n.d.).

Concerns Regarding Blockchain Privacy

1. Transparency: Blockchain provide secured and transparent platform to the users. The allowance of users to control their own data and absence of third parties is the reason behind the adoption of blockchain technology.
2. Decentralization: Blockchain technology is of decentralized nature i.e., no central point of control. Lack of single control makes the system fairer and considerably more secure.
3. Private Keys: Private key is used to protect user's identity and security through digital signatures. It is also used to access funds and personal wallets on the blockchain. Like, if any individual send

money to other user, they must provide a digital signature that is produced when provided with the private key. This procedure protects against theft.

How the System Protects Against the Following Privacy Issues

The privacy concerns face by the users while using third party services like mobile applications, application constantly collect personal data of user, of which user has no specific control or knowledge. Like this there are many such examples about which user is unaware about their information wherever it uses. To protect against such privacy issues the following point given below:

- Data Ownership: The main focus is that user has allowance to control their data. User must have the knowledge and control over their personal data.
- Data Transparency and Accessibility: The user must have complete transparency and accessibility over their own personal data.
- Fine-grained Access Control: A major concern with mobile applications is that when signing up, users are needed to grant a set of permissions. These permissions are granted on an indefinite basis and opting-out is the only way to change the agreement. Instead, the user can change the set of permissions at any given time in the framework and cancel access to previously collected data.

One application of this mechanism would be to enhance the existingpermissions dialog in mobile applications. While the user interface is likely to remain the same, the accesscontrol policies would be stored securely on a blockchain, where only the user can modify them.

Cases of Privacy Failure

- *Mt. Gox*

Mt. Gox, world's largest Bitcoin exchange during 2014 was holding around 70% of worldwide cryptocurrency. Mt. Gox suffered a huge theft of more than 450 million-dollar, initial reasons of which were unknown. This security breach was the first major hack of cryptocurrency. However, the public address of the perpetrators was identified by tracking the transactions details.

- *DAO Hack*

DAO, a digital autonomous organisation with an objective to prevent or solve data security breaching, tampering. The DAO system was hacked in 2016, while its funding window was active for a project. The loss was expected to be around $US 3.6 million.

- Coinbase

Coinbase is world's biggest digital currency exchange founded in 2012. It allows its users for storage and transactions of cryptocurrency. It was reported that the personal data of users like Telephone numbers and email address of famous individuals were used by hackers to change their account verification numbers, consequently resulting into theft of thousands of dollars from Coinbase wallets.

SECURITY OF THE BLOCKCHAIN

Security in blockchain refers to protection of transactions information and data in a block against internal, outskirts, malicious, and unexpected threat. Protection involves detection and prevention of threats, response to threat using security policies. Some important methodology related to security are given below (Prashant J. et al., 2018):

1. Defence in penetration: -This methodology uses various remedial measures to ensure the data.
2. Least authority: - In this methodology the access to data is diminished to the most minimal level to raised degree of security.
3. Manage vulnerabilities. In this methodology, manage vulnerabilities by distinguishing, authenticating, altering and fixing.
4. Manage risks: - In this methodology, manage the risks by recognizing, evaluating and controlling.
5. Oversee patches. In this methodology, patch the imperfect part like code, application, operating system, firmware and so forth by securing, testing and installing patches.

Security and Privacy Challenges and Solutions for Blockchain Applications

1. Blockchain in finance: Many Currencies such as Alter coin, Peer coin, Ethereum, Karma, Hashcash, and Binary Coin uses blockchain all across the globe. Most currency uses blockchain structure as the base while they are using use different types consensus algorithms for verification and validation of blocks. Smart contacts require the use of blockchain in the finance sector. Many organizations use blockchain to overcome from security problems, hence, blockchain are ensuring authorized parties to access correct and appropriate data. Blockchain provide the warranty of security of data and data access.
2. Blockchain in IOT: IOT is a technology that interconnects computing devices, mechanical and digital machines, objects, animals or people in order to transfer data across a network without requiring human-to-human or human-to-computer interaction. IoT is used in blockchain as to store data. So, that the user has the access to the data from any place across the world ensuring security and privacy. This can be achieved by creating an account and setting password. Then, permissions are checked and then the process of extraction of previous block number and hash value takes place, consecutively, the user creates a random unique id and sends data to storage by using this id. The life of transaction is checked and the storage availability is confirmed. In this way, IOT uses blockchain.
3. Blockchain in mobile applications: Smartphones also uses blockchain in its software applications which supports peer-to-peer data service, peer-to-peer file transfer and direct payment. Blockchain provide an immense value to the security strategies regarding mobile applications. Blockchain is more secure that it is used in different applications that deal with sensitive data, since blockchain does not have any single point of failure. Blockchain is used for authentication to protect data. One more use of blockchain is that its mobile applications enables to access digital wallets.
4. Blockchain in Defence: defence also uses blockchain technology. In the upcoming era, defense will use cyber-enabled systems and the data they contain. Blockchain technology overturns the cyber security paradigm due to its trust less, transparent and fault tolerant thereby decreasing the chance of data compromise.

Blockchain can be used in defence application by providing the operational or support roles as follows:

a)   Cyber defence- This consumes low-cost, high payoff application of blockchain. At first, blockchain helps to ensure that all digital events are widely perceived by transferring to all other nodes in the network and thereafter uses different consensus algorithms to validate and verify. Once the data is secured then it is timestamped and stored, then it cannot be manipulated. If the data is altered or updated, it is again timestamped and the log is maintained. In this way, the advanced weapon and component details can be imaged, hashed and secured in the database and continuously monitored using blockchains.

b)   Supply chain management. The day to day increment in concern regarding supply chain management in defence leads to the need of a technology to establish the origin and owner traceability

5.   Blockchain in automobile industry: technology in Modern vehicles is increasing results in connecting to online or network-based applications and which in return provide an excellent base for the use of blockchain technology. Automobiles use security architectures which help to address a few requirements to placate the future requirements for smart vehicles.

Automotive security architectures along with several advantages of smart vehicles needs to tackle some challenges to satisfy the needs of future services of smart vehicles from the perspectives listed as follows:

a)   Safety. Along with several uses of smart vehicles, there arises the need to secure the data from threats involving security breaches occurring due to malfunction as well as due to numerous autonomous driving functions.

b)   Centralization- The security of the system should be concentrated at a single point of failure. So, decentralized architecture is more appreciable due to the low scale ability of the centralized architecture.

c)   Maintainability. The automotive architecture has the property to maintain hardware and software for a long-fixed period of time along with the extend-ability option for maintainability of a vehicle.

TRUST IN BLOCKCHAIN

Blockchain technology solves the fundamental and most regular issue trust during transfers, transactions, storing and managing data. A lot of industries like healthcare, education, security, banking, real estate, voting is using blockchain technology because it is trusted (Prashant J. et al., 2018).

The reasons why blockchain technology is trusted given below ("Quora blockchain", 2017):

- Immutability of data: - Immutability means unable to change i.e., once data written in ledger nobody, not even system administrator can update or delete it. It implies once information has been kept in touch with a blockchain then no one including system administrator can transform it. This attempt disallows the fraudulent tampering.
- Verification: - Records and Tracking verified through cryptography. Blockchain verify each transaction through strong encryption.
- Unique Tokens

- Decentralized network: -There is no central authority that guarantees or validations for transactions. No one on a Blockchain network owns the ledger. Because of its decentralized nature, everyone on the network has a copy of the ledger ("Quora blockchain", 2017).
- Consensus: - The blockchain technology has consensus algorithms. The architecture or to say infrastructure has designed which has those consensus base which makes it relevant as well as a trusted approach for the businesses ("Quora blockchain", 2017).
- Distributed Ledger: - A public ledger will provide every information about a transaction and the participant. It's all out in the open, nowhere to hide.

Figure 4. Features of Trust Boundary

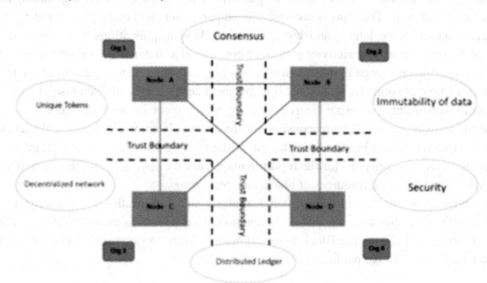

PERFORMANCE ANALYSIS AND OPTIMIZATION OF THE BLOCKCHAIN TECHNOLOGY

Blockchain technology has drawn significant attention of society in the ongoing past, as from previous of years' digital money is consistently in the news with respect to the benefits and demerits and issues identified with security. Another notable name of the Blockchain technology is Distributed Ledger Technology or DLT, which exhibit to save a lot of time and effort of the association. The Blockchain technology is utilized to produce a decentralized record system, which is responsible for the verifying the private data of the network on the channel.

In nowadays, blockchain technology isn't just utilized by different organizations in order to manage financial statement, yet additionally to ideally deal with the standardization of coordination and other supply chain programs. Therefore, broad research on the technology uncovered that achieving the throughput and inertness of the Blockchain technology is the most troublesome challenge, with the end goal that yield of the system channel can be optimal managed.

After the advancement of initial applications, it has been outputted that improvement for the blockchain framework degraded in giving optimal inertness to the system and thus, it makes its measure to solve the difficulties preceding the improvement of technology. Therefore, there are different procedures which can be utilized so as to check the presentation and improve the blockchain technology further for the advancement of society.

Above all else, parameter can be blockchain platforms and foundation arrangement which guarantee the improvement model picked for the advancement is appropriate for it or not. To exemplify, a study was led for the two blockchain technology, for example, Hyperledger Fabric and Ethereum that mirrors the advancement model and installation of essential software is a significant to rely upon the latency and transfer speed of the framework. The pre setup module plays a major role, however after the improvement the assessment depends on the workload dispatcher and execution information gathering module of the blockchain technology. These previously mentioned parameters will make the technology particular regarding the execution time, latency and throughput of blockchain applications. The difference in execution time of the transaction on various stages can be considered as the native functionalities and custom function to check the difference in information access and information management of the framework applications. From that point onward, comparing average latency can be utilized also plot to gauge the exchanges of involvement in securing the trials and stages increment for the rapid action's management. Insurance and transfer value will be responsible for the average latency assumption calculation for the optimal areas to focus for the better administration of the varying functions. Moreover, greatest simultaneous transactions are conveyed for the report management for appropriating the present version of the platform to the CPU used resources of blockchain technology.

Accordingly, suffice to say that performance analysis and optimization are fundamental thought which could effectively guarantee the present adaptation of the platforms as well as finding the present loopholes in the knowledge of the Blockchain technology. Moreover, private blockchain frameworks will be considered as effective platform for communication.

CONCLUSION

The first and foremost reason behind using any technology is that it provides secure and trustworthy result. Thanks to the advent of the blockchain, data is now being recorded, disclosed, transparent, and secured. Blockchain can be considered as sustainable and secure solution for future generations to come.

REFERENCES

Andreas, M. (2014). *Mastering Bitcoin: Programming the Open Blockchain.* Academic Press.

Hasib Anwar. (2018). *What is ZKP? A Complete Guide to Zero Knowledge Proof.* https://101blockchains.com/zero-knowledge-proof/

IntelliPaat Blogs. (n.d.). *What is Blockchain Technology?* https://intellipaat.com/blog/tutorial/blockchain-tutorial/what-is-blockchain/

Mark Gates. (2017). *Blockchain: Ultimate Guide to Understanding Blockchain*. Bitcoin, Cryptocurrencies, Smart Contracts and the Future of Money.

Pathak, N., & Bhandari, A. (2018). *IoT, AI, and Blockchain for. NET : Building a next-generation application from the ground up.* doi:10.1007/978-1-4842-3709-0

Performance Analysis and Optimization of the Blockchain Technology. (n.d.). https://assignmenthelp4me.com/article-performance-analysis-and-optimization-of-the-blockchain-technology-869.html

Prashanth Joshi, A., Han, M., & Wang, Y. (2018). *A survey on security and privacy issues of blockchain technology*. Mathematical Foundations of Computing., doi:10.3934/mfc.2018007

Quora. (2017). *What makes blockchain trusted?* https://www.quora.com/What-makes-blockchain-trusted

Wikipedia. (n.d.). *Privacy and blockchain*. https://en.wikipedia.org/wiki/Privacy_and_blockchain

Zero Knowledge Proof. (2018). *An Introduction to Zero Knowledge Proof*. https://101blockchains.com/wp-content/uploads/2018/11/Zero_knowledge_Proof_ZKP.png

Zyskind, Nathan, & Pentland. (2015). Decentralizing Privacy: Using Blockchain to Protect Personal Data. *2015 IEEE CS Security and Privacy Workshops.*

This research was previously published in Opportunities and Challenges for Blockchain Technology in Autonomous Vehicles; pages 134-146, copyright year 2021 by Engineering Science Reference (an imprint of IGI Global).

Chapter 60
Blockchain Revolution:
Adaptability in Business World and Challenges in Implementation

Archana Sharma

Institute of Management Studies, Noida, India

Purnima Gupta

Institute of Management Studies, Noida, India

ABSTRACT

As the base of bitcoin, the blockchain has received widespread consideration recently. Blockchain stands for an immutable ledger which permits transactions to occur in a decentralized ways. Applications based on blockchain are numerous for instance financial services, industrial and supply chain services, legal and healthcare services, IoT and blockchain integration, bigdata analytics, and so on. Nevertheless, there are still numerous confronts of blockchain technology like security and fork problems that have to be resolved. This research highlights an inclusive indication on blockchain technology with blockchain architecture in the first phase. And in the second phase, the security challenges and problems associated with blockchain are highlighted. It further proposes and measures up to various typical consensus algorithms used in different blockchains. Research has been concluded with the potential prospects of blockchain as future trends.

INTRODUCTION

In the current scenario, Information Technology has been playing a major role in the development of the financial industry. Financial organizations restructuring the way to interact with each other. However, the well-known practice and standards of this segment may face an all-out revamp as incredible innovations such as Blockchain is a maturing stage.

Blockchain was first described by Stuart Haber in the early nineties. In 2008, Satoshi Nakamoto(Nakamoto S.,2008), introduced the blockchain through Bitcoin as a digital cryptocurrency. Bitcoin as a cryptocurrency based on a network protocol permits the users over the network to execute the transaction with

DOI: 10.4018/978-1-6684-7132-6.ch060

digital currency or virtual money in a secure manner that must be present only in their systems. As a sequence of blocks, blockchain register and maintain the details of the transaction in a distributed public ledger crossways with various computers that are connected to peer network. A block records every recent transaction as the present component of blockchain and after completion maintained in blockchain as an eternal database. After completion of each block, another block is created. As a technology revolution of Bitcoin, blockchain maintains proof of every transaction over the network as balance and address. The transactions with Bitcoin are entered in sequential order in a blockchain as the bank transactions are maintained. Due to openness, the entire system sustains security as the public property of blockchain. The transaction is transparent and verifies the authenticity of the owner. Blockchain is considered as decentralized architecture without any verification of the transaction by third parties, it creates a serious distraction to the conventional business procedure which requires centralized architecture or verification from a trusted party. The intrinsic properties of blockchain design and architecture are robustness, transparency, auditability, and network security. Blockchain as a distributed database organizes a sequence of ordered blocks and committed blocks are set to be immutable. Due to the immutable property of the committed block, no one can alter it further. The category of blockchain decides the contents of data stored in a block. For example, Bitcoin maintains the transaction details, the amount transferred, the sender, and receiver information. For authentication, an exclusive hash is associated with each block in comparison to a fingerprint. While the creation of the block, the hash is also calculated concurrently, and in case of any alteration in the same block the hash would also be changed. There are mainly three types of blockChain:

Private Blockchain(Permissioned): Access permissions are restricted in private Blockchain. Network administrator's permission is necessary to join like a participant of blockchain or as a validator. Private organizations in general, may function as private blockchain and won't like the public communication on blocks holding perceptive company details.

Public Blockchain(Permissionless): In oppose to private Blockchain, unlimited members of the open internet can join a permissionless blockchain and perform transactions with validations.

Federated Blockchain: It is a fusion of public blockchain and private blockchain. Though Federated blockchain shares alike scalability and privacy accompanied by private blockchain, a major difference is that leader node (a series of nodes), picked in its place of a single unit for transaction verification processes.

In consideration of the application area of blockchain, renowned execution of public blockchain includes Bitcoin, Litecoin, Ethereum, and broadly the majority cryptocurrencies. The foremost advantages are self-sustained network, self-maintenance, and short of infrastructure costs, radically sinking management overheads. Whereas in private blockchains, the major applications are auditing, database management, and normally, performance-based solutions. For open platforms, Multichain may be considered as an example for constructing and arrange private blockchains. In last, federated blockchains are widely employed in the banking, business organizations, and IT sectors. There are various other application areas also where blockchain has been deployed like healthcare, supply chain, legal services.

Even though the characteristics of blockchain technology may convey additional reliable and expedient services, the security issues and challenges behind this innovative technology is also an important topic that is required to concern. The vulnerabilities include endpoint vulnerabilities,public and private key security, vendor risk, lack of standards, and regulation. Blockchain technology is a grouping of a cryptographic algorithm, peer-to-peer communication, mathematic through a consensus algorithm to determine the synchronization difficulty of distributed database. It's a built-in multi-field infrastructure building (Garay et al., 2015; Gervais et al., 2014; Nakamoto,2013). The blockchain technologies construct of six key elements.

- Decentralized: The basic characteristic of blockchain is that blockchain doesn't require to rely on centralized node any longer, the data can be documented, store, and renew in a scattered manner.
- Transparent: The recorded data by blockchain structure is transparent to all nodes, it too transparent to renew the data, due to this blockchain can be considered reliable.
- Open Source: The majority of blockchain classification is open to all, a record can be ensured publicly and the public can also employ blockchain technologies to produce any application as desired.
- Autonomy: Due to the support of consensus, all nodes on the blockchain organization can reassign or renew data securely, the proposal is to conviction from a particular person to the complete system, and nobody can interfere with it.
- Immutable: A few records will be set aside evermore, and can't be altered unless somebody can acquire control over 51% of node in the identical time.
- Anonymity: Blockchain technologies resolved the trust, trouble connecting node toward node, therefore data transfer or else transaction can be unidentified, just need to recognize the individual's blockchain address.

THEORETICAL BACKGROUND

Blockchain was introduced through Bitcoin as cryptocurrency. Bitcoin is an organism that controls electronic cash without any support of central power, so certainly there must be a system for the prevention of fraudulence of data, payment repetition, and other kinds of threats and attacks activities possible from unauthorized users. To accomplish this objective, Bitcoin makes use of numerous different essential technologies including, P2P, public-key cryptography, hashing, digital signatures, and Proof of work. The details of these underlying technologies of the blockchain are as follows:

Bitcoin: Electronic Cash in Peer-To-Peer System

As a cryptocurrency, Bitcoin consent to the transfer of digital belongings in the peer-to-peer System without any support of conviction of third parties, Bitcoin is broadly used and exceedingly treasured digital currency across the world (Nakamoto, 2008; Narayanan et al.,2016). In Bitcoin, the complete sequence of a block is vital to maintain possession of each coin. To sustain the ownership of each block, a link has been established through the pointer to form a chain by pointing to the previous correct block in the sequence of the chain. The previous block's hash is maintained to form a linked list structure.

The total count of blocks from starting to end block of the blockchain is known as a block height. Generally, the blockchain persistently grows, and due to this unremitting enhancement of blockchain, there would be a need for a massive amount of computational resources for the validation procedure. To remain the volume and computational attempt reasonable, Bitcoin proposes a simplified payment verification support on Merkle trees (Nakamoto, 2008).

Figure 1. Simplified blockchain

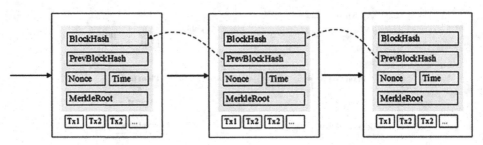

Hash Function

A hash value h is generated in the form of a fixed-size string with the input value I and assigned to hash function H. With the help of this mechanism, a similar hash value will be generated only if the right input is given. Assumption of original input value with the help of hash is tremendously complicated. Bitcoin utilizes the computation of the hash values method to assure the finding of data distortion and verify the persistence of blockchain records.

Figure 2. Hash Mechanism

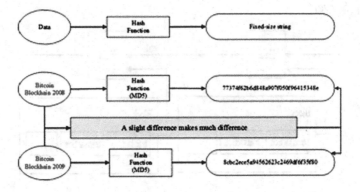

Public-Key Cryptography and Digital Signature

Public, as well as the private key, are significant components of blockchain for digital currency transfer. As asymmetric cryptography, it uses the pair of keys for encryption as well as decryption. Generally, the public key is accessible by anyone in the world and can forward a message to the receiver by encrypting the message using the receiver's public key. The private key of the receiver has been used for message decryption at the receiver's end only (Bergstra & Leeuw, 2013).

Through public-key cryptography, a digital signature verifies the legitimacy of the message sent digitally. It provides authentication, non-repudiation, and integrity, and including these features, the ownership of bitcoin transactions in addition to the bitcoin wallet addresses has been validated (Badev & Chen,2014).

Figure 3. Digital Signature

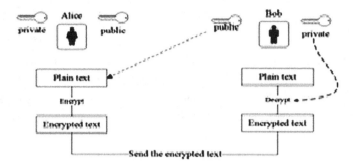

Timestamp Server

A timestamp server was proposed by Bitcoin to take a block of transactions using a hash for time-stamping and hash publication at a broad level. The timestamp establishes the association chain of transactions, and all timestamp is incorporated in the preceding timestamp inside its hash.

The timestamp server is intended to demonstrate that the data must be present all the time(Nakamoto, 2008).

Figure 4. Timestamp Server

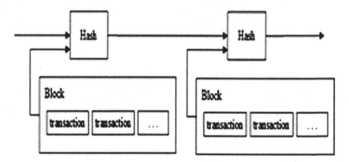

Merkle Trees

Bitcoin's every block with the support of Merkle trees maintains the summing up of each transaction within a block. Merkle tree as a data structure has been used to recapitulate and integrity verification a huge amount of data. As a binary tree, the Merkle tree may also have merely two child nodes (Liu et al., 2015). Merkle tree is created using the hash function and executed recursively on a couple of nodes till there is a single hash identified as Merkle root. Bitcoin's Merkle tree's hash algorithm SHA256 of cryptography has been applied twice, Bottom to top Merkle tree is developed. It doesn't store the transaction, instead of the transaction's data has been hashed and the outcome of the hash will be maintained in each child node. Due to the binary nature of the Merkle tree, in case of an odd figure of transactions, the last transaction will be reproduced to maintain the even figure of child nodes. Merkle tree gives the option to dispose of superfluous transactions without infringement a block's hash because the interior hashes are not maintained.

Figure 5. Merkle Tree

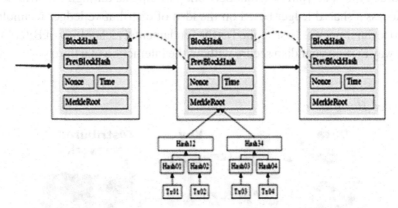

Simplified Payment Verification (SPV) becomes possible in Merkle trees for validation of payment instead of executing a complete network node. A replica of the block header of the longest Proof-of-Work chain is needed to be maintained by the user. The user has no transaction access permission other than network acceptance of it.

As a peer-to-peer network, a network of blockchain also maintains the network of nodes and functions with cryptographic algorithms. The communications and verification process of transactions have been handled by network nodes, and these nodes also resist for revenue (transaction fee) by producing a legitimate block from end to end procedure of getting transactions and determine a resource inducement task (PoW). The bitcoin network runs the following steps:

- Digitally marked fresh transactions are transmitted to every single one node.
- A block contains the fresh transactions collected by each node.
- PoW(Proof-of-Work) is being computed by a node for its block.
- After confirmation of Pow by node, it transmits the block to rest all nodes

Distributed Hash Table

Distributed Hash Table as a disseminated data structure is generally used to accumulate entries related to a key. Moreover, as two major components, the key which is considered to be an address, and value could be the file contents that are linked to that address. Thus, users are permitted to find a key through an entry, as with contacts in a phone as soon as a user looks for a phone number (key) via names (address). DHTs are broadly used to build and manage complex services. For illustration, BitTorrent is employing DHTs for the purpose have hash tables at the top of the mind for any problem as a potential method to resolve the problem." (Figure 6)

Distributed Ledger Technology

As a catalog, the distributed ledger is to facilitate several locations or along with many participants. Blockchain technology also comes under the name DTL. DLT mentions an innovative and fast mechanism for sharing, recording, and store data beyond multiple ledgers. This technology allows us to share, transact, and recorded the data from different network participants through a distributed network. Each participant can access a shared ledger based on the idea of distributive ledger technology. The idea of Blockchain-based technology was first applied as the fundamental technology of Bitcoin cryptocurrency. It also provides a way to keep your data secure without the interaction of a third party (Mills et al., 2016).

Figure 6. Distributed Hash Table

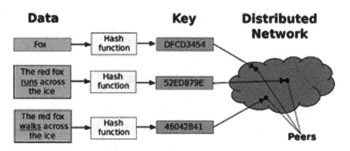

Distributed Ledger Type

Distributed ledger technology can be permissionless (Public) or permissioned (Private) and there are basic differences between the two. Ethereum and Bitcoin are the most popular examples of completely permissionless blockchains, whereas Codra and Hyperledger fabric are a prominent example.

Public Ledger

The public ledger also called the non-permissioned ledger, No one needs permission to create and validate blocks as well as to modify the ledger state by storing and updating data. It provides transparency to everyone for accessing and storing data. In this technique there is no requirement of pre-approval by any entity, network participants can join or leave the network as they will. There is no owner to control it. The homogenous copies of the records are distributed to all network participants. This raises privacy concerns for particular scenarios where the privacy of such data needs to be protected.

Private Ledger

Private ledger, also known as the permissioned ledger, as the name suggests it is restricted that means only trusted and authorized entities are allowed to take part in ledger activities. Distributed Ledgers members are selected prior by someone who is an owner or an administrator of the ledger. They also control network access and sets the ordinance of the ledger. It is restricted unlike its public counterpart in the sense that only authorized and trusted entities can participate in the activities within the ledger. By allowing only authorized entities, a private ledger can ensure the privacy of ledger data, which might be desirable in some use-cases.

Private ledger, also known as the permissioned ledger, as the name suggests it is restricted that means only trusted and authorized entities are allowed to take part in ledger activities. Distributed Ledgers members are selected prior by someone who is an owner or an administrator of the ledger. They also control network access and sets the ordinance of the ledger. It is restricted unlike its public counterpart in the sense that only authorized and trusted entities can participate in the activities within the ledger. By allowing only authorized entities, a private ledger can ensure the privacy of ledger data, which might be desirable in some use-cases.

Table 1. Public ledger vs Private ledger

	Public Ledger	**Private Ledger**
Access	Read & Write public to everyone	Read & Write public to everyone
Central Party	No central owner or administrator	Has some degree of administration or control
Network actors	Don't know each other	Know each other
Speed	Slow	Fast
Identity	User identity anonymous	Identity verification required by the owner
Native Token	Yes	Not necessary
Security	Security through wide distribution in large scale network	Security through access control combined with DLT in small scale network
Openness	Ledger is open and transparent	Different degree of openness and transparency
Level of Trust	Network member is not required to trust each other	A higher degree of trust among members required
Example	• Bitcoin • Ethereum • Manero • Zcash • Steemit • Dash • Litecoin • Stellar etc.	• R3(Banks) • EWF(Energy) • Corda • Hyperledger Fabric Etc.

Hyperledger Fabric

Hyperledger Fabric is emerged by IBM beneath the Hyperleger project. Hyperledger is a project of open-source blockchains. It has been evolved by the foundation of Linux. Hyperledger Fabric was first implemented in 2015. Hyperledger Fabric provides a high privileged network on which members can interact, exchange, and track with digitized data. The fabric is designed to support implementations of a different function, it also allows to use of various programming languages like GO language to implement chain codes, and commonly run within Docker containers. It is a distributed platform for running the chain code. In the hyperedge fabric, transactions follow permissioned ledger and confidential. Since the network is private, every user who wants to participate in the transaction must have registered in the network for getting their corresponding ids. Fabric ledger also provides auditability to meet regulatory needs. The modular architecture delivers a high proportion of resiliency, flexibility, confidentiality in implementation, and design. (Sajana et al., 2018).

Corda

It is a DLT(distributed ledger technology) that focuses on the finance application. It aims to provide support for finance use-cases structure. Various degrees of openness and transparency of the records is possible. It is a permissioned network that means all participants must have corresponding verifiable identities to participant in any transaction. A higher degree of faith among members required. One of the major differences between Corda and other public Distributed Ledger platforms like Ethereum and Bitcoin is the use of a blockchain to record the transaction. Corda is also a DLT platform but does not use a blockchain to record transactions. Corda Govern By private company R3, consortium of over 70 financial institutions. It provides a very high level of trust. One of the powerful features that make Corda different than some renowned financial networks such as Ripple and Stellar is its smart contract facilities. It consists of a large developer community who can write codes in Kotlin and Java to develop DApps in Corda(Chowdhury et al., 2019).

IOTA

IOTA is a freely available distributed ledger designed for the IoT(Internet of Things). It is built to enhance the power of future IoT. It provides secure communications between IoT devices. A distributed technology of IOTA is not a chain of block propel transaction. Its consensus-building structure is made of a DAG (Directed Acyclic Graph) that is based on Tangle. A network of vertices joined by an edge each vertex represents a transaction. IOTA has no cost for transaction and scalability. Its transaction is very fast. IOTA uses Tangle that solving the transaction fee and the scalability both issues faced by most distributed ledgers. IOTA avoids centralization it grows via a transaction, not miners or stacker. IOTa aims to become the backbone of the m2m economy of the Internet of things (Chowdhury et al.,2019).

Blockchain Applications

Digital Currency: Bitcoin

Bitcoin's transaction system and its data structure were developed based on blockchain technologies which built Bitcoin as a digital currency for an online payment system. Funds transfer can be accomplished in a secure manner using an encryption technique without trusting any third party bank. Public keys have been employed for sending as well as receiving the bitcoin, transaction recording, and the individual ID was unsigned. The transaction processes authenticate needs further the user's computing power to acquire consensus and then account for the transaction to the network.

Smart Contract: Ethereum

Smart Contract as a digital contract organize user's digital belongings, devise the participant's right and responsibilities, which will be executed automatically by a computer system. It can be considered as a contract among participants and allow them to receive and respond to messages besides storing the data. Further, a smart contract may send a message to outside also. As a trusted authority or person, a smart contract can also embrace assets for a temporary period and pursue the instructions which have already been programmed (Kosba et al., 2016). As an open-source blockchain, the Etherium platform to handle the contract combines the smart contract and offers a decentralized virtual machine. By the use of ETH, which is called the digital currency of it, users on this platform may create various applications, services, or contracts (Watanabe et al.,2016).

Hyperledger

As Ethereum, Hyperledger blockchain is also an open-source platform to maintain the distributed ledger, initiated by Linux Foundation in December 2015. It is paying attention to ledgers considered to maintain worldwide business transactions, together with foremost financial, supply chain companies and technologies to enhance numerous aspects of performance and reliability. To build up open protocol and set of standards, various independent efforts have been put together to provide a modular framework that maintains dissimilar components for various purposes. This would comprise a mixture of blockchains with their storage models and consensus, and identity, contract, and access control services.

Other Applications

Financial Services

Presently, blockchain technology has been used in a broad level of financial areas, along with business services, financial assets settlements, economic transactions, and prediction markets. An essential role has been expected by blockchain in the global economy's sustainable expansion, consumers benefits in present banking structure and the entire world in common (Nguyen, 2016).

The worldwide financial organizations are looking the procedure of employing blockchain-built application for financial resources, such as fiat money, securities, and imitative contracts (Peters et al., 2016; Fanning & Centers, 2016; Kosba et al.,2016). For example, blockchain technology recommends an enormous alteration to the capital marketplace and a more proficient method for performing processes like derivatives transactions, securities, and digital payments.

Insurance Claims Processing

Claims processing can frequently be an unsolved and a problematical task for the claims processing staff. Insurance workstation requires to go from beginning to end, staged incidents, fake cases, and difficult to deal with clients, etc. which extensively widen the risks of inaccuracy and misclassifications. An ideal framework can be present by Blockchain in such kind of situation administration without any hazard and openness in dealing out with cases. Its encryption (Mota,et al.,2017) feature facilitates guarantor to ensure that dispensation is secure and reliable.

Legal Services

A "Smart Contract" is a computer code for the automation of an agreement, an auto- executing digital agreement that records and implement an agreement between two or more person. Unlike a traditional contract, it is self-enforcing in nature, that is, a smart contract's outcome is inherently and directly coded into the contract itself (Legalwise,2019). A traditional Blockchain allows for a network of computers to build a trusted decentralized and automatic system that is an authority for such Smart Contracts. These digital contracts can be executed more efficiently and without human involvement, resulting in the potential for increased certainty of outcomes.

Healthcare Management

The Healthcare industry is another area of application where blockchain technology could participate an important role in the numerous applications of various regions like public healthcare management, automated health asserts settlement, longitudinal healthcare reports, sharing patients' health check-up data, online patient access, user-oriented remedial research, drug forged, clinical experiment, and precision medicine (Juneja&Marefat, 2018). Normally, blockchain technology along with the SCs could find the solution of problems of the scientific authority of verdict(endpoint switching, missing data, selective publication, and data search) in the clinical examination as well as a matter of patients' informed permission.

Business and Industrial Applications

Blockchain has the prospective to be converted into a significant foundation of troublesome advancements in industry and management through getting better and automate business processes. IoT and blockchain are rising in the current scenario and based on that numerous e-business models have been developed. Blockchain applications materialize to propose substantial performance enhancement and commercialization prospects, recovering reliability in e-commerce and facilitating IoT corporations to optimize their process while reduction of time and cost. blockchain-dependent applications could provide decentralized trade process organization for numerous enterprises. In such examples, all business process illustration may be retained on the blockchain, and the workflow direction-finding could be carried out by SCs, thereby reformation and mechanize intra-organizational procedure and cost reduction (Mendling et al.,2018)

Supply Chain Management

Blockchain technology is likely to raise transparency and liability in supply chain systems, therefore enabling additional flexible worth chains. Particularly, blockchain-dependent applications have the prospective to produce advancements in three areas of the supply chain: optimization, visibility, and demand. Blockchain can be employed in logistics, recognizing bogus products, declining paper load processing, facilitating source tracking, and allow buyers and vendors to perform directly without maneuvering by intermediaries (Subramanian, 2017). Besides, it has been verified that the blockchain-based applications handling within supply chain networks would be able to take care of security, show the way to more vigorous contract management system between 3rd and 4th party logistics (3PL, 4PL) for combating information irregularity, improve tracking system and traceability assertion, offer better information organization across the whole supply chain, offer improved customer facility through highly developed data analytics (i.e. encrypted consumer data) and original recommender system, get better inventory and performance administration across compound supply chains, and at last, it can get better smart transportation arrangement and propose novel decentralized developed design.

VARIOUS PROBLEMS ASSOCIATED WITH BLOCKCHAIN IMPLEMENTATION

Blockchains are digital blocks consisting of records of transactions over public or private networks. The blockchain record security can be ensured through cryptography. The concepts of consensus and immutability are the core security and privacy concern in the blockchain network however blockchain network security depends on the infrastructure of the network. Infrastructure has capabilities like preventing all type of users from accessing sensitive information, preventing illicit data change requests or attempts, and using the highest security mechanism to guard security keys form hackers, are the basic security requirements of infrastructure within blockchain network public, private and hybrid blockchains are different so deliver the different intensity of security. Public blockchains are in communication with public networks like the internet so that any independent node can join it but private networks only let known networks to join. Anonymity is the principle design on which blockchains have typically been designed and identity is the key term that is used by private blockchain to confirm access privileges (Zhang et al., 2019).

Attacks on Blockchain

Majority Attack

An attacker can cause severe network disruption through a majority attack (51% attack), which is a potential attack on a blockchain network, in which the attacker attempts to manage the main part of the hash fee. Transactions over the blockchain network can be prevented if the attack is successful but the attack does not permit the invader to reverse the transactions from other parties. New transaction creation and submission over the blockchain network, cannot be prevented through this attack.However, changing the previously confirmed block gets more difficult when the chain grows because the more confirmation a block gets, it is getting tougher for altering and reverting the transaction. Historical blocks cannot be changed due to the hard coding of the previous transactions. Krypton and Shift are the two blockchain networks based on Ethereum and suffered from majority assault in August-2016. Bitcoin Gold also suffered a majority attack held in May 2018, in which the attacker was successful in double-spend (Lin&Liao,, 2017; Saad et al.,2019).

Double Spending

Double spending is an application-oriented attack, which refers to the spending currency twice through a conflicting transaction in a quick session over the blockchain network which would destroy the trust in the service provider. It is very essential to verify the ownership of the transactions to stop double-spending and other frauds. The outcome of previous researches shows that to execute a double-spending attack over a large blockchain network like Bitcoin would require a very large amount of computational power which would not possible for any individual. the security risk for smaller blockchain networks still exists. The attacker's identity could be revealed after planting this attack over the network and if there are two transactions sequentially generated to impose an attack, then those transactions would be transferred to the unconfirmed transaction pool. the first transaction will be authorized and the second will be flagged as an invalid transaction. in case of both transactions are verified as legal and pulled from the group, then transaction having a maximum numeral of confirmations will be incorporated into the chain, and other would-be discarded(Vokerla et al.,2019).

Finney Attack

Finney attack is launched by the miner in which he mines or controls the content of his block with his transaction and this block is not broadcasted over the network. The coins related to the previous transaction are now used in the second transaction and after that previously mined block is released again. This action would cause some time lag in the rejection of a second transaction by the other miners. If the seller does not wait for enough confirmation, the supply may occur twice. This type of attack gets successful only if the seller accepts the unconfirmed transaction. suppose the time required between finding the block and seller accepts the payment is t, as well as the average time for searching the block is T, then there will be a probability of t/T time unit to find another block on the same network. the attack would not be successful and the attacker will not get any benefit against block B. The standard cost of attempting an attack is (t/T)*B. Suppose V is the value of the transaction, then the seller has to wait at least t=V*T/B before releasing the supply. The Finney attack has a low success probability due to short block intervals and time-sensitive attack procedures. The Bitcoin and Ethereum have 10 minutes and 15 seconds of block time(Saad, et al.,2019).

Brute-Force Attack

In such kind of attack, the invader tries the massive number of possible passwords for digital signature secret keys of existing wallets and checks the returned paint-text for its accuracy. Attack time and the number of attempts depend on the key size. This type of attack is used to steal bitcoins from honest users. First of all, the attacker creates the list of bitcoin addresses having some funds into them using the current set of unused transaction outputs associated with the current status of the blockchain. After that, the attacker selects some set of secret keys from the extracted transaction list and build the secret key list. After that a secret key is selected from the secret key list, and generates a corresponding address. the generated address is then get matched with the addresses from the address list generated in the first stage. If the address is found, then the attacker publishes a transaction to get the benefit of the funds from the compromised address to their address. All these operations are repeated for all secret keys from the list (Vokerla et al.,2019).

Selfish Mining Attack

This attack is also known as Block Withholding Attack. In this attack, an attacker having malicious intentions harms the integrity of the network. In the case of selfish mining, only malicious miners are being referred. The malicious miner hides/withhold the mined block and harms the other honest miners and lets them loos the trust in the integrity of the blockchain network. In this scenario, honest miners get confused and waste their assets in fruitless courses. It becomes very tough to add valid blocks because of the addition of invalid blocks or withholding the valid blocks by the miners. Selfish miners will maintain their private chain and reveal it for getting more rewards that will be assured because of their contributive approach. A random assignment of blockchain branch to the miners and setting threshold limit for mining pool can eliminate this type of attack (Vokerla et al., 2019; Saad, et al.,2019).

Sybil Attack

An attacker compromises the client system and performs the transaction over the blockchain in this category of attack. A dummy software or multiple fake accounts, nodes, or computers can be treated as a medium to compromise the part of the blockchain. It is a community-based attack performed by a group of compromised nodes. The word "Sybil" comes from the name of a woman having a disease named multiple personality disorder"Sybil Dorsett". If an attacker creates many fake accounts, they can refuse to receive or transmit blocks to prevent other users to perform block transmission. If multiple account creation gives the ability to control the maximum required hash rate of computing strength, then the majority attack can be initiated by the attackers. Elimination of security enforcement against this type of malicious activity over the blockchain association can be performed to make the attack process very impractical by using different types of consensus algorithms like proof of stake, proof of work, or delegated proof of stake. Raising the cost of creating a new identity, implementing trust management protocol before new identity creation, and weighting the user power based on reputation can highly reduce the possibility to launch the attack over a blockchain network (Vokerla et al.,2019).

Fork Problem

Blockchain network is based on a decentralized group of parties (nodes) in collaboration with each other. This problem of Fork comes into existence when blockchain software is involved in an update process. Each node of a blockchain network verifies the public ledger of blockchain and ensures the blockchain network security. When a new software update is launched, the agreement rules also get changed for each node participating in the blockchain system. This event causes the partition of all nodes into two groups. one group accepts the updates and agreed to follow newly updated transaction rules and the other group discards the update and continues to follow the old transaction rules. This conflict arises the chain to be split (Fork) into two parts (Lin, I. C., & Liao, T. C.,2017).

The opinion difference about new protocol in the community results in two different types of approaches (problems). The Hard Fork problem refers to the part of a community that does not agree on the upgraded version of the protocol or new agreement. If there is enough strength of old nodes rejecting software upgrades, they could continue to follow the completely different chain even when the computation power of new nodes is stronger in comparison to old nodes.

Soft Fork can be represented as backward compatible. When the community accepts the new agreement, it is not compatible with the old protocols and refuses to mine the old chain. The majority of nodes should be upgraded with the new protocol to get the Soft Fork work and make the network more secure after Fork. Due to the difference between the computation power of both types of nodes, new nodes never agreed to approve blocks mined by old nodes as well as the same chain is continued to be held by both types of nodes. like a hard fork, the soft fork never reduces the effectiveness and integrity of the system at the time of upgrade. Soft Fork is being used in both Bitcoin and Ethereum blockchain(Lin & Liao,2017).

SUGGESTIONS

Blockchain as a disseminated decentralized network intends to offer immutability and data security. With no central power to authenticate and validate the transactions, all transactions in a blockchain are measured to be protected and validated. As blockchain has been built in a decentralized model and accounts for huge volume transactions in instantaneous, there may be the possibility of the complexity of what is the reality. The key is to obtain consensus on one approach or another, or else malevolent possessions like double-spending assault can occur. Thus, there is a role of the consensus algorithm arrive.

A consensus algorithm is a method in computer science to set up agreement lying on a single data value crossways distributed evolution of systems. As a protocol, in a consensus algorithm, all the team or users of the blockchain network move towards a general agreement (consensus) lying on the current data position of the ledger and be able to believe unidentified peers in a distributed computing background. The consensus algorithms are very much essential in blockchain networks as an essential element because they maintain the integrity and security of these distributed computing systems. In the blockchain, the way to accomplish consensus surrounded by unreliable nodes is a revolution of the Byzantine Generals (BG) Problem(Lamport et al.,1982). In this trouble, a group of generals controls a segment of the Byzantine army on all sides of the city. Various generals are in favour to attack whereas other generals have a preference to retreat. Nevertheless, the assault would be unsuccessful if barely part of the generals assaults the city. Consequently, they have to accomplish conformity (or agreement) to attack otherwise retreat. The way to achieve a consensus in distributed surroundings is a challenge. Same confront for blockchain also due to its network is distributed. There would be a need to make sure ledgers in unlike nodes are consistent.

There are several general approaches to get to a consensus in the blockchain.

Approaches to Consensus

Proof of Work (PoW)

Proof of work is a consensus approach applied in the Bitcoin Net (Nakamoto S., 2008). In a decentralized set of connections, somebody has to be chosen for the documentation of the transactions. The best way is random selection. Nevertheless, a random choice is vulnerable to assault. Subsequently, in case of node desire to bring out a block of transactions, a large number of labor has to be done to establish that the node is not probable to attack the system.

Figure 7. Proof of Work process

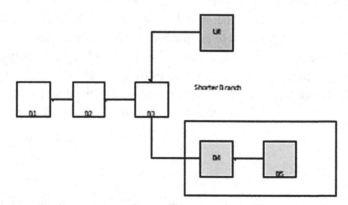

Table 2. Typical Consensus Algorithms Comparison

Property	PoW	PoS		PBFT	DPOS		Ripple			Tendermint
Node identity management	open	open	[21]	permissioned	open	[22]	open	nodes	in	permissioned
Energy saving	no	partial		yes	partial		yes	[23]		yes
Tolerated power of the adversary	<25%	<51%		<33.3%	<51%		<20%			<33.3%
Example	computing power	stake		faulty replicas	validators		faulty			byzantine voting
	Bitcoin [2]	Peercoin		Hyperledger Fabric [18]	Bitshares		UNL Ripple			power Tendermint [24]

Figure 7 shows the development of blockchain branches (the branch which would be longest to be admitted as the major chain whereas the shorter one would be abandoned) calculations. In PoW, the network's each node computes a block header's hash. A nonce and miners of the block header would modify the nonce very often to get dissimilar hash values. The consensus has desirable that the computed value necessarily equal to or lesser than a certain specified value. As soon as one node accomplishes the objective, it would transmit the block to additional nodes and every single node must mutually finalize the accuracy of the hash value. In case of the block is validated, supplementary miners would add on the validated block to their blockchain. Nodes that compute the hash describes the miners and the PoW process has been known as *mining* in Bitcoin.

Decentralized network's validated blocks might be produced all together when numerous nodes find the appropriate nonce just about at a similar time. Due to this, branches possibly will generate as shown in Figure 7. Though, it is doubtful that two opposing forks will produce the next block concurrently.

Proof of Stake

Proof of Stake as consensus may be at variance with the PoW mining consensus utilizing a method wherever blocks are authenticated based on the venture of the network applicants. At this time, dissimilar executing hash functions, authenticators stake resources principally in the appearance of tokens or digital money or tokens. Every block's authenticator is further randomly chosen from the stakeholders due to the quantity of computational power owed.

All PoS scheme may put into practice the algorithm in unlike ways, usually, the blockchain is protected by a pseudo-random selection process with the aim of a node's allotment and the distribution– determining the assurance of the party to make sure the network secure. The Ethereum blockchain, which has been considered as largest blockchain network in the world in terms of developer actions, has begun to move from PoW algorithm to PoS to put an effort to improve the network's scalability in addition to reduce unnecessary electricity wastage.

Practical Byzantine Fault Tolerance

It is a replication algorithm to accept byzantine faults (Miguel & Barbara,1999). In this algorithm, Hyperledger Fabric makes use of the PBFT like its consensus algorithm as PBFT could hold up to 1/3 malevolent byzantine limitation. A novel block is identified in around. In all rounds, a man would be chosen according to a variety of rules. Besides, it is accountable for organizing the transaction. The entire process could be separated into three segments: *pre-prepared*, *prepared,* and *commit*. In all phases, a node would come into the next phase if it has acknowledged votes from over 2/3 of all nodes. As a result, PBFT has needed that each node is to be recognized to the network. Similar to PBFT, (SCP) Stellar Consensus Protocol (Mazieres D.,2015) is as well a Byzantine fault-tolerant protocol. Within PBFT, all nodes have to inquiry other nodes where as SCP gives contributors the right to select other contributors set to believe. Customers need not be concerned about the fraudulent entrust as they could be designated out without a doubt. DPOS is the spine of bit shares.

Ripple

Ripple is a consensus protocol that makes use of jointly-trusted subnetworks surrounded by the larger network (Schwartz et al., 2014). In this case network's nodes are separated into two categories: *server* for taking part in consensus procedure and *client* for just transporting funds. all servers have a Unique Node List (UNL). It is essential to the server. As soon as determining whether to set a transaction keen on the ledger, the server would inquiry the nodes in UNL, and in case of acknowledged agreements have accomplished 80%, the transaction would be filled into the ledger in support of a node, the ledger will remain accurate provided that the percentage of damaged nodesinUNLisbelow20%.

Tendermint

Tender mint is a byzantine consensus that identifies afresh block in around. A proposer is probably chosen to broadcast the not finalized block in the current round. It might be subcategorized into three steps: 1) *the Prevote step*. Certification authorities choose whether to transmit a pre-vote for the projected block.2) the *Pre-commit step*. In case of the node has received above 2/3 of votes lying on the projected block, it transmits a pre-commit in favor of that block. Otherwise in case of the node has acknowledged more than 2/3 of recommits, it goes through the entrust step. 3) *Commit step*. The node authenticates the block and transmits a commit for the validated block. In case of the node has acknowledged 2/3 of the commits, it admits the block. In distinction to PBFT, nodes need to restrict their coins to turn into validators. Once an authenticator or validator is brought into being to be fraudulent, it would be penalized.

A high-quality consensus algorithm indicates safety, efficiency, and expediency.in recent times, several accomplishments have been over to get better consensus algorithms within the blockchain. Fresh consensus protocols are developed intending to resolve some particular of blockchain. The foremost proposal of PeerCensus(Decker et al.,2016) is to decouple block formation and transaction finalization so that the consensus speed can be significantly improved.

POSSIBLE FUTURE DIRECTIONS

Blockchain has revealed its prospective in business and academia. The research focuses its potential future guidelines concerning four fields: blockchain testing, the tendency to centralization, big data analytics, and IoT with blockchain.

Blockchain Testing

In recent times, a different category of blockchains has come into view and more than 700 cryptocurrencies are recorded in Crypto-currency market capitalizations, 2017 so far. Nevertheless, several developers might forge their blockchain presentation to pull towards investors determined by the enormous profit. In addition to that, as soon as users desire to merge blockchain into trade, It must be clear that which blockchain fits their requirements. So blockchain testing method desires to be in a position to examine dissimilar blockchains.

Blockchain testing could be segregated into two segments: standardization and testing stage. In the standardization segment, every criterion has to be completed and settled. Even as a blockchain is intuitive, it could be experienced with the approved criteria to apply if the blockchain efforts are fine as developer desire. Since for testing segment, blockchain testing requirements to be performed with unlike criteria. For instance, a user who is responsible for online trade be concerned regarding the blockchain's throughput, thus the examination needs investigation of the average time from a client to send a transaction to another transaction and is bundled into the blockchain.

Tendency to Centralization

Blockchain is intended to be a decentralized system. Though, there is a tendency that miners be federal in the mining group. So far, the top 5 mining groups together own superior to 51% of the inclusive hash control in the Bitcoin network. Excluding that, the selfish mining approach demonstrated that groups over 25% of whole computing control could obtain more profits than fair distribution. Balanced miners would be involved in the selfish group and at last, the group could without difficulty exceed 51% of the entire power. Since the blockchain is not projected to serve a small number of organizations, several techniques should be projected to resolve this trouble.

Big Data Analytics

Blockchain could be well shared with big data. Now, it is just about to classify the grouping into two categories: data management addition to data analytics. In support of data management, blockchain could be employed to accumulate important data since it is dispersed and safe. Blockchain may perhaps also ensure the data is novel. For instance, in the case of blockchain is employed to accumulate patients' health details, this information could not have interfered and it would be very difficult to steal an individual's private contents. While as it moves toward data analytics, blockchain transactions could be applied for big data analytics.

IoT and Blockchain

IoT represents the interconnection of disparate things. The term object refers to a human, sensor, or possibly anything that can request or provide a service. The purpose of IoT is to connect an object to object, the object to human, and human to human (Mosenia & Jha,2016). It's convenient for identification, management, and control. Various IoT applications main focus on automating their tasks and empower the objects. Automating the things to perform a different task to support various IOT applications. Main focus to make the object empower, to operate without any human involvement.

IoT Security Goal

IoT applications promise to bring cosmic change into our lives. If we remove the obstacle of security threat then IOT could help to make our life smart and convenient. With the aid of exhaustive computing technology, wireless network, and superior sensor IoT has become the next frontier. The security triad, distinguished technique put into services by use of three main regions which are: data integrity confidentiality, and availability. Data confidentiality is the ability to provide confidence to the user about the privacy of the confidential data by using the different technique so that its disclosure to the unapproved party is prevented and can be ingresses by the authorized users only. Data confidentiality is usually supported through different mechanisms such as data encryption or access control (Zhang et al,,2019). Data integrity refers to the accuracy and consistency of data over its lifecycle. It can be indicated by the absence of modification between two objects or between two upgrades of stored data information. Data integrity can be verified through checksum and cycle redundancy check. Data availability ensures the immediate access of authorized party to their information resources not only in the normal conditions but also in adverse conditions (Sharma et al. 2019; Adat & Gupta,2018)

IoT Security Using Blockchain

Today 5 billion devices have been connected through IoT accounts, and this number will continue to increase and reach 29 billion by 2022 (Reyna et al., 2018). Every object generates and transfers data on the Internet. As IoT has distributive architecture and it is an essential summons for security. Typically, in an IoT network, each node is a possible point of risk that can be utilized to launch cyber attacks. In the presence of a data vulnerability attack, IoT data cannot be exploited properly. Besides, with the involvement of much smart application of IoT where devices exchange data, computational power or other resources, data security becomes critical (Sridhar & Smys,,2017). Blockchain technology has become a very effective solution for all security issues. Blockchain and IoT are two attractive technologies that focus on improving the overall transparency, visibility, level of comfort, and level of trust for the users. The implementation of blockchain into IoT brings some refinements such as decentralization and scalability, identity, autonomy, reliability, security, and market of services The basic idea behind the blockchain is simple, it used distributed ledger technology. The entries in the blockchain are chronological and time-stamped. Each entry in the ledger is tightly coupled with the previous entry using cryptographic hash keys (Panarello et al., 2018).

IoT and Blockchain Integration

IoT can get benefits from the various features delivered by blockchain and can help to further improvement of existing IoT technologies. Blockchain can perform an important role in securing data in IoT applications. At the current time, these two technologies have the most prominent topics in research. The combination of this approach can bring the revolution. (Reyna et al., 2018). Few benefits of IoT and Blockchain integration are as follows:

- Identity: Participants can identify every single device using a common block system. Data provided and store in the system is unchangeable and uniquely recognize actual data that was provided by a device. Subsequently, for IoT applications, a blockchain can provide an authorized and trustful environment.

- Decentralization and scalability: decentralization of the architecture help in the improvement of fault tolerance and system scalability. Other benefits of the shift from a centralized architecture to a Peer-2-Peer distributed will remove central points of failures and tailback.
- Autonomy: Blockchain helps IoT devices to interrelate one device to another without the assistance of any server. Blockchain technology empowers next-generation IOT application features, making it an autonomous object.
- Reliability: With the support of blockchain, IoT information can remain as it has been uploaded. Blockchain systems are capable to check the data integrity and provide the satisfaction that no one has altered the data. The most important aspect of blockchain is to bring reliable IoT.
- Speed: Within a minute, A blockchain distributes the transaction across the whole network and any time throughout the day it can be processed.
- Safely code deployment: Blockchain provides unchangeable storage. Relevant code can be uploaded on the device safely.

Figure 8. Benefits of IoT and Blockchain Integration

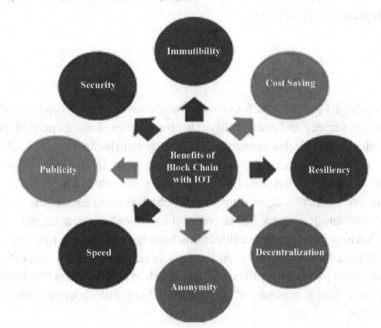

When integrating IoT with blockchain, it has to be determined wherever these interactions will take place. There are varieties of integration scheme:

IoT-IoT

As it can work offline therefore it fastest in terms of security as well as latency. IoT transactions can happen without using blockchain because barely a component of IoT data stored in the blockchain as shown in figure 9. This approach is useful when with secure IoT data where IoT interaction does perform with low data latency.

Figures 9. IOT-IOT to IOT –Blockchain Integration

IOT-IOT   **IOT-BLOCKCHAIN**

IoT-Blockchain

When this approach has been applied, all interactions happen via blockchain. All selected interactions are traceable as their record can be accessed in the blockchain by using this approach. It also ensures the autonomy of IoT devices. One of the popular complications in blockchain to record all transactions that increase bandwidth and data. Even all IoT data associated with this transaction should also be stored in the blockchain as represented in Figure 9.

CONCLUSION

Blockchain has revealed its prospective for transforming conventional business with its key features: devolution, persistency, secrecy and audit ability. This research explores a comprehensive summary on blockchain. In first phase, it highlights a general idea of blockchain technologies together with blockchain architecture and main characteristics of blockchain.. Furthermore, in next phase research briefs several security challenges and problems that would hinder blockchain development. In addition to that, research discusses the distinctive consensus algorithms used in blockchain to sustain the integrity and security of these distributed computing systems. These conscious protocols were analyzed and evaluated in different perspective. Various potential future directions have been discussed like big data analytics with blockchain, IoT and blockchain integration. At the present time blockchain supported applications are rising up and this research put an effort to conduct in-depth explorations on blockchain-based applications in various business area at present and in the future along with security challenges.

REFERENCES

Adat, V., & Gupta, B. B. (2018). Security in Internet of Things: Issues, challenges, taxonomy, and architecture. *Telecommunication Systems*, *67*(3), 423–441. doi:10.100711235-017-0345-9

Badev, A., & Chen, M. (2014). *Bitcoin: Technical Background and Data Analysis*. Academic Press.

Bergstra, J. A., & de Leeuw, K. (2013). *Questions related to Bitcoin and other Informational Money*. arXivPrepr. arXiv1305.5956.

Chowdhury, M. J. M., Ferdous, M. S., Biswas, K., Chowdhury, N., Kayes, A. S. M., Alazab, M., & Watters, P. (2019). A comparative analysis of distributed ledger technology platforms. *IEEE Access: Practical Innovations, Open Solutions*, 7, 167930–167943. doi:10.1109/ACCESS.2019.2953729

Decker, C., Seidel, J., & Wattenhofer, R. (2016). Bitcoin meets strong consistency. In *Proceedings of the 17th International Conference on Dis- tributed Computing and Networking (ICDCN)*. Singapore: ACM.

Fanning, K., & Centers, D. P. (2016). Blockchain and its coming impact on financial services. *Journal of Corporate Accounting & Finance*, 27(5), 53–57. doi:10.1002/jcaf.22179

Juneja, A., & Marefat, M. (2018). Leveraging blockchain for retraining deep learning architecture in patient-specific arrhythmia classification. *2018 IEEE EMBS International Conference on Biomedical and Health Informatics, BHI 2018*, 393–397. 10.1109/BHI.2018.8333451

Kosba, A., Miller, A., Shi, E., Wen, Z., & Papamanthou, C. (2016). Hawk: The blockchain model of cryptography and privacy-preserving smart contracts. *2016 IEEE Symposium on Security and Privacy (SP'16)*, 839–858. 10.1109/SP.2016.55

Lamport, L., Shostak, R., & Pease, M. (1982). The byzantine generals problem. *ACM Transactions on Programming Languages and Systems*, 4(3), 382–401. doi:10.1145/357172.357176

Legalwise. (2019). *Rise of Smart Contracts with Blockchain Technology in Australia and New Zealand.* Available at: https://www.legalwiseseminars.com.au/news/smart-contracts-and-the-law/

Lin, I. C., & Liao, T. C. (2017). A survey of blockchain security issues and challenges. *International Journal of Network Security*, 19(5), 653–659.

Liu, C., Ranjan, R., Yang, C., Zhang, X., Wang, L., & Chen, J. (2015). MuR-DPA: Top-down Levelled Multi-replica Merkle Hash Tree Based Secure Public Auditing for Dynamic Big Data Storage on Cloud. *IEEE Trans. Comput.*

Mazieres, D. (2015). *The stellar consensus protocol: A federated model for internet-level consensus.* Stellar Development Foundation.

Mendling, J., Weber, I., Aalst, W. V. D., Brocke, J. V., Cabanillas, C., Daniel, F., Debois, S., Ciccio, C. D., Dumas, M., Dustdar, S., Gal, A., García-Bañuelos, L., Governatori, G., Hull, R., Rosa, M. L., Leopold, H., Leymann, F., Recker, J., Reichert, M., ... Zhu, L. (2018). Blockchains for business process management-challenges and opportunities. *ACM Transactions on Management Information Systems*, 9(1), 4. doi:10.1145/3183367

Miguel, C., & Barbara, L. (1999). Practical byzantine fault tolerance. *Proceedings of the Third Symposium on Operating Systems Design and Implementation*, 99, 173–186.

Mills, D. C., Wang, K., Malone, B., Ravi, A., Marquardt, J., Badev, A. I., ... Ellithorpe, M. (2016). *Distributed ledger technology in payments, clearing, and settlement.* Academic Press.

Mosenia, A., & Jha, N. K. (2016). A comprehensive study of security of internet-of-things. *IEEE Transactions on Emerging Topics in Computing*, 5(4), 586–602. doi:10.1109/TETC.2016.2606384

Mota, A. V., Azam, S., Yeo, K. C., Shanmugam, B., & Kannoorpatti, K. (2017). Comparative analysis of different techniques of encryption for secured data transmission. *IEEE International Conference on Power, Control, Signals and Instrumentation Engineering, ICPCSI*. 10.1109/ICPCSI.2017.8392158

Nakamoto, S. (2008). *Bitcoin: A peer-to-peer electronic cash system*. Academic Press.

Narayanan, A., Bonneau, J., Felten, E., Miller, A., & Goldfeder, S. (2016). *Bitcoin and Cryptocurrency Technologies: A Comprehensive Introduction*. Princeton University Press.

Nguyen, Q. K. (2016). Blockchain-A Financial Technology for Future Sustainable Development. *Proceedings – 3rd International Conference on Green Technology and Sustainable Development, GTSD 2016*, 51–54.

Paech, P. (2017). The governance of blockchain financial networks. *The Modern Law Review*, *80*(6), 1073–1110. doi:10.1111/1468-2230.12303

Panarello, A., Tapas, N., Merlino, G., Longo, F., & Puliafito, A. (2018). Blockchain and iot integration: A systematic survey. *Sensors (Basel)*, *18*(8), 2575. doi:10.339018082575 PMID:30082633

Peters, G. W., & Panayi, E. (2016). *Understanding modern banking ledgers through blockchain technologies: future of transaction processing and smart contracts on the internet of money. New Economic Windows*. doi:10.1007/978-3-319-42448-4_13

Reyna, A., Martín, C., Chen, J., Soler, E., & Díaz, M. (2018). On blockchain and its integration with IoT. Challenges and opportunities. *Future Generation Computer Systems*, *88*, 173–190. doi:10.1016/j.future.2018.05.046

Saad, M., Spaulding, J., Njilla, L., Kamhoua, C., Shetty, S., Nyang, D., & Mohaisen, A. (2019). *Exploring the attack surface of blockchain: A systematic overview*. arXiv preprint arXiv:1904.03487.

Sajana, P., Sindhu, M., & Sethumadhavan, M. (2018). On blockchain applications: Hyperledger fabric and ethereum. *International Journal of Pure and Applied Mathematics*, *118*(18), 2965–2970.

Schwartz, D., Youngs, N., & Britto, A. (2014). *The ripple protocol consensus algorithm*. Ripple Labs Inc White Paper.

Sharma, P., Tripathi, S. S., & Panda, R. (2019). *A Survey of Security Issues in Internet of Things*. Academic Press.

Sridhar, S., & Smys, S. (2017, January). Intelligent security framework for iot devices cryptography based end-to-end security architecture. In *2017 International Conference on Inventive Systems and Control (ICISC)* (pp. 1-5). IEEE. 10.1109/ICISC.2017.8068718

Subramanian, H. (2017). Decentralized blockchain-based electronic marketplaces. *Communications of the ACM*, *61*(1), 78–84. doi:10.1145/3158333

Vokerla, R. R., Shanmugam, B., Azam, S., Karim, A., De Boer, F., Jonkman, M., & Faisal, F. (2019). An Overview of Blockchain Applications and Attacks. In *2019 International Conference on Vision Towards Emerging Trends in Communication and Networking (ViTECoN)* (pp. 1-6). IEEE. 10.1109/ViTECoN.2019.8899450

Watanabe, H., Fujimura, S., Nakadaira, A., Miyazaki, Y., Akutsu, A., & Kishigami, J. (2016). Blockchain contract: Securing a blockchain applied to smart contracts. *IEEE International Conference on Consumer Electronics (ICCE'16)*, 467–468. 10.1109/ICCE.2016.7430693

Zhang, R., Xue, R., & Liu, L. (2019). Security and privacy on blockchain. *ACM Computing Surveys*, *52*(3), 1–34. doi:10.1145/3316481

Chapter 61

Blockchain and the Research Libraries:
Expanding Interlibrary Loan and Protecting Privacy

Anthony L. Paganelli
Western Kentucky University, USA

Andrea L. Paganelli
Western Kentucky University, USA

ABSTRACT

This chapter will examine the theoretical uses of blockchain technologies in research libraries. Technology has enhanced the services and operations of research libraries since the early implementation of computerized cataloging systems. Blockchain technology provides research libraries with the opportunity to decentralize services, while also maintaining and strengthening digital rights management. Research libraries will be able locate services that can be decentralized to provide patrons with a more effective and efficient service. The blockchain technology has the potential to expand library collections through distributed verifiable sovereign identity, which would allow patrons to securely access information from multiple libraries while maintaining their privacy. Libraries will be able to evaluate services and programs to determine best uses for blockchain technology.

INTRODUCTION

When people mention technology, most would relate the term technology with computers or some form of electronic device. However, libraries have embraced technology as a broader term that is inclusive of pre-digital tools implementing various forms of technology well before computers. Libraries have utilized technology for centuries that includes the Gutenberg printing press that increased library collections. Due to the increase of collections, print book catalogs were created for librarians and patrons to access books.

DOI: 10.4018/978-1-6684-7132-6.ch061

Eventually, the catalog books were changed to cards that would provide accurate record of the collection without having to reprint the catalog book as books were acquired or withdrawn. The card catalogs were enhanced with the invention of the typewriter, which the Library of Congress created in 1902.

A major technological advance for libraries was the implementation of the Machine Readable Cataloging (MARC) format in the mid-1960s that automated the cataloging process and eventually led to the creation of catalog cards. Because of the Machine Readable Cataloging format, libraries were able to use that format to create the Online Public Access Catalog, which is what most people are familiar with as the library's online catalog of the library's collection. From this technological format, libraries later created the database management systems that allows users to go directly to the data entry or record for the information, whether it be a book in the collection or an electronic source. The computer technology has provided libraries to process, manage, and access information effectively and efficiently.

While this internal technological transformation for libraries was beneficial for libraries to maintain the needs of patrons, computer technology also altered workflows and traditional services. Many of these traditional services, such as reference services, processing print books and materials, and cataloging were drastically changed. In some instances, these jobs were eliminated or greatly reduced Again, technology is on the verge of changing how research libraries operate with the introduction of Blockchain technology. The technology has the potential to alter the ways research libraries will acquire academic materials, collaborate with publishers and vendors, and conduct scientific research.

Since the introduction of computer technology in the library, academic library leaders have continued to predict the technological trends and innovations that will prepare the library to meet the needs of their patrons and the institution. With the advent of new technology implementations, libraries have embraced technology that will have an impact on many facets of library organizations' operations. Currently, Blockchain has been considered as disruptive technology that will have an impact on many facets of organizations' operations Therefore, library administrators are carefully considering how to better understand Blockchain prior to attempting implementation.

Blockchain technology is another innovation that library administrators are viewing as a possible important technological tool. The importance of library administrators' perspective of technology will provide a foundation in the future of how the technology will be used and create best practices to be more effective for the organization and patrons. Some library administrators view technology as transformational, which is often the case as technology can be disruptive to an organization's operations (Cox, Pinfield, & Rutter, 2019). As a librarian you can't help but wonder, is Blockchain the next revolution in library practice or just a passing trend?

Why Blockchain and the Research Libraries?

According to Cox, Pinfield, & Rutter (2019), technology drives social change, which pressures libraries to stay abreast of new technology to meet the needs of patrons. Major industries are implementing the technology for various reasons, such as to aid in fraud prevention, which can cost companies millions of dollars. Lindenmoyer and Fischer (2019) noted that "the following industries are implementing some type of Blockchain: the diamond industry, medical industry, retail law offices, energy management, accounting, and education to a small extent" (p. 77). This includes the health sector that has increased usage of Blockchain in regards to supply-chain management (Bhargava, 2019; Hirsh & Alman, 2019).

If this many fields that manage large amounts of data are having success using Blockchain technology how could it aid or impact library function and technology programming? As libraries are continually striving to remain relevant in our increasingly technology savvy society by utilizing the latest technology that includes the implementation of Virtual and Augmented Reality devices, Makerspaces, 3D printers, and eBooks. The need and drive to increase technology availability for patron in librarian use can be a costly endeavor. In a political climate that sees a continual reduction in funding from federal and state agencies maximizing available resources is a must. As such, libraries are seeking more efficient ways to provide services and programming.

The urgency to keep libraries relevant due to the decrease funding has also changed library operations towards an entrepreneurship approach. Basically, libraries are being pushed more toward an operating model that resembles a business like organization. Creating opportunities and challenges for libraries to become more cost effective. This drive to utilize technology and operate more as a business model begins with the use of technology. Libraries and librarians can use technology to support functional operations in an efficient and effective manner. Blockchain has the promise to deliver as both efficient and effective tool.

Blockchain technology has reached significant attention due to the use of Blockchain to create cryptocurrency. The draw of interest has further increased around Blockchain technology because organizations are identifying uses outside of cryptocurrency. These uses such as smart contracts and supply chain management have potential to be revolutionary. The technology has received attention from government agencies, which are implementing legislation and regulation regarding Blockchain technology. The impact for libraries and Blockchain technology is heavily influenced by the government's implementation, perspective, and regulation of the budding technology. In other words, as governments continue to recognize and implement the technology, the potential for research and public libraries to utilize Blockchain technology may become a reality.

A recent survey by the Deloitte accounting firm released data from 1,386 international senior executives that noted over 50 percent viewed Blockchain as a new technology that would be needed in their organizations (Hirsh & Alman, 2019). The same expectations are also noted in government organizations that are beginning to realize the potential of Blockchain technology. Based on the increase usage of the technology in the financial sector and the business community, eventually libraries will have to consider whether the technology will be a feasible and practical technological tool.

In other words, libraries will have to remain diligent about how and when to use Blockchain technology. For instance, library administrators will have to think about what type of data needs to be stored on a Blockchain, the type of information that maybe significant in changing the organization's operations, the impact of the technology in regards to users, and the expenditures (Hirsh & Alman, 2019). Research libraries will also have to consider security by maintaining confidentiality, integrity, and user availability of data, because of the Family Educational Rights and Privacy Act (FERPA).

The utilization of Blockchain Technology has the possibility to positively impact research libraries' services and operations. Primarily, libraries have to consider the fundamental elements of Blockchain in regards to implementing the technology. Most importantly, Blockchain is an option for library administrators to change operational workflows by removing a centralized system, preserving and archiving metadata, and research publications, as well as other opportunities to reduce expenditures and enhance services and operations. Overall, Blockchain could be a useful tool for research libraries.

HIEARCHY OF IMPLEMENTING BLOCKCHAIN INTO RESEARCH LIBRARIES

To implement Blockchain technology in the research library, there are a few factors that library administrators will have to note, such as costs, privacy, security, and trust. However, the technology may be implemented based on the hierarchy of government institutions. For libraries to fully utilize Blockchain technology, libraries will examine and review how technology is used in other government agencies, which begins with legislation that provides regulations, universities implementation and assessment of the technology, and a universal standard that is agreed upon by the library community. Therefore, the hierarchy begins and moves from government officials, to government agencies, to higher educational institutions, and then research libraries. By examining and reviewing the outcomes of these other organizations, research libraries will have a better understanding of how the technology works, determine best standards and practices, and best uses for Blockchain in research libraries.

Legislation

Because most research libraries are funded through federal and state government agencies, libraries will have to abide governmental regulations, such as FERPA or information technological restrictions. Therefore, the implementation of Blockchain technology will be regulated by governmental legislation, which numerous state governments are researching and approving legislation regarding Blockchain technology. The government's interest in Blockchain began with the trend of cryptocurrency and regulating the financial aspects of the currency. Afterwards, the introduction of smart contracts associated with Blockchain caused state governments to determine how to best regulate and eventually utilize the technology in their own organizations.

Government agencies "have recognized the technology's potential for the delivery of public services, and are at various stages of implementation" (Ray, p. 10). The Delaware Blockchain Initiative introduced by former Governor of Delaware Jack Markell, "Smart Contracts offer powerful innovative way to streamline cumbersome back office procedures, lower transactional costs for consumers and businesses, and manage and reduce risk" (Ray, p. 10). Delaware's Blockchain Initiative allows corporate registration and other Uniform Commercial Code (UCC) filings. Illinois and Arizona are also implementing some form of Blockchain technology. Illinois has a series of pilot programs that want to "transform the delivery of public and private services, redefine the relationship between government and the citizen in terms of data sharing, transparency and trust, and make a leading contribution to the State's digital transformation" (Ray, p. 10). Arizona has made legislation and regulations regarding contract signatures, transactions, and contracts that will allow their residents to pay their income tax in cryptocurrencies (Ray, 2019).

On February 14, 2018, the U.S. House of Representatives Committee on Science, Space, and Technology held a joint hearing stated, "This hearing is an opportunity to learn more about the standards, guidelines and best practices that may be necessary to ensure effective appropriate implementation of Blockchain technology" (Ray, p. 11). The hearing also resulted in the discussion of "ways to improve government efficiency and private sector success with this technology" (Ray, p. 11). A form of efficiency is the use of Blockchain in voting, because the technology would provide full transparency and accurately count each vote (Bhargava, 2019).

Smart Contract is the actual code on the Blockchain that determines the agreement between two or more parties (Beraducci, 2019). Beraducci (2019) provided an example of a Smart Contract by describing a person who creates a Smart Contract that states "if the Cleveland Browns win a game next year, I will buy everyone a lunch" (p. 25). According to Beraducci (2019), the contract "would be open, available, inspectable, and I could not tamper with the rules set in the code" (p. 25). Once the code has been completed, it cannot be changed.

While the smart contract appears to be a legal contract, Rohr (2019) notes that smart contracts are "not necessarily legal contracts" (p. 68). He stated that once the code was completed it cannot be altered or ended, which is a challenge when the parties involved have a dispute about the contract that would make the agreement an expensive breach of contract. In these instances, the courts will have to review and interpret Smart Contracts.

Despite the concept that Smart Contracts are not actually a contract, state legislatures are recognizing smart contracts as legal entities. The State of Tennessee approved legislation in 2018 that stated, "smart contracts may exist in commerce. No contract relating to a transaction shall be denied legal effect, validity, or enforceability solely because that contract is executed through a smart contract" (Beraducci, 2019, p. 70). California, New York, Arizona, and Nevada have also passed legislation since 2017 regarding the language and usage of Blockchain technology and smart contracts.

In Beraducci's article (2019) he uses Nick Szabo's analogy that a vending machine represents the Blockchain concept, which describes any person can place money in a vending machine that is coded to only accept the payment terms. Once the money has been entered into the vending machine the transaction cannot be breached by the purchaser. Plus, if there is a breach it would be extremely expensive to undo the transaction.

The vending machine analogy also brings into account that smart contracts at this particular stage of implementation struggles with open-ended phrases, because the code of the vending machine relies on closed-ended terms that is easily understood by both parties. In other words, the owner of the vending machine and the purchaser agree on the exchange of goods for a set price. More complicated contracts that would require open-ended terms and phrases could be subject to debate, which would be difficult to add to a Blockchain. Basically, more research is needed to implement traditional contracts into the new smart contract concept.

Higher Education

As government agencies continue to recognize this technology as a tool and resource, they will begin to utilize Blockchain more frequently, which may include the transactions between government agencies, universities, libraries, and other sources in the future. This type of involvement with Blockchain could be more noted in library administrative and leadership roles. However, Lindenmoyer and Fischer (2019) stated, "Higher education is an industry where Blockchain has not been implemented on a major scale" (p. 78). Yet, higher education has the potential for numerous areas to utilize Blockchain technology, because Blockchain's basic structure of a ledger system will greatly enhance the various record keeping systems of a higher educational institution.

Of course, FERPA is the major issue that universities would have the most challenge implementing the Blockchain technology. Therefore, higher education would have to rely mostly on a consortium Blockchain. The consortium closed Blockchain that allows restrictions on those who read the data and create data on the Blockchain (Lindenmoyer and Fisher, 2019). Due to the Blockchain's ability to prevent external sources from altering the data and the technology is immutable, Blockchain is a tool that could be a keeper of data that could not be altered or corrupted.

According to Tapscott &Tapscott (2018), four aspects of higher education will be affected by Blockchain technology that include "Identity and student records, new pedagogy, costs (student debt), and the meta-university (new models of universities). There will be several uses for higher education to utilize Blockchain that will include the ability for students to verify and control their academic progress and achievements. According to Hoy & Brigham (2017), "Early in 2016, Sony announced plans to build a Blockchain for the 'open and secure sharing of academic proficiency and progress records'" (p. 276).

In other words, students will be able to access all of their academic information that would include all assignments, tests, courses completed, and submitted works. The technology would also prevent academic dishonesty. For instance, tests and assignments on a student's Blockchain could be activated to prevent students from printing or sending to other students. The Blockchain could also send an alert if a student attempted to access an old test or assignment (Lindenmoyer & Fischer, 2019).

Most importantly, Blockchain uses the Self-Sovereign Model that gives the user complete control over their data. Due to this control, students have the opportunity to control their information as they progress through their college tenure. Basically, students will be able to review their academic progress, financial records, and other school related materials.

The current concept of Blockchain in higher education is verifying certificates and degrees. Massachusetts Institute of Technology (MIT) offers students that are graduating in finance and obtaining a masters in media arts the option to receive a digital diploma following graduation, which would allow potential employers to verify degree completion utilizing Blockcerts. Similar opportunities exist with verifying certificates or completion of training programs for government and businesses. By providing this type of information on a Blockchain, universities could reduce costs, remove the centralized workflow (transcript offices or departments), and provide a secure platform for the student's diploma and data (Hirsh and Alman, 2019; Bhargava, 2019).

According to Alammary, et al. (2019), listed numerous other opportunities for higher education to utilize Blockchain that includes fees and credit transfers, obtaining digital guardianship consent, the evaluation of student's professional skills in regards to workforce demands, and Digital Rights Management. The final item, Digital Rights Management is a service that will impact research libraries should Blockchain technology be utilized, along with other library services.

Research Libraries

Libraries will need to assess the need for Blockchain technology before spending time and expenditures on technological equipment and personnel. The purpose for the assessing the needs is to determine whether the technology would be best option to serve the institution, the library, and the patrons. They will have to look for areas in the library that can be decentralized and become transparent. The use of blockchain technology in the library must be understood that this a closed-term system. In other words, if the library would like to implement the blockchain technology then the system must be setup so that any agreement with another party is clearly understood between both parties, such as the vending machine concept noted earlier (Berraducci, 2019).

Library leaders and experts have discussed other factors to consider when planning for Blockchain technology, such as the creation of universal standards, implementation of the technology internally, understanding that data entered on the Blockchain is immutable, and public and private keys are irreplaceable (Smith, 2019; Hirsh & Alman, 2019).

In regards to transparency, the supply-chain management is a concept that provides transparency and would be useful for research libraries in regards to acquisitions or metadata. Sissman & Sharma (2018) noted that "Supply chains are made up of network of individuals, organizations, technology, resources and activities that spread from the initial creation of a product to delivery. Therefore, Blockchain would useful for research libraries creating a Blockchain for archiving and preservation of materials.

Hirsh and Alman (2019) noted several options where Blockchain technology can be implemented into libraries that include interlibrary loan services, universal library cards, archiving records. Other experts in the library profession seeking other uses for Blockchain. For instance, the utilization of Blockchain for scholarly communications, Digital Rights Management, securing contracts with publishers, maintain patrons' records, and creating metadata (Hirsh & Alman, 2019; Alammary, et al., 2019).

BLOCKCHAIN TECHNOLOGY IN THE RESEARCH LIBRARY

Preparing for Blockchain

Despite the numerous potential opportunities, research libraries must prepare for Blockchain technology. Most importantly, research libraries will need to keep in mind that Blockchain technology will rely on trust between more than one organization, if a library is entering a consortium or some type of collaboration with other organizations. In addition, this decentralization system must rely on an agreement by all parties. Therefore, research libraries collaborating with other research libraries will have to create a set of standards for sharing the data entered into the Blockchain.

The creation of standards must consider the fundamentals of Blockchain technology, which is a distributed ledger that is transparent, but maintains security and integrity. Based on the fundamental properties of a Blockchain, research libraries collaborating with other libraries or even internally will have to agree to how the data is entered, shared, and interpreted. The agreement or standards that are created must include any legal implications, because the information entered on the Blockchain is immutable. Due to the inability to change data on a Blockchain, legal experts and legislators are determining ways to interpret these issues.

Once research libraries create a plan that includes an agreement or set of standards and guidelines, library administrators can begin planning for implementation. Due to the recent introduction of this technology in governmental agencies and libraries, library administrators or other personnel may begin a small internal project to fully understand the Blockchain process. By starting on a small scale, stakeholders will have a better understanding of the technology needed and the personnel required to enter information and maintain the technology.

Other factors to include in this pre-planning stage is how Blockchain technology will either benefit or hinder the libraries' mission to provide services to patrons and meet the goals of the institution. First factor to consider is whether the technology is necessary to complete the mission of the library and will the technology efficiently enhance library services. Organizations that are implementing this technology have realized the potential Blockchain and have invested in the personnel and the equipment. Financial costs is a factor some experts have noted about utilizing Blockchain, due to the equipment needed to mine the text and data. Therefore, library administrators will have to determine if the expenditures to implement Blockchain is beneficial to providing services to patrons and the operations of the library.

Metadata

The premise of Blockchain is to remove an authoritative centralized unit, which libraries have a centralized unit in creating metadata. Therefore, the potential disruptive technological service that Blockchain would have an impact on for research libraries is creating and preserving metadata. Librarians have been creating metadata for decades, therefore libraries are familiar with the concept of metadata, which is the basis of Blockchain technology. Yet, research libraries rely mostly on a third party to assist with creating metadata primarily due to the continuous budget cuts to libraries. For instance, most research libraries utilize the Online Computer Library Center (OCLC) to provide metadata on materials purchased.

OCLC is the largest Online Public Access Catalog that provides bibliographic metadata for libraries that are members of the OCLC. The standards that research libraries utilize is the Library of Congress Classification system, which is a system that has the metadata standards for archiving preserving, and retrieval of information. The Library of Congress is another source that librarians receive metadata information due to the classification system. In 2012, the Library of Congress began to change the source for bibliographic metadata from MARC to the 2016 version BIBFRAME (Bibliographic Framework). The newest version to create metadata was based on new technology being introduced into libraries.

Research libraries have the opportunity to collaborate with other libraries to create a standards based on the Library of Congress Classification system utilizing Blockchain. The collaboration and creation of bibliographic metadata would decentralize the need of a third party, such as OCLC and the Library of Congress. Libraries could create and distribute the metadata that could be updated and tracked. This would mean that libraries did not have to pay a membership fee to OCLC to have their metadata included through acquisitions or through an external source. Through this system libraries could share their MARC or bibliographic metadata with other libraries.

OCLC is a large corporation that has been a producer and owner of metadata since 1971, therefore libraries may have a difficult decision whether to discontinue a reliable service and use Blockchain to create and share bibliographic metadata. However, Blockchain does provide the option for research libraries to create a metadata system. Blockchain could provide the opportunity to create an international metadata system (Hirsh & Alman, 2019). This system could offer libraries the position of the selling and purchasing of metadata, which could generate revenue or even reduce costs of utilizing a third party. In addition, using Blockchain to create metadata could alter the workflow of an organization's operation.

Another purpose that research libraries would utilize Blockchain for metadata is the preservation and archiving items (Hirsh & Alman, 2019). Special collection libraries are responsible numerous items that include historical artifacts and documents. By utilizing Blockchain technology, archivist will be able to create metadata that could be shared with other institutions for research and other preservation needs.

Digital Rights Management

Digital Rights Management is an element of libraries that can be better maintained through Blockchain. Since research libraries act as providers of scientific digital content for patrons, libraries are held accountable of copyrighted digital works and bound by the works' legal permission to use (Abu Sirhan, et al., 2019). Current Digital Rights Management tools includes the encrypted conversion of text and decoding encrypted text in digital media, identification and authenticity systems, digital signatures, digital watermarks that are created in the work, digital fingerprints that allow access through identification, copy detection systems, and payment methods (Abu Sirhan, et al., 2019).

Through Blockchain, publishers and authors will have more control of their works. First of all, Blockchain can create the verifiable transaction, which authors and publishers can establish specific licensing fees for the works. Secondly, owners of the works can control how the work is utilized or even reproduced. According to Hoy & Brigham (2017), Blockchain can assist in the reproduction of digital materials. Hoy & Brigham (2017) stated, "Because the Blockchain creates a unique, verifiable record that can be accessed by anyone, it could be tied to digital materials and used as a method to show 'provable scarcity' of that resource. This would allow digital materials to be uniquely identified, controlled, and transferred" (pp. 276-277).

The Music Modernization Act was signed into law on October 11, 2018 that created the Mechanical licensing Collective to create and maintain an open database by January 1, 2021 of copyrighted works. The database will provide copyright owners' works that will make it easier for licensing agreements to be established between owners and consumers. The purpose of the act was to increase more control to the copyright owners, primarily due to the large streaming platforms, such as Amazon, Apple, Google, Pandora, YouTube, and Spotify.

The open database is also aligned with new technology such as AI and Blockchain. According to Panay, Pentland, & Hardjono (2019),

Layered on top of open, shared standards, new technologies like Blockchain and AI have the potential to allow all participants in the digital music supply chain – songwriters, performers, producers, labels, publishers, music services, rights societies, licensors and critically, consumers - to safely and securely transact and collaborate with each other, offering unprecedented access to information and data and giving rise to rich new consumer experiences that are currently out of reach due to an antiquated, centuries-old infrastructure.

This is another way in which Blockchain can impact research libraries, because libraries will be able to assist patrons with identifying digital works and establish licensing agreements with the copyright owner, which could be a best practice. Of course, Blockchain also creates other opportunities for copyright owners that includes authors and owners of copyrighted works being able to sell or license their works directly to the consumer. Through Blockchain technology, authors or creators of works are not bound to a third party, such as a publisher or other organization to sell their works to consumers, because Blockchain will allow a secure transaction of the work.

Scholarly Communication and Publishing

Blockchain can provide researchers the opportunity to collaborate with other researchers on specific topics. Researchers could be given a problem that multi researchers can contribute through Blockchain by tracking and providing data pertinent to the research, while maintaining a peer-reviewed system. In addition, researchers will not have to rely on publishers to publish the research, because the work would exist on the Blockchain, which is easily available for those seeking information on the topic instead of searching multiple databases. This form of collaboration would also reduce redundancies in research topics being conducted and published by different researchers in multiple locations (Hirsh & Alman, 2019; Smith, 2019).

In regards to scholarly communication, van Rossum (2018) mentions two platforms that have the potential to disrupt scholarly communication. Scienceroot and Plato are platforms for researchers to collaborate on research topics and to publish their findings. According to van Rossum (2018), "Scienceroot is an open access Blockchain-based scientific ecosystem that combines all of the functionalities required during the scientific discovery process – from funding through research to publishing" (p. 98). The Plato platform is an etherium Blockchain that does not rely on the traditional centralized workflow process to conduct and publish research.

Authors and researchers also have the opportunity to sell their works directly to the buyer, thus again avoiding publishers and providing freedom to openly share information. Digital first sale can be important for libraries if it is an open platform that allows authors to have more control of their works. In other words, libraries could purchase works directly from the authors. The platform DECENT is a Blockchain application that would allow libraries to purchase works directly from the author, which would avoid costs set by publishers or subscription fees from digital subscribers. Through this platform it would provide the consumer with the transparency to know the source of the work, which address issues of credibility.

Open Educational Resources, Supply-Chain Management, and Smart Contracts

Supply-Chain Management would be utilized in the acquisition of Open Educational Resources (OER), which are textbooks or educational materials that are free or at a reduced costs to students. Based on the supply-chain management system, Blockchain could assist with the demand to reduce college student debt by offering OER. Based on the supply-chain's transparency, textbook materials could be produced through Blockchain where faculty could follow the OER chain to determine if the resource is a credible source to support the course curriculum. Basically, the supply-chain management concept offered by the Blockchain technology will allow faculty to trace the origins of information entered in the chain to better evaluate the source for the educational purposes.

In addition, the supply-chain management that Blockchain offers will enhance the record keeping of research libraries in regards to operational expenditures. Due to the budget regulations by government agencies, libraries can be more transparent of their purchases to their stakeholders through the use of Blockchain technology. According to Sissman & Sharma (2018), "Blockchain provides an increased level of transparency across the production of goods in supply chain management" (p. 46). Currently, the U.S. Department of Commerce and the U.S. Department of Defense are utilizing Blockchain to be more transparent and increasing knowledge to track supplies (Sissman & Sharma, 2018). Libraries could also purchase materials with cryptocurrency, as well as purchase international goods or services, such as Interlibrary Loans using cryptocurrency that would be more efficient than using international exchange rates.

In addition, the smart contract concept allows libraries to utilize Blockchain in the place of an Integrated Library System. The Integrated Library System is the primary system that interacts with patrons' services, such as checking out a book or using the Interlibrary Loan service. Through Blockchain, library administrators can maintain patron data and library services. The concept of smart contracts that Blockchain technology offers can be created to place holds on patron's account and accept payments. The technology will also allow libraries the opportunity to set fines, restrictions on borrowing materials, and create a patron history database. The smart contract concept will also allow libraries to analyze patron data effectively by the transparency of the patrons' usage of library services, that includes reference, computer, printer and Interlibrary Loan usages.

Interlibrary Loan and Distance Education

Interlibrary Loan is a library service that libraries provide when patrons request materials that are not in their main library collection, which libraries will then borrow books from other libraries on behalf of the patron. This service is a centralized system, wherein the patron has to request the service from an Interlibrary Loan department or specialist. Through Blockchain, libraries can remove the centralized system by authenticating patron's credentials to borrow books from any library within the consortium Blockchain.

The concept could also apply to Distance Education Library Services where some institutions require a centralized entity, typically a distance education library department or distance education librarian provides the materials to students at satellite campuses or other locations. These entities are third parties that interact as an agent for the library and provides services to distance education students. Basically, if libraries created a consortium Blockchain with other libraries then a student would be issued a library card that would work at any of those libraries through the Distributed Verifiable Sovereign Identity.

Annie Norman, State Librarian of Delaware and Director, Division of Libraries stated that Blockchain could expand stronger securities for patron identity and open several opportunities for public libraries to increase the value of libraries. She noted, "New technological solutions such as a distributed ledger could provide the necessary authentication and privacy capabilities for public libraries to support a universal library card, a union catalog with provenance and ownership verification, data sharing, and more" (Hirsh & Alman, 2019, p. 52).

If libraries could create the standards and a consortium to provide patrons with a universal library card with Blockchain, then this would decentralize Interlibrary Loan and Distance Education services. Of course, the standards for a universal library card would have to ensure patron's data was secure and complied with FERPA regulations. Strengthening personal data is being implemented in the health care field, as health care organizations are attempting to use Blockchain to exchange patient's health information within other health care organizations.

Universal library cards that allow patrons to access multiple library collections through a secure authentication system will increase available collections for patrons and eliminate the need for an Interlibrary Loan department or librarian, as well as Distance Library Education services. By removing the centralized Interlibrary Loan and Distance Education services, research libraries will be able to reduce costs associated with personnel and other operational expenditures.

Educate Students and the Community

If research library administrators determine that Blockchain is not needed for their libraries or cannot justify implementing Blockchain technology into their organization, the library can provide educational workshops or provide information about Blockchain technology to students, faculty, or even the community (Hirsh & Alman, 2019; Smith, 2019). As Blockchain continues to increase usage in businesses and governmental agencies, the demand to gain knowledge of the new technology will increase.

Libraries have an opportunity to provide patrons and the community the best information regarding Blockchain technology. The information can be presented to patrons in workshops or through reference services, as well as the library's collection. Overall, libraries will need to have information about Blockchain as the technology continues to be utilized in other organizations. For research libraries, educating students on the technology is significant in giving students the necessary education about Blockchain to be knowledgeable of Blockchain's potential use in the workforce.

PROBLEMS

While there are numerous possibilities to implement Blockchain technology into a research library, the risk factors do need to be stated. The first and most noted issue with Blockchain technology is the cost. In order to implement and maintain a Blockchain system is to have costly equipment, which requires a server or many servers depending on the size of Blockchain. The servers are expensive and they also require a facility that can store and maintain the correct temperature of the room. Opponents of Blockchain have concerns that the amount of energy used to utilize Blockchain technology is not sustainable and hazardous to the environment. Also, bandwidth is an issue noted by library professionals, due to the amount of bandwidth required to store data.

Secondly, data entry error and immutable is an issue when interacting with Blockchain technology. If information is entered and accepted into the chain, the information could no longer be changed. While the technology is significant in providing data that cannot be altered, the issue of needing to change the data can cause several issues. Due to this problem with Blockchain, attorneys and legislatures are addressing these concerns.

Thirdly, Blockchain is a decentralized concept, yet if a majority is recognized on a Blockchain then an authoritative unit that emerges can control the Blockchain. This creation is also called the 51% Rule, where a person or organization that gains 51 percent of the Blockchain then they are the majority and would have the ability to control the data in the chain. Choo, Yong Park, & Lee, (2017) state that the integrity of the Blockchain can be held if the 51% are good nodes and have no intention of breaking the integrity of the chain. The 51% can also allow for hackers to take control.

Additionally, accessing the Blockchain requires a private or public key, which is the main authentication of the user. If a user loses the key or the information to access the Blockchain, the user cannot access the information on the chain. There have been instances where people invested in cryptocurrency and lost their key along with the money invested in the cryptocurrency. Unlike a third party or centralized system where users that lost their password can request access. Therefore, this would be an issue if a user or an organization loses access to the Blockchain, which could affect library patrons.

Finally, privacy issues for research libraries is concern for library administrators as they comply with FERPA regulations. Despite the secure infrastructure that Blockchain provides, the concept of shared student personal data with external organization is a problem that research libraries and higher educational institutions will have to address.

CONCLUSION

Library administrators have many facets of technology to consider as new technology is being introduced at a rapid rate. For example, Artificial Intelligence (AI) is already being assessed for usages in the library. Cox, Pinfield, & Rutter (2019) noted that AI has the potential to be a disruptive technology for reference services. As AI improves, the opportunities to implement AI in reference services will become more frequent, because AI has the ability to search and retrieve information. This implementation in regards to reference services could change the workforce, as AI could be used to answer reference questions 24 hours a day, seven days a week.

While Blockchain technology is being implemented in various businesses, government organizations, and education, research libraries will have the opportunity to evaluate the role Blockchain will have in their institutions. Furthermore, libraries will be able to create standards and guidelines that will dictate how Blockchain will be utilized in the future. Due to the early inception of Blockchain technology being implemented in organization, research libraries have the opportunity to participant in the design and provide valuable insight as to the usage Blockchain technology will have in research libraries and other libraries. Libraries have been noted as late adopters, therefore library administrators will need to determine when or if they want to implement Blockchain.

As for Digital Rights Management, libraries have the opportunity to be involved in the creation of industry standards as publishers and copyright owners begin to negotiate best practices for using Blockchain technology. Without input from libraries, publishers, copyright owners, and vendors of scientific information could increase costs or even establish restrictions regarding the use of copyrighted works. Therefore, library administrators have the opportunity to be involved in the technology or at least be aware of trade practices.

REFERENCES

Abu Sirhan, A., Abdrabbo, K., Ahmed Ali Al Tawalbeh, S., Hamdi Ahmed, M., & Ali Helalat, M. (2019). Digital rights management (DRM) in libraries of public universities in Jordan. *Library Management*, *40*(8/9), 496–502. doi:10.1108/LM-05-2018-0044

American Library Association. (2017). Blockchain. *Library of the Future*. Retrieved from http://www.ala.org/tools/future/trends/blockchain

Berarducci, P. (2019). Collaborative approaches to blockchain regulation: The Brooklyn Project example. *Cleveland State Law Review*, *67*(1), 22–30.

Bhargava, R. (2019). Blockchain technology and its application: A review. *IUP Journal of Information Technology*, *15*(1), 7–15.

Choo, S., Yong Park, S., & Lee, S. R. (2017). Blockchain consensus rule based dynamic blind voting for non-dependency transaction. *International Journal of Grid and Distributed Computing*, *10*(12), 93–106. doi:10.14257/ijgdc.2017.10.12.09

Coghill, J. G. (2018). Blockchain and its implications for libraries. *Journal of Electronic Resources in Medical Libraries*, *15*(2), 66–70. doi:10.1080/15424065.2018.1483218

Cox, A. M., Pinfield, S., & Rutter, S. (2018). The intelligent library: Thought leaders' view on the likely impact of artificial intelligence on academic libraries. *Library Hi Tech*, *37*(3), 418–435. doi:10.1108/LHT-08-2018-0105

Cox, A. M., Pinfield, S., & Rutter, S. (2019). Academic libraries' stance toward the future. *Portal (Baltimore, Md.)*, *19*(3), 485–509.

Griffey, G. (2018). Blockchain & libraries from Carnigie Mellon – Qatar. *Pattern Recognition*. Retrieved from http://jasongriffey.net/wp/2018/03/22/blockchain-libraries-from-carnegie-mellon-qatar/

Hirsh, S., & Alman, S. (Eds.). (2019). *Blockchain*. Neal-Schuman.

Hoy, M. B., & Brigham, T. J. (2017). An introduction to the Blockchain and its implications for libraries and medicine. *Medical Reference Services Quarterly*, *36*(3), 273–279. doi:10.1080/02763869.2017.13 32261 PMID:28714815

Lindenmoyer, J., & Fischer, M. (2019). Blockchain: Application and utilization in higher education. *Journal of Higher Education Theory & Practice*, *19*(6), 71–80.

Ojala, M. (2018). Blockchain for Libraries. *Online Searcher*, *42*(1), 15.

Panay, P. A., Pentland, A., & Hardjono, T. (2019). Why success of the Music Modernization Act depends on open standards. *Open Music Initiative*. White Paper. Retrieved from https://static1.squarespace.com/static/56d5e44060b5e9e20a94b16c/t/5bd7199e8165f5a5e9241ae9/1540823454789/Open+Music-Music+Modernization-Open+Standards+White+Paper.pdf

Ray, B. (2019). Blockchain symposium introduction: Overview and historical introduction. *Cleveland State Law Review*, *67*(1), 1–21.

Rohr, J. G. (2019). Smart contracts and traditional contract law, or: The law of vending machine. *Cleveland State Law Review*, *67*(1), 67–88.

Sissman, M., & Sharma, K. (2018). Building supply management with blockchain: New technology mitigates some logistical risks while adding for a few others. *Industrial and Systems Engineering at Work*, *50*(7), 43–46.

SJSU iSchool. (2019). Ways to use blockchain in libraries. *Blockchains for the Information Profession*. Retrieved from https://ischoolblogs.sjsu.edu/blockchains/blockchains-applied/applications/

Smith, C. (2019). Blockchain reaction: How library professionals are approaching Blockchain technology and its potential impact. *American Libraries*, *50*(3/4), 26–33.

Tapscott, D., & Tapscott, A. (2017). The blockchain revolution & higher education. *EDUCAUSE Review*, *52*(2), 10–24.

Van Rossum, J., & Lawlor, B. (2018). The Blockchain and its potential for science and academic publishing. *Information Services & Use*, *38*(1/2), 95–98.

Zalatimo, S. (2018). Blockchain in publishing: Innovation or disruption? *Forbes.Com*. Retrieved from https://www.forbes.com/sites/forbesproductgroup/2018/05/03/blockchain-in-publishing-innovation-or-disruption/#2b632a2a5456

ADDITIONAL READING

Agnew, G. (2008). Digital rights management: A librarian's guide to technology and practice (Chandos information professional series). Oxford, UK: Chandos Publishers.

Assessing Blockchain applications for the public sector: Blockchain basic for governments. (2019). Deloitte. Retrieved from https://www2.deloitte.com/us/en/insights/industry/public-sector/blockchain-public-sector-applications.html

Bashir, I. (2018). *Mastering blockchain: Distributed ledger technology, decentralization, and smart contracts explained* (2nd ed.). Packt Publishing.

Blanchard, D. (2010). *Supply chain management best practices*. John Wiley & Sons.

De Filippi, P., & Wright, A. (2018). *Blockchain and the law: The rule of code*. Harvard University Press. doi:10.2307/j.ctv2867sp

Suber, P. (2012). *Open access*. MIT Press Essential Knowledge Series. MIT Press. doi:10.7551/mitpress/9286.001.0001

KEY TERMS AND DEFINITIONS

Decentralization: The removal of an authoritative central system.

Digital Rights Management: A systematic approach for authors and publishers to protect digital media copyrights.

Immutable: Information stored on a Blockchain cannot be changed.

Integrated Library System: A system that maintains library data for the library's collection and patron information.

Interlibrary Loan: A service provided to library patrons, where the patron's library borrows materials from other libraries.

Metadata: A format that provides data regarding data, such as a bibliographic record that includes data about the author, title, date, information about the work, etc.

Open Educational Resources: A textbook or other educational resources that is accessible for students for free or at a reduced cost.

Scholarly Communication: The research process where research is conducted, evaluated, and preserved for the scholarly community.

This research was previously published in Transforming Scholarly Publishing With Blockchain Technologies and AI; pages 232-250, copyright year 2021 by Information Science Reference (an imprint of IGI Global).

Chapter 62
Millennials vs. Cyborgs and Blockchain Role in Trust and Privacy

Hamid Jahankhani
 https://orcid.org/0000-0002-8288-4609
Northumbria University, London, UK

Stefan Kendzierskyj
 https://orcid.org/0000-0001-6407-8585
Northumbria University, London, UK

Ionuț Octavian Popescu
Northumbria University, London, UK

ABSTRACT

Over recent years, technology has rapidly advanced and is accelerating the emergence to Industry 4.0, particularly due to the connectivity abundance, volume increase of smart devices, and a growing inter-connectivity between humans and technology. Within the last two years, 90% of the data in the world today was generated and in the next few years the volume of IoT interactions is said to reach approximately 4800 per day, which equates to a human interaction every 18 seconds. This correlates well with research undertaken regarding how consumers are exchanging information through smart devices and behavioural changes due to the technology adoption. The Generation Y and Z demand for smart devices, consumer behaviour online, and almost immediate data experiences is seeing fast consumption and data exchange without any preconceived concerns of trust, privacy, security, data profiling, or how data is used without their knowledge by third parties. This chapter will also analyse technology innovations to better protect identity data and processing of data through blockchain technology.

DOI: 10.4018/978-1-6684-7132-6.ch062

INTRODUCTION

This chapter takes a deeper look into themes such as smart retailing in the internet era, the adoption of new technologies, and the differences between generations Y and Z and the notion of the millennial versus cyborg. There are differences between generations in terms of the decision-making process regarding smart retailing, which covers the comprehensive idea of young generations of consumers are behaving differently in the era of smart retailing. This also means how they access through devices in decision making and how freely data is given.

To help with an understanding of how generations are labeled, the following Table 1 gives the status and description of each:

Table 1. Labelling of generations

Type	Year of Birth	Description
Baby Boomers	1944 - 1964	After World War II, Population was enjoying new-found prosperity, so the term "baby boom."
Generation X	1965 – 1979	Illustrating the undetermined characteristics that followed Baby Boomers so why 'X' was used
Generation Y	1980 – 1994	Generation Y followed as alphabet but was coined by the phrase 'Millennials' and although tech-savvy not as fully reliant on smart devices as Generation Z
Generation Z	1995 - 2015	The newest Generation and different from Millennials as having truly grown up with in the hyper-connected world, heavily reliant on smart devices

THEORIES AND PRINCIPLES AND EVOLUTION OF MARKETING CHANNELS IN DIGITAL ERA

It is useful to understand marketing transitions so human interactions may be further analysed. During the past couple decades, humanity has experienced the most revolutionary inventions such as the growth of the Internet and World Wide Web which had a very powerful impact on the printed press, eventually leading to the digitalization era. The development of new technologies imposed a powerful impact on organizations, transforming the strategies of the businesses and the way of creating awareness for products and services, moving from traditional advertising (TV ads, direct marketing, etc.) to a digital approach (Pomirleanu, 2013).

The development of new technologies created new opportunities and challenges for education and academic research, likewise for industry practitioners (Weiss, 2011), and the global adoption of digital marketing strategy, has automatically contributed to the growth of marketing for organizations and communication with individual consumers, receiving individual feedback to provide the optimum decision for actual and potential customers for goods and services (Simons, 2008).

"Traditional Marketing" evolved to "Digital Marketing", through the development of communication and marketing channels and has been described as a powerful adaptive process to promote brand awareness, to increase sales for an organization, to create a strong relationship with existent and potential customers, and to satisfy customer's needs (LexiconFT, 2018).

In Kung (2008) perspective, the digitalization of communication channels and media will impact a substantial change in the direction for communication and interactions, and the consumer behaviour and the development of technologies have always been the main elements of developmental direction in marketing strategy.

Theories of Marketing Channels

Watson et al. (2015) describe that the evolution of marketing channels is divided in in two categories "Pre-1980" and "Modern Developments". Previous studies describe a marketing channel as "a set of interdependent organizations involved in the process of making a product or service available for use or consumption" (Palmatier et al., 2016), which is perceived as a flow of goods or services before 1980. In Modern Developments, the literature shows that theories from sociology, social psychology or political science has been adopted in marketing, emerging to a behavioural based approach illustrating the benefits of behavioural theories in marketing channels domain (Palmatier, Dant, & Grewal, 2007). Recent research describes a new era of marketing, reflecting the maturation and diversification of the domain, with the substantial disruption caused by the internationalization of marketing and the amplification of e-commerce approach (Grewal, Kumar, Mallapragada, & Saini, 2013). The development of marketing channels strategy is based on a range of *Marketing channels theories* (see Table 1) Based on Stern and Reve (1980) study, the evolution of marketing channels has been studied by using two different frameworks (see Table 2):

- **Economic**: To emphasize the performance and economic efficiency
- **Behavioural:** To understand the disagreements that develop from rational statements in an economic framework, as they are presented in Table 2 (Watson et al., 2015).

TECHNOLOGY DEVELOPMENT AND ADOPTION THEORY

The development in technology or adoption of new technology is a key element for the process of growth and development, and for the unaccountable income in the world. However, any barriers implemented will not allow the process of development. Studies show that there are different types of barriers due to technology development such as cost-adoption (Leung & Tse, 2001) or "appropriate technology" concept for the slow diffusion of technology as a consequence of productivity differences across countries (Lahiri, Ding & Chinzara, 2018). Cobin and Hobijn (2010) state that, the diffusion of new technologies is the main contributor to economic development, and the differences in use cases of technology lead to inequality between countries.

The nature of products and services today has radically changed due to the adoption of digital technologies, implementing the digital capabilities that in the physical world will allow companies to reach new opportunities and for creating unique experiences for customers. Currently, in the era of digital transformation, products, services, and organization activity are controlling the world markets. To manage innovations in an unpredictable and highly dynamic environment, organizations have to understand the diffusion of developments to generate proper decisions, because innovations could become very quickly outdated, and competitors will create market advantage from this situation where organisations do not adapt quickly enough. Companies have to create products or services with a high level of adoption to perform and guarantee profit and growth. This phenomenon of diffusion of technology without a clear understanding may lead to late adoptions generating a slow diffusion and can consequently create a loss of market share to competitors and negative financial outcomes. Hence, it is crucial to develop digital innovations with a high rate of advancement and to address to a wide market segment (Jahanmir & Cavadas, 2018).

Table 2. Marketing channels theories (Source: Watson et al., 2015)

Economic Framework	
Transactions Cost Economics Theory	Describes the transaction-specific asset (TSA) as tangible and intangible with the purpose to exchange relationship at the end of the transaction (Heide & John, 1988). The channel design decisions should be targeted at minimizing transaction costs.
Agency Theory	Describes an efficient contract as one that delivers the leading outcome for the receiver of the contract with given constraints imposed by circumstances, with unrevealed information that refers to the agent knowledge which is favorable for the agent, and the receiver does not know (Bergen, Dutta, & Walker, 1992). The relationship between different levels of channels members can be seen as principle and agents based relationship. The relationship of different members of distribution should be determined and settled by considering the agency theory and any channel members' conflicts should be resolved accordingly.
Game Theory	State that all the possible actions or decisions in a game is defined as a strategy for the available options given to "the payoffs and expectations of other players actions" (Watson J., 2013). The channel strategies are a win/lose game. The options should be decided with a winning game move.
Resource-Based Theory	Illustrate the organization resources are valuable, rare and ineffectively imitable and other organization could exploit the resources to generate a considerable competitive advantage for potential competitors (Barney & Clark, 2007). The channel members and their skills, knowledge, culture, etc can create rare, non-copiable, value for the customers. Such values can be the basis of the core competency of a company.
Behavioral Framework	
Power Conflict and Dependence Theory	Describes the distribution of power among group members which could lead to conflicts, and the use and response to power are effective in explaining the outcomes such as performance and structure (Gaski & Nevin, 1985). The channel relationships can be determined as per this theory.
Relational Norms Theory	State that, norms are "expectations about attitudes and behaviors parties have in working cooperatively together to achieve mutual and individual goals" (Cannon, Achrol, & Gundlach, 2000, p. 183).
Commitment Trust Theory	Presents the commitment and trust as the fundamentals of intern-organizational performance, both promoting mutual goals and prevent the members of an organization to act in their own interest (Morgan & Hunt, 1994). The Supply chain relationship will enhance commitment, and trust and relationship of the channel members with the organisation.
Network Theory	Highlights the social structure and standardizing in which exchanges are fixed providing an appropriate approach to understand how one ecosystem part influence the others (Baron & Hannan, 1994). This theory explains and prescribes the basis of designing distributed channel networks, efficiently.

During the development stage, organizations considered as decision makers/leaders, have to understand the problems that may influence the consumer's decisions by using a specific pattern or strategy. To understand why people, accept new technologies, researchers and practitioners have to create a better method for evaluation and prediction for users accepting new technologies (Dillon & Morris, 1996).

Theories and technology adoption frameworks have been applied in a wide range of sectors to analyse, understand, and predict the consumer's behaviour, to explain the adoption of new technologies and the cause that can influence the consumer's acceptance. Based on Venkatesh et al. (2003) research, eight models of adoption have analysed the differences and similarities regarding the information system, which all of these models had origins from communication, sociology, and psychology. These eight models are,

Theory of Reasoned Action, Social Cognitive Theory, Diffusion of Innovations Theory, Motivational Model, Technology Acceptance Model, Theory of Planned Behaviour, Model of PC Utilization, and mix between TAM and TPB in Figure 1 below (Taherdoost, 2018).

However, the *Unified Theory of Acceptance and Use of Technology* (UTAUT), is developed from the previous eight theories and has a construct on performance and effort expectations, social influence and facilitating conditions, anxiety, computer self-efficacy, and attitude towards technology adoption; which generate significant moderating variables such as age, gender, experience and action of use. These variables demonstrate the behavioural intention and certain use case (Venkatesh et al., 2003). In Bgozzi (2007) view, UTAUT consolidates aspects and functions of the Adoption Model with different models from IT adoption research but being extremely complex and the so applicability is difficult to appraise. Van der Haijden (2006) also believes that UTATUT is limited regarding the applicability in voluntary use of technology such as mobile applications, ecommerce and mobile banking.

Figure 1. Adoption theories (Bgozzi,(2007)

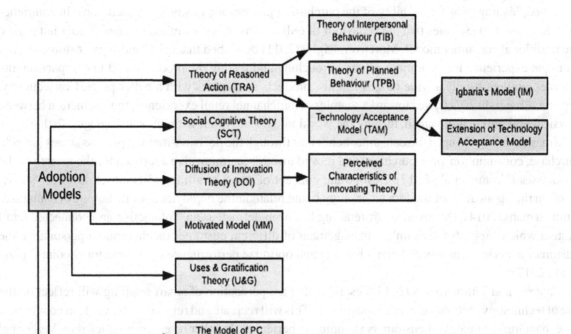

Venkatesh et al. (2012) introduced an extension in the UTAUT model, specifically UTAUT2 by introducing hedonic motivation, habit and price value as independent variables to create a more suitable adoption model regarding use of technology for consumers. Hedonic motivation is considered as an important driver of behavioural intention. Therefore, the adoption model of UTAUT2 can be used to analyze the main determinants of e-commerce usage regarding different generations, specifically Y and Z, to contribute to the diffusion of e-commerce.

Generations Y and Z And Adoption Of Smart Retail Interactions

During the Internet decade, retailing and communication technologies innovated the way of purchasing, allowing consumers to become technology-dependent (Zhitomirsky-Geffet & Blau, 2016). Retailing has changed due to development and adoption of new technologies in digital channels, specifically mobile and social media, having a very powerful impact on the customers and changing the perspective of shopping behavior and the business models of the organizations (Verhoef, Kannan, & Inman, 2015). Sorescu et al. (2011) state that, the customers started to behave differently, and many retailers have innovated the retail mix offered, according to the digitalization of marketing.

In a recent study, Fotiadis and Stylos (2017) analysed the way that consumers exchange information and interact through smart devices such as smartphones, laptops, tablets and PC's that resulted with online shopping developing as a continuous expansion of traditional services. Also, the customer experience improved, leading to better usability of the purchasing process and customer expectations. In contradiction, Kourafis (2003) states that the behaviour of online consumers is limited because it does not pursue the traditional consumer model. Moreover, Rigby (2011) described that brick-and-mortar stores offered a unique experience for customers, allowing touching and feeling the products, and in comparison, the internet retailers supply a wide range of items, products or services with a better price. Consequently, the "retailing industry evolves toward a seamless omnichannel retail experience, the distinction between physical and online will vanish, turning the world into a showroom without walls" (Rigby, 2011).

Smart retailing changed the consumer behaviour through the decision-making process stages (search, purchase, consumption, post-purchase) and moved towards an innovative approach for the growth of the businesses (Vrontis et al., 2017). Beyond the concept of smart retailing exists a high level of "smartness" in the application of modern technology being relatedtothe deployment of technology (Pantano & Timmermans, 2014). However, smart retailing has been defined as an "interactive and connected retail system which supports the seamless management of different customer touchpoints to personalize the customer experience across different channels and optimize performance over these touchpoints" (Roy et al., 2017).

Pantano and Timmermans (2014) describes that the perception of smart retailing will reflect on the use of technology for companies and consumers. This will recreate and reinforce a new role in economies, by enhancing the quality of customers shopping experiences. In other research conducted by Verhoef et al. (2015) it emphasizes on the importance of the customer experience and hedonic motivation, which plays a major part in retail strategy. When compared with traditional retail, smart retail brings both flexibility and challenges, as the consumer behaviour is evolving due to the process of technological changes and in the future, the interface of retail consumers may be completely different from current interactions (Roy et al., 2017).

Inman and Nikolova (2017) highlight that, from smart technologies, both customers and businesses can benefit, which will lead to business profitability and customer satisfaction. They described that mobile app, self-checkout, and scan and go technologies have a powerful impact on consumer's behaviour. However, the development of smartphones has innovated the way of purchasing, starting from mobile apps to geographic areas with same interests, creating a continuous connection with online environments which will change the consumer expectations and the ability to connect with consumers for retailers

(Grewal et al., 2017). A recent study demonstrated the forecast of smartphone users worldwide increased from 1.57 bn in 2014 to 2.87 bn in 2020 which will further create the opportunity for companies to invest in smart technologies (Statista, 2018).

Decision-Making Process and Cohort Theory on eCommerce

It is known that the decision-making process has at the foundation of it, a purchase decision with a particular pattern that a consumer will decide and follow, comparing the alternative viewpoints and opportunities to reach a decision (Erasmus, Boshoff, & Rousseau, 2001). In past research, Van der Heijden et al., (2003) adopted the Nicosia and Mayer (1976) framework for the online consumer behaviour methodology and established that the decision-making process follows next stages: recognition need, information search, alternatives, purchase and post-purchase. (Figure 2)

Figure 2. Adapted online decision-making process framework (Karimi et al., 2015)

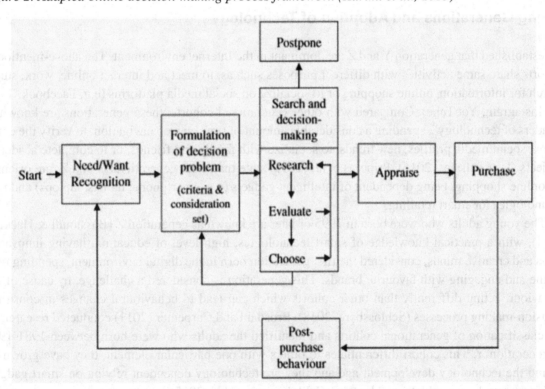

In the primary stage, recognition need, the consumers are aware of different needs or acknowledgment of certain types of products or services. The following stage, information search, consumers search and analyse the information to generate relevant decisions. The alternatives stage, consumers compare alternative products, prices or different retail websites to create appropriate judgments and suitable decisions. Furthermore, the purchase stage involves the consumer's actions or specific activities to accomplish the purchase process. The last stage, post-purchase, involves specific activities such as delivery process, reviews, ratings and recommendations for products or services, refunding or cognitive dissonance

(Liang & Lai, 2002). This is the most common framework of consumer purchase behaviour and has been extensively used in consumer research, however, the decision-making process literature describes that "decision-makers are flexible and construct decision-making processes as they adapt and respond to decision tasks" (Karimi et al., 2018). Thus, this framework of decision-making process does not accurately display the complexity of the system is too simplistic and does not illustrate the modification in the process flow (Karimi et al., 2018), because while shopping online or in stores some decisions are spontaneously initiated (Grewal et al., 2017).

De Pelsmacker et al. (2005) highlights that cohort theory using generational cohorts will allow achieving a better understanding of the decision-making process for consumers who were born in distinct period with similar values, priorities, and experiences (Bento et al., 2018). In Lee (2009) perspective, the most important variable in the digital environment is age, which creates a distinction between categories of cohorts, with various assumptions. Furthermore, lifestyle, values or other priorities or social behaviour are uniquely relative from one cohort to another, and shopping behaviours are different regarding retail format, based on purchasing drivers (Gindi et al., 2016).

Young Generations and Adoption of Technology

It's established that generation Y and Z are dominant in the Internet environment. The above-mentioned cohorts share same activities with different purposes such as, to meet and interact online, work, study, search for information, online shopping or to socialize on social media platforms (e.g. Facebook, Twitter, Instagram, YouTube). Compared with other generational cohorts, these generations are known as "leaders of technology", spending a considerable amount of time on web navigation, to verify the email inbox, social media profiles, new trends, to socialize with family and friends, or to complete academic projects (Issa & Isaias, 2016). Priporas et al. (2017) state that, both generations Y and Z, are oriented for online shopping, being dependent of intelligent gadgets (e.g. smartphone, tablets, laptops) and new technologies for smart retailing.

The young adults who were born in 1995 or later are known as generation Z (Bassiouni & Hackley, 2014), with a practical knowledge of smart technologies, high level of education, having innovative ideas and creative minds, considered the first generation born in the digital environment, spending time online and engaging with favourite brands. This generation is considered a challenge, by cause of the behaviour, acting differently than other cohorts which can lead to behavioural changes in consumer decision-making processes (Schlossberg, 2018). Brosdahl and Carpenter (2011) conducted research on the classification of generational cohorts and identified the adults who were born between 1981-1995 as generation Y. This cohort differentiates to others with one particular element, they have grown up during the technology development age and they are technology dependent relying on smart gadgets such as smartphones, tablets, and laptops (Çelikdemir & Tukel, 2015).

Recent research by Bilgihan (2016), describes generation Z as a young generation, being high consumers of customizable online shopping apps, with a perspective towards smart retailing, in which they extensively use technology for smart retailing. In Wood (2013) view, generation Z consumers had been characterized in four trends:

- **Innovation**: Interest in new technologies
- **Convenience:** Insistence in ease of use
- **Security**: Desire to feel safe

- **Escapism**: Desire to temporarily escape the reality they encounter.

Regarding social engagement, younger generations are using more often the features of social media platforms such as uploading photos, content writing, socializing and creating posts, compared with older generations (Hayes et al., 2015).

Internet's Influence on Generations

Generations Y and Z are aware of local and global events, as they are connected to the internet, social media, cable television or other sources of information, and are obsessed with new technologies, devices, having an unmeasurable desire to obtain highly advanced knowledge and skills around them (Freestone & Mitchell, 2004). However, the internet could create challenges, opportunities, and threats for these cohorts, increasing their knowledge, developing their skills for study, work or social environment, leading to independence. On the other hand, it could lead to damaging health and cause stress, anxiety or depression (Issa & Isaias, 2016).

It's noted that the internet will facilitate the communication, collaboration, involvement, becoming more aware of local and global issues, and will replace the face to face interaction, cooperating to meet new people, developing relationships and maintain actual friendships (Sun, 2011). Additionally, most importantly it will allow developing independent learning, to become self-regulating learners possessing the ability to solve problems easily, allowing to perform well in their studies and work developing their communication, reading and writing skills (Pujazon-Zazik & Park, 2010). Contrarily, as mentioned before the internet could have a negative impact on people and, the influencing factors can be easily identified which is considered to be caused by computer addiction leading to isolation, stress and depression, since the interaction face to face is no longer present in a digital environment and people have fewer reasons to leave their homes (Tyler, 2002).

Online Activities and Shopping Behaviour

Regarding online activities, both generations Y and Z are using, on a daily basis, Facebook, YouTube, and Instagram for pictures and fashion to access social media platforms and the preferred method to navigate online being through their own smartphone. However, there are more social media platforms, which they are accessing such as Snapchat, LinkedIn and various blogs. Most preferred posting across social media platforms such as lifestyle posts, while IT&C posts are more available on Facebook, beauty and personal care on YouTube and fashion-oriented on Instagram. Young generations select Facebook for promotional content adopting promotional articles, product trial, and presentation videos. Similarly, YouTube content related to video products, presentation videos and vlogs are preferred. After acknowledging the advertising on Facebook and YouTube young consumers are often searching for in-depth information on that particular product or brand and are most likely to recommend the products or brands they have seen online via advertisements (Starcom, 2018).

Concerning shopping behaviour, young generations are keen on online shopping, as a result of saving time to do other activities. However, on a weekly basis, neighbourhood stores and supermarkets are favourite places to purchase the necessary goods, being more reasonable to have a fast trip to the nearest shop to their living location, whenever they are in need for different goods. Furthermore, from typical ecommerce websites, young consumers purchase clothes, IT&C products, and books and from foreign websites, women purchase clothing and beauty care products. Young generations when they choose the online retailer, the first condition is price followed by terms of delivery. In terms of payment methods, men opt for online payment via the website and women prefer payment on delivery whether it is cash or card (Starcom, 2018).

DIGITAL FOOTPRINTS AND THE VALUE OF DATA

Data is the new currency of value. Mostly all online activity captured either is a passive or active manner and users may not even be aware of the digital footprint they leave, how they can be targeted through ads, etc. It's willingly shared by users in a way that sometimes has no thought to the consequences and actually it is the data that is being left unintentionally that offers more value to those collating and profiling than the fixed type of data one might see for example on LinkedIn employment history. To help understand the differences between Passive and Active can be explained as follows:

Passive: This is usually data that organisations harvest in an admin function such as purchasing habits or browsing data, operating system used, etc. It's collected to build profiling on its audience and perhaps used for advertising targeting. VPNs may be a way around this issue to minimise footprint.

Active: This can be publicly traceable data which can be a cause of concern. This type of digital footprint is information shared on the web and can be as example Twitter or Facebook updates, messages or rants. A classic example of this may be prospective employers undertaking a search on a job candidate across these social media platforms to detect behaviours past anything a CV will tell about how a person may be.

Data Harvesting and Mining

A huge amount of data and wealth of information is regularly generated about our lives with or without knowing. A digital footprint is established that stays forever and mostly cannot be erased. Whilst individuals think on obvious places such as credit card, banking, purchases, social interactions, etc., that builds this picture of preferences and routines, there is the aspect of data mining that is going on in the background that is more cause for concern. Forrester undertook research and output of a report in 2014, *Big Data's Big Meaning for Marketing*, and some highlights discussed by Kramer (2015) with regards to personal data protection, financial liabilities, and ethical dilemmas. Methods of protecting an individual's identity may not go far enough in the case of identity protection in the data mining process. Forrester outlines how Netflix released data after believing it had anonymised the data, but University of Texas researchers were able to identity Netflix users for anonymous reviews, but by knowing some parameters such as movies rented then it was possible to reverse-engineer the data and find out all viewing history; Pepitone (2010).

Whilst many would be in favor of healthcare providers mining data to ensure best-placed precision-based healthcare, where data mining is used to predict health needs. This sounds good but could raise ethical questions on privacy invasion. An example of Carolinas Healthcare System who manages 900 care centers and purchase data collected from credit card purchases, store loyalty programs, etc., to allow identification of high-risk patients in attempts to intervene prevention on any health issues developing, Kramer (2015). This identification by medical practitioners would enable gaining insight into patients' lifestyles and habits. A risk score is used so doctors can see flagged up issues. The data is collected from credit card purchases, store loyalty programs, and other public records. In theory, medical practitioners can learn more about their patients—and their patients' lifestyles—from their shopping habits than from brief, or sometimes non-existent, consultations. Although the data doesn't yet identify individual purchases, it does provide a risk score doctors can use to highlight potential problems. The issue could become a more trust-based issue between medical providers and patients if the data mining intrudes into the privacy and questions even healthy patients about their habits and digital footprints they leave. Or it may not take too long before insurance companies also start to review this mined data and risk score and that influences the service a patient receives, or worst case is refused if deemed too high a risk.

Or perhaps the case of Target, a retail organisation, that through a number of factors was able to identify and assign shoppers with a pregnancy prediction score (due to the array of 25 products when analysed together) and estimate a birth delivery due date to a small window. It allowed Target to provide coupons to the specific stages of pregnancy and highlighted a case of a dad who discovered his teen daughter was pregnant because Target mined her purchased data and sent her ads for baby products, Hill (2012).

Social Media Data Misuse

The widespread success of online social networking sites (OSNS) such as Facebook is a tempting resource for businesses engaged in electronic commerce. Using personal information, willingly shared between online friends' networks, OSNS appear to be a natural extension of current advertising strategies such as word-of-mouth and viral marketing. However, the use of OSNS data for business marketing purposes has provoked outrage amongst social network users and highlighted issues over privacy. Within such environments, OSNS users disclose information that would be potentially rich sources of data mining for commercial organisations because it includes information that can personally identify an individual in rich detail (Krishnamurthy and Will 2010). Such 'personally rich' information includes attributes such as name, location (city), telephone numbers, email addresses, photos, interests, and purchases, etc. This rich online social network data together with electronic word-of-mouth (eWOM) communications of OSNS users represents a tempting resource for viral and word-of-mouth marketing unlike other online and offline data which has to be prepared before systematically explored for patterns of use meaningful to commercial organisations (Kohavi et al. 2002, Zhang et al. 2011). A qualitative investigation of 861 blog comments from 715 individual online users was collected during the launch of Beacon, an unsuccessful third party marketing initiative by Facebook. Results show that business integrity, transparency of data use, user control, automatic disclosure, and data leakage were key privacy concerns posing significant challenges to using business analytics in online social networks. However, attempts to leverage personal information and eWOM communications for commercial gain have provoked outrage amongst OSNS users because of privacy concerns. Privacy concerns of online social network users include use of personal information by unknown others for potential harmful purposes (e.g. by sexual predators), use and selling of personal information without notice and consent, access of personal information by unwanted audiences (Young and Quan-Haase 2009), involuntary disclosure of personal information, damaged reputation because of rumours and gossips, unwanted contact and harassment or stalking, third party use of personal information, and identity theft (Boyd and Ellison, 2008). Consequently, privacy concerns challenge the classic thinking outlined by Kohavi and Provost (2001) that online (social) environments are particularly suitable domains for data mining because of the rich and large volume of data publicly available. Rather, issues of privacy concerns have emerged that overshadow the commercial potential of OSNS data (Hoadley et al. 2010) and highlight the boundaries of acceptance and use of business analytics in social networks. Privacy concerns have emerged as a critical factor determining the willingness, or not, of internet users to divulge personal information to online companies. Many studies have used 'privacy concern' construct to understand privacy in online contexts. Therefore 'privacy concern' has become a central construct to study privacy in information systems research. Likewise, it is a useful construct for business analytics because it provides theoretical guidance in defining and measuring privacy-related issues in the context of mining social network data for business marketing.

Facebook's personalised marketing tool "Beacon" was initially withdrawn by Facebook due to users' backlash because of privacy concerns and ultimately shut down due to the settlement of a lawsuit of $9.5 million. What should have been a successful innovation, however, was damaged and ultimately withdrawn because the nature and form of privacy concerns in OSNS were poorly understood.

Biohacking and the Arrival of the Cyborg

Biohacking, or sometimes labeled as 'do it yourself' biology, are essentially ways to enhance human abilities. This futuristic thinking has become a reality with more humans seeking to turn themselves into cyborgs with additions, for example, USB drives in their fingertips, or growing third ears on their forearms; Wainwright, 2015. The idea of the third ear which is part surgically modeled and partly has grown from the person's flesh is to turn this into a remote listening device and even add a GPS tracker so movements can be monitored and followed. This community of biohackers terms themselves as 'grinders' and information shared in how to attempt these practices are openly shared in online forums and wetware implants (biological equipment) offered. However, the term cyborg is not new as Professor Kevin Warwick was declared the worlds first cyborg in 1998 after he implanted an RFID tag in his arm and tracked his movements around the University campus, opened doors without physical touch and so on. His projects went further by implanting a 100 electrode chip into nerve fibers of his arm that transmitted signals from his wrist to computer, Warwick (2002).

There may be benefits to the advancement of humanity as some participate as a method for alternatives to large pharmaceuticals. Some may argue that trying to uncover drugs through biohacking can be undermining scientific research without following procedures to detect toxicity before patients would be administered any drugs. But the government are not able to stop individuals from experimenting on themselves even though there seems a lot of risks as the methods appear unregulated.

THE ROLE OF PRIVACY AND TRANSPARENCY IN THE DIGITAL ERA

Data is growing at exponential rates and there is no sign of any slowing down or resistance to technology enablers, such as smart devices, Internet of Things, etc. There are also other considerations regarding interoperability of data interchange since data is mainly kept in silos and other factors that give rise to concerns of non-transparency due to the nature in the way that data is stored and accessed. There is also the risk of cyber-attacks that cause data breaches and identity data theft due to a number of reasons in the way data are managed by trusted third parties and types of sophisticated cyber-attacks and those who are undertaking the attack. The ownership of data is also becoming a question of trust and looks to have abuses and exploitation as part of daily normal activities.

However, the properties of blockchain can offer a solution to give immutability, audit trail, traceability, offer better security and importantly a method for transparency and privacy. If we consider the way millennials interact with data, especially in retail or social media, then there are concerns over exactly what type of data is kept or profiled on them and where that data is further sent or analysed. If blockchain can be the mechanism to protect identity then the purposes of these faster interactions by millennials may be more protected. This also covers protecting privacy in newer concepts such as 'smart cities or societies.'

BLOCKCHAIN BACKGROUND

Blockchain is being viewed as a mechanism to provide further protection and enhance the security of data by using its properties of immutability, auditability, and encryption whilst providing transparency amongst parties who may not know each other, so operating in a trustless environment. In the view of Benchoufi & Ravaud (2017) some characteristics that have helped blockchain to withstand itself from the previous inventions are that it has greater velocity, wider implications and vast areas of implementation enabling all the modern features of the technology. Clauson et al., (2018) added to this by stating that blockchain is counted as one of the top 10 trends in the business world relating to technological emulation, enabling a great platform for extending peer to peer decentralised connectivity. Blockchain can be a great way to enable and bring a dynamic and drastic change in the business world enhancing the productivity dynamics, changing the employment pattern and transforming the ways present industries operate. Hill (2018) added that the overall concept of blockchain is to create a unique platform towards a fully digitalised, flexible, secure, immutable and fixed way of making business operations that are expected to transform the sub-systems and support activities of the business to a large extent as well. This would take care of some of the issues hanging around the privacy and ownership of data. Particularly in the retail world where identity data is shared and re-shared across third parties and there appears to be a loss in the ownership of how the data should be used, what is being stored on individuals and impacts on how they are profiled or targeted.

Forming Decentralization and Distributed Ledger

Blockchain is the method of maintaining digitalization and distributed way of data recording and handling. By implementing blockchain technology the retail business owners can effectively form a peer to peer communication hub reducing the costs regarding human resources and also allowing less intervention of the third parties. Blockchain can lead to a decentralized distributed ledger through creating unique nodes and safeguard the records of the ledger through enabling encryption option (Dixit, 2017). This can help the retail companies to reduce the roles of the third parties, reduce the theft of the trade secrets and handle the entire transactions in a more secure and safe way via soundproofing and verifying options. The best thing with the decentralized and distributed ledger is that it can protect the company for the manual modification of the records which can stop fraud and enable more transparency in the operation and also can enable the users to access the data from anywhere and anytime.

Different Aspects of Blockchain Technology

According to Clauson et al., (2018), the context and aspects of blockchain technology are huge and difficult to cover as the use and application of the blockchain technology is immense. Many are familiar with blockchain being associated with cryptocurrency or financial transactions, but the real benefits look to be far wider and reaching into the different sectors. Santos (2017) listed some of the major companies that have already enabled different forms blockchain in the market by adding that Bitcoin, Ethureum, NEO, NEM, Qtum, Zcash, Hyper ledger, and Quorum are some of the forms of blockchain available in the market. Kaal (2017) mentioned that one of the major advantages of blockchain technology is the wide ranges of transformation provision that it provides and means it can be in different forms that allow taking advantage of the key properties of blockchain that suit to the specific task. Ishmaev (2017) added to this discussion by adding that though there can be different forms of blockchain technology, their implications remain almost similar as they allow the same sets of benefits but appear in different forms. Kaal (2017) mentioned while describing different aspects of blockchain technology not only can it be used in banks and financial institutions, but applied to manufacturing organisations, public services, hospitals/healthcare and so on. Blockchain offers some obvious benefits in banking and financial applications by bringing safer and faster transactions and in the manufacturing and retail sector blockchain is expected to bring changes in the supply chain management, utilising its traceability, transparency and saving costs, reducing wastages and deterring identity data thefts.

Types of Blockchain

Asnit (2014) had the view that cryptocurrencies are going to change the entire face of banking transactions as it involves digital currency and fast transmission of the money peer to peer in real-time, without the intervention of the third party. It can also cover the world percentage that has no bank account or do not want to pay the higher transaction cost of trusted third parties. Casado-Vara, R et al (2018) noted that the main advantage of cryptocurrency is that it allows safer and faster transmission without any real transaction costs and help to facilitate cross-border trade in much faster and safer ways. The following are a few popular blockchain types.

Ethereum

Ethereum is a version of blockchain technology that mainly involves smart contracts between parties in a safe, faster and flexible way by developing a unique set of algorithms that automatically creates a shared ledger and can be accessed by the parties involved from anywhere anytime. Cocco et al., (2017) mentioned the major advantage of a smart contract is that it removes the time lags and also helps to remove the transaction costs in the contract as well to a large extent. With regards to chronological ordering or time-stamping, this is extremely helpful for auditability and trackability.

NEO

Dash & Behera (2017) mentioned that NEO is the latest addition of smart contract which is mainly China-based and the core aim of it is to facilitate the establishment of the smart economy by enabling faster and safer transaction through the use of smart contracts and deal. Dixit (2017) added that this technology involves the issuance of the business ICOs to the token owners and allow them fast peer to peer transaction to help to create a decentralised economy.

NEM

In the view of Dos Santos (2017) NEM is an upcoming blockchain technology that is the idea which will lead to the creation of the smart asset based on the proof of algorithm through a fast, flexible and secure way. Halaburda (2017) suggests that NEM involves the record of the how many coins and transactions users do and also helps to establish smart pools of assets and systems that can have wider implications in the financial asset management, documents handling and supply chain-related operations.

Qtum

Hayes (2009) stated that Qtum is a technology that has combined the Bitcoin and Ethereum technology together to form an improved all-around package for blockchain technology as it involves the use of smart contract through the UTXO technology and proof stake mechanism that can be customised for the enterprise functions. John (2017) mentioned that Qtum technology adds more areas of implementation for blockchain technologies in different industry segments.

Hyperledger

Dos Santos (2017) mentioned one of the major advantages of the blockchain technology is the immutable record opportunity that it provides and Hyperledger is exactly the solution to it as it is an umbrella organisation formed by Linux that incubate different blockchain technologies in a single platform to integrate the use of blockchain technology in different operations. Dixit (2017) state that Hyperledger allows the instant and simultaneous safe and unbreakable recording of business transactions.

BLOCKCHAIN IMPACTS IN DIFFERENT SECTORS

Kawa and Maryniak (2018) listed the major segments where blockchain can be implemented by articulating that blockchain can be used in supply chain management and manufacturing. Its main purposes for recording the transactions, stopping fraud and can be used for reducing the lags and delays in operations and give assurances to its traceability. This was also the case with Benchoufi & Ravaud (2017) who mentioned that in supply chain management blockchain can be very useful, allowing control and tracking of the inventories in every step of the supply chain and can be a great aid in stopping theft and inconsistencies while the shipment and storing of the goods can be effectively monitored.

Halaburda (2017) added that the major shipping companies have already shown their interest in the blockchain technology investing around $150m and it is predicted that the technology is going to reduce 85% of the paper use and 90% of the time delays helping the companies to save at least 10-15% costs in each transaction. Ishmaev (2017) explained the implications of the blockchain technology from the macroeconomic perspective by describing and marking it as a way of introducing digital currencies and already some emerging countries like Tunisia and Senegal have initiated their digital currencies such as E-Diner and E-CFA taking the concept from this technology.

IMPORTANCE OF BLOCKCHAIN APPLICATIONS IN THE RETAIL SECTOR

The size of the UK retail market has grown significantly over the last few years and shows no sign of slowing down. See Figure 3 below that explains the growth cycle.

Figure 3. Retail growth 2015-2020

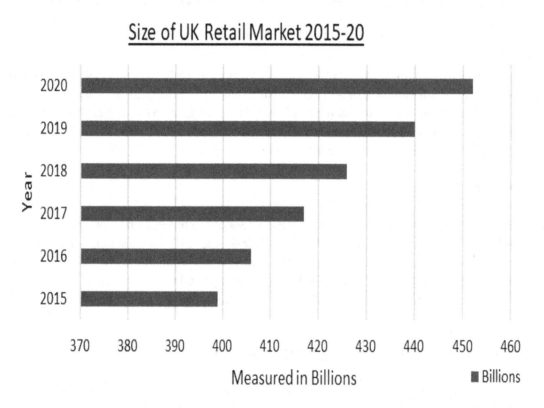

While commenting about the application of the blockchain technology in the retail segment, Ishmaev (2017) mentioned some of the major challenges that the retail companies are now currently dealing with, are regarding more transparency with their consumers whom more recently have become cautious on the origin of the goods, whom the products have been produced by and ethics concerning this. Tracking and traceability are relied upon in more conventional methods and where trust is not certain. Kaal (2017) added that aside from the customer viewpoint blockchain has real use cases in some of the core operational areas for the retail companies especially in handling their supply chain management operation which is proven to be the most crucial for the retail companies. Contamination in the supply chain can be not just financially uncomfortable and damaging to credibility, but potentially fatal if processes are not tracked and provide the trust and immutability around this.

Kane (2017) added to this discussion by stating that blockchain can be an all-around solution for supply chain management enabling the companies to monitor and control their physical goods flow in the most effective way possible involving the companies with the entire journey and real-time monitoring. In the view of Stratopoulos (2018) blockchain can have countless positive consequences and can help the retail companies to connect with their customers more intensely, gaining trusts in their transparency statement.

However, on the other hand, the collation of retail data without fully understanding its intent or purposes can have significant effects in profiling consumers and assumptions made by those controlling the data sets.

The following sub sections discuss the properties of blockchain and use cases with examples of benefits.

Transparency And Ethical Trading

One of the recent trends in the UK retail industry is that customers want to engage themselves with every stage of the production journey and requiring to ethically consume viable products. They want to know from where exactly the raw materials have been sourced, who is the producer and how it has been served and observe this information perhaps from a QR code on the packaging that is the immutable footprint of information stored on the blockchain. There have already been some situations where contamination of meat products has infiltrated the production line and ended up in the consumer purchase point. Such as the horse meat scandals by major UK retailers (Clowes, 2014). Companies and blockchain technology organisations are investigating this need for end-to-end traceability for its quality and assurance that what is being delivered is 100 percent and the single version of the truth.

Authenticity and Intellectual Property Protection

Intellectual property rights or ownership are a concern as to how records are maintained and its authenticity. This is more apparent in the high street fashion retailers, as it has been noticeable that there have been many replicas of expensive fashion brands and it's become difficult for consumers to recognize the actual authentic product. Blockchain technology can become a potential solution for enabling consumers to have authentic and original products. An example of this is the popular fashion brand Babyghost, who is experimenting with the Chinese company Bitse to form NFC tags for each cloth to enable consumers to check the authenticity (Cocco, et al, 2017).

Logistic Consideration

A study conducted by Dudek (2017) reveals that 15% of the total operating expenses of the top 5 retailers of the UK are derived from the theft and poor handling of the shipment and its workflow process. Blockchain can enable a better logistical solution as it can make the shipment easier to verify and any information regarding the status of the products at every stage of shipment with all rich data available around what happens at these milestone stages. For a retail business, this technology can effectively solve the food safety and contamination and give an added layer of prevention as blockchain can trace the temperature and airflow throughout the shipment journey and any issue is flagged and recorded. The blockchain technology has already been practiced by major retailers and there has been evidence that blockchain technology has potentially helped to overcome the UK egg crisis enabling the process to track the origin of eggs and handle and destroy them accordingly.

Ecommerce, Payment and Ownership Verification

Cross-border transactions have always been lengthy and costly because of different documentation requirements and blockchain is expected to provide an alternative with the introduction of crypto-currencies in the transaction process and so can make the cross-border barter trade a lot easier. The introduction of cryptocurrency payment can make ecommerce more secure, fast and flexible way of handling the transactions as it can lead towards the creation of an immutable record of transactions, protecting the interest of the related stakeholders. Already companies have been experimenting with the crypto-currency payments as travel giants like Expedia is accepting hotel booking payments through the use of Bitcoin. E-commerce giants such as Shopify is also expecting the bitcoin payment (Dash, & Behera, 2017) to take place.

Chronological Recording And Immutability And Security

One of the core reasons behind the poor customer satisfaction in the retail industry is that there is a great deal of time wasted in finding out the desired products and it happens as most of the retail business can't afford to make the chronological recording of the goods because of the flow of the huge product as found by study conducted by Dixit (2017). Blockchain can help to redeem this problem by allowing the effective categorisation and recording of the goods in a chronological manner. Another benefit that blockchain can provide to the retail companies is that it can help with the immutable record feature as once it is recorded on the blockchain platform, it is there forever. The data is protected by encryption and can only be accessed by those authenticated or allowed through the key exchange. This is one of the core reasons for the growing popularity of blockchain technology through its security properties. As retail businesses hold personal sensitive information, so hence the majority of this information always remains vulnerable to cyber-attacks. Blockchain solves this issue by enabling encryption option for the stored information and by not allowing any alteration and destruction of the recorded information at the same time, Hayes (2009).

Transparency and Auditability

The transparency of data is a key aspect from both the context of the retailers and also from the viewpoint of the consumer. Blockchain solves this problem by allowing greater transparency through real-time control, time-stamping of data and chronological ordering. In the blockchain system, no third-party can enter into the system without the consent of the controlling parties or access the data without correct authentication approvals. The suitability and evaluation of the stored information become a lot easier in the blockchain system because it helps to represent the data in an organised and structured way with parties that have the authentication rights to view and access all data.

Allowing Better Traceability and Faster Response Time

As there are millions of products and huge numbers of suppliers involved with the retail industry it becomes often difficult for the retail companies to exact trace which products have been received from which supplier. There is a great deal of cost factor associated with manual recording and data handling. The tracking of the shipment products has also become costly and difficult for the retail business as well.

Blockchain technology can allow real-time traceability, removing the paper use and can ensure the just in time response regarding the status of the products of the retail business on an instant basis. Take the pharmaceutical retail industry, as an example, of where traceability is both key and important. It is mostly about the strong chain of custody in the manufacturing and supply of drugs to a patient and blockchain heralds itself as the answer to the issue where things have gone wrong and act as the block to fake drugs entering the supply chain. As it stands counterfeit drugs are estimated to be at 50% in low-income countries with a global market range of $200 billion (DrugPatentWatch, 2017). As well as counterfeit drugs being a failure to treat the patient, it may also kill/harm the patient. Blockchain will create a place where the ecosystem of a supply chain would interact and record all transactions without being able to tamper the records. The result is a transparent method to secure the chain of custody and data.

Removal of Fraud and Quickening up the Pace of Tracking

Fraud, in the context of the retail business, happens mainly because of the selling from the expiry of the products, wastages, and theft of the goods in the shipment process and also theft from the store. A study conducted by John (2017) reveals that 2.5% of the global import gets counterfeited that amounts up to half a trillion dollars. Around 6% of the imported products get pirated and 24.72% of the major retail products such as handbags, perfumes, and chemicals get duplicated. From the research conducted by Kane (2017) shows that this rate can be reduced as low as 3% and 74% of the counterfeit trade can be stopped if blockchain can implement in the system as blockchain allows the quick tracking enabling optimum traceability and control from the source of intellectual property (IP) to its end point. Inventory management has also become a major cause of concern for retailers as the costs associated with it has become intensified and also companies are facing difficulties in serving their customers according to their exact needs. Due to the constant demand fluctuations either retail businesses are facing the threat of over inventory storage or a shortage of inventory storing. A study conducted by Karame and Androulaki (2017) reveals that 25% of the overall operational costs for the retail business comes from the inventory management operation. As described earlier, blockchain can enable the provision for the digital flow of the physical goods allowing the companies with optimum inventory management operations. Another benefit that blockchain can enable in the context of retail business is that it can contribute to reducing the overall courier costs for the retail companies. Kane (2017) discusses how the implementation of the blockchain in the shipment of goods around the world can reduce the courier costs by 80% as it will effectively stop the time lags in delivery and the use of lengthy documentation. Kawa and Maryniak (2018) confirm that in a year almost £5billon is lost because of the poor documentation and also the failure of the timely delivery of products arising from this poorly kept documentation. The smart contracts feature helps to create digital documentation through the use of unique codes and the comprehensive blockchain software can enable the completion of the contract and detection of the contract with ease.

DIGITAL IDENTITIES AND BLOCKCHAIN

The concept of digital identities is not an entirely new idea and has been approached with ID cards but this is not digital identity in a true sense. Digital identities originate from activity online or via the web and shadow data is generated as a collective body of data and recorded as individuals carry out various tasks that may be automated rather than intentionally purposed. This shadow data may mean a collation of data taken from IP surveillance, communication metadata, sensors and so on. This creates a risk in terms of data being clearly associated with an individual. With online activity, a normal interaction on a frequent basis means potentially many interactions where data is given without necessarily receiving or purchasing a product. For example, purchasing car insurance can require all identity data points before the individual selects a vendor from a series of quotes or smart data interactions in the concept of smart cities. This means there needs to be a greater demand for trust and security due to the highly mobile activity an individual undertakes.

Even in website login and creation of that initial registration either generating a new login ID and password on the site or through universal login features such as through Facebook or Google. Both methods carry a risk since the former can be subjected to a cyber-attack and identity data loss or in the latter case the data is being collated by the Universal login feature and not entirely known as to what action is being taken on the data being parsed through as third-party trackers embedded on the site are accessing this data as well. Also, the concept of KYC (Know Your Customer) presents an issue each time for due diligence a financial institution has to start afresh with onboarding the process of documents of identity and proof such as passport, identity card, driver's license, etc.

The concept of blockchain playing a part in securing digital identities looks a valid and viable option to offer enhancement of privacy and security. The choice is given more to the individual in that they can access it at anytime and cannot be accessed without their consent. There can be many use cases of how to incorporate digital identities into everyday activities. For government they could consider introducing into voting elections or in the case of KYC, blockchain makes it viable for financial institutions to access customer information without having to start from the beginning with taking in personal data. The same can be said for digital identities being used for loan requests, social media interaction and even in property auction where the example can be the buyer's identity being used as the digital identity and so not revealing true identity until a decision on purchase is agreed.

Digital identity systems look to provide the trust, privacy, and transparency a digital world will need to protect its citizens from events of cyber-attacks and loss of data. Also, to protect the invisible profiling undertaken so that sensitive personal data remains personal and not for public consumption without an individual's consent.

CONCLUSION

This chapter looked at the main differences between the different generations and interactions made in how online activity is undertaken. Without a doubt, the volume of data is exponentially increasing and daily interactions with smart data becoming the normal mode of interaction. The gap between humans and technology has never been so close and now with the advent and acceptance of biohacking has made this transition to the term cyborg. However, so is the abundance of data being created around individuals from their online activity and retail interactions. This makes it more accessible for social media misuse and data profiling undertaken from analyzation that may use tools of machine learning and artificial intelligence. This is one of the reasons that blockchain is becoming more valued for its various use cases in industry and the retail sector is interesting since there is a high instantaneous response in data interactions (especially with millennials) that can cause a potential risk in how that data is profiled and used by third parties and other. The use of digital identities can make a layer of protection to offer better security and privacy. Using blockchain in a commercial way explained in this chapter also takes care of the transparency issues and with its properties of immutability, auditability, and traceability add to making this mechanism a powerful addition to any organisation.

REFERENCES

Asnit, A. (2014). Collective Intelligence based Supply Chain Planning Process Considering Supply Chain Uncertainties. *Korean Journal of Logistics*, 22(4), 15–26. doi:10.15735/kls.2014.22.4.002

Barney, J. B., & Clark, D. N. (2007). *Resource-based theory: Creating and sustaining competitive advantage*. New York: Oxford University Press.

Baron, J. N., & Hannan, M. T. (1994). The impact of economics on contemporary sociology. *Journal of Economic Literature*, 32(3), 1111–1146.

Bassiouni, D. H., & Hackley, C. (2014). 'Generation Z' children's adaption to digital consumer culture: A critical literature review. *Journal of Customer Behaviour*, 13(2), 113–133. doi:10.1362/14753921 4X14024779483591

Benchoufi, M., & Ravaud, P. (2017). Blockchain technology for improving clinical research quality. *Trials*, 18(1), 335. doi:10.118613063-017-2035-z PMID:28724395

Bergen, M., Dutta, S., & Walker, O. C. Jr. (1992). Agency Relationships in Marketing: A Review of the Implications and Applications of Agency and Related Theories. *Journal of Marketing*, 56(3), 1–24. doi:10.1177/002224299205600301

Bilgihan, A. (2016). Gen Y customer loyalty in online shopping: An integrated model of trust, user experience and branding. *Computers in Human Behavior*, 61, 103–116. doi:10.1016/j.chb.2016.03.014

Brosdahl, D. J., & Carpenter, M. J. (2011). Shopping orientations of US males: A generational cohort comparison. *Journal of Retailing and Consumer Services*, 18(6), 548–554. doi:10.1016/j.jretconser.2011.07.005

Cannon, J. P., Achrol, R. S., & Gundlach, G. T. (2000). Contracts, norms, and plural form governance. *Journal of the Academy of Marketing Science*, (28): 94–180.

Casado-Vara, R., Prieto, J., la Prieta, F., & Corchado, J. (2018). How blockchain improves the supply chain: Case study alimentary supply chain. *Procedia Computer Science*, 134, 393–398. doi:10.1016/j.procs.2018.07.193

Çelikdemir, D. Z., & Tukel, I. (2015). Incorporating Ethics into Strategic Management with regards to Generation Y's view of Ethics. *Procedia: Social and Behavioral Sciences*, 207, 528–535. doi:10.1016/j.sbspro.2015.10.123

Clauson, K., Breeden, E., Davidson, C., & Mackey, T. (2018). Leveraging Blockchain Technology to Enhance Supply Chain Management in Healthcare. *Blockchain In Healthcare Today*. doi:10.30953/bhty.v1.20

Clowes, R. (2014). Thinking in the Cloud: The Cognitive Incorporation of Cloud-Based Technology. *Philosophy & Technology*, *28*(2), 261–296. doi:10.100713347-014-0153-z

Cocco, L., Pinna, A., & Marchesi, M. (2017). Banking on Blockchain: Costs Savings Thanks to the Blockchain Technology. *Future Internet*, *9*(3), 25. doi:10.3390/fi9030025

Dash, C., & Behera, P. (2017). Blockchain Technology: A Revolutionary Bitcoin Technology. *International Journal Of Information Science And Computing*, *4*(1), 27. doi:10.5958/2454-9533.2017.00004.7

De Pelsmacker, P., Geuens, P., & Van den Bergh, J. (2005). *Marketingcommunicatie*. Amsterdam: Pearson Education Benelux.

Dillon, A., & Morris, M. (1996). User Acceptance of Information Technology: Theories and Models. *Annual Review of Information Science & Technology*, 3–32.

Dixit, R. (2017). Multi-Cloud for Improving Cloud Data Security. *International Journal For Research In Applied Science And Engineering Technology*, *5*(11), 2696-2700. doi:10.22214/ijraset.2017.11371

Dos Santos, R. (2017). On the Philosophy of Bitcoin/Blockchain Technology: Is it a Chaotic, Complex System? *Metaphilosophy*, *48*(5), 620–633. doi:10.1111/meta.12266

DrugPatentWatch. (2017). *Can Blockchain Technology put an end to Counterfeit Drugs*. Available at https://medium.com/drugpatentwatch/can-blockchain-technology-put-an-end-to-counterfeit-drugs-c4087e652fe0

Dudek, D. (2017). Possibilities of using blockchain technology in the area of education. *Informatyka Ekonomiczna*, (45), 55-65. doi:10.15611/ie.2017.3.05

Erasmus, A. C., Boshoff, E., & Rousseau, G. G. (2001). Consumer decision-making models within the discipline of consumer science: A critical approach. *Journal of Family Ecology and Consumer Science*, *29*, 82–90.

Fotiadis, A., & Stylos, N. (2017). The effects of online social networking on retail consumer dynamics in the attractions industry: The case of 'E-da' Theme Park, Taiwan. *Technological Forecasting and Social Change*, *124*, 283–294. doi:10.1016/j.techfore.2016.06.033

Freestone, O., & Mitchell, V. W. (2004). Generation Y Attitudes Towards E-ethics and Internet-related Misbehaviours. *Journal of Business Ethics*, *54*(2), 121–128. doi:10.100710551-004-1571-0

Gaski, J. F., & Nevin, J. R. (1985). The Differential Effects of Exercised and Unexercised Power Sources in a Marketing Channel. *JMR, Journal of Marketing Research*, *22*(2), 130–142. doi:10.1177/002224378502200203

Gobo, G. (2014). Glocalizing methodology? The encounter between local methodologies. *International Journal of Social Research Methodology*, *14*(6), 417–437. doi:10.1080/13645579.2011.611379

Grewal, R., Kumar, A., Mallapragada, G., & Saini, A. (2013). Marketing Channels in Foreign Markets: Control Mechanisms and the Moderating Role of Multinational Corporation Headquarters–Subsidiary Relationship. *Journal of Marketing Research*, (50), 378-398.

Halaburda, H. (2017). *Blockchain Revolution Without the Blockchain*. SSRN Electronic Journal. doi:10.2139srn.3133313

Hayes, J. (2009). The clout of the cloud (cloud computing). *Engineering & Technology*, *4*(6), 60–61. doi:10.1049/et.2009.0611

Heide, J. B., & John, G. (1988). The Role of Dependence Balancing in Safeguarding Transaction-Specific Assets in Conventional Channels. *Journal of Marketing*, *52*(1), 20–35. doi:10.1177/002224298805200103

Hill, T. (2018). Blockchain for research [Review]. *Learned Publishing*, *31*(4), 421–422. doi:10.1002/leap.1182

Hofmann, E., Strewe, U., & Bosia, N. (2016). *Supply Chain Finance and Blockchain Technology*. Academic Press.

Inman, J. J., & Nikolova, H. (2017). Shopper-Facing Retail Technology: An Adoption Decision Calculus. *Journal of Retailing*, *93*, 7–28. doi:10.1016/j.jretai.2016.12.006

Ishmaev, G. (2017). Blockchain Technology as an Institution of Property. *Metaphilosophy*, *48*(5), 666–686. doi:10.1111/meta.12277

Issa, T., & Isaias, P. (2016). Internet factors influencing generations Y and Z in Australia. *Information Processing & Management*, *52*(4), 592–617. doi:10.1016/j.ipm.2015.12.006

Jahanmir, S. F., & Cavadas, J. (2018). Factors affecting late adoption of digital innovations. *Journal of Business Research*, *88*, 337–343. doi:10.1016/j.jbusres.2018.01.058

John, A. (2017). Blockchain and Its Applications. *International Journal of Recent Trends in Engineering and Research*, *3*(4), 143–145. doi:10.23883/IJRTER.2017.3123.ZS1WM

Kaal, W. (2017). *Blockchain Technology and Race in Corporate America*. SSRN Electronic Journal. doi:10.2139srn.3071378

Kane, E. (2017). *Is Blockchain a General Purpose Technology?* SSRN Electronic Journal. doi:10.2139srn.2932585

Karame, G., & Androulaki, E. (2017). *Bitcoin and blockchain security*. Academic Press.

Kawa, A., & Maryniak, A. (2018). *SMART Supply Network*. Cham: Springer.

Lee, S. (2009). Mobile internet services from consumers' perspectives. *International Journal of Human-Computer Interaction*, *25*(3), 390–413. doi:10.1080/10447310902865008

Leung, C. K., & Tse, C. Y. (2001). Technology choice and saving in the presence of a fixed adoption cost. *Review of Development Economics*, *5*(1), 40–48. doi:10.1111/1467-9361.00105

Lexicon, F. T. (2018). *Financial Times*. Retrieved from LexiconFT: http://lexicon.ft.com/Term?term=digital-marketing

Liang, T., & Lai, H. (2002). Effect of store design on consumer purchases: Van empirical study of on-line bookstore. *Information & Management*, *39*(6), 431–444. doi:10.1016/S0378-7206(01)00129-X

Morgan, R. N., & Hunt, S. D. (1994). The Commitment-Trust Theory of Relationship Marketing. *Journal of Marketing*, *58*(3), 20–38.

Nicosia, F. M., & Mayer, R. N. (1976). Toward a sociology consumption. *The Journal of Consumer Research*, *3*(2), 65–75. doi:10.1086/208653

Palmatier, R. W., Dant, R. P., & Grewal, D. (2007). A Comparative Longitudinal Analysis of Theoretical Perspectives of Interorganizational Relationship Performance. *Journal of Marketing*, *71*(4), 94–172. doi:10.1509/jmkg.71.4.172

Pantano, E., & Timmermans, H. (2014). What is smart for retailing? *Procedia Environmental Sciences*, *22*, 101–107. doi:10.1016/j.proenv.2014.11.010

Pomirleanu, N. S., Schibrowsky, J. A., Peltier, J., & Nill, A. (2013). A review of internet marketing research over the past 20 years and future research direction. *Journal of Research in Interactive Marketing*, *7*(3), 166–181. doi:10.1108/JRIM-01-2013-0006

Priporas, C.-V., Stylos, N., & Fotiadis, A. K. (2017). Generation Z consumers' expectations of interactions in smart retailing: A future agenda. *Computers in Human Behavior*, *77*, 374–381. doi:10.1016/j.chb.2017.01.058

Pujazon-Zazik, M., & Park, M. J. (2010). To Tweet, or Not to Tweet: Gender Differences and Potential Positive and Negative Health Outcomes of Adolescents' Social Internet Use. *American Journal of Men's Health*, *4*(1), 77–85. doi:10.1177/1557988309360819 PMID:20164062

Pujazon-Zazik, M., & Park, M. J. (2010). To Tweet, or Not to Tweet: Gender Differences and Potential Positive and Negative Health Outcomes of Adolescents' Social Internet Use. *American Journal of Men's Health*, *4*(1), 77–85. doi:10.1177/1557988309360819 PMID:20164062

Rigby, D. (2011). The Future of Shopping. *Harvard Business Review*, *89*(12), 65–76.

Rouse, S. V. (2015). A reliability analysis of Mechanical Turk data. *Computers in Human Behavior*, *43*, 304–307. doi:10.1016/j.chb.2014.11.004

Schlossberg, M. (2018). *Teen Generation Z is being called 'millenials on steroids', and that could be terrifying for retailers*. Retrieved from Business Insider UK: http://uk.businessinsider.com/millennials-vs-gen-z-2016-2

Simons, G. (2008). Marketing to postmodern consumers: Introducing Internet chameleon. *European Journal of Marketing*, *42*(3/4), 299–310. doi:10.1108/03090560810852940

Sorescu, A., Frambach, R. T., Singh, J., Rangaswamy, A., & Bridges, C. (2011). Innovations in Retail Business Models. *Journal of Retailing*, *87*, 3–16. doi:10.1016/j.jretai.2011.04.005

Starcom. (2018). *Starcom România lansează ediția 2017 a studiului Consumer Report*. Retrieved from IQAds: https://www.iqads.ro/articol/40927/starcom-romania-lanseaza-editia-2017-a-studiului-consumer-report

Statista. (2018a). *eCommerce Romania*. Retrieved from Statista: https://www.statista.com/outlook/243/148/ecommerce/romania#market-age

Statista. (2018b). *Number of smartphone users worldwide from 2014 to 2020 (in billions)*. Retrieved from Statista: https://www.statista.com/statistics/330695/number-of-smartphone-users-worldwide/

Stern, L., & Reve, T. (1980). Distribution Channels as Political Economies: A Framework for Comparative Analysis. *Journal of Marketing*, *44*(3), 52–64. doi:10.1177/002224298004400306

Stratopoulos, T. (2018). *Blockchain Technology Adoption*. SSRN Electronic Journal. doi:10.2139srn.3188470

Sun, J., Yan, J., & Zhang, K. (2016). Blockchain-based sharing services: What blockchain technology can contribute to smart cities. *Financial Innovation*, *2*(1), 26. doi:10.118640854-016-0040-y

Sun, S. (2011). The Internet Effects on Students Communication at Zhengzhou Institute of Aeronautical Industry Management. Advances in Computer Science, Environment. *Ecoinformatics and Education*, *5*(11), 418–422.

Taherdoost, H. (2018). A review of technology acceptance and adoption models and theories. *Procedia Manufacturing*, *22*, 960–967. doi:10.1016/j.promfg.2018.03.137

Tyler, T. (2002). Is the Internet changing social life? It seems the more things change, the more they stay the same. *The Journal of Social Issues*, *58*(1), 195–205. doi:10.1111/1540-4560.00256

Van der Haijden, H. (2006). User Acceptance of Hedonic Information System. *Management Information Systems Quarterly*, *28*(4), 695–704. doi:10.2307/25148660

Van der Heijden, H., Verhagen, T., & Creemers, M. (2003). Understanding online purchase intentions: Contributions from technology and trust perspectives. *European Journal of Information Systems*, *12*(1), 41–48. doi:10.1057/palgrave.ejis.3000445

Venkatesh, V., Morris, M. G., Davis, G. B., & Davis, F. D. (2003). User acceptance of information technology: Toward a unified view. *Management Information Systems Quarterly*, *27*(3), 425–478. doi:10.2307/30036540

Venkatesh, V., Thong, J. Y., & Xu, X. (2012). Consumer acceptance and use of information technology: Extending the unified theory of acceptance and use of technology. MIS Quarterly: Management. *Information Systems*, *36*(1), 157–178.

Verhoef, P. C., Kannan, P. K., & Inman, J. J. (2015). From Multi-Channel Retailing to Omni-Channel Retailing: Introduction to the Special Issue on Multi-Channel Retailing. *Journal of Retailing*, *91*(2), 174–181. doi:10.1016/j.jretai.2015.02.005

Wainwright, O. (2015). Body-hackers: the people who turn themselves into cyborgs. *The Guardian*.

Warwick, K. (2002). *Project Cyborg 2.0: The next step towards True Cyborgs*. Available at: http://www.kevinwarwick.com/project-cyborg-2-0/

Watson, G. F. IV, Worm, S., Palmatier, R. W., & Ganesan, S. (2015). The Evolution of Marketing Channels: Trends and Research Directions. *Journal of Retailing*, *91*(4), 546–568. doi:10.1016/j.jretai.2015.04.002

Watson, J. (2013). *Strategy: an introduction to game theory* (3rd ed.). New York: W. W. Norton and Company.

Weiss, M. A. (2011). The use of social media sites data by business organizations in their relationship with employees. *Journal of Internet Law*, *15*(2), 16–27.

Wood, S. (2013). Generation Z as consumers: trends and innovation. Institute for Emerging Issues: NC State University.

Zhitomirsky-Geffet, M., & Blau, M. (2016). Cross-generational analysis of predictive factors of addictive behavior in smartphone usage. *Computers in Human Behavior*, *64*, 682–693. doi:10.1016/j.chb.2016.07.061

KEY TERMS AND DEFINITIONS

Biohacking: Sometimes labelled as 'do it yourself' biology, is essentially ways to enhance human abilities.

Blockchain: This is viewed as a mechanism to provide further protection and enhance the security of data by using its properties of immutability, auditability and encryption whilst providing transparency amongst parties who may not know each other, so operating in a trustless environment.

Cyborg: The gap between humans and technology has never been so close and now with the advent and acceptance of biohacking has made this transition to the term cyborg.

Data Harvesting: A huge amount of data and wealth of information is regularly generated about our lives with or without knowing and through a set of preferences and routines using data mining a pattern can be harvested.

Digital Footprint: Is the track of data created and left behind while using the digital platforms.

Digital Identity: Digital identities originate from activity online or via the web and shadow data is generated as a collective body of data and recorded as individuals carry out various tasks that may be automated rather than intentionally purposed.

Digital Marketing: The digitalization of communication channels and media will impact a substantial change in the direction for communication and interactions, and the consumer behaviour and the development of technologies is the main elements of developmental direction in marketing strategy in the digital era.

Social Media: During the Internet decade the social arrangements made up of many actors in the virtual environment/ media which is called social media.

Chapter 63
Decentralizing Privacy Using Blockchain to Protect Private Data and Challanges With IPFS

M. K. Manoj
VIT University, India

Somayaji Siva Rama Krishnan
VIT University, India

ABSTRACT

Blockchain technology is a distributed framework for sharing data that is validated through crypto-graphic functions. The nodes of the network come to a consensus regarding addition of data to the blockchain. Every blockchain operation requires a processing fee. This fee makes storing of large data on the blockchain infeasible. An indirect alternative for this challenge could be use of IPFS, which is a decentralized peer-peer network that facilitates storage of file. This is accomplished by storing the hash of the IPFS as data on the blockchain.

WHAT IS BLOCKCHAIN?

A blockchain is a time-stamped series of immutable records of data that is managed by a cluster of computers. Information held on a blockchain exists as a shared and continually reconciled database. This means that data of a blockchain is not owned by a single entity. Each of these blocks of data is secured and bound to each other using cryptographic principles (Rosic, 2016).

If all the data is shared then this means that there is no centralized version of this information. Thus, a blockchain has no centralized authority. The information on the chain is open for anyone and everyone in the network to see. Hence, anything that is built on blockchain is very transparent by nature and everyone involved is accountable for their actions (Hales, 2019).

DOI: 10.4018/978-1-6684-7132-6.ch063

WHY BLOCKCHAIN?

The blockchain is considered a disruptive technology; one that significantly alters the way businesses or entire industries operate. It often forces companies to change the way they approach their business or fear losing market share and to become irrelevant.

Blockchain brings into picture something truly unique. It gives a new no trust mechanism. Imagine a situation where a transaction made by a person A is shown to be done but due to a malicious intruder (hacker) or software error it does not show up but the amount is lost, or a case where the bank balance of A is different from the actual balance that A thinks it is. For situations like these, the third party trust is a must. A person trusts a bank and uses its features. If in case know that a bank is not trustworthy or is fraudulent then the obvious choice is to not use that particular bank's services. If an unfortunate error happens, the bank is held liable for any mistakes made.

Such situations will never arise with blockchain being similar to a public ledger with so many people acting as proof of one's transaction. There is no need to rely on a third party and hence it has become a huge concept seeking attention. The blockchain provides a trust and authentication protocol that has already disrupted banking and is on the verge of revamping healthcare, financial services, social apps and more.

Blockchain brings the proof of trust in the form of cryptographic functions i.e. mathematical equations that are solvable and can give a definitive analytical proof and not in the form of a developer who developed it (prone to human error) or any other means. So, for the first time in human existence, blockchain brings about a trust mechanism that is trustless. In other words, it is independent of where it resides and who operates it, as the trust mechanism is mathematically proven. This removes the need for human intervention in the system altogether. That is the major problem that blockchain solved for the world, which no one was able to solve before it.

HOW DOES A BLOCKCHAIN WORK?

Blockchain works mainly on the basis of hashing. Hashing is a technique used to map data of arbitrary size into a fixed size. Hashing is a one-way function. It means that once converted to a hash it is not possible to get back the previous data. Now this means that sharing of a hash of a password to anyone, it would not be possible to find the original password from it.

Hashing has a lot of advantages. It is used widely in password store where a database stores the hash of a person's password in a database, so even if the database is compromised, there is no actual leakage of confidential information to a third party. When requires the site can then hash the input password and check if it matches with the one in the database to let the user have access.

Some Properties of Hashing

Deterministic: This means that no matter how many times a single input is passed through a hash function, the output will always be the same. This is critical because if there is different output over time for the same input then it will be impossible to keep track of input.

Quick Computation: The hashing function must be able to return the hash of an input quickly. If the process is not fast enough the system won't be efficient to use.

Pre-Image Resistance: What pre-image resistance states is that, given Hash A it is infeasible to determine A, where A is the input and Hash A is the output hash.

Small Changes in the Input Changes the Hash: Even if a single small change in input, the hash must have a significant change in output.

Collision Resistant: Given two different inputs A and B where Hash A and Hash B are their respective hashes, it is not possible to have Hash A equal to Hash B. This means that for each input there will be a unique output (hash).

Figure 1.

Message	This is a hash text for test
Hash	f7fcdae4c05d3f5860b0f1c9dd6af4c2b53afad7ffdb6d8386ea2f920fe9a66e

In the above examples, it is clear that the only difference of the two string inputs is the lower case and upper case at the start but then the output is unique and differ a lot form the other. It should also be noted that the hash of a string is not impossible to crack. One may always brute force all possibility and may end up with the same hash thereby finding input. But this is very inefficient, time-consuming and cannot yield many benefits. Since resource for computation is very high and time taken is also painfully high. As an example, a popular hashing algorithm SHA - 256 has a 256-bit output which may have binary values (0 or 1). Thus, making it have 2^{256} outputs.

Figure 2.
2^{256} = 115792089237316195423570985008687907853269984665640564039457584007913129639936

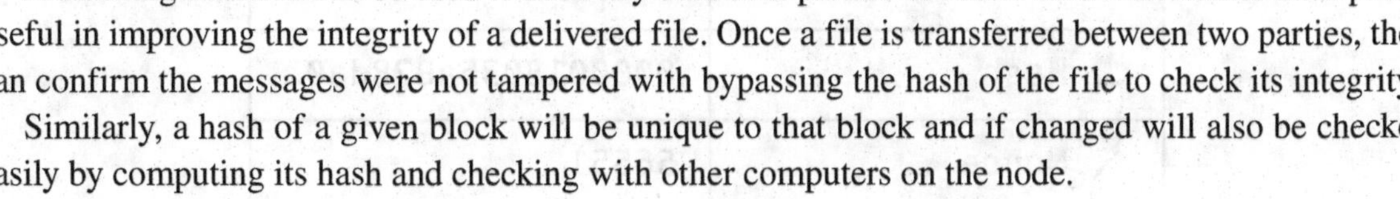

Message	this is a hash text for test
Hash	4b8f89a381611387b493fd816686774ef90d74fa685b3ecd3b2aeb21c094936a

This number is exponentially big. So brute forcing this is not a very likely option.

A Hashing function can be used to hash any data be it picture or file or text. This makes hash pretty useful in improving the integrity of a delivered file. Once a file is transferred between two parties, they can confirm the messages were not tampered with bypassing the hash of the file to check its integrity.

Similarly, a hash of a given block will be unique to that block and if changed will also be checked easily by computing its hash and checking with other computers on the node.

CONTENTS OF A BLOCK IN BLOCKCHAIN

Index: Position of the block in the blockchain. Index of genesis block (or starting block) is 0.

Timestamp: The exact time when that particular block was created.

Hash: A hash value of that block in the blockchain.

Previous Hash: Hash value of the previous block in the chain. Through this mechanism, we can link all the blocks of a blockchain. For genesis block, this value is 0.

Data: Data stored on the node. For example, transactions.

Nonce: It is a number used to determine a valid hash. To generate this number, the processing power or resources are used.

A valid hash is a term used to state a particular format of hash that is considered to be correct for a given blockchain. An example of having a hash with 5 zero's at the start is considered valid. Then, it might not be possible to have such a hash with the given/existing data input. This does not mean it is impossible to get one. Enter nonce, a random number generated and added with the data of a block to generate a hash. By changing the nonce value we can end up with a particular value for the nonce that produces a valid hash (it has 5 zero is start according to example).

This process requires a lot of computation power and this adds latency in addition of a new block to the chain.

A key point here is to see that having a timestamp as an entry in the block makes it very unlikely that someone else can have even a minor possibility to produce the same hash. Since one can produce that particular hash only if all data, previous block hash and timestamp match. It is very unlikely this is possible since one cannot go back in time to get the same timestamp. An example of the same is shown in figure below.

Figure 3. Genesis block (Han, 2017)

🏆 Genesis Block	
⏮ Previous Hash	0
📅 Timestamp	Thu, 27 Jul 2017 02:30:00 GMT
Data	Welcome to Blockchain CLI!
🔥 Hash	0000018035a828da0…
⚔ Nonce	56551

Merkle Tree: Merkle tree takes a large amount of data and makes it more manageable for processing.

Figure 4. Merkle Tree (Asolo, 2018)

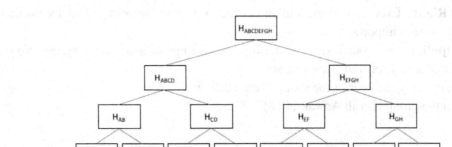

A transaction in the blockchain is represented a T_A. The hash value for the same is represented as H_A. After each transaction has been hashed individually, the corresponding hash values are combined and hashed to produce H_{AB}. If there are odd number of hash values then the odd hash element is simply hashed with itself to obtain a new hash. Example if 5th hash value is H_E then it is hashed with itself to obtain H_{EE}.

This process is repeated to obtain the last hash value also known as a Merkle Root. Here the merkle root is $H_{ABCDEFGH}$.

Advantages of Merkle Tree Structure

- **Tamper Proof**: Organising transaction into a merkle root makes it easy to check if a transaction has been tampered with. If a transaction has been changed then its corresponding hash will also change leading to a completely different merkle root.
- **Uses Less Resources**: Organising transactions into a merkle tree uses fewer resources when compared to having to add each individual transaction hash into the block header.
- **Verification**: A merkle tree allows one to check if a transaction has been added to a block without having to download the entire blockchain (Asolo, 2018).

CONSENSUS ALGORITHM

A consensus algorithm is the root of a blockchain. It helps facilitates decision making based on the algorithm applied. It is used to arrive at a decision that helps ease the majority of the participants of the chain.

Consensus algorithms do not merely agree with the majority votes, but it also agrees to one that benefits all of them. So, it's always a win for the network.

Blockchain consensus models are methods to create equality and fairness in the online world. The consensus systems used for this agreement is called a consensus theorem.

These consensus models consist of some particular objectives, such as:

Coming to an agreement: The mechanism collects all the agreements from the group as much as it can.

- ○ **Collaboration**: Every one of the group aims toward a better agreement that results in the group's interests as a whole.
- ○ **Co-Operation**: Every individual will work as a team and put their own interests aside.
- ○ **Equal Rights**: Every single participant has the same value in voting. This means that every person's vote is important.
- ○ **Participation**: Everyone inside the network needs to participate in the voting. No one will be left out or can stay out without a vote.
- ○ **Activity**: Every member of the group is equally active. There is no one with more responsibility in the group (Hasib Anwar, 2018).

Figure 5. Different types of consensus algorithms (Anwar, 2018)

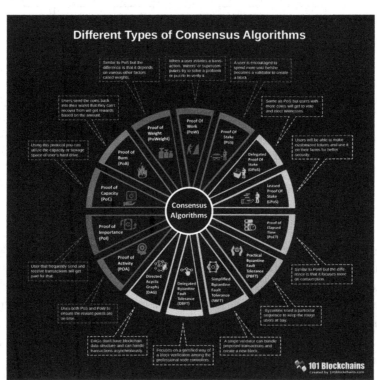

The major algorithms are:

Proof of Work

It is used in the Bitcoin network and the first algorithm to be used in a blockchain. The duty to add a block to a blockchain falls on to people called miners and the procedure they use is termed as mining. This technology works to solve complex mathematical problems.

In this method, the amount of work done by a miner decides that miner's possibility of mining a single block and the reward for mining (receiving an equivalent value of winning done in terms of the coin of the network).

What Are the Main Issues With Proof of Work Consensus Algorithm?

The majority of the Consensus algorithms have drawbacks and Proof of work is no different. The main drawbacks of the system are:

Greater Energy Consumption

Blockchain network contains huge number of microchips that hashes constantly. This process requires a lot of energy. Bitcoin currently offers 20 billion hashes per second. This procedure enables the network to add a layer of protection from a botnet attack.

The security level of the blockchain network based on proof of work requires a lot of energy, and it is intensive. The greater consumption is becoming a problem in a world where we are running out of energy. This incurs a large sum of cost due to electricity consumption.

Centralization of Miners

With the energy resource constraints, proof of work will move toward cheaper electricity solutions. However, the primary problem would be if a bitcoin miner-manufacturer rises. Within a certain time, the manufacturer can become more power hungry and try to create new rules in the mining system.

This situation will lead towards centralization within the decentralized network. That's why it's another great problem these Blockchain algorithms are facing.

The 51% Percent Attack

This attack would mean a possible control of majority of the users and taking over most of the mining power. In this scenario, the attackers will get enough power to control everything in the network.

They can stop other people from generating new blocks. Attackers can also receive rewards based on their tactics.

Less reward as chain increases in size:

This means as the chain grows it reaches a point where more resources are used mine a block than the reward obtained. Hence a loss.

Proof of Stake

Proof of stake is a blockchain algorithm that deals with the major drawbacks of the proof of work algorithm. In this, every block gets validated before the network adds another block to the blockchain. The difference is, the miners can join the mining process using their coins to stake.

The proof of stake is a new type of concept where every individual can mine or validate new blocks only based on their own coin possession. So, in this scenario the more coins one has, the better the chances are.

Although the process is entirely random, still not every miner can participate in the staking. All the miners of the network are randomly chosen. A specific amount of coins must be stored in a wallet, to be qualified to enter the staking process. New blocks will get created proportional to the number of coins based on the wallet. For example, if A owns 10% of all the coins, then A gets to mine 10% of the new blocks.

There are lot of blockchain technologies that use a variety of proof of stake consensus algorithm. However, all of the algorithms work the same for mining new blocks. Every miner will receive a block reward as well as a share of the transaction fees.

The mining capability of a miner is determined by the number of coins staked. The proof of stake community is majorly decentralized and the 51% attack is very expensive to pull off.

Proof of stake consensus algorithm blockchain is very energy efficient when compared to proof of work.

The main drawback of the system is that full decentralization is not possible ever. This is because, only a handful of nodes get to participate in the staking on the network and individuals with the most coins will eventually control most of the system.

How Much Would be the Cost Incurred for Adding a Block to the Blockchain?

One of key factors in the cost of adding a block to the blockchain is the amount of data stored in that particular block. For a block in a blockchain, the typical amount of data one can store is roughly capped at 1 MB (taking bitcoin as an example).

Why Is Storing Data on Blockchain Not Viable?

Because the amount of data one stores has to be stored by every node on the network. Everyone who is a part of the blockchain will have a copy of the data. This is why even storing KB can cost a lot.

When storing data on the blockchain, one has to pay for the base price for the transaction itself, plus an amount per byte of data stored. If smart contracts are involved, payment for the execution time of the smart contract is also added.

Every operation on a blockchain whether it is adding a block or checking an entry or finding a block, requires payment in the form of that particular coin base used in that blockchain.

Hence, storing a large amount of data would mean incurring a large sum of payment for processing it, which makes storing of data on blockchain not feasible. (CanYa, 2018).

What Is the Alternative for Storing a File on Blockchain If It Is Not Possible Directly?

Enter IPFS: [Interplanetary File System]

IPFS or Interplanetary File System, developed by the Protocol Labs is a peer-to-peer protocol where every node stores a group of hashed files. A client who wants to retrieve any of file enjoys access to an abstraction layer, where it simply needs to call the hash of the file it wants. IPFS then combs through the nodes and supplies the client with the file.

It's a decentralized way of storing and referring to files but gives more control and refers to a file by its hash (Coral Health, 2018).

If one wants to upload a file to IPFS, it is enough to put the file in the working directory and tell IPFS to add the file, which generates a hash of that file (starts with Qm for IPFS hashes). This file is then available on the IPFS network.

Now when this file has to be accessed by someone else, the hash of that file is enough for the other party to call the original file from IPFS and get a copy of the file.

There is an obvious security challenge here. As long as anyone has the hash of the file, they can retrieve it from IPFS. So sensitive files are not well suited for IPFS in their native states.

To overcome this challenge one must secure the file before uploading to IPFS. Asymmetric encryption allows us to encrypt a file with the public key of the intended recipient so that only they can decrypt it when they retrieve it with IPFS. A malicious party who retrieves the file from IPFS can't do anything with it since they can't decrypt it.

Figure 6. Asymmetric encryption (Information Commissioner's Office, n.d.)

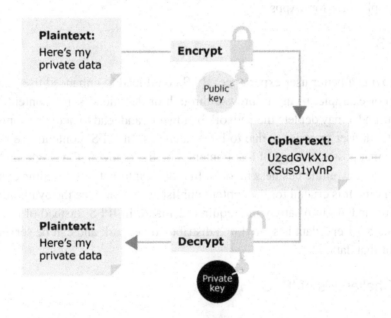

So the process changes such that before the file is uploaded to IPFS it is encrypted with the other party's public key and the encrypted file is sent to IPFS. This hash is then shared to the other party who then downloads the encrypted file and can decrypt the file using their private key to gain access to the file. A malicious party cannot decrypt the file because they lack the private key to it.

This is the reason why IPFS is powerful when coupled with blockchain. Instead of simple text, one just needs to store the hash of the IPFS file. Thus, achieving the simplicity of data that's required on the blockchain but gets to enjoy the file storage and decentralized peer-to-peer properties of IPFS.

Storing files securely on a distributed network. What does that actually mean?

It means that one can then reimagine the way one can think about how the internet itself works. For example:

- There's going to be no servers hosting websites. All the content will be served from IPFS and data pulled from the blockchain directly.
- One won't have to sign up for accounts. One's private key will grant permission and validate the identity of users to the websites/providers.
- Direct communication with another party without anyone middle man. Truly secure and private communication based applications are possible.

IPFS allows for distributed storage of data which is immune to altering and forgery. Data stored on the IPFS network cannot be altered without changing the data identifier (Hash of that file). This means non-critical data can be stored to IPFS while storing the identifier on the blockchain.

IPFS is an optimal storage platform for Decentralized applications (dApps) which are a class of applications that leverage decentralization to achieve exceptional benefits. This decentralization helps in eliminating or reducing any trading fee. Such dApps require the storage of a significant amount of data. IPFS allows this data to be stored in a distributed manner. For these reasons, IPFS is turning into a preferred storage platform for dApps.

Benefits of IPFS

- IPFS can provide a better user experience: IPFS could lead to enhanced user experience in multiple cases. For example, trying to browse through or download some content using the typical client-server model may deplete the network bandwidth and lead to network congestion. This may result in difficult user experience due to large latencies. In IPFS, contents are rendered from the closest peers that possess a copy of that content thereby removing the single-node pressure.
- IPFS allows for new online business models: In today's internet, every online content is hosted on dedicated servers. It is crucial for the content publisher to guarantee the availability of the content and adequate bandwidth to satisfy the required demand. In IPFS, instead of having a single host server serving all users, data is shared in a distributed network and can be served by any node in possession of that data.

What Are the Challenges of IPFS

IPFS is a new technology undergoing development. Yet, there are several challenges that need to be resolved in order to achieve greater usage.

- **Bandwidth Requirements**: Running an IPFS node currently takes significant bandwidth that may not be feasible for many users. Excessive bandwidth usage may harm the adoption of IPFS. One solution to this problem may be, financial incentives. Gaining rewards for hosting content on IPFS can help overcome the costs of running the nodes and encourage usage of IPFS.
- **Availability**: The current implementation of IPFS cannot guarantee data availability upon request due to lack of IPFS nodes. One way to ensure availability is through content pinning which means constantly saving copies of the published content on the node. This node is required to be online every time to ensure availability of the file.

- **Private Content**: Content published to IPFS is public by design. Anyone in possession of the content hash can access the file. Currently, IPFS does not provide a built-in solution for storage of private data. Encryption can be used to store private data on IPFS. Another solution might be to deploy a private network (zk Capital, 2018).

CASE STUDY

E- File Sharing Using Blockchain on Ethereum DAPP and IPFS for Personal or Private Data

In this concept, the user may upload a file to IPFS and have it encrypted so that once downloaded by the recipient, only the decryption key (Asymmetric key) can help view the original contents. It is of importance to understand that this may be extended to important business files so that one server or hard disk does not contain all the required personal data and that it actually chunked and decentralized among many peers who can gain access only if authorised. Storing the hash of the file in a blockchain can help in reducing the trust issues of the file handling since IPFS makes use of hashing function thereby providing a different hash value for a different file. This helps easily track malicious changes done to file by an intruder.

The main reason as to why blockchain is of prime importance is because it makes the issue of trusting a third party unnecessary. This means all users have access to the public data ledger (blockchain) and that any changes done to a block is reflected to every block on the chain. Thus making a decentralized block-chain storage a viable option with no single point of failure and hence one will not lose any private data.

REFERENCES

Anwar. (2018). *Consensus Algorithms: The Root Of The Blockchain Technology*. Retrieved from https://101blockchains.com/consensus-algorithms-blockchain/

Asolo. (2018). *Merkle Tree & Merkle Root Explained*. Retrieved from https://www.mycryptopedia.com/merkle-tree-merkle-root-explained/

Coral Health. (2018). *Learn to securely share files on the blockchain with IPFS*. Retrieved from https://medium.com/@mycoralhealth/learn-to-securely-share-files-on-the-blockchain-with-ipfs-219ee47df54c

Hales. (2019). *What is Blockchain Technology? A Beginner's Guide*. Retrieved from https://www.uplarn.com/what-is-blockchain-technology-a-beginners-guide/

Han, S. (2017). *How does blockchain really work? I built an app to show you*. Retrieved from https://medium.freecodecamp.org/how-does-blockchain-really-work-i-built-an-app-to-show-you-6b70cd4caf7d

Information Commissioner's Office. (n.d.). *What Types of Encryption Are There?* Retrieved from https://ico.org.uk/for-organisations/guide-to-data-protection/guide-to-the-general-data-protection-regulation-gdpr/encryption/what-types-of-encryption-are-there/

Rosic. (2016). *What is Blockchain Technology? A Step-by-Step Guide For Beginners.* Retrieved from https://blockgeeks.com/guides/what-is-blockchain-technology/

Ya. (2018). *Why IPFS is the Future of Decentralised File Storage.* Retrieved from https://medium.com/canyacoin/why-ipfs-is-the-future-of-decentralised-file-storage-8958f3bd02c5

zk Capital. (2018). *IPFS: A Complete Analysis of The Distributed Web.* Retrieved from https://medium.com/zkcapital/ipfs-the-distributed-web-e21a5496d32d

This research was previously published in Transforming Businesses With Bitcoin Mining and Blockchain Applications; pages 207-220, copyright year 2020 by Business Science Reference (an imprint of IGI Global).

Chapter 64

Blockchain and IoT Integration in Dairy Production to Survive the COVID-19 Situation in Sri Lanka

ruwandi Madhunamali
Sabaragamuwa University of Sri Lanka, Sri Lanka

K. P. N. Jayasena
Sbaragamuwa University of Sri Lanka, Sri Lanka

ABSTRACT

The epidemic crises place massive burdens on our economies. The risk of food supplies is also pushing massive stress on food vendors around the world. There are big problems associated with supply chains framework. Farmers do not receive payment upon delivery of their supplies. The buyers do not have access to finance that will enable them to pay farmers on time. To solve this problem, the authors proposed a dairy production system integration with blockchain and IoT. Blockchain is a decentralized digital ledger technology that allows network participants to trust each other and interact. The dairy product system can check the temperature of the product in real-time by using the website application. Moreover, customers can get notifications when the policy found problems related to temperature values. The blockchain database confirms the information security of the system by using the proof of work algorithm to create the transactions and the blocks. Therefore, the proposed methods can use sensitive data with reasonable time consumption, and no block creation fees are needed.

DOI: 10.4018/978-1-6684-7132-6.ch064

INTRODUCTION

Every day we consume food products on the basis of the confidence because that providers are produced, warehouse and transported in agreement with the internal and government regulations on food safety. Before reaching the end consumer, food product moving through different phases of supply chain from suppliers to retailers. These intermittent stages contribute to product design, manufacture, delivery, and sales. Although food safety measurements do periodic and provide certifications of the quality, it is often difficult to trust when searching a supply chain scaling across countries with the distribution of technology. For example, The United States stopped imports of meat from Brazil due to the acceptance of bribes by food examiners in Brazil, the horsemeat scandal in Europe, the milk powder of babies' scandal in China and the growing problem of food pollution in India. Over the past decade, these incidents have occurred periodically, pushing consumers and governments to request greater transparency throughout the food supply chain(Bosona & Gebresenbet, 2013)(Aung & Chang, 2014).

Based on Food and Drink research, organizations decide, increasing consideration of the food provenance as a business challenge. They are finding business opportunities through increasing health awareness. Nowadays consumers highly consider the quality of food product so they hesitate to purchase. It is because there is no way to ensure the quality of the food product and less transparency through the supply chain process of the product. So the organizations are identified that customers are always looking for trusted products with verified sources. For that, they are plan to get a competitive advantage by providing service with transparent food supply chain and sustainable manufacturing. For example, Walmart has joined with IBM to study. They were together from February 2018 to test whether the organization can guarantee the Health of food products that they sell in their retail stores. Nevertheless, contemporary repositories for each silo stage of the logistic transportation are ineffective in giving unparalleled trust to the client, because they are not dishonest. A lot of food supply chains today only check their product end of the logistic transportation processes and still there is no way to map their product in source and stages between customers.

Although the different phases of the food supply chain contain many possible adverse results such as Irreversible disruption to the environment, abuse of working conditions, unethical manufacturing practices, counterfeiting and large quantities of agricultural waste attributable to imbalanced sourcing and storage strategies. End users tend to use these programs without realizing the repercussions that they create by their footprint and food supply chains are easily kept hidden with little effort to provide end-to-end access to their stakeholders. Although these challenges, the idea of requiring a single agency to provide data and transaction control in food supply chain was the only realistic solution until recently when a modern system called blockchain provided a whole modern way of addressing food provenance.

BACKGROUND

Supply Chain

Throughout the years, global supply chains are getting increasingly complicated. Therefore, it is very difficult to manage continuously within the industry as sustainable, because the problems many foreign buyers (including large retailers and brand owners) and consumers are concerned about, where monitoring and analysis of their transportation supply networks relies on many suppliers, distributors and delivery centers, some of them uncommon or even one-time. (Venkatesh, Kang, Wang, Zhong, & Zhang, 2020a)(Petri Helo & Shamsuzzoha, 2020). Supply chains are not fixed. It develops and changes in size, shape, and configuration, and in how they are coordinated, controlled and managed. Not only the economic drivers but also the technological drivers affect the changes in the supply chain. As a result of that, digital technology integrates with supply chain management. The new step introduces as "Supply Chain Digitization". Digitization may play a leverage role in aligning current sourcing strategies as well as developing new sourcing strategies to enhance long-term efficiency, productivity, and competitive advantage overall organizational objectives.

In a dairy supply chain, a network of stakeholders transacts to the end consumer in the form of rising, storing or selling foods. Transport companies act as links which connect these stages and ensure that the right quantity and quality product reaches the right destination at the right time

The stakeholders include:

1. Milk suppliers.
2. The milk processors engaged in the manufacture and sometimes distribution of the milk commodity
3. The distributer active in the sale to end consumers and dealers of the finished product.
4. The end customers engaged in shopping the items, which consists of individuals and markets.

Blockchain

Considered one of the most innovative innovations available, the blockchain first showed up in 2008 when published "Bitcoin: A Peer-to-Peer Electronic Cash System". The scheme suggested was based on cryptographic proof rather than dependency, allowing any two parties to perform transactions without the need of a trustworthy third party. The plan solved the issue of double spending(Kosba, Miller, Shi, Wen, & Papamanthou, 2016)(Wright & De Filippi, 2015). This is the first application of blockchain, Created by Satoshi Nakamoto (Nakamoto, 2008). There are many critical features, that blockchain provides. Such as Decentralized, Traceability, Consensus mechanism, Immutability, Smart contract(Yumna, Murad, Ikram, & Noreen, n.d.)(Madumidha, Ranjani, Varsinee, & Sundari, 2019). Blockchain application contain distributed architecture. That mean of distributed architecture is the program does not rely on any centralized authority but uses a peer-to - peer application server network operated by the owners of decentralized interests (P. Helo & Hao, 2019)(Tezel, Papadonikolaki, Yitmen, & Hilletofth, 2019). Today blockchain is applications further than finance, as in government, health, science, arts and culture(Frizzo-barker et al., 2019)(Pilkington, 2016). A number of applications are already being discussed in the energy market, such as a blockchain based smart grid (Scully & Hobig, 2019). Within that network, Blockchain technology enforces transparency and ensures ultimate, system-wide agreement on the validity of a full transaction history. No major group controls the data in the Blockchain. Any party can see the entire data infrastructure. So that it helps to minimize the bias errors.(Treiblmaier, 2018) Every atutharized person in blockchain can confirm the detail of its transaction followers directly, without a Mediator or ledger unauthorized access or manipulation. Though many are speculating about the effect of blockchain technology on supply chains, the present accepting of its potential remains limited. As this technology is still in its infancy, developing and diffusing (Wang et al., 2018).

Every node inside a blockchain have encrypted keys named public and private key, and each transaction within two nodes contains some important facts about the sender and the receiver, asset information, date, and identifier for the sender 's previous transaction. An asset may be any commodity within a supply chain, or a buyer-seller exchange. A cryptographic hash function named SHA 256 (Secure Hash Algorithm 256) uses the sender's public key and transactional information to produce a 16-digit hexadecimal string called the "tag". The hash done is special to a combination of a public key and transaction information. A group of randomly clustered transactions is one block. This authenticated transaction details is decoded to verify the validity of the transactions and their origin, which can be deciphered only by brute force. The cycle of hash resolution is called mining, and miners are called nodes that validate certain transactions. When the network generates a block from the pool of unchecked transactions, available miners will be competing to validate the transactions by resolving the cryptographic hash

A consensus algorithm maintain the method of choosing a miner at a blockchain. Some network systems such as the Ethereum and Hyperledger projects are special. Every block within a blockchain contain of 3 important components - a hash (a unique digital identifier), a timestamp, and the hash of the previous block (to compute the account balance). The previous block hash ties the whole block chain together and thus stops any block being changed or added between two authenticated chains. When a transaction is checked, the blockchain records it. Changing a reported transaction value in a decentralized blockchain network such as Bitcoin is quite difficult because an intruder must obtain nearly 51 percent of the entire computing power existing in the framework. Therefore, each subsequent block enhances the verification of the preceding block and ultimately blockchain as a whole. This mechanism holds the blockchain resistant to malicious activities, contributing to the essential immutability attribute. Figure 1 shows blockchain structure.

In Ethereum, the blockchain system is controlled by rules decided upon by the participants in the network in the method of smart contracts and was firstly implemented in Bitcoin for running the mutual accounting ledger. It is commonly used after this initial financial use, when many players with little to no confidence are part of a transaction; for example, fragmented supply chains. Blockchain's three basic features make it an attractive choice for tracking supply chain assets

Figure 1. Blockchain structure

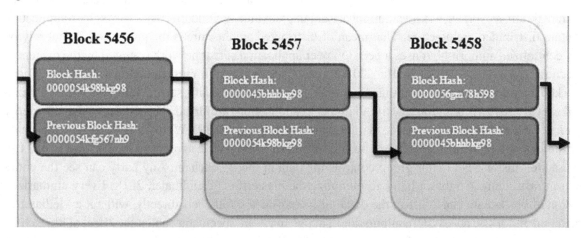

- **Distributed processing:** Does not require a central control system. The process is distributed to all processors or network members inserted in the process.
- **Synchronized records:** The ledger is circulated to all players and so it is fraud-proof.

- **Smart information:** We can build cloud applications that run within the blockchain architecture, allowing us to customize the data format that is available in the supply chain at every point.

Smart contracts

A smart contract is a program that is developed by programmer. Smart contract can activate certain functions robotically if anything predetermined happens. Intelligent contract contacts with the blockchain, the criteria are stored in "contracts" and must be met by the users in order to build a new block. The smart contract is not an integral part of the blockchain protocol itself, but a function on the network that is stored on a database within blockchain in a completely distributed way (Mattila, Seppälä, & Holmström, 2016).

Blockchain Technology in Supply Chain

Blockchains are already generating advantages on supply chains around the world. Real-time visibility can be considered an important benefit to supply chain management (Sheel & Nath, 2019). Furthermore, all transactions can be observable, and consequently. The data is organized into blocks which form a chain. All the transaction of a blockchain operate in a peer-to-peer network, in a decentralized way. Smart contracts inside distributed ledger are responsible for the validate and store transaction data, and it is not needed to have a central person that validates the transactions(Petri Helo & Shamsuzzoha, 2020). Almost all organizations need to take profit of several improvements carried about by blockchain, which spans improved process and operations over the whole supply chain, safer, efficient transactions with transparent and (Kshetri, 2018) and trust and reliability through the network, all processes and captured details being shared by all network members.

Blockchain and Internet of Things(IOT) Combination

With the implementation of Blockchain and IoT technologies combined, the supply chain problems addressed so far can be solved or minimized. Blockchain and IoT merge the physical world details directly into the computing environment and store it in a distributed ledger in a multi partner situation thereby bridging the confidence gap. Whilst various IoT sensor systems can be combined. It system ensures open and auditable traceability of properties by automatically extracting and processing important information from the IoT systems along the entire supply chain and maintaining these data directly in its underlying ledger.

Related Studies

The last couple of years also seen an eruption in research and development activities surrounding blockchain technology. Most of the research are done within the financial technology market. In fact, its intrinsic capacity to deliver immutable and manipulative records, together with its potential of enabling trust and reliability among untrusted peers represents too attractive features, preventing this technology to stay relegated into a single vertical sector. With the population of blockchain characteristics, several industries start researching this. Blockchain technology has already been identified as a driver for a paradigm shift in the financial sector.

Figure 2. Publication year of the selected primary papers

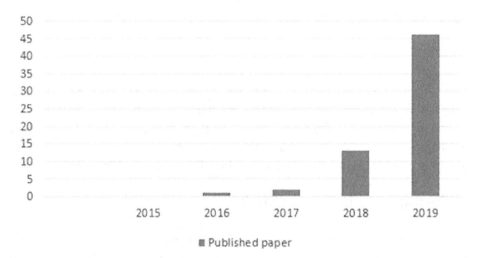

Figure 2 Noteworthy, after the year 2015 all selected papers were published. It indicates that selected area to do the research is both new and original. Through all the papers selected, 1 paper (1.61%) has been published in 2016, 2 papers (3.22%) in 2017, 13 papers (20.96%) in 2018 and 46 papers (74.19%) in 2019 when zooming into the distribution year. Which represents increase in blockchain interest.

Blockchain technology is still in its infancy of marketing and while there are many industry experts who agree that there is a promising future for the deployment of this technology through industry, many others claim that there is an unrealistic assumption of blockchains that could, in turn, intensify the impact of the inability to implement blockchains in industry. However, while many unsuccessful attempts have been made to use blockchain technology, several successful business cases, such as those listed in this article, have also occurred. The latter provides a rather optimistic view that as more progress is made in overcoming the limits of blockchains, like many other emerging technologies, blockchains can find a position in operation and become popular.

Papers on blockchain, supply chain and blockchain integrated with supply chain management were read and the following results were obtained including the gaps in current studies, requirements in blockchain technology within supply chain management.

Table 1 represent what are the existing research topic and application area of them on supply chain on blockchain

For several specific supply chain scenarios, there are various deployed and conceptual systems, among them the food supply chain has become the hottest topic. The issues relating to food origin and safety are important problems that need to be addressed. There are some ongoing food supply chain projects or food traceability projects. More challenging applications are involving wine and agricultural foods. Pharma and drug industry, Blockchain also helps the electronics industry, since healthcare is also a major social problem.

Table 1. Existing research topics on Blockchain technology with supply chain

Research topic	Applied areas	Research Paper	Key finding
Transparency and Traceability: In Food Supply Chain System using Blockchain Technology with Internet of Things	Food industry	(Madumidha et al., 2019)	An effective system incorporating RFID and Blockchain technology is a technical mechanism for monitoring and locating products
A Blockchain-based decentralized system to ensure the transparency of organic food supply chain	Food industry	(Basnayake & Rajapakse, 2019)	Preparing an efficient and fair food certification architecture
The Rise of Blockchain Technology in Agriculture and Food Supply Chains	Food industry	(Kamilaris, Fonts, & Prenafeta-Boldú, 2019)	Applying blockchain technology to build reliable and secure farm and food supply chains
Framework Design of Financial Service Platform for Tobacco Supply Chain Based on Blockchain	Financial	(Liu, Li, & Cao, 2018)	Build system design for a tobacco supply chain financial service platform based on blockchain
Blockchain-Based Secured Traceability System for Textile and Clothing Supply Chain	Textile and clothing	(Agrawal, Sharma, & Kumar, n.d.)	Blockchain based Secure Traceability System with Textile and Clothing Supply Chain Implementation
Blockchain Framework for Textile Supply Chain Management	Textile	(Elmessiry & Elmessiry, 2018)	A full blockchain-based clothing quality assurance platform that allows cross-chain facts sharing with assured validity and precision in almost real time, allowing for the detection of product faulty lots in all networks as soon as they are identified in a few.
A Blockchain-Based Supply Chain Quality Management Framework	Global supply chains	(Chen et al., 2017)	Using blockchain technology to solve problems caused by lack of trust in the quality management of the supply chain and to achieve sophisticated product quality management
Blockchain in Supply Chain Trading	Global supply chains	(Al Barghuthi, Mohamed, & Said, 2019)	A well-functioning system of supply using a blockchain
Blockchain-based Soybean Traceability in Agricultural Supply Chain	Agriculture	(Salah, Nizamuddin, Jayaraman, & Omar, 2019)	Blockchain and Ethereum smart contracts will map and monitor effectively and make it possible to incorporate busy transactions and workflows in the agricultural supply chain without presence
Blockchains everywhere - a use-case of blockchains in the pharma supply-chain	Pharmaceutical industry	(Bocek, Rodrigues, Strasser, & Stiller, 2017)	Blockchain lets pharmaceutical supply chain to observer temperature and humanity over the distribution of medical products
How the Blockchain Revolution Will Reshape the Consumer Electronics Industry	Electronics industry	(Madhunamali, 2017)	Blockchain can improve efficiency and alignment of processes in consumer electronics supply chain management. Areas in which block chains can impact supply chains include a temper-proof history of product manufacture, handling and maintenance, digital ownership and packaging identification, smart contract sand interaction with customers in the supply chain
Can Blockchain Strengthen the Internet of Things?	Manufacturing/ physical distribution	(It, 2017)	Blockchain can play an important role in tracking sources of insecurity in supply chains and in managing crisis situations such as product recalls that arise after vulnerabilities in safety and security are identified

The Importance of Blockchain Within any Supply Chain Industry

Supply chain management is a term that interaction together for controlling a distribution channel 's total process (Petri Helo & Szekely, 2005). Manage the supply chain is difficult as it involves dispersed practices from upstream, interacting with individuals, physical resources and manufacturing processes to downstream, covering the entire process of marketing; i.e. contracts, sales to customers, distribution and disposal (Tian, 2016). Aim of the supply chain is to create a multi stakeholder collaborative background through mutual trust, for eliminate communication problems, and ensure that the various companies are connected to pursue routinely the integration of the whole supply network. In the end, linked supply chain stakeholders will increase overall performance and add larger value and benefits to their business (Azzi, Chamoun, & Sokhn, 2019).

Blockchain can solve supply chain problems and even lead to numerous critical objectives of the supply chain management, such as cost, quality, speed, dependability, risk reduction, sustainability and flexibility (Kshetri, 2018)(Basnayake & Rajapakse, 2019)(Al Barghuthi et al., 2019)(Tönnissen & Teuteberg, 2019). Therefore, among the many other operations that are likely to be changed by blockchain the supply chain needs special consideration. Identified profits of applying blockchain in supply chain management are: Improve overall quality, Reduce cost, Shorten delivery time, Reduce risk, and Increase trust. In the following describe problems that address by blockchain in the supply chain.

1. **Differential Pricing:** Companies prefer keeping their pricings a secret, since this allows them to pay lower prices when outsourcing to developing countries.
2. **Numerous Parties Involved:** Mediating between so many parties can be a big problem for logistics-providers, slowing down the delivery of services and creating a large overhead for logistics. Furthermore, a centralized mediator of these parties can misuse power to prefer some parties over others.
3. **Quality & Compliance issues:** Procuring a replacement for defective parts is a long drawn and uncomfortable process.
4. **Inevitable Disruptions:** LEAN "on-demand" manufacturing falls flat in a situation where natural disasters and socio-economic problems are common. For example, Japan (frequently affected by earthquakes) has outsourced most of it's supply chain logistics to other countries.
5. **Centralization:** A central mediator for parties is required, which centralizes power in the hands of a few and is a gateway to misuse of resources.
6. **Fraud by Middlemen:** As number of interacting parties increase, there is a proportional increase in middlemen. They lead to fraud and slow down the supply without adding anything to the network.
7. **Tracking history of any product:** Validating identity vendor and checking for tampering by middlemen is not possible.

Blockchain Characteristic for Supply Chain

1. **Quality assurance:** In the perspective of investigation & guidance to adopt required steps for the flawless high-quality production of goods & services, quality assurance makes a remarkable impact to make the business processes easier. (Yadav & Singh, 2019).

Table 2. How to resolve them by applying blockchain

Problems	Solution
Differential Pricing	Permissioned ledger for confidential transactions between parties
Numerous Parties Involved	Consensus between multiple parties is maintained through Smart contracts
Quality & Compliance issues	Smart contract stores money while all solutions are checked and tested
Inevitable disruptions	Digital ledger is free of geographical constraints like natural disasters, socio-economic issues
Procuring replacements for defective pieces	Smart contract only lets out payments once both parties satisfied
Centralization	Risk of fraud is mitigated by using decentralized nodes for checking delivery status
Fraud by Middlemen	Because of using doubly-signed smart contracts, no financial fraud by middlemen can occur in the system
Tracking history of any product	Using network anyone can verify vendor identity and validity of product

2. **Scalability in Supply chain management:** When facts noted in a block of the block chain, this characteristic ensures that it is non-variable & non-volatile. This leads to integrate blockchain without a risk of losing the data consistency.(Tönnissen & Teuteberg, 2019)(Madavi, 2008).
3. **Transparency:** Ensure peer to peer transactions are certified by minor at the end and make sure that the modified data not allow to changed or hacked. Also the assets of changing anything in the ledger stays on it makes the blockchain a transparent system. (Yumna et al., n.d.)(Pe & Llivisaca, n.d.)(Wu et al., 2019)(Casino, Dasaklis, & Patsakis, 2019)
4. **Integrity:** Provides management for the flow of physical goods in supply chain using integration of serial numbers, bar codes, sensors, digital tags like RFID, etc. Following this the flow of blockchain became smoother from manufacturer to end-user.(Yadav & Singh, 2019)(Litke, Anagnostopoulos, & Varvarigou, 2019)
5. **Solving the double spend problem:** Solves the issue of data transaction which cannot be sent to two or more people at the same time. With the help of authenticated peer to peer transaction after the verification by a minor. (Yadav & Singh, 2019)(Bartling & Fecher, 2016)
6. **Immutability and encryption**: After confirming the transaction or data flow from one center to another, changes are not allowed since any change on the block chain cannot be stored without the solidarity of the network (Yumna et al., n.d.)(Schmidt & Wagner, 2019)(Wu et al., 2019).
7. **Efficiency:** The high rate of data flow speed without an intermediator, smart contracts easily traceable and further, it streamlines the process considerably saving time and money. (Pe & Llivisaca, n.d.)(Ahram, Sargolzaei, Sargolzaei, Daniels, & Amaba, 2017).
8. **Security:** Once the creation of block is completed changes or deletion is not applicable. This feature makes the safety of Supply Chain more refine after the adoption of blockchain in the existing traditional methods. (Pe & Llivisaca, n.d.)(Tönnissen & Teuteberg, 2019)(Casino et al., 2019)
9. **Removal of intermediaries:** Blockchain create the platform for a straight business deal eliminating the involvement of intermediaries or a third party(Yadav & Singh, 2019)(Weber et al., 2016)
10. **Reduction in administrative cost:** Reduction in cost of the paper and other consumable items, time-saving, quick discussion, better management, administration & shared databases ease administrative work. (Tönnissen & Teuteberg, 2019)(Osei, Canavari, & Hingley, 2018)

11. **Decentralization:** Blockchain is a system of teaming up gatherings with a database that is decentralized. This implies that most of the gatherings team up on a blockchain have their own duplicate of the considerable number of exchanges that put away on the blockchain.(Yumna et al., n.d.)(Schmidt & Wagner, 2019)(Wu et al., 2019)(Kharlamov, Parry, & Clarke, n.d.)(Lai, 2019)

12. **Traceability and visibility:** Trust-worthy system is imparted by blockchain technology by knowing the origin of a product by offering real-time, live and consistently connected updates(Yumna et al., n.d.)(Kharlamov et al., n.d.)(Venkatesh, Kang, Wang, Zhong, & Zhang, 2020b)(Kamilaris, Fonts, Prenafeta-Boldú, et al., 2019)

The Blockchain based supply chain network focused in reference implementation. This research methodology was chosen in this research because blockchain is still in its infancy. Our goal is to create a model to satisfy the demand for supply chain related operations, while at the same time ensuring that records are safe and transparent across all activities. Nonetheless, it is difficult to transit from modern supply chain to the Blockchain based supply chain as it is not smooth.

Companies must pose the knowledge and capability in blockchain to adopt it. Furthermore, blockchain technology is still in its early stage in terms of industrial application development. It is full of uncertainties such as whether the blockchain is suitable for the required process, whether the practitioners have the working out and required technical development. Moreover, It is important to realize that industrial solutions based on blockchain should start with the willingness of the stakeholders to cooperate and to be involved. They need to reach consensus on building knowledge and capabilities in blockchain with a focus on providing value for all stakeholders. So, creating a culture of collaboration is critical. Scalability is holding back early adoptions of blockchain in supply chains or in other similar areas. By definition, each computer that is connected to the same network will process the transactions. Organizations must compromise productivity to achieve protection. Therefore, in terms of technical infrastructure there is a high demand which will be more expensive than traditional approach.

According to the characteristics of blockchain, stakeholders who use this blockchain based supply chain system will advantage more when the number of joining users grows in this community. When more and more players in the supply chain participate, blockchain becomes more relevant and credible, and develops into market practice. This can be especially difficult as there are legacy processes, regulations and laws that regulate different facets of the company as stakeholders can incur costs as transitioning from legacy systems and combining with new systems and practices. In the future, due to the competitive nature of industry, many companies will be putting effort into the blockchain based logistics network, not just in the private sector but also in public agencies. To ensure interoperability between different blockchain based platforms, it is therefore necessary to establish standards and agreements.

Gaps in Existing Research

If considering the all researches of the study, Most of the identified gaps had to do with outside reasons such as administrative and technical sides.

- The first obstacle is conformity with the laws and the legal barriers restricting Blockchain technology implementation. Common standards for completing transactions are missing (Tribis, El Bouchti, & Bouayad, 2018).

- The second difference is the failure to adapt and acceptance. Mostly society are unaware about how to operates and produce the great difficulty of getting together all parties concerned and convincing supply chain players to change their traditional supply chain to the current blockchain based system(Tribis et al., 2018)(P. Helo & Hao, 2019).
- The third difference relates to scalability and scale. Most of the proposed blockchain-based architectures have been evaluated in a laboratory environment only on a limited scale; including a number of nodes, certain difficulties that occur in scaling blockchains network.
- The latest blockchain implementations are basically small in size. Next gap that identified is Strong computerization demand. Nevertheless, many supply chain participants are not able to adopt blockchain in the developing countries.
- Complexity and uncertainty of the development is the next gap. The delay of transactions that last for several hours until all parties upgrade their ledgers and a smart contract can be access to the public, but the details needed for authentication may or may not be available to everyone.
- Implementation cost of the adaptation is high. For blockchain process, it requires a virtual network and it depends on the electricity, infrastructure and hardware computing systems. These gaps are that most of the frameworks proposed systems were not tested for real world design applications, Researchers should therefore find the viability of blockchain based solutions and test their applicability to industry (Salah et al., 2019).

However, work on t blockchain supply chain management is only in its early stages and should find future applications (Longo, Nicoletti, Padovano, d'Atri, & Forte, 2019)(Yadav & Singh, 2019). Most of the supply chain operations, especially small and medium-sized companies, state they know nothing about blockchain technology, and that they find the influence of blockchain as a menace. To increase understanding of blockchain, a prototype of a blockchain-based logistics monitoring system, frameworks based solution have real performance evaluation in the industrial context(Tribis et al., 2018)(Wamba, 2019).

In Sri Lanka, there is no measurement to measure the readiness to accept blockchain in supply chain management. And also there is less researches have done in this area. This research aims to solve supply chain management challenges with blockchain implementation in the Sri Lankan food supply chain industry. Therefore, for filling some gaps in the literature, this research will be a great support.

MAIN FOCUS OF THE CHAPTER

While the challenges involved in implementing a transparent supply chain are huge, the benefits of applying blockchain to the dairy supply chain far outweigh the disadvantages (initial capital investment cost and maintenance). The advantages of an active blockchain can be narrowly defined as a financial advantage, the benefits of the authorities and the benefits of the food companies. For simplicity's sake, however, the benefits can be classified as enhancing consumer loyalty, improving food crisis management, improving dairy supply chain management, expertise and technical innovation, and contributing to sustainable agriculture. There is an emerging rich network of devices and sensors that build an ecosystem rich in data for efficient monitoring and analysis of properties, which was unlikely in supply chains several years ago. This evolution has now allowed us to use this technology to create a blockchain network that provides as mentioned in this research a lot of possible benefits.

Many of the potential risks and the lack of demonstrable evidence the implementation of blockchain in the supply chain is currently sluggish. Nonetheless, businesses are trying to consider the positives or drawbacks of blockchains in supply chains.

Problem Definition

The emergence of digital businesses transforms conventional market models and, mainly, how we do it. The flow of industry has intensified in a environment today running 24 hours. This has changed the way businesses collaborate, trade and connect with customers, vendors and partners. Suppliers and the supply chain have an effect on everything: from efficiency, distribution and expense, to customer support, loyalty and benefit. Enterprise globalization expanded the difficulty of the supply chain processors. Now it is a main component to improve and integrate the information system. The difficulty of taking decisions needs real-time data sharing (Yu, Wang, Zhong, & Huang, 2016). When information moved in a linear form in conventional supply chains and inefficiencies in one stage influenced the following cascade stages, Digital supply networks are now capable of building interconnected networks capable of overcoming the action-reaction cycle with real-time data and facilitating cooperation. The figure 3 shows the move from the traditional supply chain to the digital supply network (Mussomeli, Gish, & Laaper, 2015).

Figure 3. The evolution of Supply chain

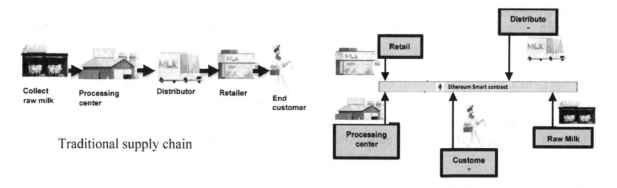

Traditional supply chain

Digital supply chain network

According to this, emphasis on how blockchain affects the supply chain. To have this done, Possible applications and implementation of blockchain are discussed in the supply chain to help businesses understand how to achieve their business goals. Furthermore, A logistics management program based on blockchain is applied to evaluate the viability of applying blockchain in the food supply chain. Accordingly, the major objective of this research is to fill current research gaps, new approaches to integrate blockchain and IoT technology within food supply chain, and food quality management in the Sri Lankan food supply chain system. This study has following objectives also.

- Improve the scalability of any business by increasing customers' experience and more awareness about blockchain.
- Provide Trust for the entire supply chain network through blockchain agreement(consensus)
- Improve the privacy of the supply chain system by facilitating access control over who will have access to the information in the block.
- Reduce costs by ignoring additional payment for third-party persons.
- Make consumers happier than traditional food supply chain system in terms of transparency of the product and price.

Table 3. Current problems and blockchain impact in supply chain system

Supply chain actor	Current Problems	Blockchain impact
Famer/Supplier	Capability to prove the origin and quality metrics of goods using a global and clear process.	Benefits from the improved trust by maintaining track by raw material production and supply chain from the raw material to the end customer.
Processor	Poor ability to track the goods produced to the final destination. Small ability to analyze measured content from raw material.	Value added from shared facts system with suppliers of raw materials and distribution networks.
Distributor	Customized monitoring devices with limited ability to work together. Limited certification skills and confidence issues.	Ability to have proof of position recorded in the database, and conditions certifications.
Wholesaler	Lack of confidence, and certification of the product path.	Capacity to test the origin of the products and the conditions for transformation or transportation.
Retailer	Lack of confidence, and certification of the product path.	Tracking any single commodity between the wholesaler and the final customer. Capacity to manage the returns of malfunctioning goods efficiently.
Consumer	Lack of trust about the product's compliance with the requirements and origin defined for the origin, quality and enforcement of the product.	Complete and clear view of the sources of the product and its entire journey from the raw material to the purchased finished product.

SOLUTIONS AND RECOMMENDATIONS

This segment describes the suggested solution that using blockchain within ethereum network and smart contracts to trace, track, and perform transactions in dairy supply chains. This approach eliminates the need for a trustworthy centralized authority and allows transactions and store the transaction information for food supply chain management. Table 4 describe how blockchain based model address the issues in current dairy supply chain.

The suggested approach would concentrate on the use of autonomously implemented smart contracts on the decentralized blockchain Ethereum network. Functions of the smart contract execution and conduct by thousands of mining nodes. The mining nods are globally distributed, and the execution outcome is agreed by all of the mining nodes.

Additionally, any actor or participant must have an Ethereum account in blockchain and they have to have a unique Ethereum address. This helps to identify the actor in a unique way. The Ethereum account basically consists of the Ethereum address with public and private keys that are used to sign and verify the data integrity within each transaction cryptographically and digitally, and associate each transaction with a specific Ethereum address or account.

Table 4. Problems that address by blockchain in the dairy supply chain

Issues in the existing Supply chain system	The solution is given by proposed mechanism
Lack of trust about the product's compliance with the requirements and origin defined for the origin, quality and enforcement of the product.	Complete and clear view of the sources of the product and its entire journey from the raw material to the purchased finished product.
Require a central party to maintain the dairy supply chain transactions.	facilitate the platform for do the transaction directly without the interference of intermediaries or a third party IoT sensors track the data and smart contract validate them and added to the blockchain.
Have to manually enter the data about dairy transaction.	Reduction in paper and another consumable item, time saving. automatically detect and store the data in to blockchain
In traditional dairy supply chain, manually check temperature, volume and quality of milk. It is time consuming.	Information flow speed, no intermediary, smart contracts, simple traceability and ultimately streamlining the processes considerably

Figure 4 shows how combination of IoT blockchains within the food supply chain. This chart describes the process of tracking information from raw milk, processing details, transport information, quality of manufactured product, etc. That will finally bring value in the customer's hands to the finished product.

This architecture captures information regarding traceability using a range of IoT devices based on the type of event to be recorded. A transaction could be a movement of milk product, processing or store of milk, Distribute. Multiple data recorded from an IoT checkpoint is converted into a transaction and pushed to the Ethereum network. All the transaction data check and validate within the smart contract and then publish to the public ledger. The contract layer monitors every transaction data, to execute the smart contracts when an initial event takes place and it ensures expected data about the raw milk or milk product from the supplier, manufacture and distributor in the supply chain according to terms of trade agreed upon connecting to the blockchain network.

Each entity involved plays a role, relationship, and interactions with the smart contract. Propose model contain only five participating entities. Here describe their role:

Milk Supplier: As per the depiction milk suppliers have access to web applications. Through that application they can view information that they using IoT sensor. IoT will play a key role in the capture and transmission of this information from raw milk to the Blockchain.

Milk Processor: In these premises and storage locations, IoT sensors can significantly improve traceability and support end consumers with information of product storage requirements such as physical density, temperature, volume, etc. The status of several environmental or physical and product related characteristics can help to assess the quality of the finished product before and after manufacture, its freshness and other consuming characteristics. Aberrations can be very dangerous during production and this information isn't available today. This can be made available and evaluated with the IoT network system, which help to determine the root cause causes if anything goes wrong or any complications found through random sample checks.

Distributer: Nowadays consumer can get only few information about transporting these products. Capturing IoT data at the time of travel or factory exit analysis will greatly help close this significant gap. The sensors will capture the physical storage conditions in the trucks / ocean freight warehouse and make it accessible in the blockchain network. Diverse partners can access this information and produce informed product decisions based on smart contracts. Where authenticity and transparency are required, and also this information can be rendered to end customers.

Retailer: The emphasis on product safety and freshness is of vital importance for a retailer. Data are available in blockchain that can be traced and analyzed right from farm to fork. In addition to that, the IoT Blockchain architecture can help to obtain the information from source / origin until final consumption.

Customer: The customer is the end user who buys and uses the retailer's product.

Figure 4. Supply chain solution with IoT Blockchain model architecture

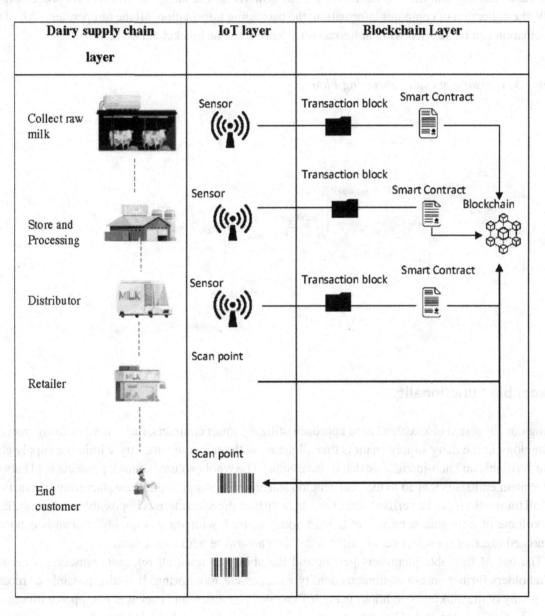

Transaction Data Processing Flow

Figure 5 describe the transaction data processing flow of storing data in the blockchain. IoT devices generate data such as density, temperature, volume, etc. After digital signing and the hashing, such data will be sent directly or through the IoT gateways to the entire blockchain network nodes, where they are verified, connected to the Transaction Pool and stored in blockchain.

Customers can access and validate all transaction data via their laptops or mobile phones. For example, one buys a package of milk from a supermarket and then he or she can use a mobile to check the 2-D barcode to gather all the transaction data relevant to it, including the farm from which the milk was made, the day and time it was delivered, the cow ID on the farm, the workers ID processing the milk, the collection of computer information, the packaging information, all the temperature. All of that information can be verified without human intervention by the blockchain system.

Figure 5. Transaction Data Processing Flow

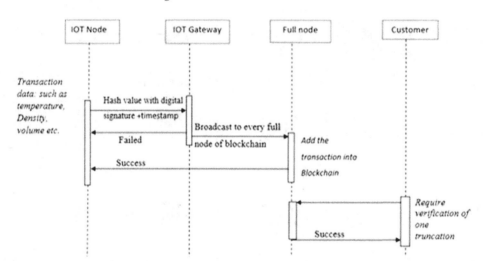

Traceable Functionality

Using our suggested blockchain based approach utilizing smart contracts, the benefit of using traceable technology in the dairy supply chain is that all actors without a core authority within the supply chain have verifiable and non-modifiable details accessible. The whole volume of milk products sold between subsequent entities is logged to the next echelon starting with supplier and manufacturing transactions, and all transactions can be verified. For example, with the agreed terms, it is impossible to alter or change the volume of milk sold between entities. In addition, milk with various quality standards cannot be combined together for sale, because all stakeholders are aware with total quantity.

The use of traceable identifiers per lot and the ability to trace all relevant transactions between stakeholders further ensure continuous quality enforcement monitoring. It is also possible to monitor the quality of the milk and conditions using IoT enabled containers and packages equipped with sensors, cameras, GPS locator, and 4G communication with blockchain, such knowledge and verification cannot be changed or tampered with, and usable automatically and open to all stakeholders in a transparent and decentralized way, without intermediaries.

It should be remembered that a stakeholder can steal or may transact and record fraudulent data. The blockchain, in this situation, marks the data as such with a validated reference to the source data (i.e. the real stakeholder). If the data were caught to be incorrect at a later stage, the judges and all participants can attribute the data to a given actor or stakeholder with 100 percent certainty. Blockchain can identify fraud in that scenario. To resolve this kind of theft, blockchain can be configured by smart contracts to provide additional functionality for the whole supply chain process, and any steps can be taken to enforce fines on dishonest suppliers or take appropriate and punitive action. This will create new corrective data and activities to be produced and connected to deceptive data, maintaining reliable and unchallenged traceability and audit capabilities.

Proposed blockchain based model have three different smart contract named FamerRoal, Processor-Role and DistributerRole. System creates a new batch which is initial stage of dairy supply chain. Milk supplier initiate the process of dairy supply chain. Before the milk is delivered to the dairy manufacturer, capture the temperature of the raw milk, volume, time and date, famer ID into smart contract.

Figure 6 shows FarmerRole smart contract. The initial contractual state is determined, the smart contract checks to confirm that the applicant farmer is already registered, the temperature of the raw milk and volume. If the scenario is successful, then the contractual state will change to ProcessorRole. Famer state changes to manufacture and first block added to the blockchain. ProcessorRole smart contract same as the farmer role contract in this stage describes the process of milk product. Most important criteria to consider in this stage are packaging date time, processor name, unique Id of the milk product and check the temperature of raw milk for the product. At this stage, the contract has to check two condition. First one is the requesting milk processor is a registered entity and second one is the quality of the milk is agreed (temperature, volume). If these two requirements are valid or met, the contract state will be changed to DistributorRole. Manufacture state change to distributer. In the other case, if the above two conditions are not fulfilled, change the contract state to ProcessorRoleFail, processor state changes to RequestFailure, the cancel the process.

At the distributor stage retailer buy the product from distributer. The date of manufacture of the product and the amount sold are some important parameters to keep a check. The distributor and retailers will have their Ethereum addresses identified. For execute the DistributerRole smart contract, authorized distributer have to input date about transport information and warehouse information of the milk product. Then smart contract check and validate distributor role. Above each and every success transaction add a new block to the blockchain. This is how the dairy supply chain complete for one batch. In this way store all the batch information into blockchin database. Using smart tag with barcode reader batch information can show for the outside user. Retailer and customer are final role of the system. They can verify the entire history of a product before buying it in a transparent manner. Each package may be associated with smart tags, so retailers and consumers can easily retrieve the entire product history.

Figure 6. FarmerRole smart contract

```
uint256 public temp;
using Roles for Roles.Role;
event FarmerAdded(address indexed account);
event FarmerRemoved(address indexed account);
Roles.Role private farmers;

constructor() public {
  _addFarmer(msg.sender);
}
modifier onlyFarmer() {
  require(isFarmer(msg.sender), "Caller is not a farmer.");
  _;
}
function isFarmer(address account) public view returns (bool) {
  return farmers.has(account);
}
function addFarmer(address account) public onlyOwner {
  _addFarmer(account);
}
function renounceFarmer() public onlyOwner {
  _removeFarmer(msg.sender);
}
function _addFarmer(address account) internal {
  farmers.add(account);
  emit FarmerAdded(account);
}
function _removeFarmer(address account) internal {
  farmers.remove(account);
  emit FarmerRemoved(account);
}
function setTemperature(uint256 temp) public {
    temp = temp;
}
function getTemperature() external view returns (uint256) {
    return temp;
}
function checkTemp() external view returns (string){
    if(temp<=5 ){
        return "Correct temperature";
    }else{
        return "Incorrect temperature";
```

FUTURE RESEARCH DIRECTIONS

Future research efforts can concentrate on defining the different compensation mechanisms to be used within the blockchain network to promote a consistent transfer of power as to how the transactional data can be used within the food supply chain. A major technological transition such as the introduction of blockchains is only possible if it is driven by the company in certain stages of the value chain with a larger impact on the sector. Therefore it would be interesting to find out how the power balance between retailers and food processors would change the blockchain model proposed. Another possible research problem to answer is blockchain scalability.

CONCLUSION

Food provenance is one of the most challenging questions that companies in the food supply chain are trying to solve today and this research is a small contribution to answering that question. The primary aim of this research is to establish a blockchain platform that can be applied within a food supply chain and include its advantages and disadvantages in terms of food provenance and product traceability over conventional tracking systems It is clear from this research initiative that blockchains can be more effective in monitoring food provenance, avoiding significant degradation of food items, detecting and eliminating the source of foodborne disease in seconds, whereas contemporary systems may take as many weeks. It would also provide greater customer confidence that reflects the satisfaction of sales and customers.

REFERENCES

Agrawal, T. K., Sharma, A., & Kumar, V. (n.d.). *Blockchain-Based Secured Traceability Chain*. Academic Press.

Ahram, T., Sargolzaei, A., Sargolzaei, S., Daniels, J., & Amaba, B. (2017). Blockchain technology innovations. *2017 IEEE Technology and Engineering Management Society Conference. TEMSCON, 2017,* 137–141. Advance online publication. doi:10.1109/TEMSCON.2017.7998367

Al Barghuthi, N. B., Mohamed, H. J., & Said, H. E. (2019). Blockchain in Supply Chain Trading. *ITT 2018 - Information Technology Trends: Emerging Technologies for Artificial Intelligence,* 336–341. doi:10.1109/CTIT.2018.8649523

Aung, M. M., & Chang, Y. S. (2014). Traceability in a food supply chain: Safety and quality perspectives. *Food Control, 39*(1), 172–184. doi:10.1016/j.foodcont.2013.11.007

Madhunamali, A. T. H. E. (2017). *How the Blockchain Revolution Will Reshape the Consumer Electronics Industry*. Academic Press.

Azzi, R., Chamoun, R. K., & Sokhn, M. (2019). Computers & Industrial Engineering The power of a blockchain-based supply chain. *Computers & Industrial Engineering, 135*(August), 582–592. doi:10.1016/j.cie.2019.06.042

Bartling, S., & Fecher, B. (2016). Could Blockchain provide the technical fix to solve science's reproducibility crisis? *Impact of Social Sciences Blog*.

Basnayake, B. M. A. L., & Rajapakse, C. (2019). A Blockchain-based decentralized system to ensure the transparency of organic food supply chain. *Proceedings - IEEE International Research Conference on Smart Computing and Systems Engineering, SCSE 2019,* 103–107. 10.23919/SCSE.2019.8842690

Bocek, T., Rodrigues, B. B., Strasser, T., & Stiller, B. (2017). *Blockchains Everywhere - A Use-case of Blockchains in the Pharma Supply-Chain*. Academic Press.

Bosona, T., & Gebresenbet, G. (2013). Food traceability as an integral part of logistics management in food and agricultural supply chain. *Food Control, 33*(1), 32–48. Advance online publication. doi:10.1016/j. foodcont.2013.02.004

Casino, F., Dasaklis, T. K., & Patsakis, C. (2019). A systematic literature review of blockchain-based applications: Current status, classification and open issues. *Telematics and Informatics, 36*, 55–81. doi:10.1016/j.tele.2018.11.006

Chen, S., Shi, R., Ren, Z., Yan, J., Shi, Y., & Zhang, J. (2017). A Blockchain-Based Supply Chain Quality Management Framework. *Proceedings - 14th IEEE International Conference on E-Business Engineering, ICEBE 2017 - Including 13th Workshop on Service-Oriented Applications, Integration and Collaboration, SOAIC 207*, 172–176. 10.1109/ICEBE.2017.34

Elmessiry, M., & Elmessiry, A. (2018). *Blockchain Framework for Textile Supply Chain Management.* doi:10.1007/978-3-319-94478-4

Frizzo-barker, J., Chow-white, P. A., Adams, P. R., Mentanko, J., Ha, D., & Green, S. (2019). International Journal of Information Management Blockchain as a disruptive technology for business : A systematic review. *International Journal of Information Management, 0–1*(April). Advance online publication. doi:10.1016/j.ijinfomgt.2019.10.014

Helo, P., & Hao, Y. (2019). Blockchains in operations and supply chains: A model and reference implementation. *Computers & Industrial Engineering, 136*(July), 242–251. doi:10.1016/j.cie.2019.07.023

Helo, P., & Shamsuzzoha, A. H. M. (2018, December). Real-time supply chain—A blockchain architecture for project deliveries. *Robotics and Computer-integrated Manufacturing, 63*, 101909. doi:10.1016/j. rcim.2019.101909

Helo, P., & Szekely, B. (2005, January). Logistics information systems: An analysis of software solutions for supply chain co-ordination. *Industrial Management & Data Systems, 105*(1), 5–18. Advance online publication. doi:10.1108/02635570510575153

It, S. (2017). *Can Blockchain Strengthen the Internet of Things?* Academic Press.

Kamilaris, A., Fonts, A., & Prenafeta-Boldú, F. X. (2019). The rise of blockchain technology in agriculture and food supply chains. *Trends in Food Science & Technology, 91*, 640–652. doi:10.1016/j. tifs.2019.07.034

Kamilaris, A., Fonts, A., Prenafeta-Boldú, F. X., Kamble, S. S., Gunasekaran, A., Sharma, R., ... Beynon-Davies, P. (2019). How the blockchain enables and constrains supply chain performance. *Supply Chain Management, 24*(4), 376–397. doi:10.1108/IJPDLM-02-2019-0063

Kharlamov, A., Parry, G., & Clarke, A. C. (n.d.). *Advanced Supply Chains : Visibility, Blockchain and Human Behaviour.* Academic Press.

Kosba, A., Miller, A., Shi, E., Wen, Z., & Papamanthou, C. (2016). Hawk: The Blockchain Model of Cryptography and Privacy-Preserving Smart Contracts. *Proceedings - 2016 IEEE Symposium on Security and Privacy, SP 2016*. 10.1109/SP.2016.55

Kshetri, N. (2018). Blockchain's roles in meeting key supply chain management objectives. *International Journal of Information Management, 39*(June), 80–89. doi:10.1016/j.ijinfomgt.2017.12.005

Lai, J. (2019). Research on Cross-Border E-Commerce Logistics Supply under Block Chain. *Proceedings - 2nd International Conference on Computer Network, Electronic and Automation, ICCNEA 2019*, 214–218. 10.1109/ICCNEA.2019.00049

Litke, A., Anagnostopoulos, D., & Varvarigou, T. (2019). Blockchains for Supply Chain Management: Architectural Elements and Challenges Towards a Global Scale Deployment. *Logistics, 3*(1), 5. doi:10.3390/logistics3010005

Liu, H., Li, Z., & Cao, N. (2018). *Framework Design of Financial Service Platform for Tobacco Supply Chain Based on Blockchain* (Vol. 2). doi:10.1007/978-3-030-05234-8

Longo, F., Nicoletti, L., Padovano, A., d'Atri, G., & Forte, M. (2019). Blockchain-enabled supply chain: An experimental study. *Computers & Industrial Engineering, 136*(July), 57–69. doi:10.1016/j.cie.2019.07.026

Madavi, D. (2008). *A Comprehensive Study on Blockchain Technology*. International Research Journal of Engineering and Technology.

Madumidha, S., Ranjani, P. S., Varsinee, S. S., & Sundari, P. S. (2019). Transparency and traceability: In food supply chain system using blockchain technology with internet of things. *Proceedings of the International Conference on Trends in Electronics and Informatics, ICOEI 2019*, 983–987. 10.1109/ICOEI.2019.8862726

Mattila, J., Seppälä, T., & Holmström, J. (2016). Product-centric Information Management. *A Case Study of a Shared Platform with Blockchain Technology*.

Mussomeli, A., Gish, D., & Laaper, S. (2015). The Rise of the Digital Supply network. *Deloitte*.

Nakamoto, S. (2008). *Bitcoin: A Peer-to-Peer Electronic Cash SyNakamoto, S. (2008). Bitcoin: A Peer-to-Peer Electronic Cash System. Consulted*. Consulted. doi:10.100710838-008-9062-0stem

Osei, R. K., Canavari, M., & Hingley, M. (2018). An Exploration into the Opportunities for Blockchain in the Fresh Produce Supply Chain. doi:10.20944/preprints201811.0537.v1

Pe, M., & Llivisaca, J. (n.d.). Advances in Emerging Trends and Technologies. *Blockchain and Its Potential Applications in Food Supply Chain Management in Ecuador., 3*, 101–112. doi:10.1007/978-3-030-32022-5

Pilkington, M. (2016). Blockchain technology: Principles and applications. Research Handbooks on Digital Transformations. doi:10.4337/9781784717766.00019

Salah, K., Nizamuddin, N., Jayaraman, R., & Omar, M. A. (2019). Blockchain-Based Soybean Traceability in Agricultural Supply Chain. *Blockchain-based Soybean Traceability in Agricultural Supply Chain, 7*(May), 73295–73305. Advance online publication. doi:10.1109/ACCESS.2019.2918000

Schmidt, C. G., & Wagner, S. M. (2019). Journal of Purchasing and Supply Management Blockchain and supply chain relations : A transaction cost theory perspective. *Journal of Purchasing and Supply Management*, *25*(4), 100552. doi:10.1016/j.pursup.2019.100552

Scully, P., & Hobig, M. (2019). Exploring the impact of blockchain on digitized Supply Chain flows: A literature review. *2019 6th International Conference on Software Defined Systems, SDS 2019*, 278–283. 10.1109/SDS.2019.8768573

Sheel, A., & Nath, V. (2019). Effect of blockchain technology adoption on supply chain adaptability, agility, alignment and performance. *Management Research Review*, *42*(12), 1353–1374. Advance online publication. doi:10.1108/MRR-12-2018-0490

Tezel, A., Papadonikolaki, E., Yitmen, I., & Hilletofth, P. (2019). *Preparing Construction Supply Chains for Blockchain : An Exploratory Preparing Construction Supply Chains for Blockchain : An Exploratory*. Academic Press.

Tian, F. (2016). An agri-food supply chain traceability system for China based on RFID & blockchain technology. *2016 13th International Conference on Service Systems and Service Management, ICSSSM 2016*. 10.1109/ICSSSM.2016.7538424

Tönnissen, S., & Teuteberg, F. (2019). Analysing the impact of blockchain-technology for operations and supply chain management: An explanatory model drawn from multiple case studies. *International Journal of Information Management*, *0–1*(January). Advance online publication. doi:10.1016/j.ijinfomgt.2019.05.009

Treiblmaier, H. (2018). The impact of the blockchain on the supply chain: A theory-based research framework and a call for action. *Supply Chain Management*, *23*(6), 545–559. doi:10.1108/SCM-01-2018-0029

Tribis, Y., El Bouchti, A., & Bouayad, H. (2018). Supply chain management based on blockchain: A systematic mapping study. *MATEC Web of Conferences, 200*. 10.1051/matecconf/201820000020

Venkatesh, V. G., Kang, K., Wang, B., Zhong, R. Y., & Zhang, A. (2020). System architecture for blockchain based transparency of supply chain social sustainability. *Robotics and Computer-Integrated Manufacturing, 63*(November), 101896. doi:10.1016/j.rcim.2019.101896

Wamba, S. F. (2019). *Continuance Intention in Blockchain-Enabled Supply Chain Applications : Modelling the Moderating Effect of Supply Chain Stakeholders Trust*. doi:10.1007/978-3-030-11395-7

Wang, Y., Han, J. H., Beynon-davies, P., Wang, Y., Han, J. H., & Beynon-davies, P. (2018). *Understanding blockchain technology for future supply chains : a systematic literature review and research agenda*. doi:10.1108/SCM-03-2018-0148

Weber, I., Xu, X., Riveret, R., Governatori, G., Ponomarev, A., & Mendling, J. (2016). *Untrusted business process monitoring and execution using blockchain*. Lecture Notes in Computer Science. Including Subseries Lecture Notes in Artificial Intelligence and Lecture Notes in Bioinformatics. doi:10.1007/978-3-319-45348-4_19

Wright, A., & De Filippi, P. (2015). Decentralized Blockchain Technology and the Rise of Lex Cryptographia. SSRN *Electronic Journal*. doi:10.2139/ssrn.2580664

Wu, H., Cao, J., Yang, Y., Tung, C. L., Jiang, S., Tang, B., . . . Deng, Y. (2019). Data management in supply chain using blockchain: challenges and a case study. *Proceedings - International Conference on Computer Communications and Networks, ICCCN,* 1–8. 10.1109/ICCCN.2019.8846964

Yadav, S., & Singh, S. P. (2019). *Blockchain critical success factors for sustainable supply chain Resources, Conservation & Recycling.* doi:10.1016/j.resconrec.2019.104505

Yu, Y., Wang, X., Zhong, R. Y., & Huang, G. Q. (2016). E-commerce Logistics in Supply Chain Management: Practice Perspective. *Procedia CIRP, 52,* 179–185. Advance online publication. doi:10.1016/j.procir.2016.08.002

Yumna, H., Murad, M., Ikram, M., & Noreen, S. (n.d.). *Use of blockchain in Education: A systematic Literature Review.* Academic Press.

KEY TERMS AND DEFINITIONS

Cryptography: The practice and study of secure communication techniques in the presence of third parties known as adversaries.

Decentralization: Process by which an organization's activities, in particular those relating to planning and decision-making, are distributed or delegated from a central, authoritative place or group.

Distributed Ledger: A consensus of geographically spread replicated, shared, and synchronized digital data across multiple sites, countries, or institutions.

Double Spend: Potential flaw in a digital cash scheme where the same digital token can be spent more than once.

Ethereum: Decentralized open source blockchain featuring smart contract functionality.

Immutability: Design pattern where something can't be modified after being instantiated.

Smart Contract: Computer program or transaction protocol that is intended to automatically execute, control, or document events and actions legally relevant under the terms of a contract or agreement.

This research was previously published in Blockchain and AI Technology in the Industrial Internet of Things; pages 198-220, copyright year 2021 by Engineering Science Reference (an imprint of IGI Global).

Section 6
Managerial Impact

Chapter 65
Applying Blockchain Security for Agricultural Supply Chain Management

Amarsinh V. Vidhate

(iD) https://orcid.org/0000-0003-4954-7560

Ramrao Adik Institute of Technology, India

Chitra Ramesh Saraf

Ramrao Adik Institute of Technology, India

Mrunal Anil Wani

Ramrao Adik Institute of Technology, India

Sweta Siddarth Waghmare

Ramrao Adik Institute of Technology, India

Teresa Edgar

University of Houston, USA

ABSTRACT

Blockchain technology permits a highly secured record keeping and digital transaction. Blockchain technology is changing the digital world and industry by bringing a new view to security, transparency, and efficiency of systems. It provides a safe way for the exchange of products, services, or transaction. Blockchain will enable more agile value chains, faster product innovations, closer customer relationship sector. This paper provides an overview of blockchain technology and its potential in developing a secure and reliable agriculture supply chain management. Agriculture supply chain management systems are vital for getting food products delivered from farmers to the consumers. Blockchain technology can also be used to achieve better prices and payment options, land title registration and for transparent disbursement of subsidies to farmers.

DOI: 10.4018/978-1-6684-7132-6.ch065

INTRODUCTION

In recent years, the security concern is increasing exponentially and the technologies being developed for the same are also advanced. Blockchain can a futuristic technology and it will be particularly used for secure end-to-end transactions in terms of payments, values, trades in the supply chain, etc.. The blockchain technology can be implemented in various sectors like retail, healthcare, logistics, manufacturing, and communication. Technology can be simply characterized as a decentralized, distributed ledger system. Blockchain sometimes is also termed as Distributed Ledger Technology (DLT). Nowadays, blockchain technology is also implemented and been used in various government sectors for administrative purposes like land deals and land authentication. The government of Kerala has implemented various methods to use blockchain technology to the technologies purchase process and provide a network of vegetables, fish, and various other small scale retail networks. Blockchain technology originated from the bitcoin technology in 2008, having various characteristics such as decentralized, distributed, providing asymmetric cryptography, smart contract, and time stamp. The blockchain technology has a key contribution to allow building confidence and trust among people without any centralized body, by providing mathematical solutions to the problem of trust. The main aim of blockchain technology is to confirm that the information is authentic and not tampered by a group of hackers on the net by "sharing" and "checking" all accounts within the network. Blockchain technology can be summed up as decentralization, consensus trust, collective maintenance, and a reliable database.

With inspiration for blockchain technology and a bitcoin system, the agricultural supply chain system can be developed with a distributed network of the participants including the farmers, end-users, distributors, retailers, small scale business owners. The key component of such supply chain systems is replicable and shared data encrypted and decrypted using SHA-256 algorithms. In an agricultural supply chain using blockchain technology, we can put all the knowledge and information about the crop produced by a farmer and transactional details and event onto blockchain nodes within a network to enable transparent, reliable authenticated and trusted source of data for the farmers. Farmers can put data associated with the food such as quality, payments, the demand of the crop and selling price of the crop, etc. all at one platform(single network)Blockchain will help in setting up a direct link between farmers and consumers, retailers and small scale business owners. It will empower and encourage small farmers to prepare themselves and acquire together to achieve the market without any help from third-party elements like distributors and retailers. The peer-to-peer network is used in blockchain technology and everybody is allowed to affix.

LITERATURE SURVEY

Fran Casino et al. (Casinoa, 2019) has proposed a survey-based application of blockchain and its tremendous usage in various categories. The team has classified in terms of privacy & Security, Education, Health, IoT, Governance, integrity verification, financial, data management & business. This field is wide open with full of research issues enlisted in this paper. There is another survey given by Marco Conoscenti et al. (Conoscenti, 2016) where they have discussed the Use Cases of the Blockchain beyond Cryptocurrencies, along with various categories based on implementation differences.

A paper by Satoshi Nakamoto (Lin, 2018) has given a concrete solution in terms of bitcoin. It is a purely peer-to-peer version of electronic cash which will allow online payments to be sent directly from one party to another without going through a financial institution.

The paper (Nallapaneni & Mallick, 2018) Jun Lin et al. have proposed the blockchain and IoT based on Food Traceability System. In this paper, they propose a trusted, self-organized, open, and ecological food traceability system base on blockchain and IoT technologies, which involves all parties of the smart agriculture ecosystem, even if they may not trust each other. In this paper, IoT devices used to replace manual recording and verification as many as possible, which can reduce human intervention to system effectively.

Nallapaneni Manoj Kumara et al. (Khaled, 2019) has proposed the probabilistic security and privacy conceals related to component communication in the Internet of things and studies as well as implement the distributed ledger-based blockchain (DL-BC) technology. The application areas of blockchain in different sectors and categories are studied. Numerous challenges related to the internet of things and with blockchain are also studied and discussed to understand the blockchain technology and its contribution.

Blockchain-Based Soybean Traceability in Agricultural Supply Chain by Khaled Salah(Sidhu, 2017) et al., this paper introduces Agri Block IoT, a redistributed, Blockchain technology-based traceability resolution for Agri-Food supply chain management, ready to integrate IoT devices into manufacturing and overwhelming digital information on the chain. To effectively evaluate Agri-Block IoT, they outline a classical use-case at specific intervals in the given vertical domain, namely from-farm-to-fork. Where they have developed and deployed use-case, achieving traceability pattern of completely different blockchain implementations, significantly Ethereum and Hyperledger Serration Lastly, the performance of each deployment is evaluated and compared concerning network usage, latency, CPU utilization and lastly highlighted the pros and cons.

A white paper (Conoscenti, 2018) discusses how the bitcoin has solved the double-spend problem and provided work with timestamps on a public ledger, the author has extended the vision of Nakamoto by creating a set of commercial-grade services supporting a wide variety of business use cases, including a fully developed blockchain-based decentralized marketplace, secure data storage, and transfer, and unique user aliases that link the owner to all services controlled by that alias.

The author of (Hua, 2018) has highlighted that blockchain has a strong capacity to monitor and check the confidentiality of the education records. An expansion of blockchain in terms of educational document verification can cut down the possibility of fake certificates which shall not be caught by digital forensics. Blockchain plays a vital role. The University or The Educational Institute is responsible for issuing the certificates, mark-sheets, transcripts, etc. and mining it over the blockchain. The student is provided with the hash number which is the reference number. This number serves the reference of the data. The Organization or the Industry Personal using the hash number checks for the integrity of the submitted document.

Jing Hua et al. (Mukri, 2018) has discussed the provenance (tracing) system of agricultural products is important for ensuring food safety. However, the stakeholders (growers, farmers, sellers, etc.) are numerous and physically dispersed, making it difficult to manage data and information with a centralized approach, a decentralized approach like blockchain can scale up this problem due to its unique decentralized feature.

Bushra Mukri (Jayand & Akutsu, 2015) also discussed a supply chain is a system of services and dispersal options that performs the task of acquisition of materials, transformation of these materials into intermediate and finished deliverables, and the circulation of these finished products to customers.

The author has put a light on how blockchain is revolutionizing the benefits and making a supply chain management more efficient.

Similarly K. Jayand et al. (Preneel, 2010), Sushmita Ru et al.(Aida Kamiali & Heriko, 2018), Aida Kamali et al. (Green, 2018), Gill green et al. (Badr, 2019), Ahmed Badr at el. (Nakasumi, 2017), M. Nakasumi (Matsui & Zuccherat, 2004) discussed the various applications under a blockchain category.

Few of the review points that are deduced from the above papers as

- A supply chain is using a blockchain is one of the very powerful an application domain which can be applied to agricultural supply chain management
- Blockchain technology can reduce inefficiencies while saving time and energy in the agriculture value chain.
- Blockchain technology would allow farmers to store allow their data in one place so that it can easily be accessed by those who need it, simplifying the entire process, and saving valuable time and energy.
- With the block chain's ability to improve automation, digitization, and food tracking, there's no doubt that technology is a must for modern agriculture.
- In Blockchain the information is highly secure and tamperproof. With Blockchain, we can expect an efficient supply of products, fair pricing, efficient supply, and improved product tracking. It will also enable farmers to do real-time management of the stock.

PROJECT DESCRIPTION

Problem Statement

Presently the agriculture supply chain management system is not secure against the tampering and fraudulent activities. The present system does not provide quality parameters of the crop produce also misleading information can be generated and circulated within the network. The current system is also prone to attack where the transaction between the farmer and the consumer can be captured and modified by an attacker. This proposed methodology proposes a system that is to be developed using smart contracts. The farmer uploads the data of the food in the blockchain; transparency is maintained at the end-user that is the consumer can check for the integrity of the food or crop. Also, the consumer and farmer transact directly and efficiently and achieving a goal of paperless and quick business.

Proposed Methodology

The system consists of 3 main processes; generation and validation process.

1. **Generation Process:** In this process, initially the farmer registers on the agriculture supply chain management system. The registration process is followed by a login process. The farmer updates all the relevant information on the crop and other necessary documents. The information and records consist of the name of the crop, certificate name, category, quality of the crop, rate of the crop, etc. All the information is saved in a block and hashed using hashing operation.

The block is subsequently verified and validated by nodes within a network through cryptography techniques and methods. The block is authenticated, dated, and later added to the blockchain so that all consumers can have access to the information and blocks in a Chain as each node builds it's own exemplary independently and the hash is generated using above information.

2. **Validation Process:** Once the data has been generated and stored in a block, the consumers as well the farmer can access and use the data in various cases. The users can access the data to ensure whether the integrity of the food is maintained.

3. **Transaction:** In the last process, once the consumer access the quality control analysis data, generates a request for the crop. Once the farmer receives the request a successful transaction occurs between farmer and the consumer.

Algorithm Used

The national security agency has designed SHA-2 [19] cryptographic hash functions which consist of the SHA 256 algorithm as one of the members. The computations inside SHA 256 hashing algorithm are performed on 32 bit long words consisting of eight factors as A, B, C, D, E, F, G, and H which are 32 bit long as well. SHA 256 computations also generate the word length of 32 bits. At each round, the quality of working factors is calculated and the procedure is preceded till 64 rounds. In all aspects, it is noticed that all the increases are performed on modulo 232 in SHA 256 hashing algorithm. A 256 piece initialization vector fixed for the principal message square is used in SHA 256 hashing computation. A transitional message digest is obtained at the end of 64 rounds which is added following the message square. The SHA 256 hash work is congregated by davies-Meyer development in which the initialization vector is added to the end of 64 rounds. After 64 rounds, a halfway message condensation of 256 bits is generated due to the message pressure capacity and expansion of the calculation. Once the entire message square is been hashed, a 256-bit incentive is earned as the last message review. Thus, the SHA-256 hashing algorithm is similar to square figure with 256 piece message size and 512-bit key which is outlined in sixty-four 32 bits round keys using message scheduler for each round. SHA 256 has the following technical parameters-

*   64-byte block size indicator.
*   33 bytes maximum message length
*   32 byte characteristic of a message digest
*   4-byte word size
*   64 number of iterations within a single cycle
*   Approximately 140 Mb/s speed accomplished by protocol

IMPLEMENTATION AND RESULT

The agriculture supply chain includes various entities in a system. The various entities may include distributors, retailers, farmers, consumers, small scale business owners, etc.

Figure 2 shows the wallet generator where farmers can create a wallet followed with the generation of public and private keys which can be used for a transactional purpose.

Figure 1. System architecture

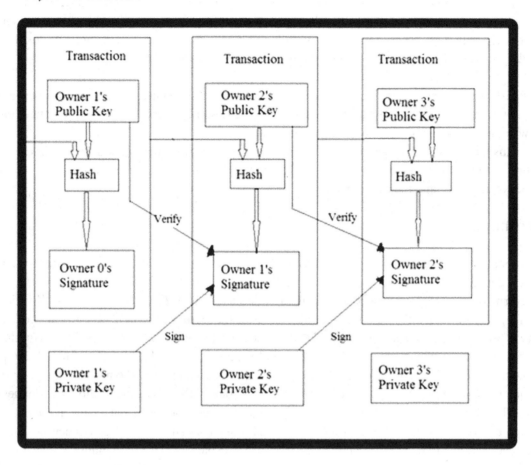

Figure 2. Generation of hash value

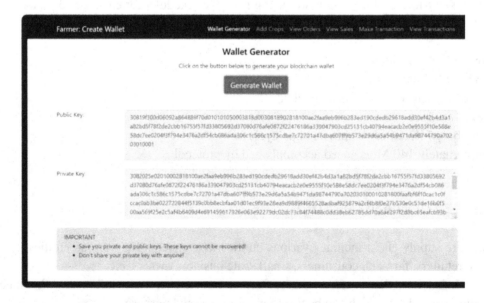

Figure 3 shows add crop tab allowing a farmer to add all the crop details such as the name of the crop, quality, a quantity of the crop required, rate of crop per kg, and lastly the provision to upload the picture of the crop produced.

Figure 3. Farmer adds the crop details

In figure 4, the farmer can view all the requested orders under the view all orders tab describing details of the crop required. The view order tab is beneficial for maintaining the history of crops sold so far.

Figure 4. View all orders

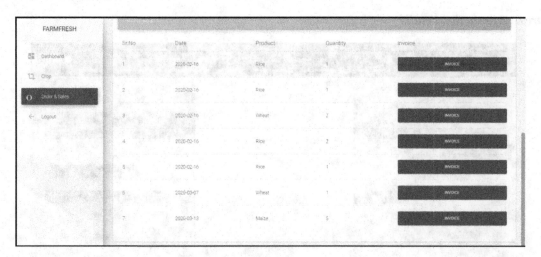

Figure 5, indicates the view all sales tab which can be used by a farmer to view all the sales and relevant information such as farmer id, client id, quality, and quantity of the crop. The sales tab also has an additional feature to export all the sales data.

Figure 5. A farmer can view all the sells

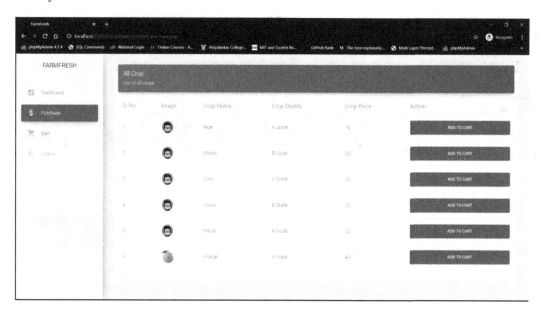

Figure 6, shows all the transactional details of the sender as well as receiver such as sender address, recipient address, amount to be paid, transaction signature generated for the particular transaction, and can be used for verification as well, and lastly the blockchain node URL address.

Figure 6. Transaction details

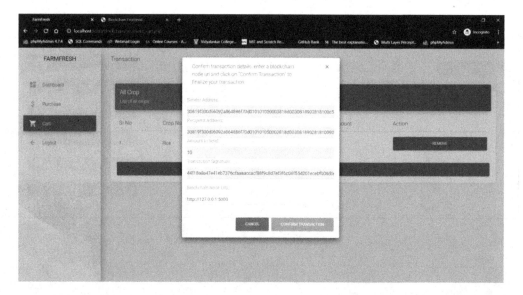

The system can also be enhanced and improved for land authentication and verification for additional security and information like the origin of the food and also for traceability purposes.

Figure 7. A successful transaction dialog box appears after purchase completion

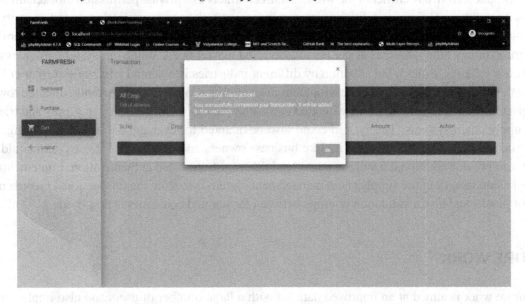

Figure 8. Analysis graph

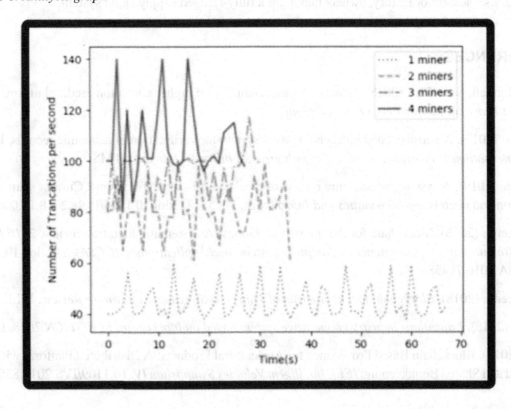

CONCLUSION

This system presents a solution to the challenge of transferring and proposes a system to verify the integrity of food and crops between the farmer and the end consumer. The system can intelligently do the trading of food products from any corner of the world. Smart contracts as a private permission blockchain can be used as it provides real-time visibility, accuracy, transparency, clear communication, speed, security, and efficiency. The system is also open and can be extended for any food supply type, fertilizers, chemicals, eggs, milk, or any other products as per the industry and market need. While our system provides a fast and secure solution, widespread adoption by different industries is essential and could further enhance this methodology leading to further development in technology. While this is currently directed towards the agriculture sector, it can be easily extended to include various sectors wishing to supply and transact over supply chain systems. The system could also be adapted to leverage and enhance existing solutions, such as to include various entities like business owners and distributors. The system could also enhance to provide additional features such as land title registration and authentication. Implementation of blockchain in agriculture supply chain management system is to store the transactional records in the form of blocks and also a validation of crops between farmer and consumer is proposed

FUTURE WORK

Our future work is aimed at an improved data set with a large number of users and also implementing different other technologies. Also, the system can be improved to include various entities like retailers, distributors, industry or factory, owners making it a fully-fledged supply chain system.

REFERENCES

Aida Kamiali, & Heriko. (2018). Eductx: A blockchain-based higher education credit platform. *IEEE Access : Practical Innovations, Open Solutions*.

Badr, A. (2019). A permissioned blockchain based system for verification of academic records. In *10th IFIP International conference on new Technologies, Mobility & security*. NTMS.

Casinoa. (2019). A systematic literature review of blockchain-based applications: Current status, classification and open issues. *Telematics and Informatics, 36*, 55–81. doi:10.1016/j.tele.2018.11.006

Conoscenti. (2016). Blockchain for the Internet of Things: A systematic literature review. *2016 IEEE/ACS 13th International Conference of Computer Systems and Applications (AICCSA),* 1-6. doi: 10.1109/AICCSA.2016.7945805

Conoscenti. (2018). *Blockchain for the Internet of Things: a Systematic Literature Review*. IEEE.

Green. (2018). *Education- industry cooperative system based on blockchain. In HOTICN 2018*. IEEE.

Hua. (2018). Blockchain Based Provenance for Agricultural Products: A Distributed Platform with Duplicated and Shared Bookkeeping. *IEEE Intelligent Vehicles Symposium IV*. 10.1109/IVS.2018.8500647

Jayand, & Akutsu. (2015). *The blockchain-based digital content distribution system.* ICBDC IEEE.

Khaled. (2019). Blockchain-Based Soybean Traceability in Agricultural Supply Chain. *IEEE Access : Practical Innovations, Open Solutions.*

Lin. (2018). Blockchain and IoT based Food Traceability System. *International Journal of Information Technology, 24*(1).

Matsui, & Zuccherat. (2004). *Security Analysis of SHA-256 and Sisters.* Springer.

Mukri. (2018). Blockchain Technology in Supply Chain Management: A Review. *International Research Journal of Engineering and Technology, 5*(6).

Nakasumi. (2017). *Information sharing for supply chain management based on block chain technology.* IEEE CBS.

Nallapaneni & Mallick. (2018). Blockchain technology for security issues and challenges in IoT. *International Conference on Computational Intelligence and Data Science, ICCIDS.*

Preneel. (2010). *Cryptographic Hash Functions: Theory and Practice.* Springer-Verlag.

Rane. (2020). Integrity and Authenticity of Academic Documents Using Blockchain Approach. *ICACC-2020, ITM Web of Conferences, 32,* 03038.

Ruj, & Lam. (2018). *A Blockchain framework for insurance processes.* BSC. IEEE.

Sidhu. (2017). *Syscoin: A peer-to-peer electronic cash system with blockchain- based services for e-business.* IEEE.

This research was previously published in the International Journal of Applied Evolutionary Computation (IJAEC), 11(4); pages 28-37, copyright year 2020 by IGI Publishing (an imprint of IGI Global).

Chapter 66

Security Issues of Blockchain–Based Information System to Manage Supply Chain in a Global Crisis

Kamalendu Pal

iD https://orcid.org/0000-0001-7158-6481

City, University of London, UK

ABSTRACT

Global supply chain crisis management has become increasingly crucial for tackling unusual incidents (e.g., natural disaster, terrorism, pandemic). While crisis management has focused on a few organizations involved in supply chain operations (manufacturers, governments, carriers, and the consuming public), it has primarily received a functional focus. Due to their decentralized network structure, supply chains are prone to suffer from disruptive events solved by supply chain crisis management. This chapter presents the blockchain technologies' possibilities and limits used in an integrated IoT-based information system architecture. The chapter describes how the scalability limits of blockchain technology affect the proposed architecture performance that uses it. Also, the chapter presents a review of the academic literature, pointing out how some solutions use a centralization process to improve response time and security of the blockchain-based architecture. Finally, the chapter provides security threat models, which consider by blockchain protocols in IoT networks.

INTRODUCTION

In recent decades, many academics and practitioners have conducted empirical and conceptual research studies on various business crisis (Lagadec, 1990) (Lagadec, 1993) (Shrivastava, 1993). However, as with many new research areas, these studies lack adequate integration (Shrivastava, 1993). The interdisciplinary nature of organizational crisis has explicitly resulted in this lack of integration (Shrivastava, 1993). Mainly, organizational crisis inherently are phenomena for which psychological, social-political, and

DOI: 10.4018/978-1-6684-7132-6.ch066

technological-structural issues act as motivational sources in their creation and management (Pauchant & Douville, 1994). Because the study of organizational crisis involves many disciplines, researchers believe that crisis must be researched and studied using a systems approach (Pauchant & Mitroff, 1992). Also, academics and practitioners believe that psychological, socio-political, and technological issues should be explicitly considered and used when studying and managing organizational crisis.

Some researchers, in their studies, wholeheartedly pursue a multidisciplinary research approach (Shrivastava, Mitroff, Miller & Miglani, 1988). However, some other researcher uses causal reasoning, and management techniques to understand organizational crisis (Shrivastava, 1993). This chapter assumes that this lack of integration has kept research on organizational crisis at the management theory periphery. To take a required step toward a multidisciplinary approach to the study of organizational crisis (Lagadec, 1993) (Shrivastava, 1993), the chapter illustrates an alternative view on organizational crisis by handling the situation with a scenario planning activity. This scenario planning is not a prediction about what will happen, but it represents hypotheses about what could happen and the effect on the manufacturing (e.g., apparel, automobile) business world.

This chapter serves as a beginning point to help businesses and policymakers think through the potential implications for manufacturing industry operations management and success in the marketplace. The disruption had always existed in the manufacturing supply chain network operations even before the term supply chain management (SCM) became part of today's business (Pal, 2017). Disruptions have changed their abilities and types over centuries from supply chain disruptions due to ecosystem changes, business model transformation, and security attacks in emerging information and communication technologies (ICT).

Global manufacturing supply networks' fragility is increasing due to disruption risks that directly or indirectly endanger the industry's stability and security. As an example, the spread of coronavirus globally has affected the movement of people and materials worldwide. The resulting manufacturing business network disruptions have led to delivery delays and shortages of products and essential items. Simultaneously, demands for objects utilized for pandemic control have increased dramatically, and the forecasting of demand patterns for many consumer goods has become more challenging (Taghipour, 2020) (Radhouri et al., 2018) (Cliché et al., 2020).

In addition, the apparel manufacturing industry inclines to worldwide business operations due to the economic advantage of the globalisation of product design and development. In this way, a typical apparel manufacturing network consists of organisations' sequence, facilities, functions, and activities to produce and develop an ultimate product or related services. This activity starts with raw materials purchase from selective suppliers and products produced at one or more production facilities (Pal, 2019). Next, these products are moved to intermediate collection points (e.g., warehouse, distribution centres) to store temporarily to move to the next stage of the manufacturing network and finally deliver the products to intermediate storages or retailers or customers (Pal, 2017).

The connecting path from supplier to the customer can include several intermediaries, such as warehouse, wholesalers, and retailers, depending on the ultimate products and markets. Global apparel manufacturing networks are becoming increasingly complicated due to a growing need for inter-organizational and intra-organizational connectedness, which enabled by advances in modern technologies and tightly coupled business processes. The essential strategic asset in apparel business operational information has been a critical strategic asset. Also, apparel business networks use information systems to monitor manufacturing network activities (Pal, 2020).

The new digital technologies (e.g., Internet of Things (IoT), Blockchain Technology, Service-Oriented Computing, Big Data Analytics) have attracted attention from academics and practitioners as a growing area of research (Okorie et al., 2017). This research focuses on how data derived from various manufacturing sources can produce a better product life cycle management. In this life cycle management initiative, researchers are looking for ways to increasing the manufacturing products utilization and environmental compliance of the manufacturing of the product.

A group of researchers (Pagorpoulos et al., 2017) advocated three primary information and communication technology (ICT) application areas in manufacturing: (i) integration of heterogeneous data along with the global operations, (ii) data collection, and (iii) analysis of collected data. Within heterogeneous data integration, service-oriented computing (SOC) plays a dominating role, given that intelligent perception and collection from the various computer networks of physical manufacturing resources and abilities. Also, SOC provides reliable security solutions and technologies under the wider internet environment. At the same time, new technologies have emerged. They have wide use in different manufacturing applications, such as the IoT. The data collected by Radio Frequency Identification (RFID) tags and sensors for their underlying assets can help find the circular attributes (e.g., location, condition, availability) that form the essential ingredient for the modern apparel manufacturing economy. Therefore, IoT-enabled manufacturing assets can improve their real-time data gathering abilities to act as a vital enabler for modern manufacturing.

Standard IoT systems are built on a centralised computing environment, which requires all devices to be connected and authenticated through the central server. This framework would not be able to provide the needs to outspread the IoT system in globalised operation. Therefore, moving the IoT system into the decentralised path may be the right decision. One of the popular decentralisation platforms is blockchain technology.

In simple, a blockchain technology is based on a distributed database management system which keeps recods of all business-related exchange information (i.e., transactions) that have been executed and shared among participating parties in the network. This distributed database system is known as a distributed ledger technology (DLT). Individual business exchange information is stored in the distributed ledger and must be verified by the consent of the majority of the participating-members of this network. All business realted transactions that have ever made are contained in the block. Bitcoin, the decentralised peer-to-peer (P2P) digital currency, is the most popular example that uses blockchain technology (Nakamoto, 2008).

The convergence of IoT with blockchain technology will have many advantages. The blockchain's decentralisation model will have the ability to handle processing a vast number of transactions between IoT devices, significantly reducing the cost associated with installing and maintaining large, centralised data centres and distributing computation and storage needs across the devices that form IoT networks. Besides, working with blockchain technology will eliminate the single point of failure associated with the centralised IoT architecture. In addition, convergence of blockchain with IoT will allow the P2P messaging, file distribution and autonomous coordination between IoT devices with no centralised computing model.

This chapter presents an overview of integrating blockchain with the IoT system; this involves examining the advantages resulting from the integration process and the implementation challenges encountered. The ultimate goal of this work is to provide a framework, and its description of the benefits and challenges that result from combining blockchain with IoT to decide whether to go with the decentralisation for the IoT.

Below, this chapter introduces first the basic idea of blockchain technology. Next, the chapter presents the use of blockchain technology in the manufacturing industry. This section also analyses the issues (e.g., traceability, security, flexibility, and smart contracts) related to the blockchain-based manufacturing system. The chapter presents related research work in the manufacturing industry in recent years. Then the uses of blockchain-based technology in the manufacturing industry have been discussed. Next, it discusses the critical issues that need consideration in designing industry-specific reference architecture. It also includes different secure manufacturing problems in business process automation. Finally, the chapter discusses the experimental results and concludes with the scope of future research.

INTERNET OF THINGS AND ITS APPLICATIONS IN APPAREL INDUSTRY

The IoT idea was õrst created in 1999 by Kevin Ashton (Keertikumar et al., 2015). IoT technology uses in apparel industries for different business process automation purpose. This area of computing has recently focused on enterprise automation, and there is a handful of evidence of the successful use of this technology in supply chain operations. IoT based information system aims to improve organisational communication and collaboration activities. In recent decades, World Wide Web technologies are getting prominence for business use, and the number of Internet-based IoT services are increasing rapidly for supply chain communities. These services, which human users can access using devices. The main form of communication is human-to-human. IoT attempts to not only have humans communicating through the Internet but also have objects or devices. These things are to exchange information by themselves over the Internet, and new forms of Internet communication forms: human-to-things and things-to-things.

The apparel (i.e., textile and clothing) industry is an integral part of the world economy and society (Pal & Ul-Haque, 2020) (Pal, 2020). In recent decades, global apparel manufacturing businesses incline to worldwide activities due to the economic advantage of the globalisation of product design and development (Pal, 2020a). Global apparel supply chains are becoming increasingly heterogeneous and complicated due to a growing need for inter-organisational and intra-organizational connectedness by advances in modern technologies and tightly coupled business processes. Hence, information has been an essential strategic asset in apparel business operational management. The apparel business networks are also using information systems to monitor supply chain activities.

Despite the increasing applicability of IoT applications in supply chains, there are many challenges to using this technology. For example, IoT-related technical issues experienced when operating at the ecosystem level, such as security, authenticity, confidentiality, and privacy of all stakeholders (Tzounis et al., 2017). Academics and practitioners consider that privacy and security issues are mainly related to IoT system applications' vulnerability. Besides, problems such as physical tampering, hacking, and data theft might increase business partners' trust-related issues (Kshetri, 2017). Therefore, IoT applications must be secure against external security, particular protections that only authorised entities can access and change data in the application layer.

Moreover, most IoT devices are limited in power, data processing capability, small sizes, and low inherent design cost. Academics and practitioners are urging to design IoT devices and their protocols to data using IoT data communication network. IoT data reliability can achieve by using distributed information processing methods that execute a verification method between the parties among all its participants to ensure that data remain immutable and untampered. Considering these technical issues and realising today's blockchain technology's essential characteristics now offers several potential solutions to address known disadvantages related to IoT applications in apparel business networks.

Blockchain technology is a distributed network for orchestrating transactions, value, and assets between peers without intermediaries' assistance. Blockchain technology helps record transactions or any digital interaction designed to be secure, transparent, highly resistant to outages, auditable, and efficient. These characteristics provide impetus to blockchain-based IoT architecture for secure data processing in a distributed environment. In order words, IoT-based information systems to improve their IoT networked infrastructure to blockchain complimented technology. It is a distributed ledger managed by a peer-to-peer (P2P) network to provide internode communication and verify new blocks. A convergence of IoT and blockchain technologies can lead to a verifiable, secure, and robust mechanism of storing and managing data processed by smart connected devices. This network of connected devices will interact with their environment and make decisions without any human intervention. However, integrating blockchain technology in IoT-based information systems will enhance the security, data privacy, and reliability of IoT devices, it creates a new set of challenges.

This chapter presents how apparel businesses can leverage IoT applications in combination with blockchain technology to streamline their supply chains business information. When combined, these enabling technologies will help global textile and clothing companies to overcome difficulties related to data collection d integrity, address security challenges, and reduce information asymmetry. This chapter will demonstrate areas of disadvantages towards safety and privacy in blockchain technology. The rest of this chapter organised as follows. Section 2 presents an introduction of IoT and its applications in the apparel industry. It includes IoT applications in apparel supply chain management and IoT applications' drawbacks in the apparel supply chain. Section 3 describes blockchain technology in apparel business management applications. Section 4 explains blockchain applications for the IoT. Section 5 describes the background related to security and privacy for enterprise computing and research challenges. Then Section 6 reviews some of the threat models for blockchain technology. Finally, Section 7 concludes the chapter by discussing relevant research issues.

INTERNET OF THINGS AND ITS APPLICATIONS IN APPAREL INDUSTRY

The IoT idea was õrst created in 1999 by Kevin Ashton (Keertikumar et al., 2015). IoT technology has used in apparel industries for different business process automation purpose. This area of computing has recently focused on enterprise automation, and there is a handful of evidence of the successful use of this technology in supply chain operations. IoT based information system aims to improve organisational communication and collaboration activities. In recent decades, World Wide Web technologies are getting prominence for business use, and the number of Internet-based IoT services are increasing rapidly for supply chain communities. These services, which human users can access using devices. The main form of communication is human-to-human. IoT attempts to not only have humans communicating through the Internet but also have objects or devices. These things are to exchange information by themselves over the Internet, and new forms of Internet communication would form human-to-things and things-to-things.

Simplistically, the IoT technology characterised by three types of visions:

1. **Things Oriented Vision**: This vision supported by the fact that this technology can track anything using sensors. The advancement and convergence of microelectronic systems technology, wireless

communications and digital electronics have resulted in the development of miniature devices having the ability to sense, compute and communicate wirelessly in an effective way. The basic philosophy is uniquely identifying an object using specifications of Electronic Product Code (EPC). It is worth considering that the future of 'Things Oriented Vision' will depend upon sensor technology evolution for accurate sensing (without any error) and its capabilities to fulfil the "thing" oriented other issues.

2. **Internet Oriented Vision**: This vision realises upon the need to make smart objects which are connected.
3. **Semantic Oriented Vision**: This vision is power because the number of sensors used in the apparel industry is vast. The data that these IoT infrastructures collect is massive. Thus, the industry needs to process this data in a meaningful way to form value-added services using semantic technologies (e.g., ontology, knowledge-based reasoning), efficient, secure, scalable, and market-oriented computing.

In this way, the IoT application builds on three pillars, related to the ability of smart objects to (i) be identifiable (anything identifies itself), (ii) to communicate (anything communicates), and (iii) to interact (anything interacts) – either among themselves, building networks of interconnected objects, or with end-users or other entities in the network. Furthermore, cloud computing and fog computing provide computing resources and scalability to connect, store and analyse IoT data (often labelled as big data).

According to Barreto et al. (Barreto et al., 2017), the three distinguishing features of IoT are context, omnipresence and optimisation. The context describes IoT's capability to provide real-time monitoring, to interact, and enable an instant response to speciõc situations that are controlled. Omnipresence lies in the technology's pervasiveness and its broad applicability, while optimisation refers to the speciõc functionalities and characteristics each physical object has (Witkowski et al., 2017).

IoT Applications in Apparel Supply Chain Management

The application of IoT promises significant operational improvements in the manufacturing industry. The advantages result primarily from real-time information exchange, reducing time wastage caused by the bullwhip effect (Wang et al., 2008) (Zhou, 2012). Moreover, IoT can help to revolutionize supply chains by improving operational efficiencies and creating revenue opportunities. Three areas in the manufacturing industry that can benefit from IoT use include (1) inventory management and warehouse operations, (2) production and manufacturing operations, and (3) transportation operations (See Table 1). For example, smart forklifts and racks, and novel usage of *smart glasses* (i.e., wearable devices using sensors and camera technologies to locate objects in the warehouse), monitoring cameras, and other intelligent warehouse management software.

Also, in warehouse operations – reusable assets (e.g., inventory storage totes and pallets) can be attached to IoT-enabled tags or devices that help guide and direct the warehouse pickers to their storage locations. In this way, IoT technologies help automate the warehouses' operational activities, but they reduce human intervention (and error) linked with manual storage management. This advantage results from using industrial-grade RFID-tags and RFID-readers that send a radio signal to identify correctly tag-embedded on pallets, totes, or the product cartons leading to a reduction in the time spent in collecting, recording, and retrieving business operational data.

Table 1. IoT levers in apparel supply chain business

Inventory Management and Warehouse Operations	
Enablers	Processes
• Smart racks • Smart glasses • Monitoring cameras • Smart forklifts • Smart warehouse management system (SWMS)	• Route optimization, elimination of in-process collisions • Fast, cost-efficient, and flexible operations
Production and Manufacturing Operations	
Enablers	Processes
Embedded machine sensors Machine analytics	• Real-time condition monitoring • Predictive maintenance: Detection of physical stress levels, pileups, and prevention of failures • Enhancement of both machine-to-machine and machine-to-human interactions
Transportation Operations	
Enablers	Processes
GPRS sensors RFID tags Routers GPS satellites	• Real-time shipment tracking • Remote sensing (e.g., temperature, humidity, vibrations) • Maximizing fuel efficiency and optimize routing strategies.

IoT technologies are common to use in apparel production and manufacturing activities. Apparel manufacturing processes consist of spinning and knitting. Spinning is the conversion of fibers into yarn, while knitting is a process of making fabric by intermeshing a series of loops of one or more yarn. It generally contains three major phases, i.e., producing raw materials, processing materials, and making clothes. Therefore, IoT-based technologies can lead to more efficient machine utilization, reduce bottlenecks in production, and optimize production planning and scheduling at varying levels within an apparel business. As a result, this improved insight into key manufacturing processes will enable more vital collaboration and value co-creation with suppliers and improved machine-to-machine and machine-to-human interaction.

Moreover, when it comes to transportation activities in apparel supply chain management, IoT-based technology can also provide potential advantages. For example, a GPS (Global Positioning System) helps to position vehicles (e.g., trucks) from remote distribution centers and optimize routing and delivery time., GPS, RFID technology, and attached sensors increase the in-transit visibility by precisely localizing vehicles on public roads or shipping port using large-scale mapping, data collection from traffic, and analysis of this data. The business processes data collected from these IoT devices will improve the forecasting of delivery times, fleet availability, and routing efficiency (Waller & Fawcett, 2013). Moreover, these devices can enhance the sharing of underutilized resources among vehicles in the parking space or on the road (Barreto et al., 2017).

Drawbacks and Threats of IoT Applications in Apparel Supply Chain

The apparel manufacturing process consists of spinning and knitting. Spinning is the conversion of fibers into yarn, while knitting is a process of making fabric by intermeshing a series of loops of one or more yarn. The use of IoT-based applications in the apparel supply chain has proved to be effective in operational efficiency. IoT technology addresses different apparel manufacturing chain challenges (i.e., the right products, at the right time, in the right place, incorrect quantity, and at the right price). In this way, as IoT systems generate massive volumes of data across the apparel network business environment, this data often resides in silos, often the potential for security and privacy-related risks.

There are different types of IoT security issues that need to be addressed, including IoT device trust, access control, data integrity, physical tampering, and user privacy. An IoT technology deployment survey concluded that 70 percentage of IoT devices are vulnerable due to encryption-related issues, unprotected interfaces, and inappropriate authorization (Lee & Lee, 2015). In highlighting different privacy and security issues, a group of researchers (Cam-Winget et al., 2016) comment on the recent system security solutions are insufficient due to scalability issues in processing and analyzing data generated from vast networks of heterogeneous IoT-based devices and the need to fulfil real-time requirements. Proper security and privacy approaches are considered unusable to IoT-based information system environment due to their dynamic topology and distributed nature. The current Internet architecture with its server-based computing platform might not be able to deal with an enormous number of devices and vast data because individual servers may pose a single point of failure for cyber-attacks and physical damage. For example, IoT devices are at risk from DDoS attacks, data theft, and remote hijacking. Also, Marjani and colleagues (Marjani et al., 2017) argue that some IoT-based applications lack a service level agreement (SLA) to safeguard 'Personally Identiðable Information' (PII) demanded by privacy laws. Therefore, it can have a negative influence on data integrity. Hence, system security may suffer in privacy protection for individuals and enterprises (Suresh et al., 2014).

Moreover, apparel supply chain business-partners may have concerns regarding the physical security and conðdentiality of product information as it moves along the enterprise value chain. Even though IoT-based information system helps supply chain exchange partners validate and verify the authenticity of items in the supply chain. There are still some concerns about IoT devices' vulnerability to counterfeiting, cloning, and fraudulent practices, access authorization, tampering with existing data, and manipulation. For instance, if RFID tags are compromised,, it may be possible to bypass security measures and introduce new vulnerabilities during automatic veriðcation processes (Kumar & Iyengar, 2017). Besides, the manual retrieval and storage of information regarding unique tag identities in a centralized database permits the reproducing or forging of this information at any time (Lin et al., 2017). Hence, it is difficult to identify counterfeit products accompanied by misleading provenance histories (Hua et al., 2018).

In the end, centralized systems may pose a disadvantage for IoT-based system deployments in the apparel manufacturing business for traceability operations. The existence of centralized business organizations may lead to mistrust, which may curb the futuristic enhancement of supply chains (Tse et al., 2017). A centralized approach for data storing and processing can lead to several business risks and operation related issues to the integrity of data, privacy, and security. For example, cloud-computing based IoT systems need to consider data privacy-related issues (Khetri, 2017) (Kamilaris et al., 2019). Moreover, these solutions may create obscurity and enhance information asymmetry between supply chain exchange partners. An additional factor is that centralised information systems act as a black box, and the collaborating business nodes do not know how their data is stored, managed, utilised, and secured (Galvez et al., 2018). Blockchain technology can help to prevent e several of these problems.

BLOCKCHAIN TECHNOLOGY IN APPAREL BUSINESS

Since the innovation of Bitcoin, a digital cryptocurrency, in 2008 (Nakamoto, 2008), blockchain technology has positioned itself as the focal point of interest among a diverse range of researchers and practitioners. Blockchain is a decentralised ledger that stores all transactions that have made on top of a peer-to-peer (P2P) network in a secure, verifiable, and transparent way. The significant advantage of blockchain over the existing technologies is that it enables the two parties to make transactions over the Internet securely without any intermediary party's interference. The omission of the intermediate party can reduce the processing cost while improving the security and efficiency of transactions.

Due to the benefits that blockchain can bring in information processing, this technology expands its applicability to new territories such as supply chain management and logistics management. Today, blockchain also stands as a gatekeeper in the emerging "trust economy", in which the global apparel supply chain operates to serve its suppliers and customers. The efficiency of a global apparel supply chain relies on trust between the different stakeholders. The integration of blockchain and IoT technologies can increase the traceability and reliability of information and the business network. The IoT technology should integrate with enterprise resource planning (ERP) and point of sales (POS) systems of apparel business to share and monitor real-time information at each stage, as shown in Figure 1.

Blockchain technology offers a mechanism to record transactions, or any digital interaction designed to secure, transparent, highly resistant to outages, auditable, and efficient. In other words, blockchain technology has introduced an effective solution to IoT based information systems security. A blockchain enhances IoT devices to send inclusion data in a shared transaction repository with the tamper-resistant record. It improves business partners to access and supply IoT data without central control and management, which creates a digital fusion.

Figure 1. RFID tagging level at different stages in the apparel manufacturing network

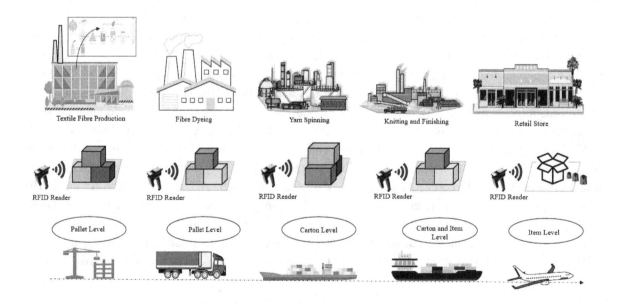

Therefore, blockchain is now a vital technology for different enterprise applications in the apparel business. A *blockchain* is a certain class of data structure used in some distributed manner (known as '*distributed ledger*' - DL) that stores and transmits data in packages called '*blocks*' connected in a digital '*chain*'. The idea of distributed ledger originated from the concept of a '*shared ledger*'. A shared ledger can be a single ledge with *layered permissions* or a distributed ledger, consisting of multiple ledgers supported by a distributed network of nodes (or *business activities*). Distributed Ledger Technology (DLT) refers to an evolving storage method and sharing data across many data stores. It helps data to record, shared, and synchronised across a distributed network of different network participants. Blockchains employ '*cryptographic*' and algorithmic methods to record and synchronise data across a network in an '*immutable manner*'. A simple diagrammatic representation of blockchain is present in Figure 2.

A blockchain is a connected list of blocks in a real-world, and each block keeps the hash function value of a previous block in the chain. The hash function computation uses a cryptographic technique to maintain the integrity of the system. Individual block also digitally signs their contents by using the hash function of their contents inside the block. An important design strategy is to create a Merkle tree (Katz & Lindell, 2007) to store and verify the hashes efficiently. Thus, each block only stores the root of the Merkle tree, as, given the root, it is easy to verify the immutability.

DLs are categorised as '*permissioned*' or '*permissionless*', depending on whether network participants (nodes) require permission from any entity to make updates to the ledger. The DLs can be classified as '*public*' or '*private*' based on the accessibility of the participating nodes. '*Public Key Cryptography* (PKC)*' techniques are often used in blockchain technology-based implementation. PKC is an asymmetric encryption scheme that uses two sets of keys: a public key that widely disseminates and a private key known to the owner. PKC can be used to create digital signatures and uses in a wide array of applications, such as '*HyperText Transmission Protocols*' (HTTP) used in the Internet operation, for authentication in critical applications in chip-based payment cards.

Transactions in a blockchain system are identical to their traditional database counterparts. A blockchain transaction could be visualised as a set of reading/write operations performed on each node of a replicated distributed database in its vanilla form.

Figure 2. Basic blockchain representations

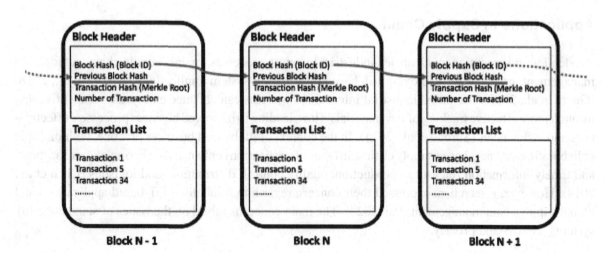

In a blockchain-based infrastructure, every node of the chain maintains a local copy of transaction information. The copy is identical to the original copy and updated in the global information sheet as it distributed within the database with well-built constancy support. Once data entered within the blockchain ledger in this database, no one can change this data in the future. However, this mechanism is known as *tamperproof*, a systematic effort required for building a *reliable* blockchain-based information infrastructure. The main features of these systematic efforts are as follows: (i) Blockchain Protocols for Commitment: The *protocol of commitment* makes sure that valid transaction from apparel business processes are committed and stored in the blockchain information storage with appropriate *validation mechanism* and within a *stipulated time*; (ii) Consensus: Consensus consists of two things: First, it permits blockchain to be updated while making sure that every block in the network is valid as well as keeping participants incentivised and second, it safeguards any single entity from controlling or crashing the whole blockchain system. The consensus aims to create a distributed network without central authorities with participants who do not necessarily need to trust each other. The consensus is an essential part of blockchain technology. Each node runs a programmed mechanism called a consensus. The consensus is how nodes agree on how to update the blockchain because of a set of transactions. Achieving consensus ensures that most network nodes have validated the same set of transactions; (iii) Security: Safety is an essential aspect of the blockchain-based transaction processes. All the data within the blockchain ecosystem needs to be secured and tamperproof. Ensures that there are no malicious nodes within the blockchain-based enterprise ecosystem. (iv) Privacy and Authenticity: Privacy in blockchain enables the client/user to perform transactions without leaking its identification information in the network; and (v) Smart Contracts: In 1994, Nick Szabo (Szabo, 1994) presented the basic concept of a smart contract.

In recent years, blockchain technology ushered a massive range of industrial applications, and many similar information exchange schemes have developed for different industrial business process automation purposes.

BLOCKCHAIN APPLICATIONS FOR THE IoT

Blockchain technology uses in different application areas in SCM. Some of these applications described in this section.

Applications in Supply Chain

Academics and practitioners identified industrial business processes, mainly supply chain and logistics management, essential for deploying IoT based information system applications (Atkore et al., 2018) (Gubbi et al., 2013). IoT-based industrial information systems can enhance enterprise competitiveness through more effective tracking of raw materials' flow, leading to improved business processes' effectiveness and efficiencies (Shroud et al., 2014). In the context of globalised business practice, with multiple collaborating-partners based supply chains, IoT-based applications enhance the sharing of more accurate and timely information relevant to production, quality control, distribution, and logistics (Chen et al., 2014). However, researchers expressed their concern regarding standalone IoT-based applications and global supply chain management (Pal, 2020). The main concerns raised on the issues of standalone IoT systems security and privacy.

The research community has proposed different hybrid information system architectures (e.g., IoT with blockchain, cloud based IoT and blockchain technology). A blockchain enhances IoT-based applications tamper-resistant characteristics. In recent years, different blockchain-based information management systems have reported by researchers. For example, IBM has developed a new blockchain-based service designed to track high-value items through complex supply chains in a secure cloud-based application system (Kim, 2016). Another exemplary industrial application is a fine-wine Provence-tracking service, known as the Chai Wine vault, developed by London-based Company Ever ledger (Finextra, 2016) in business-partnership with fine-wine expert Maureen Downey. An innovative anti-counterfeit application, called Block Verify, is designed, and deployed for tracking anti-counterfeit products (Hulse apple, 2015) to create a sustainable business world. A start-up company from Finland (i.e., Kouvola), in partnership with IBM, developed a smart tendering application for supply chain management. The reported application built on an automatic blockchain-based smart contract (Banker, 2016). Another blockchain-based smart contract, called SmartLog, launched by Kouvola in recent years (AhIman, 2016).

In recent decades, due to globalisation, manufacturing supply chain networks are going through an evolutionary change through their business practices' continued digitisation. These global manufacturing chains evolve into value-creating networks where the value chain becomes an essential competitive advantage source. Simultaneously, developments are in progress to integrate blockchain technology with other technologies solutions (e.g., IoT-based applications, cloud-based solutions, and fog computing-based automation): modern manufacturing supply chains and holistic collaboration mechanisms value-enhancing applications for the global business.

Applications on the Internet of Things Devices Management

In IoT, devices management relates to security solutions for the physical devices, embedded software, and residing data on the devices. Internet of Things (IoT) comprises of "Things" (or IoT devices) that have remote sensing and data collecting capabilities and can exchange data with other connected devices and applications (directly or indirectly). IoT devices can collect data and process the data either locally or send them to centralize servers or cloud-based application back-ends for processing. A recent on-demand model of manufacturing that is leveraging IoT technologies is called Cloud-Based Manufacturing (CBM). It enables ubiquitous, convenient, on-demand network access to a shared pool of configurable manufacturing business processes information collection and use it service provision.

However, attackers seek to exfiltrate IoT devices' data using malicious codes in malware, especially on the open-source Android platform. Gu et al. (Gu et al., 2018) reported a malware identification system in a blockchain-based system named CB-MDEE composed of detecting consortium chain by test members and public chain users. The CB-MDEE system uses a soft-computing-based comparison technique and more than one marking function to minimise the false-positive rate and improve malware variants' identification ability. A research group (Lee et al., 2017) uses a firmware update scheme based on blockchain technology to safeguard the IoT system's embedded devices.

Applications on the Internet of Things Access Management

Access control is a mechanism in computer security that regulates access to information system. The access control systems face many problems, such as third-party, inefficiency, and lack of privacy. These problems can be address by blockchain, the technology that received significant attention in recent years, and many potentials. Jemel and other researchers (Jemel & Serhrouchni, 2017) report a couple of centralised access control systems problems. As there is a third party with access to the data, the risk of privacy leakage exists. Also, a major party is in charge to control the access, so the risk of a single point of failure also exists. This study presents an access control mechanism with a temporal dimension to solve these problems and adapts a blockchain-based solution for verifying access permissions. The attribute-based Encryption method (Sahai & Waters, 2005) also has some problems, such as privacy leakage from the private key generator (PKG) (Hur & Noh, 2011) and a single point of failure as mentioned before. Wang and colleagues (Wang et al.,2018) introduce a framework for data sharing and access control to address this problem by implementing decentralised storage.

Blockchain can be classified either as private (permission) or public (permissionless). Both classes are decentralising and provide a certain level of immunity against faulty or malicious users for blockchain technology. The significant differences between private and public blockchains lie in the consensus protocol's execution, the ledger's maintenance, and the authorisation mechanism to join the distributed network.

Recently, there has been a tremendous investment from the industries and significant interest from academia to solve significant research challenges in blockchain technologies. For example, consensus protocols are the primary building blocks of blockchain-based technologies. Therefore, the threats targeting the consensus protocols become a significant research issue in the blockchain.

BLOCKCHAIN SECURITY AND PRIVACY ISSUES

Blockchain technology offers an approach to storing information, executing transactions, performing functions, and establishing trust is secure computing without centralised authority in a networked environment. Although blockchain has received growing interest in academia and industry in recent years, blockchains' security and privacy continue to be at the centre of the debate when deploying blockchain in different industrial applications.

Key Security Risk Areas of Blockchain

The main areas of security on blockchain technology are (i) Ledger, (ii) Consensus Mechanism, (iii) Networking Infrastructure, (iv) Identity Access Management, and (v) Cryptography. A diagrammatic representation is present in the risk areas in Figure 4.

Ledger: The ledger uses to register all transactions and changes in the status of the data. The ledger distributed by smart design and shared between the blockchain participating nodes. Two challenging problems (or hazards) generally threaten the applicability of the ledger technology in blockchain applications: (a) unauthorised entry into the ledger; and (b) unauthorised (or improper, or illegal) operations on recorded ledger data.

Consensus Mechanism: A consensus mechanism is a protocol (i.e., set of rules) to ensure that all the blockchain network participants comply with the agreed rules for day-to-day operations. It makes sure that the transactions originate from a legitimate source by having every participant consent to the distributed ledger's state. The public blockchain is a decentralised technology, and no centralised authority is in place to regulate the required act. Therefore, the network requires authorisations from the network participants to verify and authenticate any blockchain network activities. The whole process is done based on the consensus of the network participants, and it makes the blockchain a trustless, secure, and reliable technology for digital transactions. Distinct consensus mechanisms follow different principles, which enables the network participants to comply with those rules. Several consensus mechanisms have introduced considering the requirements of secure digital transactions. However, proof of work (PoW), proof of stake (PoS), and delegated proof of stake (DPoS) are the few consensus protocols used by the industries. In this way, the blockchain relies on the distributed consensus mechanism to establish mutual trust. However, the consensus mechanism itself has a vulnerability, which attackers can exploit to control the entire blockchain. Although a few approaches, e.g., (Muhammad et al., 2018), are highlighted in blockchain-related research to deter and prevent attacks. Due to the inherent characteristics of openness, the PoW-based permissionless blockchain networks may not be completely secure.

Network Infrastructure: The network infrastructure requirements for both blockchain and Distributed Ledger Technology (DLT). The network infrastructure threats can detect in nodes being stopped by a malicious attacker using good anticipatory mechanisms. In August 2016, nearly 120,000 Bitcoin (over US $60mn at the time) were stolen from Bitfinex (Nagaraj & Maguire, 2017). Based in Hong Kong, Bitfinex is one of the world's largest digital and cryptocurrency exchanges. The incident exploited security vulnerabilities within individual organisations. The blockchain network itself remained fully functional and operated as envisioned. The incident may have prevented a detailed end-to-end review of security, using scenarios, meaning there would have been a higher chance of identifying risks upfront and mitigating them at that point.

Identity Access Management: Privacy in blockchain enables the client/user to perform transactions without leaking its identification information in the network. Also, blockchain technology uses numerous techniques to achieve the highest level of privacy and authenticity for transactions. As information comes from different users within the blockchain industrial ecosystem, the infrastructure needs to ensure every user privacy and authenticity. Blockchain-based information system often employs a combination of public and private key to encrypt and decrypt data securely.

Cryptography: The records on a blockchain are secured through cryptography. Network participants have their private keys assigned to the transactions they make and act as a personal digital signature. If a record is altered, the signature will become invalid, and the peer network will know right away that something has happened. However, there could be software bugs and glitches in cryptography coding. These could include anything from developers' coding mistakes, inappropriate design, and an underlying defect in the cryptography routines. Also, trained coders can make a mistake in putting together well-known and tested cryptographic tools to not secure. Hackers can take advantages of this weakness.

Safety is an essential aspect of blockchain-based transaction processes. All the data within the blockchain ecosystem needs to be secured and tamperproof. The security ensures that there are no malicious nodes within the blockchain-based enterprise ecosystem. As mentioned earlier, the data inserted into a public ledger or inside the blockchain is distributed to individual users, and everyone maintains their local copy of the blockchain. In that local copy, that individual cannot tamper but upgrade the data and retransmit the network's data. However, for the transaction to be validated, the other nodes should be convinced that the broadcasted information is not malicious, and the system security is ensured.

Figure 3. Various Security Risk Areas of Blockchain

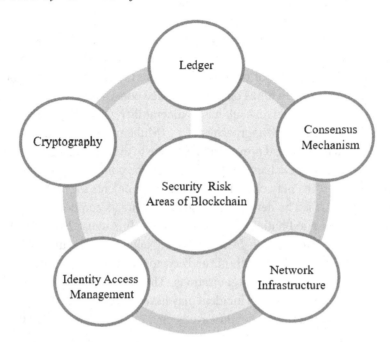

THREAT MODELS FOR BLOCKCHAIN

This section explains the threat models that are considered by the blockchain protocols in IoT networks. Threat agents are mostly malicious users whose intention is to steal assets, break functionalities, or disrupt services. However, threat agents might also be inadvertent entities, such as developers of smart contacts who unintentionally create bugs and designers of blockchain applications who make mistakes in the design or ignore some issues.

Threats facilitate various attacks on assets. Threats arise from vulnerabilities at the network, smart contracts, consensus protocol deviations or violations of consensus protocol assumptions, or application-specific vulnerabilities. Countermeasures protect owners from threats. They involve various security and safety solutions and tools, incentives, reputation techniques, best practices, and so on. Threats and their agents cause risks. They may lead to a loss of monetary assets, a loss of privacy, a loss of reputation, service malfunctions, and disruptions of services and applications (i.e., availability issues).

The blockchain-based information systems owners wish to minimise the risk caused by threats that arise from threat agents. This section presents five types of attacks: *identity-based attacks*, *manipulation-based attacks*, *cryptanalytic attacks*, *reputation-based attacks*, and *service-based attacks*. A diagrammatic representation of these attacks is shown in Figure 5.

Identity-Based Attacks

The emergence of DLT based upon a blockchain data structure has given rise to new approaches to identity management, aiming to upend dominant approaches to providing and consuming digital identities. These new approaches to identity management (IdM) propose to enhance decentralisation, transparency and user control in transactions that involve identity information. In identity-based attacks, the attacker forges identity to masquerade as an authorised user to access the system and manipulate it. Again, identity-based attacks can be broadly classified into four different types, and they are (i) Key attack, (ii) Replay attack, (iii)Impersonation attack, and Sybil attack.

Key attack: In blockchain technology, certificates and identities are validated and protected in Hyperledger Fabric by asymmetric cryptography. How each participant chooses to store and protect their private key is up to them. A wide range of wallets and management methods available as Hyperledger Fabric requires no cohesive management scheme. An outside attacker obtaining private key(s) could lead to any number of attacks. To deal with this attack, LNSC (Lightning Network and Smart Contract) protocol (Huang et al., 2018) provides an authentication mechanism between the electric vehicles and charging piles. It uses elliptic curve encryption to calculate the hash functions, ensuring resiliency against the critical leakage attack.

Replay attack: This attack aims to spoof two parties' identities, intercept their data packets, and relay them to their destinations without modiдcation. To resist this attack, LNSC (Huang et al., 2018) uses the idea of elliptic curve encryption to calculate the hash functions. On the other hand, BSein (blockchain-based system for secure mutual authentication) (Lin et al., 2018) uses a fresh one-time public/private key pair.

Impersonation attack: An attacker tries to masquerade as a legitimate user to perform unauthorised operations. As presented in Table II, three methods are proposed to protect against this attack. The elliptic curve encryption idea to calculate the hash functions is proposed by LNSC protocol (Huang et al., 2018). Wang et al. (Wang et al., 2018) propose a distributed incentive-based cooperation mechanism, which protects the user's privacy and a transaction veriдcation method. On the other hand,

BSein (Lin et al., 2018) uses the concept of attribute-based signatures (i.e., legitimate devices can produce a valid signature, and hence any impersonation attempt will be detected when its corresponding authentication operation fails.

Sybil attack: A sybil attack is when an attacker creates multiple accounts on a blockchain to deceive the other blockchain participants. A successful Sybil attack increases the reputation of some agents or lowers the reputation of others by initiating interactions in the network. These attacks should not be an issue on a permissioned blockchain since the members are clearly identified and wallets are not normally used. TrustChain (i.e., capable of creating trusted transactions among strangers without central control) (Otte et al., 2017) addresses this issue by creating an immutable chain.

Whitewashing: When an agent has a negative reputation, it can eliminate its identity and make a new one. There is no remedie to prevent this behaviour. However, it is suggested in (Otte et a., 2017) to give lower priorities to new identities agents when applying the allocation policy.

Service-based attacks: The attacker try either to make the service unavailable or make it behave differently from its speciдcations. Under this category, we can дnd the following attacks:

DDoS/DoS attack: A distributed denial-of-service (DDOS) attack is a prevalent type of network attack against a website, a communication network node, or even a membership service provider. The objective of this attack is to slow down or crash the system. The concentrated attack and subsequent shut down of the system result in a "denial of service" for legitimate users. Denial of Service (DoS) and DDoS are common security problems. DoS attacks on the connectivity of consensus nodes may result in a loss of consensus power, thus preventing consensus nodes from being rewarded. It involves sending a huge number of requests to cause the failure of the blockchain system. CoinParty (Ziegeldorf et al., 2018) proposes the idea of decentralised mixing service. Liu et al. (Liu et al., 2018) employ a ring-based signature with the Elliptic Curve Digital Signature Algorithm (ECDSA). The resilience against DoS in BSeIn (Lin et al., 2018) is achieved by limiting the block size, and using the *'multi-receivers'* encryption technique to provide conðdentiality for authorised users.

Figure 4. Classification of threat models for blockchain

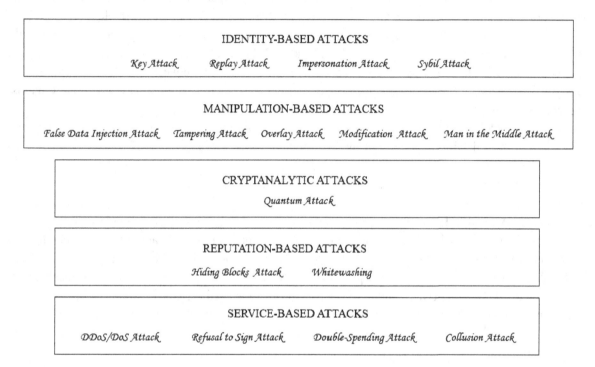

Manipulation-Based Attacks

Manipulation-based attacks can occur when the attacker is near the information system's device or data communication network. General types of physical layer attacks are as follows:

Tampering: Physical damage to device (e.g., RFID tag, Tag reader), or communication network (Andrea et al., 2015).

Malicious Code Injection: The attacker physically introduces a malicious code onto an IoT system by compromising its operation. The attacker can control the IoT system and launch attacks (Ahemd et al., 2017).

Radio Frequency Signal Interference (Jamming): The predator sends a particular type of radio-frequency signal to hinder communication in the IoT system, and it creates a denial of service (DoS) from the information system (Ahemd et al., 2017).

Fake Node Injection: The intruder creates an artificial node and the IoT-based system network and access the information from the network illegally or control data flow (Ahemd et al., 2017).

Sleep Denial Attack: The aim of the attacker is to keeps the battery-powered devices awake by sending them with inappropriate inputs, and this causes exhaustion of battery power that leads to shutting down of nodes (Ahemd et al., 2017).

Side Channel Attack: In this attack, the intruder gets hold of the encryption keys by applying malicious techniques on the devices of the IoT-based information system (Andrea et al., 2015), and by using these keys, the attacker can encrypt or decrypt confidential information from the IoT network.

Permanent Denial of Service (PDoS): In this attack, the attacker permanently damages the IoT system using hardware sabotage. The attack can be launched by damaging firmware or uploading an inappropriate BIOS using malware (Foundry, 2017).

Refusal to Sign attack: An attacker can decide not to sign a transaction that is not in his favour. Although preventing this attack is not possible, punishment measures can be taken against the refusal agents. It is proposed in (Otte Et al., 2017) to not interact with the malicious agent or split the transactions into smaller amounts. If an agent refuses to sign a transaction, the interaction is aborted.

Double-spending attack: It means that the attackers spend the same bitcoin twice to acquire extra amounts. In (Wang et al., 2017), the Timestamp and the Proof-of-Work mechanism is used. In (Aitzhan & Svetinovic, 2016), a multi-signature transaction is employed, where a minimum number of keys must sign a transaction before spending tokens.

Collusion Attack: Nodes can collide with each other and behave selõshly to maximise their proõt. In (He et al., 2018), an incentive mechanism and pricing strategy are proposed to thwart selõsh behaviours.

CONCLUSION

Today's manufacturing operation faces significant volatility, uncertainty and complexity imposed by a dynamic business environment. Changes in customer buying pattern, the demand for a low price, higher service levels, mobile commerce, and so on – necessitate customer intelligence and varying fulfilment models. These have introduced significant stress on manufacturing supply chain networks, compelling, relevant businesses to revisit their supply chain design practice. It includes the deployment of appropriate information systems that enhance supply chain execution. In such scenarios, enterprise information systems architecture plays a significant role.

The IoT-based system is a smart, more comprehensive network of interconnected objects, which through unique address schemes (e.g., EPC-based address), can cooperate and interact with their neighbours to collect data, process data, and convert it to daily business-related decisions. The data obtained from the IoT applications along manufacturing business processes can make operational decision-making much more comfortable. However, standalone IoT application systems face different security problems ranging from attacks on IoT devices to attacks on transit data that have drawn interest from academics and practitioners. The tight integration of the digital world with the physical world using automated information systems has further created IoT systems' vulnerabilities.

IoT device data often stored in the service-oriented computing storage in the cloud, but they are not protected against compromised integrity devices or tampering at the source. In contrast, the blockchain is an evolving technology that can help with IoT systems resiliency. However, the extensive use of IoT technologies and blockchain-based linked data results in new security, privacy, and policy-related problems; at the same time, they can also be part of the solution. For example, more accurate models for figuring out security issues can be built using the data's contextual semantic interpretation. Besides, the purposeful interpretation of personal data exchanged among business partners could be used to improve the ability of IoT based manufacturing network users to control over interactions, and hence better manage their online privacy. The machine-processable and machine-readable representation of data-related policies can also provide different benefits to manufacturers by automation of tasks related to policy-management.

REFERENCES

Ahemd, M. M., Shah, M. A., & Wahid, A. (2017). Iot security: a layered approach for attacks and defenses. *2017 International Conference on Communication Technologies (ComTech),* 104–110.

AhIman, R. (2016). *Finish city partners with IBM to validate blockchain application in logistics.* https://cointelegraph.com/news/finish-city-partners-with-ibm-to-validate-blockchain-application-in-logistics

Aitzhan, N. Z. & Svetinovic, D. (2016). Security and Privacy in Decentralized Energy Trading through Multi-signatures, Blockchain and Anonymous Messaging Streams. *IEEE Transaction on Dependable and Secure Computing,* 1–1.

Andrea, I., Chrysostomou, C., & Hadjichristofi, G. (2015). Internet of things: security vulnerabilities and challenges. *2015 IEEE Symposium on Computers and Communication (ISCC),* 180–187.

Atzori, L., Iera, A., & Morabito, G. (2018). The Internet of Things: A survey. *Computer Networks, 54*(15), 2787–2805. doi:10.1016/j.comnet.2010.05.010

Banker, S. (2016). *Will blockchain technology revolutionise supply chain applications?* https://logisticsviewpoints.com/2016/06/20/will-block-chain-technology-revolutionize-supply -chain-applications/

Barreto, L., Amaral, A., & Pereira, T. (2017). Industry 4.0 implications in logistics: An overview. *Procedia Manufacturing, 2017*(13), 1245–1252. doi:10.1016/j.promfg.2017.09.045

Cam-Winget, N., Sadeghi, A.-R., & Jin, Y. (2016). INVITED: Can IoT be Secured: Emerging Challenges in Connecting the Unconnected. *Proceedings of the 53rd Annual Design Automation Conference (DAC '16).* 10.1145/2897937.2905004

Chen, R., Guo, J., & Bao, F. (2014). Trust management for service composition in SOA-based IoT systems. *Proceedings of the 2014 IEEE Wireless Communications and Networking Conference (WCNC),* 3444–3449. 10.1109/WCNC.2014.6953138

Cliche, Taghipour, & Canel. (2020). An Improved Forecasting Approach to Reduce Inventory-Levels in Decentralized Supply Chains. *European Journal of Operational Research, 287*(2), 511–527.

Cui, Y. (2018). Supply Chain Innovation with IoT. In Multi-Criteria Methods and Techniques Applied to Supply Chain Management. Intech Open. doi:10.5772/intechopen.74155

Deloitte. (2017). *Digital Procurement: New Capabilities from Disruptive Technologies.* Deloitte Development LLC.

Dorri, A., Kanhere, S. S., Jurdak, R., & Gauravaram, P. (2017). Blockchain for IoT security and privacy: The case study of a smart home. *Proceedings of the 2017 IEEE International Conference on Pervasive Computing and Communications Workshops (PerCom Workshops).*

Finextra. (2016). *Everledger secures the first bottle of wine on the blockchain.* https://www.finextra.com/pressaritcle/67381/everledger-secures-the-first-bottle-of-wine-on-the-blockchain

Foundry, D. (2017). *What Is a Permanent Dos (Pdos) Attack?* https://www.datafoundry. com/blog/what-is-permanent-dos-pdos-attack/t

Galvez, J. F., Mejuto, J. C., & Gandara, J. S. (2018). Future challenges on the use of blockchain for food traceability analysis. *Trends in Analytical Chemistry, 107*, 222–232. doi:10.1016/j.trac.2018.08.011

Garg, S., Gentry, C., Halevi, S., Sahai, A., & Waters, W. (2013). *Attribute-Based Encryption for Circuits from Multilinear Maps.* Academic Press. doi:10.1007/978-3-642-40084-1_27

Gu, J., Sum, B., Du, X., Wang, J., Zhuang, Y., & Wang, Z. (2018). Consortium Blockchain-Based Malware Detection in Mobile Devices. *IEEE Access: Practical Innovations, Open Solutions, 6*, 12118–12128. doi:10.1109/ACCESS.2018.2805783

Gubbi, J., Buyya, R., Marusic, S., & Palaniswami, M. (2013). Internet of Things (IoT): A vision, architectural elements, and future directions. *Future Generation Computer Systems, 29*(7), 1645–1660. doi:10.1016/j.future.2013.01.010

He, Y., Li, H., Cheng, X., Liu, Y., Yang, C., & Sun, L. (2018). A Blockchain based Truthful Incentive Mechanism for Distributed P2P Applications. *IEEE Access: Practical Innovations, Open Solutions, 6*, 1–1. doi:10.1109/ACCESS.2018.2821705

Hua, J., Wang, X., Kang, M., Wang, H., & Wang, F. (2018). Blockchain based Provenance for Agricultural Products: A Distributed Platform with Duplicated and Shared Bookkeeping. *Proceedings of the IEEE Intelligent Vehicles Symposium (IV).* 10.1109/IVS.2018.8500647

Huang, X., Xu, C., Wang, P., & Liu, H. (2018). LNSC: A security model for electric vehicle and charging pile management based on blockchain ecosystem. *IEEE Access: Practical Innovations, Open Solutions, 6*, 13565–13574. doi:10.1109/ACCESS.2018.2812176

Hulse Apple, C. (2015). *Block Verify uses blockchains to end counterfeiting and making world more honest.* https://cointelegraph.com/news/block-verify-uses-blockchains-to-end-counterfeiting-and-make-world-more-honest

Hur, J., & Noh, D. K. (2011). Attribute-based access control with efficient revocation in data outsourcing systems. *IEEE Transactions on Parallel and Distributed Systems, 22*(7), 1214–1221. doi:10.1109/TPDS.2010.203

Jemel, M., & Serhrouchni, A. (2017). Decentralised access control mechanism with temporal dimension based on blockchain. *2017 IEEE 14th International Conference on e-Business Engineering (ICEBE),* 177–182.

Kamilaris, A., Fonts, A., & Prenafeta-Boldv, F. X. (2019). The rise of blockchain technology in agriculture and food supply chain. *Trends in Food Science & Technology, 91,* 640–652. doi:10.1016/j.tifs.2019.07.034

Katz, J., & Lindell, Y. (2007). *Digital Signature Schemes. In Introduction to Modern Cryptography.* Chapman & Hall/ CBC Press. doi:10.1201/9781420010756

Keertikumar, M., Shubham, M., & Banakar, R. M. (2015). Evolution of IoT in smart vehicles: An overview. *Proceedings of the International Conference on Green Computing and Internet of Things (ICGCIoT)*, 804–809. 10.1109/ICGCIoT.2015.7380573

Kim, N. (2016). IBM pushes blockchain into the supply chain. *Wall Street Journal.*

Kshetri, N. (2017). Can Blockchain Strengthen the Internet of Things? *IEEE IT Professional*, *19*(4), 68–72. doi:10.1109/MITP.2017.3051335

Kumanduri, R., & Romero, C. (1998). *Number Theory with Computer Applications*. Prentice Hall.

Kumar, M. V., & Iyengar, N. C. S. N. (2017). A Framework for blockchain technology in rice supply chain management. *Advanced Science and Technology Letters*, *146*, 125–130. doi:10.14257/astl.2017.146.22

Lagadec, P. (1990). Communication strategies in crisis situations. *Industrial Crisis Quarterly*, *1*, 19–26.

Lagadec, P. (1993). *Preventing chaos in a crisis*. McGraw-Hill.

Lee, B., & Lee, J. H. (2017). Blockchain-based secure firmware update for embedded devices in an Internet of Things environment. *The Journal of Supercomputing*, *73*(3), 1152–1167. doi:10.100711227-016-1870-0

Lee, I., & Lee, K. (2015). The Internet of Things (IoT): Applications, investments, and challenges for enterprises. *Business Horizons*, *58*(4), 431–440. doi:10.1016/j.bushor.2015.03.008

Liang, G., Weller, S. R., Luo, F., Zhao, J., & Dong, Z. Y. (2018). Distributed Blockchain-Based Data Protection Framework for Modern Power Systems against Cyber Attacks. *IEEE Transactions on Smart Grid*, 1–1.

Lin, C., He, D., Huang, X., Choo, K. K. R., & Vasilakos, A. V. (2018). Bsein: A blockchain-based secure mutual authentication with ðne-grained access control system for industry 4.0. *Journal of Network and Computer Applications*, *116*, 42–52. doi:10.1016/j.jnca.2018.05.005

Lin, I. C., Shin, H., Liu, J. C., & Jie, Y. X. (2017). Food traceability system using blockchain. *Proceedings of the 79th IASTEM International Conference.*

Liu, Y., Liu, X., Tang, C., Wang, J., & Zhang, L. (2018). Unlinkable Coin Mixing Scheme for Transaction Privacy Enhancement of Bitcoin. *IEEE Access: Practical Innovations, Open Solutions*, *6*, 23261–23270. doi:10.1109/ACCESS.2018.2827163

Mahjabin, T., Xiao, Y., Sun, G., & Jiang, W. (2017). A survey of distributed denial-of-service attack, prevention, and mitigation techniques. *International Journal of Distributed Sensor Networks*, *13*(12), 155014771774146. doi:10.1177/1550147717741463

Muhammad, S., Aziz, M., Charles, K., Kevin, H., & Laurent, N. (2018). Countering double spending in next-generation blockchains. IEEE ICC 2018.

Nagaraj, K., & Maguire, E. (2017). *Securing the Chain*. KPMG International. https://assets.kpmg.com/content/dam/kpmg/xx/pdf/2017/05/securing-the-chain.pdf

Okorie, O., Turner, C., Charnley, F., Moreno, M., & Tiwari, A. (2017). A review of data driven approaches for circular economy in manufacturing. *Proceedings of the 18th European Roundtable for Sustainable Consumption and Production.*

Otte, P., de Vos, M., & Pouwelse, J. (2017, Sept.). TrustChain: A Sybil-resistant scalable blockchain. *Future Generation Computer Systems.*

Paillisse, J., Subira, J., Lopez, L., Rodriguez-Natal, A., Ermagan, V., Maino, F., & Cabellos, A. (2019). *Distributed Access Control with Blockchain.* Academic Press.

Pal, K. & Ul-Haque, A. (2020). Internet of Things and Blockchain Technology in Apparel Manufacturing Supply Chain Data Management. *Proceeding of 11th International Conference on Ambient Systems, Networks and Technologies (ANT-2020).*

Pal, K. (2017). Supply Chain Coordination Based on Web Services. In H. K. Chan, N. Subramanian, & M. D. Abdulrahman (Eds.), *Supply Chain Management in the Big Data Era* (pp. 137–171). IGI Global Publication. doi:10.4018/978-1-5225-0956-1.ch009

Pal, K. (2017). *A Semantic Web Service Architecture for Supply Chain Management.* The 8th International Conference on Ambient Systems, Networks and Technologies, Portugal.

Pal, K. (2019). Algorithmic Solutions for RFID Tag Anti-Collision Problem in Supply Chain Management. *Procedia Computer Science,* 929-934.

Pal, K. (2020). Information sharing for manufacturing supply chain management based on blockchain technology. In *Cross-Industry Use of Blockchain Technology and Opportunities for the Future.* IGI Global.

Pal, K. (2020a). Ontology-Assisted Enterprise Information Systems Integration in Manufacturing Supply Chain. In Handbook of Research on Developments and Trends in Industrial and Material Engineering. IGI Global.

Pal, K. (2020b). Information Sharing for Manufacturing Supply Chain Management Based on Blockchain Technology. In Cross-industry Use of Blockchain Technology and Opportunities for the Future. IGI Global.

Pal, K., & Yasar, A. (2020). Internet of Things and blockchain technology in apparel manufacturing supply chain data management. *Procedia Computer Science, 170,* 450–457.

Pauchant, T., & Mitroff, I. (1992). *Transforming the crisis-prone organization.* Jossey-Bass.

Pauchant, T. C., & Douville, R. (1994). Recent research in crisis management: A study of 24 authors' publications from 1986 to 1991. *Industrial and Environmental Crisis Quarterly, 7,* 43–61.

Radhoui, Taghipour, & Canel. (2018). *The distribution and pickup of goods- a literature review and survey in Hierarchical Planning and Information Sharing Techniques in Supply Chain Management.* IGI Global.

Rejeb, A. (2018). Blockchain Potential in Tilapia Supply Chain in Ghana. *Acta Tech. Jaurinensis, 11*(2), 104–118. doi:10.14513/actatechjaur.v11.n2.462

Sahai, A., & Waters, B. (2005). Fuzzy identity-based encryption. In *Annual International Conference on the Theory and Applications of Cryptographic Techniques*. Springer.

Sharma, P. K., Singh, S., Jeong, Y. S., & Park, J. H. (2017). DistBlockNet: A Distributed Blockchains-Based Secure SDN Architecture for IoT Networks. *IEEE Communication Management, 55*(9), 78–85. doi:10.1109/MCOM.2017.1700041

Shrivastava, P. (1993). Crisis theory/practice: Towards a sustainable future. *Industrial and Environmental Crisis Quarterly, 7,* 23–42.

Shrivastava, P., Mitroff, I., Miller, D., & Miglani, A. (1988). Understanding industrial crises. *Journal of Management Studies, 25,* 285–303.

Shrouf, F., Ordieres, J., & Miragliotta, G. (2014). Smart factories in Industry 4.0: A review of the concept and of energy management approached in production based on the Internet of Things paradigm. *Proceedings of the IEEE International Conference on Industrial Engineering and Engineering Management,* 679–701. 10.1109/IEEM.2014.7058728

Szabo, N. (1994). *Smart Contracts.* Available online: https://archive.is/zQ1p8

Taghipour. (2020). *Demand Forecasting and Order Planning in Supply Chains and Humanitarian Logistics.* IGI Global.

Tse, D., Zhang, B., Yang, Y., Cheng, C., & My, H. (2017). Blockchain application in food supply information security. *Proceedings of the IEEE International Conference on Industrial Engineering and Engineering Management (IEEM 2017),* 1357–1361. 10.1109/IEEM.2017.8290114

Tzounis, A., Katsoulas, N., Bartzanas, T., & Kittas, C. (2017). Internet of things in agriculture, recent advances, and future challenges. *Biosystems Engineering, 164,* 31–48. doi:10.1016/j.biosystemseng.2017.09.007

Waller, M. A., & Fawcett, S. E. (2013). Data science, predictive analytics, and big data: A revolution that will transform supply chain design and management. *Journal of Business Logistics, 34*(2), 77–84. doi:10.1111/jbl.12010

Wang, Q., Qin, B., Hu, J., & Xiao, F. (2017, Sept.). Preserving transaction privacy in bitcoin. *Future Generation Computer Systems.*

Wang, S., Zhang, Y., & Zhang, Y. (2018). A blockchain-based framework for data sharing with fine-grained access control in decentralised storage systems. *IEEE Access: Practical Innovations, Open Solutions, 6,* 38437–38450. doi:10.1109/ACCESS.2018.2851611

Wang, S. J., Liu, S. F., & Wang, W. L. (2008). The simulated impact of RFID-enabled supply chain on pull-based inventory replenishment in TFT-LCD industry. *International Journal of Production Economics, 112*(2), 570–586. doi:10.1016/j.ijpe.2007.05.002

Washington, L. C. (2008). *Elliptic Curves: Number Theory and Cryptography* (2nd ed.). Chapman & Hall/CRC. doi:10.1201/9781420071474

Witkowski, K. (2017). Internet of Things, Big Data, Industry 4.0 - Innovative Solutions in Logistics and Supply Chains Management. *Procedia Engineering, 2017*(182), 763–769. doi:10.1016/j.proeng.2017.03.197

Yan-e, D. (2011). Design of intelligent agriculture management information system based on IoT. *Proceedings of the 2011 Fourth International Conference on Intelligent Computation Technology and Automation, 1*, 1045–1049. 10.1109/ICICTA.2011.262

Yin, W., Wen, Q., Li, W., Zhang, H., & Jin, Z. (2018). An Anti-Quantum Transaction Authentication Approach in Blockchain. *IEEE Access: Practical Innovations, Open Solutions, 6*, 5393–5401. doi:10.1109/ACCESS.2017.2788411

Zhou, Z. (2012). Applying RFID to reduce bullwhip effect in a FMCG supply chain. *Proceedings of the Advances in Computational Environment Science.*

Ziegeldorf, J. H., Matzutt, R., Henze, M., Grossmann, F., & Wehrle, K. (2018). Secure and anonymous decentralized Bitcoin mixing. *Future Generation Computer Systems, 80*, 448–466. doi:10.1016/j.future.2016.05.018

Chapter 67
Blockchain and IoT–Based Diary Supply Chain Management System for Sri Lanka

K. Pubudu Nuwnthika Jayasena
Sbaragamuwa University of Sri Lanka, Sri Lanka

Poddivila Marage Nimasha Ruwandi Madhunamali
Sabaragamuwa University of Sri Lanka, Sri Lanka

ABSTRACT

The central problem to be addressed in this research is to investigate how blockchain technology can be used in today's food supply chains to deliver greater traceability of assets. The aim is to create a blockchain model in the dairy supply chain that can be implemented across any food supply chains and present the advantages and limitations in its implementation. Blockchain allows monitoring all types of transactions in a supply chain more safely and transparently. Acceptance of blockchain in the supply chain and logistics is slow right now because of related risks and the lack of demonstrable models. The proposed solution removes the need for a trusted centralized authority, intermediaries and provides records of transactions, improving high integrity, reliability, and security efficiency and protection. All transactions are registered and maintained in the unchangeable database of the blockchain with access to a shared file network.

INTRODUCTION

Every day we consume food products on the basis of the confidence because that providers are produced, transported and warehouse in accordance with the internal and government regulations on food safety. Before reaching the end consumer, food product moving through different phases of supply chain from suppliers to retailers. These intermittent stages contribute to product design, manufacture, delivery, and sales. Although food safety measurements do periodic measure of food safety and provide certifications of the quality, it is often difficult to trust when searching a supply chain scaling across countries with

DOI: 10.4018/978-1-6684-7132-6.ch067

the distribution of technology. For example, The United States stopped imports of meat from Brazil due to the acceptance of bribes by food examiners in Brazil, the horsemeat scandal in Europe, the milk powder of babies scandal in China and the growing problem of food pollution in India. Over the past decade, these incidents have occurred periodically, pushing consumers and governments to request greater transparency throughout the food supply chain(Aung & Chang, 2014)(Bosona & Gebresenbet, 2013).

Based on Food and Drink research, organizations decide, increasing consideration of the food provenance as a business challenge. They are finding business opportunities through increasing health awareness. Nowadays consumers highly consider the quality of food product so they hesitate to purchase. It is because there is no way to ensure the quality of the food product and less transparency through the supply chain process of the product. Nowadays organizations are identified that customers are always looking for trusted products with verified sources. For that, they are plan to get a competitive advantage by providing a transparent supply chain and sustainable manufacturing. For example, Walmart has joined with IBM to study as of February 2018 to test whether the organization can guarantee the Health of food products that they sell in their retail stores. Nevertheless, contemporary repositories for each silo stage of the logistic transportation are ineffective in giving unparalleled trust to the client, because they are not dishonest. A lot of food supply chains today only check their product end of the logistic transportation processes and still there is no way to map their product in source and stages between customers.

Although the different phases of the food supply chain has many possible adverse results such as Irreversible disruption to the environment, abuse of working conditions, unethical manufacturing practices, counterfeiting and large quantities of agricultural waste attributable to imbalanced sourcing and storage strategies. End users tend to use these programs without realizing the repercussions that they create by their footprint and food supply chains are easily kept hidden with little effort to provide end-to-end access to their stakeholders. Although these challenges, the idea of requiring a single agency to provide data and transaction control in food supply chain was the only realistic solution until recently when a modern system called blockchain provided a whole modern way of addressing food provenance

BACKGROUND

Supply Chain

Global Supply Chains are becoming progressively difficult over the years. Therefore, it has become more challenging to manage social sustainability problems which are concerned by many foreign buyers (including large retailers and brand owners) and consumers, where monitoring and analysis of their transportation supply networks relies on many suppliers, distributors and delivery centers, some of them uncommon or even one-time. (Venkatesh, Kang, Wang, Zhong, & Zhang, 2020a)(Petri Helo & Shamsuzzoha, 2020). Supply chains are not fixed. It develops and changes in size, shape, and configuration, and in how they are coordinated, controlled and managed. Not only the economic drivers but also the technological drivers affect the changes in the supply chain. As a result of that, digital technology integrates with supply chain management. The new step introduces as "Supply Chain Digitization". Digitization may play a leverage role in aligning current sourcing strategies as well as developing new sourcing strategies to enhance long-term efficiency, productivity, and competitive advantage overall organizational objectives.

In a dairy supply chain, a network of stakeholders transacts to the end consumer in the form of rising, storing or selling foods. Transport companies act as links which connect these stages and ensure that the right quantity and quality product reaches the right destination at the right time

The stakeholders include:

1. Milk suppliers.
2. The milk processors engaged in the manufacture and sometimes distribution of the milk commodity
3. The distributer active in the sale to end consumers and dealers of the finished product.
4. The end customers engaged in shopping the items, which consists of individuals and markets.

Blockchain

Considered one of the most innovative innovations available, the blockchain first showed up in 2008 when published "Bitcoin: A Peer-to-Peer Electronic Cash System". The scheme suggested was based on cryptographic proof rather than dependency, allowing any two parties to perform transactions without the need of a trustworthy third party. The plan solved the issue of double spending(Kosba, Miller, Shi, Wen, & Papamanthou, 2016)(Wright & De Filippi, 2015). This is the first application of blockchain, Created by Satoshi Nakamoto (Nakamoto, 2008). There are many critical features, that blockchain provides. Such as Decentralized, Traceability, Consensus mechanism, Immutability, Smart contract(Yumna, Murad, Ikram, & Noreen, n.d.)(Madumidha, Ranjani, Varsinee, & Sundari, 2019). Blockchain application contain distributed architecture. That mean of distributed architecture is the system does not depend on any centralized authority but uses a peer-to-peer network of computer servers maintained by decentralized interest owners(P. Helo & Hao, 2019)(Tezel, Papadonikolaki, Yitmen, & Hilletofth, 2019). Today blockchain is applications further than finance, as in government, health, science, arts and culture(Frizzo-barker et al., 2019)(Pilkington, 2016).A range of implementations is already being explored such as a blockchain based smart grid in the energy sector(Scully & Hobig, 2019).In such a network, blockchain technology enforces transparency and guarantees ultimate, system-wide accord on the validity of a complete history of transactions. In the blockchain, no single party controls the data. The whole data infrastructure is visible to all parties. So that it helps to minimize the bias errors. (Treiblmaier, 2018) Every party can confirm the records of its transaction followers directly, without an intermediary or ledger unauthorized access or manipulation. Although many speculate about the impact of blockchain technology upon supply chains, the current understanding of its potential remains limited. As the development and diffusion of this technology is still in its infancy (Wang et al., 2018).

Every node inside a blockchain have encrypted keys named public and private key, and each transaction within two nodes contains some important information about the sender and the receiver, asset information, date, and identifier for the sender 's previous transaction. An asset may be any commodity within a supply chain, or a buyer-seller exchange. A cryptographic hash function named SHA 256 (Secure Hash Algorithm 256) uses the sender's public key and transactional information to produce a 16-digit hexadecimal string called the "tag". The hash done is special to a combination of a public key and transaction information. A group of randomly clustered transactions is one block. This authenticated transaction information is decoded to verify the validity of the transactions and their origin, which can only be decrypted by brute force. The cycle of hash resolution is called mining, and miners are called nodes that validate certain transactions. When the network generates a block from the pool of unchecked transactions, available miners will be competing to validate the transactions by resolving the cryptographic hash

A consensus algorithm controls the method of choosing a miner at a blockchain. Some network systems such as the Ethereum and Hyperledger projects are special. Every block within a blockchain contain of 3 important components - a hash (a unique digital identifier), a timestamp, and the hash of the previous block (to compute the account balance). The previous block hash ties the whole block chain together and thus stops any block being changed or added between two authenticated chains. When a transaction is checked, the blockchain records it. Changing a reported transaction value in a decentralized blockchain network such as Bitcoin is quite difficult because an intruder must obtain nearly 51 percent of the entire computing power existing in the framework. Therefore each subsequent block enhances the verification of the preceding block and ultimately blockchain as a whole. This mechanism holds the blockchain resistant to malicious activities, contributing to the essential immutability attribute.

In Ethereum, the blockchain system is controlled by rules decided upon by the participants in the network in the method of smart contracts and was firstly implemented in Bitcoin for running the mutual accounting ledger. It is commonly used after this initial financial use, when many players with little to no confidence are part of a transaction; for example, fragmented supply chains. Blockchain's three basic features make it an attractive choice for tracking supply chain assets

- **Distributed processing:** Does not require a central control system. The process is distributed to all processors or network participants embedded in the process.
- **Synchronized records:** The ledger is circulated to all players and so it is fraud-proof.
- **Smart information:** We can build cloud applications that run on top of the blockchain architecture, allowing us to customize the data format that is available in the supply chain at every point.

Figure 1.

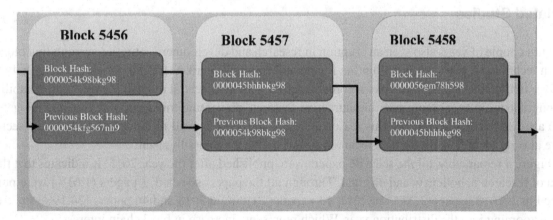

Smart Contracts

A smart contract can be defined as a program which can activate certain functions automatically if anything predetermined happens. Intelligent contract contact with the blockchain, the criteria are stored in "contracts" and must be met by the users in order to build a new block. A smart contract is not an intrinsic part of the blockchain protocol itself, but a function on the network that is stored on a blockchain database in a completely distributed manner (Mattila, Seppälä, & Holmström, 2016).

Blockchain Technology in Supply Chain

Blockchains are already generating advantages on supply chains around the world. Real-time visibility can be considered an important benefit to supply chain management (Sheel & Nath, 2019). Moreover, all transactions can be traceable, and consequently. The data are organized into blocks that shape a chain. Blockchain transactions operate in a peer-to-peer network, in a decentralized way. In other words, the transactions are validated and stored by a distributed ledger, and it is not necessary to have a central entity that validates the transactions(Petri Helo & Shamsuzzoha, 2020). Almost all organizations need to take profit of several improvements brought about by blockchain, which spans improved process and operations over the whole supply chain, safer, transparent and efficient transactions(Kshetri, 2018) and trust and reliability through the network, all processes and related information being shared by all network participants.

Blockchain and Internet of Things(IOT) Combination

With the implementation of Blockchain and IOT technologies combined, the supply chain problems addressed so far can be solved or minimized. Blockchain and IOT merge the physical world details directly into the computing environment and store it in a distributed ledger in a multi partner situation thereby bridging the confidence gap. Whilst various IoT sensor systems can be combined. It system ensures open and auditable traceability of properties by automatically extracting and processing valuable information from the IoT systems along the entire supply chain and maintaining these data directly in its underlying ledger.

Related Studies

The last couple of years also seen an eruption in research and development activities surrounding blockchain technology, particularly within the financial technology market. Indeed, its intrinsic capacity to deliver immutable and manipulative records, together with its potential of enabling trust and reliability among untrusted peers represents too attractive features, preventing this technology to stay relegated into a single vertical sector. For this reason, several industries beyond the financial technology sector have already identified Blockchain technology as a driver for a paradigm shift.

Figure 3 remarkably, all the selected papers were published after the year 2015. It indicates that this area of research is both new and original. Through all the papers selected, 1 papers (1.61%) were published in 2016, 2 papers (3.22%) in 2017, 13 papers (20.96%)in 2018 and 46 papers (74.19%) in 2019 when zooming into the distribution year. Which represents increase in blockchain interest.

Blockchain technology is still in the early stages of marketing and while there are many industry experts who agree that there is a promising future for the deployment of this technology through industry, many others claim that there is an unrealistic assumption of blockchains that could, in turn, intensify the impact of the inability to implement blockchains in industry. However, while many unsuccessful attempts have been made to use blockchain technology, several successful business cases, such as those listed in this article, have also occurred. The latter provides a rather optimistic view that as more progress is made in overcoming the limits of blockchains, like many other emerging technologies, blockchains can find a position in operation and become popular.

Figure 2. Publication year of the selected primary papers

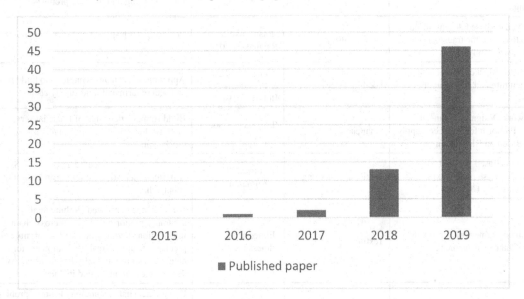

Papers on blockchain, supply chain and blockchain with supply chain management were read and the following results were obtained including the gaps in current studies, requirements in blockchain technology within supply chain management.

Table 1 represent what are the existing research topic and application area of them on supply chain on blockchain

For several specific supply chain scenarios, there are many deployed and conceptual systems, among them the food supply chain is the hottest topic. The issues of food provenance and safety are important issues that need to be addressed. There are some ongoing food supply chain projects or food traceability projects. More challenging applications are involving wine and agricultural foods. Pharma and drug industry, Blockchain also helps the electronics industry, since healthcare is also a major social problem

The significance of blockchain for the supply chain

Supply chain management is an integrative term for controlling a distribution channel 's total process (Petri Helo & Szekely, 2005). The supply chain is complex as it involves dispersed practices from upstream, interacting with individuals, physical resources and manufacturing processes to downstream, covering the entire process of selling; i.e. contracts, sales to customers, distribution and disposal(Tian, 2016). The supply chain aims to create a multi-stakeholder collaborative environment through mutual trust, to eliminate communication problems, and ensure that the various companies are connected to pursue routinely the integration of the whole supply network. In the end, linked supply chain stakeholders will increase overall performance and add greater value and benefits to their business (Azzi, Chamoun, & Sokhn, 2019).

Table 1. Existing research topics on supply chain based on blockchain

Research topic	Applied areas	Research Paper	Key finding
Transparency and Traceability: In Food Supply Chain System using Blockchain Technology with Internet of Things	Food industry	(Madumidha et al., 2019)	An effective system incorporating RFID and Blockchain technology is a technical mechanism for monitoring and locating products
A Blockchain-based decentralized system to ensure the transparency of organic food supply chain	Food industry	(Basnayake & Rajapakse, 2019)	Preparing a transparent and efficient architecture for food certification
The Rise of Blockchain Technology in Agriculture and Food Supply Chains	Food industry	(Kamilaris, Fonts, & Prenafeta-Boldó, 2019)	Applying blockchain technology to build reliable and secure farm and food supply chains
Framework Design of Financial Service Platform for Tobacco Supply Chain Based on Blockchain	Financial	(Liu, Li, & Cao, 2018)	Build framework design of financial service platform for tobacco supply chain based on blockchain
Blockchain-Based Secured Traceability System for Textile and Clothing Supply Chain	Textile and clothing	(Agrawal, Sharma, & Kumar, n.d.)	Blockchain-Based Secured Traceability System with implementation for textile and clothing supply chain
Blockchain Framework for Textile Supply Chain Management	Textile	(Elmessiry & Elmessiry, 2018)	A full blockchain-based clothing quality assurance platform that allows cross-chain information sharing with assured validity and precision in almost real time, allowing for the detection of product faulty lots in all networks as soon as they are identified in a few.
A Blockchain-Based Supply Chain Quality Management Framework	Global supply chains	(Chen et al., 2017)	Using blockchain technology to solve problems caused by lack of trust in the quality management of the supply chain and to achieve sophisticated product quality management
Blockchain in Supply Chain Trading	Global supply chains	(Al Barghuthi, Mohamed, & Said, 2019)	A well- function supply system using a blockchain technology
Blockchain-based Soybean Traceability in Agricultural Supply Chain	Agriculture	(Salah, Nizamuddin, Jayaraman, & Omar, 2019)	Blockchain and Ethereum smart contracts will map and monitor effectively and make it possible to incorporate busy transactions and workflows in the agricultural supply chain without presence
Blockchains everywhere - a use-case of blockchains in the pharma supply-chain	Pharmaceutical industry	(Bocek, Rodrigues, Strasser, & Stiller, 2017)	Blockchain allows pharmaceutical supply chain to monitor temperature and humanity over the transport of medical products
How the Blockchain Revolution Will Reshape the Consumer Electronics Industry	Electronics industry	(Jayasena, 2017)	Transparency and process integration in consumer electronics supply chain management will be enhanced by blockchain. Areas where blockchains can affect supply chains include a tamper-proof history of product manufacturing, handling and maintenance, digital identity for ownership and packaging, tendering across the supply chain through smart contract sand engagement with consumers
Can Blockchain Strengthen the Internet of Things?	Manufacturing/ physical distribution	(It, 2017)	Blockchain can play a key role in tracking the sources of insecurity in supply chains and in handling crisis situations like product recalls that occur after safety and security vulnerabilities are found

Blockchain can solve supply chain problems and even lead to numerous critical supply chain management objectives, such as cost, quality, speed, dependability, risk reduction, sustainability and flexibility(Kshetri, 2018)(Basnayake & Rajapakse, 2019)(Al Barghuthi et al., 2019)(Tönnissen & Teuteberg, 2019). Therefore, among the many other operations that are likely to be changed by blockchain the supply chain needs special consideration. Identified profits of applying blockchain in supply chain management are Improve overall quality, Reduce cost, Shorten delivery time, Reduce risk, Increase trust. In the following describe problems that address by blockchain in the supply chain.

1. **Differential Pricing:** Companies prefer keeping their pricings a secret, since this allows them to pay lower prices when outsourcing to developing countries.
2. **Numerous Parties Involved:** Mediating between so many parties can be a big problem for logistics-providers, slowing down the delivery of services and creating a large overhead for logistics. Furthermore, a centralized mediator of these parties can misuse power to prefer some parties over others.
3. **Quality & Compliance issues:** Procuring a replacement for defective parts is a long drawn and uncomfortable process.
4. **Inevitable Disruptions:** LEAN "on-demand" manufacturing falls flat in a situations where natural disasters and socio-economic problems are common. For example, Japan (frequently affected by earthquakes) has outsourced most of it's supply chain logistics to other countries.
5. **Centralization:** A central mediator for parties is required, which centralizes power in the hands of a few and is a gateway to misuse of resources.
6. **Fraud by Middlemen:** As number of interacting parties increase, there is a proportional increase in middlemen. They lead to fraud and slow down the supply without adding anything to the network.
7. **Tracking history of any product:** Validating identity vendor and checking for tampering by middlemen is not possible.

Table 2. How to resolve them by applying blockchain

Problems	Solution
Differential Pricing	Permissioned ledger for confidential transactions between parties
Numerous Parties Involved	Consensus between multiple parties is maintained through Smart contracts
Quality & Compliance issues	Smart contract stores money while all solutions are checked and tested
Inevitable disruptions	Digital ledger is free of geographical constraints like natural disasters, socio-economic issues
Procuring replacements for defective pieces	Smart contract only lets out payments once both parties satisfied
Centralization	Risk of fraud is mitigated by using decentralized nodes for checking delivery status
Fraud by Middlemen	Because of using doubly-signed smart contracts, no financial fraud by middlemen can occur in the system
Tracking history of any product	Using network anyone can verify vendor identity and validity of product

Blockchain Characteristic for Supply Chain

1. **Quality assurance:** In the perspective of investigation & guidance to adopt required steps for the flawless high-quality production of goods & services, quality assurance makes a remarkable impact to make the business processes easier. (Yadav & Singh, 2019).

2. **Scalability in Supply chain management:** When an information recorded in a block of the block chain, this characteristic ensures that it is non-variable & non-volatile. This leads to integrate blockchain without a risk of losing the data consistency.(Tönnissen & Teuteberg, 2019)(Madavi, 2008).

3. **Transparency:** Ensure peer to peer transactions are verified at the minor end & make sure that the updated data cannot be changed/hacked. Also the property of *changing anything in the ledger stays on it* makes the blockchain a transparent system. (Yumna et al., n.d.)(Pe & Llivisaca, n.d.) (Wu et al., 2019)(Casino, Dasaklis, & Patsakis, 2019)

4. **Integrity:** Provides management for the flow of physical goods in supply chain using integration of serial numbers, bar codes, sensors, digital tags like RFID, etc. Following this the flow of blockchain became smoother from manufacturer to end-user.(Yadav & Singh, 2019)(Litke, Anagnostopoulos, & Varvarigou, 2019)

5. **Solving the double spend problem:** Solves the issue of data transaction which cannot be sent to two or more people at the same time. With the help of authenticated peer to peer transaction after the verification by a minor. (Yadav & Singh, 2019)(Bartling & Fecher, 2016)

6. **Immutability and encryption:** After confirming the transaction or data flow from one center to another, changes are not allowed since any change on the block chain cannot be stored without the solidarity of the network (Yumna et al., n.d.)(Schmidt & Wagner, 2019)(Wu et al., 2019).

7. **Efficiency:** The high rate of information flow speed without an intermediary, smart contracts easily traceable & further, it streamlines the process considerably saving time & money. (Pe & Llivisaca, n.d.)(Ahram, Sargolzaei, Sargolzaei, Daniels, & Amaba, 2017).

8. **Security:** Once the creation of block is completed changes or deletion is not applicable. This feature makes the security of Supply Chain more refine after the adoption of blockchain in the existing traditional methods. (Pe & Llivisaca, n.d.)(Tönnissen & Teuteberg, 2019)(Casino et al., 2019)

9. **Removal of intermediaries:** Blockchain create the platform for a direct transaction eliminating the interference of intermediaries or a third party(Yadav & Singh, 2019)(Weber et al., 2016)

10. **Reduction in administrative cost:** Reduction in cost of the paper and other consumable items, time-saving, quick discussion, better management, administration & shared databases ease administrative work. (Tönnissen & Teuteberg, 2019)(Osei, Canavari, & Hingley, 2018)

11. **Decentralization:** Blockchain is a system of teaming up gatherings with a database that is decentralized. This implies that most of the gatherings team up on a blockchain have their own duplicate of the considerable number of exchanges that put away on the blockchain.(Yumna et al., n.d.)(Schmidt & Wagner, 2019)(Wu et al., 2019)(Kharlamov, Parry, & Clarke, n.d.)(Lai, 2019)

12. **Traceability and visibility:** Trust-worthy system is imparted by blockchain technology by knowing the origin of a product by offering real-time, live and consistently connected updates(Yumna et al., n.d.)(Kharlamov et al., n.d.)(Venkatesh, Kang, Wang, Zhong, & Zhang, 2020b)(Kamilaris, Fonts, Prenafeta-Boldú, et al., 2019)

The blockchain-based supply chain system focused in this research is a very explorative in reference implementation. This research approach was chosen because blockchain is still in its nascent stage. Our purpose is to set up a platform to meet the demand of supply chain related operations, and at the same time to guarantee the security and transparency of the records in all activities. However, it is difficult to transit from traditional supply chain to the blockchain-based supply chain as it is not smooth.

Companies must poses the knowledge and capability in blockchain to adopt it. Moreover, blockchain technology is still in its early stage in terms of industrial application development. It is full of uncertainties such as whether the blockchain is suitable for the required process, whether the practitioners have the training and required technical development. Furthermore, it is important to realize that blockchain-based industrial solutions should start from the stakeholders' willingness to collaborate and be involved. They must reach a consensus on building blockchain knowledge and capabilities with a focus on driving value for all stakeholders. So that it is critical to create a culture of collaboration. Scalability is holding back early adoptions of blockchain in supply chains or in other similar areas. By definition, every computer connected to the network needs to process the transactions. Organizations have to sacrifice efficiency to obtain security. Therefore, there is a high demand in terms of the technical infrastructure which will be more expensive than the traditional approach.

According to the characteristics of blockchain, stakeholders who use this blockchain based supply chain system will benefit more when the number of participating users grows in this community. As more and more supply chain stakeholders participate, blockchain becomes more valuable and more authentic, evolving into industry practice. This will be particularly tricky when there are legacy processes, regulations and laws governing various aspects of the business, as stakeholders will incur costs when migrating from legacy systems and integrating with new systems and practices. In the future, many organizations, not only in the private sector but also in public departments, will put effort into the blockchain-based logistics system, due to the competitive nature of business. Therefore, itis important to determine standards and agreements to ensure the interoperability between different blockchain-based platforms.

Gaps in Existing Research

If considering the all researches of the study, Most of the identified gaps had to do with outside reasons such as administrative and technical aspects.

- The first obstacle is conformity with the laws and the legal barriers restricting Blockchain technology implementation. Common standards for completing transactions are missing (Tribis, El Bouchti, & Bouayad, 2018).
- The second difference is the failure to adapt and acceptance. Mostly society are unaware about how to operates and produce the great difficulty of getting together all parties concerned and convincing supply chain players to change their traditional supply chain to the current blockchain based system(Tribis et al., 2018)(P. Helo & Hao, 2019).
- The third difference relates to scalability and scale. Most of the proposed blockchain-based architectures have been evaluated in a laboratory environment only on a limited scale; including a number of nodes, certain difficulties that occur in scaling blockchains network.
- The latest blockchain implementations are basically small in size. Next gap that identified is Strong computerization demand. Nevertheless, many supply chain participants are not able to adopt blockchain in the developing countries.

- Complexity and uncertainty of the development is the next gap. The delay of transactions that last for several hours until all parties upgrade their ledgers and the smart contract can be accessible to the public, but the details needed for authentication may or may not be available to everyone.
- Implementation cost of the adaptation is high. For blockchain process, it requires a virtual network and it depends on the electricity, infrastructure and hardware computing systems. These gaps are that most of the frameworks proposed were not evaluated to design systems for real-world applications, Researchers should therefore find the viability of blockchain based solutions and test their applicability to industry (Salah et al., 2019).

However, work on blockchain supply chain management is still in its early stage and should find future applications (Longo, Nicoletti, Padovano, d'Atri, & Forte, 2019)(Yadav & Singh, 2019). Most of the supply chain oparations, especially small and medium-sized companies, state they know nothing about blockchain, and that they find the impact of blockchain as a menace. To increase understanding of blockchain, a prototype of a blockchain-based logistics monitoring system, Frameworks-based solution have real performance evaluation in the industrial context(Tribis et al., 2018)(Wamba, 2019).

In Sri Lanka, there is no measurement to measure the readiness to accept blockchain in supply chain management. And also there is less researches have done in this area. This research aims to solve supply chain management challenges with blockchain implementation in the Sri Lankan food supply chain industry. Therefore for filling some gaps in the literature, this research will be a great support.

MAIN FOCUS OF THE CHAPTER

While the challenges involved in implementing a transparent supply chain are huge, The benefits of applying blockchain to the dairy supply chain far outweigh the disadvantages (initial capital investment cost and maintenance). The advantages of an active blockchain can be narrowly defined as a financial advantage, the benefits of the authorities and the benefits of the food companies. For simplicity's sake, however, the benefits can be classified as enhancing consumer loyalty, improving food crisis management, improving dairy supply chain management, expertise and technical innovation, and contributing to sustainable agriculture. There is an emerging rich network of devices and sensors that build an ecosystem rich in data for efficient monitoring and analysis of properties, which was unlikely in supply chains several years ago. This evolution has now allowed us to use this technology to create a blockchain network that provides as mentioned in this research a lot of possible benefits.

Many of the potential risks and the lack of demonstrable evidence the implementation of blockchain in the supply chain is currently sluggish. Nonetheless, businesses are trying to consider the positives or drawbacks of blockchains in supply chains.

Problem Definition

The emergence of digital businesses transforms conventional market models and, mainly, how we do it. The flow of industry has intensified in a environment today running 24 hours. This has changed the way businesses collaborate, trade and connect with customers, vendors and partners. Suppliers and the supply chain have an effect on everything: from efficiency, distribution and expense, to customer support, loyalty and benefit. Enterprise globalization expanded the difficulty of the supply chain processors.

Now it is a main component to improve and integrate the information system. The difficulty of taking decisions needs real-time data sharing (Yu, Wang, Zhong, & Huang, 2016). When information moved in a linear form in conventional supply chains and inefficiencies in one stage influenced the following cascade stages, Digital supply networks are now capable of building interconnected networks capable of overcoming the action-reaction cycle with real-time data and facilitating cooperation. The figure 3 shows the shift from the traditional supply chain to the digital supply network(Mussomeli, Gish, & Laaper, 2015).

Figure 3. The evolution of Supply chain

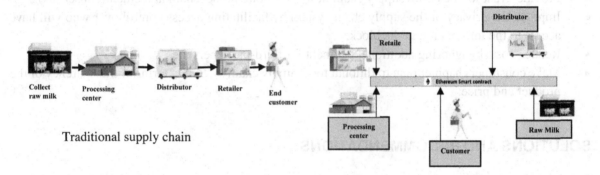

Traditional supply chain

Digital supply chain network

Table 3. Current problems and blockchain impact in supply chain system

Supply chain actor	Current Problems	Blockchain impact
Famer/Supplier	Capability to prove the origin and quality metrics of goods using a global and clear process.	Benefits from the improved trust by maintaining track by raw material production and supply chain from the raw material to the end customer.
Processor	Poor ability to track the goods produced to the final destination. Small ability to analyze measured content from raw material.	Value added from shared facts system with suppliers of raw materials and distribution networks.
Distributor	Customized monitoring devices with limited ability to work together. Limited certification skills and confidence issues.	Ability to have proof of position recorded in the database, and conditions certifications.
Wholesaler	Lack of confidence, and certification of the product path.	Capacity to test the origin of the products and the conditions for transformation or transportation.
Retailer	Lack of confidence, and certification of the product path.	Tracking any single commodity between the wholesaler and the final customer. Capacity to manage the returns of malfunctioning goods efficiently.
Consumer	Lack of trust about the product's compliance with the requirements and origin defined for the origin, quality and enforcement of the product.	Complete and clear view of the sources of the product and its entire journey from the raw material to the purchased finished product.

According to this, emphasis on how blockchain affects the supply chain. To have this done, Possible applications and implementation of blockchain are discussed in the supply chain to help businesses understand how to achieve their business goals. Furthermore, A logistics management program based on blockchain is applied to evaluate the viability of applying blockchain in the food supply chain. Accordingly, The major objective of this research is to fill current research gaps, new approaches to integrate blockchain and IoT technology within food supply chain, and food quality management in the Sri Lankan food supply chain system. This study has following objectives also.

- Improve the scalability of any business by increasing customers' experience and more awareness about blockchain.
- Provide Trust for the entire supply chain network through blockchain agreement(consensus)
- Improve the privacy of the supply chain system by facilitating access control over who will have access to the information in the block.
- Reduce costs by ignoring additional payment for third-party persons.
- Make consumers happier than traditional food supply chain system in terms of transparency of the product and price.

SOLUTIONS AND RECOMMENDATIONS

This segment describes the suggested solution that using blockchain within ethereum network and smart contracts to trace, track, and perform transactions in dairy supply chains. This approach eliminates the need for a trustworthy centralized authority and allows transactions and store the transaction information for food supply chain management.. Table 4 describe how blockchain based model address the issues in current dairy supply chain.

Table 4. Problems that address by blockchain in the dairy supply chain

Issues in the existing Supply chain system	The solution is given by proposed mechanism
Lack of trust about the product's compliance with the requirements and origin defined for the origin, quality and enforcement of the product.	Complete and clear view of the sources of the product and its entire journey from the raw material to the purchased finished product.
Require a central party to maintain the dairy supply chain transactions.	provides the platform for a direct transaction without the interference of intermediaries or a third party IoT sensors track the data and smart contract validate them and added to the blockchain.
Have to manually enter the data about dairy transaction.	Reduction in paper and another consumable item, time-saving. automatically detect and store the data in to blockchain
In traditional dairy supply chain, manually check temperature, volume and quality of milk. It is time consuming.	Information flow speed, no intermediary is required, smart contracts, easily traceable and finally it streamlines the processes considerably

The suggested approach would concentrate on the use of autonomously implemented smart contracts on the decentralized blockchain Ethereum network. Functions of the smart contract execution and conductby thousands of mining nodes. Mining nods are globally distributed, and the execution outcome is agreed by all of the mining nodes.

Additionally, any actor or participant must have an Ethereum account in blockchain and they have to have a unique Ethereum address. This helps to identify the actor in a unique way. The Ethereum account basically consists of the Ethereum address with public and private keys that are used to sign and verify the data integrity within each transaction cryptographically and digitally, and associate each transaction with a specific Ethereum address or account.

Table 5 shows how combination of IOT blockchains within the food supply chain. This chart describe the process of tracking information from raw milk, processing details, transport information, quality of manufactured product, etc. That will finally bring value in the customer's hands to the finished product.

This architecture captures information regarding traceability using a range of IoT devices based on the type of event to be recorded. A transaction could be a movement of milk product, processing or store of milk, Distribute. Multiple data recorded from an IoT checkpoint is converted into a transaction and pushed to the etheteum network. All the transaction data check and validate within the smart contract and then publish to the public ledger. The contract layer monitors every transaction data, to execute the smart contracts when an initial event takes place and it ensures expected data about the raw milk or milk product from the supplier, manufacture and distributor in the supply chain according to terms of trade agreed upon connecting to the blockchain network.

Each entity involved plays a role, relationship, and interactions with the smart contract. Propose model contain only five participating entities. Here describe their role:

Milk Supplier: As per the depiction milk suppliers have access to web applications. Through that application they can view information that they using IOT sensor. IOT will play a key role in capturing this information from the raw milk and transmitting it to the Blockchain.

Milk Processor: IOT sensors in those premises and storage locations can greatly enhance the traceability and help end customers with information of products storage criteria like the physical conditions of density, temperature, volume, etc. The status of various environmental / physical and product-related characteristics can help to assess the quality of the finished product before and after manufacture, its freshness and other consuming characteristics. Aberrations can be very dangerous during production and this information isn't available today. This can be made available and evaluated with the IOT network system, which help to determine the root cause causes if anything goes wrong or any complications found through random sample checks.

Distributer: Nowadays consumer can get only few information about transporting these products. Capturing IOT data at the time of travel or factory exit analysis will greatly help close this significant gap. The sensors will capture the physical storage conditions in the trucks / ocean freight warehouse and make it accessible in the blockchain network. Various partners can access this information and make informed product decisions based on smart contracts. Where authenticity and transparency are required, even this information can be rendered to end customers.

Retailer: The emphasis on product safety and freshness is of vital importance for a retailer. Data are available in blockchain that can be traced and analyzed right from farm to fork. In addition to that, the IOT Blockchain architecture can help to obtain the information from source / origin until final consumption.

Customer: The customer is the end-user who buys and uses the retailer's product.

Table 5. Supply chain solution with IOT Blockchain model architecture

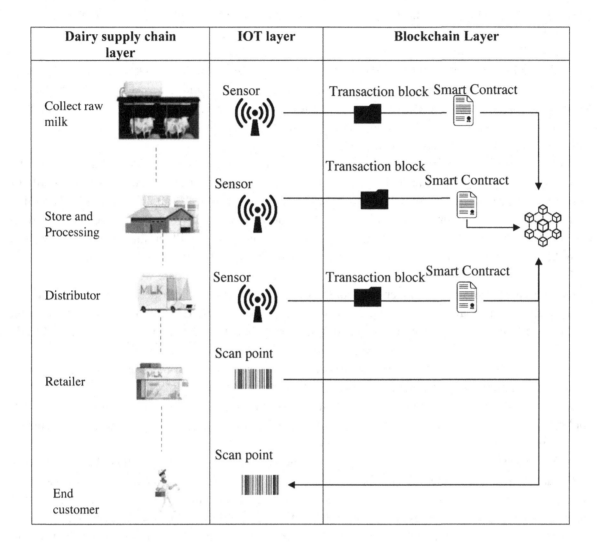

Dairy supply chain layer	IOT layer	Blockchain Layer
Collect raw milk	Sensor	Transaction block Smart Contract
Store and Processing	Sensor	Transaction block Smart Contract
Distributor	Sensor	Transaction block Smart Contract
Retailer	Scan point	
End customer	Scan point	

Transaction Data Processing Flow

Figure 4 describe the transaction data processing flow of storing data in the blockchain. IoT devices generate data such as density, temperature, volume, etc. After digital signing and the hashing,

Such data will be sent directly or through the IoT gateways to the entire blockchain network nodes, Where they are verified, connected to the Transaction Pool and stored in blockchain.

Customers can access and validate all transaction data via their laptops or mobile phones. For example, one buys a package of milk from a supermarket and then he / she can use a mobile to check the 2-D barcode to gather all the transaction data relevant to it, including the farm from which the milk was made, the day and time it was delivered, the cow ID on the farm, the workers ID processing the milk, the collection of computer information, the packaging information, all the temperature. All of those information can be verified without human intervention by the blockchain system.

Figure 4. Transaction Data Processing Flow

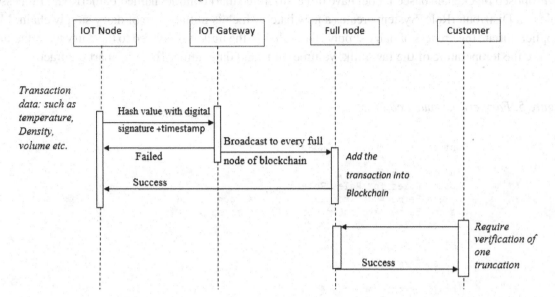

Traceable Functionality

Using our suggested blockchain-based approach utilizing smart contracts, the benefit of using traceable technology in the dairy supply chain is that all actors without a central authority within the supply chain have verifiable and non-modifiable details accessible. The total volume of milk products sold between subsequent entities is logged to the next echelon starting with supplier and manufacturing transactions, and all transactions can be verified. For example, with the agreed terms, it is impossible to alter or change the volume of milk sold between entities. In addition, milk with various quality standards cannot be combined together for sale, because all stakeholders are aware with total quantity.

The use of traceable identifiers per lot and the ability to trace all corresponding transactions between stakeholders further ensure continuous monitoring for quality compliance. It is also possible to monitor the quality of the milk and conditions using IoT-enabled containers and packages equipped with sensors, cameras, GPS locator, and 4G communication With blockchain, such knowledge and verification cannot be changed or tampered with, and usable automatically and open to all stakeholders in a transparent and decentralized way, without intermediaries.

It should be remembered that a stakeholder can steal or may transact and record fraudulent data. The blockchain, in this situation, marks the data as such with a validated reference to the source data (i.e. the real stakeholder). If the data were caught to be incorrect at a later stage, the judges and all participants can attribute the data to a given actor or stakeholder with 100 percent certainty. Blockchain can identify fraud in that scenario. To resolve this kind of theft, blockchain can be configured by smart contracts to provide additional functionality for the whole supply chain process, and any steps can be taken to enforce fines on dishonest suppliers or take appropriate and punitive action. This will create new corrective data and activities to be produced and connected to deceptive data, maintaining reliable and unchallenged traceability and audit capabilities.

Proposed blockchain based model have three different smart contract named FamerRoal,, Processor-Role and DistributerRole. System creates a new batch which is initial stage of dairy supply chain. Milk supplier initiate the process of dairy supply chain. Before the milk is delivered to the dairy manufacturer, capture the temperature of the raw milk, volume, time and date, famer ID into smart contract.

Figure 5. FarmerRole smart contract

```
contract FarmerRole is Ownable {

  uint256 public temp;
  using Roles for Roles.Role;
  event FarmerAdded(address indexed account);
  event FarmerRemoved(address indexed account);
  Roles.Role private farmers;

  constructor() public {
    _addFarmer(msg.sender);
  }
  modifier onlyFarmer() {
    require(isFarmer(msg.sender), "Caller is not a farmer.");
    _;
  }
  function isFarmer(address account) public view returns (bool) {
    return farmers.has(account);
  }
  function addFarmer(address account) public onlyOwner {
    _addFarmer(account);
  }
  function renounceFarmer() public onlyOwner {
    _removeFarmer(msg.sender);
  }
  function _addFarmer(address account) internal {
    farmers.add(account);
    emit FarmerAdded(account);
  }
  function _removeFarmer(address account) internal {
    farmers.remove(account);
    emit FarmerRemoved(account);
  }
  function setTemperature(uint256 temp) public {
      temp = temp;
  }
  function getTemperature() external view returns (uint256) {
      return temp;
  }
function checkTemp() external view returns (string){
    if(temp<=5 ){
        return "Correct temperature";
    }else{
        return "Incorrect temperature";
    }
```

Figure 5 shows FarmerRole smart contract. The initial state of the contract is established, the smart contract checks to confirm that the requesting farmer is already registered, the temperature of the raw milk and volume. If the scenario is successful, then the state of the contract changes to ProcessorRole. Famer state changes to manufacture and first block added to the blockchain. ProcessorRole smart contract same as the farmer role contract in this stage describes the process of milk product. Most important criteria to consider in this stage are packaging date time, processor name, unique Id of the milk product and check the temperature of raw milk for the product. At this stage, the contract has to check two condition. First one is the requesting milk processor is a registered entity and second one is the quality of the milk is agreed (temperature, volume). If these two conditions are true or satisfied, the contract state changes to DistributorRole. Manufacture state change to distributer. In the other case, if the above mentioned two conditions are not satisfied, contract state changes to ProcessorRoleFail, processor state chenges to RequestFailure, the cancel the process.

At the distributor stage retailer buy the product from distributer. Date of product manufacture and quantity sold are some important parameters to keep a check. The distributer and retailers will be identified with their Ethereum addresses. For execute the DistributerRole smart contract, authorized distributer have to input date about transport information and warehouse information of the milk product. Then smart contract check and validate distributor role. Above each and every success transaction add a new block to the blockchain. This is how the dairy supply chain complete for one batch. In this way store all the batch information into blockchin database. Using smart tag with barcode reader batch information can show for the outside user. Retailer and customer are final role of the system. They are able to transparently verify the whole history of a product before buying it. Smart-tags can be associated to each package, so that retailers and consumers can easily retrieve the whole history of the product.

IoT Implementation

The proposed system contain two type of IoT devices to integrate. One of them is sensors that used to collect data like temperature, volume, density. Although preparations were being made for integrating actuators into the system, the work performed here ended up only covering sensor usage for readings. Nevertheless, theoretically, the same kind of platform used for sensor-Blockchain connectivity may also be used for actuators.

For the purpose of integrating IoT devices into proposed model, first need to resolve the question about where our Blockchain client should be operating. Most IoT sensors are intended to have low processing capacity due to energy usage and cost constraints. Clients of Blockchain, moreover, are heavy programs that need massive quantities of data and computing capacity to run. As a result, the simplest way to integrate an IoT device to a Blockchain at the moment is by a gateway machine running the Blockchain client and connecting only with IoT device through another protocol.

Second one is to connect with the Blockchain, each system contain user account or a private and public key combination. Then system have to decide where it keep the secret keys that is used to sign transfers and invest the currency of the account. Realizing that executing transactions are challenging in terms of computing capacity, and that keeping a private key in the system itself can prove dangerous because there is no access control over its memory storage, system have opted to use a Blockchain wallet program in the gateway module of its own to improve the protection of that key.

When create a new batch, when parsing each and every process, it access a method in the smart contract, next fire event to start reading input data. Then gateway unit is listening to the Blockchain network. Store the data received into the system when reserved it. Finally before moving to the next phase. Consider the tracked data and it validate automatically by smart contract according to the requested quality of food.

The proposed system architecture integrate with NodeMCU for IoT implementation. It has ability receive real time data from different censers at the different level, store that data and process them into actionable insights. Using nodeMCU can store data in a place where it can be readily accessed for further analysis. It is open source, interactive, programmable, low cost, simple to complement, smart and Wi-Fi enabled device. Not only has that it also taken advantage with the building-in API to data transmit.

Here use only Waterproof a LM35 temperature sensor. That have selected in proposed model to track the temperature of raw milk and milk product in different stage of the dairy supply chain. Temperature sensor module LM35 has been selected because it needs no calibration and is compatible with NodeMCU, waterproof and even low power consumption. Other important factors of dairy supply chain can track using different sensors as the measure temperature.

3.7. Implementation Process

The proposed Blockchain-based model has three different smart contracts named FamerRoal,, ProcessorRole and DistributerRole. The system creates a new batch which is the initial stage of the dairy supply chain. Milk supplier initiates the process of the dairy supply chain. Before the milk is delivered to the dairy manufacturer, capture the temperature of the raw milk, volume, time and date, famer ID into a smart contract.

Figure 6. Algorithm 1

Algorithm 1 FarmerRole

1: **INPUT:**
2:      F is the list of registered farmers
3:      EthereumAddress(EA) of Farmer
4:      t is the TemperatureOfRawMilk
5: Contractsate is **FarmerRole**
6: Restrict access to only

$$farmer \in F$$

    i.e., registered Farmer
7: **if** farmer = registered **then**
8:      Change State of farmer to WaitForMilk
9:      **if** $t \geq 5C^0$ **then**
10:         Create a notification message stating the success of process
11:      **end if**
12: **end if**

Figure 6 Algorithm 1 shows FarmerRole smart contract. The initial contractual state is determined, the smart contract checks to confirm that the applicant farmer is already registered, the temperature of the raw milk and volume. If the scenario is successful, then the contractual state will change to Processor-Role. Famer state changes to manufacture and first block added to the Blockchain. Figure 7, Algorithm 2 describes ProcessorRole smart contract. It the same as the farmer role contract in this stage describes the process of milk production. The most important criteria to consider in this stage are packaging date-time, processor name, unique Id of the milk product and check the temperature of raw milk for the product. At this stage, the contract has to check two conditions. The first one is the requesting milk processor is a registered entity and the second one is the quality of the milk is agreed (temperature, volume). If these two requirements are valid or met, the contract state will be changed to DistributorRole. Figure 7, Algorithm 3 describes DistributorRole. In the other case, if the above two conditions are not fulfilled, change the contract state to ProcessorRoleFail, processor state changes to RequestFailure, the cancel the process.

Figure 7. Algorithm 2

Algorithm 2 ProcessorRole

1: **INPUT:**
2:      P is the list of registered Processors
3:      EthereumAddress(EA) of Milk Processors
4:      t TemperatureOfRawMilk
5:      DatePurchesed , Quality
6: Contractsate is **ProcessorRole**
7: Restrict access to only

$$Processor \in P$$

8: **if** Processor = registered **then**
9:      Change State of processer to WaitForMilkProduct
10:      **if** $t \geq 5C^0$ AND Quality **then**
11:          Create a notification message stating the success
12:              of process
13:      **end if**
14: **end if**

At the distributor, stage the retailer buys the product from the distributor. The date of manufacture of the product and the amount sold are some important parameters to keep a check. The distributor and retailers will have their Ethereum addresses identified. To execute the DistributerRole smart contract, authorized distributors have to input date about transport information and warehouse information of the milk product. Then smart contract checks and validates the distributor role. Above each and every success transaction add a new block to the Blockchain. This is how the dairy supply chain complete for one batch. In this way store all the batch information into the Blockchain database. Using a smart tag with barcode reader batch information can show for the outside user. Retailers and customers are final roles of the system. They can verify the entire history of a product before buying it in a transparent manner. Each package may be associated with smart tags, so retailers and consumers can easily retrieve the entire product history.

Figure 8. Algorithm 3

Algorithm 3 DistributorRole

1: **INPUT:**
2:        D is the list of registered Distributors
3:        EthereumAddress(EA) of Distributors
4:        TransportCondition, WarehouseCondition,
5:        DateManufactured
6: Contractsate is **DistributorRole**
7: Restrict access to only

$$Distributor \in D$$

8: **if** Distributor = registered **then**
9:      Change State of distributor to WaitForDistribute
10:      Create a notification message stating the success of process
11: **end if**

RESULT AND FINDING

An overview of the framework built and applied will be made in this portion. First, the experiments presented here will establish whether the reference implemented system performs as it should when users communicate with its processes. An overview of the built web applications is given here. That provides ability to track the origin of the milk product.

For validate the proposed model, create simple web application. If permissioned user want to gain information form Blockchain network. It provide admin dashboard and it display Total Number of User, Total Roles, Total Batch, and Batch Overview. Figure 9 shows admin dashboard.

In batches overview section provide information about the progress of each batch. By clicking on button Create Batch, system can create new batch for dairy supply chain. Complete that process user have to provide basic information of batch like Supplier Registration Number, Supplier's Name, and Supplier's Address.

Figure 9. Admin Dashboard

Figure 10. Create New Batch

Each and every process detail of the particular batch in the supply chain, user can find by pressing on eye icon. It shows as figure below. Here user can read complete details of each transaction.

With the complete details of each transaction, create RFID tag for each and product. Customers can access and validate all transaction data using that RFID tag.

Figure 11. Batch Details

Raw Milk

Registration No:	xyz ✓
Farmer Name:	xyz ✓
Form Address:	xyz ✓
Raw Milk Temperature:	xyz ✓

Milk Product

Processor name:	xyz ✓
Processor No:	xyz ✓
Product Id:	xyz ✓
Packaging Date-Time:	xyz ✓
Density:	xyz ✓

Distributor

Distributor name:	xyz ✓
Distributor No:	xyz ✓
Date-Time:	xyz ✓

Distributor

Distributor name:	xyz ✓
Distributor No:	xyz ✓
Date-Time:	xyz ✓

FUTURE RESEARCH DIRECTIONS

Future research efforts can concentrate on defining the different compensation mechanisms to be used within the blockchain network to promote a consistent transfer of power as to how the transactional data can be used within the food supply chain. A major technological transition such as the introduction of blockchains is only possible if it is driven by the company in certain stages of the value chain with a larger impact on the sector. Therefore it would be interesting to find out how the power balance between retailers and food processors would change the blockchain model proposed. Another possible research problem to answer is blockchain scalability.

CONCLUSION

Food provenance is one of the most challenging questions that companies in the food supply chain are trying to solve today and this research is a small contribution to answering that question. The primary aim of this research is to establish a blockchain platform that can be applied within a food supply chain and include its advantages and disadvantages in terms of food provenance and product traceability over conventional tracking systems It is clear from this research initiative that blockchains can be more effective in monitoring food provenance, avoiding significant degradation of food items, detecting and eliminating the source of foodborne disease in seconds, whereas contemporary systems may take as many weeks. It would also provide greater customer confidence that reflects the satisfaction of sales and customers.

REFERENCES

Agrawal, T. K., Sharma, A., & Kumar, V. (n.d.). *Blockchain-Based Secured Traceability Chain*. Academic Press.

Ahram, T., Sargolzaei, A., Sargolzaei, S., Daniels, J., & Amaba, B. (2017). Blockchain technology innovations. *2017 IEEE Technology and Engineering Management Society Conference. TEMSCON, 2017*, 137–141. Advance online publication. doi:10.1109/TEMSCON.2017.7998367

Al Barghuthi, N. B., Mohamed, H. J., & Said, H. E. (2019). Blockchain in Supply Chain Trading. *ITT 2018 - Information Technology Trends: Emerging Technologies for Artificial Intelligence*, 336–341. doi:10.1109/CTIT.2018.8649523

Aung, M. M., & Chang, Y. S. (2014). Traceability in a food supply chain: Safety and quality perspectives. *Food Control*, *39*(1), 172–184. doi:10.1016/j.foodcont.2013.11.007

Jayasena. (2017). *How the Blockchain Revolution Will Reshape the Consumer Electronics Industry*. Academic Press.

Azzi, R., Chamoun, R. K., & Sokhn, M. (2019). Computers & Industrial Engineering The power of a blockchain-based supply chain. *Computers & Industrial Engineering*, *135*(August), 582–592. doi:10.1016/j.cie.2019.06.042

Bartling, S., & Fecher, B. (2016). Could Blockchain provide the technical fix to solve science's reproducibility crisis? *Impact of Social Sciences Blog*.

Basnayake, B. M. A. L., & Rajapakse, C. (2019). A Blockchain-based decentralized system to ensure the transparency of organic food supply chain. *Proceedings - IEEE International Research Conference on Smart Computing and Systems Engineering, SCSE 2019*, 103–107. 10.23919/SCSE.2019.8842690

Bocek, T., Rodrigues, B. B., Strasser, T., & Stiller, B. (2017). *Blockchains Everywhere - A Use-case of Blockchains in the Pharma Supply-Chain*. Academic Press.

Bosona, T., & Gebresenbet, G. (2013). Food traceability as an integral part of logistics management in food and agricultural supply chain. *Food Control*, *33*(1), 32–48. Advance online publication. doi:10.1016/j.foodcont.2013.02.004

Casino, F., Dasaklis, T. K., & Patsakis, C. (2019). A systematic literature review of blockchain-based applications: Current status, classification and open issues. *Telematics and Informatics*, *36*, 55–81. doi:10.1016/j.tele.2018.11.006

Chen, S., Shi, R., Ren, Z., Yan, J., Shi, Y., & Zhang, J. (2017). A Blockchain-Based Supply Chain Quality Management Framework. *Proceedings - 14th IEEE International Conference on E-Business Engineering, ICEBE 2017 - Including 13th Workshop on Service-Oriented Applications, Integration and Collaboration, SOAIC 207*, 172–176. 10.1109/ICEBE.2017.34

Elmessiry, M., & Elmessiry, A. (2018). *Blockchain Framework for Textile Supply Chain Management*. doi:10.1007/978-3-319-94478-4

Frizzo-barker, J., Chow-white, P. A., Adams, P. R., Mentanko, J., Ha, D., & Green, S. (2019). A systematic review. *International Journal of Information Management*, *0–1*(April). Advance online publication. doi:10.1016/j.ijinfomgt.2019.10.014

Helo, P., & Hao, Y. (2019). Blockchains in operations and supply chains: A model and reference implementation. *Computers & Industrial Engineering*, *136*(July), 242–251. doi:10.1016/j.cie.2019.07.023

Helo, P., & Shamsuzzoha, A. H. M. (2018, December). Real-time supply chain—A blockchain architecture for project deliveries. *Robotics and Computer-integrated Manufacturing*, *63*, 101909. doi:10.1016/j.rcim.2019.101909

Helo, P., & Szekely, B. (2005, January). Logistics information systems: An analysis of software solutions for supply chain co-ordination. *Industrial Management & Data Systems*, *105*(1), 5–18. Advance online publication. doi:10.1108/02635570510575153

It, S. (2017). *Can Blockchain Strengthen the Internet of Things?* Academic Press.

Kamilaris, A., Fonts, A., & Prenafeta-Boldú, F. X. (2019). The rise of blockchain technology in agriculture and food supply chains. *Trends in Food Science & Technology*, *91*, 640–652. doi:10.1016/j.tifs.2019.07.034

Kamilaris, A., Fonts, A., Prenafeta-Boldú, F. X., Kamble, S. S., Gunasekaran, A., Sharma, R., ... Beynon-Davies, P. (2019). How the blockchain enables and constrains supply chain performance. *Supply Chain Management*, *24*(4), 376–397. doi:10.1108/IJPDLM-02-2019-0063

Kharlamov, A., Parry, G., & Clarke, A. C. (n.d.). *Advanced Supply Chains : Visibility, Blockchain and Human Behaviour*. Academic Press.

Kosba, A., Miller, A., Shi, E., Wen, Z., & Papamanthou, C. (2016). Hawk: The Blockchain Model of Cryptography and Privacy-Preserving Smart Contracts. *Proceedings - 2016 IEEE Symposium on Security and Privacy, SP 2016*. 10.1109/SP.2016.55

Kshetri, N. (2018). Blockchain's roles in meeting key supply chain management objectives. *International Journal of Information Management, 39*(June), 80–89. doi:10.1016/j.ijinfomgt.2017.12.005

Lai, J. (2019). Research on Cross-Border E-Commerce Logistics Supply under Block Chain. *Proceedings - 2nd International Conference on Computer Network, Electronic and Automation, ICCNEA 2019*, 214–218. 10.1109/ICCNEA.2019.00049

Litke, A., Anagnostopoulos, D., & Varvarigou, T. (2019). Blockchains for Supply Chain Management: Architectural Elements and Challenges Towards a Global Scale Deployment. *Logistics, 3*(1), 5. doi:10.3390/logistics3010005

Liu, H., Li, Z., & Cao, N. (2018). *Framework Design of Financial Service Platform for Tobacco Supply Chain Based on Blockchain* (Vol. 2). doi:10.1007/978-3-030-05234-8

Longo, F., Nicoletti, L., Padovano, A., d'Atri, G., & Forte, M. (2019). Blockchain-enabled supply chain: An experimental study. *Computers & Industrial Engineering, 136*(July), 57–69. doi:10.1016/j.cie.2019.07.026

Madavi, D. (2008). *A Comprehensive Study on Blockchain Technology. International Research Journal of Engineering and Technology*.

Madumidha, S., Ranjani, P. S., Varsinee, S. S., & Sundari, P. S. (2019). Transparency and traceability: In food supply chain system using blockchain technology with internet of things. *Proceedings of the International Conference on Trends in Electronics and Informatics, ICOEI 2019*, 983–987. 10.1109/ICOEI.2019.8862726

Mattila, J., Seppälä, T., & Holmström, J. (2016). Product-centric Information Management. *A Case Study of a Shared Platform with Blockchain Technology*.

Mussomeli, A., Gish, D., & Laaper, S. (2015). The Rise of the Digital Supply network. *Deloitte*.

Nakamoto, S. (2008). *Bitcoin: A Peer-to-Peer Electronic Cash System. Consulted*. Consulted. doi:10.100710838-008-9062-0stem

Osei, R. K., Canavari, M., & Hingley, M. (2018). An Exploration into the Opportunities for Blockchain in the Fresh Produce Supply Chain. doi:10.20944/preprints201811.0537.v1

Pe, M., & Llivisaca, J. (n.d.). Advances in Emerging Trends and Technologies. *Blockchain and Its Potential Applications in Food Supply Chain Management in Ecuador., 3*, 101–112. doi:10.1007/978-3-030-32022-5

Pilkington, M. (2016). Blockchain technology: Principles and applications. Research Handbooks on Digital Transformations. doi:10.4337/9781784717766.00019

Salah, K., Nizamuddin, N., Jayaraman, R., & Omar, M. A. (2019). Blockchain-Based Soybean Traceability in Agricultural Supply Chain. *Blockchain-based Soybean Traceability in Agricultural Supply Chain, 7*(May), 73295–73305. Advance online publication. doi:10.1109/ACCESS.2019.2918000

Schmidt, C. G., & Wagner, S. M. (2019). A transaction cost theory perspective. *Journal of Purchasing and Supply Management, 25*(4), 100552. doi:10.1016/j.pursup.2019.100552

Scully, P., & Hobig, M. (2019). Exploring the impact of blockchain on digitized Supply Chain flows: A literature review. *2019 6th International Conference on Software Defined Systems, SDS 2019*, 278–283. 10.1109/SDS.2019.8768573

Sheel, A., & Nath, V. (2019). Effect of blockchain technology adoption on supply chain adaptability, agility, alignment and performance. *Management Research Review, 42*(12), 1353–1374. Advance online publication. doi:10.1108/MRR-12-2018-0490

Tezel, A., Papadonikolaki, E., Yitmen, I., & Hilletofth, P. (2019). *Preparing Construction Supply Chains for Blockchain : An Exploratory*. Academic Press.

Tian, F. (2016). An agri-food supply chain traceability system for China based on RFID & blockchain technology. *2016 13th International Conference on Service Systems and Service Management, ICSSSM 2016*. 10.1109/ICSSSM.2016.7538424

Tönnissen, S., & Teuteberg, F. (2019). Analysing the impact of blockchain-technology for operations and supply chain management: An explanatory model drawn from multiple case studies. *International Journal of Information Management, 0–1*(January). Advance online publication. doi:10.1016/j.ijinfomgt.2019.05.009

Treiblmaier, H. (2018). The impact of the blockchain on the supply chain: A theory-based research framework and a call for action. *Supply Chain Management, 23*(6), 545–559. doi:10.1108/SCM-01-2018-0029

Tribis, Y., El Bouchti, A., & Bouayad, H. (2018). Supply chain management based on blockchain: A systematic mapping study. *MATEC Web of Conferences, 200*. 10.1051/matecconf/201820000020

Venkatesh, V. G., Kang, K., Wang, B., Zhong, R. Y., & Zhang, A. (2020). System architecture for blockchain based transparency of supply chain social sustainability. *Robotics and Computer-Integrated Manufacturing, 63*(November), 101896. doi:10.1016/j.rcim.2019.101896

Wamba, S. F. (2019). *Continuance Intention in Blockchain-Enabled Supply Chain Applications : Modelling the Moderating Effect of Supply Chain Stakeholders Trust*. doi:10.1007/978-3-030-11395-7

Wang, Y., Han, J. H., Beynon-davies, P., Wang, Y., Han, J. H., & Beynon-davies, P. (2018). *Understanding blockchain technology for future supply chains : a systematic literature review and research agenda*. doi:10.1108/SCM-03-2018-0148

Weber, I., Xu, X., Riveret, R., Governatori, G., Ponomarev, A., & Mendling, J. (2016). *Untrusted business process monitoring and execution using blockchain*. Lecture Notes in Computer Science. Including Subseries Lecture Notes in Artificial Intelligence and Lecture Notes in Bioinformatics. doi:10.1007/978-3-319-45348-4_19

Wright, A., & De Filippi, P. (2015). Decentralized Blockchain Technology and the Rise of Lex Cryptographia. SSRN *Electronic Journal*. doi:10.2139/ssrn.2580664

Wu, H., Cao, J., Yang, Y., Tung, C. L., Jiang, S., Tang, B., . . . Deng, Y. (2019). Data management in supply chain using blockchain: challenges and a case study. *Proceedings - International Conference on Computer Communications and Networks, ICCCN,* 1–8. 10.1109/ICCCN.2019.8846964

Yadav, S., & Singh, S. P. (2019). *Blockchain critical success factors for sustainable supply chain Resources, Conservation & Recycling*. doi:10.1016/j.resconrec.2019.104505

Yu, Y., Wang, X., Zhong, R. Y., & Huang, G. Q. (2016). E-commerce Logistics in Supply Chain Management: Practice Perspective. *Procedia CIRP, 52*, 179–185. Advance online publication. doi:10.1016/j.procir.2016.08.002

Yumna, H., Murad, M., Ikram, M., & Noreen, S. (n.d.). *Use of blockchain in Education : A systematic Literature Review*. Academic Press.

KEY TERMS AND DEFINITIONS

Cryptography: The practice and study of secure communication techniques in the presence of third parties known as adversaries.

Decentralization: Process by which an organization's activities, in particular those relating to planning and decision-making, are distributed or delegated from a central, authoritative place or group.

Distributed Ledger: A consensus of geographically spread replicated, shared, and synchronized digital data across multiple sites, countries, or institutions.

Double Spend: Potential flaw in a digital cash scheme where the same digital token can be spent more than once.

Ethereum: Decentralized open source blockchain featuring smart contract functionality.

Immutability: Design pattern where something can't be modified after being instantiated.

Smart Contract: Computer program or transaction protocol that is intended to automatically execute, control, or document events and actions legally relevant under the terms of a contract or agreement.

This research was previously published in Blockchain and AI Technology in the Industrial Internet of Things; pages 246-273, copyright year 2021 by Engineering Science Reference (an imprint of IGI Global).

Section 7
Critical Issues and Challenges

Chapter 68
A Comprehensive Review of the Security and Privacy Issues in Blockchain Technologies

Mangesh Manikrao Ghonge
(iD) https://orcid.org/0000-0003-0140-4827
Sandip Foundation's Institute of Technology and Research Centre, India

N. Pradeep
(iD) https://orcid.org/0000-0001-7351-5265
Bapuji Institute of Engineering and Technology, India

Renjith V. Ravi
(iD) https://orcid.org/0000-0001-9047-3220
MEA Engineering College, India

Ramchandra Mangrulkar
(iD) https://orcid.org/0000-0002-9020-0713
Dwarkadas J. Sanghvi College of Engineering, India

ABSTRACT

The development of blockchain technology relies on a variety of disciplines, including cryptography, mathematics, algorithms, and economic models. All cryptocurrency transactions are recorded on a digital and decentralized public ledger known as the blockchain. Customers may keep track of their crypto-transactions by looking at a chronological list rather than a centralized ledger. The blockchain's application potential is bright, and it has already produced results. In various fields, blockchain technology has been incorporated and deployed, from the earliest days of cryptocurrencies to the present day with new-age smart contracts. No comprehensive study on blockchain security and privacy has yet been done despite numerous studies in this area over the years. In this chapter, the authors talked about blockchain's security and privacy issues as well as the impact they've had on various trends and applications. This chapter covers both of these topics.

DOI: 10.4018/978-1-6684-7132-6.ch068

INTRODUCTION

In the business network, a Blockchain is a distributed, decentralized ledger or database that makes it easier to record commercial transactions. It can also be explained as an open-source, decentralized database that is accessible to all members of the network at all times. A majority of the network's participants must agree on every transaction before it can be recorded in the public ledger. A transaction uploaded to the blockchain can't be deleted or tampered with once the block contains verification information about it. Blockchain was first used in 2009 with the introduction of Bitcoin. This electronic payment system or cryptocurrency is cryptographically safe because it makes use of peer-to-peer (P2P) network technology. Payments cannot be made to any central institutions, such as a bank, because there is no trusted third-party authority to whom payments can be made. The owner of a Bitcoin is free to use it whenever and wherever they want without having to deal with a centralized authority. Bitcoin's arrival has sparked a lot of interest in Blockchain, which has now garnered the attention of academics as well as industry. The Blockchain's features enable security, privacy, and data integrity without the involvement of a third party in transaction control, which is why it's attracting attention.

Although the financial industry has embraced blockchain as its foundational technology, customers have expressed reservations about the platform's inherent security. Integrity, confidentiality, and availability are common concepts used to describe security. Public blockchain systems are mostly based on distributed networks and have limited levels of confidentiality, but their integrity and availability are guaranteed by these systems. In these blockchain systems, data accessibility is always on the higher end. Data replication for distributed systems increases readable data availability, but it decreases write availability. Despite the fact that the blockchain's underlying architecture is extremely safe, implementations of cutting-edge technologies have taken use of the blockchain's security features. Because all of the network's public keys are visible to everyone, the blockchain system is likewise susceptible to the leaking of transactional privacy. Ethereum and smart contracts have recently been found to have a number of security flaws. For instance, thieves exploited a smart contract recursive calling vulnerability in June 2016 and stole $60 million. Blockchain security and privacy issues have been investigated in several research, however, none have provided answers for enhancing security. In this chapter, we'll examine blockchain technology from a broader perspective, including the security concerns that go along with it. In this chapter, we'll go over the numerous security issues associated with popular blockchain systems, including a real-world assault and an analysis of the vulnerabilities exploited. For the sake of data security and preventing vulnerabilities, we'll also cover various encryption approaches in this chapter.

As you can see, the chapter is organised in the following manner. Our definition of blockchain technology and related concepts and techniques is found in Section 1. Blockchain is discussed in Sections 2 and 3, while Section 4 focuses on security-related issues. Finally, in Section 5, we talk about blockchain privacy issues. Sections 6 and 7 then present blockchain applications and challenges. Section 6 then wraps up the chapter.

STRUCTURE OF BLOCKCHAIN

While relational databases can be shared between various users, blockchains are decentralised electronic ledgers that produce an immutable record of transactions, each of which is time-stamped and connected to the one before it. In the digital ledger, each block is referred to as a digital record or transaction, and it allows anyone to contribute. Once new data is added to the blockchain, it cannot be modified or re-moved, ensuring high data integrity. Only network participants can update the blockchain. It is possible to verify every transaction on the blockchain. (Nakamoto, 2008)

Cryptocurrency bitcoin was the first to employ blockchain technology, and bitcoin Using distributed ledger technology, such as the blockchain, you can be confident that your financial transactions are com-pletely private and secure. Creator of Bitcoin Satoshi Nakamoto calls it a peer-to-peer electronic cash system that allows payments to be sent directly from one party to another without the use of a financial institution. From the standpoint of the network, Blockchain is a distributed file system where members keep copies of the file and agree on the updates by agreement. These blocks are made up of transactions as well as main data such timestamps and cryptographic signatures (hashes) of previous blocks, as well as hashes for current blocks and other information. The file is divided into these blocks. Previous blocks are linked by the hash, and subsequent blocks will also need the previous block's hash, so all of these blocks are chained together. If anything in the block is changed, the hash value will be different from the specified one, and the block will be rejected. As a result, adding the hash from the prior block in the current block combines the complete system history. (Mearian, 2018)

Figure 1. Blockchain structure
(Sultana et al., 2020)

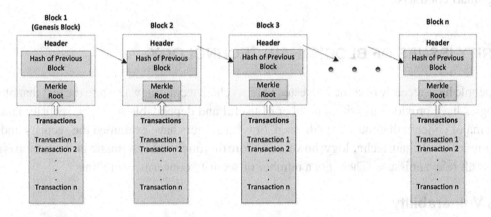

ELEMENTS OF BLOCKCHAIN

Blockchain technology consists of six key elements.

- Distributed: Every node (participant) receives and applies the same rules because the standard network protocol groups transactions into blocks for processing.
- Decentralization: Each node (participant) has a copy of all the data in the system, so a central authority is unnecessary. This helps to ensure that there isn't a single point of failure or vulner-ability. Every transaction in the traditional centrally managed system must be validated by a cen-tral authority (for example, the financial institution) and is therefore subject to service fees, time constraints and performance bottlenecks on central servers No middle man/authority service fee

is required in the blockchain network, but this also speeds up transactions. Data consistency in a distributed, decentralised network is maintained using consensus algorithms. (Kuo et al., 2020)

- Immutability: Data can't be manipulated on a blockchain. Delete or rollback transactions are nearly impossible once the participants have agreed on them and they have been recorded in the blockchain.
- Consensus: To eliminate the requirement for a trusted third party, all nodes must agree on the integrity of transaction data using a common algorithm/mechanism. The validity of the transaction must be agreed upon by all participants prior to its execution. As a result of this "consensus" process, fraudulent or inaccurate transactions are kept out of the blockchain. Invalid transactions in blocks could be exposed right away.
- Anonymity: Using a randomly created address, any user may engage with the blockchain without exposing his or her actual identity. However, the transaction history is publicly available to all users. While the bitcoin blockchain cannot ensure privacy owing to its intrinsic restrictions, other blockchain protocols promise to give the maximum level of anonymity.
- Smart Contracts: The blockchain can be used to implement scripts that run on demand when certain conditions are met. If you utilise Ethereum– Ether exchange, for example, you must meet established criteria that indicate you possess cryptocurrency and have the permission to transmit the money you claim to own. Multiple inputs can be required before a transaction is triggered using smart contracts.

SECURITY ISSUES OF BLOCKCHAIN TECHNOLOGY

A lot of people have recently become interested in blockchain technology. Despite the fact that blockchain technologies have provided us with a number of useful and dependable services, security and privacy remain a major concern that must be addressed. Several authors have examined the security and privacy implications of blockchain technology; however, a more thorough and systematic investigation is required to address all relevant issues. There are a number of security concerns, including:

1. 51% Vulnerability

To establish trust, the blockchain makes use of a distributed consensus mechanism. As long as data miners are willing to participate, the system distributes computing power equally among them. Processor cycles generate hashes, and these data miners' job is to examine those hashes. Combined, all of these miners can build a massive mining operation with unmatched processing capacity. An attack by a mining pool with 51% or more computing power could compromise the blockchain's security and compromise the entire cryptocurrency network. To use an example from POW-based blockchains, for example, if one miner's hashing power is 50% higher, that miner can easily launch a 51% attack and cause. Changing or manipulating the blockchain system's information is possible for an attacker with 51% of the total coins. This is referred to as a 50% assault. (Courtois & Bahack, 2014) (Eyal & Sirer, 2013)

Figure 2. Security threats to blockchain

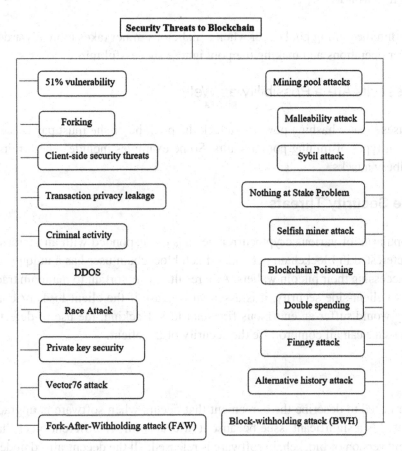

2. Double Spending

When a customer makes multiple purchases with the same cryptocurrency, this is known as double spending. An attacker who employs race attacks can start the double-spending process. As the attacker can take advantage of the time that elapses between two transactions, implementing these attacks on a POW-based blockchain is relatively simple. That way, the attacker got their hands on the first transaction's results before they expired, which could lead to fraud.

3. Mining Pool Attacks

Mining pools are created to rise a block's computation or hash power. The time it takes to verify a block is directly influenced by these pools. There is also a greater chance to win the mining reward when using these mining pools. As mining pools change, so does the risk of an attacker being able to exploit them. There are two types of attacks on a mining pool:

a. Attacks on the Inside

Attacks from within the mining pool occur when a malicious miner takes more rewards than necessary, disrupting regular operations and making the pool ignore successful mining efforts.

b. External Assaults Are a Possibility as Well

When a miner uses greater hashing power to attack the pool, he or she must pay twice as much. There are many different types of mining pool assaults. Some examples include selfish mining, block withholding, and bribery attacks.

4. Client-Side Security Threats

The surge in popularity of various cryptocurrencies has corresponded with an increase in the number of individuals interested in blockchain networks. Each blockchain user has a unique set of private and public keys for accessing their bitcoin wallets. As a result, it's important to maintain track of these keys. When it comes to client-side security, it is essential because if the client loses or compromises their wallet keys, they would suffer an enormous financial loss. Hacking, the use of defective software, or improper wallet usage can all compromise the security of the client.

5. Forking

Forking is a term used to describe the agreement that occurs when software is upgraded between decentralised nodes. It's a significant issue because it affects so many different blockchains at the same time. When a new version of blockchain software is released, all the decentralised nodes come to a new agreement on the consensus rule. As a result of this procedure, nodes in the blockchain are split into two groups: old nodes and new nodes. New nodes established in this manner may or may not agree with the transaction blocks of the existing nodes. While fresh nodes may accept transaction blocks, older nodes may not. As a result of this, we're now dealing with the fork problem.

There are two types of fork issues:

1.   Soft fork
2.   Hard fork.

A system upgrade that destroys compatibility with prior versions results in a hard fork. Both blockchains split when new version nodes' mining became incompatible with old version nodes' mining. A network's old nodes are compelled to update to the new agreement when a hard fork occurs. If the old nodes do not update and function as a separate chain, a fork will occur, resulting in two distinct networks. In case new nodes disagree with the old nodes' transaction mining, then there will be a soft fork. Soft forks do not require rapid network node upgrades; the process happens gradually and has no impact on the system's stability or efficacy during this time period The soft fork has just one chain. A soft fork can form as a result of a brief divergence. If a miner's nodes are running outdated software, clients on those nodes are breaking a new consensus rule that the nodes don't comprehend.

6. Ransomware

Criminals frequently extort money with ransomware and trade it for Bitcoin. CTB-Locker, a ransomware, was distributed via email attachment in July 2014. After clicking on the attachment, a background process encrypts 114 different types of files in the user's system. Victims are required to make a payment in Bitcoin Wi to the attacker within 96 hours of being notified of the attack. The encrypted les will be lost if this is not done.

7. Money Laundering

It's less likely that Bitcoin will be used for money laundering because of the anonymity it provides and the virtual network payment features it offers. When Cody and his colleagues created Dark Wallet, they claimed it was capable of hiding and protecting Bitcoin transactions from prying eyes. By encrypting and combining the user's transaction information with actual currency, Dark Wallet makes money laundering considerably easier.

8. Private Key Security

No 3rd party is intricate in the process of verifying the security and authenticity of a user's private key in blockchain systems. Whenever someone makes a cryptocurrency wallet, they have to include the private key as well. To ensure the safety and authenticity of the cryptocurrencies, this private key is bring in into the file. If the user's private key is stolen or lost, there is no way to recover it, and as a result, the wallet and all of the user's cryptocurrencies are no longer available. Because third-party institutions have no control over blockchain systems, data can be altered by untraceable attackers in the event of a lost or stolen private key.

9. Transaction Privacy Leakage

It is important to protect user privacy in blockchain systems because their activities can be tracked. The received cryptocurrency is stored in one-time accounts in the cryptocurrencies Bitcoin and Zcash. A private key is also required for each transaction, which must be assigned by the user. If the cryptocurrency is recovered in several transactions, the attacker will have no way of knowing if it was stolen by the same user. When initiating a transaction in Monero, users have the option of including chaff coins (referred to as "mixins"), making it impossible for an attacker to govern the link among the real coins spent during the transaction.

10. Malleability Attack

A transaction's unique ID is changed before the network confirms it, resulting in an attack. Alteration of transaction signature is the most common method of obtaining a new transaction ID. If the transaction ID is changed after this signature is altered, the previous transaction ID is no longer valid. As a result of this modification, an attacker can now pretend that a transaction never occurred. This attack was a complete and utter resounding success. (Lin et al., 2020)

11. Nothing at Stake Problem

As far as blockchain networks using PoS are concerned, this is a theoretical issue. when there are two validators proposing the same block at the same time, a fork occurs. The validator has a vested interest in casting a vote in both chains. Because mining doesn't have any associated costs. Mining both chains ensures that voters will receive their mining reward regardless of which fork is selected. The attacker can create a fork in the blockchain before spending any money and then exploit it. By mining both chains, the miners will create a shorter chain, while mining only the attacker's chain, the longest chain will be created. This means you'll end up paying twice.

12. Selfish Miner Attack

Mining pools and individual miners can commit this attack by finding the solution but failing to distribute it to the rest of the network. Once the selfish miner has gained control of this block, he or she will continue to mine on top of it in order to stay ahead of the pack. When everyone else on the network has finally caught up. A selfish miner then publishes the solved blocks so that others can benefit from it. The longest chain rules in PoW determine that their chain is the winner, and as a result, they claim the block reward. All of the other miners' hard work is in vain, and they suffer as a result. However, if such an attack is successful, the chain's value would plummet and the attacker's staked coins would lose all of their purchasing power. On the other hand, the amount of money required to gain such a significant amount of influence is usually prohibitive.

13. Sybil Attack

During a Sybil assault, an attacker uses several aliases to gain control of a peer-to-peer network. To gain control of the network, the attacker must gain a majority of the votes cast. This attack can be used against a Proof-of-stake blockchain network, which has a voting scheme that allows the attacker to validate invalid blocks. However, due to the high stakes, this attack is rarely successful. (Dorri et al., 2017)

14. DDOS Attack

An attack known as a distributed denial of service (DDoS) occurs when an attacker uses malicious traffic to inundate the target or related infrastructure. This is accomplished using zombies, which are remotely controlled hacked computers or bots. Botnet is the term for the network they create. This is used to launch a distributed denial-of-service attack, with the primary objective of preventing legitimate users from accessing the targeted resources. Botnets can contain anywhere from a few hundred computers to tens of millions. Because the attack traffic looks so much like legitimate traffic, it's hard to tell which is which in a DDoS attack. Attackers and defenders are squabbling over resources in DDoS attacks. The more resources an attacker has at his disposal, the better his chances are of succeeding. Encryption is used to protect all communications between the handler and the attack, ensuring that it cannot be detected. Attackers use MAC spoofing to their advantage (Gupta et al., 2020). DDoS attacks can be classified into three categories. Attacks on the application layer, resource exhaustion, and a volumetric attack are all possibilities.

15. Blockchain Poisoning

Private information (such as names, addresses, and credit card numbers) and illegal files have been injected into the blockchain in this attack (malware, malicious content). By forcing nodes to download harmful files, a bad actor can launch a variety of other attacks on the blockchain, including denial of service (DoS) and distributed denial of service (DDoS). As a result, the network may be in violation of government regulations. Because blockchain is immutable, it's difficult to remove these files. As a result of this attack, the compromised chain will be unable to be used unless costly and time-consuming measures are taken to remove the offending files.

16. Race Attack

Hackers can launch a race attack on the Bitcoin network by simultaneously submitting two transactions. This sort of attack is straightforward to implement on PoW-based blockchains. Businesses that accept payments with 55 "0/unconfirmed" immediately are at risk of having the transaction reversed. Counter-measures that might be employed include the following: The following are the three methods of detection:

Time allotted for hearing: Each received transaction has a "listening period" associated with it, and the vendor keeps track of all incoming transactions during this time. During the listening period, the vendor will only deliver the product or provide the service if he sees no attempt to double-spend.

It's possible for vendors to use "observers" to relay all of the transactions they receive directly to themselves via a node or a group of nodes that they control within the Bitcoin network. This aids the vendor in spotting any attempts by him or his observers to engage in double-dipping within seconds.

A good countermeasure to double-spending on fast Bitcoin payments is to forward the attempts to spend twice. If the Bitcoin network receives two more transactions with the same input but different outputs, the peers propagate an alert.

17. Finney Attack

\The attacker pre-mined one transaction in the block and spent the same coins to invalidate it before releasing it to the public network. Attacks like these are referred to the 58 Finney attacks. Once a block has been mined, a miner must participate in the Finney attack to commit fraud. Only in the presence of a single confirmation vendor can an adversary perform a double-spending.

There is only one confirming vendor for a Finney assault. The seller should wait for numerous confirmations before releasing or supplying a service to the customer in order to avoid the Finney attack. However, waiting for several confirmations will lessen the chance of a double-spending assault by reducing the attacker's motivation.

18. Vector76 Attack

A double-spending attack against Vector76's exchanges, also known as a one confirmation attack, is carried out using the attacker's own privately mined block. It's possible to undo even a single confirmation transaction using the race and finney attacks together. It's feasible to launch a vector76 attack against bitcoin exchanges that have nodes that permit direct connections. The attacker will have no problem discovering this node if it has a static IP address. Protection measures include waiting for several confirmations, not allowing any new connections, and only sending outbound connections to well-connected nodes, as well as inserting network observers and notifying the merchant of any new double-spend attempts.

19. Alternative History Attack

The attacker will have to pay a high hash rate and risk wasting energy if they attempt an alternate history attack despite several confirmations of a transaction. Protective measures include not allowing incoming connections, making clear outbound connections to well-connected nodes, adding network monitors, and alerting the merchant to the ongoing double-spend.

20. Block-withholding Attack (BWH)

Block withholding attacks, which prevent dishonest miners from publishing a mined block, undermine the pool's earnings. Dishonest miners, on the other hand, waited until the right moment to release mined blocks when engaging in selfish mining. Infiltrating another pool is the most typical method of launching a block withholding attack.

21. Fork-After-Withholding Attack (FAW)

The FAW assault is another guise for the BWH attack mechanism. For any pool of players, using an FAW assault is four times more feasible since it offers a reward at least as big as that offered by a BWH attacker. The problem has yet to be solved, and developing a low-cost yet effective countermeasure is still an open one.

PRIVACY ISSUES OF BLOCKCHAIN TECHNOLOGY

A lot has been written about the potential applications of blockchain technology in recent years. These industries include everything from banking and healthcare to property and law enforcement. Legal privacy specialists are currently focused with three major categories as a result of various blockchain applications presenting a wide range of data security and privacy concerns and potential. To begin, there's a crucial link between the physical and digital worlds that must be built; second, private information must be stored on the blockchain; and third, blockchains must exist. These options all have trade-offs, and different blockchain networks are needed for different applications to function properly based on the requirements of each one.

Physical Cyberspace Boundary

Using an "online identifier," a flesh-and-blood person can communicate in cyberspace without crossing the "physical cyberspace boundary." Creating a username and logging in is a prerequisite for using Facebook's social networking features, such as messaging. Any online interaction, such as banking, purchasing concert tickets, or downloading music, necessitates the establishment of an association between you and your online identifier before you can take part. To ensure that the ID is secure, it must cross the physical cyberspace boundary at some point (e.g. a bank account or email address without a real name attached to it). At the moment, this framework is being developed primarily through the usage of users and secret keys, with other verification approaches added as necessary. In the near future, we'll require something other than a username and password to traverse the physical cyberspace gap. However, the system contains a flaw: in order for a physical person to log in, the network must have a copy of both their log-in credentials and their online identity. A centralised system (such as Facebook or the central servers of your bank) must only keep these credentials once. These credentials will be kept on a blockchain network and will be accessible to any nodes hosting the blockchains with which you wish to interact.

Because stolen biometric IDs can't be simply replaced, it's critical when it comes to biometric identifiers. It will soon become clear that, when blocks are added to a chain of transactions, all information entered onto a certain blockchain remains intact. This means that private information can be kept for all time on the internet. It's tough to safeguard you against hackers gaining access to critical data once a user's login credentials have been compromised because blockchain has no strong central authority.

In the event that your bank account or credit card information is compromised, you may be able to contact your bank to have your login passwords reset or to have an expired credit card cancelled. Hackers could even shut you out of the system by changing your login credentials once they gain access to the network without the help of an authoritative central authority. In spite of the fact that hacking this private information poses a security risk, it also raises concerns about who is responsible for informing users whose login credentials have been compromised, if anyone. According to data breach notification legislation in the majority of states, organisations that hold personal information about people are now required to tell those individuals when that information's security has been breached ("PII"). Even if the rules are well-written, it's unclear how they'll be implemented in a decentralised network like blockchain.

Information Storage and Inference

Blockchains will hold data such as genetic sequences and biometric credentials, but some of the data stored on them will be exceedingly sensitive. Blockchains will be used to (as discussed above). Hackers may target specific nodes that are easier to enter so that they can gain access to encrypted data for whatever purpose they like, or when the law forbids this form of hacking. Having government-employed hackers use physical node placement in countries where information is more easily hacked or where legislation against such hacking are inadequate, this becomes much more of an issue." Closed networks reduce privacy threats, yet some blockchains carrying sensitive data must run in open networks because of the advantages of open networks. Furthermore, open networks increase the risk of sensitive data from transactions being accessed even if the data is encrypted. In the event that two large banks carry out a high number of transactions in a short period of time, other banks or private persons can draw conclusions from this data. So, if a doctor alters a patient's health data, a hacker who knows the patient's and doctor's online identities can see the transaction. Unless health records are collected and encrypted, they cannot be accessed or edited; however, a hacker may be able to discover which doctor saw a patient on a certain day, information that a patient may wish to keep hidden. Furthermore, no one knows who may be held responsible for harm made to the owner of the information or a third party as a result of unauthorised use, which is worrisome at this point.

Nature of the Blockchain—Eternal Records

The combined developments in data retention, cataloguing, and search capabilities in the twenty-first century represent a serious threat to data protection. More data about our lives is being collected and catalogued than ever before, making it more available to the general public. Blockchain technology is anticipated to accelerate this tendency. Because a blockchain records all transactions all the way back to the genesis block, it's said to be an advantage because it provides for near-perfect evidence of future transactions. As transaction types expand, blockchains will store an increasing number of records of each transaction. It is possible that in the future, every transaction you make will be saved on a blockchain, with you having no influence over where or how that information is utilised, or even if it remains there. Many people are concerned about the impact of these enduring records on their privacy (and the laws that govern it). To begin, the availability of these records may present difficulties for those who do not prefer to have a permanent record of all financial transactions. It is unknown who legally owns the information included in these documents at the moment. As a result, the participants to the transactions would be unable to stop the blockchain networks from selling the data contained in these records. If ownership rules are unclear, anybody — including private citizens and government organisations — might have access to this information without the agreement of the parties involved in the transaction. It may be difficult, if not impossible, to delete an inaccuracy from a blockchain once data has been uploaded with a weak or no central authority.

BLOCKCHAIN APPLICATION

The Bitcoin network is a large-scale digital currency system that operates independently throughout the entire time, enabling global, real-time, reliable transactions. These transactions can be implemented in a standard banking system. This is due to the fact that the possibilities for blockchain applications are limitless. To ensure that all transactions are completed efficiently and reliably, the blockchain-based business value network must become a reality in the future. As a result, the entire business system is managed at a lower cost, and social communications and collaboration are more effective. A new industrial revolution could be sparked by blockchain technology in this way.

In fact, we need to start with the blockchain's characteristics to find the best use case. Furthermore, the reasonable limits of the blockchain solution must be considered. Examples of blockchain applications for mass consumers include those that are available in a public chain with no borders or in a blockchain supported by multiple data centre nodes and are open, transparent, and auditable (Oh & Lee, 2017). Today, promoters distribute products all over the world.

It's extremely difficult right now to get anything done after a global securities trade. An estimated $5-10 billion will be required. More than $20 billion is spent each year on analysis, reconciliation, and processing. According to a European Central Bank report, distributed ledger technology is similar to blockchain. Changing the owner of a security is achievable in nearly all circumstances. In the midst of the ICO frenzy, "decentralisation of the Internet," and the crazies who are trying to get everything they can think of onto the blockchain, it's vital to stand back and look at the broader picture. In our opinion, the blockchain contains the following four punch-app usefulness:

1. Payments on the darknet and on the black market

There was a clear issue with darknet markets prior to the introduction of Bitcoin. If buyers and sellers on the darknet do not trust each other and do not want their identities revealed, how can payments be made between them?

As he got closer, Bitcoin appeared. Unlike other forms of digital currency (such as fiat), bitcoin does not require users to have any trust in each other. It is also pseudonymous, which means it is unaffected by governments. Darknet markets like The Silk Road, AlphaBay, and their successors used Bitcoin as the unofficial currency. Although Bitcoin is now primarily used for benign transactions, the darknet is largely responsible for its inception. There is a promotion phase for all cryptocurrencies, and this phase offers very little security. The Darknet was responsible for the initial influx of Bitcoin users and miners, which gave the entire ecosystem a boost. The darknet's annual turnover is well over $1 billion, according to most estimates. Darknet is, of course, only a small part of the global black market. As the adoption and use of cryptocurrencies increases, so will the acceptance of these digital currencies by the black market. If the darknet needs a currency, Monero or ZCash (and potentially Mimblewimble later) are better equipped than Bitcoin to fill that role.(Buxton & Bingham, 2015) (Oksiiuk & Dmyrieva, 2020)

2. Digital gold

Gold is of limited use on its own. Only a tiny fraction of the world's gold is used in industrial or production settings. Yet, everyone agreed that gold is extraordinarily valuable despite this fact. What makes you think that way?

Gold has several useful economic properties even if we ignore the irrational reasons people are drawn to it. The supply of gold has a low inflation rate because it is a difficult metal to mine and new deposits are rarely discovered. Because gold does not tarnish or corrode, it will continue to be available for purchase. As a result, there are very few price fluctuations, which makes it an appealing way to save. As a result, the ups and downs of gold's price are independent of any particular country. People gravitated toward gold as Schelling's focal point for a stable form of savings for all of these reasons and more. Gold is a hedge against global economic downturns because of its steadfast nature as a store of value. Gold remains gold, regardless of economic ups and downs, and its behaviour is, for the most part, independent. In this way, gold has served as a global decentralised means of saving for millennia. For this reason, it has a lot of value to us. (Mougayar, 2016)

3. Payments (macro and micro)

Peer-to-peer payments are impossible with blockchains, whereas precise key management is required of cryptocurrency users. Regular darknet users may be able to spend the time and risk it takes to grasp the nuances of the technology. However, real, practical security is required for blockchains to function in the mass market before they can be considered a success.

For the average person on the street, money should be simple to use, so that they aren't misled and endanger their finances. Now, the majority of people are technologically incompetent. Until then, cryptocurrencies will be unsuitable for use in a peer-to-peer payment system for the general public. Many economies are also simplifying traditional payments, which is encouraging. Venmo in the U.S., M-Pesa in Africa, or AliPay and WeChat Pay in China are all examples of similar services. As long as traditional financial technologies keep moving forward at their current rates, the blockchain will be largely irrelevant in the near future.(Sikorski et al., 2017)

4. Tokenization

Millions of people use tokenization every day, and it's the backbone of today's digital economy. Tokenization is the process of replacing value with tokens that reflect these values (such as money, stocks, credit card numbers, and medical records) in order to make trading them more convenient and secure. Tokenization As a result of tokenization, our lives have changed significantly, and it has the ability to do so again.

Tokenization makes paying for goods online much safer than it would be otherwise. Banks complete payments using a digital token created from the customer's private credit card information. This token is useless to hackers. Because digital securities are more secure and efficient than paper ones, companies are beginning to issue them as an alternative to paper certificates of ownership and other securities. Despite the fact that people already utilise tokens on a daily basis, the blockchain is only now revealing the full tokenization potential (most do not know this). There are new benefits and uses in many industries, including art and healthcare, due to the potential of blockchain to tokenize a wide range of real assets and enterprises safely and efficiently. That's why security tokenization on the blockchain has produced a brand-new trading and fundraising instrument. A wide number of businesses have found use for blockchain technology because of its decentralisation and lack of trust as well as its tamper-resistance, security, and reliability. Depending on the situation, blockchain either solves or reduces the risks and costs associated with traditional industries.(Liu, 2016)

BLOCKCHAIN CHALLENGES

- **Scalability:** The blockchain network's scalability problem has been exposed as a result of the enormous success of Bitcoin. Block size and block creation time are prefixed for a predetermined number of transaction processing in order to combat the aforementioned attacks. When there are multiple transactions to process, the processing speed can be slowed down. Both Bitcoin and Ethereum, which have 1MB blocks and confirmation times of 10 minutes on average, have scaling difficulties. The block confirmation time must be short for a large number of transactions to be processed, but the average time must be long to prevent an attack. Scalability is by far the biggest problem that blockchain is currently facing. trilemma According to Vitalik Buterin (the creator of Ethereum), it's not possible to maximise decentralisation, scalability, and security at the same time. Trilemma theorists assert that by sacrificing the third, any two can be improved upon. The electricity consumption of blockchains based on the PoW consensus, such as bitcoin, has also increased because these systems require a lot of computing power. The scalability problem has already been addressed by the authors of (Miller et al., 2017).
- **Storage Management:** It is more secure to have all nodes of the network share a blockchain ledger. Every block on the chain is recorded in the ledger from the genesis block to the most recent block. As a result of this duplication, a huge amount of space is required. According to recent estimates, the Bitcoin blockchain is growing at a rate of about 1MB per hour. Nearly 1.5736 Petabytes of space has been taken up by Bitcoin nodes, which now number over 1,000,000.
- **Lack of governance and regulation:** Permissionless blockchain networks need third-party certification since blockchain is a decentralised network. Many people have had to deal with a variety

of problems and have incurred substantial financial losses as a result. In fact, standardising the blockchain network is necessary for reasons like integration, governance, and long-term viability.

- **Throughput:** Ethereum's transaction pace is roughly twenty times faster than Bitcoin's average of seven transactions per second. PayPal conducts 193 transactions per second, which is more than VISA's 1667 transactions per second average. Because of this, Bitcoin and Ethereum need to boost their throughput if they want to compete with more established payment systems like VISA and PayPal. Blockchain networks' throughput will need to be increased once the number of transactions per second approaches that of VISA.

- **Latency:** A block of transactions is mined or created on the Bitcoin network in around 10 minutes, based on current data. Using information from Ethereum's network, we can estimate the duration to be around 14 seconds. To increase security efficiency, more time must be spent creating and validating blocks to verify that transaction inputs haven't been reused earlier, which leads to double-spending attacks. Existing blockchain systems must speed up block production and validation if they want to process transactions quickly while still preserving security.

CONCLUSION

Numerous researches on blockchain security and privacy have been conducted, however a complete study of blockchain security remains lacking. We aimed to show a systematic illustration of blockchain security vulnerabilities by examining prominent blockchain systems and providing a full description of the associated real-world assaults. Throughout this chapter, we've talked about blockchain's security and privacy features and their various applications and challenges. The chapter has concentrated on the most important blockchain security and privacy issues.

REFERENCES

Buxton, J., & Bingham, T. (2015). The rise and challenge of dark net drug markets. *Policy Brief, 7,* 1–24.

Courtois, N. T., & Bahack, L. (2014). On subversive miner strategies and block withholding attack in bitcoin digital currency. CoRR, vol. abs/1402.1718.

Dorri, Steger, Kanhere, & Jurdak. (2017). Blockchain: A distributed solution to automotive security and privacy. *IEEE Commun. Mag., 55,* 119-125. /MCOM.2017.1700879 doi:10.1109

Eyal, I., & Sirer, E. G. (2013). Majority is not enough: Bitcoin mining is vulnerable. CoRR, vol. abs/1311.0243.

Gupta, S., Sinha, S., & Bhushan, B. (2020). Emergence of Blockchain Technology: Fundamentals, Working and its Various Implementations. *International Conference on Innovative Computing and Communication (ICICC 2020).*

Kuo, T.-T., Gabriel, R. A., Cidambi, K. R., & Ohno-Machado, L. (2020). EX pectation P ropagation LO gistic RE g R ession on permissioned block CHAIN (ExplorerChain): Decentralized online healthcare/genomics predictive model learning. *Journal of the American Medical Informatics Association: JAMIA*, *27*(5), 747–756. doi:10.1093/jamia/ocaa023 PMID:32364235

Lin, Khowaja, Chen, & Hardle. (2020). *Blockchain mechanism and distributional characteristics of cryptos*. IRTG 1792 Discussion Paper 2020-027.

Liu, P. T. S. (2016). *Medical record system using blockchain, big data and tokenization. in international conference on information and communications security*. Springer.

Mearian, L. (2018, January 18). *What is blockchain? The most disruptive tech in decades*. Retrieved February 23, 2018, https://www.computerworld.com/article/3191077/security/what-is-blockchain-the-most-disruptivetech-in-decades.html

Miller, A., Moser, M., Lee, K., & Narayanan, A. (2017). *An empirical analysis of linkability in the monero blockchain*. arXiv:1704.04299

Mougayar, W. (2016). *The business blockchain: promise, practice, and application of the next Internet technology*. John Wiley & Sons.

Nakamoto. (2008). *Bitcoin: A peer-to-peer electronic cash system*. Academic Press.

Oh & Lee. (2017). Block chain application technology to improve reliability of real estate market. *Journal of Society for e-Business Studies, 22*(1).

Oksiiuk, O., & Dmyrieva, I. (2020). Security and privacy issues of blockchain technology. In *2020 IEEE 15th International Conference on Advanced Trends in Radioelectronics, Telecommunications and Computer Engineering (TCSET)*. IEEE.

Sikorski, J. J., Haughton, J., & Kraft, M. (2017). Blockchain technology in the chemical industry: Machine-to-machine electricity market. *Applied Energy, 195*, 234–246. doi:10.1016/j.apenergy.2017.03.039

Sultana, T., Almogren, A., Akbar, M., Zuair, M., Ullah, I., & Javaid, N. (2020). Data Sharing System Integrating Access Control Mechanism using Blockchain-Based Smart Contracts for IoT Devices. *Applied Sciences (Basel, Switzerland), 10*(2), 488. doi:10.3390/app10020488

This research was previously published in Blockchain Technologies and Applications for Digital Governance; pages 180-199, copyright year 2022 by Information Science Reference (an imprint of IGI Global).

Chapter 69
A Review on the Importance of Blockchain and Its Current Applications in IoT Security

Manjula Josephine Bollarapu

Koneru Lakshmaiah Education Foundation, India

Ruth Ramya Kalangi

Koneru Lakshmaiah Education Foundation, India

K. V. S. N. Rama Rao

Koneru Lakshmaiah Education Foundation, India

ABSTRACT

In recent years, blockchain technology has attracted considerable attention. As blockchain is one of the revolutionary technologies that is impacting various industries in the market now with its unique features of decentralization, transparency, and incredible security. Blockchain technology can be used for anything which requires their transactions to be recorded in a secure manner. In this chapter, the authors survey the importance of the blockchain technology and the applications that are being developed on the basis of blockchain technology in area of IoT and security.

BLOCKCHAIN IN IOT

Decentralized Framework for IoT Digital Forensics for Efficient Investigation: A Blockchain-based

Jung Hyun Ryu et.al.(2019) proposed 2 outlines the diagram of proposed advanced legal sciences system for IoT condition. The proposed structure is partitioned into three layers: cloud; blockchain; and IoT gadgets. For the most part, in an IoT domain, gadgets speak with the cloud. By 2020, the quantity of IoT gadgets is relied upon to increment to 26 billion . For this situation, it is practically difficult to examine count-

DOI: 10.4018/978-1-6684-7132-6.ch069

less IoT gadgets utilizing existing advanced measurable strategies. Figure 2 shows a review of proposed computerized criminological structure for IoT condition in this paper. Each IoT gadget stores information produced during the time spent speaking with different gadgets in the blockchain as an exchange. The IoT condition incorporates every little condition utilizing IoT gadgets: sensors; keen vehicle; savvy building; shrewd industry; brilliant home; brilliant matrix. In these conditions, cybercrime can happen whenever, and legitimate criminological system for it must be built up. In the IoT gadget classification, gadgets have different purposes, administrations, makers, advances, and information types. IoT gadgets send and receivelarge measures of information paying little heed to gadget client's will. For this situation, if the current criminological strategy is applied to every gadget framing an enormous number of connections, the examination turns out to be very difcult. Along these lines, in the proposed structure, the information created during the time spent correspondence of each IoT gadget are put away as an exchange in the blockchain. The computerized scientific agent abuses the put away trustworthiness of squares and the simplifed chain of guardianship process.

Secure Firmware Update for Embedded Devices in an IoT Environment: A Block chain Based

Boohyung Leeet.al.,(2017) In this paper, we center around a safe firmware update issue, which is an essential security challenge for the implanted gadgets in an IoT domain. Another firmware update conspire that uses a blockchain innovation is proposed to safely check a firmware adaptation, approve the accuracy of firmware, and download the most recent firmware for the installed gadgets. In the proposed plot, an inserted gadget demands its firmware update to hubs in a blockchain arrange and gets a reaction to decide if its firmware is modern or not. If not most recent, the implanted gadget downloads the most recent firmware from a distributed firmware sharing system of the hubs. Indeed, even for the situation that the variant of the firmware is upto-date, its respectability, i.e., accuracy of firmware, is checked. The proposed conspire ensures that the inserted gadget's firmware is state-of-the-art while not altered. Assaults focusing on known vulnerabilities on firmware of installed gadgets are in this manner moderated.

Blockchain Mechanisms for IoT Security

MatevžPustišeka(2018) et.al.,present three potential designs for the IoT front-end BC applications. They vary in situating of Ethereumblockchain customers (nearby gadget, remote server) and in situating of key store required for the administration of active exchanges. The functional limitations of these structures, which use the Ethereum arrange for believed exchange trade, are the information volumes, the area and synchronization of the full blockchain hub and the area and the entrance to the Ethereum key store. Consequences of these tests demonstrate that a full Ethereum hub isn't probably going to dependably run on a compelled IoT gadgets. In this manner the design with remote Ethereum customers is by all accounts a feasible methodology, where two sub-alternatives exist and contrast in key store area/the executives. Likewise, we proposed the utilization of designs with an exclusive correspondence between the IoT gadget and remote blockchain customer to additionally diminish the system traffic and improve security. We anticipate that it should have the option to work over low-power, low-bitrate portable innovations, as well. Our exploration explains contrasts in compositional methodologies, yet ultimate conclusion for a specific record convention and front-end application design is at emphatically dependent on the specific planned use case.

Securing Academic Certificates Through Block Chain

One of the incredible promising application of the blockchain innovation is that it can serve as a decentralized, changeless, and completely secure store for a wide range of benefits not just as a currency That is the thing that makes it intriguing likewise for public sector use. A University can safely store its scholarly archives utilizing block chain technology. The accompanying fundamental necessities were set up before the venture of putting the academic certificates on the blockchain starts a) the process should involve no other services or products other than the Bitcoinblockchain, b) the process should allow someone to authenticate a University of Nicosia certificate without having to contact the University of Nicosia, and c) The process should allow someone to complete the process even if the University of Nicosia, or more likely their website, no longer existed. The University of Nicosia is a private university, but this use case is just as relevant for a public university. The process of storing the academic certificates on the blockchain followed these steps Hash of the individual certificates. A hash of an certificate is at the center of the procedure. A hash function is a single function that accepts any arbitary information as input and produces a string with a fixed number of characters .The index document containing the hashes of all the individual declarations is published on the University of Nicosia home page. But if this was all, there would be no use for the blockchain. For the procedure to be genuinely decentralized individuals ought to have the option to find a copy of the index document anywhere on the web and compare it to the index document on the blockchain.

Discover a duplicate of the list record anyplace on the web and contrast it with the list archive on the blockchain. The check procedure is done in two stages; one for confirming the file archive and the second for confirming the specific endorsement: Verifying the file report. Guarantee that a legitimate record report from the University of Nicosia is utilized. The hash of the file archive ought to be equivalent to the hash put away on the blockchain, in the predefined time period. Check the declaration. When the file archive has been checked, a SHA-256 hash of the declaration (in pdf) ought to be contrasted with the hash of a similar authentication recorded in the list report. On the off chance that the hash esteems are comparative, the declaration is real. Obviously, the examination of the hash esteems just ensures the legitimacy of the testament, not that the individual who sent the authentication is equivalent to the individual on the declaration.

That must be approved in different manners. The utilization case above has given one potential utilization of the Bitcoinblockchain innovation for open segment. All associations giving declarations, licenses and so forth could profit by the new innovation, as this utilization case appears. The utilization case from the University of Nicosia has highlighted a few difficulties that ought to be researched more top to bottom so as to show up at a best practice for putting away declarations and licenses on the blockchain. The Bitcoin innovation fits the meaning of an advanced stage and the attributes of a data framework can likewise be found in the innovation, as appeared in table 3. Its scattered and disseminated "possession" is in accordance with the focal trait of an II. Introduced base is another key component in a data framework and indicates specialized and non-specialized components delineating the system impacts deciding the improvement of the foundation . The introduced base for this situation is the authoritative, monetary, and lawful components overseeing the present open help II. The legitimate elements are of exceptional significance, as is likewise examined in a large number of the distributions recorded in area three. Be that as it may, the lawful and regulatoryfactors examined in these papers are for the most part about controlling the cash and the installment framework. The utilization case portrayed above, and comparable employments of Bitcoin, gets away from these concerns since the installment part is only an essential reaction and not simply the objective. That is the situation with all utilization cases having a place with purported "keen agreements" utilization of Bitcoin. The money is utilized uniquely as a token in these cases. A data framework without direct Government control may appear to be unnerving for open part. While considering Bitcoin as an intriguing innovation with regards to eGovernment we have to survey history and be helped to remember the "fight" between worldwide system gauges toward the finish of the 1980s, start of 1990s. Governments had the decision between the controlled OSI convention and the Internet convention, and the greater part of them picked the OSI convention. USA's Government OSI Profile – GOSIP – turned into the standard for some other countries' OSI profiles, for example NOSIP – Norwegian OSI Profile. Web's ascent in prominence made it a true standard that before long invade the OSI convention, not least on the grounds that the OSI norms attempted to convey working and interoperable administrations (in the same place.). Web turned into the national and worldwide standard for worldwide correspondence not as a result of national needs, however notwithstanding them. This is something to hold up under at the top of the priority list while considering an innovation that utilizes the equivalent appropriated model that Internet itself.

In each popular government, the security of a political decision involves national security. The PC security field has for 10 years considered the potential outcomes of electronic democratic frameworks, with the objective of limiting the expense of having a national political decision, while satisfying and expanding the security states of a political race. From the beginning of fairly choosing up-and-comers, the democratic framework has been founded on pen and paper. Supplanting the conventional pen and paper conspire with another political decision framework is basic to restrict misrepresentation and having the democratic procedure recognizable and obvious . Electronic democratic machines have been seen as defective, by the security network, principally dependent on physical security concerns. Anybody with physical access to such machine can undermine the machine, in this way influencing all votes cast on the previously mentioned machine. Coming up next are the jobs and parts recognized for an e-Voting framework.

BLOCK CHAIN FOR EDUCATION

Patrick Ochejaet.al.,(2019), It is a typical practice to give a synopsis of a student's learning accomplishments in type of a transcript or authentication. Be that as it may, point by point data on the profundity of learning and how learning or lessons were directed is absent in the transcript of scores. This work presents the principal pragmatic usage of another stage for monitoring learning accomplishments past transcripts and authentications. This is accomplished by keeping up advanced hashes of learning exercises and overseeing access rights using keen agreements on the blockchain. The blockchain of learning logs (BOLL) is a stage that empower students to move their taking in records starting with one organization then onto the next in a protected and undeniable arrangement. This principally takes care of the chilly beginning issue looked by learning information logical stages when attempting to offer customized understanding to new students. BOLL empowers existing learning information logical stages to get to the taking in logs from different organizations with the authorization of the students as well as establishment who initially have responsibility for logs. The fundamental commitment of this paper is to examine how learning records could be associated across establishments utilizing BOLL. We present a diagram of how the usage has been done, examine asset prerequisites, and look at the focal points BOLL has over other comparative instruments.

Guang Chen et.al(2018)., Blockchain is the center innovation used to make the cryptographic forms of money, as bitcoin. As a major aspect of the fourth modern insurgency since the innovation of steam motor, power, and data innovation, blockchain innovation has been applied in numerous zones, for example, money, legal executive, and trade. The current paper concentrated on its likely instructive applications and investigated how blockchain innovation can be utilized to take care of some training issues. This article previously presented the highlights and points of interest of blockchain innovation following by investigating a portion of the current blockchain applications for training. Some imaginative utilizations of utilizing blockchain innovation were proposed, and the advantages and difficulties of utilizing blockchain innovation for instruction were additionally talked about.

REFERENCES

Anand, Conti, Kaliyar, & Lal. (2019). *TARE: Topology Adaptive Re-kEying scheme for secure group communication in IoT networks*. Springer Science+Business Media, LLC.

Bistarelli, S., Mercanti, I., Santancini, P., & Santini, F. (2019). *End-to-End Voting with Non-Permissioned and Permissioned Ledgers*. Springer Nature B.V. doi:10.100710723-019-09478-y

Chen, G., Xu, B., Lu, M., & Chen, N.-S. (2018). Exploring blockchain technology and its potential applications for education. *Smart Learning Environments*, 5(1), 1–10. doi:10.118640561-017-0050-x

Huh & Seo. (2018). *Blockchain-based mobile fingerprint verification and automatic log-in platform for future computing*. Springer Science+Business Media, LLC.

Karaarslan & Adiguzel. (n.d.). Blockchain Based DNS and PKI Solutions. In *Standards for Major Internet Disrutors: Blockchain, Intents and Related Paradigm*. Academic Press.

Kshetri & Voas. (2018). Blockchain-Enabled E-Voting. *IEEE Software*, 95-99.

Lee, B., & Lee, J.-H. (2017). Blockchain-based secure firmware update for embedded devices in an Internet of Things environment. *The Journal of Supercomputing*, 73(3), pp1152–pp1167. doi:10.100711227-016-1870-0

Li, H., Tian, H., Zhang, F., & He, J. (2019). Blockchain-based searchable symmetric encryption scheme. *Computers & Electrical Engineering*, 73, 32–45. doi:10.1016/j.compeleceng.2018.10.015

Liu, J., Jager, T., Kakvi, S. A., & Warinschi, B. (2018). How to build time-lock encryption. *Designs, Codes and Cryptography*, 86(11), 2549–2586. doi:10.100710623-018-0461-x

Minoli, D., & Occhiogrosso, B. (2018). Blockchain mechanisms for IoT security. *Internet of Things*, 1-2, 1–13. doi:10.1016/j.iot.2018.05.002

Ocheja, P., Flanagan, B., Ueda, H., & Ogata, H. (2019). *Managing lifelong learning records through blockchain*. Research and Practice in Technology Enhanced Learning. doi:10.118641039-019-0097-0

Pustišeka. (2018). Approaches to Front-End IoT Application Development for the Ethereum Blockchain. *Procedia Computer Science*, 129, 410–419.

Ryu, Sharma, Jo, & Park. (2019). *A blockchain-based decentralized efcient investigation framework for IoT digital forensics.* Springer Science+Business Media, LLC.

Shahzad. (2019). Trustworthy Electronic Voting Using Adjusted Blockchain Technology. *IEEE Access: Practical Innovations, Open Solutions*, *7*, 24477–24488.

Turkanovic. (2018, January 5). EduCTX: A Blockchain-Based Higher Education Credit Platform. *IEEE Access: Practical Innovations, Open Solutions*, 5112–5127.

Wang, B., Sun, J., He, Y., Pang, D., & Lu, N. (2018). Large-scale Election Based On Blockchain. *Procedia Computer Science*, *129*, 234–237. doi:10.1016/j.procs.2018.03.063

Zhou, L., Wang, L., Sun, Y., & Lv, P. (2018). BeeKeeper: A Blockchain-Based IoT System With Secure Storage and Homomorphic Computation. *IEEE Access: Practical Innovations, Open Solutions*, *6*, 43472–43488. doi:10.1109/ACCESS.2018.2847632

This research was previously published in Blockchain Applications in IoT Security; pages 121-127, copyright year 2021 by Information Science Reference (an imprint of IGI Global).

Chapter 70
Blockchain With IoT and AI:
A Review of Agriculture and Healthcare

Pushpa Singh

iD https://orcid.org/0000-0001-9796-3978

KIET Group of Institutions, Delhi-NCR, Ghaziabad, India

Narendra Singh

iD https://orcid.org/0000-0002-6760-8550

GL Bajaj Insitute of Management and Research, Greater Noida, India

ABSTRACT

Blockchain, Internet of Things (IoT), and Artificial Intelligence (AI) are remarkable emerging technologies in the coming few decades. Blockchain technology makes the application more secure and transparent, AI offers analyses the application, and IoT makes the application connected, flexible, and efficient. This paper studies the literature, formulates the research question, and summarizes the contribution of block-chain application, particularly targeting AI and IoT in agriculture and healthcare sectors. This study reveals that 20% of papers are available in agriculture and 14% available in healthcare that integrates blockchain with IoT and AI. Furthermore, the objective of the paper is to study the role of blockchain with IoT and AI in agriculture and healthcare systems in light of the literature review. The integration of blockchain with IoT and AI are playing important roles in agriculture and healthcare fields to man-age food supply chains, drug supply chains, traceability of products, smart contracts, monitoring the products, connected, and intelligent prediction.

1. INTRODUCTION

A recent paradigm shift in engineering and technology has completely moving towards Artificial Intelli-gence, IoT and Blockchain. Mobile-broadband access devices, IoT, smart networks, big data analytics, AI and Blockchain have provided a new vision and aspect in the field of Agriculture and Healthcare sector. These key tools and technologies used to magnify the production, marketing processes and wellbeing of humanity. IoT is a system where each real world entity is provided with unique identifiers and able

DOI: 10.4018/978-1-6684-7132-6.ch070

to communicate over an Internet (Singh and Agrawal, 2018). AI offers analytical and decision making capability to machine like a human being. AI and IoT brings the application smart and intelligent, for example, smart city (Dubey et al., 2020), smart health (Tian et al., 2019) and smart agriculture (Saiz-Rubio & Rovira-Más, 2020). The Blockchain technology refereed as a decentralized, distributed ledger that records the origins of a digital asset. These three technologies are combining together and reforming the various sectors including healthcare, agriculture, food supply, real estate, retail, etc.

The Blockchain is defined as a chain of Blocks that comprises information. Every block registers all of the current transactions, and after completion stores into the Blockchain as a permanent database. Each time a block gets completed and a new block is created. This technique is based on timestamp of a digital document which is unable to backdate or temper. Block in Blockchain is both a time-and date-stamped, secured server, and at the same time, a secured peer-to-peer database. Earlier Blockchain was only underlying technology used for cryptocurrency or bitcoin. Blockchain technology has the skill to automate payment in crypto currency and access to a shared ledger of data, transactions, and logs in a decentralized, secure, and trusted manner (Salah and Rehman, 2019). The Blockchain provides a direct communication between two specific parties to exchange of data or initiate the peer-to-peer transactions. Ethereum provides an open and distributed public Blockchain platform in which smart contracts can be deployed (Buterin, 2016). These contracts are functional to a broader range of business circumstances like contract processing, ownership changes, and economy sharing (Wu et al., 2019). Blockchain technology offer service mainly to trace and track of transaction to streamline and quicken the transaction and validation process. These services are not only used in cryptocurrency but also proving remarkable in other field where quick and rapid transaction required between a series of entity. There are various application areas of Blockchain like cryptocurrency, healthcare, Agriculture, food supply, copyright, banking (Chen et al., 2018; Casino et al., 2019), and real estate (Dijkstra, 2017).

Agriculture and health sectors are really two important areas that need to be focused and have the opportunity to integrate with recent technology like IoT, AI along with Blockchain. Blockchain play a significant role in agriculture and health areas to supply product and services from source to destination.

AI and IoT have already proven its importance in the field of Agriculture and Healthcare system. IoT is generating a global network of smart connected devices that can enrich Agriculture and Healthcare system. AI coupled with pervasive connectivity, is empowering exponential value being generated by IoT through its analyzing, classification and prediction ability. The interconnection of a huge number of IoT devices is suffering from the numerous privacy and security concerns (Ali, 2019). The IoT-based healthcare applications often end up monitoring and gathering sensitive personal data of patients. When such data or information is visible to third parties, such as health-care providers, the prospects of inadvertent or malicious privacy compromise become greatly probable (Yin et al, 2019). Compliance with the privacy and security concerns for a specific application is a substantial challenge in IoT-based systems (Lin and Bergmann, 2016). Blockchain based solutions can help in addressing the issues related to security and privacy. A significant advancement in Blockchain and its ability to integrate with AI and IoT provides a transparent transaction system to business (Briggs and Buchhols, 2019).Blockchain technology with IoT and AI technology can quickly track and process information related to food items right from their source to the end consumer.

Presently, Supply chain Management (SCM) has been also growing in Agriculture and Healthcare. Blockchain offers excellent capability of supply chain management in a transparent and distributed manner. The blockchain has the prospective to convert all types of digital transactions, comprising in procurement, logistic and supply chain. Blockchain capability assists worldwide manufacture to solve challenges of procurement and supply chain (Brody,2017).The IoT, AI can be integrated with the Blockchain to expand the performance of the real world application. Integration of IoT, AI and Blockchain fulfill the dynamic requirement of supply chain stakeholders in Agriculture (Lezoche el al., 2019) and Healthcare system (Rabah et al., 2018).

This paper investigates the Agriculture and Healthcare application of Blockchain that utilize IoT and AI both or solely based on Blockchain. The choice of the literature review methodology focused firstly on key words related to the Blockchain with IoT and AI in Agriculture and Healthcare system mainly from Jan 2017 to 2020. This paper structured as follows. Section 2 relates research methodology. Section 3 and section 4 review and tabulated the findings of IoT, AI, and Blockchain in the field of Agriculture and Healthcare system. Role of Blockchain with IoT and AI on Agriculture and Healthcare system is discussed in section 5 as a result and discussion section. Section 6 concludes the paper.

Figure 1. Applications areas of blockchain

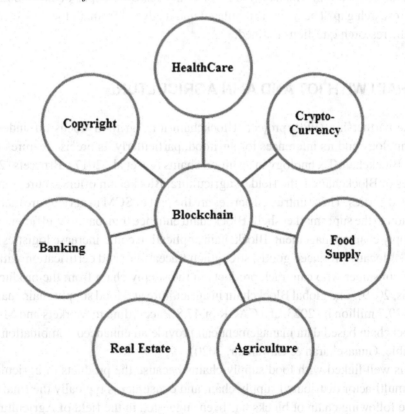

2. REASEARCH METHODOLOGY

This paper mainly presents the contribution of Blockchain technology in Agriculture and Healthcare along with IoT and AI. A systematic review of Blockchain on Agriculture and Healthcare is followed in the formulation and evaluation of research questions. The focus of the current research work is to express the research questions that are answered in detail by keeping the objectives of questions in mind. These research questions are RQ-1 and RQ-2.

RQ-1: What is the role of Blockchain with IoT and AI in Agriculture?
RQ-2: What is the role of Blockchain with IoT and AI in Healthcare?

Search strategy starts with identification of key terms. The keywords are "IoT," "AI", "Machine Learning", "Healthcare", "Smart hospitals", "Agriculture", "Smart Farming", "Supply Chain", and "Blockchain". The search string is formed based on joining the keywords in the following ways for stated research question.

RQ-1: (IoT) or (AI) or (Machine Learning) or (supply chain) and (Healthcare) or (Smart hospitals) and (Blockchain)
RQ-2: (IoT) or (AI) or (Machine Learning) or (supply chain) and (Agriculture) and (Blockchain)

The aforementioned search string was checked on www and examined the document 'contribution, author and year of publication. This study includes only research paper of 2017-2020 to understand recent role and research gap. The result is tabulated and analyzed from all the collected research paper for addressing the research questions defined.

3. BLOCKCHAIN WITH IOT AND AI IN AGRICULTURE

A public private partnership (PPP) project 'Blockchain for Agrifood' focus on understanding of the Blockchain technology and its inferences for agrifood, particularly its precise features of SCM and necessity to apply Blockchain Technology in agrifood chains (Ge et al., 2017). Brussels (2019) elaborated the opportunities of Blockchain in the field of agriculture. Blockchain offers secure transactions among different untrusted parties. These untrusted parties are the part of SCM in agriculture that associated from the raw production to the supermarket shelf. Blockchain enhance transparency, efficiency and security in Agricultural supply chain management. Blockchain application could increase logistics (Chris and Ken, 2017), delivery of locally produced goods, strengthen traceability and certification with information of farm to table of consumer who can track products in the supply chain from the producer, supplier and buyer (Kamilaris, 2019). The global Blockchain in agriculture and food supply chain market is estimated to extent USD 429.7 million by 2023, at a CAGR of 47.8% according to Markets and Markets (2019). In agriculture, Blockchain based data management can provide an enhanced combination of supply chain resources (Kamble, Gunasekaran & Gawankar, 2020)

Agriculture is well linked with food supply chains because the products of agriculture are used as inputs in some multi-actor distributed supply chain and consumer is typically the final client (Maslova 2017). There are following chain of blocks has been suggested in the field of Agriculture (Kamilaris et al., 2019) as shown in figure 2.

Block 1: Block 1 is Provider that offers information about crops, fertilizers, pesticides, soil condition etc. The transaction is recorded between producer and farmer.
Block 2: Information about the farm, crop cultivation process, farming policies is suggested by producer.
Block 3: It is Processing block that provides information about the processing techniques and tools. The financial transaction between producers and distributors are also recorded here.

Block 4: Block 4 is the distribution block that entails shipping details, trajectories followed, storage conditions, and time in transit at every transport method etc. All transactions between the distributors and retailers are recorded on the Blockchain.

Block 5: Block 5 is retailer block that provides information about each food item such as present quality, quantity, expiration dates, storage conditions and time spent on the shelf are recorded on the chain.

Block 6: Block 6 is a final consumer block. A consumer can use a mobile phone connected to the Internet in order to scan a QR code associated with some food item. All the information related to the product, from the provider to producer and producer to retailer is visible to the consumer.

Figure 2. Supply chain of block in agriculture

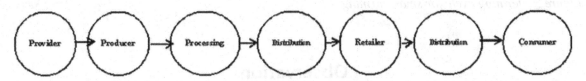

Lin et al. (2018) presented a trusted, self-organized, open and ecological food traceability system based on Blockchain and IoT technologies that comprises all parties of a smart agriculture ecosystem. IoT devices are performing well instead of physical recording and verification, which reduces the human intervention to the system effectively. Surasak et al. (2019) proposed OurSQL Blockchain that offers unchanged data when the data stored into the database. A smart contract that was used for real agreement between the seed Company and the farmer with the help of IoT. The Ethereum Blockchain, is a recognized Blockchain technology that is used for traceability system (Caro, 2018). Blockchain provides farmers with access to information on current transactions,the stock price of goods, and buyer's information. Author suggested design architecture by integration of IoT and Blockchain for Smart Agriculture (Devi et al., 2018). Tian (2017) proposed a real time monitoring system for food safety based on Hazard Analysis and Critical Control Points (HACCP), Blockchain and IoT.

The Blockchain is used to create a digital identity for a physical product/service and finally form traceability to verify origin and movement of product/services from agriculture farm to the food table. AI engine offers the inclusive aggregation of data at several points in supply chain management to proactively guidance farmers on sowing, pest control, harvesting etc. and alert the farmers by using IoT based smart devices. Blockchain help to control future food safety crises, such as the e.coli outbreak that caused people in 25 states to become sick after eating contaminated lettuce. Companies that use IoT devices, AI systems, and Blockchain stand to improve their yields, reduce costs, and enhance their profits. Walmart and Kroger constitute examples of the first companies to hold Blockchain and comprise the technology into their supply chains (CB Insights, 2017), working primarily on case studies that emphasis on Chinese pork and Mexican mangoes. Artificial intelligence enables a smart farming iterating cycle with 4 successive and recurring steps: 1) Observation, 2) Diagnostic 3) Decisions 4) Actions, as shown in figure 3:

MYbDAIRY (2019) discussed Artificial Intelligence and Blockchain Based Dairy Products in MYbDAIRY farms. MYbDAIRY farm is characterized by conscious farming, efficient production, high quality dairy products, lower pricing (in comparison with other organic products), innovative marketing, sales and distribution channels and, and a vision focused on health and social benefits. Author discussed various challenges related to technical aspects, farmer education, and government policies and regulations. However, through the use of underlying technologies, above challenges are not so much prominent. Agriculture 4.0 is an integration of Blockchain, IoT, AI and big data and provides the following advantages (Clercq, Vats & Biel, 2018):

a)   Smart uses of natural resources, for example amount of water supply for irrigation
b)   Increase the productivity in Agriculture and no impact of sudden climate change.
c)   Increase the market efficiency and manage the massive waste food.
d)   Increase the efficiency of food chain supply management.
e)   Reduce the hunger and poverty

Figure 3. Iterating cycle for smart farming

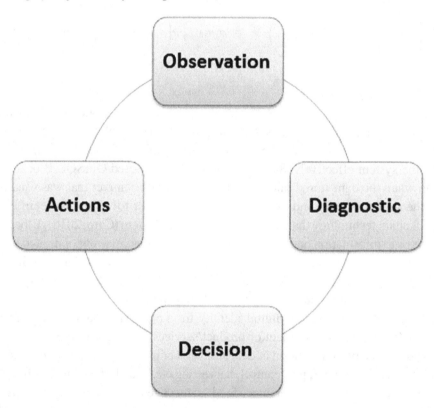

Blockchain technology applied in the making and supply chain delivery for eggs from farm to the consumer table by a company based in the Midwestern USA (Bumblauskas et al., 2020). Further integration of IoT and AI with Blockchain are making Agriculture field more smart, predictive, trackable and transparent. Food industry and Dairy industry implement Blockchain technology platform to ensure transparency in their food supply chain. Following paper has been reviewed to represent the role of IoT or AI/Machine Learning with the Blockchain frome 2017 to 2020. The major contribution of literature is extracted and represented in table 1.

Table 1. Blockchain with IoT and AI in agriculture

S. No.	Author (s)	Contribution	IoT	AI
1.	Borah et al.(2020)	To secure food supply chain using Blockchain	Yes	
2.	Bumblauskas et al.(2020)	To tack products from farm to fork using Blockchain and IoT	Yes	
3.	Khan et al. (2020)	Focus on Food Industry 4.0 with Blockchain	Yes	Yes
4.	Torkya & Hassaneinb (2020)	Reviewed sub-sectors of in precision agriculture such crops, livestock grazing, and food supply chain with Blockchain and IoT.	Yes	
5.	Antonucci et al. (2019)	Focused on smart contracts, typology of the supply chain implementation in Agri-food sector with blockchain and IoT	Yes	
6.	Awan et al. (2019)	Food Supply chain management from food source to end consumer with IoT and Blockchain.	Yes	
7.	Baruah (2019)	AI in Indian Agriculture with Blockchain		Yes
8.	Lezoche el al. (2019)	Supply chain management is examined with IoT, AI and Blockchain	Yes	Yes
9.	MYbDAIRY (2019)	Blockchain and AI based Dairy Product		Yes
10.	Surasak et al. (2019)	Smart Agreement between seed company and the farmer using Blockchain	Yes	
11.	Clercq,Vats & Biel, (2018)	Focus on Agriculture 4.0 with Blockchain	Yes	Yes
12.	Devi et al., (2018)	Smart Agriculture System with Blockchain	Yes	
13.	Lin et al.,(2018)	Ecological food traceability system using Blockchain	Yes	
14.	Lin et al., (2017)	ICT E-Agriculture System with Blockchain	Yes	
15.	Tian (2017)	Food safety based on HACCP	Yes	

4. BLOCKCHAIN WITH IOT AND AI IN HEATHCARE

Block chain is restructuring the traditional Healthcare system to a more consistent means, in terms of effective diagnosis and treatment through safe and secure data sharing. AI and machine learning in the healthcare system is used to accurate prediction, disease diagnosis and medicine suggestion (Singh et. al., 2020). The potential of Blockchain technology can be witnessed in the fields of medicine, genomics, telemedicine, tele-monitoring, e-health, neuroscience, and personalized healthcare applications and offers secure data with which users can interact through different types of transactions.The healthcare is considering in intense for new and innovative applications of Blockchain to assist the issue of supply chain. A Blockchain could manage, particularly Pharmacy department and track each step of the supply chain of the individual drug by using Hyperledger Fabric (Jamil et al., 2019). The healthcare industry will soon be taken by storm with the applications of Blockchain, accompanied by AI and IoT. IoT based sensor devices are monitoring the pulse rate (Pandey et al., 2020), blood glucose level (Agrawal, Singh, & Sneha, 2019) and various health care services such as Ambient Assisted Living, Adverse Drug Reaction, Wearable Device Access, Semantic Medical Access and Indirect Emergency Healthcare (Nogueira & Carnaz, 2019). Peterson (2016) suggested Blockchain applications to Health Information Exchange Networks to facilitate data interoperability and sharing for the complex problem of sharing healthcare data.

Gary Leeming (2019) proposed a Blockchain-based health record solutions and reference architecture for a "Ledger of Me" system that encompasses Personal Heath Record (PHR) to create a new platform merging the collection and access of medical data and digital interventions with smart contracts. AI and

Blockchain algorithms guarantee safe verification of medical institution PHR data (Kim & Huh, 2020). Various eHealth organization are emerging Blockchain techniology target the potential of patients and sell their health data on personal Electronic Health Records (EHRs) and wellness routine profiles collected by wearable sensor devices (Zajc, 2018; Dimitrov, 2019).

Siyal (2019) discussed various applications of Blockchain Technology in Medicine and Healthcare. Author revealed various challenges like interoperability, storage, scalability and social acceptance; and also explored opportunities like secure, Irreversible transaction, transparency etc. Dwivedi (2019) combined of the private key, public key, Blockchain and many other lightweight cryptographic primitives are used to design a patient-centric access control for electronic medical records. Any health care model must require the characteristics of security, robustness and privacy to support the Nationwide Interoperability Roadmap and national healthcare delivery priorities such as Patient-Centered Outcomes Research (PCOR). Kuo (2018) proposed Patient-centered SCAlable National Network for Effectiveness Research (pSCANNER) model with enhanced security and robustness of distributed privacy-preserving healthcare predictive modeling using Blockchain technology. A secure technique was suggested to provide confidentiality, authenticity and integrity of data transmission in IoMT with Blockchain technology by Diawar (2019). With IoMT technology, healthcare equipment such as heart monitor, body scanners, and wearable devices could collect, process and share data over the Internet in real time. Khezr (2019) presented further research on innovative solutions that promote Blockchain as a service that permits several parties of the IoMT prototype to access basic infrastructures of Blockchain.

For any AI based project, a datasets are key point of success. Data is coming from the heterogeneous sources and the integrity of a dataset is complex. Blockchain is very secure storage medium that provides a technological quantum leap in sustaining data integrity (Sgantzos, 2019). Hence, Blockchain ensure the data integration of patient data in the Healthcare sector. The smart contract offers an immutable log of authentication and permissions for healthcare data access. IoT and AI particularly when paired with Blockchain provide more possibilities for healthcare. Following paper has been reviewed to represent the role of IoT or AI/Machine Learning with the Blockchain since 2017 to 2020. The major contribution of literature is extracted and represented in table 2. The Blockchain technology is estimated to restructure the healthcare ecosystem. Blockchain provides transparent and secure healthcare with improved quality and reduced cost.

5. RESULT AND DISCUSSION

This section evaluated the research questions from table 1 and table 2 and answered in detail by keeping the objectives of questions in mind.

5.1 RQ-1: Role of Block chain with IoT and AI in Agriculture

In order to address this question, total 15 relevant research papers were selected according mention keyword in section 2. From 15 papers, 66.67% papers integrate IoT with Blockchain, 13.33% papers integrate AI with Blockchain and 20% papers integrate both IoT and ML with Blockchain as shown in figure 4 in the field of agriculture.

Table 2. Blockchain with IoT and AI in Healthcare

S. No.	Author(s)	Main contribution	IoT	AI
1.	Kim & Huh (2020)	Focus on PHR with blockchain and AI		Yes
2.	Dwivedi et al. (2019)	Joint the advantages of the private key, public key, Blockchain with IoT to control patient health record.	yes	
3.	Diawer et al. (2019)	provide confidentiality, authenticity and integrity of data transmission in IoMT with Blockchain	Yes	
4.	Khezr et al. (2019)	Focus on secure communication system by Blockchain and IoT.	yes	
5.	Sgantzos and Grigg (2019)	Integration of data with Blockchain and AI		Yes
6.	Singh, Rathore, and Park (2019)	BlockIoTIntelligence: A Blockchain-enabled Intelligent IoT architecture with AI	Yes	Yes
7.	Siyal et al., (2019)	Opportunities and challenges of Blockchain technology in medicine & Health care		Yes
8.	Zubaydi (2019)	Discuss of Blockchain technology and their challenges and implementation in the healthcare system	Yes	
9.	Caro et al., (2018)	Focus on AgriBlockIoT by using IoT and Blockchain	yes	
10.	Kuo and Ohno-Machado (2018)	security and robustness of distributed privacy-preserving healthcare predictive modeling using Blockchain technology		Yes
11.	Rabah (2018)	Focus on Merging of AI, IoT, Big Data and Blockchain in Healthcare and other domain	Yes	Yes
12.	Mamoshina et al., (2018)	Present an innovative solution to amplify the biomedical research to profit from patient 'data with Blockchain and IoT.		Yes
13.	Simić et al., (2017)	Deal with storage capacities using Blockchain and IoT in health sector	Yes	
14.	Peterson et al. (2016)	To enable data interoperability and sharing for the complex problem of sharing healthcare data by Blockchain.		Yes

Figure 4 represent that majority of paper (66.67%) available that integrate Blockchain with only IoT in Agriculture and play a crucial role in our day-to-day lives. IoT devices such as sensors can monitor the weather conditions, soil health; detect crop disease due to pesticides and traceability of products. These sensors directly feed information to a set of block Smart Contract. Predefined conditions are already written on the Smart Contract. AgriBlockIoT for Agri-Food supply chain management integrate IoT devices to produce and consume digital data along the chain. IoT, Blockchain, and AI, enhanced supply chain provenance system for Industry 4.0 in the food sector.

Blockchain Technology in association with IoT devices and machine learning can provide a bigger and valuable picture of the overall agriculture sector. Integration of IoT, AI and Blockchain has potential to enhance efficiency of SCM, traceability of information, smart Farming, logistic etc. The item/product will be well linked to the materials and products on the each phase of supply chain by IoT. AI can evaluate the circumstances for sowing, right crop timing, assessment of agriculture land suitability etc.

Figure 4. Paper distribution of IoT and AI with Blockchain in Agriculture

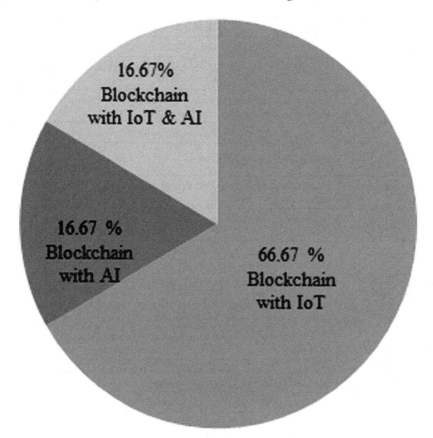

5.2 RQ-2: Role of Blockchain with IoT and AI in Healthcare

In order to address impact of Blockchain with IoT and AI, total 14 relevant research papers were selected with keyword IoT, AI and Blockchain in Healthcare. From 14 papers 43% papers integrate IoT with Blockchain and 43% papers integrate AI with Blockchain and 14% papers integrate IoT and AI with Blockchain as shown in figure 5.

According to figure 5, Blockchain is equally using either IoT or AI in Healthcare. However, integration of Blockchain, IoT and AI is still in its initial phase. IoT enables the fast communication between doctors and patients by offering several healthcare applications like remote monitoring, smart sensors, and medical device like ECG, pulse monitoring device, body wearable device integration help in constant monitoring of patient data in real time. This data is collected and analyzed by the AI technique. Machine Learning (ML) approach is one of the most prominent techniques of AI that is used to automate the system without explicit programmed. ML allows healthcare professionals to move to a personalized care system, which is known as precision medicine. ML and deep learning became one of the most amazing revolutions in the healthcare industry. Foremost companies in the healthcare industry are trying to integrate IoT, AI and Blockchain to help develop advanced precision medicines. By using Blockchain technology, regulatory bodies can create a shared stream of de-identified patient information. Blockchain technology offers transparent, secure health chain supply, Healthcare Payment, and Claim Management, drug supply chain management. AI analyses the data, and IoT makes Data more connected. Blockchain application enables supply chain used to prevent losses from pharmaceutical counterfeiting, reduction in Medicare fraud, clinical trials, and data security predictive capabilities and demand forecasting with AI and IoT.

The literature based results showed, that the integration of Blockchain with IoT, Blockchain with AI are playing important role in Agriculture and Healthcare field to manage supply chain, traceability of product, offer smart contract, monitor the products, activities, and intelligent prediction. Integration of IoT, AI and Blockchain have potential to enhance efficiency of SCM and fulfill the dynamic requirement of supply chain stakeholders in Agriculture and Healthcare system Blockchain with IoT and AI implementation research in Agriculture have slightly higher percentage rather than Healthcare.

Figure 5. Paper distribution of IoT and AI with Blockchain in Health Care

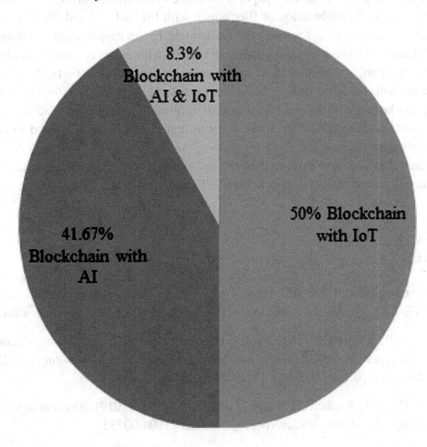

5.1 Limitation

Blockchain with AI in Agriculture is still deployed in limited aspect and hence need more exploration to discover the challenges in this direction. This research is limited to Agriculture and Healthcare system. There are many other areas presented in figure 1, can be a good candidate to incorporate Blockchain with IoT and AI

6. CONCLUSION

This paper surveyed and studied the existing state of-the-art related to the use and applicability of Blockchain with AI and IoT in Agriculture and Healthcare system. Author provided an outline of Blockchain technology with IoT and AI in Agriculture and Healthcare system. Safe data storage, protected transactions, secure data exchanges between organizations, immutable data record, and transparent data flow are all advantages of Blockchain integration with IoT and/or AI. A smart contract is one of the Blockchain features that can be used as a real agreement in Agriculture and Healthcare system. Agriculture 4.0 is an integration of Blockchain, IoT and AI. Blockchain will ensure that data is distributed in a transparent way and efficient transaction system. The role of Blockchain with IoT or AI leverages Agriculture and Healthcare more smart and intelligent. This study concludes that 20% research paper is available in the field of Agriculture and 14% research paper is available in the Healthcare system. 66.67% reported text present the successful collaboration of Blockchain with IoT. IoT, AI and Blockchain adoption in agriculture and healthcare focus on food supply management, health supply chain and drug supply chain management. IoT enable connectivity and data transfer between the assets across the supply chain, monitor the weather conditions, soil health and AI can detect crop disease due to pesticides in Agriculture in transparent manner and also offers new opportunities for smart healthcare providers in order to patience care. Adopting Blockchain with AI and IoT in various applications is in its early stages, and there may exists various research challenges to be addressed and undertaken in areas related to privacy, smart contract security, interoperability etc.

Future research direction is to explore the practical challenges that occur during the integration of three heterogeneous technologies i.e. Blockchain, IoT and AI in a common platform and distributed environment.

REFERENCES

Addison & Lohento. (2108). CTA. ICT Update issue 88. Unlocking the potential of Blockchain for Agriculture. *2017, CTA organised a workshop on blockchain opportunities for agriculture.*

Agrawal, V., Singh, P., & Sneha, S. (2019, April). Hyperglycemia Prediction Using Machine Learning: A Probabilistic Approach. In *International Conference on Advances in Computing and Data Sciences* (pp. 304-312). Springer. 10.1007/978-981-13-9942-8_29

Ali, A., Latif, S., Qadir, J., Kanhere, S., Singh, J., & Crowcroft, J. (2019). *Blockchain and the future of the internet: A comprehensive review.* arXiv preprint arXiv:1904.00733

Antonucci, F., Figorilli, S., Costa, C., Pallottino, F., Raso, L., & Menesatti, P. (2019). A Review on blockchain applications in the agri-food sector. *Journal of the Science of Food and Agriculture*, *99*(14), 6129–6138. doi:10.1002/jsfa.9912 PMID:31273793

Awan, S. H., Ahmed, S., Safwan, N., Najam, Z., Hashim, M. Z., & Safdar, T. (2019). Role of Internet of Things (IoT) with Blockchain Technology for the Development of Smart Farming. *Journal of Mechanics of Continua and Mathematical Sciences*, *14*(5), 177–188.

Ayushman, B. (2019). Artificial Intelligence in Indian Agriculture – An Industry and Startup Overview. *Business Intelligence and Analytics*. Accessed on https://emerj.com/ai-sector-overviews/artificial-intelligence-in-indian-agriculture-an-industry-and-startup-overview/

Boldú & Fonts. (2018). *The Rise of the Blockchain Technology in Agriculture and Food Supply Chain*. Institute of Agrifood Research and Technology (IRTA).

Borah, M. D., Naik, V. B., Patgiri, R., Bhargav, A., Phukan, B., & Basani, S. G. (2020). Supply Chain Management in Agriculture Using Blockchain and IoT. In *Advanced Applications of Blockchain Technology* (pp. 227–242). Springer. doi:10.1007/978-981-13-8775-3_11

Brody, P. (2017). How blockchain is revolutionizing supply chain management. *Digitalist Magazine*, 1-7.

Brussels. (2019). *Opportunities of Blockchain for agriculture*. Accessed on 18 June 2020 https://brusselsbriefings.files.wordpress.com/2019/07/cta295-bb55-highlights-english-01_rev2.pdf

Bumblauskas, D., Mann, A., Dugan, B., & Rittmer, J. (2020). A blockchain use case in food distribution: Do you know where your food has been? *International Journal of Information Management*, *52*, 102008. doi:10.1016/j.ijinfomgt.2019.09.004

Buterin, V. (2016). What is Ethereum? *Ethereum Official webpage*. Available: http://www. ethdocs. org/ en/latest/introduction/what-is-ethereum. html

Caro, Ali, Vecchio, & Giaffreda. (2018). Blockchain-based traceability in agri-food supply chain management: A practical implementation. *2018 IoT Vertical and Topical Summit on Agriculture - Tuscany (IOT Tuscany),* 1–4.

Caro, M. P., Ali, M. S., Vecchio, M., & Giaffreda, R. (2018, May). Blockchain-based traceability in Agri-Food supply chain management: A practical implementation. In *2018 IoT Vertical and Topical Summit on Agriculture-Tuscany (IOT Tuscany)* (pp. 1-4). IEEE.

Casino, F., Dasaklis, T. K., & Patsakis, C. (2019). A systematic literature review of blockchain-based applications: Current status, classification and open issues. *Telematics and Informatics*, *36*, 55–81. doi:10.1016/j.tele.2018.11.006

Chen, W., Xu, Z., Shi, S., Zhao, Y., & Zhao, J. (2018, December). A survey of blockchain applications in different domains. In *Proceedings of the 2018 International Conference on Blockchain Technology and Application* (pp. 17-21). 10.1145/3301403.3301407

De Clercq, M., Vats, A., & Biel, A. (2018). Agriculture 4.0: The Future of Farming Technology. *Proceedings of the World Government Summit*, 11-13.

Devi, M. S., Suguna, R., Joshi, A. S., & Bagate, R. A. (2019, February). Design of IoT Blockchain Based Smart Agriculture for Enlightening Safety and Security. In *International Conference on Emerging Technologies in Computer Engineering* (pp. 7-19). Springer.

Diawar, N., Rizwan, M., Ahmad, F., & Akram, S. (2019). Blockchain: Securing Internet of Medical Things (IoMT). *International Journal of Advanced Computer Science and Applications*, 82-89.

Dijkstra, M. (2017). Blockchain: Towards disruption in the real estate sector. In *An Exploration on the Impact of Blockchain Technology in the Real Estate Management Process*. University of Delft.

Dimitrov, D. V. (2019). Blockchain Applications for Healthcare Data Management. *Healthcare Informatics Research*, 25(1), 51–56. doi:10.4258/hir.2019.25.1.51 PMID:30788182

Dubey, S., Singh, P., Yadav, P., & Singh, K. K. (2020). Household Waste Management System Using IoT and Machine Learning. *Procedia Computer Science*, 167, 1950–1959. doi:10.1016/j.procs.2020.03.222

Dwivedi, A. D., Srivastava, G., Dhar, S., & Singh, R. (2019). A decentralized privacy-preserving healthcare blockchain for iot. *Sensors (Basel)*, 19(2), 326. doi:10.339019020326 PMID:30650612

Ge, L., Brewster, C., Spek, J., Smeenk, A., Top, J., van Diepen, F., & de Wildt, M. D. R. (2017). *Blockchain for agriculture and food: Findings from the pilot study (No. 2017-112)*. Wageningen Economic Research.

Insights, C. B. (2017). *How Blockchain Could Transform Food Safety*. https://www.cbinsights.com/research/blockchain-grocery-supply-chain/

Jamil, F., Hang, L., Kim, K., & Kim, D. (2019). A novel medical blockchain model for drug supply chain integrity management in a smart hospital. *Electronics (Basel)*, 8(5), 505. doi:10.3390/electronics8050505

Kamble, S. S., Gunasekaran, A., & Gawankar, S. A. (2020). Achieving sustainable performance in a data-driven agriculture supply chain: A review for research and applications. *International Journal of Production Economics*, 219, 179–194. doi:10.1016/j.ijpe.2019.05.022

Kamilaris, A., Fonts, A., & Prenafeta-Boldú, F. X. (2019). The rise of blockchain technology in agriculture and food supply chains. *Trends in Food Science & Technology*, 91, 640–652. doi:10.1016/j.tifs.2019.07.034

Khan, P. W., Byun, Y. C., & Park, N. (2020). IoT-Blockchain Enabled Optimized Provenance System for Food Industry 4.0 Using Advanced Deep Learning. *Sensors (Basel)*, 20(10), 2990. doi:10.339020102990 PMID:32466209

Khezr, S., Moniruzzaman, M., Yassine, A., & Benlamri, R. (2019). Blockchain Technology in Healthcare: A Comprehensive Review and Directions for Future Research. *Applied Sciences*, 9(9), 1736. doi:10.3390/app9091736

Kim, S. K., & Huh, J. H. (2020). Artificial Neural Network Blockchain Techniques for Healthcare System: Focusing on the Personal Health Records. *Electronics (Basel)*, 9(5), 763. doi:10.3390/electronics9050763

Kuo, T. T., & Ohno-Machado, L. (2018). *Modelchain: Decentralized privacy-preserving healthcare predictive modeling framework on private blockchain networks*. arXiv preprint arXiv:1802.01746

Lago & Tayeb. (2018). *Blockchain Technology: Between High Hopes & Challenging Implications*. Academic Press.

Lee, M. Rammohan, & Srivastava. (2017). Value Chain Innovation Initiative. Academic Press.

Leeming, G., Cunningham, J., & Ainsworth, J. (2019). A ledger of me: Personalizing healthcare using blockchain technology. *Frontiers in medicine*, 6. PMID:31396516

Lezoche, M., Hernandez, J. E., Díaz, M. D. M. E. A., Panetto, H., & Kacprzyk, J. (2020). Agri-food 4.0: A survey of the supply chains and technologies for the future agriculture. *Computers in Industry, 117*, 103187. doi:10.1016/j.compind.2020.103187

Lin, H., & Bergmann, N. W. (2016). IoT privacy and security challenges for smart home environments. *Information, 7*(3), 44. doi:10.3390/info7030044

Lin, J., Shen, Z., Zhang, A., & Chai, Y. (2018). Blockchain and IoT based Food Traceability System. *International Journal of Information Technology, 24*(1), 1–16.

Lin, Y. P., Petway, J. R., Anthony, J., Mukhtar, H., Liao, S. W., Chou, C. F., & Ho, Y. F. (2017). Blockchain: The evolutionary next step for ICT e-agriculture. *Environments, 4*(3), 50. doi:10.3390/environments4030050

Mamoshina, P., Ojomoko, L., Yanovich, Y., Ostrovski, A., Botezatu, A., Prikhodko, P., ... Ogu, I. O. (2018). Converging blockchain and next-generation artificial intelligence technologies to decentralize and accelerate biomedical research and healthcare. *Oncotarget, 9*(5), 5665–5690. doi:10.18632/oncotarget.22345 PMID:29464026

Markets and Markets. (2019). *Blockchain in Agriculture Market: Growth Opportunities and Recent Developments.* Accessed on 18 June 2020: https://www.openpr.com/news/1977139/blockchain-in-agriculture-market-growth-opportunities

Maslova, A. (2017). *Growing the Garden: How to Use Blockchain in Agriculture.* https://cointelegraph.com/news/growing-the-garden-how-to-use-blockchain-inagriculture

Maslova. (2018). *Blockchain: Disruption and Opportunity.* Strategic Finance.

MYbDAIRY Farms Ltd. (2019). *Artificial Intelligence and Blockchain Based Dairy Products.* https://mybdairy.com/document/MYbDAIRY-Whitepaper.pdf

Nogueira, V., & Carnaz, G. (2019). *An overview of IoT and healthcare.* Academic Press.

Pandey, R. S., Upadhyay, R., Kumar, M., Singh, P., & Shukla, S. (2020). IoT-Based HelpAgeSensor Device for Senior Citizens. In *International Conference on Innovative Computing and Communications* (pp. 187-193). Springer. 10.1007/978-981-15-0324-5_16

Peterson, K., Deeduvanu, R., Kanjamala, P., & Boles, K. (2016, September). A blockchain-based approach to health information exchange networks. In *Proc. NIST Workshop Blockchain Healthcare* (*Vol. 1*, pp. 1-10). Academic Press.

Rabah, K. (2018). Convergence of AI, IoT, big data and blockchain: A review. *Law Institute Journal, 1*(1), 1–18.

Saiz-Rubio, V., & Rovira-Más, F. (2020). From smart farming towards agriculture 5.0: A review on crop data management. *Agronomy (Basel), 10*(2), 207. doi:10.3390/agronomy10020207

Salah, K., Rehman, M. H. U., Nizamuddin, N., & Al-Fuqaha, A. (2019). Blockchain for AI: Review and open research challenges. *IEEE Access : Practical Innovations, Open Solutions, 7*, 10127–10149. doi:10.1109/ACCESS.2018.2890507

Sgantzos, K., & Grigg, I. (2019). Artificial Intelligence Implementations on the Blockchain. Use Cases and Future Applications. *Future Internet*, *11*(8), 170. doi:10.3390/fi11080170

Simić, M., Sladić, G., & Milosavljević, B. (2017, June). A case study IoT and blockchain powered healthcare. *Proc. ICET*.

Singh, N., Singh, P., Singh, K. K., & Singh, A. (2020). Diagnosing of Disease using Machine Learning, accepted for Machine Learning & Internet of medical things in healthcare. *Elsevier Publications*.

Singh, P., & Agrawal, R. (2018). A customer centric best connected channel model for heterogeneous and IoT networks. *Journal of Organizational and End User Computing*, *30*(4), 32–50. doi:10.4018/JOEUC.2018100103

Singh, S. K., Rathore, S., & Park, J. H. (2019). Block iot intelligence: A blockchain-enabled intelligent IoT architecture with artificial intelligence. *Future Generation Computer Systems*.

Siyal, A. A., Junejo, A. Z., Zawish, M., Ahmed, K., Khalil, A., & Soursou, G. (2019). Applications of blockchain technology in medicine and healthcare: Challenges and future perspectives. *Cryptography*, *3*(1), 3. doi:10.3390/cryptography3010003

Surasak, T., Wattanavichean, N., Preuksakarn, C., & Huang, S. C. H. (n.d.). Thai Agriculture Products Traceability System using Blockchain and Internet of Things. *System*, *14*, 15.

Tian, F. (2017, June). A supply chain traceability system for food safety based on HACCP, blockchain & Internet of things. In *2017 International conference on service systems and service management* (pp. 1-6). IEEE.

Tian, S., Yang, W., Le Grange, J. M., Wang, P., Huang, W., & Ye, Z. (2019). *Smart healthcare: making medical care more intelligent*. Global Health Journal.

Torkya, M., & Hassaneinb, A. E. (2020). *Integrating Blockchain and the Internet of Things in Precision Agriculture: Analysis, Opportunities, and Challenges, Computers and Electronics in Agriculture*. Elsevier.

Wu, K., Ma, Y., Huang, G., & Liu, X. (2019). A first look at blockchain based decentralized applications. *Software, Practice & Experience*, spe.2751. doi:10.1002pe.2751

Yin, X. C., Liu, Z. G., Ndibanje, B., Nkenyereye, L., & Riazul Islam, S. M. (2019). An IoT-Based Anonymous Function for Security and Privacy in Healthcare Sensor Networks. *Sensors (Basel)*, *19*(14), 3146. doi:10.339019143146 PMID:31319562

Zajc, T. (2018). *F020 Blockchain, value of data, and the role of legislation with adoption (Ray Dogum, Health Unchained)*. https://medium.com/faces-of-digital-health/f020-blockchain-value-of-data-and-the-role-of-legislation-withadoption-ray-dogum-health-80919d909e97

Zubaydi, H. D., Chong, Y. W., Ko, K., Hanshi, S. M., & Karuppayah, S. (2019). A review on the role of blockchain technology in the healthcare domain. *Electronics (Basel)*, *8*(6), 679. doi:10.3390/electronics8060679

This research was previously published in the International Journal of Applied Evolutionary Computation (IJAEC), 11(4); pages 13-27, copyright year 2020 by IGI Publishing (an imprint of IGI Global).

Index

A

Academic Certificates 1309, 1311

Access Control 28, 37, 42-47, 56-59, 62, 68, 70-71, 75, 83, 89, 93-98, 105, 165, 187, 191-192, 205-206, 220, 233, 329, 353, 371, 375, 384, 393, 399, 401, 485, 492, 498, 510-511, 515, 517, 520, 529, 531-532, 546, 549, 563, 568, 616, 631, 642-643, 645-646, 666, 681, 690, 695, 697, 710, 718, 739, 747, 749, 814, 820, 822, 824, 827, 839, 869, 873, 876, 881-883, 885, 888, 932, 939, 966, 972, 981-982, 984, 991, 1016, 1024, 1036, 1058, 1062-1064, 1073, 1078, 1097, 1103-1104, 1118, 1122, 1137, 1146, 1151, 1217, 1247, 1251-1252, 1259-1262, 1276, 1281, 1308, 1322

Adaptive Trade Systems 556

analytic framework 421, 423, 437

Anonymity 18, 52, 88, 90-91, 116, 167-168, 203, 224, 238, 256, 279, 477, 539, 541, 568, 683, 691, 820, 823, 834, 849-850, 875, 880, 884-885, 895, 909, 919-920, 923, 926, 933, 1032, 1072, 1130, 1139, 1296, 1299

Apparel Business 242, 352, 354, 359, 362, 960-962, 964, 967-969, 979, 1241, 1243-1244, 1246, 1248-1250

Artificial and Natural Intelligence Technologies 556-557

Artificial Intelligence 80, 110-111, 216, 227, 244, 418-419, 421, 423, 426, 442, 444, 480, 487, 511, 521, 550, 558-561, 565-567, 608, 644, 690, 716, 754, 777, 792, 837, 869, 931, 952, 958, 1031, 1038, 1040-1041, 1044, 1046, 1049-1050, 1052, 1098, 1110, 1112, 1163-1164, 1186, 1223, 1226, 1287, 1290, 1315, 1319, 1327, 1329-1330

Attack Surface 314, 322, 327, 442, 535, 864, 979, 1150

Authentication 21, 37, 51-52, 58, 61-62, 65, 68, 70-71, 76, 83, 88-89, 92, 96-97, 100, 118, 166, 178, 181, 184-185, 190-193, 203, 205-206, 208, 218, 222, 225, 236, 253, 256, 266, 268, 289, 303, 320-321, 328, 333, 335, 376, 386, 388-389, 401, 423, 426, 432, 435, 442, 476, 479-480, 484, 498, 507, 509-510, 513-516, 518, 520, 522, 529-530, 532-533, 539, 541, 545, 547-549, 551, 563-564, 571, 585, 593, 616, 666, 671-680, 682-684, 689, 691-697, 699-700, 725, 734, 736, 739, 748, 751, 766, 801, 819, 822, 827, 829-830, 841, 844, 859, 862-867, 869-870, 873, 876, 882, 888, 892, 896, 898-899, 901, 912, 915, 917, 923-924, 927-928, 932, 968, 973, 975-977, 982, 984, 995, 1010, 1012-1013, 1019-1020, 1023-1025, 1031-1032, 1035, 1058, 1062-1064, 1072, 1074-1076, 1080-1081, 1083, 1097-1098, 1101, 1104, 1112-1113, 1115, 1121, 1123, 1129, 1131, 1162-1163, 1184, 1194, 1215, 1230, 1237-1238, 1249, 1255, 1260, 1263, 1274, 1311-1312, 1322

autonomous vehicle 588, 590-592, 604, 883

B

BCIoT 928

BCS 588, 594-595, 667-668, 683

Big Data 19-20, 62-64, 88-89, 100, 106, 125, 128, 141, 160-163, 165, 168, 180, 190, 238, 245-246, 257, 278-281, 283-285, 289-290, 313-315, 317, 319-320, 322-324, 328-329, 348, 363, 379-380, 400, 419, 443, 447, 450, 459, 465-466, 481, 483-486, 497, 499, 517, 521, 526, 534, 546, 550, 557, 559-561, 565-567, 571, 586, 628, 682, 692, 696, 701, 703, 705, 707, 710-712, 715-718, 720, 736, 766, 776, 792, 796-797, 800, 804, 813, 816, 830, 837, 851, 856, 874, 912, 916, 920, 926, 928, 953, 959, 963, 983-984, 999, 1005, 1007, 1021, 1031-1032, 1035, 1038-1040, 1045, 1050, 1052, 1056, 1059, 1081, 1096, 1109, 1111-1112, 1144-1145, 1148-1149, 1176, 1242, 1245, 1261-1263, 1308, 1315, 1320, 1329

biohacking 1178, 1186, 1192

Bitcoin 1, 3-5, 7-8, 10-15, 17-22, 24-26, 33, 38-41,

43, 48-49, 53-54, 56, 58-59, 63-66, 90, 113-114, 130, 134-135, 137-138, 141-142, 145, 157, 161, 166-169, 171, 176, 179-180, 182, 186, 201-202, 206, 208-209, 226, 230, 234, 245, 248, 250-252, 257, 262, 277, 282, 290, 295-299, 304, 321, 331, 334, 347-348, 354, 363, 403-404, 406-407, 416-418, 430, 488, 490, 495-497, 502, 504-505, 507, 512, 536-539, 541, 543-544, 567, 570, 572, 577, 579, 581-584, 587, 589-590, 598, 600-602, 605, 608, 622, 656, 667, 687, 741, 769, 771, 774, 776-777, 794, 796-797, 800, 805-806, 815, 837, 841, 844, 846-849, 851, 874, 877-878, 883, 896, 901, 905, 910-911, 914, 917, 920-921, 927, 932, 937, 955, 957-958, 967, 973, 976, 978, 982-984, 991, 1070, 1080, 1086, 1088, 1093, 1097, 1101, 1103-1107, 1113, 1121-1122, 1126-1134, 1136, 1139-1143, 1145, 1148-1150, 1180-1181, 1184, 1188-1189, 1198-1200, 1204, 1207-1208, 1225, 1230-1231, 1242, 1248, 1253, 1257, 1260, 1262-1263, 1266-1267, 1289, 1294-1296, 1298-1299, 1301, 1304-1309, 1311-1313, 1316

Block Chain Technology 105, 489, 556, 1103, 1239, 1311

Blockchain 1-8, 10-68, 76, 78, 84-86, 88-100, 103-109, 113-131, 133-145, 148-162, 164-171, 174-195, 201-212, 215-217, 219-228, 230-248, 250-260, 262-263, 265-268, 271-273, 276-285, 289-292, 295-300, 302-308, 310-315, 317-334, 337-343, 345-358, 360-366, 368, 375-376, 378-382, 384-385, 390, 392-400, 402-407, 409, 411-419, 434, 436, 438, 445, 449-450, 452, 467, 472-474, 477-486, 488-527, 532, 535-579, 581, 583-625, 642-644, 647-651, 655-663, 665, 667-669, 687, 689-701, 708, 711-712, 717-718, 721-723, 725-726, 731, 733-735, 738-739, 741-744, 747-748, 752-753, 766, 768-777, 794, 796-797, 799-803, 805-816, 818-842, 844-852, 854, 869-870, 873-875, 877-896, 900-904, 906-930, 931-940, 942-960, 962, 966-1012, 1019-1045, 1047-1056, 1058, 1060, 1064-1070, 1072, 1075-1131, 1133, 1136-1167, 1178-1189, 1191-1194, 1196-1227, 1229-1233, 1236, 1238-1240, 1242-1244, 1247-1281, 1283-1284, 1287-1291, 1293-1330

Blockchain Classification 133, 1130

Blockchain Headers 984

Blockchain Mining 90, 285, 1029

Blockchain of Internet of Things 108, 118, 131

Blockchain safety 1115

blockchain security attacks 1293

blockchain security problems 1293

Blockchain Technology 6-7, 18-22, 24, 26, 28-32, 34, 36, 39, 42, 47, 57, 62-64, 68, 76, 78, 84, 88-91, 93-95, 97-99, 104-107, 115-117, 119-122, 125, 127-128, 130-131, 133-134, 136, 138-145, 148, 153-161, 164-167, 178, 192, 194-195, 201-210, 216, 223, 226-228, 230, 232-238, 240-248, 250, 253-256, 258, 262-263, 265, 267, 276, 289, 292, 295-296, 303-305, 308, 310, 312-315, 317-318, 320-321, 323, 327, 330, 332-334, 337-338, 345-358, 360-365, 368, 376, 378, 399-400, 419, 450, 467, 472-473, 477, 479, 482, 484, 488-489, 492-494, 496-500, 502-503, 507-513, 516, 522, 524-525, 527, 535-536, 539, 541-545, 551, 556-560, 562-563, 565-567, 569, 572, 577, 587, 589-591, 593, 599-608, 610-611, 614-625, 656, 660, 663, 693-695, 697, 701, 721, 741-742, 752, 766, 769-771, 774, 776-777, 801, 813, 815-816, 818, 824, 837-841, 844, 847-848, 850-851, 874, 879, 889-890, 892-893, 895-896, 900, 902-903, 906, 908-914, 917-921, 923-928, 930, 932-934, 943, 946, 953, 959-960, 962, 966-967, 969-973, 975, 979-983, 991, 1004-1006, 1008-1010, 1021-1022, 1025, 1028-1029, 1038-1039, 1041-1042, 1045, 1047-1049, 1052-1056, 1058, 1060, 1064-1067, 1069-1070, 1072, 1075-1080, 1082-1083, 1093, 1097-1104, 1106, 1108, 1110-1113, 1115-1116, 1119, 1121, 1123-1129, 1133, 1137-1138, 1146-1147, 1149, 1152-1165, 1167, 1179-1185, 1187-1189, 1191, 1193, 1203-1204, 1207, 1209-1211, 1214-1215, 1223-1226, 1229-1232, 1239-1240, 1242-1244, 1247-1248, 1250-1253, 1255, 1258-1261, 1264, 1266, 1268-1269, 1272-1273, 1287-1291, 1293-1296, 1302, 1304, 1306-1309, 1313-1324, 1326-1328, 1330

Building Information Modeling (BIM) 366-369, 371, 379, 381

C

Centralized System 2, 7, 43, 156, 164, 167, 293, 337, 502, 533, 841-842, 844, 927, 1154, 1162-1163

Certificate Authority (CA) 39, 314-316, 318, 321-323, 326, 328, 394, 398, 648, 650, 652, 658

chain blocks 221

Chaincode 220, 356, 395-396, 808, 811

Clinical Trial 121-122, 128, 131, 607-608, 610-611, 614-625, 1054

Cloud Computing 76, 161, 172, 194-195, 198, 208-209, 247, 276, 279, 290, 312, 319, 331, 375, 380, 424, 426, 434-435, 445-447, 453, 457-459, 464-470, 474, 483, 486, 501, 515, 517, 529, 546, 559-560, 565-566, 568, 627, 630-631, 643-646, 665,

687, 701, 705, 711-712, 715-720, 736, 748-749, 792-793, 800, 813-814, 823-825, 827, 831-832, 839, 857, 863, 871, 890, 906, 915, 918, 950, 959, 963, 1030, 1059, 1098, 1101-1102, 1111-1113, 1189, 1245

cloudlet 1102, 1104, 1111, 1113

computation algorithm 488-489

Consensus Algorithm 10, 12, 27, 39-40, 57, 94, 100, 234, 236, 239, 245, 256, 375, 418, 507, 519, 538-539, 543, 548, 608, 669, 680, 684, 686, 695-696, 831-832, 844, 878, 904-905, 917-918, 920-921, 929, 931, 934-937, 939-940, 942-943, 945, 951, 959, 1000, 1069, 1076, 1083, 1108-1109, 1129, 1142-1144, 1150, 1193, 1197, 1199-1200, 1208, 1267

Consensus Mechanism 2-3, 8-9, 15, 38-41, 78, 90, 98, 100, 238, 252, 303, 403, 483, 511, 519, 538, 548, 558, 561, 566, 661, 684, 687, 769, 805-806, 808, 869, 878, 885-886, 903, 926, 931-932, 934, 937-944, 951-956, 973, 976, 1021, 1036, 1207, 1252-1253, 1266, 1296

Corruption 230, 588, 590-591, 596-600, 603-604, 625, 909, 1045

COVID-19 108-109, 111-112, 122-124, 126-131, 243, 557, 622, 1038, 1043, 1053-1054, 1205

Crowdsourcing 179, 1101-1102, 1112

Cryptocurrencies 3, 5-6, 8, 13, 17-19, 21, 25, 37, 55, 59, 107, 113, 138, 142-143, 160, 179, 208, 226, 234, 247-248, 279, 295, 299, 304, 311, 489, 583, 690, 821, 832, 841, 849, 874, 915, 928, 956, 991, 1049, 1097, 1099, 1105, 1107, 1110, 1119, 1127, 1129, 1144, 1155, 1180, 1230, 1293, 1298-1299, 1305

Cryptocurrency 1, 3-4, 7, 13, 17, 21-22, 25, 28-29, 33, 40-41, 56, 59, 90, 105, 142-143, 154, 157, 160, 180, 209, 247, 256, 262, 279, 282, 290, 299, 307, 323-324, 330, 334, 354, 403-404, 415-416, 418, 477, 489, 493, 504, 512, 536, 543, 572, 608, 644, 667, 741, 773, 824, 839, 841, 844, 846-849, 851, 921-922, 927, 967, 973, 1067, 1070, 1099, 1101, 1104-1105, 1113, 1122, 1128, 1130, 1134, 1150, 1154-1155, 1161, 1163, 1179-1180, 1184, 1248, 1253, 1293-1297, 1299, 1305, 1316

Cryptography 3-4, 8, 22, 25, 32, 39, 41, 48, 51, 54, 58, 78, 90, 103-104, 108, 114, 128, 131, 133, 136, 143, 148, 150, 152-153, 157, 171, 179, 182, 184, 201, 204, 217, 234, 245-246, 258-259, 266, 276, 284, 294-295, 298, 300, 304, 324, 334, 356, 364, 406, 408, 411, 496, 507, 509, 511-513, 537, 539, 554, 563, 568, 572, 577-578, 581, 597, 630, 633, 648, 677, 682, 686, 696, 738, 742, 773, 802, 823, 838, 841, 845, 847, 851, 869, 877, 899-900,

919, 928, 931, 934, 939, 954, 968, 971-975, 981, 984, 1019, 1063, 1067, 1074, 1105, 1119, 1124, 1130-1132, 1139, 1149-1150, 1224, 1227, 1230, 1233, 1249, 1252-1253, 1255, 1259, 1262, 1289, 1291, 1293, 1313, 1330

cyber resilience 799-803

Cybercrime 748, 818, 1051, 1091, 1099-1100, 1167, 1310

Cyber-Physical Systems 229, 429, 437, 445, 466, 521, 526, 529, 550, 695, 800, 986-987, 989, 998, 1005, 1099, 1104

Cybersecurity 67, 84, 94, 105, 125, 142, 154-156, 209, 225-226, 421, 424, 437, 446, 451, 465, 509-510, 533, 567, 587, 687, 738, 799, 815-816, 818-820, 822-826, 828, 830-840, 859, 882, 893, 957, 972, 1037, 1039, 1045-1046, 1048, 1050-1053, 1055-1056, 1064, 1081, 1084, 1100, 1167

cyborg 1168, 1178, 1186, 1191-1192

D

DAaps 570, 575

DAG 5, 27-28, 264, 493, 544, 561, 683, 931, 937-939, 943, 953, 1001, 1003, 1136

Data Access and Verification 382, 395

data assets 162, 242

Data Communication 205, 210, 222, 228, 233, 246, 335, 350, 352-353, 364, 499, 502, 526, 528-530, 532-533, 540, 554, 705, 860, 962, 984, 1063, 1243, 1256

Data Compression 702-704, 709-710, 712, 715-718, 910, 944

Data Harvesting 1176, 1192

Data Market 162-168, 170-179, 279, 560, 717

Data Mining 231-232, 277, 314, 402-405, 413, 417-419, 441, 449, 560, 703, 708, 712, 715, 718-719, 797, 830, 952, 1102, 1176-1177, 1192

Data Prediction 778-784, 787-793, 795

Data Privacy 61, 68, 70-72, 83, 92, 96-97, 110-111, 117, 121, 126, 162-163, 168, 175, 210, 214, 238, 242, 374, 405, 407-409, 413, 495, 532, 542, 616, 645, 671, 768, 803, 879, 881, 883, 896, 909, 962, 973, 980, 1031, 1099, 1244

Data Provenance 250, 543, 611, 619, 1005, 1010, 1021, 1032, 1035-1036, 1096

Data Security 3, 64, 97-99, 103, 121, 141, 163, 179, 193, 224, 291, 298, 347, 376, 403, 451, 454-456, 465, 468, 483, 495, 500, 515, 527, 529, 568, 573, 577, 607-613, 616, 618, 623, 625, 643, 662, 674, 709, 711, 742, 766, 774, 794, 812, 857, 863, 883, 887, 928, 955, 1006, 1044, 1083, 1090, 1122,

1141, 1146, 1188, 1294, 1302, 1325

Data Sharing 88-89, 91-107, 122, 162-163, 165, 168, 180-181, 186, 190-191, 233, 243, 278-285, 289-290, 369, 510-511, 519-521, 524, 532, 548, 550, 554, 569, 608-611, 617, 619, 621, 626, 630, 640-646, 681, 701, 721, 776, 810, 885-886, 893, 932, 945, 950, 972, 984, 1021, 1026, 1065, 1076, 1083, 1090, 1099, 1155, 1162, 1216, 1252, 1262, 1275, 1308, 1321

data sharing architecture 278, 281

Data Transmission 71, 99-100, 104, 166, 168, 172, 175, 223, 258, 266, 658, 661, 675, 690, 693, 860, 906, 931, 934, 937, 945, 953, 987, 1061, 1103, 1150, 1322

Ddos 43, 72, 74, 80, 98, 118, 129, 211, 249, 330-336, 339-348, 386, 388, 400, 429, 514, 516, 524, 533, 545, 553-554, 601, 671, 675, 682, 699-700, 829, 859, 862, 869-870, 875-876, 879, 947, 966, 978, 1016, 1023, 1072-1076, 1082, 1096, 1098, 1247, 1255, 1300-1301

Decentralised System 841-842

Decentralized Computing Infrastructure 246, 364, 555, 985

Decryption 88, 100, 169, 171, 201, 218, 414, 454, 465, 578, 628-631, 633-637, 641-642, 811, 820, 856, 863, 1131, 1193, 1203

Device Addressing 382

Diary Supply Chain Management System 1264

Digital Certificate 314, 316, 811, 867

Digital Economy 130, 556-557, 560-561, 567, 569, 813, 910, 1039, 1056, 1100, 1306

Digital Footprint 1176, 1192

Digital Identity 29, 59, 153, 156-157, 203, 508, 819, 1112, 1185-1186, 1192, 1319

Digital Information 166, 178, 308, 488, 569, 741, 749, 801, 1106, 1231

Digital Marketing 1168, 1192

Digital Rights Management 1152, 1157-1159, 1164, 1166

Digital Transactions 142-143, 154-155, 157, 242, 511, 973, 1042, 1050-1051, 1253, 1316

Digital Transformation 108, 142-143, 161, 347, 367, 482, 766, 799, 816, 995, 1037, 1039, 1043, 1045, 1047, 1050, 1053-1056, 1155, 1169

Distributed AI 421

Distributed Ledger 2, 4-5, 10, 21, 25, 35, 49, 60-61, 88-90, 96, 99, 103, 114, 125, 131, 134-135, 148, 152-153, 216-217, 220, 236-237, 242-243, 250, 254, 259-260, 291, 333-334, 354-356, 362, 375, 390, 392-395, 403, 477, 482, 496, 502, 504, 509, 511, 536-537, 539, 542, 544, 574, 577-579, 625,

667, 683-684, 741, 743, 770, 773, 776, 818, 830, 842, 874, 877, 879, 890-891, 896, 920, 931-932, 957, 962, 968, 973, 991, 1005, 1025-1026, 1030, 1039, 1041-1042, 1047, 1049, 1066, 1069, 1071, 1081, 1102, 1116, 1118, 1125, 1128, 1133-1134, 1136-1137, 1146, 1149, 1158, 1162, 1166, 1179, 1209, 1227, 1230, 1242, 1244, 1249, 1252-1253, 1264, 1268, 1291, 1295, 1304, 1316

Distributed Network 22, 53-54, 154, 216, 290, 301-302, 324, 335, 350, 382, 386, 388-389, 397-398, 473, 490, 508-509, 539-540, 559, 572, 583, 608, 741, 934, 962, 968-969, 972, 1019, 1038, 1052, 1115, 1134, 1201-1202, 1230, 1244, 1249-1250, 1252

Distributed Processing 28, 492, 885, 1208, 1267

Distributed Systems 2, 58, 106, 160, 164, 179, 191, 195, 290, 338, 402, 421, 561, 691, 735, 778, 794, 836, 843-844, 915, 958, 981, 1032, 1035, 1112, 1259, 1294

Double Spend 334, 1213, 1227, 1272, 1291

E

ECC 49, 58, 686, 899, 1072, 1076

Edge Computing Security 78

Effective Use 110, 665, 799, 802, 805, 813

Electronic Commerce 160, 248, 556-557, 569, 1177

Electronic Data Interchange (EDI) 569

Electronic Health Records (EHR) 97, 104, 110-111, 117, 483, 773, 776, 799-800, 803, 805, 813-814, 886, 1039, 1047, 1058, 1083, 1322

EMR 129, 588, 593-594, 605, 1009, 1047, 1054

Encryption 3, 20, 61, 71, 74, 76, 78, 82, 88-89, 93-100, 104, 106-107, 114, 118, 125, 169, 171-173, 175, 185, 190, 201, 217-218, 220, 222, 225, 249, 280, 283, 310, 319, 329, 407, 413, 417, 420, 454, 465, 476, 479, 492, 505, 511, 514, 517, 519, 522, 524, 532, 537, 546, 548, 551, 554, 564-565, 568, 573, 575, 578, 628-631, 633-636, 638, 640-643, 645-648, 650-655, 658, 660-662, 672-673, 677, 679-681, 684, 686, 711, 725, 728, 734, 771, 773, 806, 811, 820, 822-823, 827, 829, 833, 853-854, 858, 862-863, 865-867, 876, 879, 882, 899, 909, 924, 932, 968, 972, 975-978, 981, 983, 990, 999, 1001, 1013, 1019, 1024, 1047, 1049-1050, 1066, 1074-1076, 1096-1097, 1099, 1103-1104, 1121, 1124, 1131, 1136-1137, 1146, 1150, 1179, 1184, 1192-1193, 1201, 1203, 1213, 1249, 1252, 1255-1257, 1259, 1262, 1272, 1294, 1300, 1309, 1313

End-Point Security 839

Energy Consumption 80, 100, 103, 210, 212, 216, 223, 225, 266, 275, 375, 377, 475, 507, 617, 621,

685-688, 703-704, 709-710, 712, 719-720, 752, 870, 939, 979, 999, 1011, 1019-1020, 1027-1028, 1060, 1199

Energy Efficiency 251, 320, 382-383, 475, 705, 712, 718, 750, 1028, 1031

Enhanced use 803, 813

Enterprise Information System 240, 349-350, 359, 515, 525

Ethereum 1, 3, 5, 7-8, 12-13, 20-21, 26, 40-41, 48, 50, 53, 56, 58-59, 62, 64, 87, 90, 94, 97-100, 113-114, 119, 137, 140, 142-143, 159, 161, 167-168, 171-173, 175-177, 184, 186, 231, 241, 244, 252, 255, 299, 304, 306-308, 310, 312, 317, 321, 323-324, 326-327, 331, 404, 413-415, 418, 436, 538, 543-544, 569, 575, 578-579, 583, 587, 598, 616, 667-668, 680, 696-697, 700, 774, 800, 805-806, 815, 824, 877-878, 881-882, 901, 910, 917, 932, 957, 991, 1001, 1003, 1007, 1025, 1075, 1079, 1086, 1088, 1100-1101, 1103, 1107-1108, 1113, 1118, 1121, 1123, 1126, 1129, 1134, 1136-1137, 1139-1141, 1143, 1150, 1180-1181, 1203, 1208, 1217-1218, 1221, 1227, 1231, 1264, 1267, 1276-1277, 1281, 1283, 1291, 1294, 1296, 1306-1307, 1310, 1313, 1316, 1319, 1327

F

FANET 664-665, 670, 677, 679-680, 685-688, 696, 701

flying ad-hoc networks 663, 696

Fog Computing 67-68, 76-78, 80, 82, 84-85, 99, 103, 195, 209, 258, 265, 267, 276-277, 337, 469, 524, 529, 553-554, 650, 662, 681, 684, 690, 694, 705-706, 711, 715, 717-719, 735, 789, 792-793, 804, 815, 907, 950, 954, 958, 963, 1006, 1032, 1036, 1056, 1102, 1245

Fog computing security 67

Forensics 209, 329, 529, 553, 699, 738-742, 744, 747-749, 918, 1231, 1309, 1314

G

Generation Y 1167, 1174, 1187-1188

Generation Z 1167, 1174, 1187, 1190, 1192

Global Crises 1240, 1263

Green System 382

H

Hash Value 8, 38, 50-51, 58, 90, 97, 115, 170, 174-175, 211-212, 216, 220, 296, 298, 506, 537, 603, 648, 656-658, 723, 730, 733, 744, 877, 895, 902,

944, 1067-1068, 1070, 1106, 1123, 1131, 1143, 1196-1197, 1203, 1234, 1295

Hashing 13, 23-24, 49, 51, 58, 61, 78, 114, 153, 181, 188, 217, 234, 267, 296-298, 317, 354, 410, 505, 537, 570, 573, 578, 580-584, 647, 655-656, 740, 743-744, 770, 808, 810-811, 874, 902, 910, 913, 928, 985, 1001, 1069, 1072, 1103-1104, 1117, 1130, 1193-1195, 1203, 1220, 1232-1233, 1278, 1296, 1298

Hashing auxiliary device 647

Hashing Function 296, 505, 537, 582, 1193, 1195, 1203

healthcare and blockchain 768

healthcare environments 748, 778-779, 793-794

Healthcare privacy and security 768

horizontal integration 986, 995-997, 1002, 1007

Hyperledger Fabric 41, 47, 59, 65, 90, 223, 226-227, 231, 241, 252, 255, 310, 394-395, 397, 399, 495, 513, 748, 801, 805, 807-811, 814-815, 880, 942, 955, 958, 975, 991, 1126, 1134-1135, 1143, 1150, 1255, 1321

I

IIoT Merkle root 647

IIoT-arranged system 648, 650, 658

Immutability 2, 18, 30, 37, 53, 89-94, 96-97, 103, 115, 120-121, 123, 148, 150-151, 246, 248, 296, 327, 333, 337-338, 354, 356, 364, 392, 477, 507, 539-540, 543, 555, 604, 607-608, 611, 618-619, 621, 625, 667-668, 683-684, 688, 739, 742, 744, 799, 819-820, 822-823, 826-827, 829, 835, 840, 874, 877, 880, 883, 895, 903, 919-920, 923, 926-928, 968, 985, 1072, 1075-1076, 1078, 1083, 1103, 1119, 1124, 1139, 1141, 1178-1179, 1182, 1184, 1187, 1192, 1207-1208, 1213, 1227, 1249, 1266-1267, 1272, 1291, 1296

Immutable 2, 34, 58, 62, 89, 114, 118, 126, 142, 150-151, 237, 247, 250, 255, 279, 295, 305, 311, 317-318, 327, 333, 339, 355, 358, 375, 384, 477, 505, 514, 537, 540, 542-543, 573, 576-578, 593, 597-598, 603-604, 616, 619, 741, 753, 800-801, 804-805, 811, 819, 823, 826-830, 833, 835, 844, 869, 877, 880, 901, 909-910, 920, 925-926, 960, 962, 968, 976-977, 994, 1021-1022, 1065, 1067, 1069, 1071, 1080, 1110, 1117, 1128-1130, 1156-1158, 1163, 1166, 1179, 1181, 1183-1184, 1193, 1209, 1243, 1249, 1255, 1268, 1294, 1301, 1322, 1326

Implementation Multi chain 556-557

Incentive Mechanism 89, 93-94, 103, 107, 278-279, 285, 318, 426, 885, 928, 979, 981, 1257, 1259

Industrial Internet Of Things (Iiot) 64, 84, 100, 140-141, 166, 178, 190, 227, 245, 257, 290, 440, 472-473, 484-487, 516-517, 520, 522-524, 545-546, 549, 551-554, 644-645, 660-662, 700, 721, 736, 882, 892, 956-957, 986-987, 1004-1005, 1007-1009, 1227, 1291

Industrial Process Automation Systems 986-987, 1006

Information Security 19, 49, 65, 208, 225, 277, 379, 439, 451, 466-467, 644, 799, 801, 804, 807, 815, 822-823, 825-826, 830, 835, 983, 1005, 1045, 1050-1051, 1058, 1092, 1097, 1205, 1262

Information Systems 84-86, 116, 159, 193, 230-234, 241, 243, 347, 350, 352, 361-362, 371, 399, 401, 417, 426, 431, 433, 440, 442, 498-503, 507-508, 513, 515, 525-527, 532, 534, 539, 606, 609, 719, 734, 796, 801-803, 813, 873, 961-963, 966-967, 970, 975, 979, 983, 988, 1007, 1035, 1056, 1098, 1149, 1178, 1191, 1224, 1241, 1243-1244, 1247-1248, 1250, 1254, 1257, 1261, 1288

Integrated Library System 1161, 1166

Intellectual Capital 569

interests of use 607-608, 611

Interlibrary Loan 1152, 1158, 1161-1162, 1166

Internet Of Things (Iot) 17-19, 21, 28, 35, 37, 48-49, 54, 64-65, 67-68, 72, 76, 83-87, 89, 92, 100, 103, 105-106, 108-113, 117-118, 127-131, 133-134, 137-138, 140-141, 165-166, 178-180, 190-196, 207-213, 215-216, 223-228, 230, 242-247, 256-260, 262-263, 265, 276-278, 289-292, 307, 312-313, 315, 329-332, 345-350, 352-353, 363-364, 366-367, 379-382, 399-401, 429, 436, 440, 445, 448, 466-470, 472-473, 483-487, 493, 495-496, 498-499, 501, 510, 516-526, 530, 532, 545-556, 558-561, 567, 573, 586, 603, 606, 608, 617, 626, 631, 643-646, 660-665, 688-702, 715-721, 734-738, 747-755, 758-759, 766-767, 776, 778-784, 787, 792-800, 813, 815, 825-826, 833, 837-838, 840, 852-854, 865, 871-874, 882, 889-897, 906, 908, 913, 915-919, 924, 928-930, 932-934, 952, 955-958, 960-963, 971-972, 980-987, 1003-1005, 1007-1010, 1024, 1032-1035, 1037-1043, 1046, 1050-1052, 1054, 1056, 1058-1060, 1080, 1082, 1096-1101, 1104, 1111, 1113, 1136, 1148, 1150, 1178, 1209, 1224-1225, 1227, 1231, 1238, 1242-1244, 1251, 1258-1263, 1268, 1288-1289, 1291, 1313, 1315, 1326, 1330

Internet-of-things hashing 181

Intrusion Detection 67-68, 76, 81-87, 195, 207-209, 330, 332, 335-336, 339, 341-343, 345-346, 348, 423, 426, 436-437, 441-443, 529, 545-546, 550, 677-678, 694, 700, 724-725, 727, 734-737, 869,

876, 885, 890, 932, 990

Intrusion Detection Systems 67-68, 81-82, 84, 86-87, 207-208, 332, 336, 346, 426, 436, 529, 545-546, 677, 876, 890, 990

Iot And Cloud 208, 263, 319, 702-703, 705, 712, 716, 736

Iot Architecture 55, 83, 119, 127, 196, 198, 207, 210, 227, 231, 254, 258, 338, 368, 445, 499, 502, 527, 530-531, 535, 559, 671, 674, 703, 711, 752, 803, 852, 859, 865, 880, 932, 949-950, 958, 962, 1030, 1242, 1244, 1330

IoT arData privacy 67

IoT Data Management In Cloud 702

Iot Security 19-20, 36, 42, 55, 57, 59, 62, 67-68, 70, 72, 76-78, 80-81, 83, 85-86, 135, 137-139, 141, 191, 193-195, 207-208, 212, 226, 245, 248, 250, 253, 256, 262, 312, 330, 334, 364, 386, 400, 428, 443, 448, 452-454, 483, 496-497, 516-517, 519-521, 527, 529-530, 541, 545, 547, 549-550, 554, 628, 644, 663-667, 671-672, 674, 679, 681-682, 691, 696, 734-735, 742, 748, 765, 828, 836, 871-873, 879, 890, 892, 894, 897, 913, 916, 925, 933, 956, 966, 980, 985, 1035, 1063, 1072-1074, 1083, 1090, 1092, 1111, 1146, 1247, 1258, 1309-1310, 1313-1314

Iot Technology 111, 123-124, 194-196, 199, 202-203, 205, 207, 230-233, 237, 240, 256, 319, 352, 372, 498, 501, 515, 530, 680, 703, 712, 747, 960-963, 965-967, 1045, 1064, 1075, 1216, 1243-1244, 1247-1248, 1276

IoT threats 67

IPFS 59, 98, 167, 170, 172, 174, 177, 279, 282-285, 407, 409, 412-413, 495, 1100, 1193, 1200-1204

K

K.P.N Jayasena 1205

KNN 723, 750-753, 756, 760

L

LBPH 750-751, 757, 766

lightweight cryptography 931, 954, 1063

Limitations 18, 33, 36, 47, 55, 67, 78, 81-82, 84, 93, 108, 111, 171, 195, 206, 239, 248, 256, 279, 286, 315, 318-320, 392, 473, 509, 533, 593, 605, 607-608, 611, 702-703, 705, 712, 773, 775, 818-819, 824, 829-831, 834-836, 856-857, 891, 904, 907, 914, 920, 923, 943, 950-951, 960, 987, 1006, 1011, 1039, 1041, 1063, 1103, 1264, 1310

M

Machine Intelligence 402, 417, 952
Machine Learning 67, 76, 80, 83-84, 86, 99, 165, 170,
    172, 256, 328, 346, 367, 383, 400, 402-405, 414,
    417-419, 421-422, 430, 441-443, 446, 487, 522,
    552, 561, 678, 691, 698, 707, 711, 719, 736, 750,
    752, 754-756, 759, 765-767, 796, 852, 854, 869-
    871, 920, 926, 1006, 1018, 1029, 1036, 1038-1040,
    1042-1043, 1049-1050, 1052, 1055, 1073, 1076,
    1099, 1186, 1318, 1320-1324, 1326, 1328, 1330
Machine-To-Machine Communication 719, 875, 891,
    986
Malicious 9, 33, 40, 56, 74-75, 77, 81, 88, 93-94, 98,
    115, 138, 172, 199, 201, 211, 220-221, 235, 279,
    281-284, 293-294, 315, 327, 331-332, 335-336,
    338-339, 343, 377, 386-387, 403, 411, 428-429,
    432-433, 436-437, 441, 478, 480, 489, 494, 499,
    503, 509-510, 512-513, 515, 526, 532-534, 560,
    590, 620, 640, 667, 671-679, 684-686, 701, 726,
    742, 830, 832, 852, 858-866, 869-870, 874-875,
    879, 883, 885, 887, 898, 909, 918, 921, 924,
    926, 936, 942, 946, 969, 971-975, 978, 1013,
    1016, 1018-1020, 1023, 1026-1027, 1032, 1034,
    1045, 1062, 1064, 1073-1076, 1106, 1108, 1123,
    1140-1141, 1194, 1201, 1203, 1208, 1250-1254,
    1256-1257, 1267, 1298, 1300-1301, 1316
MANET 487, 628, 664, 669-670, 699, 701
Manufacturing Industry 41, 228, 230-233, 236, 238,
    240, 242, 245, 349-351, 475, 498-502, 507, 509,
    515, 522, 525-527, 529-534, 542, 551, 747, 1005,
    1241, 1243, 1245
markle tree 1128
Metadata 23, 120, 284, 296-297, 488, 772, 775, 846,
    888, 1021, 1036, 1103, 1152, 1154, 1158-1159,
    1166, 1186
Mining 3-4, 8, 10, 13, 19, 25-26, 28, 33, 35, 38-40, 42,
    44, 48, 56, 63, 66, 90, 98, 100, 115, 136-138, 141,
    167, 176, 182, 185, 203, 209, 219, 231-232, 234,
    238, 252, 271-273, 277, 283, 285, 297, 303-304,
    314, 322-323, 325-328, 347, 380, 402-405, 411-
    413, 416-419, 441, 449, 491, 537, 544, 560-561,
    567, 579, 584, 587, 601, 620, 648-649, 651, 655,
    669, 687, 702-703, 707-708, 712, 715, 718-719,
    741-743, 769, 771, 797, 829-830, 844, 846-849,
    851, 874, 877, 882, 886, 895, 903, 905, 910, 914,
    916, 920-922, 927, 934-935, 939, 952, 980, 990,
    1001, 1028-1031, 1070-1071, 1083, 1102, 1106,
    1108-1109, 1140, 1143, 1145, 1176-1178, 1192,
    1198-1200, 1204, 1208, 1217, 1231, 1266, 1277,
    1296-1298, 1300, 1302, 1307

Mitm 249, 588, 593, 671, 1016
mobile ad-hoc networks 475, 481, 485, 663

N

near-ring 626, 631-634, 637-640, 642, 644
novel use 799, 801, 803, 807

O

oil and gas industry 472, 474-475, 478, 482, 484
Open Educational Resources 1161, 1166
Open Source Platform 556-557, 1118

P

P.M.N.R.Madhunamali 1205
Peer To Peer (P2P) 319, 840, 1059
Peer-To-Peer Networking 488-489, 667, 851, 1019
Performance Analysis 210, 290, 482, 485, 640, 1007,
    1125-1127
Performance Optimization 436, 440, 661, 953, 957,
    1115
Pharmaceutical Supply Chain 119, 128-129, 131,
    609, 879
Physical Things 258, 666
Power industry 474
Predictive Analytics 402, 963, 983, 1262
Privacy And Security 68, 86, 95, 97, 103, 111, 117,
    119, 121-122, 126-127, 137, 194, 201, 237, 256,
    259, 261, 320, 331, 476, 498, 526, 593, 631, 643,
    645, 675, 681, 768, 800, 812, 848, 871, 873, 875,
    879, 887, 896, 920, 928, 961, 966, 1080, 1186,
    1243, 1247, 1316, 1329
Privacy Issues 19, 54, 162, 195, 206-207, 209, 211, 242,
    245, 346, 436, 448, 470, 511, 524, 553-554, 826,
    838, 853, 869, 894, 918, 972, 991, 1102, 1122,
    1127, 1163, 1252, 1293-1294, 1302, 1307-1308
Privacy Management 194, 438, 1099, 1115
Privacy Protection 104, 162-163, 171, 178, 289, 453,
    541, 563-564, 566, 616, 661, 695, 871, 932, 966,
    1035, 1062, 1077, 1247
privacy through blockchain 768
Private Blockchain 7-8, 24-25, 39-42, 45, 52-53, 56-57,
    90, 95, 97-98, 134, 141, 145, 151, 201-202, 250,
    253, 304, 331, 478, 491, 507, 539, 558, 570, 577,
    667, 697, 821, 887, 901-903, 976, 991, 1007, 1075,
    1088-1089, 1118, 1121, 1126, 1129, 1139, 1328
Private Ledger 570, 576, 1134-1135
Proof Of Work 3, 8, 11, 22, 90, 94, 136, 167, 186, 212,
    220, 235, 244-245, 268, 281, 291, 303, 331, 337,

417, 511, 542, 544, 573, 579, 581, 584, 665, 669, 682, 692, 806, 822, 847, 902-904, 914, 921, 928, 955, 973, 990, 1063, 1083, 1105, 1108, 1111, 1130, 1141-1142, 1198-1200, 1205, 1253

Proof-of-Useful-Work 402-403, 405, 411

Property Rights 588, 590-591, 596, 1183

Provenance 121, 123, 236, 246, 250, 364, 377, 392, 478, 540, 543, 555, 598, 611, 617, 619, 621, 625, 883, 887-888, 966, 981, 985, 1005, 1010, 1021, 1032, 1035-1036, 1096, 1162, 1206, 1223, 1231, 1238, 1247, 1259, 1265, 1269, 1287, 1323, 1328

Proxy Re-Encryption 94, 96-97, 99, 105, 520-521, 550, 626-631, 633-634, 641-646, 1099

Public Blockchain 7-8, 24-25, 39-40, 42, 52-53, 56-57, 90, 97, 107, 134, 141, 145, 169, 182-183, 187-189, 201-202, 231, 238, 250, 253, 255, 331, 392, 491, 505, 507, 511, 536, 539, 558, 570, 577, 579, 619, 650, 667, 699, 742, 821, 848, 901-903, 927, 973, 990, 1021, 1024, 1088-1089, 1118, 1121, 1129, 1252, 1294, 1316

public databases 488

Public Key Infrastructure (PKI) 154, 314-315, 563, 1020

Q

Quality Of Service 76, 487, 533, 705, 1014, 1083

R

Radio Frequency Identification 230, 331, 476, 487, 501, 530, 542, 671, 789, 859, 911, 960-961, 1242

random space learning 721

Real-Time Systems 251, 986-989, 991, 995, 997-998, 1000, 1006, 1033

Reinforcement Learning 98, 104, 290, 421-424, 426-430, 433, 437-444, 520, 549, 649, 661, 679, 687, 689, 696, 755-756, 869, 942-943, 952, 957, 1010, 1020-1021, 1029, 1033-1036

Reliability blockchain 647

RFID 49, 55, 69-70, 73, 75, 110-111, 130, 196, 198, 205, 215, 230-232, 245, 308-311, 320, 331, 350, 352-353, 364, 447, 449, 476, 487, 499, 501-502, 521, 526, 530-531, 541-542, 551, 671, 703, 789, 838, 858-859, 888, 918, 939, 955, 960-961, 965-967, 983-984, 1059-1060, 1063, 1074, 1178, 1213, 1226, 1242, 1246-1248, 1256, 1261, 1263, 1272, 1285, 1290

S

Sabaragamuwa University of Technology 1205

Scholarly Communication 497, 1160-1161, 1166

SDN 263, 336, 375, 380-381, 464, 480-481, 484-485, 487, 671, 682, 721-724, 727-728, 730-735, 978, 983, 1010-1011, 1014-1017, 1022-1025, 1032-1034, 1262

Security And Privacy 18-19, 65, 70, 97, 104, 106, 119, 126, 135, 140, 159, 162, 165, 168, 175, 179-180, 190, 195, 203-204, 206-207, 209-211, 225, 241, 245, 256, 329, 346, 348, 352, 361, 363, 400, 403, 418-419, 436, 438, 445-448, 453, 455, 465-466, 468, 470, 483-484, 498, 511, 517, 520, 523-524, 533, 541, 547, 549, 553-554, 587, 590-591, 593, 610, 626, 628, 630, 642-646, 660, 662, 666-667, 689, 694, 696, 701, 705, 712, 734-735, 754, 766, 768, 777, 794, 813-814, 829, 838-839, 853, 857, 862, 872, 885-886, 890, 893-894, 896, 899, 912, 915, 918, 920, 925-926, 928-930, 934, 950, 956-957, 962, 966, 970, 972, 979-980, 990, 1005, 1009-1010, 1026, 1044, 1053, 1066, 1072, 1075, 1079, 1101, 1103, 1111-1112, 1115, 1123, 1127, 1139, 1149, 1151, 1186, 1224, 1231, 1244, 1247, 1250, 1252, 1258, 1289, 1293-1294, 1296, 1302, 1307-1308, 1316, 1330

Security Attack 859, 1058

security countermeasures 67-68, 76

Security Issues 1, 21, 28, 32-33, 47, 88, 97, 99, 111, 122, 131, 139-140, 154, 160, 194-195, 198-200, 202-203, 207, 225-226, 248, 319, 331, 334, 337, 366, 368, 380, 386, 463, 465, 469, 485, 492, 498, 500, 518, 527, 529-530, 533, 547, 587, 600-602, 605, 617, 621, 671, 673, 675, 677, 681, 685, 688-689, 692, 694, 696, 719, 738, 766, 837, 852, 855, 857, 869, 873-875, 880, 889, 895, 897-900, 914, 919-920, 961, 966, 1005, 1018-1020, 1025, 1032, 1035, 1045, 1055, 1091-1092, 1107, 1129, 1146, 1149-1150, 1239-1240, 1243, 1247, 1257, 1293-1294, 1296

Service-Oriented Computing 228, 233, 239, 353, 467-468, 499, 515, 526, 533, 541, 1242, 1257

SHA-256 Hashing 49, 58, 1233

Sinknode/Base Station 192

Smart Agriculture 199, 204, 383, 399, 474, 476, 478, 703, 716, 864, 932, 1231, 1316, 1319, 1327

Smart Application 382, 850, 1146

Smart Building 320, 383-385, 397, 474-475, 478

Smart Cities 64, 67, 87, 103, 107, 179, 194, 198-199, 207-208, 330, 367, 371, 379, 381, 446-449, 456, 459, 464-465, 467, 469, 522, 552, 626, 669, 671,

691, 698, 712, 717, 719-720, 766, 832-833, 853, 881, 888, 892, 912, 924, 1031, 1060, 1062, 1064-1065, 1072-1073, 1076, 1078-1082, 1097, 1100, 1112, 1179, 1186, 1191

Smart Contract 40-41, 44-47, 59, 63-64, 88, 91-93, 95-99, 113, 119, 128-130, 136, 153, 166-168, 170-174, 176-177, 184, 187, 220, 230, 236-237, 239, 242, 305-306, 308, 310, 312, 317, 321, 323-327, 356-357, 361, 390, 392-396, 414, 513, 557-559, 565, 574-575, 579, 595, 597, 620, 680, 683-684, 697, 753, 806, 818, 832, 836, 884, 894, 910, 912, 920, 932, 970-971, 975, 985-987, 991, 994-995, 1001-1002, 1008, 1070, 1075, 1078, 1083, 1086, 1112-1113, 1136-1137, 1155-1156, 1161, 1180-1181, 1200, 1207, 1209, 1215, 1217-1218, 1221-1222, 1227, 1230, 1250-1251, 1255, 1264, 1266-1267, 1274, 1277, 1280-1283, 1291, 1294, 1319, 1322-1323, 1325-1326

Smart Devices 89, 111, 138-140, 206, 212, 254, 258-262, 265, 280, 336, 367, 378, 446, 492, 528, 543, 559, 628, 856, 885-886, 926, 933, 1010, 1167, 1172, 1178, 1319

Smart Iot 206, 757-758, 869, 931

Smart Meter 1062, 1083

Social Media 33, 150, 796, 875, 976, 1102, 1172, 1174-1177, 1179, 1186, 1192

Software-Defined Networking 464, 485, 671, 1033, 1035-1036

SoK 423

Spectrum Sensing 693, 1010, 1017, 1026, 1028, 1036

Storage Optimization 238, 702, 953

strategic distance 649, 651

Supply Chain 16, 29-32, 42-43, 55-56, 59-60, 62, 65, 68, 91, 94, 99, 103, 105, 119-120, 123-124, 128-129, 131, 150, 160-161, 201, 203, 228-230, 232-233, 237, 240-246, 255, 291-293, 305, 308-313, 334, 347, 349-352, 354, 357-365, 368, 375, 472-474, 476-479, 481-485, 495, 498-499, 502, 517, 520-522, 526, 531, 540-541, 546, 550-551, 555, 567, 609-610, 850, 879, 882, 886, 888, 893, 918, 960-967, 970, 979-986, 988-989, 991, 993-994, 996-997, 999, 1004, 1007, 1009, 1041-1042, 1053-1055, 1061-1063, 1066, 1074, 1076-1083, 1093-1094, 1097, 1124-1125, 1128-1129, 1137-1138, 1154, 1160-1161, 1166, 1180-1182, 1185, 1187, 1189, 1206-1227, 1229-1233, 1238-1241, 1243-1248, 1250-1251, 1257-1282, 1284-1285, 1287-1291, 1315-1321, 1323-1328, 1330

Supply Chain Management 55, 62, 94, 105, 201, 203, 228, 230, 232, 240-243, 245-246, 291-293, 310, 312, 349-350, 352, 357-359, 361-365, 482-483,

521-522, 526, 540-541, 551, 555, 567, 886, 888, 893, 960, 962, 964, 967, 970, 979-980, 982-983, 985, 1004, 1053-1054, 1061-1062, 1066, 1076, 1079, 1081-1082, 1097, 1124, 1138, 1154, 1161, 1166, 1180-1182, 1187, 1207, 1209-1210, 1212-1213, 1215, 1217, 1224-1227, 1229, 1231-1232, 1238-1241, 1244-1246, 1248, 1250-1251, 1258, 1260-1261, 1264-1265, 1268-1269, 1271-1272, 1274, 1276, 1288-1291, 1316, 1318-1319, 1323-1324, 1326-1327

SVM 80, 408, 433, 750-753, 756-757, 760, 1076

systematization-of-knowledge 423

T

Taxonomy 50, 53, 194-195, 200, 207, 484-485, 568, 624, 665, 671, 674, 680, 688, 690, 696, 712-713, 715, 778, 780-781, 787-788, 795, 797, 871-872, 875, 897, 960, 1035, 1114, 1148

Time-Stamped 21, 201, 234-235, 246, 354, 554, 618, 774, 985, 1103, 1146, 1193, 1294

Traceability 29, 31-32, 53, 91, 93-94, 116, 118, 120, 127, 129, 231, 243, 279, 284, 291, 293, 305, 308, 310-313, 318, 351-352, 358, 360-361, 478, 482, 485, 495, 502, 510, 533, 541, 577, 607, 611, 614, 616, 619-621, 623, 625, 664-665, 667, 683, 769-770, 774, 822, 834, 880, 887-888, 892, 908, 911-912, 918, 926, 950, 966-967, 981-982, 994, 998, 1008, 1019, 1021-1022, 1024, 1029, 1066, 1072, 1077-1078, 1080, 1103, 1109, 1111, 1124, 1138, 1167, 1178, 1180-1185, 1187, 1207, 1209-1210, 1214, 1218, 1221, 1223-1226, 1231, 1237, 1239, 1243, 1247-1248, 1259-1260, 1264, 1266, 1268-1269, 1272, 1277, 1279, 1287-1290, 1315, 1318-1319, 1323, 1325, 1327, 1329-1330

Transaction Data 15, 94, 98, 143, 168, 170, 251, 260, 283, 302-303, 310, 314, 322-323, 326, 541, 563, 681, 806, 1072, 1209, 1218, 1220, 1277-1279, 1285, 1296

Transparency 2, 6, 16, 18, 53, 88-94, 96-98, 103, 115, 120-121, 123, 126-127, 142-143, 164, 167, 201, 228, 231, 239, 243, 247, 250, 291-293, 305, 308, 310, 334, 350-352, 359, 363, 376, 416, 477-478, 481, 499, 509, 513, 526, 537, 539, 543, 564, 567, 573, 598-601, 604, 607, 609, 611, 614, 616, 618-619, 621, 623-625, 668, 794, 802, 877, 884, 887-888, 920, 923, 933, 965, 970, 973, 975, 979, 985, 996, 1005, 1026, 1029, 1031, 1038, 1041, 1046, 1066, 1072, 1075-1078, 1080, 1083, 1111, 1116-1117, 1119, 1121-1122, 1129, 1134, 1136, 1138, 1146, 1155, 1158, 1161, 1177-1180, 1182-

1184, 1186-1187, 1192, 1206-1207, 1213, 1217, 1219, 1223, 1225-1226, 1229, 1232, 1238, 1254, 1265-1266, 1272-1273, 1276-1277, 1288-1290, 1309, 1318, 1320, 1322

twisted root extraction problem 626, 628-629, 632, 637, 639

V

validating device 647, 658
VANET 56, 429, 438, 481, 484-487, 522, 552, 664-665, 669-670, 675-676, 679, 683-684, 687-688, 694-696, 698, 700-701, 839, 1024, 1075-1076
Vehicular Ad-Hoc Networks 475, 481, 663, 892, 1026
Vehicular Networks 472, 474-475, 478, 481, 524, 553, 684, 691, 693, 706, 896, 971

vertical integration 986-988, 993, 995-998
Virus 109, 111, 122, 124, 341, 510, 533, 557, 677, 1046
Vulnerabilities And Attacks 701, 1074

W

Warehouse 229, 237, 246, 309, 351, 365, 451, 479, 499-500, 502, 526, 528, 531, 555, 587, 650, 758, 771, 961, 964, 985, 1206, 1218, 1221, 1241, 1245, 1264, 1277, 1281, 1283
web administration 648, 650, 658
Web of Trust (WoT) 315, 319
Wireless Communication 211, 258, 262, 265, 436, 448, 475-476, 481, 518, 547, 550, 870, 896, 909, 920, 1006

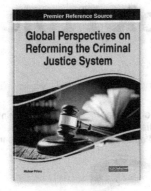

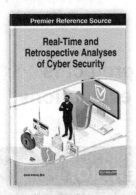

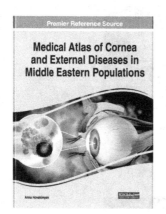

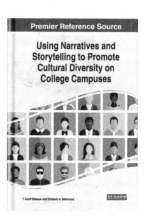

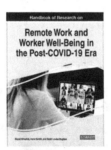

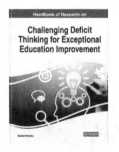

Printed in the United States
by Baker & Taylor Publisher Services

Printed in the United States
by Baker & Taylor Publisher Services